KRLA ARCHIVES

KRLA
Chronological Archives
Volume 7
April 22, 1967, to September 9, 1967

KRLA ARCHIVES

The issues of KRLA Beat running collected in this archive volume were published bi-weekly and ran 24 pages. That was a huge difference from the newsletter that started as 4 pages and covered mostly radio station happenings and a good bit of Beatle news.

Bands like the Seeds, Blues Magoos, The Yellow Balloon, Smokey Robinson, The Bee Gees, Jefferson Airplane, Of course, Sonny and Cher, The Monkees, the Mamas and Papas, The Beatles, The Rolling Stones stayed in the spotlight. Second stringers like Paul Revere and the Raiders, the Buckinghams, Eric Burdon, The Turtles, The Association, and Don and the Good Times also got coverage...although naturally a lot less than the A list performers.

The Beat had added album reviews a short time back (why that wasn't done from the beginning is anyone's guess) and events like Monterey Pop were just made for Beat coverage.

And as prior, it wasn't just music-related events that were covered: rock stars' private lives were good for articles, as well. Gary Lewis' wedding received coverage, as did Carl Wilson defying the draft.

Non-music related things were also covered: Twiggy, College Suicide, getting summer jobs, bending to the establishment and censorship all got coverage of one type or another.

In presenting these original issues, we've moved a few of the pages around to ensure that the spreads still lined up. Not a big deal to most people unless you are severly OCD and have access to the original issues.

Copyright © 2016 White Lightning Publishing

KRLA ARCHIVES

America's Pop Music NEWSpaper
KRLA Edition BEAT
25¢ MFP

Volume 3, Number 3 — LOS ANGELES, CALIFORNIA — April 22, 1967

JAMESON
COLOR HIM IN

KRLA ARCHIVES

KRLA BEAT

Los Angeles, California — April 22, 1967

Frank Sinatra To Go On Tour

HOLLYWOOD — Frank Sinatra, the man who grabs all the top club bookings, has decided to go back to regular old personal appearance tours. Accordingly, Sinatra has signed contracts for a seven-city concert tour during July.

Sinatra has not done a concert tour since the summer of '65 but perhaps he feels that now is a good time to begin touring again since he seems to be coming up with hit after hit on the pop charts. His latest is, of course, "Somethin' Stupid," which he sings with daughter, Nancy.

Mr. Sinatra's schedule begins at the Pittsburgh Civic Arena on July 2 and then moves on to Cleveland on July 6 at the Public Auditorium; July 8, New Auditorium, Dade County Fair Grounds; July 9, Detroit, Cobo Hall; July 11, Chicago, International Amphitheatre; July 13, Philadelphia, Convention Center; and July 15, Baltimore Civic Center.

Promoters feel that the potential audience for Sinatra's entire tour will run close to the 86,000 mark. Top ticket prices will be $12.50 with the bottom price set at $4.50. According to Sinatra's spokesmen, the bottom price was insisted upon by Sinatra in order to afford an opportunity to attend for those who could not pay the $7.50 to $12.50 prices.

It will be interesting to see just what age-bracket attends Sinatra's concerts. All of a sudden Sinatra began receiving air play on the pop stations and his records similarly climbed up the pop charts; however, no one can quite decide if it is the young adults or the "old" adults who are purchasing Sinatra's singles. This concert tour should decide the issue once and for all.

SINATRA TO hit the road.

...KEITH RICHARD AND MICK JAGGER will appear in court on May 10. *BEAT Photo: Robert Young*

Stones Jagger, Richard Receive Court Summonses

CHICHESTER, England — Two members of the Rolling Stones, Mick Jagger and Keith Richard have received summonses to appear in court on May 10.

Several weeks ago, eight people (including Mick Jagger and girlfriend Marianne Faithfull) were searched at Keith Richard's house by fifteen policemen who entered the house with a search warrant issued under the Dangerous Drugs Act. Substances were taken from Keith's house but no arrests were made.

No Charges

No formal charges have been filed against the two Stones but the summonses were delivered and Mick and Keith will appear in court.

Before their appearance in court, the Stones are on an extensive European tour which includes a stop-off behind the Iron Curtain. The Stones will appear by government invitation in Warsaw, Poland. They will also visit Oerbro, Sweden; Athens, Halsenborg, Bremen, Cologne, Dortmund, Hamburg, Vienna, Bologna, Rome, Milan, Genoa, Paris, Zurich and The Hague.

The group also has a British tour lined up but it is possible that they will not be appearing in the United States this summer as was originally thought. Speculation is running very high that the U.S. Government will refuse to grant work permits to the Stones.

However, as far as is known the Stones have not even applied for work permits and until they do it will be impossible to know whether or not they will in fact be refused.

Since 1965, the Stones have sold more than ten million singles and eight million albums. Last year, their albums grossed an estimated $20 million in the United States alone.

Despite all their trouble in England, their record sales have not been affected in the slightest. Their only album release of 1967, "Between The Buttons," has already grossed $6 million.

No Blackout

It's hardly likely that there will be a complete Stones' blackout in the States, even if they are not granted a work permit. They would still be able to appear on our television shows via tapes shot in England.

Stones' representatives here in the States have refused to comment on the Jagger/Richard summonses but admit that the Stones currently have no plans to tour the U.S.

DAVY JONES FORMS OWN RECORD FIRM

Davy Jones and his manager, Hal Cone, are going into the disc business. They formed Davy Jones Records, Ltd., and signed Vinnie Basile as the company's first recording artist.

Vinnie, 21, has been blind since the age of eight. He writes much of his own material and is a self-taught drummer and singer. His first single on the Davy Jones label will be out soon.

Old Hand

Jack Angel, an old hand in many facets of the music business including management and publishing, will be executive vice president for the East Coast. He started Herald and Ember Records. Two of Angle's biggest hits on the label were "Shake A Hand" and "Paradise Hill."

New Talent

Angel is now scouting for new talent to record on the Jones label and is searching for distributors for the company.

Davy will keep working with the Monkees who record for RCA Victor.

DAVY'S FORMED A disc firm. *BEAT Photo: Dwight Carter*

LATE NEWS
BEATLES MANAGER SIGNS THE MONKEES
(Story on Page 8)

JIM HARPO VALLEY DROPS RAIDERS TO GO AS SOLO

A member of Paul Revere & The Raiders has split with the group and is now going it alone as a single. Jim "Harpo" Valley makes his solo debut with a new single release on the Jerden label, "There Is Love," backed with "I'm Real." Harpo wrote both numbers.

Harpo's departure was with no hard feelings. Paul Revere is very fond of Harpo and wished him the best of luck. He was sorry to be losing a valuable member of the group, but appreciates Harpo's desire to succeed on his own.

Before he joined the Raiders, Harpo played with Don & The Goodtimes, who just released a new single on the Epic label, "I Could Be So Good To You."

HARPO NO longer a Raider.

KRLA ARCHIVES

Letters TO THE EDITOR

DEATH OF 'ACTION'

Dear *BEAT*:
How many teen shows are the television stations going to take off? I just found out that "Where The Action Is" isn't anymore. Oh, great! So now what happens to the Raiders, Tina Mason, Steve Alaimo and people who were "made" by this show and by Dick Clark?

I imagine they will make a personal appearance or two occasionally and they will probably make a few records. I'm concerned because I've seen too many talented people disappear into the pages of history because of this kind of an unfortunate occurrence.

Because "Action" is going off, I have a question or two to ask you. My first is what will Paul Revere and the Raiders do? Just records and a few concerts mixed with an occasional television appearance? That's hardly a compensation for the weekly pay check and the exposure "Action" provided.

My second question is, do you know of any shows that are scheduled to replace "Action" for teens? I would appreciate it if you could answer my questions.
Thank you.
Nancy Parry

In answer to your first question, Paul Revere and the Raiders are one of the biggest touring groups in the United States! They're forever on the road and, as a matter of fact, they probably make more money on tours than any other group with the exceptions, of course, of the Beatles, Stones and now the Monkees. It's quite safe to say that they will not starve because of the loss of an "Action" paycheck.

As for replacing "Action" with another national teen show, there is nothing definite but there is a very hot rumor that "Go," filmed as a special, will become a weekly show. However, nothing is yet confirmed.

It seems that the television networks are not about to touch a teen show because of the cancellation of such shows as "Hullabaloo," "Shindig," and now "Action." So, instead of devoting a full show to teens they book pop acts on their variety shows. Ed Sullivan has been regularly utilizing this means of picking up a young audience ever since he booked the Beatles.
The Editor

APOLOGY TO MONKEES

Dear *BEAT*:
Recently I did an extremely dumb thing. I wrote a letter to an English pop paper (the name of which shall remain nameless) and said some extraordinary things. Being the kind who has a tendency to run off at the mouth, they were extremely "witchy" things... the kind of things normally said by juveniles. Or something.

Anyway, having said them, I now regret them profoundly. My apologies to the Monkees. The funny thing is, I like the Monkees. I like their music and frankly, I like them. It isn't simply a question of "not knocking success" and their music is good; it's interesting and well done. The show, well to be honest, I can't really take it every week. But for what it is, it's acceptable.

Maybe it was because I had a typewriter and was feeling a need to try out the various little buttons. Maybe it was because being a Beatle fan (they are not my number one fave rave group... that dubious honor having to go to the "out" Lovin' Spoonful – but they are okay too. More or less), I felt a need to say something profound (I like "Penny Lane," but I can understand the dull reaction both here and in England. Some musical excitement is needed and if I had been able to condense my thoughts into smaller sentences, maybe the English paper would have printed the "digs" I included against the fab four.) Or maybe it was (and is?) a case of "feet going in where the brain fears to tread."

In any event, why am I writing to *The BEAT*? Well, you must certainly be aware of this English paper and seeing the name of one of your faithful readers "knocking" one of your favorite groups might cause a reaction – a highly negative one. And my real gripe with the English paper and I suppose with all pop papers currently is why kill a golden goose by over-exposing it?

Reading about nothing but the Monkees... seeing them every week... hearing their records until you are ready to fall to pieces is a bore. Honest. And having barely survived that kind of thing with the Beatles, do you really think I *want* to go through it again with the Monkees? Especially when Micky Dolenz insists on sounding like chubby cheeks Paulie? Sob. Not to mention scream and climb up the wall.

I said it; I'm not glad and if *The BEAT* staff sees it, please (for my sake, please) just forget it.

I'll tell you something. I read the tribute to the Monkees with glazed eyes and afterwards I did a lot of giggling. Then I think I went around for days seeing Monkee faces everywhere I looked. Ugh. It was a horrifying experience, and I don't wish to go through it again. So, please, from a faithful, loyal, highly pro-*BEAT* dedicated reader – please don't feel you have to engage in some kind of retributive (derivative of "retribution") act. Please, please, please.
Brenda

AIRING HER POP VIEWS

Dear *BEAT*:
I would like to air my views about groups (as if you cared!). My fave group is the Beatles. They are so extremely talented and luvable.

The Monkees are good too, but why do people insist that they are carbon copies of the Beatles? They are two completely different groups. Personally, I think the Beatles are more talented, but to each his own. I think the Monkees are awfully funny, though.

The Monkees' humor is sort of TV humor, whereas the Beatles' humor is a little more sophisticated and many times harder to understand. I think that's why the Beatles have lost many of their younger fans – because the kids don't understand them. I think their mustaches are glorious (I understand Micky has grown a beard) and their latest record is great!
Connie Howell

MONKEES ADDRESS

Dear *BEAT*:
I would like to write to the Monkees. Will you be kind enough to send me their address? I would appreciate it a lot.
Juana Carter
You can write to the Monkees at 1334 North Beachwood Drive, Hollywood 28, California 90028.
The Editor

HERMAN'S SCHEDULE

Dear *BEAT*:
Do you have any information on Herman's Hermits probably tour this summer? Any tentative dates, places, or anything?

If you do, could you either print the information or send it to me? Thank you.
Susan Mills
The Hermits are due to tour Stateside for four or five weeks during June and July. However, the exact dates depend entirely on their movie schedule. They're filming "Mrs. Brown You've Got A Lovely Daughter" and until they get further along with the shooting they will not be able to make even tentative dates.
The Editor

'MUSIC IS TO ENJOY'

Dear *BEAT*:
I'm sick of the whole business – the constant battle of who is the greatest, what group is "in," what group is "out," what country is "in," what country is "out" – greatest, worstest, in, out, on. Who needs it?

Man, I thought the music scene was to enjoy, enjoy, enjoy, and all I hear is "I hate this, ugh that, phew on them, a heck there, a yech everywhere." Or "I love them so much, I don't see how you can dare compare them to those creeps!"

Every single group is the greatest and all the countries in the world are "in" and every song and sound echoing around this world is the "fabbiest," "raviest" ever!

The Monkees are cute and funny and put out fantastic records and a hilarious television show.

The Beatles made their name and deserve to keep it – what's earned is earned. Their albums are works of art, their films are larfy, Paul is cute and a great person, Ringo is a kind, good person, George is georgeous and interesting, John Lennon is John Lennon.

The Rolling Stones are exciting and unpredictable. Their music is well done and sometimes funny, sometimes serious, always worthwhile.

The Spoonful are a bucketful of new songs; the Raiders are where some of the action is and made the show what it was – action-packed.

The Mamas and Papas have a different sound, a great sound. The Association are a bunch of great guys and always have something great to say.

Anyway, my point is that if you would rather have just your faves and no one elses – great. Then make it that way and see if things don't get extremely, unbearably... yawny. I'm not sure one or several groups *couldn't* carry the sound scene but who wants to take a chance on losing it all?

Just my being able to list all the groups and their attitudes goes to show the diversity and interesting people that make the music scene what it is. A moving, exciting, thrilling, unbelievable, unpredictable, artistic, magnificent, sparkling, fabby, ravey, geary, soul-stirring, sensational, wild, frantic, seething, warm, spirit-moving and overwhelming part of everyone's life (or should be).

As John Lennon said: "Pop music gets through to all people, all over the world, that's the main thing."

And all I really want to say is ENJOY! Please?
Victoria Bowen

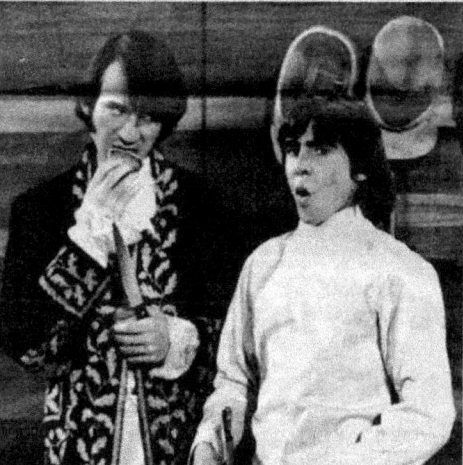

OPEN LETTER TO ELVIS

Dear *BEAT*:
This letter is really not directed to you. It's an open letter to Elvis Presley:
Dear Elvis:
My friends and I feel that it's our duty to give you some advice. We have always until now though you were great. You have a beautiful voice but you ruin your voice with the music you play to go with your songs. It always has the same beat. Your music and songwriters must be out to ruin you. I have never heard such awful music in my life.

In your movies you always sing at the wrong time. You always sing to the girl. Don't you know it's old fashioned to sing to the girl? This may sound a little silly, but why don't you go mod? Grow your sideburns again and get some Carnaby Street clothes and get with it.

Remember you're not a fogie! Look at Petula Clark. She is married, has kids and is on radio, television and the whole bit. If she can do it, so can you. So, go before you wear out your qualities by letting them rust.

Don't let us fans leave you. Don't disappoint us.
Carmen Zavala

KRLA ARCHIVES

Beach Boys Wind Up Tour

HOUSTON — The Beach Boys wound up a ten-city tour of one night stands here. Their gross earnings for the performances promoted by Irving Granz totaled over $198,000.

Stops en route included Fort Worth, Texas; Dallas, Texas (where top earnings of more than $40,000 were taken at the gate); Austin, Texas; Memphis, Tenn.; Tulsa, Okla.; St. Louis, Mo.; Kansas City, Mo.; Davenport, Iowa and McCool, Ill.

Other box office attractions splitting the bill were Keith & The Wild Kingdom, The Casinos and Harpers Bizarre with the Buckinghams stepping in for the Bizarre after Memphis.

The Casinos have been signed to compose and record the title song for "Winchester For Hire," a film featuring Edd Byrnes and Guy Madison.

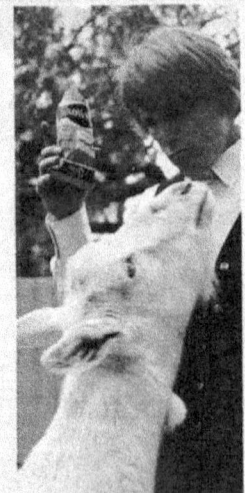

Gordon Solos With 'Speak'

Gordon Waller, half of the Peter & Gordon team ("Lady Godiva," "Night in Rusty Armour," "Sunday For Tea") has just released his first solo single, "Speak For Me," on the Capitol label.

The single was produced in England by John Brugess who produced the group's other hits. "Speak" is backed with "Little Nonie," an original number by Gordon.

GOLD DISC FOR RAWLS

Chicago blues artist Lou Rawls received a Gold Record award from the RIAA for his "Lou Rawls 'Live'" album. Lou has two other LPs which are nearing the million dollar mark — "Soulin'," and his latest, "Carryin' On."

His latest single, "Dead End Street," is moving fast and his tenth album on the Capitol label is scheduled for release in early summer.

Fats Domino Rocks London

LONDON — Around the time when Jerry Lee Lewis was creating stage hysteria with "Great Balls of Fire" and Elvis was gyrating into a new chapter of rock 'n' roll history, Fats Domino was racking up an impressive list of million-plus records with "Blueberry Hill," "Goin' Home," "I'm In Love Again" and "Ain't That A Shame."

Now Fats Domino is making his first visit here. The veteran pioneer of rock from New Orleans will headline at London's Saville Theater starting Easter Monday in a week-long series of stage shows presented by Brian Epstein.

Then "The Fats Domino Show" moves to Manchester for a pair of concerts. After that the master piano thumper leaves immediately for Germany.

YARDBIRDS DUE IN U.S.

The Yardbirds are scheduled for their fifth American tour hitting major state fairs and resorts from July 14 to September 1. They go to Rotterdam for TV, concert and radio appearances followed by a 10-day tour in Scandinavia.

The groups new single, "Little Games," has been released in England.

Joannie Will Sing Capitol

Singer Joannie Sommers has signed an exclusive recording contract with Capitol Records. Since the vocal artist began her recording career in the early 1960's, Joannie has been under contract with Warner Brothers and Columbia.

Her best-selling singles include "One Boy," from the Broadway musical "Bye, Bye Birdie," and "Johnny Get Angry." Joannie has also built up a following as a top nightclub attraction.

Her producer, Nick Venet, has not yet set the date for first recording sessions.

Righteous Brothers Head Out On Nation-Wide Tour

The Righteous Brothers will be joined by Sergio Mendes and Brasil '66 for a 10-city tour starting April 17 in Buffalo, N.Y. and winding up in Vancouver, B.C. The two acts have previously split the bill in two California engagements.

Their schedule is:
April 17, Buffalo, N.Y.; 18, Onondaga, Syracuse, N.Y.; 19, Raleigh, N.C.; 20, Greenville, S.C.; 21, Baltimore, Md., or Richmond, Va.; 22, Pittsburg, Pa.; 23, Washington, D.C.; 26, Alberta, Canada; 27, Calgary, Alberta, Canada; 28, Spokane, Wash.; 29, University of Oregon, Eugene, Ore.; 30, Portland, Ore.; May 2, Seattle, Wash.; 3, Vanoucver, B.C. and 5, Oregon State University, Corvallis, Ore.

From May 29 through June 12, the Righteous Brothers will play the Coconut Grove in Hollywood's Ambassador Hotel.

The duo has also been booked for eight shows at Toronto's O'Keefe Music Centre starting July 31.

ASSOCIATION WRITE BOOK

The Association has just written its first book called *Crank Your Spreaders*. It's full of stories, poetry, photographs and a variety of literary forms without category.

Beechwood Music, the publishing firm, will distribute the first press run of 50,000 copies to newsstands.

PAUL JONES IN NEW FILM

LONDON — Paul Jones will leave for the U.S. at the end of the month to promote his new film, "The Privilege," co-starring Jean Shrimpton, which premiered here. The film's LP soundtrack will be released by Decca. "Bad, Bad Boy," "Free Me," "Breaking Up," and the title song are some of the numbers on the disc.

Paul's next LP is scheduled for summer release. He has completed eight numbers for it and plans to finish after his current tour with The Hollies and Spencer Davis. The album includes four original compositions including "Along Came Jones."

KRLA ARCHIVES

DC5 HAVE SMASH HIT

It looks like they are going to do it again! The Dave Clark Five's "You Got What It Takes" sold over 100,000 copies less than a week after its release and could easily go on to win the group its fifteenth gold platter.

"You Got What It Takes," represents an important singing style for the DC 5, one of the most consistently successful British pop groups. The song experiments with a rhythm and blues treatment. The group flew in from England to debut the song on the Ed Sullivan Show.

WHO'S TJB?
Irving's mother

Bobby Elliot Out Of Tour

Hollie drummer Bobby Elliot, first taken ill in mid-February, has suffered a relapse and will be out of the group for several months, missing their current world tour.

Bobby first collapsed in Germany with an inflamed appendix but was supposedly recovering until he suffered another collapse last week at his home in Lancashire, England.

Tony Mansfield, formerly a drummer for the Dakotas, is taking over drumming chores until Bobby is able to return to the group.

UNCLE Hosts Rock Group

"The Man From U.N.C.L.E." is threatening to become a rock 'n roll showcase. Illya and Napoleon, who recently played host to Sonny and Cher, will soon share billing with Every Mother's Son, a new rock combo.

The group will debut in a two-part episode titled "The Five Daughters." They will perform a song from their album.

UK STARS PACK SHOW

LONDON – The Beatles and the Rolling Stones were only a few of the top pop celebrities among the star-studded capacity crowd of 10,000 people at the opening here of the Stax-Volt Revue titled, "The Memphis Sound."

Star performers turned out to view the show featuring Otis Redding, Sam and Dave, Eddie Floyd, Booker T and the MG's and the Mark-Keys. South African singer Sharon Tandy won a five-minute standing ovation from the enthusiastic crowd. Sharon, who now lives in England, has shot to the top of the U.K. charts with, "Toe-Hold," on the Stax label.

Carla Thomas, who appeared in the revue, made a special appearance at the Bag O' Nails Club. In her audience were some highly appreciative fans, themselves British pop groups – the Who, the Hollies and the Kinks.

Trini Lopez Set For National Tour

Trini Lopez is currently on an extensive U.S. tour which will take him to over 40 cities. A series of one-nighters, concerts and night club engagements will keep the entertainer virtually booked solid through November 5, according to a recent announcement by his agent manager, George (Bullets) Durgom.

The one-shot appearances kicked off in Denver. Trini is also slated to appear in Salt Lake City, Utah; Dallas, Texas; South Orange, N.J.; Troy, Rochester and West Point, N.Y.; Rutherford, N.J.; Scranton, Pa.; Jersey City, N.J.; Bronx, White Plains and Syracuse, N.Y., Iowa City and Chicago, Ill.

Then the singer starts a tight schedule of club engagements at the Latin Casino, Cherry Hill, N.J. followed by appearances at Blinstrub's in Boston, Mass. from May 18-28; New York City's Basin Street East from June 1-24 and Harrah's in Reno from July 13-August 2.

He is also set for several concerts in theaters-in-the-round and a continuing concert tour running from October 5 through November 5.

PEOPLE ARE TALKING ABOUT the latest thing with the hippies being buying bananas—that good old mellow yellow . . . spokesmen for the **Raiders** denying that anyone other than **Harpo** has even a thought of leaving the group but the rumor persists that two other members are thinking of taking their leave . . . **Lee Hazelwood** investing his money in an almond and raisin ranch . . . **Don McKinney** being taken ill and **Jeff Hawks** substituting for him with **Don and the Goodtimes**

. . . **Eric Burdon** and his new Animals arriving Stateside and wondering when, or if, Eric will ever get his book published . . . the owners of the famous Gold Star Recording Studios, Stan Ross and Dave Gold, forming their own label, Gold Star Records, and signing the **Raving Madd** for their first artists . . . what has prompted **Frank Sinatra** to hit the road again . . . when **Herman** will decide it's time to leave the **Hermits** behind him

. . . the great pains Texas took to welcome **Sonny and Cher's** "Good Times" . . . the **Supremes'** "Happening" . . . everyone being so hard-up for new **Beatle** pictures that some publications are even penciling in mustaches to make their old pictures look new . . . how many pop groups are going to make headlines before the British get finished with their huge drug crackdown and one group which is not going to be touched . . . whatever happened to the **Turtles'** famous Cisco Kid Fan Club and deciding that it has gone the way of the Buffalo Bill Fan Club

. . . **Tommy James** and the **Shondells** and wondering if they've dropped off the face of the earth . . . whether or not **Davy Jones** will really be drafted and coming to the conclusion that everyone can relax – he's safe . . . why **Nancy Sinatra** turned down interviews with Saturday Evening Post and Esquire . . . **Elvis Presley** buying radio time everywhere for his religious album . . . the **Association** on the **Smothers Brothers** Show being a perfect booking – two groups of craziness together

. . . the **Troggs** manager pulling them out of London clubs because "it has reached the point where if you are in the pop business people think you are going to offer them LSD. I don't want the **Troggs** to be involved in that sort of publicity" . . . **Micky Dolenz** saying that "it's (the **Monkees'** humor) not the same kind of humor as the **Beatles'**"

. . . the extensive security precautions being planned for the **Monkees'** visit to London equalling that which we set up for the President

. . . **Jimmy Darren** getting back into the pop bag with "Since I Don't Have You" and wondering why he doesn't re-release "Gidget" . . . when the **Yardbirds** are going to get another hit . . . the

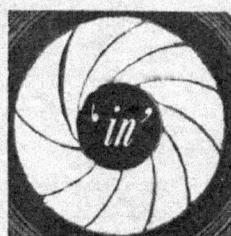

Dave Clark Five's latest, "You Got What It Takes" being the best thing they've ever done and wondering why it's taken so long for the group to let their soul come out

. . . whether or not the **Royal Guardsmen** are the figments of somebody's imagination or a real live group

. . . **Dusty Springfield** trying anything to get a hit and getting it . . . **Sky Saxon** getting mobbed so much that it's a wonder he has enough nerve to keep getting back on the stage . . . **Simon and Garfunkel** being extremely creative and talented . . . **Spencer Davis'** "I'm A Man" rivaling the **Yardbirds'** hit of the same title . . . why no one has had a hit with "Better Man Than I," which has the best lyrics of all-time . . . "Alfie" coming back—this time with **Dionne Warwick** . . . more entertainers doing commercials than albums . . . the **4 Seasons** being the perennial group though many people don't realize it

. . . **Gary Lewis** being anything but a "Loser" . . . **Davy Jones** crowning Miss Teenage America of 1967 . . . **Bill Cosby's** quote being the truest thing ever uttered: "You have to do more than make people laugh; you have to entertain them" . . . how far underground is the underground . . . the Merry-Go-Round going up instead of around . . . whatever happened to the **Leaves** . . . how long it will take before the **Mama's** and **Papa's** go in for movie-making

. . . the **4 Tops** singing "On The Street Where You Live" like its never been sung before — even by Professor Higgins . . . the **Monkees** hitting with so many different songs that you can turn on every pop station in a large city and hear a different one at the same time . . . the **Buckinghams** having three songs on the nation's charts at once . . . **Lesley Gore** working very hard to get her record on all the stations.

Beat Publications, Inc.
Executive Editor . . . . Cecil L. Tuck
Publisher . . . . Ouyie Tuck
Editor . . . . Louise Criscione
Staff Writers
Carol Deck   Bobby Farrow
Ron Koslow   Shirley Poston
       Rochelle Reed
Contributing Writers
Tony Barrow   Sue Barry
Lawrence Charles   Eden
Tommy Hitchcock   Rochelle Sech
Bob Levinson   Jamie McCluskey, III
Photographers
Chuck Boyd   Dwight Carter
Advertising
Dick Jacobson   Jerry Loss
Winona Price   Dick Stricklin
       Ron Woodlin
Business Manager . . . . Judy Felice
Subscriptions . . . . Nancy Arena
Distribution
Miller Freeman Publications
500 Howard Street, San Francisco, Calif.
The BEAT is published bi-weekly by BEAT Publications, Inc., editorial and advertising offices at 6290 Sunset Blvd., Suite 504, Hollywood, California 90028. U. S. bureaus in Hollywood, San Francisco, New York, Chicago and Nashville; overseas correspondents in London, Liverpool and Manchester, England. Sale price 25 cents. Subscription price U.S. and possessions, $5 per year; Canada and foreign rates, $9 per year. Second class postage prepaid at Los Angeles, California

KRLA ARCHIVES

BEATLES WIN TOP NOVELLO AWARDS: 'MICHELLE' MOST PERFORMED WORK

LONDON — The Beatles cleaned up at the 12th annual Ivor Novello Awards presentation here. Prizes go to writers, publishers and exploiters of British pop music. Chairman Paddy Roberts of the Songwriters Guild of Great Britain, presented the winners bronze statuettes during a special BBC concert.

The most performed work of the year was "Michelle," written by John Lennon and Paul McCartney and published by Northern Songs Ltd. John and Paul took second place too for "Yesterday."

The 1966 record which achieved highest British sales was another Beatle composition, "Yellow Submarine," on the EMI label.

Britain's international song of the year, "Winchester Cathedral," which also grabbed off the top rock 'n' roll song of the year Grammy Award, won a statuette for writer Geoff Stephens and Meteor Music Publishing Co., Ltd.

MANDALA IS HIT IN N.Y.

NEW YORK — The Mandala has brought its new religion of "Teen-age Soul" straight from Canada and is serving it up here at Steve Paul's, the Scene.

George Oliver starts off stomping and clapping and then the high "priest" of the group bellows at the teen-agers who cram the Scene. "Have you any faith?" The audience gets caught up in all the shouting and stomping with the group which consists of two electric guitarists, a drummer and an electric organist in addition to Oliver. Their treatment is generally R&B and soul treatment.

The Mandala is scheduled for a 10-city tour soon. Its first single on the Chess label, "Opportunity," is number three in Canada.

Walker Bros. Fans Shocked

The Walker Brothers shocked their fans with the news that their April British tour will be their last. The tour with Cat Stevens, Jimi Hendrix and Engelbert Humperdinck opens in London and runs through the end of April.

Lead singer Scott Engel said the group's touring days are over. They'll concentrate on cabaret performances and tours outside Britain, unless they come up with a flood of hit records.

"I think the fact that we haven't had any big hits recently is due mainly to the fact people are tired of the sound," he said.

Scott wants to change their sound by introducing a beat sound and using some Andrew Oldham material.

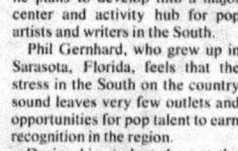

MOVE OVER TJB HERE COMES MQCB!

Pop Center For South

ST. PETERSBURG — The man who created "Snoopy vs. the Red Baron" and its follow up, "Return of the Red Baron," has set up what he plans to develop into a major center and activity hub for pop artists and writers in the South.

Phil Gernhard, who grew up in Sarasota, Florida, feels that the stress in the South on the country sound leaves very few outlets and opportunities for pop talent to earn recognition in the South.

During his student days at the University of Tampa in Florida, Phil established a full-time office in downtown St. Petersburg for Gernhard Enterprises, his own company which handled pop music exclusively. While still a student, Phil was a consistent chart-rider. In 1961 he both published and produced "Stay" which has been recorded by the Dave Clark 5, the Four Seasons and other pop groups.

ON THE BEAT BY LOUISE CRISCIONE

It very well may be that the Rolling Stones have toured the U.S. for the last time. This is only speculation, of course, but our Government takes a very dim view of granting work permits to foreign artists who have so much as had their names *mentioned* in the same breath with drugs. As you know, Keith Richard's house in England was searched under the Dangerous Drugs Act and Keith and Mick have been summoned to court.

No arrests have been made; yet they *are* going to court and this may be enough to insure a denial of work permits for the Stones.

There is, at this moment, a very well-known British pop artist who has had (and continues to have) hit records over here but who has been denied a work permit ever since his name was linked with drugs. The same thing could conceivably happen to the Stones despite the fact that they have not been formally charged with the possession of dangerous drugs.

Again, let me say that I'm purely speculating on this work permit situation. There is no denying the fact that the Stones are a big group who make enormous amounts of money in the States and perhaps for this reason they may be granted work permits.

It's great to see Don and The Goodtimes come up with a winner in "I Could Be So Good To You." A nicer group of guys you couldn't find anywhere. Even personnel of rival record companies are keeping their fingers crossed for the Goodtimes — secretly, of course!

...DON & THE GOODTIMES

Seriously, they are a fantastic group and if they play a date within a hundred miles of you, do yourself a favor and see them perform. They put on quite a show and very nicely succeed in giving everyone their money's worth.

Pop For Movies

The entire recording industry seems to be turning into plants this month. I think the Seeds' leader, Sky Saxon, was the first to come up with "flower music" and then "flower children." But now we have the Flower Girl and Capitol Records sending everyone packs of flower seeds and RCA delivering baby Christmas trees with planting instructions! Now if someone will just send dozens of roses...

Have you noticed how many motion picture executives have discovered the value of having a pop artist sing the title song from a movie? It's a clever idea if for no other reason than the cold hard fact that each time the record is played on the air the movie receives three minutes of musical advertisement for free. How many hours of free publicity do you think "Alfie" received just because Cher recorded it?

Then, of course, there is the press. "You're A Big Boy Now" received space in publications which ordinarily would never have mentioned it simply because the Lovin' Spoonful had their name on it.

Naturally, it's great for the pop people too because it means that another entertainment media has finally recognized them. And the Turtles are the latest group to be so recognized. They sing the title tune from "A Guide For The Married Man."

The Turtles, who seem to change group members everytime you blink, have taken their newest member, Jim Pons, and hit the road. Their schedule for May has been set and includes dates in Chicago, Milwaukee, St. Paul, Des Moines, Davenport, Hinsdale, Beneld, Battle Creek and winds up with the Memorial Day weekend in Atlantic City.

The Turtles then fly off for their first European tour beginning June 1 in London. They'll continue on to Copenhagen, Paris and Rome and then return Stateside on June 23.

In closing, MGM would like you all to know that Every Mother's Son is "loyal, steadfast and knows who won the Series in 1923." Every Mother's Son also brushes his teeth three times a day and drinks plenty of milk. At least, that's what their daily post cards say!

...HOWARD KAYLAN

KRLA ARCHIVES

...HERMAN'S HERMITS (left to right) Keith Hopwood, Herman, Lek Leckenby, Karl Green and Barry Whitwam arriving Stateside.

The Kaleidoscope That Is Peter Noone

By Louise Criscione

He's actually a kaleidoscope. Young, old, funny, serious. A businessman, a clown, an extremely competent actor. Formally known as Herman, he now prefers to be called by his real name, Peter Noone.

He looks young; in fact, is young and in front of a teen audience he acts it. Making faces and clowning around, you'd never believe that Peter is quite the serious businessman. Cunning and calculating, he turns his career over and over in his mind until he decides which way it will move best and then he wastes no time in speeding in that direction. And so far he's been right.

Follows Market

From the Heartbeats to the Hermits, from "Hold On" to "The Canterville Ghost," Herman hits where the market is. With the British group craze at its peak, with London the focal point of the young adult world, Herman donned a Cockney accent and sold a million records. With that peak now over, Herman's accent has become noticeably less Cockney and reverted back to his original Manchester accent.

You can scream "phony" if you want, but the fact still remains that Peter Noone is smart and blessed with a considerable amount of foresight. The entire trick to show business longevity lies not especially in talent but in versatility and the ability to lay your finger on what the public is next going to buy.

Entertainers who refuse to bend even slightly never last long because the market becomes saturated and the public demands novelty and freshness. This Peter knows—and knows well. He watches and gauges the public as a driver watches the white lines in the street. If you move over the double-line you're dead. If you disregard the public for long, your career is referred to in the past tense.

Taking it from the top, Peter Noone is an actor. He began as an actor and those wise in such things predict that he will end up an actor. He got mixed up with the rest of it because in 1964 that's where the market was. In a youth club in Manchester, England, a boy nicknamed Herman got up on stage to sing a song with a group called the Heartbeats. What started out as a song became a whole new career.

Almost immediately Herman became the center of attraction in the group. He was already an experienced actor and so it was with little trouble that his stage presence showed through and enabled him to establish spontaneous rapport with his audience. It was only natural then that the group change their name to read Herman and the Hermits and later shorten it simply to Herman's Hermits.

With the invasion of the British groups into the American charts, Herman's Hermits lost no time in releasing "I'm Into Something Good," "Can't You Hear My Heart Beat" and "Silhouettes." But it wasn't until he dug up "Mrs. Brown You've Got A Lovely Daughter" that Herman's Hermits made a huge and definite impact on America.

The decision to cut "Mrs. Brown" was one of the smartest recording moves ever made. The British could not believe that their American cousins would buy it and even Herman admitted that he would never dream of doing in England the things which won him a name in the U.S.

Clever Phony

But the biggest shock was to come in the form of "Henry The VIII." Donning a thick Cockney accent, Herman recorded the song which caused the English to reel in laughter at the fact that Americans were buying such a "phony." It would be something like Frank Sinatra singing "Old Man River" with a Southern accent and selling it to the British supposing that they did not know the difference between a Hoboken, New Jersey accent and a New Orleans drawl. But Herman knew what the American market was buying. He knew he could hit with a Cockney "Henry" and, of course, he was right.

With the success of "A Hard Day's Night" paving the way, the next thing to do was to make a movie. Accordingly, Herman and his Hermits launched into "Hold On." It certainly was not the biggest box-office smash the world has known—but it was not the biggest bomb either.

Television offers from the top U.S. variety shows came the group's way and picking and choosing carefully Peter the businessman landed on just the right ones. He did his clowning and face-making and the girls did their screaming and Ed Sullivan did his best to shut them up during the commercials.

Hidden Below

Making it big as an entertainer usually means being a hit in as many medias as your talents will allow and to as wide an audience as possible. Accordingly, Peter Noone decided that it was about time the world discovered that beneath all the amplified guitars and longish hair he had a very decent singing voice. He chose to demonstrate his vocal ability with the oldie, "Jezebel." It received a fantastic reception and Peter had proven his point. He could sing.

It was about time for something else too—time that the public learned that Peter Noone was first an actor. So he left his Hermits behind and signed to play in the "Stage 67" segment, "The Canterville Ghost." He had already decided that he would be billed as Peter Noone for acting purposes.

Now Peter along with the Hermits are in London filming "Mrs. Brown You've Got A Lovely Daughter." The market having already changed, it's doubtful that "Mrs. Brown" will hold any resemblance to the group's first effort, "Hold On."

He's proven his ability as an actor, a singer, a personality. If you still think that Peter Noone is a wet-eared kid with nothing going for him except an ability to make faces to a television camera, you're crazy.

KRLA ARCHIVES

Bobby Jameson: Prophet In Leather

One takes, the other one gives
One must die and the other one live

JAMESON IS...

To you what you would believe...
In your mind is the key...
There is love or none at all
There is truth or none at all
Beauty is and ugliness is your own decision.
There is need always—a need to feel—a need to live.
I bring you only myself, for that is all I am worth.
That worth must be decided by you.
For you—I have made my decision.
I have lived only 21 years
But I see into forever—if I lie then speak openly of where
Hair is only hair that God gave—that life gave.
I am not a freak—unless to you by your decision.
I am not unreal unless by your decision.
I am no more than me — JAMESON
I believe in belief
To believe in love—to believe in truth—to believe in life
I believe in you—and we are all a part of each other.
Again it is YOUR decision.
YOUR decision is you—and I
  can only be to you what you decide.
I want you to want me...
I already want you—I always have—I always will
My music is where I have been
what I have seen
how I feel and who I am.

— BOBBY JAMESON

By Ron Koslow

Yes, he has a beard, and long hair, and his leather suit is adorned with various beads and charms—and in biblical times he would have fit right into the picture—no one would have given him a second glance. But he doesn't seek this title out, in fact, Bobby claims to be a spokesman for nobody but himself, but it seems that he is able to express the problems and desires of his generation in terms that prove quite articulate and moving.

Bobby Jameson is a product of the times, the result of an ever-widening generation gap and an increasingly unified group of young prophets and sages, wise beyond their years, who are now announcing and prescribing drastic social change.

Bobby has found the most effective channel to the people to be in music—and his music is charged with his feelings and ideas. His new album on the M.G.M. label (all original songs by Bobby) should be required listening for any young person wishing further insight on the current scene, and all adults who fail to comprehend the basic problems.

A resident of the Sunset Strip for the past five years, Bobby's outspokenness and active participation in the recent Sunset Strip riots has acquired him the honorary title of "Mayor of the Sunset Strip." He did not seek this title out, in fact, Bobby claims to be a spokesman for nobody but himself, but it seems that he is able to express the problems and desires of his generation in terms that prove quite articulate and moving.

Bobby Jameson's mind operates in Kaleidoscopic fashion, taking fragments of various ideas and concepts and unifying them into original ideas which quickly reform and reshape themselves into other areas.

Rather than try to relate Bobby's thoughts second hand—let's let Bobby speak for himself—listen—he has a lot to say:

On being a spokesman:
"I don't mind being called the spokesman for my generation because I believe what I say is the truth—and anyone who wants to relate to it is welcome to."

The Sunset Strip:
"The problem's been growing for the last two years and it's beginning to show signs of explosion. We don't like to riot, but it became imperative for the kids to get up and voice their opinions and risk getting their heads knocked in, because that's the only way people take notice. It's a very serious situation; I can see a violent situation arising unless someone takes the time to try and understand instead of just dismissing it."

On the Police:
"The police *are* society. They're society's tool—but they overstep their bounds. Law should be used for the benefit of man, but the police would not hesitate to break 10 laws themselves in order to uphold one. In my opinion, they are not acting as public servants.

The loitering law allows you to stand in any given place for 15 minutes, but if you've got long hair or a beard you can be standing on a corner for 30 seconds and a policeman will order you to move. That's a violation of man's basic rights."

Society:
"I'm not going to tell anyone to relate to society; I'm going to tell them *not* to relate to society because it's a game — a competitive, economic state of being — it's not living — it's being dead.

Everyone's fighting with one another to get ahead, to get more of this or beat the next guy out of that... or do something better than someone else.

No, you've got to relate to yourself—do what's best for you. I'm not telling everyone to "freak-out"—the most important value is self-discipline.

Society is trying to impose its values on the individual. They tell us to grow-up and act normal. But what's growing up and what's acting normal?"

His present life:
"My day is a very long day. I'm up about 20 hours and sleep the rest. I stay up all night every night. I write all the time—I've got four books ready to be published and I'm working on the fifth. I write music and I've recently gotten into photography. I think a great deal—about what's happening and what's going to happen. I do exactly what I want to do."

On England:
"I was in England for eight months and learned a great deal there.

The young people over there have become a big part of the economy. The whole atmosphere caters to young people—fashions, movies, music—of course English music changed the whole world. The kids over there have a lot more freedom.

I would parallel what's happening now in the U.S. as a reaction by the American youth to the English youth. The American kids saw what beautiful freedom the English kids have, and wanted it too.

But England reacted to the psychedelic revolution which originated here—and soon spread over there. It's a reciprocal action."

On America:
"Americans are totally unprepared for what's going to happen to them: America is on the verge of a nervous break-down—so is the whole world.

I see evidence of this everywhere I go. Everybody is weary and afraid and unknowing and unable to straighten themselves out. They refuse to face the problems.

It's a computerized world—nobody is really themselves and when someone tries to be themselves they are the subjects of scorn and ridicule, because the others are afraid of them."

On the generation gap:
"A lot of young people are looking at their parents and saying, 'I'm supposed to be like my parents, but I don't want to because they're all hung-up —they're unhappy,' so they decide to do something different—they disagree—and by disagreeing they have to be disagreed with. And they realize that there's going to be a fight—a psychological and sometimes physical battle which creates an ever-growing gap—a generation gap."

My friend there's no one gonna tell you
More than you know about yourself
And all those thoughts that are inside you
Are not controlled by someone else

Everyday we live we should find something new
And everyday we live we should give something too
I know that life can surely bring you down
But I know too that only you can keep you down

KRLA ARCHIVES

U.K. POP NEWS ROUND-UP
Brian Epstein Signs Monkees

By Tony Barrow

THE MONKEES WILL STAR IN A SERIES OF THREE STAGE SHOWS AT BRITAIN'S LARGEST INDOOR CONCERT VENUE THIS SUMMER. THE DEAL TO BRING THE MONKEES TO THE U.K. HAS BEEN FIXED BY VIC LEWIS, A DIRECTOR OF BRIAN EPSTEIN'S LONDON-BASED NEMS ORGANIZATION.

It is the outcome of concentrated discussions which took place in Hollywood several weeks ago between Vic Lewis, representing NEMS, Steve Blauner, SCREEN GEMS executive, and Bert Schneider, manager of THE MONKEES.

The concerts—one show each evening—will take place at London's Wembley Empire Pool on June 30, July 1 and July 2. Top price for tickets at the massive 9,500-seater venue will be 30-shillings—which is about 4 dollars—but the cheapest seats will sell at seven shillings and sixpence (about one dollar) each.

Announcing that he had clinched the deal via a London/Los Angeles phone call, Vic Lewis said: "The Monkees will give their own hour-long show which will fill the entire second half of each concert performance. These will be the only British concerts by The Monkees and we're expecting fans to travel from all parts of the country for the occasion."

BECAUSE THE MONKEES WILL NOT BE APPEARING OUTSIDE LONDON, THE NEMS ORGANIZATION PLANS TO SET UP AN UNPRECEDENTED SYSTEM OF SPECIAL TRAINS AND BUSES WHICH WILL BRING FANS TO WEMBLEY AND RETURN THEM TO THEIR HOMETOWNS THE SAME DAY. "MONKEES SPECIALS" WILL OPERATE FROM KEY CITIES UP AND DOWN THE U.K.

According to Lewis, The Monkees will fly into London on Thursday, June 29, the day before their first Empire Pool appearance. They are expected to give just one king-size Press News Conference in London the day they arrive.

On behalf of THE BEATLES, who were tied up in the recording studio completing the final tracks for their upcoming summer LP album, I had the pleasure of collecting a bundle of Ivor Novello Awards at a ceremony held in the BBC Playhouse Theatre in London.

Awarded each year by the Songwriters Guild of Great Britain, the Novello trophies are the U.K. equivalent of your American "Grammy" presentations. As composers of "Yellow Submarine," John and Paul were awarded a Novello statuette for achieving highest 1966 record sales in the U.K.; in the "Most Performed Work Of The Year" section they had the first and second places with "Michelle" and "Yesterday."

The Novello Award for "Britain's International Song Of The Year" went to "Winchester Cathedral" written by Geoff Stevens, recorded by THE NEW VAUDEVILLE BAND.

DON BLACK and JOHN BARRY came top of the "Film Song Of The Year" section with their composition "Born Free."

Inside London pop circles the entertainment bombshell of the month must be the bid by EMI to take over the Grade Organization. EMI is the largest recording organization in the world whose roster of stars ranges from The Beatles and The Seekers to Herman's Hermits and The Hollies. Grades represent a host of top American stars plus artists as varied as Sir Laurence Olivier and Albert Finney, Dusty Springfield and The New Vaudeville Band, The Dave Clark Five and The Hollies, The Animals and Cat Stevens, Paul & Barry Ryan and Cliff Richard.

CLIFF RICHARD AND THE SHADOWS are to make a full-length feature movie with a dramatic screenplay based on the war in Vietnam . . . Clipped from his current album, new TOM JONES single in the U.K. is "Those Funny Familiar Forgotten Feelings" . . . Songstress SHIRLEY BASSEY will make her West End stage debut in the title role of "Josephine," a musical set in the times of Napoleon and his Empress . . . MANFRED MANN vocalist MICHAEL D'ABO joined by his wife Maggie on BBC Television's "Juke Box Jury" panel.

ROLLING STONES supported by THE MOVE at Paris Olympia concerts April 11 . . . After May concert tour of U.K. BEACH BOYS will take vacation in Europe with their wives . . . JOHN ENTWISTLE of THE WHO engaged to 20-year-old secretary Alison.

BARRY RYAN (Of Paul And) has 21-year-old Caroline Walker, secretary to top deejay ALAN FREEMAN, as his current steady . . . "New York Mining Disaster, 1941" self-penned ballad on first U.K. single by teenage foursome THE BEE GEES. New BILLY J. KRAMER single, "Town Of Tuxley Toy Maker, Part One," another original Bee Gees composition . . . GEORGIE FAME to make LP album in London with COUNT BASIE'S ORCHESTRA next month . . . Radio Caroline selling "Your very own authentic PENNY LANE street signs" to listeners for R1.50 . . . Probably Coconut Grove month for NEW VAUDEVILLE BAND after Las Vegas (Tropicana Hotel) appearances at the beginning of June. N.V.B. plan to spend most of summer and fall in America and may undertake October concerts with veteran LOUIS ARMSTRONG! . . . Watch for hefty promotion treatment from Warner-Reprise to push "Purple Haze" by JIMI HENDRIX EXPERIENCE . . . Former MOODY BLUE DENNY LAINE just made fantastic solo disc debut.

STEVIE WINWOOD with three-man group called The Traffic recording for Island label . . . "This Is My Song" back at Number One in Britain – this time version is by HARRY SECOMBE who is to play Bumble in colour movie of "Oliver!" and D'Artagnon in London stage musical of "The Three Musketeers."

BILL MOELLER(21), former road manager with Unit Four Plus Two, unmasked as WHISTLING JACK SMITH, star of Britain's fastest-selling non-vocal single of the year "I Was Kaiser Bill's Batman." Bill previously sang on record as Coby Wells but the "Kaiser Bill" single was the idea of his Liverpudlian Decca producer NOEL WALKER.

Current London Clubmanship rules that the Scotch Of St. James is only "in" if other fave clubs are too crowded. Bag O'Nails is still main rendezvous for pop stars and other night people, freshly-opened Speakeasy tipped as next month's "in" place – and not just because THE BYRDS played there!

MAMA CASS went back to America very suddenly! . . . New 4-man YARDBIRDS combo out with "Little Games." Group expects to undertake 7-week July/August U.S. concert tour . . . 3 saxes, 2 trombones and 1 French horn from SOUNDS, INC. called in for backing work on a BEATLES album track . . . BRIAN JONES plays sitar, organ and harmonica on soundtrack of Cannes Film Festival movie "A Degree Of Murder."

. . . PETER TORK AND MICKY DOLENZ prepare for flight to England.

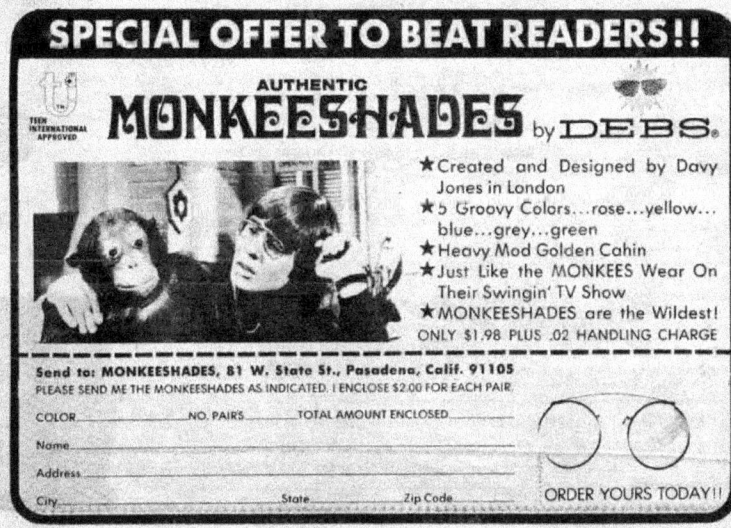

SPECIAL OFFER TO BEAT READERS!!

AUTHENTIC MONKEESHADES by DEBS

TEEN INTERNATIONAL APPROVED

★ Created and Designed by Davy Jones in London
★ 5 Groovy Colors...rose...yellow...blue...grey...green
★ Heavy Mod Golden Cabin
★ Just Like the MONKEES Wear On Their Swingin' TV Show
★ MONKEESHADES are the Wildest!

ONLY $1.98 PLUS .02 HANDLING CHARGE

Send to: MONKEESHADES, 81 W. State St., Pasadena, Calif. 91105
PLEASE SEND ME THE MONKEESHADES AS INDICATED. I ENCLOSE $2.00 FOR EACH PAIR.

COLOR_____ NO. PAIRS_____ TOTAL AMOUNT ENCLOSED_____
Name_____
Address_____
City_____ State_____ Zip Code_____

ORDER YOURS TODAY!!

KRLA ARCHIVES

KRLA ARCHIVES

TEEN PANEL
Listening to Mind Music

BEAT art by Henri Mumsford

The first half of his panel discussion appeared in a previous issue of The Beat.

The subject of "Pop Music And Drugs" was explored by Susan - 16, Marina - 19, Todd - 17 and Gary - 18. Also particpating was "Luke," member of a singing group, who volunteered to sit in on the discussion and answer whatever questions the panel might have.

The panel had many. In the course of the conversation, "Luke" freely admitted that some pop stars do use "drugs" (mainly marijuana and some LSD). He also admitted he feels that these "drugs" have, in some cases, contributed to the growth of pop music, by freeing the tensions and inhibitions of those who are creating it. He feels, however, that for the most part, the evolution of rock is a natural evolution. A field growing up and out of its childhood yeah-yeah stage.

At the conclusion of the first half of the discussion, Luke had just stated that he thinks the psychedelic bag has also done pop a lot of harm. We resume at this point.

★ ★ ★

Susan – "I don't get something you interjected into that last sentence. You said 'the psychedelic bag' – and by that I don't mean the actual taking of drugs.' I think I lost you."

Luke – "The 'psychedelic bag' has very little to do with the actual taking of drugs. No, that isn't what I mean. I mean everyone in it doesn't take drugs. The term psychedelic can be applied to so many things – clothes, art, stage productions, movies, music. Psychedelic doesn't mean drug-taking. The term is defined as "mind-manifesting" in the new dictionaries. But I'm getting off the subject. What I started to say was that this bag has done some bad things. Too many bands are passing off a lot of junk and noise under the tag of psychedelic music."

Rock Shows

Marina – "Well, I'm sure glad to hear someone in the pop field admit that. I've sat at rock shows and been in clubs and listened to records and actually wondered if I was going out of my mind. I could not believe that *anyone* could consider some of that *noise* music. There's this one band in particular. They have their first national hit now, and it's a good song, but in personal appearances, they're just one big whine and grind of instruments. But, because it's 'psychedelic,' people think it's groovy."

Todd – "Luke, as a musician, you're equipped to tell the difference between something that actually is psychedelic and something that's just a lot of clanging around. But what about the person who just listens to music? How does he learn to tell the difference between what's good and what isn't?"

Luke – "Just *really* listen. Determine first of all whether everyone in the band is playing the same song. If they are, keep *really* listening to *how* they play it. How well. Electronic composing is one of the most difficult things you can attempt in music. The Beatles are a good example of how well this can be done. I have too much respect for them to call them psychedelic, because I don't have much respect for the term, but they definitely are 'mind-manifesting.' Another group that is very good at this sort of thing is The Blues Magoos. They have a very far out sound at times, but it's well written and well performed and that's the whole difference."

Harmed Pop

Susan – "I think the psychedelic thingy has harmed the pop business in another way. There are too many records that don't make any sense. It sounds like groups are making records for each other instead of for the public. Songs are full of little key phrases that don't mean anything to the general public. I'm not sure they're referring to drugs, but I'm pretty sure. Whatever they're referring to, songs should be written for the people who are going to buy them, not in a contest to see who can go on the biggest trip."

Gary – "That's not a bad point, but it's actually the same thing Luke was talking about before. Junk and noise under the guise of psychedelic music. What you mentioned falls into that category. I think this happens with any trend. People wear out a good thing; try to get on the band-wagon."

Marina – "I see that we're running out of tape. Before we do, I'd like to ask Luke something I'm sure we've *all* wondered about. Is it the rumor that several of the best-known pop musicians get 'high' before they perform?"

Luke – "Hardly anyone does this. Not if they have any interest in performing, or care what happens. Getting 'high' either speeds you up or slows you down. When you have an instrument in your hand and you have to play it, it's very rough to do this under the influence of anything, including alcohol. The guitar, for instance, is a hard instrument to learn, and it's never what you'd call easy, no matter how long you've been at it. You can't play it well when you're not aware. Or a drum. Or any other instrument I can think of. You can't sing well either, unless you're singing completely freeform; jazz or something, where improvisation is expected. But to get up and sing a song right, one that has a steady beat you have to keep up with, forget it."

Performers

Todd – "I've seen performers who either were high or were making every possible attempt to make the audience think so. If they were just putting this on, *why* were they?"

Luke – "Because. Some audiences dig that kind of thing. I've done it myself. I hate to admit it, but I have. If you're playing in a real hippie joint, you give them what they came to see. I don't like doing it, but I figure what the heck. The whole scene – the big psychedelic wave – will be gone before we know it, and pop will still be around. I think it'll always be around."

Susan – "I agree, but what makes you think the psychedelic thing is fading so rapidly?"

Luke – "Well, it used to be fun and now it's getting to be funny. I mean, how can any person keep a straight face while smoking a banana?"

JAMESON
SINGLE JUST RELEASED
THE NEW AGE
B/W
PLACES TIMES & THE PEOPLE
ON Verve
ALBUM - APRIL 10th - V6-5010
JAMESON
COLOR HIM IN

KRLA ARCHIVES

...THEN...NOW...WHENEVER!!!

KRLA ARCHIVES

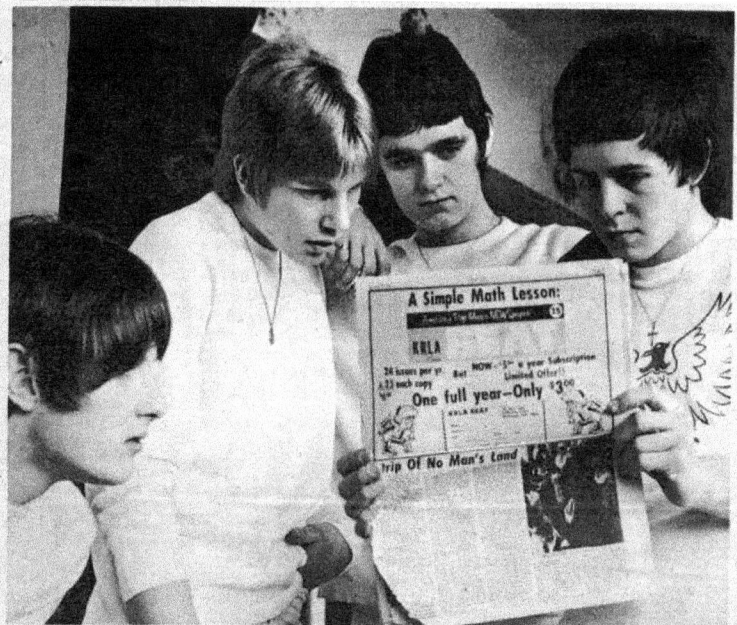

LONDON, ENGLAND — John's Children, a hit on British charts with their latest record "Just What You Want," read their airmail copy of **The KRLA BEAT**. Their disc will be released shortly in the United States by White Whale Records. Left to right, John, Andy, Chris and Marc.

Peter Bergman's 'Oz'... Happening

Peter Bergman's "Oz" program has arrived on radio KRLA!

Billed (by Bergman) as "the only radio program that is not now and never was," the "Oz" outing is clearly an experimental presentation. Even with KRLA's reputation as one of radio's leading experimenters in the areas of format development, news presentation and commercial policy, taking on Bergman's "living trip" is truly a broadcast innovation of the first water.

'Fish-In'

At this point, any non-member of the "flower children" or "love generation" is apt to ask, "what's so special or unusual about Bergman and his "Oz" thing?" In a word ... everything!

Described as "free-form radio," Bergman's formless "happening" has no format, unheard of in today's broadcasting. What KRLA and Bergman may be on the verge of developing is a paradoxical non-format format.

What is the listener likely to hear on his KRLA stanza? For one thing, a lot of verbage the unhip will not understand. He will, no doubt — but then, who can say — play some funky music. He might discuss such a typical "Oz" subject as "the incredibly good taste of Joe Pyne" with listeners via the telephone.

In A Word

Certainly one can expect provocative interviews with "Oz" devotees like Alan Ginsberg and Andy Warhol. Describing his on-air effort as "plastic and inflatible," Bergman has plans to present some original plays for radio along with several intimate "love offerings." We might also expect him to advocate a Los Angeles River "fish-in."

Now that we know what Bergman might do on KRLA, the time has come to ask if this is a put on?

To this question an annoyed Bergman answers, "Oz is that Oz is! The brown shoe is on the other foot!"

PEN PALS

LOS ANGELES pen pals wanted. Marilyn Tomori, 19, 909 Kawailani St., Hilo, Hawaii 96720.

GROUP-MANIACS!!! Please write: Alice, 11021 Noble Ave., Mission Hills, California.

KRLA+BEAT= WONDERFULNESS

KRLA TOP 40

1. SHE HANGS OUT — Monkees
2. I THINK WE'RE ALONE NOW — Tommy James & Shondells
3. YELLOW BALLOON — Yellow Balloon
4. PENNY LANE/STRAWBERRY FIELDS FOREVER — Beatles
5. NO MILK TODAY — Herman's Hermits
6. BLUES THEME — Davy Allen & Arrows
7. HAPPY TOGETHER — Turtles
8. LITTLE BIT ME, LITTLE BIT YOU/GIRL I KNEW SOMEWHERE — Monkees
9. SOMETHING STUPID — Nancy & Frank Sinatra
10. CAN'T SEEM TO MAKE YOU MINE — Seeds
11. SUNSHINE GIRL — Parade
12. LIVE — Merry-Go-Round
13. BUY FOR ME THE RAIN — Nitty Gritty Dirt Band
14. CONNECTIONS — Rolling Stones
15. WESTERN UNION — Five Americans
16. DEDICATED TO THE ONE I LOVE — Mamas & Papas
17. SHE — Monkees
18. MY BACK PAGES — Byrds
19. 59TH STREET BRIDGE SONG (FEELIN' GROOVY) — Harpers Bizarre
20. THIS IS MY SONG — Petula Clark
21. AT THE ZOO — Simon & Garfunkel
22. BERNADETTE — Four Tops
23. WHEN I WAS YOUNG — Eric Burdon & The Animals
24. SHOW ME — Joe Tex
25. SUMMER WINE — Nancy Sinatra
26. LITTLE BLACK EGG — Nite Crawlers
27. GET ME TO THE WORLD ON TIME — Electric Prunes
28. SHE'S LOOKIN' GOOD — Rodger Collins
29. THE LOVE I SAW IN YOU WAS JUST A MIRAGE — Miracles
30. I BEEN LONELY TOO LONG — Young Rascals
31. I NEVER LOVED A MAN — Aretha Franklin
32. LITTLE GAMES — Yardbirds
33. YOU GOT WHAT IT TAKES — Dave Clark 5
34. DOUBLE YELLOW LINE — Music Machine
35. SOMEBODY TO LOVE — Jefferson Airplane
36. THE HUNTER GETS CAPTURED BY THE GAME — Marvelettes
37. THE HAPPENING — Supremes
38. LOVE EYES — Nancy Sinatra
39. BREAK ON THROUGH — Doors
40. CASINO ROYALE — Herb Alpert

KRLA ARCHIVES

MICKEY AND THE INVADERS — Battle of the Bands winners at the Teen-Age Fair.

Mickey & Invaders Capture 'Battle Of Bands' Award

A southern California group whose repertoire ranges from rock 'n roll to Latin music copped first prize in the recent "Battle Of The Bands" at the Teen-Age Fair.

Mickey and the Invaders, six versatile musicians ranging in ages from 18 to 20, will also join the Dick Biondi Road Show on its future tours.

The Invaders have been together several years and have appeared with many top stars, including Sonny and Cher, The Righteous Brothers, April and Nino, The Superbs and Jody Miller.

Group Members

The group consists of:

Mickey Aversa, who hails from Montebello, is the leader of the group and generally plays lead guitar, plus his lead singing duties.

John Ortiz lives in East Los Angeles with his wife, Lydia. He has been playing organ and sax for over ten years and sings harmony with the rest of the group.

Barry Ward, drummer for the group, attended Montebello High and lives in Monterey Park. He's played drums for 10 years.

Simon Casas, a six year veteran of music, plays bass guitar, guitar, organ and sings with the Invaders.

Mario Sasa attends Mark Keppel High School in Alhambra and plays in his school band as well as the Invaders. He plays trumpet for the group.

Sonny Lathrop plays rhythm guitar in the group. He is attending Long Beach State College.

Versatile Sounds

The Invaders are a very versatile group, switching off on each other's instruments. Their sound is described as "up-to-date in all phases of music" and includes rock 'n roll, popular, jazz and Latin numbers.

By Pen
'The Land Of Oz'

The night was blurred—but thoughts were clear. The Wizard came, the Wizard saw, the Wizard conquered.

Easter Sunday night "Radio Free Oz" began, and it's unpredictable host, Peter Bergman, invited his listeners to a four hour trip filled with sounds and thoughts. The switchboard jammed, KRLA's lobby and outside stairway filled and listeners discovered a happening they never thought possible.

Music interspersed talk of brown-shoes and hippies, of love and antagonism. Peter's philosophy intertwined talk of freeway and auto designs, and conversations with Ralph Gleason of the San Francisco *Chronicle* and the proprietor of a psychedelic shop in the Haight-Ashbury District.

Questions of "what happened?" and "who was that?" filled the air and the mail. Don't you have to ask that question. Listen to "Radio Free Oz" with Peter Bergman — heard Sunday nights, 8 p.m. to 12 midnight, on KRLA.

FIGURE 8 STOCK CAR RACES
SEE SPEEDWAY RACING WITH A CRISSCROSS INTERSECTION
10,000 SEATS
PLENTY OF PARKING
Every SUN. EVE.
Gates open 6 – 1st. Race 7 pm
Pass Two 50¢

ASCOT RACES • IN COLOR • KTLA
Ascot 18400 S. Vermont-Gardena
Easily Reached — Just Off Harbor & San Diego Frwys.
PASS 2 50¢ SAVINGS PER PERSON

ICE HOUSE GLENDALE
234 So. Brand Ave. Reservations: 245-5043

April 4-16
Co-Starring
Hypnotist George Sharp
a fabulously funny act
—and—
Hearts & Flowers
with their hit "Rock 'n Roll Gypsies" and releasing a new Capitol single, "Please."

April 18-23
Dr. West's Medicine Show and Junk Band
with their hit "The Eggplant That Ate Chicago" and new Go Go label single, "Gondaliers, Shakespeares, Overseers, Playboys and Bums" as seen on the Smothers Bros. Show
—and— **Comic Pat Paulsen**

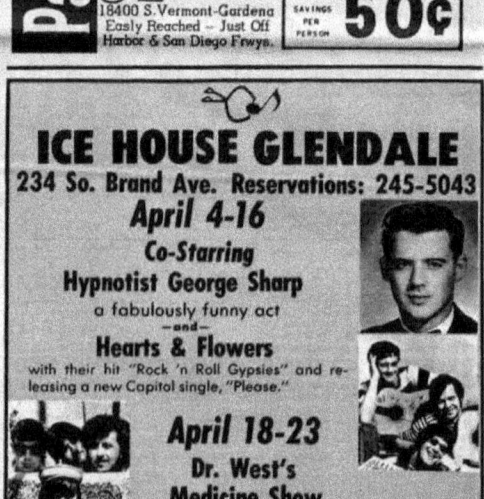

ICE HOUSE PASADENA
24 No. Mentor — Reservations: 681-9942

Thru April 16
Bob Lind
with his hit "Elusive Butterfly Of Love"

April 11-30
Comedian
George McKelvey
as seen on Johnny Carson's Tonight Show
—and—
Thomas & Turner
a striking new folk/pop duo

ATTENTION!
High Schools, Colleges, Universities and Clubs

CASEY KASEM
May Be Able To Serve You...
Casey can HELP you put on a Show or Dance
Phone: 2-7253

THE PEANUTBUTTER CONSPIRACY
&
CARL HOLMES AND THE COMMANDERS
WITH RUTHIE MAC FADDEN

JEFFERSON AIRPLANE
COME DANCE WITH ME BY THE SEA
bonus
1 NAVY STREET
P.O.P. STA. MONICA, 392-4501
CHEETAH

KRLA ARCHIVES

BEAT EXCLUSIVE
Gary's Wedding

By Lawrence Charles

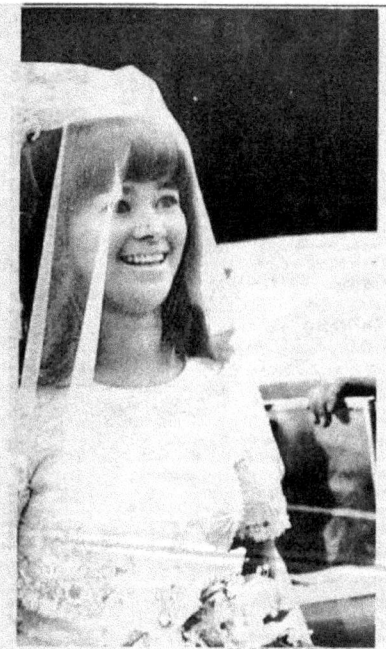

When Gary Lewis asked a friend in Manila to find him a go-go girl for his Philippines tour, he had no idea that would lead him to Jinky, his future wife. The friend set up an interview with Gemma Suzara, the dark-eyed daughter of the Philippines chief harbor pilot and one of Manila's top dancers.

Gemma, 16, brought her older sister, Sara, nicknamed Jinky, along for company. Gemma flunked the interview but wound up as her older sister's maid of honor. Gary flipped for Jinky's raven beauty. Gary whisked Jinky through a whirlwind courtship in between his night club appearances.

Gary carried on the romance via daily telephone calls to Manila after he returned to his parents' California home. The fateful phone call came on December 21st. Gary asked Jinky to make it a merry Christmas by joining him in the U.S.

Jinky arrived in time to trim the tree and delighted Patti and Jerry Lewis. Jerry finally had a girl! The funny man had always waxed poetic before the births of his five sons by wishfully singing, *Think Pink*.

However, Uncle Sam intervened and soon Gary was wearing Army olive drab. The couple was engaged after an eight-week courtship during which they could visit each other only from opposite sides of a chain link fence at Ford Ord army base where Gary was stationed.

Jinky looked resplendent in her simple white gown when Gary slipped the wedding ring on her finger at St. Paul the Apostle Church on a balmy Saturday, March 11, in Westwood. One hundred fifty close friends attended the ceremony. Later at the Lewis' Bel-Air mansion 300 people gathered to toast the newlyweds. Among the guests were long time family friends Jan Murray, Phyllis Diller and Jimmy Durante.

Gary had to leave his bride of five days to report back to Fort Ord. He is due for a two-week leave soon. He and his petite bride will jet to Hawaii for a belated honeymoon of surfing and relaxing on the beach.

BEAT Photos by Dwight Carter

... JINKY was lovely in a simple, white gown.

... NEWLYWEDS kiss outside of the church.

TWO HAPPY SETS of parents with bride and groom at reception.

WISTFUL DAD: His son grew up.

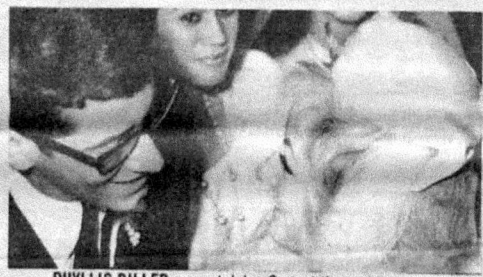

... PHYLLIS DILLER congratulates Gary at the wedding reception.

THE SHONDELLS
Sudden Explosion

By Lawrence Charles

Tommy James and the Shondells stay quiet, make few ripples and remain in the background until, suddenly, without any warning they EXPLODE! They are gone from the newspaper columns but when they come on the scene they are not a two inch story buried in the middle of the paper, they are the headline. They are a tidal wave that rises up seemingly out of nowhere and crashes on the unsuspecting heads of their fans as well as the insiders in the music industry — who are usually in the know about big developments and get to sniff out trends before records are even cut.

Chart-Topper

The Shondells have hit it big with their tremendous smash, national chart-topper, "I Think We're Alone Now." Surprisingly, even though the song is one of the biggest numbers in the country right now, we have heard no news of the group.

No new pictures have been sent to us. Although we've heard nothing to indicate the group's composition has changed, we don't know if Tommy James and The Shondells still have the same members. At last report the group consisted of Tommy James, Joe Kessler, George Magura, Vinnie Pietropaoli, Ronnie Rosman and Mike Vale.

But for the Shondells, bolting like lightning across the rock 'n' roll scene is a matter of style. They cut their first record and for three years nothing happened. Absolutely nothing!

Then one fateful day a lone disc jockey lost a contact lens somewhere in the forgotten record file room. He decided the only way to find it was to systematically pick his way through the cobwebs and accumulated dust.

In his search the DJ unearthed the old Shondells' record, the now-famous hit, "Hanky Panky," and played it. Suddenly requests from listeners and orders for the record flooded in. Overnight it was a fabulous success, bulleting up the charts and everyone was talking about this "new group!"

To say the boys were surprised would be an understatement! It was like landing on the moon and picking up your local radio station on your space suit transistor radio.

"Hanky Panky" has a happy, hand-clapping sound which was completely different from the rhythm and blues sound the group was developing when their first hit bolted on the scene. Talk about a delayed reaction!

The group are all in their late teens or early twenties. They keep their hair cropped close, not quite in the military crew cut style, but they are definitely out to put down the scruffy, hair-all-over look. At last look George and Mike were sporting neat, close-cropped beards which wouldn't spot them in the crowd as wild-looking entertainers. Their clothes, like their manners, are subdued.

We know they're not wasting their time, because they are on the top of the charts. But we like to know more about what they are doing with it.

SHONDELLS — Vinnie Pietropaoli, Ronnie Rosman, Joe Kessler, George Magura, Tommy James, Mike Vale.

KRLA ARCHIVES

'Ask Anne'

Dear Anne,
I know this sounds silly but my mother is getting to be a real problem. I can have my friends over to my house any time I want, but my mother never leaves us alone. She is always hanging around trying to be "one of the gang." We've got a big house with a wreck-room but my mother never seems to have anything else to do when my friends come over except monopolize the conversation. It's gotten to the point where my friends are noticing and saying things. How can I handle this nicely, without being mean?

Dear Teen,
It's all very well for your mom to chaperone your activities but I think she's over doing it. Your mother should know what you're doing but it's wrong of her to dominate your gatherings. You should be free to talk "girl talk" without interference from your mother. Tell your mother that you appreciate her interest in knowing your friends and making them feel at home, and that you enjoy having her "drop in" on you. But also tell her that you are old enough to act as hostess for your friends, and you'd be grateful if she would allow you to spend some time alone with them. If she doesn't get the hint you'll have to tell her straight out that when a grown woman tries to act like a teen-ager, she succeeds—in making a fool of herself.
Anne

Dear Anne,
What do you think about long hair on boys?
Dear Curly,
I think the slightly longer look is interesting. But boys with hair hanging down around their shoulders don't look like boys. I saw one "boy" in the market the other day with his hair pulled back in a sort of semi pony tail and he just looked effeminate and silly. I never thought I'd see the day when I'd be giving "beauty" advice to a guy—but if you must wear your hair long, at least keep it clean and trimmed. A shampoo at least once a week is a must—long, greasy hair is the ugliest thing in the world on a man, a woman, or a shaggy dog.
Anne

Sonny & Cher 'Good Times' You Won't Stop Laughing

By Lawrence Charles

"Good Times," Sonny & Cher's first movie is a sparkling comedy loaded with vivid sets in exciting color, a list of hit songs by the duo and a continuous fashion show of wild, mod fashions created by Cher.

The script is action-loaded with funny lines, bright, fast-moving scenes and a moral: be yourself. Sonny & Cher play themselves, a married couple who happen to be two top rock performers. They are offered a contract by a tricky and cynical film tycoon played by George Sanders. Sonny agrees to the contract although Cher is reluctant. However, when they hear the script which portrays Sonny & Cher as unsavory, backwoods folk, the couple agree the script is not for them. Yet they are committed to do the film, so they try to come up with new script ideas.

Triple Hero

Sonny imagines himself as the triple-threat hero of a cowboy shoot-up, a king-of-the-jungle sequence and a detective thriller. The result is a hilarious spoof of formula movies in which Cher and George Sanders play multiple parts.

You'll never stop laughing at Sonny when he plays, Irving Ringo, the fearless sheriff of Broken Elbow, Neb. who uses more ammunition than anyone because he misses every shot. Cher—who never wears a skirt professionally—dons a fiery red wig and a lotte-cut gown and turns up as Nell Belle, a dance hall queen of the Short Horn Saloon. Sonny's cowboy costume includes a ruffle-cuffed, red paisley shirt under a vest and six bowls of chili dumped on his head by tough guy Kelly Thordsen.

Hit Numbers

Besides starring in the film, Sonny wrote all the music for it. Their hit song, "I've Got You Babe," spruces up the score in an instrumental and Bossa Nova arrangements. Hit numbers include the title song, "Good Times," plus "Don't Talk To Strangers," "Trust Me," "Just A Name," "I'm Gonna Love You," and "It's the Little Things."

Cher started a rage with bell-bottom, hip-huggers. Now she introduces a black and white polka dot fox coat with matching hat and bell-bottom pajamas of pink and orange ostrich feathers.

"Good Times" kicked off April 12 in Austin, Texas with Sonny & Cher in person for the world premiere. By official proclamation, Austin's Mayor, Lester Palmer, re-named his city, "Good Times, Texas" and changed the name of Congress Avenue to "Sonny & Cher Boulevard!"

CLAUDINE LONGET
Las Vegas, Not The Whole U.S.

By Bobby Farrow

"I never thought of myself as a singer," says petite Paris born actress, Claudine Longet. Yet the public reaction was astounding the first time Claudine sang "Meditation" as part of her role opposite Ben Gazzara in a tragic love story aired on the NBC-TV series, "Run For Your Life," during the 1965-66 season.

One of the millions of people who heard Claudine sing for the first time on TV was Herb Alpert, owner of one of the world's largest independent record companies, A&M Records. He was so impressed by her irresistible, French-accented singing voice, he signed her to an A&M contract in 1966.

Claudine made her first visit to this country seven years ago as the lead dancer in the first Folies Bergere show presented in Las Vegas.

No English

Speaking almost no English, Claudine spent the next year in Las Vegas with the revue. Recalling her life there, she says:

"We all thought that Las Vegas was typical of America. All of us thought that every American city stayed open all night."

While in Las Vegas, Claudine renewed a friendship that had begun in France with Andy Williams.

"Shortly after I returned to France," Claudine remembers, "Andy came over and proposed. We were married in 1961. When Andy brought me to Los Angeles I was shocked to see that the city didn't look anything like Las Vegas."

Two Children

The Williams have two children, a girl Noelle, and a boy, Christian, one, and live in the fashionable Holmby Hills section of Los Angeles.

Claudine made her successful debut as a professional singer in September, 1966 on "The Andy Williams Show," and has joined her husband on all his annual Christmas shows.

In the past two years, she has been featured in episodes of "Combat," "Hogan's Heroes," "Dr. Kildare," "Mr. Novak," and three "12 O'Clock High" episodes.

For the 1966-67 TV season, Claudine will appear in a three-part "Rat Patrol" show and a sequal to her original "Run For Your Life" appearance.

Under Herb Alpert's direction, Claudine creates an unusual, pro-

CLAUDINE: second singer at home

vocative musical sound. Her LP, "Claudine," and a single, "Here, There And Everywhere," have just been released on the A&M label.

As her hard-to-ignore, soft-throated singing voice reaches the public, the Williams' household will be featuring another singing star.

A BEAT MELODRAMA
About the Teenager and the Rising Cost of Living
(or . . . How To Buy The Necessary Luxuries With As Little Work As Possible)

Gwen and Ken were sorrowfully depressed...Cokes cost 25c... The show cost $2.50...Ken's '49 Ford needed a can of oil...and Ken had already spent his meager allowance on a birthday present for his Chihuahua. Sob!

Then! In a blaze of red, white and black, out of his XKE stepped the shining BEAT Knight . . . paisley tie, double-breasted jacket, gambler's striped bell bottom pants, Cuban heels. Instantly, Gwen and Ken recognized him.

"Over here!" shouted the BEAT Knight at the twosome. "Read this page of BEAT, speared on the end of my sharp and ever-present spear."

Gwen and Ken began to grin. What did they see, speared on the end of his sharp and everpresent spear? Why are they running towards the mailbox? Why is Gwen saying, 'I want a new Monkee album, and a paper dress and a can of oil for your stupid car and a life-size picture of Herman, and . . . ?'

OK . . . we'll tell you the secret:

Work for THE BEAT and earn money for:
- Yourself
- Fraternity-Sorority
- Fan Club
- School Activities

It's fun and easy too!!

All you do is sell BEAT subscriptions to your friends and earn a commission on each order you take.

Just fill out this form and send it to:
BEAT Representatives
6290 Sunset Blvd., Suite 504
Hollywood, Calif. 90028

We'll send you the necessary information to become a successful BEAT Representative. You'll be amazed to see how much money you can earn (and have fun doing it)!

This is a brand new recruiting program. Former BEAT Representatives must sign up again.

P.S. If you aren't a subscriber, your own subscription can be your first order.

Yes! I want to be a BEAT Representative. Please send me additional information and forms for selling subscriptions so that I can start earning money right away!

Name _____
Address _____
City _____ State _____ Zip _____

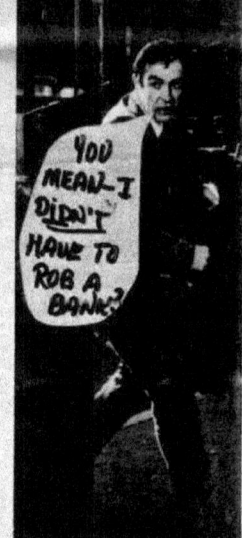

KRLA ARCHIVES

Dave Clark: 'I Only Know What I Read In The Papers'

By Bobby Farrow

HOLLYWOOD — Dave Clark and Mike Smith were in town recently to kick off a 20-day, 9-city promotional tour of this country. The Dave Clark Five's past visits to the United States were jam packed with concerts and TV appearances. Now the boys want a chance to meet informally with disc jockeys and the press.

A handful of reporters, photographers and DJ's were on hand for the cocktail party in the Five's gold and white, ninth floor suite at the Continental Hotel. A few teenagers somehow found out about the party and were dazed when Dave turned his smiling root-beer brown eyes on them and said, "Hi!"

New Single

The trip will coincide with the release of the group's new Epic Records single, "You Got What It Takes."

"It's a departure from the sort of thing we've been doing," said Dave describing the new single. "It's our first try at something in the R&B vein. We're going to see what the response to it is. If it's good we'll follow it up."

At this point Dave became a bit distracted because room service was taking an age with the refreshments. "Where's the ice, Americans love ice, let's have some ice."

One of Dave's friends at the party connected with the record's promotion described it as "A R&B, Motown, brass, sound. Right from the disc jockeys around the country without any baloney it looks awfully good."

Room service was just beginning to remove a large tray of dirty breakfast dishes from the suite which they had obviously overlooked by failing to set up for the cocktail party before the first guests arrived.

Dave mentioned that the other members of the group were scheduled to leave London in time for the group's fifteenth appearance on the "Ed Sullivan Show" March 26.

Someone made a crack about the group's weekly appearance on the Sullivan program. Dave smiled and said,

Gold Watch

"It's always a pleasure being on his show. Sullivan is a real gentleman." Breaking into a smile he said: "I guess when we reach our twentieth appearance, they'll give us a gold watch and pension us off."

At this point a photographer sticks his camera in Dave's face. With the shutter about six inches from his nose, he says to Dave, "You don't mind if I get a close-up?" Dave is obviously in a tolerant mood.

Dave resumes talking about the group's plans. "We're going to start filming a thriller in September in London for Warner Brothers. The working title is 'You'll Never Get Away With It,' but I'm sure it will change."

The film will star Dave, and the other members of the group will all have character parts. "The film is definitely centered around the Dave Clark Five," said the leader.

The group has just released a short, "Hits In Action," which will be screened in theaters around the country starting in June. The Five's first full length feature film was "Having a Wild Weekend."

Dave is interrupted again. This time by the photographer's girlfriend who said, "Hey that looks like fun. Why are you always griping about your job?" she asks her boyfriend. "It's better than typing all day like me. I think Hollywood parties are great."

Stunt Man

Dave is very eager to start the film. "I used to be a stunt man, you know. I always wanted to act but I could never afford dramatic classes. Stunts are really very safe. Everything is timed and you always wear a safety belt. And you really know your capability. If a guy tells you to jump off a 10-story building, for example, you know you really can't do that so you tell him to jump off the roof himself."

"WHERE'S THE ICE, Americans love ice, let's have some ice."

What's happening on the British pop scene? "Dusty Springfield is still very popular in England, Elvis Presley keeps coming up now and again with a hit and the Spencer Davis group is very good."

We asked Dave what he knows about all the news out of England alleging that the Rolling Stones were searched for illegal drugs. Fending off the question, Dave replied with a puzzled look, "I only know what I read in the papers."

What does Dave think about psychedelic music? First he acted like he hadn't heard the question. When he had heard the question he had an I-never-heard-of-it look on his face. Then he mumbled some subtle understatement:

"I haven't given it much thought. I guess it's supposed to have a message. People always talk about freak out. I think it's just some kind of hip talk."

From here Dave and Mike visit San Francisco, Chicago, Detroit, Cleveland and Boston.

DAVE CLARK AND MIKE SMITH at a Hollywood press party.

By Madame Zena

With this issue, BEAT begins a regular column of personal astrological predictions and advice by Madame Zena, a noted specialist in the science of teen-age horoscopic forecast. Send Madame Zena your problems and questions and she will give you an answer by reading the stars. Here is your April horoscope.

— The Editor

YOUR SIGN IS ARIES IF YOUR BIRTHDAY FALLS BETWEEN MARCH 21-APRIL 20

Pay Special Attention to: Finishing your homework and achieving success by always looking neat. If you're a girl keep hemlines appropriate for school wear. If you're a boy, cut your hair before it grows below your collar. You should avoid being unkind or unpleasant, especially where parents are concerned.

★ ★ ★

YOUR SIGN IS TAURUS IF YOUR BIRTHDAY FALLS BETWEEN APRIL 21-MAY 21

Be on your guard for: making friends jealous. Even if you have more Monkee records than your best friend, don't rub it in. Now is the time to concentrate on school. You will slip far behind unless you pay extra attention now. Avoid ruining your health by keeping late hours.

★ ★ ★

YOUR SIGN IS GEMINI IF YOUR BIRTHDAY FALLS BETWEEN MAY 22-JUNE 21

Look out for: praise in school, more dates than usual and a chance to increase your wardrobe. You will succeed by not putting off important projects. Now is the time to: cut your bangs, clean out your closet and drawers, and limit yourself to two ice creams a day.

★ ★ ★

YOUR SIGN IS CANCER IF YOUR BIRTHDAY FALLS BETWEEN JUNE 22-JULY 23

Good news is headed your way: a great summer job or chance to travel is on the horizon. Your principal has honors for you, but you must earn them first. You should avoid: loading up on hot dogs and pizza and ruining your appetite for dinner. Success will be yours by: offering to help your mother with the dishes or the shopping. Avoid: complaining unnecessarily.

★ ★ ★

YOUR SIGN IS LEO IF YOUR BIRTHDAY FALLS BETWEEN JULY 24-AUG. 23

Now is the time to: save your allowance. A great record album is coming out soon. Don't squander your money or you won't be able to afford it. You should avoid: overly tight bell bottoms. Dress conservatively and win more friends.

YOUR SIGN IS VIRGO IF YOUR BIRTHDAY FALLS BETWEEN AUG. 24-SEPT. 23

You must avoid: telling secrets and spreading gossip. You will achieve success by concentrating on studying your weak subjects. Be sure you know all the math before the exam or you will fail badly. Don't be overconfident. Hurry through your schoolwork and do extra reading. Awaiting you: is great success if you earn it by following this advice.

★ ★ ★

YOUR SIGN IS LIBRA IF YOUR BIRTHDAY FALLS BETWEEN SEPT. 24-OCT. 23

You can achieve the greatest success by: accepting advice from your parents, aunts and uncles. Avoid: motorcycles and going-steady. You want to date different people and not be tied down to one. Now is the time to read and go to the movies. Your wits are sharp and you will understand everything clearly.

★ ★ ★

YOUR SIGN IS SCORPIO IF YOUR BIRTHDAY FALLS BETWEEN OCT. 24-NOV. 22

Absolutely Avoid: risking your health by staying up too late, filling up on candy or wearing summer clothes in April. Success will be yours if you: learn to accept criticism from your parents and improve your conduct in school. You tend to be too lazy: improve your penmanship on English compositions.

★ ★ ★

YOUR SIGN IS SAGITTARIUS IF YOUR BIRTHDAY FALLS BETWEEN NOV. 23-DEC. 21

Awaiting you are: Many parties and school dances. You will enjoy yourself whether or not you are with a date. You will have a close brush with romance, but be careful. It is too soon to begin a permanent relationship. Avoid: ignoring personal neatness: Don't be lazy, shower regularly.

★ ★ ★

YOUR SIGN IS CAPRICORN IF YOUR BIRTHDAY FALLS BETWEEN DEC. 22-JAN. 20

Now is the time to join groups. Go out for the team. You are a better athlete than you think. Sororities and fraternities will expand your circle of friends. You will find many opportunities for improving your grades. Avoid: dishonesty, especially on tests and written assignments.

★ ★ ★

YOUR SIGN IS AQUARIUS IF YOUR BIRTHDAY FALLS BETWEEN JAN. 21-FEB. 19

Now is the time to abandon your old ideas. You don't think you're very attractive but you have many admirers. Concentrate on school and don't be shy. Your success lies in music. Listen to good records and write your own lyrics. Express your hidden talents.

★ ★ ★

YOUR SIGN IS PISCES IF YOUR BIRTHDAY FALLS BETWEEN FEB. 20-MARCH 20

Now is the time to: improve your personal appearance. Go on a diet or start eating sundaes to slim down or up to your right weight. Don't over-do it. Exercise properly and guard your health. Avoid: too many social activities. Turn down some dates even if it means breaking hearts.

A Girl Called Twiggy

She's skinny, she's awkward, she's knock-kneed. She has no bustline, no hips and practically no hair. She sucks her thumb, bites her nails and speaks like Eliza Doolittle before Prof. Higgins found her.

Though men call her ugly, she's the universal model of beauty, the "Now" girl, the 17-year-old who will carry one million U.S. dollars back to England this month.

Twiggy, really Leslie Hornby was an ordinary, unnoticed schoolgirl a year ago. Then the Cinderella miracle happened, coupled with much hard work. She became, though she still refuses to believe it, the follow-up to Jean Shrimpton.

It began with her "twiggies," small lines painstakingly painted underneath her bottom lashes. Then the haircut, the shearing that left her hair shorter than a man's — more feminine than the longest tresses.

Then the figure. She left it thin, so unbelievably thin that even ultra-slim models stare at her, wondering how something so frail can be healthy. She exercised to put her sparse poundage where it should go, eliminating unsightly hollows.

The awkward feet and legs—she let them stand unpoised, unnatural, but camera-perfect. She smartly covered them with stockings, but showed them off underneath mini-skirts so short they are less than mini.

She conquered her own country, England, then went on to captivate France, wowing the Paris school of design.

The English fashion press, the French press, the Italian press following her every move, Twiggy went on shopping sprees, designer showings, club appearances, and endless photo sessions.

Meanwhile, she and her young manager, Justin, developed Twiggy everything—clothes, make-up, accessories, shoes, stockings and purses.

Then the United States. She arrived here in late March, wore the latest of tent dresses, stayed mostly in New York. She soundly shook Fifth Avenue with her freshly scrubbed schoolgirl appearance.

And now it's back to England, where she'll pose for more photos, record more records, spend some of her money, maybe make a movie, design some clothes herself, stock "Twiggy Boutiques" and wait for the shutter to click that will make someone else the "Now" girl and Twiggy merely "yesterday's look."

Around The Fashion World

■ Waitresses in Liverpool are wearing outfits in red and bright pink, and every dress is covered with some 150 small, oval or rectangular mirrors.

■ U.S. students are latching onto the antique look, buying up old dresses, shoes, hats, belts and taxi-driver caps.

■ Second hand uniforms are widespread wearing apparel in England. Especially prized are American Civil War outfits, with World War I uniforms second on the most wanted list.

■ Light clothes—the Thomas Edison kind — are brightening up dresses and capri outfits from here to France. They blink, shine, twinkle and flash with the aid of rechargeable battery pack carried over the shoulder concealed like a handbag.

■ Small prints—flowers, ladybugs, what-have-you—are breaking out in bermudas, swimsuits and skirts. Very feminine, very fancy.

■ Buttons are still hanging from every lapel. The current fad is to wear just one rather than many.

> Do you have a fashion question, problem, or just something you would like to share with other BEAT readers? Send it to BEAT FASHION, 6290 Sunset Blvd., Hollywood, California 90028. We'll answer questions, advise problems and share fashion news...

■ Hose are going Renaissance! U.S. girls are wearing fishnet stocking—a different color on each leg — to match colors in their outfits.

■ Battle or military dresses are taking over in the Switched On world. Neat, trim and refined, they sport high collars and lots of buttons.

■ Bronze make-up, the type that makes you look like you've spent hours in the sun, is being worn with summer and pre-summer dresses.

■ Gold-tinted stockings go on the legs that show under the dresses that are bright, airy, colorful chiffon.

■ Nails are squared off, geometric forms—like Cher's—painted with opaque polish. And they don't chip as easily.

■ Straw purses or suitcases are carrying the items which won't fit into tiny handbags ... good for books, lunches, hair brushes and everything else.

■ Paper flowers, the kind you make yourself, have become pins, necklaces, earrings, rings.

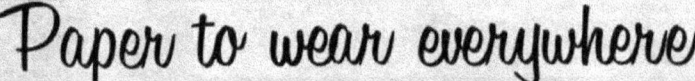

...CUT IT OUT   ...TAPE IT TOGETHER   ...ADMIRE IT   ...WEAR IT!

PAPER DRESSES have been around for awhile, and now they are gaining momentum as *the* dress for young Switched Ons. Montgomery Wards, placing a fashion eye to the future, came up with what they call the "Paper Caper," a nifty shift sold by the roll and left to the buyer to cut out, tape together and wear. Though you couldn't quite wear the "Paper Caper" to school, it's definitely great for party-time and a step in the right direction for full-time paper dress wear.

KRLA ARCHIVES

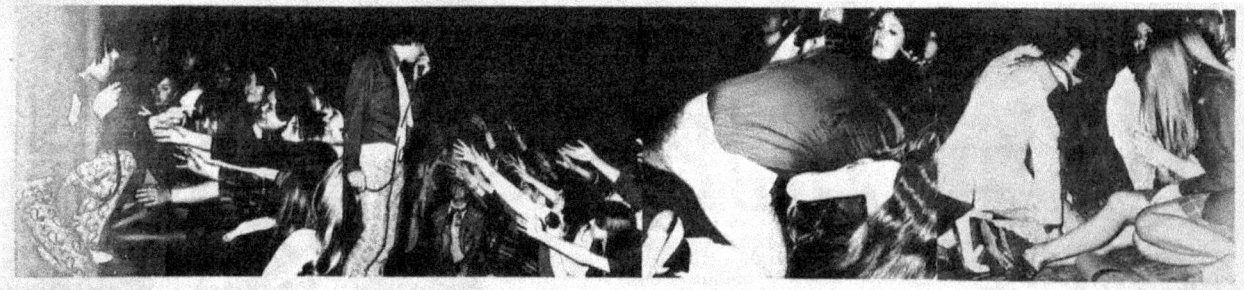

SEEDS SPROUT FLOWER POWER EVERYWHERE

BEAT Photos: Ed Caraeff

By Bobby Farrow

Flower Power! That's the cry of teenagers and disc jockeys across the country. It's the force that pulsates from flower music, the sound sensation originated by The Seeds, a Los Angeles-anchored quartet which has smashed into the nation's charts with "Pushin' Too Hard," "Mr. Farmer" and "Can't Seem To Make You Mine."

The Seeds shun all labels but their own. "Our sound is definitely not rock 'n' roll," said Sky Saxon, 22, lead singer and composer of the group's material. "Rock 'n' Roll was started by Alan Freed. It's all about baggy pants, short hair and dull colors. The sound has changed. Our music is blossoming forth with power and color. So we've given it a new name, one that fits the sound: flower music."

Teenage fans often spend their money on gifts for their singing idols, Sky continued, explaining that flowers are beautiful, simple gifts of love and happiness; they grow free and wild. "I'm just as happy with a flower as I am with an expensive gift," said Sky.

Individual

The Seeds are four highly individual performers. Daryl Hooper plays piano and organ. With his flowing brown hair and regal purple, velvet costume and billowing sleeves, he looks more like a Renaissance musician at a gold and white harpsichord.

Jan Savage, guitarist of the group, is quiet and intensive. Jan, 22, is a full-blooded Cherokee Indian from Ardmore, Oklahoma. He has jet black hair and rootbeer brown eyes. His taste runs to all kinds of music. His hobbies include sky diving and his antique '54 Corvette. One day he'd like to live off the land and run his own ranch.

Rick Andridge, 22, the Seeds' drummer, is lanky and easy-going. Rick has two years of training on a computer but lacked the college degree necessary to find a job in that field. His first love is music even though he says: "What I hope to do is make enough money to have my own computer. I'm a frustrated computer operator and I'm going to learn if it takes me the rest of my life." That's powerful determination.

Now the Seeds are happening. Together they burst forth with a sound that is exciting their young fans, all renamed "the flower children" because they are "the representatives of the flower generation."

Flower Fans

At one of the Seeds' recent concerts they had to battle their way to their dressing room through screaming flower fans who showered the group with petals. Lord Tim Hudson, the London-born, former Los Angeles disc jockey who manages the Seeds, pushed through the wild crowd by swinging a rolled up magazine like a jungle explorer clearing a swath through thick undergrowth.

The group managed to force the dressing room door shut, when Sky became terribly upset because a fan had snatched his favorite pair of 29 cent glasses right off his nose. He was totally heartbroken at the loss, but also flattered that a fan admired him enough to lift his specks.

Then Lord Tim noticed that his $400 suede jacket was grabbed off his shoulders. All was total chaos. Sky moaning over his glasses, Tim over his coat.

Later during the concert, Lord Tim had to ransome Sky's coat for $50 from a fan who had grabbed it as a souvenir from the stage. It was ripped to shreds. The flower children rushed the stage, showering the group with flowers of every color. The tour was a great success. The Seeds doubled previous attendance records at their Seattle performances.

Lord Tim at 25 is an energetic manager who thinks with and for the Seeds. He doesn't sit behind telephones and direct the group by remote control. He's always with the boys on the scene. "He's as much a part of the group as if he played tambourine for us or something," said Rick.

Lord Tim describes flower music as "pulsating and insistent" and says it's "more than the new music of the younger generation. At it's base, of course, is a sort of poetic throwback to pastoral values, the sun, the rain and earth as the bedrock of human experience. Saxon's lyrics say today's youngsters are in a state of growth, that they are the seeds of the next adult generation which will flower into something quite beautiful."

More Vocal

The group feels that today's teenagers are more vocal and better informed than their parents were. They admire honesty and love. Lord Tim says: "Flower music is the first music to really express their emotions."

The Seeds are now on tour of the Midwest, appearing in Peoria, Ill., April 8; Skokie, April 14 and Aurora, April 15. They'll split the bill with the Supremes on April 29 at the Hollywood Bowl. The Seeds new album "Future," is on the Crescendo label.

The group will headline on an extensive U.S. tour beginning in May. In July they'll head for London where they will do a series of television performers.

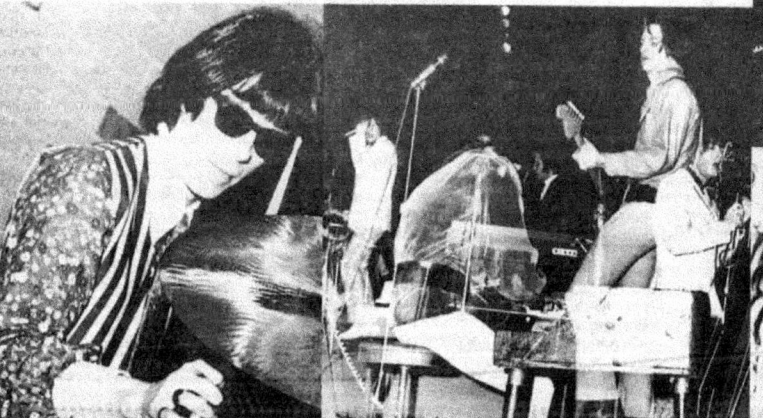

KRLA ARCHIVES

Blues Magoo's—Up From Cellar & Shaggy Fringe

By Bobby Farrow

What's in a name? To the Blues Magoo's it's everything.

"We were 15-year-old record buyers when the Beatles and the Rolling Stones exploded on the scene," said 20-year-old Ronnie Gilbert, the group's bass player. "I just flipped out of my mind at those names. Now if the Stones had called themselves something like Ronny and the Daytonas, I would have said they were good, but with a name like the Rolling Stones they were absolutely out-of-sight."

The Blues Magoo's quintet was dubbed by chance but they feel the name really fits their image. The group was working a New York club simultaneously with five other bands. The twenty or so musicians could never remember the names of all the others. So each band was nicknamed and the Magoo's members all dropped their real last names and took on the common name. "That's how I became Ronnie Magoo."

Shaggy Fringes

Currently, the group lives at the Albert Hotel in New York which lies between the shaggy fringes of Union Square and the outer limits of Greenwich Village, handy to the clubs where they have appeared and to the pads and places where they meet their friends.

"We used to practice in the basement of the Albert," said Peppy Magoo, alias Emil Thielhelm, "nobody minded much except the cleaning store upstairs. I think we jiggled the dials on their machines with our sound."

"And remember the day Peppy saw the roach?" recalled Ralph Scala, organist. "He sprayed it with 'the bomb' and millions of roaches came swarming out from everywhere to attack."

The Albert, The Blues Magoo's report, has become such a popular residence for rock groups that its basement has been renamed the New York Rehearsal Studios by all the musicians who have played there free.

We asked the group what they try to do with their music. "It's a fun-sound," said Geoff Daking, drummer, "we try to make people laugh along with us."

"All we have to do is walk down the street and people laugh at us," said Peppy, the youngest member and biggest clown in the group.

"I'd like the group to stand for something," said Ronnie. "We sing about what's happening to us. We praise some things and we put some things down."

Kind of Awareness

The group started out calling their sound psychedelic more than two years ago because of the kind of awareness they try to create in music.

"Now everyone calls themselves psychedelic. We present an electronic form of music on stage. Some groups can't produce those electronic effects in personal appearances even though they achieve them on records because they are produced in the studio by using feedback sounds," said Ralph.

The Blues Magoo's made their first musical dent at the Night Owl Cafe in Greenwich Village which had previously given rise to The Lovin' Spoonful and has proved a talent discovery showcase for emerging groups. They've also 'gigged' at The Eighth Wonder, other New York discotheque rooms and done many school performances, traveling in Geoff's Volkswagon Bus.

Bob Wyld and Art Polhemus, heads of their own aptly titled record company, "Longhair Productions," caught the Magoo's act one night in the Village and signed them with Mercury Records.

Ronnie Gilbert, born in April 1946 in Los Angeles, did most of his growing up in the Bronx. He has very long brown hair and very blue eyes. His earliest ambition was to be a hot dog vendor with a pushcart and he worked briefly as an Arthur Murray dance instructor.

Ralph Scala denies he's from the Bronx but his accent gives it all away. Born in the closing days of 1946, he is now 6'1".

Peppy is an almost graduate of the same Bronx high school, DeWitt Clinton, that Ronnie and Ralph graduated. He was born in June 1949 and is now a bushy-blond 5'9".

Mike Esposito was born in Slaughter Beach, Delaware in 1945. He is the quietest member of the group but as lead guitar he says, "I play the loudest."

Peppy started telling how Mike joined the group. "Mike came up from Delaware to buy boots and he stayed. He's still wearing the same boots."

Incredible Grin

The group needed a drummer so Mike wrote to his friend Geoff in Wilmington, Delaware. "So he drove up to New York," recalls Peppy, "with his corvair loaded with 50 tons of equipment straight out of American U. He stepped out and gave us an incredible grin and said, Hi fellows I'm here!"

BLUES MAGOOS (top to bottom) Geoff, Ronnie, Mike, Ralph and Peppy.

The Blues Magoo's followed up their first successful single, "We Ain't Got Nothing Yet," with "Pipe Dreams" which broke into the charts a week after its release. Their first album, "Electric Comic Book," has just been released on the Mercury label.

Peaches And Herb —Upholding The 'Soul Sweetheart' Image

...**PEACHES AND HERB:** "We're just good friends."

Peaches and Herb, riding high with their great success, *Let's Fall In Love*, were visiting in Hollywood recently. The duo billed as the Sweethearts of Soul, stopped off at *The BEAT* offices to say hello.

Peaches (Francine Day, 18) and Herb (Herb Fame, 21) are both from Washington, D.C. Although many of their fans think they must be childhood sweethearts, the two singers met about a year ago when Date record producer Dave Kapralik hit upon the idea of Peaches and Herb singing tandem.

Peaches launched her professional singing career as one third of an all-female group, The Sweet Things. They released two singles on the Date label.

Choir Boy

Herb's singing career began at seven in the church choir. Dave Kapralik and songwriter-singer Van McCoy visited the D.C. record shop where Herb worked after graduating from high school. Suddenly the boy behind the counter broke into song. Herb won an audition and was signed to a Date contract. He had released a single before pairing with Peaches.

'The Sweethearts,' are not steadies. "We're just good friends," insists Herb. "A lot of our fan mail asks us if we're married and so many people ask us if we've set the date. I guess to our fans we're sweethearts. That's our image so I guess we've got to uphold it."

Young Love

Peaches and Herb, believe young love is fine, although they're too busy with their singing careers to think much about it.

"Older people always think that young love is just infatuation. But it depends on the individual. Some people mature earlier than others and really do fall in love when they're young, said Peaches.

"Older people just forget sometimes," adds Herb, "how they felt when they were young."

We asked the duo who their favorite Rhythm and Blues artists are. Peaches laughed a little and exclaimed,

"Why Peaches and Herb of course!" Then she added, I really admire Dione Warwick, "her singing, her personality; just her, period."

Herb had his answer to that question all ready. "My favorite R&B artist is Mary of the Supremes. She is out of sight—but don't print that!" Herb is very polite and often shy person. For him to admit such tremendous admiration for a girl—is well—out of sight.

Much of Peaches and Herb's material on their "*Let's Fall In Love*" album is chosen from a repertoire of top 40 hits and old standards. "We enjoy singing old standards," said Peaches, "that's what made us. But now we're looking around for some original material too."

The couple's new single, "Close Your Eyes," a track off their first album, has just been released.

KRLA ARCHIVES

With Love...

Now Available At **Montgomery Ward** Record Departments

KRLA ARCHIVES

Lee Mallory — The Message Is Love

LOVE SURELY DOES, Lots...
You can't ration it out, and you can't keep it in.
You can't control it, and sometimes you can't handle it.
And you always have it, no matter how hard your
mind tries to take it away and over-arrange it for
you, it persists and carries you where you want to go...
— Lee

By Rochelle Reed

He just couldn't stay in one place. By the time he was 16, he'd run away from home three times, once hitch-hiking to New York and back. When he finally left home for good at 18, he moved through San Francisco, Denver, Chicago, Cleveland, New York City again and Maine. He tried to "disappear" in Mexico City but wound up back where it all started for him, Southern California.

For Lee Mallory had come to terms with himself. A long hair in a crew cut world, but definitely not his world. He's now 22, a young, hardworking singer-songwriter with two almost-hits behind him.

People used to find him strange, mostly because of his ideas, and he adds, "I always had a feeling I was strange too. Lots of things didn't make sense anymore in a normal suburban society. Least of all, the television set."

So he left home. "I decided it was time to stop playing around and go back East where the nitty gritty music was getting into something serious.

"The Beatles had hit and they were the first rock group that was really good. From that point on, I realized they would be here to stay. They'd made it so big, there was no reason they couldn't say anything to anyone.

"At the time," Lee says, "I didn't like rock and roll except for the Beatles. But I do now, although some parts are very good, some fair and some completely rotten."

Meanwhile, he spent his time looking for Utopia, "the perfect place to be where there were lots of happy people."

He came very close, but he didn't find it in Maine or Mexico, so on the advice of a friend, he decided perhaps what he has to say should best be said to a mass audience — the pop world.

His message is that of the Flower children, the Human Be-In's, the Now Generation. In fact, he'd just come back from a Be-In when he stopped at *The BEAT*.

"I saw 20,000 happy people there, just standing around liking each other," he said thoughtfully. It was a good thing for Lee because his message (a musical combination of folk and rock), is simply "Love." And as his poem says, *"Love surely does... lots."*

THE 5TH DIMENSION — a new dimension in sound inspired by modern harmony and soulful blues.

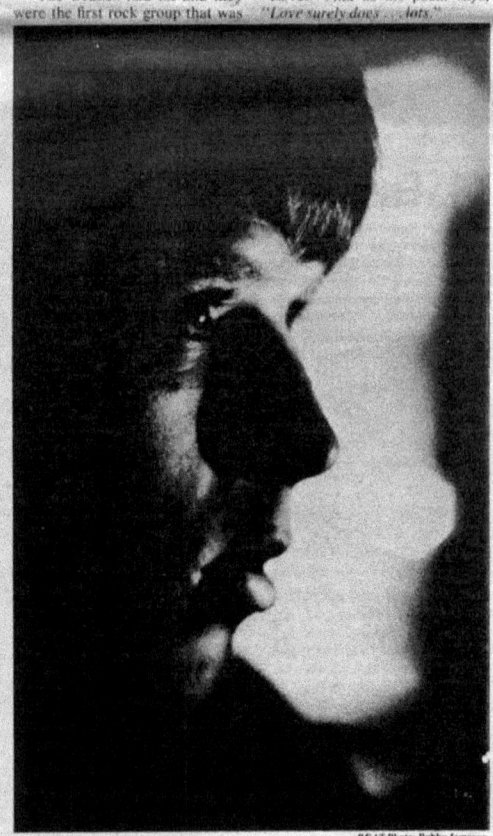

BEAT Photo: Bobby Jameson
LEE MALLORY — working and waiting for the one big hit.

5th DIMENSION — UNIQUE GROUP WITH LOTS OF ROCK AND SOUL

By Jamie McCluskey

The Fifth Dimension is a new dimension in sound. It's the new sound, a convergence of all the musical influences of the 60's embodied in a unique and talented group.

Inspired by modern harmony combined with the soulful rhythm of contemporary blues singers, the 5th Dimension have created their own dimension in pop music.

Discovered while on a Ray Charles tour, they cut a single titled "I'll Be Lovin' You Forever." But before it began to climb, their version of the Mama's and Papa's "Go Where You Wanna Go" hit the charts.

Outside of the Dimension, there is a growing phenomenon of pop music. From their inside track looking out, the 5th Dimension have many ideas on this development.

Standards

Marilyn: "When I think of the term 'pop music' I think of the standards and the well-established singers like Frank Sinatra, Nancy Wilson, the late Nat Cole — this type of a singer and this type of music.

"The way that they refer to 'pop music' nowadays — I think a better term for it would be 'commercial sound,' because that's really what it is more than a *pop* sound."

Lamont: "I think pop music is very pleasing to describe — we'll just take the term 'pop' which is short for 'popular' and popular means the majority and what is more commercial? Pop tunes sell more than any other tunes in the nation, so why not call it *pop? Popular* is *money!*"

One of the controversies currently raging in *any* dimension of the music industry is the difference between pop music and rhythm and blues, and the connection of "soul" with R&B. The only problem is that no one seems quite certain what any one of these three terms really means.

Inside Soul

For example, Billy explains that "soul music" is "something that a person has inside." He continues to explain that it must be something which is deeply felt and sincerely expressed by one individual but most important — is simultaneously deeply felt by someone else who is listening. It must be a *mutual* emotional experience.

As far as the restriction of "soul" to the Negro singers is concerned, Billy is quite emphatic: "Everybody has soul... everybody! Doctors, lawyers, businessmen... everybody." Billy feels that if a person really *believes in* and *feels* what he is doing, then he is doing it with soul. "The doctor is *operating* with *soul*, because this is his profession. *Soul* is in *every* person."

Lamont agrees with Billy as he explains: "I think *soul*, in terms of music, is not only the way the *singer* feels, but the way he makes someone else feel." For Florence, "*Soul*, in music, is whatever makes a person react emotionally." For the way they will *express* the song makes it pop."

Lighter Music

"To me there are actually *two* categories of pop music. At one time, when I thought of pop music I thought of the large bands and also groups of people singing standards. However, after listening to the pop stations on the radio, I think more of the popular tunes of today are done in a certain style which is really sort of hard to explain. It's not a very heavy rhythm type of music, but the music, to me, is more involved than, say, the R&B — the arrangements and production — and also, it's a *lighter* type music, usually, than R&B.

To Florence, soul should also be something to which the listener can relate and associate with.

But meanwhile, the 5th Dimension are working on their first album and another single which, hopefully, will spread their new dimension in sound to many more people.

KRLA ARCHIVES

SHIRLEY You Jest!
By Shirley Poston

My column is going to be different this issue. (And, pray tell, when *isn't* it?) (As in *different* is not the word.)

I usually rave about a variety of fascinating (zzzzz) subjects. Well, this time I'm going to rave about *one* fascinating (re-zzzzz) subject. Me, for instance.

I jest, I jest (Shirley I do). What I really want to babble about is something that's happened to a friend of a friend of a friend of mine. The same something is probably happening to a lot of you, and it's just recently dawned on me that part of the situation may be a little bit my fault.

Quivering Mass

Shortly after I started writing this quivering mass of insanity (not to mention inanity), I began making it perfectly clear that I was crazy. About George T. Harrison (T. as in Thrash), that is. And for almost two years I've been ranting and panting and writhing and writing about him.

I'm now starting to wonder if I should have done this. By sharing my big hang-up with you, I may have caused some to get even more hung up on their fave than they were before I came along and commenced blithering.

This friend of a friend of a friend I mentioned before is a good example of what I'm trying to point out. Two years ago, she was an avid George fan, age sixteen. Now she's an avid George fan, age eighteen, which somehow figures. But the problem is, she's *too* avid.

I think about George all the time, but George is all she thinks about. And, badly as I've put it into words, there is a difference. A sort of terrible difference. This girl is really sharp and pretty, and always has boys hanging around her, but she's reached the point where she won't even go out on dates because she feels she would be being untrue to George.

Warm Thingy

I know this feeling all too well, as I'm sure many of you do. It's a nice, private, warm thingy you experience when you really get close (even if it's only in your own mind or heart) to someone you care about. But it can also by anything *but* nice.

If it gets out of hand, it can become a wall between you and the rest of the world, and keep you from doing much about the fact that you're alive.

The reason I feel partly responsible is because the girl in question wrote and told me how my ravings have brought her even closer to George. Others who like (a conservative estimate) other stars have told me the same thing. That my rattling on has made their faves seem less far away and more real.

Such A Ball

I've always thought this was really a great compliment. Besides, it's been such a ball getting my feelings out on paper, knowing they'll not just be *read* but *understood* by people who feel the same way. Now I'm kind of panicky. This girl is sitting at home nights when she could (and should) be out having fun. Her grades have dropped and she's no longer sure

she even wants to go to college next fall. She's only sure of one thing—her love for George.

God, God, God. If I could only say a magic word or wave a wand or do *something* to make it stop hurting. Or, I should say, do something to make her stop hurting herself.

I'm going to try. I'll probably fail miserably. I often do when I'm trying to put personal experiences and things that mean a great deal to me into sentences and paragraphs. But I'm going to try anyway.

Up to a point, being in love with a star is one of the most valuable experiences that will ever occur in your whole lifetime. I know. It teaches you *how* to love, and makes you realize that love is so desperately important. It makes you more aware of yourself, and it helps you grow up.

Between The Lines

There isn't any way I can just come right out and say this in print,

BEAT Art by Woody Alexander

but if you'll read between the lines, you'll see what I mean when I say that loving a star also acquaints you with a lot of needs and feelings you may never have felt before. Those day-type dreams (as in whoppers) we all make up about h-i-m, whoever he may be. They aren't all funny things or all hearts and flowers. Sometimes they get right down to the real N.G. Again, I don't know how to say this politely, but I think this teaches you that loving and wanting go hand in hand, and equips you with a better, more aware attitude about certain subjects that are going to play a vitally important role in your future.

But, when that up-to-a-point is passed, all this loses its value. If you don't use what you've learned in your own life, I mean, and just use it in your dreams. Again, I

know. I've mostly been goofy when I gabble about George, but there have been times when I've thought I was going to absolutely *die*. There have even been times when I actually wanted to.

Danger

This is when loving a star (or anyone beyond your reach) becomes a danger; a threat to your present and your future.

You get so far into you and into him and into you *and* him, you lose contact with reality. Therefore, you lose interest in reality. Reality isn't the right word. What I mean is, you don't care enough or pay enough attention to the life you live on the outside of yourself, and you forget that it's *you*, not *him*, that you're going to have to live with the rest of your life.

God, God, God, again. I'm blithering and not getting this out at all. You've got to live now, and you've got to prepare yourself for a lot more living. You can't do this if you're all wound up in a private world.

Totally Lost

I sound like I'm preaching a sermon. Maybe I am. I should probably *completely* shatter the remnants of my cool, calm image and tell you just *how* close I came to getting totally lost in George.

But, I can't do that. Some things you just can't admit to anyone. All I can say is that if you're in the same pickle, do anything you can to get out of it, and *quick*.

If you have to force yourself to have an interest in other boys, or even *fake* the interest for awhile, until you can stop comparing everyone with your fave, do it! Even if you're miserable when you go out, you'll find you're less miserable (or that it's a different, more tolerable kind of misery) than you are when you stay at home.

Too Deep

Something I forgot to mention—when you get in too deep with a star, he can become a substance that insulates you against things you don't like. Say you're involved in a situation that really galls you. Instead of doing something about the situation, you get in deeper with him and the security of that feeling (it's not *all* bad, believe me) makes you able to tolerate the situation instead of changing it into something you can accept. The same is true if you can't accept yourself, or feel others don't accept you for some reason. You have him, so you don't try as hard to change yourself as you would if you didn't have anyone. Well, if a star is all you have, you really don't have anyone. Not to the degree you *need* someone.

Some Sense

Oh, RATS! I hope I've made at least some sense. And I hope none of you are mad at me for speaking my alleged mind. I just feel kind of guilty and wretched about the whole thing, so I had to come out and say that there's a lot of bad with the good of loving a star if you let it get that far.

Just please don't let it.

And don't think I won't be back to my old irrational self next issue. As in re-get out the nets, boys, she's plotting another escape!

Turning On

PETER & GORDON KNIGHT IN RUSTY ARMOR (Capitol) *Knight in Rusty Armor, Stranger With a Black Dove, To Show You I Love You, A Boy With Nothing* plus seven other tracks.

The duo follows through on their jolly-old-English musical style which won them top honors on the international pop charts with *Lady Godiva*. Peter Asher and Gordon Waller are two dashing young knights with oiled armor and a buoyant sound.

THAT ACAPULCO GOLD, THE RAINY DAZE (Universal City Records) *Absurd Bird, Baby I Need Your Loving, Weatherman, Out of a Calico Dream, Shake* plus nine other tracks.

The Rainy Daze have picked up more of a rock beat on their first album. Their first single, "*That Acapulco Gold*," had a more bouncy, vaudeville band sound. A highlight on the album is a medley of tunes by Sam Cooke, Otis Redding and Eddie Floyd.

TEMPTATIONS LIVE! (Motown's Gordy Label) *Girl (Why You Wanna' Make Me Blue), The Girls, All Right With Me, I'll Be In Trouble, I Want A Love I Can See* plus fourteen other songs.

The Temptations ought to whirl their way to the top of the charts with this fabulous sound from Motown. Judging by the screams and cheers of the crowd at Detroit's Upper Deck club where the album was cut, this is a top performance.

* * *

DISCussion

Motown sends us a couple of sure winners, The SUPREMES, *The Happening*, is the title song from the movie . . . It's a sweet, full of life sound from those three fabulously talented Detroit girls...

4 TOPS ON BROADWAY (Motown) *Hello Broadway, Maria, Climb Ev'ry Mountain, Mame* plus eight other tracks. The group can probably add this to their list of consecutive hit recordings. The 4 Tops have broadened their repertoire with popular ballads and show tunes. *On The Street Where You Live* and *Maria* are some of the many works of top Broadway composers and lyricists . . . BUFFALO SPRINGFIELD (Atco) *For What It's Worth, Go and Say Goodbye, Sit Down I Think I Love You, Nowadays Clancy Can't Even Sing* plus eight other tracks. *For What It's Worth* is probably the most outstanding on the album but the rest has a pleasant sound... HERB ALPERT AND THE TIJUANA BRASS, *Casino Royale*, Herb's suave horn sound promises to make this a winner for the A&M artist . . . LOU RAWLS, *Dead End Street Monologue*, Lou socks it to you with soul stirring feeling in monologue and song . . . The FOUR SEASONS, *Beggin'*. Although Frankie Valli is still featured, he doesn't come through as strong in this as in previous hits. A good sound, somewhat harder than usual... THE LIVERPOOL FIVE, *Cloudy*. This English quintet sings in pretty and beveled tones. They're looking for a hit but don't know if this is strong enough to carry them to the top of the charts . . . NEIL DIAMOND, *Girl, You'll Be A Woman Soon*, a soulful treatment of great lyrics by Diamond is backed up by an easy paced rhythm which should make it a chart topper . . . THE HAPPENINGS, *I Got Rhythm*. This very Groovy Gershwin revival has a strong vocal arrangement and great dance beat... Look for these singles to go high on the charts. DON AND THE GOODTIMES, *I Could Be So Good To You*...THE PEANUT BUTTER CONSPIRACY, *Dark On You Now* . . . THE TOKENS, *Portrait Of My Love*.

KRLA ARCHIVES

please send me
BEAT
26 issues only
$3 per year

Mail to: **BEAT Publications**
6290 Sunset Blvd. #504
Hollywood, California 90028

☐ New Subscription
☐ Renewal (please enclose mailing label from your last BEAT)
I want BEAT for ☐ 1 year at $3.00 or ☐ 2 years at $5.00
I enclose ☐ cash ☐ check ☐ money order
Outside U.S. - $9 per year
• Please print your name and address.

Name_____
Street_____
City_____
State_____ Zip_____

BEAT AT THE MOVIES

SHAKESPEARE—THE EASY WAY

Ever try to read Shakespeare in original Middle English? It's like another language, isn't it? Even in translation it's pretty rough stuff. But the drama of William Shakespeare is required in all high schools, so sooner or later we all have to try and handle it.

Well, there's an easier way—the film version of Shakespeare's *The Taming of the Shrew* would have done the old Bard proud. It has Elizabeth Taylor and Richard Burton and colors and sets that you have to see to believe.

The story takes place in Padua, Italy, a pretty rollicking town. Katherina, played by Elizabeth Taylor, is the despair of her father, Baptista; she's got a temper that scares men off. Her sister in contrast is the sweet and gentle Bianca who is pursued by every man in town. Their father decides that the only way to get Kate off his hands is to announce that no one can marry Bianca until a husband is found for Kate.

The suitors of Bianca come up with a mate for Kate in the person of Petruchio, a lusty but impoverished gentleman, played by Richard Burton. He has come to Padua to find himself a rich wife. When Petruchio learns that Kate's dowry will include 20,000 crowns and half of her father's lands, he starts to woo her at once.

Her temper tantrums and violent resistance to his embraces do not discourage Petruchio. He chases her through the house and onto the roof, finally catching her in a huge vat full of fleece. He then announces that they are to be married the following Sunday.

The rest of the film deals with Petruchio's subsequent "taming" of Kate and his incredibly successful results. It's definitely a film that should be seen and can be enjoyed by everyone. Some of the humor is fantastic.

After seeing the film, read the play in its original form. Odds are you'll end up appreciating both a lot more.

CLASSIFIED

BANDS FOR HIRE
SAM'S TRAIN—for diesel-driven sounds. 982-0166 - area 714

FOR SALE
NEW BOX BASS $200. Case included. 873-0963 (Los Angeles, Calif.)

MAMA'S & PAPA'S POSTERS 22'x28" $1.00 each postpaid. The Seper Co., 5273 Tendilla, Woodland Hills, California.

"The soul of man is not an inner pearl." Send dime for mailing for rest of MalvinaReynolds' "The Soul Book," 2027 Parker St., Berkeley, Calif. 94704.

For photographs of your favorite recording artists, call Marianne Hebert, 935-4232 (Los Angeles, Calif.)

PERSONALS
JOAN—I love Davy Moore

Cutsy: As You Like It

Gene Clark is Ann's

RUSS GIGUERE: I Love You

Down with the Monkee!!!
Up with the RAIDERS!!

Paul McCartney—I love you! Lynn

ELLEN: Happy Birthday, Dragon, Mouse

Brandon—Call Kathy

BONITA HIGH RULES!
DOWN WITH BOSCO RABBIT
PEANUTMEN REIGN!

BRYAN—HAPPY BIRTHDAY! Love ya lots - Tricia and Cha-Cha.

"BEATLES COME BACK!"

BONNIE JONES—I still love you.

Larry Mon may be reached at Box 22004, San Francisco, California 94122.

WHO IS LARRY MON?

HEY DOLO: Happy Thirteenth! My love, Jackie.

MOJO MEN RULE!!

TERRY KIRKMAN for President!!!

MONSTER, I think you're groovy...Teresa CLAUDE

Roxanne loves PAUL McCARTNEY!

JOHN PETERSEN RIDES AGAIN WITH HARPERS BIZARRE — A Younger Girl.

"Hot Lips" seek to find "Red Nose"

Mike loves—Gayle loves. From Dede.

"CODY, CYN, Balboa, Summer '66, Love"

SINCERE HAPPINESS Denis & Lyn. Your ardent fans, Dawn Lee's Club

EXPERIENCE THE HARBINGER Complex

"HEY TAHOE, WHO'S ROGER HART?" HARPO

JOHN SENNE you're outasite. a fan.

Fay Rose Donovan of Norwood, Massachusetts, please call 762-2315.

HELLO BRIAN CARRIGAN

MARK BIGGERSTAFF—I'll always cherish you. Karen.

"BANANA WONDERFUL"

Lynnea Anne Hansen and Alice Bergman are MY BEST FRIENDS.

JOYCE BECK is really groovy!

CHRIS HOVEY — Summer's comin' and I long for L.A. — DEB

GARY HOVEY — Long live Tulare Union High School! — "Tu-Lar-eKid"

DON TAYLOR — you conformist!

SAM'S TRAIN IS HAPPENING!

HOW ART THOU, DARRYL POTTER?-I love you-Cyndee.

Be aware of THE KNACK...I sure am! — Pam Dwyer

DARRELL RUSSELL HUGHES!!!!

I LOVE YOU, CARTER SMITH

CAROLYN LOVES JOHN DOERING

WANT TRADE PIX of Stones, Herman, McCallum for Paul McCartney. Write: Elaine McCartney, 3312 Red Rose Drive, Encino, Calif. 91316

DEADLINE FOR THE NEXT ISSUE: APRIL 11.

POXO is Alive, Alive!!!!!!

LYNNEA, ALICE, RANDY: If you don't stop, I'll tell everyone! Secret Pal

PAM—BANANAS RULE!!!!

DOWN WITH BOSCO RABBIT

FRED—how about BOOGA-LOO Bartholomew?

When you care enough to hear the very best—PAT MOORE!!! (Luv, your Patriotic Pat Lovers, Pam and Lisa, Downey)

FAN CLUBS
GROUP MANIACS!!! Please write: Alice, 11021 Noble Ave. Mission Hills, California.

FANTASTIC NEW SINGER!! ON VALIANT RECORDS. JOIN ART GUY FAN CLUB! RECEIVE: BUMPER STICKER, CARD, PHOTO, AND ALL INFO. SEND 50c TO: ART GUY FAN CLUB, 15947 DICKENS ST., ENCINO, CALIF. 91316. HURRY!!

LOS ANGELES pen pals wanted. Marilyn Tomori, 19. 909 Kawailani St., Hilo, Hawaii 96720

DAVE CLARK FIVE FAN CLUB, 9416 Cedar Avenue, Bloomington, Calif. 92316

HERMAN'S HERMITS OFFICIAL CHAPTER FAN CLUB. Send $1.25, name, address to: Edith Eskridge, 1900 Cabrillo St., San Francisco, Calif.

WANTED
WANTED: Teen songwriter to collaborate with. Bay Area. Alameda County (Calif.) preferred. 569-0507

WANTED: Information on the "Roadrunners" of Santa Ana, Calif. *Especially* Jan Heath. Send to Dianne Stilwell, RR #1, Baltimore, Ohio

WANTED: Sonny & Cher loyalists. JSM, 7827 Midbury, Dallas, Texas.

WHO WAS THE CUTE GIRL in "Skaterdater?" Identify yourself in next Classified.

WANTED: PHIL VOLK FOLK – ROCK – BLUES GROUP BEING FORMED Call 289-9374 (Alhambra, Cal.)

CLASSIFIEDS

BEAT is beginning a classified column, designed to buy, sell, find, lose, trade, give, announce, notify, warn, or say whatever you wish.

Ads will be accepted for just about anything, including
**for sale — wanted — pen pals
fan clubs — announcements — personals
lost guys and gals — special notices — everything else**

Prices are cheap! Only 20c a word for classifieds and a mere 10c a word for personal messages (from you to someone else without an item for sale, trade, etc. involved).

Now, what's a word? Well, it's the usual thing plus two exceptions: the city and the state count as only one word (Hollywood, California) and the number and street (6290 Sunset Blvd.) are only one word.

Send all advertisements (clearly printed or typed) along with the correct amount of money to:

Classifieds
BEAT Publications
6290 Sunset Blvd. Suite 504
Hollywood, California 90028

KRLA ARCHIVES

RECORDS FREE FROM RC®
You'll Flip at the ZZZIP in RC® Cola

while you swing to your favorite stars! RC and music, perfect partners for the perfect lift

TAKE 1 ALBUM FREE

For everyone you buy... with 6 cork liners or seals from R.C. bottle caps over 100 Capitol LP's available. Order as often as you wish. Nothing to join. Look for this display at your favorite store.

Here's your best way yet to save more on the records you want. In dollars-and-cents terms you get two albums that the Capitol Record Club sells for $3.98 each time you buy one. The savings are even bigger on stereo records! And there are no shipping charges to pay, nothing else to join or buy.

What's more, you choose from top albums by today's biggest stars, including the Beatles, David McCallum, Frank Sinatra, Lou Rawls, Buck Owens, Petula Clark, the Outsiders, Nancy Wilson, Dean Martin, Sonny James, the Beach Boys and many others.

OTHER FINE BRANDS: DIET-RITE®COLA, NEHI®BEVERAGES, PAR-T-PAK®BEVERAGES, UPPER 10®
"ROYAL CROWN" AND "RC" REG. U.S. PAT. OFF., ®1966 ROYAL CROWN COLA CO.

America's Pop Music NEWSpaper 25¢

KRLA Edition

BEAT

MAY 6, 1967

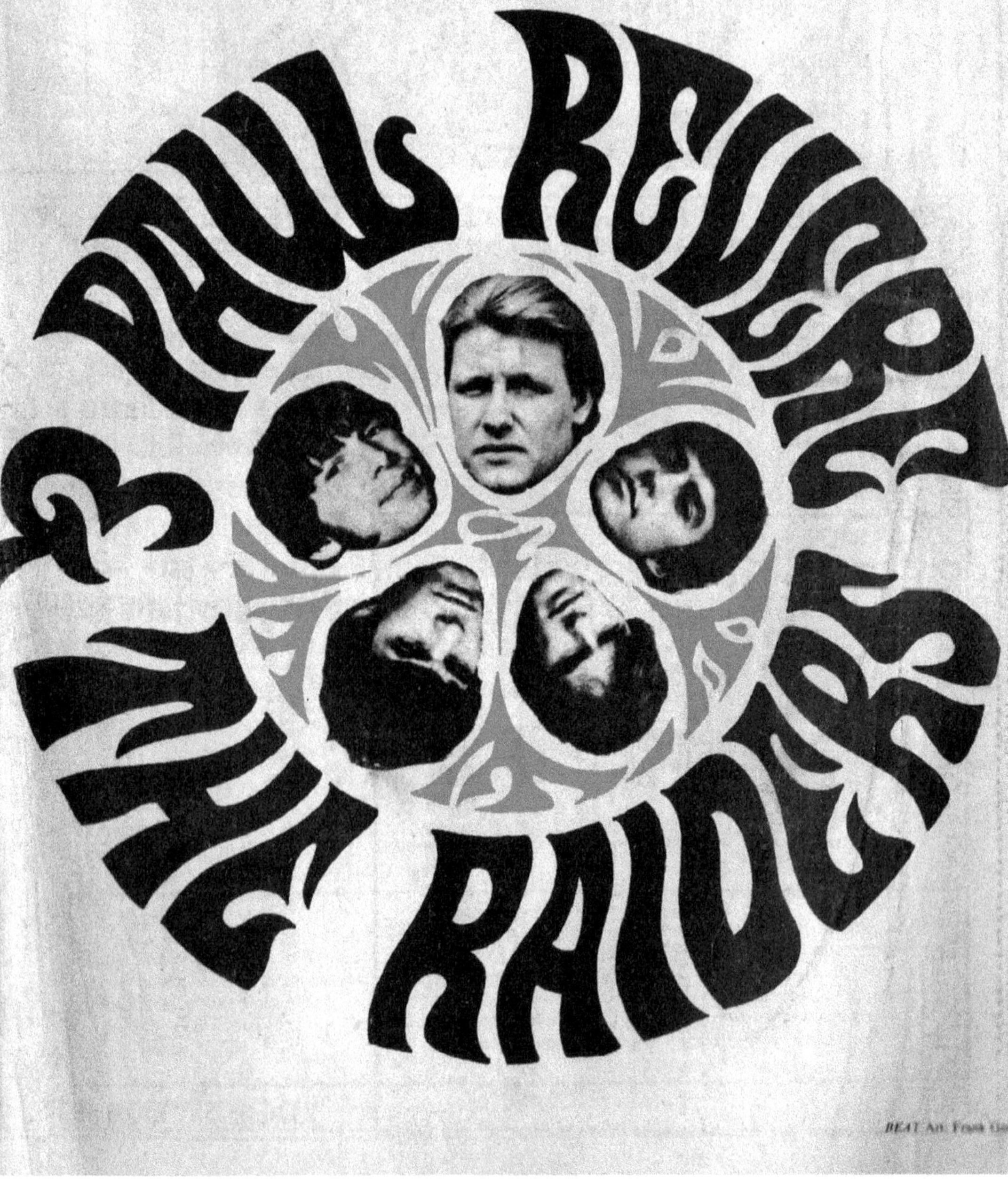
PAUL REVERE & THE RAIDERS

BEAT Art: Frank Gold

KRLA BEAT

Volume 3, Number 4 — May 6, 1967

DAVY JONES NIXS RUMORS

Rumors that Davy Jones is going to play the title role in the screen version of Lionel Bart's "Oliver" have been vigorously denied by the firm making the picture, Romulus Films. British newspapers have carried stories suggesting that Davy wants a vacation from the Monkees to accept the part.

A spokesman for Romulus said there is no truth whatsoever in these reports and that Davy's name has not even been mentioned. He called such speculation nonsense since Oliver is the role of a child.

Another rumor that the Monkees and the Beatles will split the bill in a "Battle of the Giants" concert has been strenuously denied by both Nems and Screen Gems.

Davy Jones released a single recently using Bob Dylan's "It Ain't Me Babe" backed with "Baby It's Me." Both tracks are from a previous Davy Jones LP.

MAMAS AND PAPAS DENY BREAK-UP

By Rochelle Reed

Are the Mamas and Papas breaking up?

That's the big question from Hollywood to London.

The reason stems from the fact that the group has lately gone their separate ways. John and Michelle have reportedly been spending almost all their time in Mexico. Denny is in the Virgin Islands and Cass, awaiting the birth of her child late this month, was living in England until a sudden return to the U.S.

BEAT contacted Dunhill Records for a straight-from-the-top answer to questions surrounding the top-ranked vocal group.

Mamas and Papas' producer Lou Adler denies all rumors indicating that the group is splitting, saying that "the Mamas and Papas are headlining the Monterey Pop Festival in June. That speaks for itself."

Furthermore, according to another Dunhill official, the group has just recut "Creeque Alley" and will issue it as the next single release. However, he admitted that only the instrumental tracks were actually re-done and the vocal cuts were simply spliced in places to make the song shorter. This did not necessitate attendance of the entire group at the studio.

But he added that the rumor of a break-up is absolutely untrue, indicating that the Mamas and Papas will make several personal appearances throughout the summer.

In addition, he cleared up part of the mystery surrounding the whereabouts of separate Mamas and Papas.

Cass is indeed back in Hollywood, having returned from London early this month. She is working on the Monterey Pop Festival Committee (along with Paul McCartney) and is "very happy."

Though her baby is due the last week in April, Cass will be well enough to perform at the Pop Festival in June.

Denny is vacationing in the Virgin Islands—St. Thomas Island to be exact—where the Mamas and Papas once lived.

John and Michelle are mainly sitting at home playing pool and writing songs. Their frequent sojourns to Mexico are twofold.

First, they have a Spanish maid, Esperanza, to whom they are very attached. Because she gets lonely in Hollywood, John and Michelle often take her to Mexico to visit friends and relatives.

Also, Michelle was raised in Mexico and speaks fluent Spanish. Many of John and Michelle's jaunts are to visit the people who raised her.

With that, Dunhill hopes the rumors of a Mamas and Papas break-up will be squashed, until the next time around anyway.

BEAT Photo: Dwight Carter
THE MAMAS AND PAPAS are saying the split just isn't so.

SONNY, CHER CAUSE PANIC IN HOUSTON

HOUSTON—The city of Houston has never seen anything like the tremendous welcome given pop's most popular duo, Sonny and Cher, when they landed by chartered Lear Jet for a promotional tour of Texas coinciding with the premiere of their movie, "Good Times," in Austin, Texas.

Five bands failed to drown out the screaming, waving fans, numbering over 13,000 who flocked to the airport to greet the Bonos. Near-panic forced airport security to rush in reserve officers to prevent the scene from turning into complete chaos and the crowds managed to all but completely shut-down regular commercial air traffic.

For their part, Sonny and Cher never once lost their cool in the face of the twisting, turning crowd. Instead they gratefully acknowledged their fans by signing autographs and shaking hands before being whisked away in a bannered caravan to a waiting press dinner. They were escorted by motorcycles and left the airport with no major difficulty.

CHAOS at the airport.

Paul McCartney In America; Beatles Finish 'Sgt. Pepper'

By Tony Barrow

On Monday, April 3, Paul McCartney flew from London to the West Coast of America, via Paris, accompanied by Mal Evans who is one of The Beatles' two remaining road managers. It was Mal who acted as Paul's traveling companion late last year when the Beatle took off for an unplanned vacation, driving down through France into Spain and, finally, making an on-the-spot decision to visit North Africa for a breif cine-safari in Kenya.

With Jane

The simple but important motive behind Paul's trip to America was to spend time with Jane Asher before and on her 21st birthday. His travel plans were cloaked in utter secrecy since Paul made it clear that he wanted to avoid publicity.

So that he could get away from London on time, The Beatles worked to an April 2 deadline on the final recording sessions for their next LP album. They didn't quite make it—while Paul was away extra orchestral accompaniment was added to a ballad track entitled "She's Leaving Home." Otherwise the main work remaining unfinished was that of re-balancing and finally mixing all the recordings, a long and intricate job involving a series of tape playback meetings between producer George Martin and The Beatles themselves.

Named

Now everything has been worked out and the album has a title ("Sgt. Pepper's Lonely Hearts Club Band") and a U.K. release date (early June). What's more, there is to be a most elaborate open-out album cover carrying, in addition to much highly decorative artwork, colorful new photographs of John, Paul, George and Ringo. For the photo session they hired an assortment of military gear from a theatrical costume agency in London!

The album takes its title from the song which will be heard on Side One Band One. As this issue of BEAT goes to press The Beatles have yet to decide the precise running order of the rest of the tracks but I can reveal exclusive details of at least a few recordings involved.

Ringo's track, one of the last to be written and recorded, started out with the title "Bad Finger Boogie" but this has been amended to "A Little Help From My Friends."

Two For George

George wrote and recorded two of his own original items during the 4-month series of sessions. One is to be held in the can for future use but the other, called "Within You And Without You," is amongst the "Sgt. Pepper" selections. Other tracks include "A Day In The Life" (which has full orchestral accompaniment supplied by no less than 41 top musicians), "Good Morning, Good Morning" (for which brass men from Sounds Inc. were brought in to produce the beefy R & B backing), "Being For The Benefit Of Mr. Kite" (with lyrics which John based upon the wording of an old theatrical poster he bought at an antique shop), "Rita" (all about a female traffic warden) and "When I'm Sixty-Four" (Paul's novelty specialty with a Vaudeville influence).

NEXT ISSUE — **SONNY & CHER** — **DON'T MISS IT!**

An Outasite Surprise — A Collector's Item

KRLA ARCHIVES

LETTERS TO THE EDITOR

THEM SPLIT; THANK FANS

Dear *BEAT*:
Great to hear Them still have many fans in America but unfortunately the group that toured there has been split up for some time.
As for myself, I'm going to New York to record for the Bang label as a solo artist and henceforth with my own bag shall emerge in due course.
I would appreciate it if you thanked the fans publicly for giving us such a wonderful time over there.
Hope to see you all in the near future when I go to the United States to promote my new record.
Van Morrison

PAUL/JANE RUN-AROUND

Dear *BEAT*:
I am practically dying because so many people (including untrustable magazines) have been saying that Paul McCartney and Jane Asher have broken up. I really just don't know what to believe any more.
I know she's in America touring with Old Vic and that he's busy in England. But, on the other hand, he could very well take time out to visit her.
Another rumor (or fact) is that if Paul has his way he will be married to Jane before this Spring. An article printed in the *Redwood City Tribune* said that Jane wasn't sure whether she would marry Paul. In The *BEAT*, a few issues ago, you stated that Jane said she loved Paul very deeply and that "he feels the same."
I'm tired of groping around in my own mind trying to find out the truth.
Please tell me what the real truth is and print it. You always seem to know what you're talking about and I'm sure I can trust your reply.
Yvonne Lowe

I'm afraid the only two who know the real truth, Yvonne, are Paul and Jane. Paul has remained mum on the subject but upon landing in the States Jane said: "I love Paul very deeply and he feels the same. I certainly should be very surprised indeed if I married anyone but Paul." However, during her stay in Los Angeles, Jane went to a private club several times with British actor, David Hemmings.
For the past few months, rumors have been flying around England that Paul and Jane have broken up. But Paul's recent visit to the U.S. to see Jane would seem to dispel those rumors!
The Editor

'SPREADERS' INFORMATION

Dear *BEAT*:
First of all, I want to congratulate you on the look of the "new" *BEAT*. It's fantabulous! Just keep those groovy articles coming.
Could you please tell me where I could get a copy of the Association's book, "Crank Your Spreaders?" Could I write straight to the company that puts it out? I tried a bookstore but they wouldn't order it.
Please have some articles on the Jefferson Airplane and the Buffalo Springfield. Both are great groups which deserve recognition.
Also, have more articles on the Association, Neil Diamond and the Turtles.
Thanks for reading this. Keep up the good work and LIVE!
"Trooper"

Send one dollar to Beechwood Music Corp., 1750 North Vine, Hollywood, California 90028 and they'll send you a copy of "Crank Your Spreaders."
The Editor

MICKY'S ADDRESS

Dear *BEAT*:
My name is Jeanine Ionata. I'm 12-years-old. Maybe you're not supposed to do this but I would like Micky Dolenz's address.
The reason is because he was born on the same day as I. I would also like to know what the membership card is for?
Jeanine Ionata

I'm sorry Jeanine, but we can't possibly give you Mickey's home address. We value our lives! I suggest that you write to him at 1334 North Beachwood Drive, Hollywood, California 90028.
The membership card is for their fan club and is obtainable at the same address.
The Editor

MONKEES

Dear *BEAT*:
Would you please send me a brochure about the Monkees and the prices of how much it would be to get an autographed picture of Davy Jones, Micky Dolenz, Mike Nesmith and Peter Tork. If it does not cost anything, would you please send me one?
George N. Brock

Send your request for an autographed Monkee picture to 1334 North Beechwood Drive, Hollywood, California 90028. Include a large stamped, self-addressed envelope for a faster reply. Unless Screen Gems has changed policy, there will be no cost for the picture.
The Editor

SPOONFUL CORRECTION

Dear *BEAT*:
Read your story "Power Behind The Lovin' Spoonful" in a recent issue of *BEAT*. Was very impressed with the story but I would like to point out some discrepancies. Artie Ripp did not find the Lovin' Spoonful. They were brought to the attention of Charles Koppelman and Don Rubin by their manager, Bob Cavallo, while they were appearing at The Night Owl Cafe in the Village. Charlie and Don became, and still are, the exclusive producers of the Lovin' Spoonful. You will note that on all Lovin' Spoonful recordings the legend "a product of Koppelman-Rubin Associates." They are released on the Kama Sutra label.
Dick Gersh

READER PROTESTS POP STARS JAGGER, JONES

Dear *BEAT*:
I'm writing in protest to a lot of people who support pop singers that don't do anything and the ones that don't have any talent.
The only reason that you publish the good stuff about them is that if you didn't the readers wouldn't buy your mag and you wouldn't make any money.
Why don't you print the truth about Mick Jagger, Peter Noone, Davy Jones, etc. They have no talent and you know it. What is our generation coming to when girls go for singers because they are good looking? To me they look like girls.
Even if I cut a few records of songs that I have written, made personal appearances, had a few good write-ups with pictures in your mag, I would be a sensation! Anyone would for that matter.
I don't think that it is fair for an untalented, tone-deaf, sick-looking person (such as Mick Jagger) to get a break and make millions doing nothing. What he does, to me, is nothing. He acts like he is so cool, but if he knew what he looked like when he performs he would run and hide.
Don't get me wrong. I love your mag but it gets to me when you give these people all of this recognition when it's really the guys in the back that do all the work.
Why don't you devote a couple of pages to drummers, guitarists, bass guitarists, etc., etc. This would be a change and it would be very interesting.
"Frenchie" Horn

RESENT CHARGE OF MONKEE IMITATION

Dear *BEAT*:
My group and I (and many others I'm sure) resent your "in" column stating that many groups are imitating the Monkees sound because of their success. Our group sounds exactly like the Monkees and we have been singing as a group for over two years. Since when is a sound exclusive?
We perform hits that the Monkees have done and some people have said we sing 'em better than the Monkees. At least we are not "electronically produced!"
You should hear Brian and I do "When Love Comes Knocking At Your Door" and my solo of "I Wanta Be Free." Also, the Monkees' hits—"I'm A Believer," "She," "Last Train To Clarksville" and "Let's Dance On"—we excel in.
Now that the Monkees are supposedly "in" we're being accused of using the Monkees' tracks and just mouthing the words! And actually we should sue the Monkees for stealing our sound, if we are getting technical!
Please print this as our side of the story. The groups that do sound like the Monkees are getting tired of being accused of it, especially since it isn't true.
Tony Walters of The Swiss Cheese

PRAISE

Dear *BEAT*:
Congratulations to Eden for the beautifully written history and comments on "rock and roll" titled "Into Every Gap Some Music Must Fall."
I'd like to tell you that from the first, The *BEAT* was outstanding and has developed into the best publication in the pop field. No sensationalism or Drug Store Psychology just excellent reporting, photography and a touch of insanity just for fun. I enjoy every inch of it.
Wonderful as you are, *BEAT*, I have a request. Could you start printing where to write to the artists, maybe at the end of the article on them? Please?
Keep progressing, *BEAT*, and may a curse fall upon me if I *ever* let my subscription run out.
Leona

GENE CLARK

Dear *BEAT*:
I am writing to see if you could give me information on where I could reach Gene Clark. His split was a shock but that's in the past. If you know an address where I can write him, please send it to me. I love the Byrds new record. Keep up the good work.
Carolyn Brown

Write to Gene Clark at 6121 Sunset Blvd., Hollywood, California 90028.
The Editor

Beat Publications, Inc.
Executive Editor .... Cecil L. Tuck
Publisher .... Gayle Tuck
Editor .... Louise Criscione

Staff Writers
Carol Deck — Bobby Farrow
Ron Koslow — Shirley Poston
Rochelle Reed

Contributing Writers
Tony Barrow — Sue Barry
Lawrence Charles — Eden
Tommy Hitchcock — Rochelle Sech
Bob Levinson — Jamie McCluskey, III

Photographers
Chuck Boyd — Dwight Carter

Advertising
Dick Jacobson — Jerry Loss
Winona Price — Dick Stricklin
Ron Woodlin

Business Manager .... Judy Felice
Subscriptions .... Nancy Arena

Distribution
Miller Freeman Publications
500 Howard Street, San Francisco, Calif.

The *BEAT* is published bi-weekly by BEAT Publications, Inc., editorial and advertising offices at 6290 Sunset Blvd., Suite 504, Hollywood, California 90028. U.S. bureaus in Hollywood, San Francisco, New York, Chicago and Nashville; overseas correspondents in London, Liverpool and Manchester, England. Sole price 25 cents. Subscription price: U.S. and possessions, $5 per year; Canada and foreign rates, $9 per year. Second class postage prepaid at Los Angeles, California.

the death of 'action'

1965-1967 the quiet blond leader... paul revere—the good looking singer... mark lindsay—the lovable bass "fang"... phil volk—the twin... drake levin—the insane drummer "smitty"... mike smith—the versatility of... steve alaimo—the first girl singer... linda scott—the hours of practice... action kids—paul mccartney who we thought... keith allison—beatle sounding... knickerbockers—the lookalikes... the robbs—the harpo horn... jim valley—second girl singer... tina mason—hooray for rowboat... tommy roe—the moody... hardtimes—up-coming group... don and the goodtimes—what can i say?
ayn kemling

KRLA ARCHIVES

POP FESTIVAL FOR MONTEREY

Many of the big names in contemporary music, including Paul McCartney have joined together to launch a three day pop festival in Monterey, California.

The Monterey International Pop Festival/'67 will be held June 16, 17 and 18 on the beachside fairgrounds.

Simon and Garfunkel, the Mamas and Papas, Johnny Rivers, the Beach Boys, the Byrds, the Buffalo Springfield and Jefferson Airplane will perform without fee.

Paul McCartney, along with Donovan, Andrew Oldham, John Phillips, Paul Simon, Johnny Rivers and producer Terry Melcher, is on the Board of Governors.

McCartney has spent part of his time in the U.S. in telephone conversation about the Festival with Ben Shapiro, director of the event.

A total of $40,000 has been invested so far by the Mamas and Papas, Simon and Garfunkel, Johnny Rivers and producer Lou Adler to give the Festival working capital.

The event will be a non-profit corporation with proceeds going towards a pop foundation. The board of governors, which Paul serves on, will decide how to use the money for the advancement of pop. The board will also decide which groups will perform on the concert bill.

The festival will open with a show on Friday night. Two more will be held on Saturday and on Sunday afternoon. Ravi Shankar will perform. The festival will close Sunday night with a concert by the big names in the business. Seminars and workshops will also be held.

Davy Draft Upsets U.K.

LONDON: "Dear President Johnson: We are very much against writing you this letter but it seems necessary because you plan to draft Davy Jones of the Monkees." It goes on. "We know maybe Davy won't protest but if you don't draft him, he won't have to."

It is a letter, signed by 2,000 fans and handed to the U.S. Embassy in London by a crowd of 150 angry teens. One placard read, "Singer not soldier, Monkee not guerilla."

Said an 11-year-old girl, "It's all very well to say get out there and fight, but he's too small. He only weighs about eight stones, eight pounds (120 lbs.) and what would the Monkees do without him?"

MOVIE OFFER FOR TWIGGY

HOLLYWOOD — British model Twiggy is negotiating with a film company here in hopes of starring in a movie titled "Scamp," the story of a girl who masquerades as a boy on her way to stardom, then finds it difficult to reveal the hoax.

"Twiggy is the only girl around who is able to get away with looking like a boy," said writer-producer Joseph Stefano. "At first we were stumped on whom to cast in the role but we feel Twiggy is perfect for the part."

Discussions will continue when Twiggy flys into Los Angeles. The movie is slated to begin shooting this fall in Hollywood and London.

Meanwhile, the world's most talked about model also completed details for world release of her first single. It will appear on racks in France as an album.

'Mrs. Brown' Director Signed

The director of Academy Award-nominated films "Auntie Mame" and "The Music Man" has been signed to head the next major film for Herman's Hermits.

Morton Da Costa will direct "Mrs. Brown, You've Got A Lovely Daughter," a full-length color production to be released by MGM.

The movie is described as "a hip, Walt Disney-type of comedy-drama with music" and deals with the dog-racing business in England.

Herman and his Hermits will have double duties in the film, with acting roles for each member of the group as well as opportunities for introducing a number of new songs.

Herman will report May 1 for the first day of shooting at MGM's British studios.

Director Da Costa is currently in London for conferences, including one with author-composer Trevor Peacock, who wrote a screenplay for "Mrs. Brown" for his own original story, and also composed the Hermits' hit song of the same title.

Agent & Avalon In Suit

LOS ANGELES — Singer Frankie Avalon has been charged with being "ungrateful" in a suit with his agent Robert P. Marcucci.

However, Avalon claims his agent is attempting to keep a contract that is "unconscionable, unfair and unjust."

The two men are currently involved in a suit and counter suit over a contract which both men say neither side read before signing.

Avalon says the contract was dated September 18, 1961, and was made for only three years. Marcucci says it was for five years with an option on five more years. However, a clerical error completely left out any termination date, and since neither side read the contract before signing it, the termination date was never decided.

Marcucci is asking the 26-year-old singer for $392,000 in damages in addition to a ruling that the agreement was to run for two more years.

Marcucci's attorney says that Marcucci "discovered, created and put Avalon where he is today. My client took this raw talent and developed it. This is a case of ingratitude."

In countering, Avalon cited numerous complaints about the way Marcucci alledgedly handled his business investments. He stated that he once had his salary attached while singing at New York's Copacabana because Marcucci had not repaid a $15,000 loan which he had signed for the agent.

Mia Sends A Taxi To Frank

LONDON — Poor Frank. It's bad enough that Mia has been in London for the last couple of months filming "A Dandy In Aspic." But now the London press has revealed what Mia is sending him as a present. Which is, by the way, a London taxicab.

The Sinatra bride has been getting raves all over the Kingdom, has been hailed as the "1968 girl," and some claim she has the most beautiful eyes in the world. Her movie studio also got into the act by sending out fetching pictures of a sheet-clad Mia from scenes in her movie.

Does Mia think Frank minds it — all the fuss, bother and long absences?

"There would be no point in having a wife who stayed at home and and cooked his spaghetti for him. Any number of women could have done that," she said.

Don't Miss It . . .
SONNY & CHER
(SOUVENIR EDITION)
Next Issue of BEAT

Street Singer Wins Grammy

When "Blues In The Street" was voted a Grammy Award by the record industry recently as the best folk recording of 1966, few people realized the story behind the song. And even fewer people knew the history of the singer.

The disc was recorded on a street in Nashville, Tenn. by Cortelia Clark, a 60-year-old Negro who has been blind since 1948. He's a member of the legion of men who sit or stand on street corners in every city, pencil cup in one hand or on the ground, singing and playing the old songs, the bluesy songs, literally "sing for your supper" music.

Clark's particular sidewalk seat is in front of a dime store on Fifth Avenue in Nashville. He sells shopping bags rather than pencils, and on a good week, he makes nearly $20.

When RCA taped him playing his guitar, they didn't move him into a studio. Instead, they captured Clark on tape with city noise, his rhythmic cry, "Shopping bags!" and the sound of money falling into his tin cup.

For his efforts, Clark received $940 — nearly a year's income. His record has to sell 10,000 before royalties begin to come in.

Today, Clark has spent the $940 and is back to singing on Fifth Avenue. "It's as if," said one citizen, "the city is back to normal."

MONTREAL — Hundreds of teens greeting Elvis Presley's guitar. They even stayed during the presentation to the U.S. Pavilion at Expo '67.

KRLA ARCHIVES

HAPPENING

TEENS ARE BEGINNING TO TURN OFF—NOT ON

NEW YORK—With drug usage a very real and very terrifying problem among today's younger generation, the question is no longer how to turn *on* but rather how to turn *off* the drug users.

All the way from the Federal Government to three ex-addicts, the problem of drugs is being explored and new theories tested.

The newly-formed Bureau of Drug Abuse Control has come to the conclusion that the biggest problem is the lack of communication between the old and the new generations. The minute the older generation begins moralizing against the use of drugs, the younger generation completely shuts its ears and, many times, turns to drugs as a sort of cool rebellion against the established society.

Consequently, the Bureau is attempting to solve this aspect of the drug problem by obtaining the services of such "idols" as Paul Newman to narrate films like "Bennies and Goofballs," which is now circulating among schools all across the nation.

But an even more effective method is utilized in the films which show teen addicts themselves telling of their life with drugs. Such a film is "Hooked," which shows one teen admitting that she stole her uncle's heart pills to satisfy her craving for drugs.

"Narcotics, Why Not?", is a documentary drug film which features a young teen sniffing glue and another addict being pulled from a car he smashed while under the influence of drugs.

High schools, universities and colleges are suddenly awaking to the enormous problem of drug addiction and are eagerly snatching up anti-drug literature and all the anti-drug films they can get their hands on.

In Greenwich Village another approach is being effectively used. Three young ex-addicts have formed an organization called Encounter to combat the addiction they once suffered through. Their biggest method is group therapy added to the fact that "we have been down that road too."

As Ray Charles, who is himself a cured addict, said: "Jail ain't no place for nobody." Young adults who agree with Charles are now turning off instead of on.

GO SMOKE A CANCER

PORTLAND—There is a new cigarette on the market, one designed to help smokers kick the habit. "It's no gag," declares Howard Steinbach, a Portland pharmacist who introduced the cigarettes with the brand name of Cancer.

In one month 3,100 cartons of Cancers have been sold. Promos for the cigarettes call it "the country's most whispered-about cigarette" and posters show a smoker golfing in a cemetery along with the phrase "This Is Cancer Country."

Steinbach believes that the biggest sales are from non-smokers who buy Cancers for the smoking members of their family. So far, the results have been rather good. After smoking a Cancer, a person is sorely tempted to never smoke another cigarette!

TRINI NAMED MAN OF YEAR

DALLAS—Trini Lopez has been honored by his hometown by being named Dallas' Man Of The Year. Trini was presented with his award at a special luncheon held at the Adolphus Hotel while hundreds of his friends and relatives sat applauding.

It was a particularly proud moment for his parents because it was they who demanded that Trini rise above the slum section of Dallas known as "Little Mexico" where he was born and raised. This Trini has done, mostly with the help of his parents. His career began because his father bought him a $12 guitar when he was in his early teens. That guitar led Trini to local Dallas clubs and finally to Reprise Records where he's now one of their hottest artists and the Man of Year.

DICK CLARK SIGNS MONKEES FOR EAST

LOS ANGELES—Dick Clark Productions has announced that they will promote a series of three concerts by the Monkees at the Forest Hills Tennis Station in New York.

Dick Clark will host the shows which are set for July 14, 15 and 16. The Monkees will do one show per night in the open-air 14,000-plus seat arena, which will be scaled to gross over $300,000 for the three days.

Just in case of rain, Clark has also rented the Stadium on the nights of July 17, 18 and 19.

'BATMAN' DROPPED

LONDON—Holy Batman! Britain is through with Batman and Robin! It's true, the British television viewers have had quite enough and two television companies are discontinuing the series because of low ratings.

ABC-TV, which serves viewers on the commercial channel in the Midlands and North of England, is replacing "Batman" with a spy series. Rediffusion, which transmits in the London area on weekdays, has announced that the caped wonder and his sidekick "will be gone by the summer." They have not commented on "Batman's" replacement.

Teen-Oriented Show To Air

PHILADELPHIA—May is bringing a new teen television show to the nation's viewers by way of the CBS-TV network. Only this show will not feature any dancers, singers or comedians.

"Trial By Another Jury" will allow teens from different religions, races and financial standings to act as the jury in criminal cases based on actual court proceedings.

Shirl Conway will moderate the series being produced for the CBS owned stations' Community Affairs program exchange.

SEGAL INKS TO RECORD

NEW YORK—George Segal, the actor who first received national attention with his role in "The New Interns" and who was this year nominated for an Academy Award for his performance in "Who's Afraid of Virginia Woolf," has been signed to an exclusive recording contract with Phillips Records.

Segal's first album for the label is "The Yama Yama Man." Wonder if George will let his hair grow out?

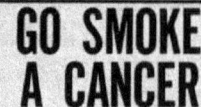

TRINI LOPEZ RECEIVES the Man of the Year award from Neal Hall.

... GEORGE SEGAL

PEOPLE ARE TALKING ABOUT how much the **Buckingham's** "Don't You Care" sounds like a **Neil Diamond** song ... "Somethin' Stupid" being a million-seller soon, probably marking the first time a father-daughter team has won a Gold Record ... Uni Records will release the soundtrack from "The Privilege," the controversial **Paul Jones/Jean Shrimpton** movie about a pop singer.

... **Ray Charles** being on a nine-month tour ... the sharp increase in the sale of bananas ... the **Beach Boys** going into movies and television ... whether or not the **Turtles** are happy together and will make no more group changes ... when, or if, the **Monkees** will embark on an extended cross-country personal appearance tour of the U.S. ... who the **Parade** are ... how much soul the pop charts have lately ... the **Mama's** and Papa's furious at the reporter who wrote they were splitting and how funny they think the thing about BEAT in Post was ... **Lou Rawls'** "Dead End Street" being paved in gold—now ... how many groups have taken to sounding like the Association and why the Association weren't on "The Smothers Brothers Show" they were scheduled to be on.

... **Jane Asher's** remarks in Dallas not setting too well with Beatle fans ... how long the "love-ins" and "be ins" are going to last ... whether or not **Fang** will really leave the **Raiders** ... when the **Spencer Davis Group** is going to come Stateside ... **Engelbert Humperdinck???** ... what a hit Petula Clark will be in the movies ... what would happen if one of the **Supremes'** wigs fell off during a performance

... why **Dusty Springfield** is not as big here as she deserves to be ..

San Francisco taking over as the happening place ... **Bobby Elliott's** illness being a tough break for the **Hollies** ... whatever happened to the **Kinks** ... the trend toward shorter hair among pop artists ... the **Nitty Gritty Dirt Band** finally going nationwide ... when, or if, the **Jefferson Airplane** are going to get a smash

... **Purify Brothers** busy shakin' a tail feather ... the return of **Fats Domino** ... how many people are now going to claim that they thought up the name "Flower Children" ... the **Montfort Singers**, all of whom attend the Montfort Seminary in St. Louis, putting out an album entitled "There'll Come A Day" ... how happy **Joey Bishop** is that **Johnny Carson** is leaving "The Tonight Show"

... whether or not **Mick Jagger** and **Marianne Faithfull** will get married and deciding that they probably won't ... the **Who** possibly touring Stateside with the **Hermits** this summer but not counting on it due to work permit trouble ... **Paul's** visit to America not really surprising to anyone ... how many girls are going to get their heads shaved like **Mia Farrow** and **Twiggy**

... a spokesman for Frank Sinatra saying that if they booked him into London and charged $25 a ticket they'd sell-out in 24 hours ... how funny it is that several male singers have recorded "Sherry" from the Broadway play ... how long **Aretha Franklin** has waited for a hit and how great it is that she finally has one ... what a gas it was to see **Brenda Holloway** on stage playing a violin

... **Frankie Laine** back on the pop charts ... how much the **Fifth Dimension** sound like the **Mamas and Papas** ... how many people don't know that the **Ed Ames** of "My Cup Runneth Over" is the Indian on "Daniel Boone" and was one of the Ames Brohers ... the surprise Dick Clark has up his sleeve for next season's television viewers ... where **Tommy James and the Shondells** are—besides high in the charts ... when the **Yardbirds** are coming back ... **Lawrence Welk** still being unable to get on the pop charts despite the fact that he recorded "The Beat Goes On."

KRLA ARCHIVES

ON THE BEAT BY LOUISE CRISCIONE

Good news for you Monkee fans this week. It looks as if Screen Gems and Columbia have finally worked out an agreement whereby the Monkees will make a movie. The deal supposedly is that Columbia will be allowed to make a Monkee movie if Screen Gems receives exclusive rights to turn "The Professionals" into a television series! The theory of "give a little, get a little" put to good use.

Award For Brian

Nice honor for chief Beach Boy, Brian Wilson. He was named the first American winner of Denmark's "Ekstrabladet's Beat Pris," the annual musical award given to the producer of the Best Foreign Recording. Brian copped the prize for "Good Vibrations."

Had to laugh at the way the press has already started the "Monkees to Split?" stories. Never takes some people long, does it? It's really amazing how a half-quote can be twisted and turned around 'til the reader doesn't know which end is up. Micky can say that the Monkees "have changed" and by the time you read the story you're convinced that the change will be in personnel rather than the intended musical change. Anyway, the Monkees are not even *thinking* of breaking up – so don't waste your mind worrying about it.

...MIKE NESMITH

According to Jeff Beck's publicist, Jeff and his new group broke the existing Rolling Stone record at the Marquee Club in England. Quite a switch from Jeff's debut which ended in his dropping out of the tour. He recently spent time in Los Angeles and then flew back to Britain to open at the Marquee.

Prejudiced Press?

Record World recently printed an article on the strict segregation policy of practically all fan publications. It set me to thinking and, sure enough, Negro recording artists are seldom, if ever, featured in typical teen publications. Of course, I distinctly remember *Seventeen* once featuring an interview with Bill Cosby. But I wonder who these publications think buy records by the Four Tops, the Supremes, the Temptations, James Brown, Martha and the Vandellas, Lou Rawls and Ray Charles?

In Hollywood, the club openings which habitually draw the biggest celebrity turn-outs are those of the Motown artists. On any given night the Four Tops or Miracles or Temptations are playing a club date, the lines run for blocks. Obviously, then, these artists are popular. Why, then, the lack of articles on Negro artists? Couldn't be a bit of prejudice left over from a hundred years ago, could it?

At least one of Herman's Hermits' dates for their summer Stateside tour has been booked. The group will play the Ohio State Fair in September. This will make the second-time-around the Fair for the Hermits, who played it last year with Perry Como. The tour will last for six weeks and will probably end in Hawaii, though the entire schedule depends on when they complete filming on "Mrs. Brown You've Got A Lovely Daughter." Shooting should begin in England on May 8 and last for approximately ten weeks.

Rascals To England

The Young Rascals are due to arrive in England on May 17 for a two-week tour and the Lovin' Spoonful are set to hit Britain in August. Originally, the Spoonful were to tour England during May but have now dropped the date back to August.

I'm still wondering if that's not the Four Seasons singing "I Got Rhythm" by the Happenings. If it isn't (which, supposedly, of course, it isn't) it certainly sounds like their twins! A good record, though, so why kick?

...YOUNG RASCALS

There is still no word on whether or not the Rolling Stones will tour Stateside this summer, though insiders believe Stone management will wait until Mick and Keith make their court appearance before deciding one way or the other.

...THE HOLLIES and Jackie DeShannon met at a party in Hollywood.

HOLLIES BOW OUT OF TOUR DUE TO ELLIOTT

The Hollies bowed out of a package tour of Australia and New Zealand which includes Eric Burdon and the Animals and Paul and Barry Ryan. The Troggs, whose biggest hit is "Wild Thing" are substituting.

The Hollies' drummer, Bobby Elliott, returned to the group after a long illness but suffered a relapse under the strain of performing. The Hollies have decided to pass up the tour rather than use a replacement drummer. They still hope to go to Japan this month.

Meanwhile the Troggs' new single, "Give It To Me," has fallen under the censor's ax for off-color lyrics. Troggs' manager, Larry Page, has withdrawn the tune and will rush-release "Any Way That You Want Me" instead.

THE WHO ARE IN U.S.

The Who, one of Britain's top pop groups, arrived on U.S. shores for a list of appearances they hope will boost their popularity with American audiences. They appeared on New York disc jockey, Murray the K's, special show in New York and are trying to arrange television appearances on Ed Sullivan and CBS Reports.

The group's spokesman, Peter Townshend, compared performing in this country favorably with that abroad. The Who are paid more for appearances in the U.S., he said, because many British youngsters can't afford the three or four dollar price usually charged for tickets in this country.

The Who have several albums and singles releases. "A Quick One," is the title of their latest LP and their newest single is "Happy Jack" on the Decca label.

Roger Daltry, lead singer; Keith Moon, drummer; John Entwhistle, bass player; and Townshend, guitarist, all compose the groups material.

Fats Rocks 50's Fans

LONDON – New Orleans pianist, Fats Domino, a great pioneer of the 50's rock 'n' roll boom, had the audience swinging on their feet when he made his European debut at Brian Epstein's Saville Theater here.

Rock fans who have grown up knowing only the Beatles and the Monkees probably never heard of Fats Domino whose last English hit was "Country Boy" back in 1960. But the pop fans of the 50's were still loyal enough to pack the hall for the entertainer's week-long engagement.

A sliver of history was recreated when Domino opened the concert with his classic, "Blueberry Hill" which received an enthusiastic ovation. Soon the audience was shouting requests to the stage for every song Domino had ever recorded.

He remained seated at the piano during the show. His one concession to showmanship, was at the wind up of the concert when, in a sparkling finale he pushed his piano across the stage with his knees without missing a note.

Gold Disc To Raiders

Paul Revere and the Raiders, former regulars on Dick Clark's "Where the Action Is," have won a gold record from the RIAA for their Columbia LP, "Midnight Ride." Earlier this year, the group earned their first gold record for million plus sales of their album, "Just Like Us."

FRIENDS THE SECRET IS OUT!

JBL BRINGS BACK THE MENDELSOHN QUINTETTE CLUB OF BOSTON YEA YEA!

NOW YOU MAY GET J. B. LANSING'S NEWEST RELEASE...THE EXPLOSIVE, UNCENSORED STORY OF "THE MENDELSOHN QUINTETTE CLUB OF BOSTON", AS NARRATED BY IRVING MENDELSOHN!

A JBL ORIGINAL

You've cherished their records ..."Meet me at the Liberty Bell Sarah, 'cause you're a ding-a-ling"..."The Boulder Colorado Rock"..."These Socks"... and many more. You've thronged to their stand-up and sit-down concerts...you've traveled miles to their appearances at corner stone layings, super market galas, quilting bee hops, AND NOW you can read the true, little-known facts about your beloved quintette club. You won't be happy until you've read it...so get it now!

MAILED FREE!!!
On receipt of 25¢ for handling.
Fill in and mail this coupon.

COUPON
Enclosed is 25¢ for handling charges. Please send me the story of "THE MENDELSOHN QUINTETTE CLUB OF BOSTON."

Name _____
Address _____
City _____ State _____

JAMES B. LANSING SOUND, INC.
3249 CASITAS AVE., LOS ANGELES, CALIFORNIA 90039
(BEAT)

KRLA ARCHIVES

HEY, HEY...

We're the Monkees

and We're at

At cut-rate prices, too!

KRLA ARCHIVES

across the board

Making The News

FROM THE EDITOR...

Beginning with this issue, I'll be letting you in on a little of the behind the scenes *BEAT* activities. How we came up with the pictures and stories, why we chose the artist or group featured on our cover, entertainers who dropped by to visit, etc.

Our Paul Revere and the Raiders cover was designed exclusively for *The BEAT* by Frank Goad, Graphics Art instructor at one of the nation's leading universities.

We felt it was high time the Raiders were our cover guests since their success in the pop field has won for them the distinction of being one of America's top musical groups.

The Raiders are one of the busiest groups in the nation, without exception. They're continually touring the country (always to sell-out crowds), guesting on the top variety shows ("Ed Sullivan," "The Smothers Brothers") and when they finally get a week off they spend it recording!

There is one disconcerting rumor which is floating around to the effect that following Harpo's example, Fang will shortly be leaving the Raiders — possibly even before they reach New York for the Sullivan Show. However, no one in the Raider camp will admit to knowing anything about Fang's alleged desire to leave the group. We'll see.

Eric Burdon, Dick Clark and Twiggy drew full-page spreads this issue. Eric because he is one of the hottest and most controversial figures on the pop scene; Dick Clark because he, perhaps more than any other individual, has influenced the popular music field; and Twiggy because she is the most talked-out, written-about and photographed model in the world.

In the next issue of *BEAT* we will be featuring a special four-page Sonny and Cher spread tracing their success all the way from their first record to their second movie.

Also, the next *BEAT* will contain an interview with the fabulous Righteous Brothers in which they answer the charges that they've left the teen market behind them in order to hit the adult clubs.

Before I sign off, I'd like to remind you that *The BEAT* belongs to you and any suggestions, criticisms (or praise!) you may have regarding the paper will be read and carefully considered.

Louise Criscione

ONCE 'ROUND THE WORLD

DALLAS — "This award has to mean something to me," said Trini Lopez upon receiving Dallas' Man of the Year Award. "I just interrupted a tour of one-nighters to make it here. And at my-going price, I don't think I can afford myself." Trini received the award at the Adolphus Hotel where he once mopped the floors in his job as an assistant to his father, the hotel's custodian. Mr. Lopez, Sr. is now retired and living in a $50,000 home purchased by his son, Trini.

DENVER — When Paul McCartney flew into town to help celebrate girlfriend, Jane Asher's, 21st birthday, neither he nor Jane would talk to the press. Denver reporters consequently tagged the Beatle a "shaggy snob." Jane, however, did tell newsmen in Dallas: "I certainly don't object to people having children when they're not married and I think it's quite sensible to live together before you're married. But I guess the idea of marriage is just ingrained in me."

LOS ANGELES — Frank Sinatra has contributed $25,000 to the Motion Picture Relief Fund. Sinatra's money will be used for construction of additional medical, housing and recreational facilities at the Country House and Hospital in Woodland Hills, California.

WASHINGTON D.C. — Controversy is brewing around the proposed John F. Kennedy Center for the Performing Arts. Groundbreaking ceremonies were held for the $55 million center over two years ago but construction has yet to begin. The conflict allegedly revolves around the New York sophisticates led by Jackie Kennedy and the Washingtonians, led by Dillon Ripley, head of the Smithsonian Institute. The New Yorkers would like the Center to showcase the nation's great dancers, singers and musicians while the Washingtonians wish the Center to develop local talent of its own. The disagreement between the two sides has caused the opening date to be pushed all the way back to late 1969.

LONG ISLAND — The Four Seasons, who seem to come up with hit record after hit record, recently played to a sell-out, standing-room-only crowd at the Westbury Music Fair Theatre in Westbury, Long Island.

BURBANK — Warner Brothers/Reprise Records has just enjoyed its biggest sales week ever, with the singles sales figure of 679,000. The Sinatra's Nancy and Frank, helped tremendously with their "Somethin' Stupid" which has sold over 850,000 to date. Bill Cosby added his share with his million-selling "Wonderfulness" album and his latest album, "Revenge," which has already reached the 266,000 mark with its first shipment.

HOLLYWOOD — Leonard Nimoy, the star of the NBC-TV series, "Star Trek," has signed a recording contract with Dot Records. The actor has already completed his first album for the label, "Leonard Nimoy Presents Mr. Spock's Music From Outer Space."

NEW YORK — While his father and sister enjoy the Reprise record label, Frank Sinatra Jr. has signed a recording contract with RCA Victor. He has cut a single and is expected to begin work on an album in the near future.

HOLLYWOOD — Robie Porter, a huge star in his native Australia, is aiming at becoming an even bigger star in the U.S. He has signed with MGM and has recorded "I Have Got Nothing Better To Do" from the Sandra Dee movie, "Dr. You've Got To Be Kidding." Robie is also going into the movies and a possible television series. "I'd like to do a comedy with real people," says Robie, "the kind of acting which Steve McQueen and David Hemmings do. The kind Bill Holden has done for years."

CHICAGO — Bob Cummings will star in "Generation" at the Drury Lane Theatre for two months beginning August 15. His two co-stars will be his daughters, Melinda and Patricia, working with their father for the first time.

The top newsmaker of the month is the 17-year-old, virtually figureless model who has made the cover of practically every publication in the world, Twiggy. Latest to honor the British model were the Seagulls who have recorded a song entitled "Twiggs." The group sang their honor to Twiggy while she was in New York — Twiggy's comment: "I love it."

Jonathan King, who first became known in the U.S. for his "Everyone's Gone To The Moon," is on a one-man campaign to discourage the taking of any form of drugs. His latest record, "Round And Round," is a clear and definite put-down of drugs. King is currently in the United States to "convince druggies and psychedelic drop-outs" that drug-taking means early death. King predicts "an era when all non-addictive drugs, which, incidentally, means physically non-addictive, are as constantly imbibed as alcohol. The only way to stop it is by logical argument."

Judy Michaud and Frank Vander Puil, both 17, have been chosen the winners in the 1967 "American Bandstand Dance Contest." Judy is from Burbank, California and Frank is from Pasadena, California. The couple will receive valuable merchandise prizes for being chosen winners by studio audience applause.

Montreal's Expo 67 put its very best and most entertaining foot forward for the $100-a-plate formal ball saluting the debut of the fair. Nominees for the Quebec Heart Foundation's "Entertainer of the Century" include Barbra Streisand, Julie Andrews, Sammy Davis Jr., Judy Garland, Jimmy Durante, Lena Horne, Danny Kaye, Joan Crawford, Frank Sinatra and Maurice Chevalier. Special awards are being made to performers in the television and recording medias. Nominees for these awards are Dean Martin, Jackie Gleason, Ed Sullivan, Perry Como, Andy Williams, Steve Lawrence, Eydie Gorme, Connie Francis, Charles Aznavour and Ella Fitzgerald.

The clean-cut "Andy Williams Show" and the not-quite-so-straight laced "Dean Martin Show" both took extreme exception to the gown which Shirley Bassey chose to wear on the shows. The sequined floor-length gown featured a halter connected to the skirt of the dress by a mere thread. Bare skin dominated the outfit and consequently producers of both shows forbade Miss Bassey's appearance unless she changed clothes — which she did. Shrugging her shoulders, Shirley admitted that she had worn the dress on British television and "nobody had any complaints."

Lynda Bird Johnson, President Johnson's 23 year old daughter, turned into something of a bomb with her third major effort for "McCalls." The article, entitled "Glossary of Campus Slang — How To Tell What in the World the Younger Generation Is Talking About," featured such "new" expressions as "cool it," "bug out" and "put on." Lynda did, however, turn up at least one expression which is relatively new ("Turn your E.B. up to Mother") since electric blankets are a comparatively recent invention.

Neil Diamond seems to be making a separate career out of penning hit records for other artists. No one can deny that he was an enormous help to the Monkees via his compositions "I'm A Believer" and "A Little Bit Me, A Little Bit You." Neil's latest "helping hand" was to Ronnie Dove in the form of a song entitled "My Babe," which Neil wrote and produced. The next step for Neil is movies.

The Sinatras apparently cannot lose. With both daddy Frank and daughter Nancy continually making the charts, it was only a matter of time before they combined their talents on a single. The result, "Somethin' Stupid," sold over 850,000 copies as of this week and is well on its way to the magic million mark. Nancy also has two other songs on the nation's charts, "Summer Wine" and "Love Eyes." And all because those boots started walking.

The perennial folk-favorites, Peter, Paul and Mary triumphed again. This time at New York's Carnegie Hall. With the obviously delighted audience joining in, Peter, Paul and Mary went through their biggest hits, "Puff The Magic Dragon," "If I Had A Hammer" and "Blowin' In The Wind." But what actually makes the trio so undyingly popular is their unique ability to draw material from every part of the world and from just about every era the world has known.

Ahmet Ertegun, Atlantic Records' President, flew to the West Coast to confer with some of the label's "old" artists as well as signing new talent. Ertegun met with Keely Smith to discuss the singer's debut album with the label; Bobby Darin regarding the promotion for his latest album, "Inside Out"; Sonny and Cher to work out a national campaign for the Sonny and Cher soundtrack album from their movie, "Good Times."

WHERE THEY ARE

PAUL REVERE AND THE RAIDERS
April 22, Cheyenne, Wyoming, Auditorium; April 25, Roswell, New Mexico, The Crater; April 28, San Diego, California; April 29, San Jose, California; April 30, New York, "Ed Sullivan Show."

THE SEEDS
April 17-24, Hollywood, recording; April 28, Honolulu, Hawaii, April 29, Hollywood, Hollywood Bowl.

THE BEACH BOYS
May 2, Dublin, Ireland; May 3, Belfast, Ireland; May 5, London, England; May 6, Birmingham, England; May 7, Manchester, England; May 9, Glasgow, Scotland; May 10, Edinburgh, Scotland.

MOTHERS OF INVENTION
Garrick Theatre, New York, thru September 4.

BILL COSBY
To Europe with co-star Bob Culp for filming of next season's "I Spy."

THE ROBBS
Thru May 4, promotional tour of the East and Midwest.

TEDDY NEELY FIVE
May 9-27, Los Angeles, Cocoanut Grove.

THE MANDALA
April 25, 26, 27, The Scene, New York; May 2, 3, 4, Westchester, New York.

BAJA MARIMBA BAND
April 29, Lafayette, Indiana, Purdue University; Atlanta, Georgia; Mobile, Alabama; New Orleans, Lousiana; Lafayette, Louisiana; Knoxville, Tennessee; Greensboro, North Carolina; May 7, Charlotte, North Carolina.

KRLA ARCHIVES

Paul Revere And The Raiders

Paul Revere and the Raiders are our featured artists in this issue of *The BEAT*. We feel that they are truly an outstanding group, one which has made a name and a future for themselves, beginning at the bottom and working their way to the top.

Their records (both albums and singles) are consistently best-sellers and their list of sell-out concerts and standing-room-only audiences prove that you feel the Raiders are one of the hottest and most popular groups in America.

They're currently on tour and the pictures which we have included here are exclusive *BEAT* photos taken on their present tour and printed for the first time anywhere. Hope you like 'em.

The Editor

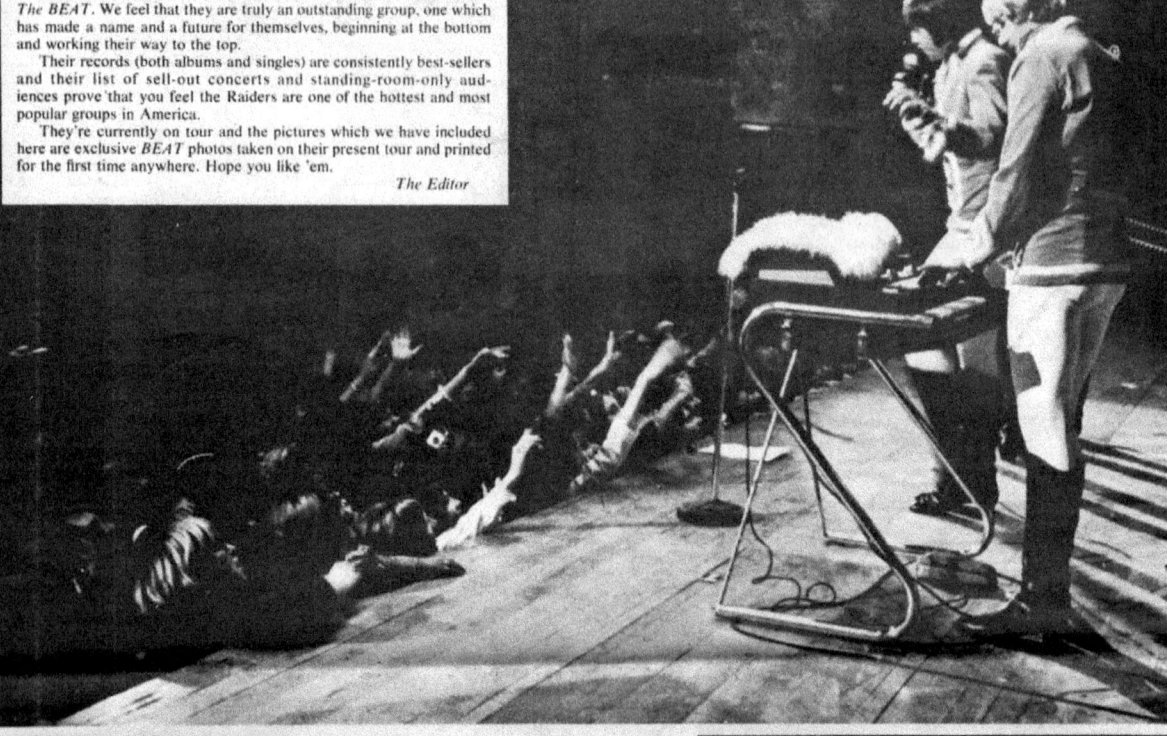

The Many Moods of The Chief Raider

HARPO TELLS REASON FOR LEAVING RAIDERS

Jim "Harpo" Valley – the happiest Raider and love's devout apostle – has recently made the most important decision of his young life. After spending exactly one fun-filled year with Paul, Mark, Fang and Smitty, Harpo decided to give up the Raider life and strike out on his own.

As he put it, "I've loved every minute of working with the Raiders. It's been a great year . . . I've learned so very much and made so very many wonderful friends; but, now I feel that the time has come for me to go out on my own. Though I dig the Raiders' sound, my own compositions and style of singing are in a different sphere."

To cite an example, the name of Harpo's new music publishing company is "Gentle Mind." The tunes he writes are more in the ethereal vein than the Raiders' style of rock and roll.

To keep the record straight, Harpo added, "Please make sure everyone understands that my separation from the Raiders is completely amicable and that we are still the closest of friends. In the past, I had an occasional thought of doing my own thing . . . and somehow the advent of my 22nd birthday on March 13, plus a series of other serendipitous events, sort of sparked the whole move off."

Harpo has written many beautiful and meaningful songs. They are songs that express his innermost feelings and deep convictions. They are songs about love and understanding. He has a profound longing to record these songs and present them to you.

Harpo's last gig with Paul Revere and The Raiders was in Seattle, Washington on March 18 . . . and though he'll always be the best of friends with his buddies Paul, Mark, Fang and Smitty . . . he is, at last, doing exactly what he wants to do.

KRLA ARCHIVES

THE RAIDERS' DAY BEGINS WITH a plane ride. AND THEN IT'S ON to meet the press, pose for photos and answer the many questions. THE WAIT BACKSTAGE for Mark.

FINALLY THE RAIDERS REACH THE STAGE and greet their many appreciative fans. THE AUDIENCE SCREAMS THEIR APPROVAL as the Raiders break into their hit songs.

OFFSTAGE, BACKSTAGE AND ONSTAGE

...FANG, HARPO AND MARK take some time out to talk to talented Carl Reiner. ...VERY SIMPLY Mr. Smith. MARK LINDSAY, "Him Or Me, What's It Gonna Be?"

  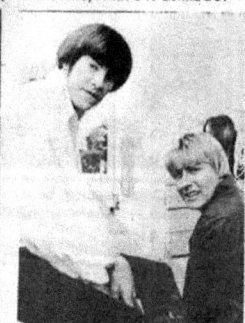

EVEN WHILE HAVING LUNCH THE RAIDERS are busy discussing their next show. PENSIVE LOOK FOR FANG while waiting to go on. TWO RAIDERS takin' it easy.

KRLA ARCHIVES

U.K. POP NEWS ROUND-UP
Jagger Hit With Food; Shaw Wins Song Contest

By Tony Barrow

In competition with new pop compositions entered by 16 other European countries, Great Britain has won the 1967 Eurovision Song Contest for the first time in 12 years!

An estimated 230 million televiewers watched the Grand Prix contest finals screened live throughout Europe from Vienna. SANDIE SHAW, British songstress who performs bare-footed, presented our winning number, "Puppet On A String," which she had already taken to third position in the U.K. charts before the date of the finals.

From juries in 17 different countries, Sadie's song gained a total of 47 votes. Her nearest rival was Ireland's SEAN DUNPHY who collected 22 votes and was placed second with "If I Could Choose."

Stones Hit

Violence seems to have been commonplace at European concerts given by THE ROLLING STONES. Mick Jagger was pelted with sandwiches, eggs and plastic cups at shows in Milan!... Screen star and cabaret balladeer DIANA DORS presented with a demand for 160,000 dollars by British tax authorities... From recently issued album of pre-Monkees solo recordings by DAVY JONES, Pye Records have now put out his version of Dylan's "It Ain't Me Babe" as a single... Unfortunately HOLLIES withdrew from tour of Far East and Australia because drummer Bobby Elliott still unable to rejoin them after his recent hospitalization. Replacing Hollies DAVE DEE group touring with PAUL AND BARRY RYAN plus ERIC BURDON'S ANIMALS... Gold disc for ENGELBERT HUMPERDINCK'S "Release Me" single. Now the chart-topping singer has turned down a lucrative summer season in Blackpool to undertake promotional visit to America... HERMAN spent Easter week vacationing in Ireland, visited mini-village of Four Mile House, Roscommon, birthplace of his grandfather.

Spring is really here with Beatle Paul crossing the Atlantic to be with Jane and BBC "Top Of The Pops" TV girl SAMANTHA JUSTE following the same route to renew her friendship with Monkee Micky!

Beatle Rumor

Most absurd American Beatle rumour of the month must be the one about Ringo planning a series of solo appearances at cafes in Europe!

What London lawyer David Jacobs described as "numerous matters during the course of performances and rehearsals since the tour began" led to the sudden cancellation of Hollywood screen star JAYNE MANSFIELD'S U.K. cabaret contract during the first week of April. And impressario Don Arden announced that he planned to sue the singing sex symbol for breach of contract. Her eight-week tour had six weeks to run and was worth a total of more than 70,000 dollars. Most of Jayne's cabaret dates were in North of England clubs at places like Newcastle, Liverpool and Blackpool.

Trogg Trouble

If they really care very much about the outcome, a lot of TROGG fans must be quite anxious about the on-off relationship between guitarist CHRIS BRITTON and the rest of the group. At first Britton gained national publicity in British newspapers and trade press by saying he was leaving The Troggs because he couldn't live with the current drugs 'n' long hair image being applied to the pop scene in general. Then, just as the group was ready to leave London for dates in Italy and Ireland, Britton turned up at the airport and claimed that he was postponing his departure. Yet he repeated that he was unhappy and wanted to quit not only the group but the entertainment business as soon as possible.

Whether Britton stays or goes the episode gave The Troggs one of their biggest slices of press publicity in ages!

VINCE HILL following example of Engelbert Humperdinck — cancelling Great Yarmouth summer season show in order to promote his "Edelweiss" single in America... HERMAN'S next single in U.K. expected to feature Neil Diamond number... THE WHO likely to tour America with HERMAN'S HERMITS... Is there no more news of MAMA CASS?

Stones Stripped

Brian Epstein's new Joint Managing Director ROBERT STIGWOOD produced new single and several album tracks with THE CREAM in New York after group's Easter stint in Murray The K's stage show... ROLLING STONES stripped and searched before being allowed to enter Sweden!

BEATLES must have paid more than 60,000 dollars in recording studio rental charges to make "Sgt. Pepper's Lonely Hearts Club Band" album... Big U.K. press stories manufactured from unfounded rumour that DAVY JONES might play "Oliver!" in movie version of the Lionel Bart musical.

ROY ORBISON buying a home in Britain... CILLA BLACK, co-starring with DAVID WARNER, just finished shooting her first full-length motion picture "Work... Is A Four Letter Word"... TOMMY STEELE joining Odetta, Petula Clark and Fred Astaire in screen version of "Finian's Rainbow."

...MICK JAGGER PELTED with sandwiches, eggs and plastic cups.

...HERMAN SPENT HIS VACATION in Ireland at Four Mile House.

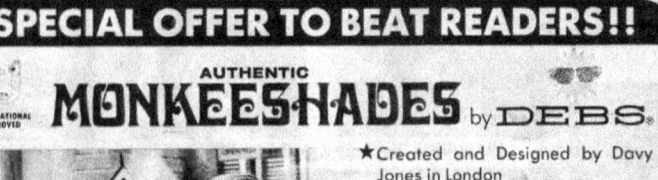

SPECIAL OFFER TO BEAT READERS!!

AUTHENTIC MONKEESHADES by DEBS

★ Created and Designed by Davy Jones in London
★ 5 Groovy Colors...rose...yellow...blue...grey...green
★ Heavy Mod Golden Chain
★ Just Like the MONKEES Wear On Their Swingin' TV Show
★ MONKEESHADES are the Wildest!

ONLY $1.98 PLUS .02 HANDLING CHARGE

Send to: MONKEESHADES, 81 W. State St., Pasadena, Calif. 91105
PLEASE SEND ME THE MONKEESHADES AS INDICATED. I ENCLOSE $2.00 FOR EACH PAIR.

COLOR_____ NO. PAIRS_____ TOTAL AMOUNT ENCLOSED_____
Name_____
Address_____
City_____ State_____ Zip Code_____

ORDER YOURS TODAY!!

KRLA ARCHIVES

Blue-eyed soul at it's righteous best.

IN THE RECORD DEPARTMENT

KRLA ARCHIVES

THE TEMPTATIONS dropped by Casey Kasem's "Shebang" recently to say "hello."

NANCY SINATRA and Lee Hazelwood, her partner on "Summer Wine."

BILL MEDLEY and Bobby Hatfield trade jokes with Casey.

KRLA TOP 40

1. I THINK WE'RE ALONE NOW — Tommy James & Shondells
2. SHE HANGS OUT — Monkees
3. YELLOW BALLOON — Yellow Balloon
4. PENNY LANE/STRAWBERRY FIELDS FOREVER — Beatles
5. LIVE — Merry-Go-Round
6. CAN'T SEEM TO MAKE YOU MINE — Seeds
7. LITTLE BIT ME, LITTLE BIT YOU/GIRL I KNEW SOMEWHERE — Monkees
8. SUNSHINE GIRL — Parade
9. BLUES THEME — Davy Allen & Arrows
10. CONNECTIONS — Rolling Stones
11. HAPPY TOGETHER — Turtles
12. NO MILK TODAY — Herman's Hermits
13. SOMETHIN' STUPID — Nancy & Frank Sinatra
14. WHEN I WAS YOUNG — Eric Burdon
15. SUMMER WINE — Nancy Sinatra
16. DOUBLE YELLOW LINE — Music Machine
17. LITTLE GIRL LOST & FOUND — Garden Club
18. RAPID TRANSIT — Robbs
19. BUY FOR ME THE RAIN — Nitty Gritty Dirt Band
20. WESTERN UNION — Five Americans
21. THIS IS MY SONG — Petula Clark
22. AT THE ZOO — Simon & Garfunkel
23. SHOW ME — Joe Tex
24. MY BACK PAGES — Byrds
25. THE HAPPENING — Supremes
26. SOMEBODY TO LOVE — Jefferson Airplane
27. LITTLE GAMES — Yardbirds
28. DON'T YOU CARE? — Buckinghams
29. I WAS KAISER BILL'S BATMAN — Whistling Jack Smith
30. HIM OR ME, WHAT'S IT GONNA BE? — Paul Revere & Raiders
31. RESPECT — Aretha Franklin
32. LISTEN GIRL — Giant Crab
33. SIX O'CLOCK — Lovin' Spoonful
34. BERNADETTE — Four Tops
35. I BEEN LONELY TOO LONG — Young Rascals
36. I NEVER LOVED A MAN — Aretha Franklin
37. THE LOVE I SAW IN YOU WAS JUST A MIRAGE — Miracles
38. SWEET SOUL MUSIC — Arthur Conley
39. JIMMY MACK — Martha & Vandellas
40. DEDICATED TO THE ONE I LOVE — Mamas & Papas

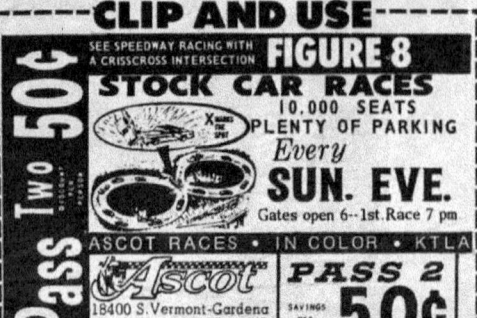

CLIP AND USE
SEE SPEEDWAY RACING WITH A CRISSCROSS INTERSECTION
FIGURE 8 STOCK CAR RACES
10,000 SEATS
PLENTY OF PARKING
Every **SUN. EVE.**
Gates open 6 — 1st Race 7 pm
ASCOT RACES • IN COLOR • KTLA
Ascot 18400 S. Vermont-Gardena
Easily Reached — Just Off Harbor & San Diego Frwys.
Pass Two 50¢ — PASS 2 50¢

KRLA ARCHIVES

KRLA REPORT
College Suicide Epidemic

In Los Angeles County 400 college students attempted suicide last year. There is an average of one suicide attempt on the University of California campus at Berkeley each day. In a recent one-month period, six students were successful in taking their own lives at Berkeley.

These and other astonishing facts on the subject of on-campus self-destruction were revealed in a special study undertaken by Los Angeles radio station KRLA entitled "The College Suicide Epidemic." Researched by special assignments editor Lew Irwin, the suicide probe is the sixth in a series of studies of contemporary social problems by the station.

The study delves into the relationship of the controversial hallucinatory drugs, barbituates and alcohol to suicides committed by college and university students.

List of Experts

Among the experts interviewed by newsman Irwin were Dr. Richard Seiden, University of California School of Public Health, Captain Hugh Brown, Commander Los Angeles Police Department Homicide Division and Dr. Sidney Cohen, University of California expert on LSD.

Looking into some of the reasons for the rise of suicide on college campuses, the report discovered that self-destruction is the number two cause of death among students.

Older Students

"Simply on the basis of the changing age distribution," states Dr. Seiden, "the fact that students are older now than they were a generation ago—primarily because of graduate school—there will be more suicides."

"The competitive pressure of student life," Seiden goes on to say, "is a major cause of attempted suicide. Berkeley and many other campuses are restricted to only the upper eight percent, the 'cream of the cream' of the graduating classes in high school and the pressure is considerable. I believe those two factors are enough to predict an increase in the future."

It appears that when students have an outlet to vent pent up

emotions few seek escape in attempts at self-destruction.

"It was rather startling to find out," says Dr. Seiden, "that there were no suicides during the time of the campus free speech movement and the number of cases that came into the student mental health clinic declined by twenty percent."

Dr. Harrington Ingham, chief psychiatrist for student health services at UCLA, defines suicide attempts as efforts to escape.

"Suicide is a retreat, an escape," according to Dr. Ingham. "The student with suicidal tendencies has two different ideas. First, he just can't handle all the pain involved in the continuation of life. The other idea is a cry for help. He thinks 'You'll be sorry!' or 'You'll notice now!'."

At the student level, a fourth year psychology student at UCLA tells Irwin of great cynicism among students about what use a college education has and that this thought can incapacitate a student to the point where suicide is the only escape.

LSD expert Dr. Sidney Cohen believes that there is no great relationship between the use of the drug and suicide attempts, pointing out that a student under the influence of LSD might just as easily decide against self-destruction as in favor of it.

"LSD," offers Dr. Cohen, "alters the values of an individual. Most suicides are committed under the influence of alcohol rather than drugs."

Legal Act

What are the legal implications in suicide? Captain Hugh Brown of the Los Angeles Police Department flatly states, "There's no law against suicide!"

"But part of our job is to protect life," he goes on to say. "We make every effort to take steps which will prevent suicide."

Whether the subject wants his life saved or not has no bearing on police action in suicide cases.

In a pioneering effort to examine and report on the problems and issues found on Southern California's many and varied college and university campuses, KRLA recently became the West's first radio station to establish an internal educational division.

By Pen

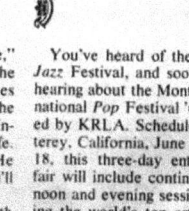

You've heard of the Monterey *Jazz* Festival, and soon you'll be hearing about the Monterey International *Pop* Festival '67 presented by KRLA. Scheduled in Monterey, California, June 16, 17 and 18, this three-day entertainment fair will include continuous afternoon and evening sessions featuring the world's top artists in the pop field.

Ravi Shankar, the Buffalo Springfield, the Jefferson Airplane, The Byrds, Hugh Masekela, the Nitty Gritty Dirt Band, the Grateful Dead—these are just a few of the stars looking forward to the June happening. Being the first event of its kind, this will be the only time top name artists from all over the world will have a chance to meet and work with each other.

These three days will mean a lot to them and to you. Tickets will go on sale in May, and packaged tours including transportation, food accommodation and tickets, leaving Los Angeles will be available. Listen to KRLA for further details.

* * *

Short of money? Call the KRLA request lines and try to cash in on the $111 prize as a "C.I.A." winner. All the KRLA "C.I.A." request lines are being "bugged" and taped segments of request callers' conversations are being played throughout the day. Do you know what your own voice sounds like?

Carol Backer of La Mirada did. Melanie Leidholt of West Covina, Mark Bech of Van Nuys and Dennis Haverty of Glendale—all were $111 winners. If you can identify your voice when you hear it on KRLA—call the station within five minutes and win $111. Call today and request your favorite song. Your request could bring you fame and FORTUNE.

APRIL 25-MAY 14
Troubadour
THE NEW & EXCITING
CHAD MITCHELL
"AMERICA'S ANSWER TO AZNAVOUR & BREL"
—THE NEW YORKER
PLUS COMEDIAN
HOWIE STORM
CR. 6-6168
9081 SANTA MONICA BLVD.
OPEN EVERY NIGHT—NO AGE LIMIT

ICE HOUSE GLENDALE
234 So. Brand Ave. Reservations: 245-5043

THRU APRIL 23
Dr. West's Medicine Show and Junk Band

with their hit "The Eggplant That Ate Chicago" and new Go Go label single, 'Gondaliers, Shakespeares, Overseers, Playboys and Bums'

NOW THRU APRIL 30
Comic Pat Paulsen
as seen on the Smothers Bros. Show

APRIL 25-30

Tim Morgon

MAY 2-7

The Yellow Balloon

with their hit "The Yellow Balloon"

A NEW MEMBER? No, the Knack hasn't added another drummer. It's KRLA's Dick Moreland sitting in.

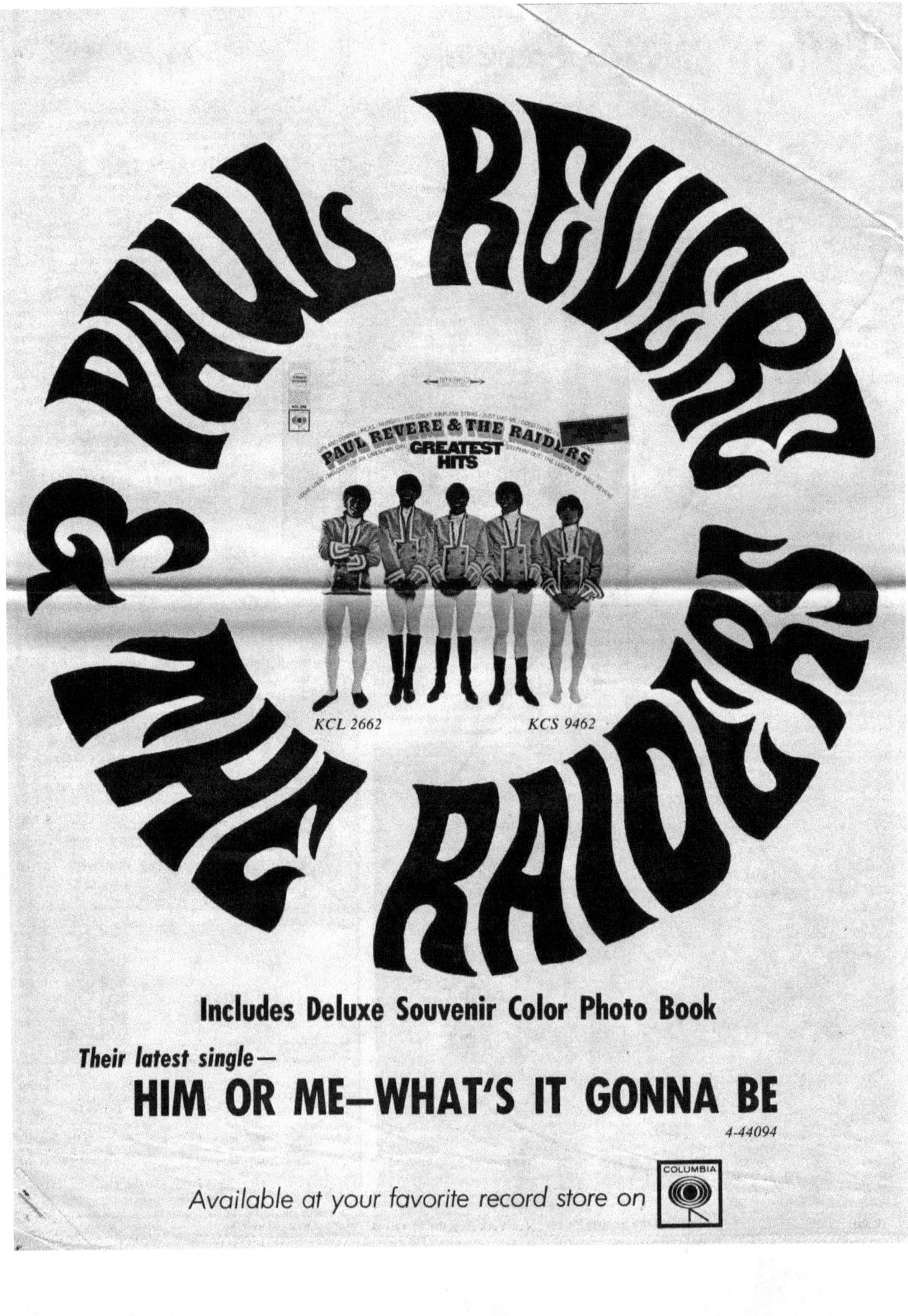

KRLA ARCHIVES

PAUL REVERE & THE RAIDERS

KCL 2662　　KCS 9462

Includes Deluxe Souvenir Color Photo Book

Their latest single—
HIM OR ME—WHAT'S IT GONNA BE
4-44094

Available at your favorite record store on

KRLA ARCHIVES

HOW TO MAKE MONEY AND ENJOY SUMMER

If you're one of the million or more teenagers looking for a summer job the time to start is—NOW! Last summer only two thirds of the army of teenagers searching for a way to pick up extra dollars during their school vacation found work.

Act fast and you can be one of the lucky ones. There are plenty of jobs available in resorts, restaurants, hotels, summer camps, beaches and summer theaters all over the country. You can combine swimming, horseback riding, hiking and a range of outdoor activities with making money by locating in one of the country's magnificent national parks.

The BEAT research staff has come up with some exciting summer job possibilities. To make your summer fascinating and profitable, the rest is up to you. Happy hunting!

The National Parks

Between roasting marshmallows at glowing campfires and enjoying the water sports at Yellowstone Lake, the Savages of Yellowstone National Park, teenagers who served as cabin maids, waitresses or garbage men (G-men to insiders), had a very groovy summer. The National Parks have to expand their staffs during the warm weather as these spots draw swelled summer crowds. Fire control, maintenance, construction work and similar chores are tucked in between folksings and sightseeing.

There are always more applicants than jobs. Act fast! To apply for Federal seasonal employment (summer jobs in the National Parks) use Standard Form 57 which is available at your Post Office or personnel office of any Federal Government Agency.

In many cases the Federal Government does not run the hotels, restaurants, shops and transportation facilities in the National Parks. Private firms operate many of the concessions and hire guides, waitresses, bellboys, maids, clerks and service station attendants. To apply, write directly to the individual companies. Here are just some of the listings: BIG BEND NATIONAL PARK, Texas, Mr. Garner B. Hanson, Pres., National Park Concessions, Inc., Mammoth Cave, Kentucky; GRAND TETON NATIONAL PARK, Jackson, Wyoming, Personnel Dept., Grand Teton Lodge Co., 209 Post St., San Francisco 8, Calif.; YOSEMITE NATIONAL PARK, Calif., Mr. Harold K. Ouimet, Personnel Mgr., Yosemite National Park, Calif.

A Christian Ministry in the National Parks hires music students to handle employee choruses and choirs and to play at services. For information write to: Warren W. Ost, Director, A Christian Ministry in the National Parks, 475 Riverside Dr., N.Y., N.Y. 10027.

If you don't mind roughing it, the more than 600 Girl Scouts Summer Camps are a fun-packed summer. You have an edge over other applicants if you have camping or counselor experience. Positions are open for waterfront assistants and counselors. Address your letter to "Girl Scouts of the U.S.A." to the national branch office in your section of the country.

The Boy Scouts of America are looking for counselors, truck drivers, unit heads, waterfront directors and kitchen help. Preference goes to ex-scouts and boys with camping experience, but if you can untie your thumbs long enough to pitch a tent write to the "Boy Scouts of America," your local regional office.

Social Skills

There's a long list of summer and part-time jobs open at the 450 Jewish Community Centers, camps, and YM & YWHAs operated by the Jewish Welfare Board around the country. And for teenagers who think they might eventually be interested in a career in social work, this is a great opportunity to test your skill in the field!

For further details write to: Henry B. Stern, ACSW, Personnel Services, National Jewish Welfare Board, 145 East 32nd St., N.Y., N.Y. 10016.

Uncle Sam hired 14,000 temporary employees last summer to replace vacationing regular employess or to work on special summer projects. In most cases you must pass a Civil Service exam to qualify. The number of jobs per agency is limited but the variety is enormous. Exciting opportunities are open to work beside engineers, librarians, biologists and writers.

To apply for these jobs use Application (Form 5000 AB) available at college replacement offices, Post Offices, or at the U.S. Civil Service Commission; or write to U.S. Civil Service Commissio Washington, D.C. 20415 and enclose a dime with your request for Pamphlet 68-November 1965, titled "Summer Vacation Jobs In Federal Agencies." It will tell you all you want to know about landing a job with Uncle Sam.

Seasonal assistant jobs are open at the Post Office. Some of the highest paying jobs for teens are to be found here! Check at your local Post Office for details on the written test for postal service work (required of all applicants).

Long List

It would take an entire issue of *The BEAT* to list all the summer jobs open to teens as bellhops, maids, counselors, etc. at Dude Ranches, summer camps, restaurants, hotels, motels, yacht marinas and summer stock theaters. Try writing to the American Association of Summer Camps for job possibilities. For a detailed listing of openings in recreation and vacation spots from Province Town to Peoria, go to your local public library and tell the librarian you are interested in seeing a guide to summer jobs for teenagers.

If you're scouting around for a fun summer and earning money is optional, you can join a group of teenagers under American Hostel auspices and enjoy a low-cost trip in unique style—hiking and bicycling. With your close-knit group of 8-10 teenagers you'll explore caves, learn about camping, frolic in National Parks and cool mountain lakes. An AYH leader who is familiar with the section of the U.S. you visit makes all necessary arrangements. Your part of the trip is to ENJOY. AYH is hiring tour leaders (minimum age 21) but the best way to beat out the competition for a leadership job is to be an ex-hostler. For information write to: Mrs. Linda Greenwood, Travel Director, American Youth Hostel, Inc., National Headquarters, 20 W. 17th St., New York, N.Y. 10011.

Want a free trip to Europe? The University Travel Company is hiring tour organizers. These are recruited from students whose job it is to book tours for the company in exchange for free passage to Europe. University Travel sponsors a wide variety of student tours to Paris, Rome, London, Madrid and a host of other glamorous European cities. All aboard! Further information is available from: University Travel Company, 18 Brattle Street, Cambridge, Mass. 02138.

THE BUCKINGHAMS

Triple Sensation

By Lawrence Charles

When a deep sea diver surfaces from the ocean bottom too quickly he suffers from an ailment called the "bends" which is a complete physical upset. The Buckinghams, five rock musicians from Chicago, have pulled a kind of musical upset this year and their heads are still spinning from it.

The Buckinghams are riding high with three smash hits at the top of the U.S. charts, "Kind of a Drag," the song which rocketed the group into national prominence, "Lawdy Miss Clawdy;" and "Don't You Care," the group's latest release.

Strong Hits

How does it feel to be cramming the charts with three strong hits? "Well it's kind of crowded," said 21-year-old Denny (Dennis Tufano), who plays harmonica, guitar, drums, and finger cymbals.

"It's all happened so fast," added Carl Giammarese, 20, lead guitarist of the group, "that we still haven't had time to react. Everyone keeps asking us how it feels to have three big hits going at the same time. I'm not sure, I still haven't had a chance to react."

The five Buckinghams were all playing with different rock groups in Chicago. They frequented the same clubs and entertainment spots around the city and decided to band together. They released several records before "Kind of a Drag" which received some local air play.

Life was kind of a drag since the group was going nowhere musically, which is sort of how their first record came about. They picked up a popular Chicago phrase which is a description of things when they're going slow and negative and molded it into a chart-rocker.

"Kind of a Drag" zoomed to the top of the Chicago charts and stayed there for seven weeks. All of a sudden it broke in the rest of the country and was number one.

The Buckinghams have drawn fans almost as quickly as they have scored hits. Even the New York police weren't ready for the group's instantaneous fame. Just a few men in blue were posted at the two N.Y. music stores where the Buckingham's made promotional appearances. The screaming fans charged the police, knocking the sturdy law enforcers to the floor and mauled the group.

Torn Clothes

"They tore at our clothes and ripped my jacket to shreds," said Jon-Jon Poulos, the group's drummer. Were they all little girls? "No," said Jon-Jon emphatically, "They were all very big girls, with muscles, maybe I still have some of the bruises and scratches," he said starting an inspection of his arm.

"But in Atlanta we had a very nice experience," said Nick Fortune, who plays bass guitar. "We met some people who were really upset that we were leaving. So they slipped into our hotel room and decorated the whole place with different colored crepe paper and tinsel. There were even bottles of champagne in buckets of ice when we came back to the hotel."

The Buckinghams are currently on a tour which will take them to thirty states and Canada. They can't wait to get to Montreal.

Clothes-City

"Montreal is really 'clothes-city,'" said Marty Grebb, fingering the collar of his electric-blue silk shirt. "They import all those groovy French and English styles," he said like a starving man discussing different cuts of steak.

The group's musical harmony seems to carry over into clothes. "We all seem to like the same things. Our taste in clothes is so similar we wind up buying the same things even when we're apart," said Nick. Like I'll come back from shopping and I'll pull a pair of pants out of a bag very excited and say 'hey guys look at these, aren't they great?' Then one of the guys will walk into the room with the same pair on and say, 'hey shove them back in the bag, look what I've got on."

. . BUCKINGHAMS (left to right) Jon Jon, Nick, Marty, Denny and Carl

The group doesn't shop, they invade a clothes store. They wind up in a tug-of-war for the same tie. One of them will be trying on a pair of shoes and another one will grab the second shoe and refuse to give it up.

The weirdest clothes purchase was Jon's: a miniskirt. Well, girls don't have a monopoly on groovy knees!

Denny was so excited after shooting $65 on mod clothes in a New York shop, that he walked out without the merchandise he had just paid for!

Clothes have even helped Marty out of tight spots. Marty was trying to explain himself out of being late to Miss Winky, his elderly teacher at Chicago's American Conservatory of Music. "But you see it was my collar. I used to wear velvet collars and Miss Winky loved to touch them and then she would forget she was angry."

Jon suffers from the rigors of being on the road. "I hate living out of a suitcase," he said. Jon also has a personal vendetta going against bellhops, whom for some reason known only to himself, he dislikes.

The rest of the group took a dislike to a pair of pants Nick used to wear and wear and wear. So while they were on tour, they hung the pants in the shower and put a match to them. "I smelled the smoke," said Nick, recalling the loss, "but by the time I got there all I saw was the zipper just hanging there."

The Buckingham's manager is discussing film plans for the group. They are very eager to act in a movie or do the score, but nothing definite has been decided yet. They're cutting an album in Hollywood which they refer to as "the album" because no title has yet been picked for the LP. When it's finished, it will be rushed out. Instant success seems to be the Buckinghams' style. Maybe they'll even break their record on single releases and produce a bunch of hit albums all at once!

KRLA ARCHIVES

OLÉ!

NOW AVAILABLE AT YOUR LOCAL

KRLA ARCHIVES

Eric Burdon

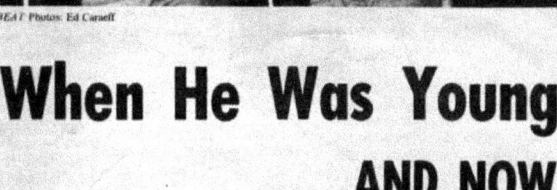

BEAT Photos: Ed Caraeff

When He Was Young ... AND NOW

"The rooms were so much colder then,
My father was a soldier then,
And times were very hard When I was young."

By Ron Koslow

Hitch-hiking down from Newcastle to London, a sleeping bag under his arm and nothing in his pockets, and not much else in his life but the music, young Eric Burdon, poor man's son, poor boy; and things are pretty gray in Newcastle.

Meeting another kid on the road, they hitch-hiked together; and this other kid was really hung up on Chicago Blues. So these two scruffy looking kids talked music, and did a bit of harmonica stuff on their way to London.

Bright lights, big city, London offered them what they wanted—not food, not shelter, not acceptance—Music. And so young Eric Burdon and even younger Mick Jagger, sang with any little blues group they could find; and when they earned a few pennies, singing in the streets, they rushed off and bought a Jimmy Reed or Bo Diddley record. They took the record back to their home towns in the North and played it until the grooves had worn out, and the music and style and soul were imbedded in their brains.

Today, Eric Burdon smiles when he thinks of the hard times. "After the war, things were tough for everybody in England; they still are. I guess I was just lucky."

But it was more than just luck. It was the years of living for nothing else but music, that molded his style and created his incredible dedication. Eric's music *is* hard time music and he knows from whence he speaks.

He is now more than just a pop star; he is respected on many levels; and it is doubtful whether any white performer on today's scene is further into the concept of Rhythm and Blues, or more aware of its social implications. His writings on the subject have been published and read world-wide.

During my three hour interview with Eric, what impressed me was his ability to speak for himself, to articulate his own opinions on a wide spectrum of topics. And what he said was spoken with candor and insight. Unlike so many personalities in public focus, he was unafraid to speak the truth.

On the racial problem in America:

"At one time in my life, nothing seemed more important than the problems the Negro people were having in America. It hurt me because I identified closely with their music; and much of their music is filled with pain.

I realize it's impossible for a white man to truly feel the problems of being Negro; but in a very small way, I was operating on their wave length. I wrote an article for *Ebony Magazine* expressing my concern for the lack of appreciation of Rhythm and Blues in America (you know in England, there's nothing more popular). But I realize now that these problems are just part of the over-all scheme of things (Yes, I believe in Destiny); and the most important thing an individual can do is deal with the problem on an individual level. Nothing I say is going to change people's minds; but at least I know where I stand."

On Los Angeles:

"I think everyone should come to Los Angeles just once. They should realize that someday the whole world could become like Los Angeles, and try very hard to prevent it. L.A. is not a happy place, and it is very easy to become lazy as things are so very easy there.

"If I had to choose an American city to live in, it would be San Francisco. Right now everything is happening there—I don't mean just the Haight-Ashbury thing, but the entire city; it's a way of life. When you live in San Francisco, you actually live.

Politically, it seems that Los Angeles had been taken over by the Conservatives. Even the hip people there are very conservatively hip. There seems to be an underlying tension between what people think they *should* be, and what they *are*.

"But for me, London is the only place; creatively it's the most dynamic city in the world."

On Psychedelic Drugs:

"In London now, the police are really cracking down on drugs. At first they just ignored them, and then the whole thing exploded and got completely out of hand.

"It's amazing to see the changes in the world today that can be directly related to drugs. Art, music, even politics have all been affected and I think this is only the beginning. One has to acknowledge the fact that certain drugs have already changed society and will continue to do so. They can't be ignored.

On The London Music Scene:

"The whole music thing started because the kids had nothing else to do. There was no significant pop music being produced in England at the time so we became absorbed with American music. It became a competitive game; America's 45's were hard to get and the kid who could get his hands on a Fats Domino or Bo Diddley record was the king of the neighborhood.

"We naturally got involved with making music too; and it seemed like all over the country kids were forming groups. This was in '62; Jagger, Keith Richard, Brian Jones, and many other big names all had their own groups. As we traveled around, the heaviest musicians naturally joined together; so when the explosion hit in 1964, we were ready. It was a case of being in the right place at the right time and having the right background.

"But since that initial explosion, when any English guy could have a hit record, the mediocre ones have dropped away and the heavies still remain. And rightfully so.

What's happening in England now is a mass experimental movement, led, of course, by The Beatles, and followed by The Who, The Cream, and I hope, The Animals.

"We're taking our influences now from international music forms (Indian, electronic, and classical) and putting them into a contemporary musical structure. The potentials of this new sound are unlimited.

"You'll notice in 'When I Was Young' we use an electric violin which gives the song a touch of the eastern classical. The great thing about the scene in London is that no one is satisfied with one particular bag, everyone wants to progress to newer and more exciting concepts.

On The Beatles:

"John Lennon is a completely changed man. He has become humble and gentle and spends most of his time sleeping; and when he's not sleeping, he's resting. The lyrics of 'Strawberry Fields' describe Lennon perfectly ("living is easy with eyes closed.")

"George and Paul are working very hard on some really exciting projects. Paul is writing a motion picture score, which is some of the most beautiful music I've ever heard. And George is very deep into Indian mysticism, attempting to incorporate it into a musical form. This is going to blow people's minds.

"And Ringo of course is busy being Ringo."

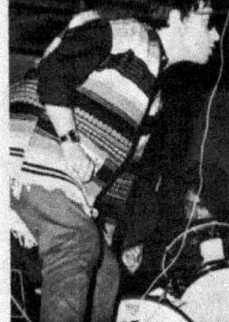

KRLA ARCHIVES

Twiggy: A Mini-Everything

BEAT Photos: UPI

By Louise Criscione

NEW YORK — The world's most in-the-news model, Britain's seventeen year old Twiggy, arrived at Kennedy International Airport to a horde of newsmen and photographers of the proportions ordinarily used to greet a visiting foreign dignitary.

Along to protect Twiggy during her six-week stay in the U.S. are four bodyguards, three policemen, her manager and a dog named Sigfried. This is not to mention a daily entourage consisting of 20 to 30 photographers, model and ad agency people who travel by five chauffeured limousines to the location of each day's shooting.

Discovered

The Twiggs' success story began two years ago when Nigel Davis — a jack-of-all-trades who has worked as a bookie's office boy, amateur boxer, antique salesman, interior designer and a hairdresser at Vidal Sasoon's Bond Street salon — spotted Lesley Hornsby at his brother's beauty shop. Nigel immediately spotted the modeling potential of the fifteen year old Lesley and set about completely changing her appearance.

The very first thing to go was her name. From Lesley Hornby it became simply Twiggy. His name was also changed to add a dash of class to what he was positive would be the triumph of Twiggy. Accordingly, Nigel Davis was tossed off in favor of Justin de Villeneuve.

An entirely new look was created for Twiggy. Justin saw to it that her original mousey-brown hair was barbered and changed to blonde. Eye makeup was "in" with three pairs of false lashes as well as painstakingly painted lower lashes.

Her makeup takes approximately one hour to apply. "Most of it's me eyes," declares the strictly Cockney Twiggy. "Justin showed me 'ow to do most of me makeup. I think he got the idea for the lines from looking at a doll."

The Launch

With a boyish-looking hairstyle, a boyish-looking figure and the three pairs of false eyelashes, Justin felt that Twiggy was ready and so launched her into British prominence by talking the *London Daily Express* into naming her "The Face of 1966."

"We both get very mad when people call me a ten-percenter," admits Justin. "I wasn't an impresario looking for a star when I met her, you know. She was beautiful and I wanted to take her out."

But at the same time, Justin felt that it was "inevitable" that Twiggy become *the* model of the now generation. "There's that lovely face — and she's a model who is also a personality. She's young and funny and she loves what she's doing," declares Justin. "She bridges pop and fashion and other girls her age love that because it could be them. She's not just a cold, perfect clotheshorse — she's a heroine."

Twiggy herself doesn't quite understand nor agree with most of the articles written about her. "It's like reading about somebody else. That's not me, I say."

Born and reared and still living in a workingclass district of London, Twiggy went to the same schools as her neighbors. She had the distinction of being called such cherished nicknames as "Sticks" and "Ox Fam" by her classmates. "The nasty school boys who lived across the street used to call me 'Ox Fam' — that's short for the Oxford Famine Relief Committee," says Twiggy.

Pancake Flat

"Can you imagine wot it was like? All the girls gettin' lovely figgers and me stayin' flat as a pancake. It was no fun, I tell you." It might not have been any fun but it was certainly worthwhile if you count your blessings with money and fame.

Because of her less-than-voluptuous measurements (31-22-32), Twiggy has been the object of highly uncomplimentary press. The editor of *Elle*, while much in favor of Twiggy, still believes she "looks pathetic." The editor of the acid-tongued *Women's Wear Daily* calls the whole thing "a massive publicity stunt."

But it matters not what adjectives (kind or unkind) are used — the fact still remains that mini-bosomed or not Twiggy has made the cover of almost every major publication in both Europe and America.

As fashion photographer Bert Stern so aptly puts it: "She is happening."

"Simply Smashing"

As for her first glimpse of the U.S. from the New York side, Twiggy exclaims: "New York is simply smashing and I love it when all the drivers say 'Hello, Twiggs.' But we 'ad about 3,000 people all pressing 'round outside a store one day. I cried — I was that scared — and 'arold (bodyguard Harold Poole) 'ad to pick me up and carry me through to the car."

The entourage shadowing her in New York is even amazing to Twiggy. "It's so organized. You'd think I was the Beatles."

Twiggy supposedly earns a fantastic $120 to $240 an hour for modeling. And if this is true, it makes her one of the highest paid models in the world today.

Besides modeling, Twiggy is here chiefly to sell a line of her clothes to deparment stores all across the nation. "They're mostly lovely colors. All bright and shiny," said Twiggy. What she didn't say was that Twiggy Enterprises predicts they'll make ten million dollars a year.

Although she has been dubbed "The mini-queen of the new British social aristocracy," Twiggy denies that she's a swinger. "I never stay out until three or four a.m. I get droopy much before that," admits Twiggy. "Besides, it isn't fair to show up for a booking looking like death warmed over and I can't work with bags under me eyes.

"I don't like these LSD people," said Twiggy. "They don't seem to do any work. They're phony. I suppose there is a crowd like that in London but we're not part of it. I like to dance, but I don't fancy the discotheques — they're too crowded."

In addition to being her discoverer and manager, Justin is also her boyfriend. "'e was the first boy I really dated," said Twiggy of the 27 year old Justin. "Before I met 'im, I just went about with a crowd."

Marriage?

Twiggy says she'll marry Justin when she's "oh, at least 24." Justin says 21 will be more like it. "We'll get married eventually," he predicts. "But she's so young that she could easily change her mind. It's not fair for her to decide now. She's not catty or shrewd and she never thinks more than a few weeks ahead. I'm the one that thinks about the future."

Twiggy has, however, given some thought to the future. She knows she will not stay on top of the fashion heap for more than a year. "Someone's always looking for a new girl, I guess. Everybody gets a turn." Her turn came only because "I 'appened along at the right time." When it's all over and no one can remember a girl they once called Twiggy, Lesley Hornby will "buy a little 'ouse in the country."

"I don't like these LSD people. They don't seem to do any work. They're phony."

TWIGGY WAVES to reporters and photographers as she arrives for six-week stay in U.S. Following Twiggy off plane is manager, Justin.

"I wasn't an impresario looking for a star when I met her, you know. She was beautiful and I wanted to take her out."

TWIGGY WEARS HER dresses eight to ten inches above knee.

KRLA ARCHIVES

BEAT SALUTES DICK CLARK ON
Eleven Years Of Success

By Ron Koslow

The name of Dick Clark and popular music are synonymous. No other individual has had more influence on the growth and development of the contemporary music scene. It is now eleven years since that June day in 1956 when Dick took over "The American Bandstand" on WFIL-TV in Philadelphia. Trends have changed; an entire generation of teenagers have come and gone; and still Dick Clark Productions corners the market on youth orientated entertainment. The reason for this can be simply attributed to Dick's personality. It is his respect for young people, coupled with his desire to present top-flight entertainment that is the secret of his success.

Rapport With Teens

His rapport with teenagers won him the immediate devotion of millions, and can be readily seen when he stages his Bandstand reunions; ex-Bandstand regulars, some even married and with children, return to honor Dick. Many have achieved success themselves in varied fields. Most prominent, however, is Jerry Blavett who is now the most popular disc jockey in Philadelphia, with a TV show of his own.

"It all started," Dick reminisces, "one summer day when we left the studio doors open and kids started to wander in off the streets. Suddenly they were dancing and we had a hit show on our hands."

After Dick's first year as Bandstand host, the show went national and a new era in teen culture was born.

"We Chew..."

In February of 1958, "The Dick Clark Saturday Night Show" went on the air nation-wide, presenting almost every pop star of consequence, with the exception of Elvis and Ricky Nelson. During the two years the Saturday Night Show was aired, Dick was responsible for the incredible success of his sponsor, Beechnut Gum, and for the creation of a new era in music—"The Philadelphia Sound" which launched the careers of Frankie Avalon, Fabian, Bobby Rydell, and Chubby Checker.

In late 1964, Dick moved his crew to Los Angeles. The music field had shifted west and he felt it was time to diversify into other areas of entertainment.

He conceived a format involving pop music and exotic locations; in 1965, "Where the Action Is" was aired and hailed as a major breakthrough in TV presentation.

It was a costly show to produce since all work was done on location, but Dick believed it was a worthwhile project. This show was responsible for a "New Wave" of pop stars: Paul Revere and the Raiders, Keith Allison, Steve Alaimo, and Don and the Goodtimes.

Bandstand Secure

Meanwhile, Bandstand switched to its present Saturday afternoon time spot; and all indications are that the show will last forever, or at least as long as Dick wants it to.

Unfortunately, "Action" was cancelled in March of this year due to its expense to the network. Its cancellation provoked a deluge of irate letters from all over the country; but, as usually is the case, they were ignored. Dick, however, has plans for a new series next season, which he predicts will be an even bigger success than "Action." In addition, Dick Clark Productions is now in the process of producing two feature films, an area that Dick ultimately hopes to achieve major recognition in. Knowing Dick, and his previous record, he cannot miss.

REMEMBER WHEN Doris Olsen and Joyce Schaefer were regulars on the old Philadelphia "Bandstand" and Frankie Avalon was tops?

...THE ACTION KIDS were all happy before the show was dropped.

...DICK CLARK signs off each week from continuing "Bandstand."

A BEAT MELODRAMA

About the Teenager and the Rising Cost of Living (or... How To Buy The Necessary Luxuries With As Little Work As Possible)

Gwen and Ken were sorrowfully depressed...Cokes cost 25¢... The show cost $2.50...Ken's '49 Ford needed a can of oil...and Ken had already spent his meager allowance on a birthday present for his Chihuahua. Sob!

Then! In a blaze of red, white and black, out of his XKE stepped the shining BEAT Knight...paisley tie, double-breasted jacket, gambler's striped bell bottom pants, Cuban heels. Instantly, Gwen and Ken recognized him.

"Over here!" shouted the BEAT Knight at the twosome. "Read this page of BEAT, speared on the end of my sharp and ever-present spear."

Gwen and Ken began to grin. What did they see, speared on the end of his sharp and everpresent spear? Why are they running towards the mailbox? Why is Gwen saying, 'I want a new Monkee album, and a paper dress and a can of oil for your stupid car and a life-size picture of Herman, and...?'

OK...we'll tell you the secret:

Work for THE BEAT and earn money for:

- Yourself
- Fraternity-Sorority
- Fan Club
- School Activities

It's fun and easy too!!

All you do is sell BEAT subscriptions to your friends and earn a commission on each order you take.

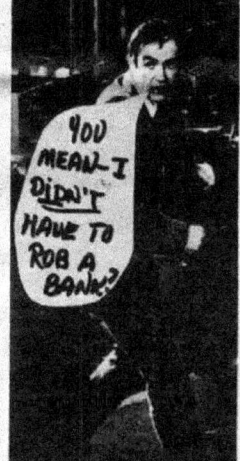

Just fill out this form and send it to:
BEAT Representatives
6290 Sunset Blvd., Suite 504
Hollywood, Calif. 90028

We'll send you the necessary information to become a successful BEAT Representative. You'll be amazed to see how much money you can earn (and have fun doing it)!

This is a brand new recruiting program. Former BEAT Representatives must sign up again.

P.S. If you aren't a subscriber, your own subscription can be your first order.

Yes! I want to be a BEAT Representative. Please send me additional information and forms for selling subscriptions so that I can start earning money right away!

Name _____
Address _____
City _____ State _____ Zip _____

KRLA ARCHIVES

Don And The Goodtimes—The Usual Overnight (Three-Year) Success Bag

THE GOODTIMES (l. to r.) Buzz, Charlie, Bobby, Don and Jeff

GOODTIMES are good enough to pose before leaving on tour

By Debbie David

"I Could Be So Good To You" is the name of the Epic Records single. It's almost prophetic, because it's proving so good to the record company, record shops, fans everywhere, and most of all the group whose song it is, Don & The Goodtimes.

The disc was enroute to hit status virtually from the moment it became available a few weeks ago, in Los Angeles, Seattle, Boise, Boston, Tulsa, San Francisco, onward and upward, everywhere!

Testimony

Reaction is testimony to the terrific fan following built by the guys from the time they became regulars on Dick Clark's "Where The Action Is" TV show. The program is off the air now—much to the dismay of everyone—but kids have stayed tuned in to the Goodtimes.

As one fan, Gina Ayala, wrote in her school newspaper, the Lions' Trail of El Monte (Calif.) High, "Don & The Goodtimes have everything it takes. In the entertainment business, personality is just as important to the record buyers as talent. They have more than enough of both."

The Goodtimes' Don Gallucci laughed recently, "I guess we're the usual overnight success story. All it took us was three years of obscurity."

Added Charlie Coe, "It's all the kids' fault. We couldn't have gotten this far, approximately the southeast corner of Sunset and Vine, without them. They've been so great to all of us."

Inquired Bobby Holden, "Did anyone happen to find a brown sock?"

Dick picked the Goodtimes after a search for new "Action" regulars that covered every state and some of Europe. Reaction when they made their first formal appearance justified the selection, boosted everyone's confidence, and produced a flood of mail to compliment the Goodtime's storm of talent.

(They try to answer every letter personally, by the way, although it's now at the point where it may take a while... The address is 9171 Wilshire Boulevard, Suite 540, Beverly Hills, Calif., 90210).

Fan comments point to their appearance, their musicianship, their distinctive vocal sound. And, most of all, the warmth, charm and friendliness radiated by Don, Charlie, Bobby, Buzz Overman and Jeff Hawks.

L'il Don

L'il Don, 19, insists he's 9'-7". His talent at the organ towers higher than that. His fingers race over the keys, his other hand shakes a tambourine, his body bounces in time to the music. His smile tells the story.

Charlie, 20, "The Clown," gets his laughs quietly. He's the lead guitar, who gets his skill through hours of daily practice. He has auburn hair, brown eyes, an honest expression, and everyone loves Charlie.

Buzzy, "The Buzzard," gives every audience his fullest on bass guitar and vocals (including "I Could Be So Good To You," on which he takes lead), and that's quite a bit. He's a muscular 5-10, the result of daily workouts, and a dedicated songwriter. He wrote the flip side on the Epic release, "And It's So Good." (Know what? It is!!).

Bobby, the drummer, turned 20 on April 16. (GLee py Birgday, Bobby!). He's the group's maker of mirth, which sells for 25¢ an ounce, and there's always a microphone near his mouth to catch the wisecracks (which fall out between his molars, he reports). Fans who don't know sometimes call him the "quiet one." Hah!

New Member

Jeff, 20, is the newest Goodtimes member. He stepped in when Don McKinney was taken ill, shortly before the cross-country tour which started in mid-March, and quickly proved himself up to the task of lead singer. He's been accepted fully and completely as a fine talent, by fans as well as the other Goodtimes.

Don & The Goodtimes have an album scheduled for release in June or sooner, and they start work on their next single when the current tour concludes this month.

NOTES FROM THE UNDERGROUND
Where Do We Stand?

By Ron Koslow

The revolution has begun. The battle between the generations is being waged full force and it's important to find out just where we stand.

It's us against the establishment, they've got the money and the power. We have the one thing their money can't buy and their power can't seize—youth. And youth is where it's at.

As the world has become ever complex and computerized, need for understanding and vitality has increased. We're a tribe, (in the words of a Los Angeles Disc Jockey) "the flower children," the most important natural resource this country possesses—and we must be allowed to "bloom."

Musical Bond

Aside from our common struggle against the "other generation," the most basic and universal bond between us is our music. Rock and Roll belongs to us. It was created by and for young people in reaction to the flat emotionless music of the 30's and 40's.

After listening (I mean *really* listening, really getting into) Bob Dylan's poetry or Mick Jagger's "hot" sounds, Benny Goodman seems "luke warm."

Can you imagine 25,000 "hippies" all loving their music and each other in the most beautiful, peaceful way at a huge outdoor picnic and freak-out—it happened at the Human Be-In in San Francisco.

Or how about 50,000 turned on kids at a Beatle concert, screaming and laughing and crying at the same time—that's happened too. This is where our power lies, and it's the best kind of power—it's the power of human emotion.

Just tune in the John Lennon's "Strawberry Fields." It speaks for

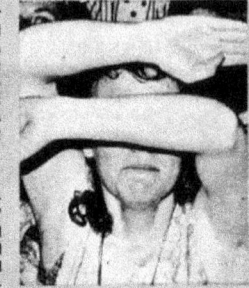

itself and even non-rock people in the business are overwhelmed by its depth and creativity. They're acting as though they've just come upon a great discovery—but we knew it all along.

We're living in the most exciting times the world has ever known—life in the 60's is one big happening and we're the ones who are making things happen.

One of our brightest and most dedicated allies is Brian Wilson of the Beach Boys. Brian had a vision one night; all of a sudden he realized that the most important way he could do to make things straight was through his music. Up till that time he had been saying things other people wanted him to say (Surfin' U.S.A., 409) but that phase had passed. He went to work and put six months of his life into a song entitled "Good Vibrations."

And wasn't it worth it? People all over the world picked up on Brian's vibrations.

Understanding

But how do we handle the problem of the "other generation" and the values they're trying so hard to impose on us? We try to understand them—that's all—just understand. We know what we've got going for us so there's no reason to get up tight. Meanwhile we've got ourselves and our music and that's plenty.

This column is for us—and it must be shared. I'll try to keep you informed about what's happening on this end and I'd like you to keep me informed about what's happening with you. If you've got a thought to share, or a poem, or a drawing, or even a bit of local news, pass it on. The only way we can make it is together.

Fast-workin' burn-stoppin' dark-tannin'

SEA & SKI

89¢ to 2.75

KRLA ARCHIVES

Shirley You Jest

Would you believe that I have waited until the last parsible (podden?) moment and that I now have approximately four seconds to write this (and I use the word in a mobile manner) (loose, too) column?

I've always been one of those "eleventh hour" people. You know the type. The kind who waits until the night before to start a big project for botany class and has to sit up all night trying to disguise weeds with clever touches of fingernail polish. Not to mention the kind who would have ended up taking botany in the first place.

Botany

Why in the you-know-what am I raving about botany? I'm not even sure I know what it is. (I'm *positive* I don't know *where* it is.) (At.) What I had intended to do was tell you why I'd put off writing this mass until the aforementioned hour of eleven. Suddenly, I was on a botany trip.

Now that I've returned, allow me to splain myself (a painful expelience). I didn't start writing earlier because I didn't know quite what to say (nothing new, nothing new). That's on account of the diatribe I went into last issue, wherein I crawled atop the nearest soap box and babbled about the pitfalls of falling in love with a star. (I should talk.) (And do, about 24 hours a day).

It isn't that I didn't mean what I say, unsolicited little lectures, I get panic-stricken and start worrying if I've opened my big mouth (which I generally open only to change feet) too far and hurt someone's feelings.

Paranoia

If I did, I didn't mean to, and I really have no reason to think this might be the case since I haven't received any poison pen letters and/or bombs. Must be my paranoia acting up again.

What it really is is this. (I hate sentences where you have to use the same word twice in a row to get a point across. (The one you usually try to wear a hat over.) I always get slightly buggy when I've said anything that might make people think that *I* think I'm some kind of authority or something.

Like I always say (I always say that), I mean far more well than I am. And, come to think of it, I *am* an authority on being in love with a star. Isn't that right, George darling? (What's new besides hope, hope, hope.)

Speaking of George (I *told* you I was going to start that again), I have another of my fascinating (as in prop up your eyelids, Mable, there she goes again) Beatle incidents to relate.

While riding in a car driven by a rational, sensible adult type person, I suggested that we turn the radio to a pop station, instead of the "good music" thingy we were listening to.

Arctic Quality

That suggestion was met by a glare of Arctic quality and quantity, but the day was suddenly saved as I heard the strains of "Strawberry Fields Forever" beginning to pour forth from the aforementioned "good music" thingy.

The rational, sensible adult smiled pleasantly and listened rather intently until the song, which was an instrumental version came to an end.

The adult then turned to me (barely missing the car in front of us) (am-day it) (it's my turn to have a whiplash) and smugly said, "tell me that wasn't beautiful."

Just then, before I had time to answer, the announcer came on the air and said the tune number was 'Strawberry Fields Forever,' currently a big hit for the Beatles."

Me: "*Beautiful.*" (A very effective word when echoed in a perfectly *simpering* tone of voice.)

Adult: "Well - ahh - er - no *wonder* it's a big hit for them. *Anyone* could record a beautiful song like that and be successful. The credit goes to the *writer* in this case. I'll bet *you* can't tell me who wrote it!"

The Beatles

Me: "The Beatles." (*Two* particularly effective words whether echoed in a perfectly simpering tone of voice or whispered reverently while bowing toward the Mecca.) (As in Surrey.)

To get away from the Beatles for a moment (pardon me while I tear myself) (as in away, as in away), Cathy, a friend of mine in Oregon wrote and told me that she and her friends have made up a new dance called "The Odor." You dance it the same way you do "The Chicken" except you don't wear new ban spray deodorant.

Nothing but class in this column, nothing but class. However, while I'm on the subject of such pleasant thingies, I must say I do wish they'd stop having all those television commercials about all the horrible things a person might have without even knowing it. I'm getting so I'm afraid to even breathe on anyone for fear they'll go home, stand in front of the mirror and say: "I don't care if you *are* Shirley Postum – you smell *nasty*." I realize these commercials are designed to do just that – get you wondering about yourself so you'll buy a whole bunch of products, but jeez . . . do they have to make you feel so un-confident (making up words again) that you wonder if you could get a male type person to even look at you. Maybe *I* could if I showed up at Sing-Sing with a handful of pardons, but I'm not sure.

Funny Bit

Here's a funny bit you can use the next time someone corrects your grammar. Smile and tell them you didn't know they were an English major. When they admit proudly that they were, ask them what regiment they were with. (And that is how you play Get The Guests.) (Yes, yes, I know. A stolen line, a stolen line.)

Have you ever had the strange feeling that something is going to happen no matter what happens? (Speaking of strange feelings, that sentence just gave me a stranger one.) Like that, frinstance, you were going to end up liking someone you don't really like or don't like someone you really like (confusing, but surely making sure your path crosses with someone elses, at which time you'll get all involved whether you want to or not?)

Right now, I have this feeling so strongly it scares me. I even got melodramatic about three weeks ago and wrote down "No matter how they toss the dice" and hid the piece of paper to look at when the thingy finally happens, and say I-told-you-so. (As in nya-nya-nya.)

And you know what really galls me? The person isn't *George*.

Curses, re-foiled.

EXCLUSIVE BEAT photo shows Peter Tork talking to Russian poet, Yevgeny Yevtushenko, when they met in Hawaii. L. to r., Toby Rafelson, Yevtushenko, Peter, Bob Rafelson (co-producer of "The Monkees").

Turning On

THE PEANUT BUTTER CONSPIRACY IS SPREADING (Columbia) *It's a Happening Thing, Then Came Love, Twice is Life, Dark on You Now, Second Hand Man* plus five other tracks.

This LP definitely establishes the Peanut Butter Conspiracy as an important rock group. Sandi, the group's female vocalist, has a great, powerful sound. Two of their big singles hits are cuts off the album.

PSYCHEDELIC PSOUL THE FREAK SCENE (Columbia) *A Million Grains of Sand, Rose of Smiling Faces, Behind the Mind, The Subway Ride Thru Inner Space* plus eight other tracks.

Throw away all your guide books because they'll never help you find your way around this LP. It's a very sharp musical criticism of a world where too many people are getting blown apart, choking in smog and starving.

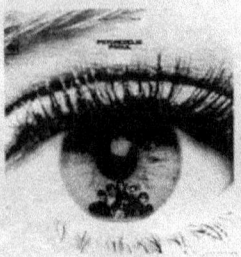

JAMES DARREN/ALL (Warner Brothers) The LP features Jimmy's hit rendition of *All* plus nine other happy listening tracks.

All rocketed Jimmy back onto the best selling charts and this new album should face no difficulties. happy easy listening treatment to his tunes, which are all proved winners. With a big band backing up his smooth vocal performace, Jimmy's new LP is all good listening.

ELECTRIC COMIC BOOK, The Blues Magoos (Mercury) *Pipe Dream, Gloria, Albert Common Is Dead, Lets Get Together* plus other tracks.

The group's latest hit, Pipe Dream, is one of the featured numbers and characteristic of the group's wailing, electronic sound. Amplified sounds scream back and forth in a wild volley of driving electronic sounds.

THE INMATES, *Local Town Drunk,* The happy, springy tempo recalls early Beatle sounds and could bounce this one to the top of the charts . . . **BAJA MARIMBA BAND** . . . Georgy Girl, a compelling, Latin-type instrumental of the Seeker's smash hit Oscar nominee . . . **THE BROTHERS FOUR** *Shenandoah.* Sweet, harmonizing rendition of a classic ballad that could catch enough heart strings to catch on . . . **SMOKEY AND HIS SISTER,** *Creators of Rain,* The two sing with the beveled, innocence of tender children. Their hushed quality could rocket this to the top of the charts . . . **THE GRATEFUL DEAD,** *The Golden Road,* Hard driving, up-tempo, freaky rock beat that's happening out of San Francisco with a good thumping dance rhythm . . . **THE CARNABY STREET SET,** *I Was Kaiser Bill's Batman,* An instrumental. Whistling Jack Smith parade music, novelty number interspersed with parody German command shrieks . . . **RONNIE DOVE,** *My Babe,* with lyrics by Neil Diamond, has a dynamic, constant throb that sure to vibrate the charts. . . **SONS OF CHAMPLIN,** *Sing Me a Rainbow,* groovy, steady, driving rock adventure could pick up fans for this new group . . . **YELLOW BALLOON,** An easy, frothy, light fun sound that could climb very high in weeks to come. . . **PARADE,** *Sunshine Girl,* Easy listening, happy, swing sound. With a little more air play this one could bullet to the top . . . **THE WHO,** *Happy Jack,* This top British group could have found a solid follow-up to their first big American hit, Wild Thing . . **JEFFERSON AIRPLANE,** *Somebody To Love,* very solid lyrics backed up by wild blending of electronic sounds . . . **THE SEA GULLS,** *Twiggs,* Musical tribute to guess which top British fashion model . . .

KRLA ARCHIVES

please send me
BEAT

26 issues only

$3 per year

Mail to: **BEAT Publications**
6290 Sunset Blvd. #504
Hollywood, California 90028

☐ New Subscription
☐ Renewal (please enclose mailing label from your last BEAT)
I enclose ☐ cash ☐ check ☐ money order $3.00 or ☐ 2 years at $5.00
Outside U.S. - $9 per year

* Please print your name and address.

Name_____
Street_____
City_____
State_____ Zip_____

ELVIS PRESLEY recently received his latest award from 21-year-old Lyn Hook, Adelaide, Australia, for success in that country. Lyn also presented Elvis with a scrapbook containing 2500 pictures of fan club members. Lyn has seen some of his pictures as many as 60 times.

CLASSIFIED

FOR SALE

NEW VOX BASS $200. Case included. 837-0963. (Los Angeles, Calif.)

FAT CITY. Magazine of rock 'n roll. Send 50c to FAT CITY, Box U, Old Chelsea Station, New York, New York 10011 for sample.

GUILD F-20. Acoustic, $125. 438-4095 (Long Beach, Calif.)

MUSICAL FLASH CARDS: Every group needs a good musician — why not you? Easiest way to learn notes, time values, and just good basic knowledge of music. Over 400 facts included in two sets, beginning and intermediate. This is not just a card game for kids! Enclose $1.65 for each set ordered. Immediate delivery. Hollingworth Publishing Co., Rush, Colorado 80833.

PERSONALS

Long Live the Kinks...
BILL — I love you... KATHIE
THE LOST CAUSE
LINDA LOVES WALLY BARNICK
EXPERIENCE THE HARBINGER COMPLEX
EAST BAY MUD IS COMING.
FOR FREDDIE: THE FLIPSIDE?!
DAVE ELLIS IS MY BROTHER "sis"
Want to trade records from people from different parts of country. Write Jim Kendrick, 2242 73rd Ct., Elmwood Park, Ill. 60635
USC Trojans Rule Right Felix?
Union Square Beatle People! Another Rally!
Long Live Berkeley
NO ONE I THINK IS IN MY TREE, YOU OTHER NUTS FELL TO THE GROUND. THE BEATLES AND MR. SPOCK RULE.
MICHAEL T. CORBETT
Arthur: Beat it! From Cathy M.
Don't let hebrelatation out of site.
RITA NAQUIN, MOUSEY, I LOVE Y'ALL! DIANNE
P. TORK, M. DOLENZ — 18 & cute, dying to meet you. CHERI, Rt. 2, Box 728, Sonora, 95370, 532-9259. GAIL, Star Rt. Box 1090, Sonora, 95370, 586-4443.
BOSCO RABBIT is more alive than any of you clods think!!!
I am alive.
BOSCO RABBIT has squashed all of those hypocrites!!! And now they believe!!!!
Where Is The S.P.C.A.?
LOVE TO Debby, Lila, Sheila, Mowier Group; psychedelic peanut butter.
TOOTS LOVES Peter Sunshine
BEATLES RULE YOU!!!!!
SEE ELVIS in "Easy Come, Easy Go." Great!
KEITH AND DEBBIE
Del Pierce Is Out — The S.P.C.A. Is In!
the "CREAM" is turnin' on!!! Sheilla and Darrylin
BEATLES FOREVER — Carol
John — I LOVE YOU and think you're outasite!!!! - Jackie
UGLINESS RULES!!! CUTEY
"BEATLES FOREVER — THE ORIGINAL FLOWER CHILDREN"
The Mucky Duck crowd is outasite!!! Jackie, Sandra and Andrea
KATHY loves THE POOR
Sharon — Nice talking to you.
KNACK are the grooviest! Judy
GREETINGS COALINGA! LOVE FROM JANE.
PAUL J. ROBBINS is groovy, Jamie
Randy & Robin, Randy & Robin, Randy & Robin, Randy & Robin, Randy & Robin.
TOSB luvs Cougar
Personal to BRIAN WILSON — Did you get our chicken? If so, please answer enclosed letter. IF NOT — Personal to BEACH BOYS — Why didn't you give BRIAN his chicken, huh? LOVE — DEBBIE KEIL, 4344 No. Denver, Kansas City, Mo. 64117, GL 3-2619 (Area Code 816) and KATHY WINDERS, 5315 NE 44 St., Kansas City, Mo. 64117, GL 3-6646 (Area Code 816).
Long Live HIPPIES
YATAHAE!
"KAREN LOVES DAVE SELSKI"
Come Fly With Us! The LADYBIRDS
BEWARE WESTMOOR... Laura is coming
PAM and LISA, Downey. You are the Supremest. Luvpat.
DAVID SERNA loves his guitar, and his girl, KAREN SCHAFER
OXO WHITNY
TERRY KNIGHT is happening.
BEAT THE PUD. — SHNOOK
THE GIANT CRAB is catching on. Write to 448 West Las Tunas Drive., San Gabriel, Calif.

HOW ABOUT THAT "SMILE" BRIAN?

PEN PALS

GROUP-MANIACS!!! Please write: Alice, 11021 Noble Ave. Mission Hills, California.

WANTED

Want to trade records from people from different parts of country. Write Jim Kendrick, 2242 73rd Ct., Elmwood Park, Ill. 60635
Wanted — one outasite guy, answers to name JOHN SENNE.

FAN CLUBS

FOR INFORMATION ON THE ROBBS NATIONAL FAN CLUB, WRITE P.O. BOX 350, BEVERLY HILLS, CALIFORNIA 90213.

Write to the S.P.C.A., 304 Raymond Avenue, Glendale, Calif. 91201

Official WHO Fan Club. Send self-addressed stamped envelope 2410 So. Springfield Ave., Chicago, Ill. 60623

BIRTHDAYS

HAPPY BIRTHDAY Paul.
HAPPY BIRTHDAY JOYCE GOMEZ of San Leandro, Calif. from her secret admirer.
HAPPY BIRTHDAY SKIP (fantastic) BAGDASARIAN FROM BIG "T"
HAPPY BIRTHDAY Sherry! Micky. (Chuckle, Chuckle).
HAPPY BIRTHDAY to a real outasite girl — Cathy Di Santis ... B.B.
KEN — Happy Birthday Darling. Blue Eyes Rule My Heart. — B.J.
HAPPY 14th BIRTHDAY to Joan Stolz, from Cathy and Cheryl
HAPPY BIRTHDAY, Patty Yanakeff, Utica, Michigan. From Bob and Kathy Gale.

CLASSIFIEDS

designed to buy, sell, find lose trade, give away, announce, notify, warn, or say whatever you wish.
Ads will be accepted for just about anything, including
for sale — wanted — pen pals
fan clubs — announcements — personals
lost guys and gals — special notices — everything else
Prices are cheap! Only 10c a word for personal messages (from you to someone else without an item for sale, trade, promotion, etc. involved). Other classifieds — just 20c a word.
Now what's a word? Well, it's the usual thing plus two groovy exceptions: the number and street (6290 Sunset Blvd.) are one word and the city and state count as only one word (Hollywood, California). Telephone numbers are one word (please include city or area code).

ABSOLUTE DEADLINE FOR NEXT ISSUE: APRIL 26
Send all advertisements (clearly printed or type) along with the correct amount of money to:

Classifieds
BEAT Publications
6290 Sunset Blvd. Suite 504
Hollywood, California 90028

KRLA ARCHIVES

KRLA BEAT

Volume 3, Number 5 — May 20, 1967

NEW STARR TO DEBUT

RINGO AND MAUREEN STARKEY are expecting their second baby in August or early September. Says Ringo: "When Zak was on the way we said all along it would be a boy. I do want another boy but it doesn't matter as much this time. We'll both be very happy whether it's a boy or a girl this time. Before we had a baby of our own, children were not all that important to me. Now it's entirely different. Every new stage of growing up gives us a lot of pleasure. Zak has just started joining words together. He's been chattering and saying the odd word for several months. Now he says whole phrases. It makes us feel just great to hear him."

Ringo and Maureen became parents in September, 1965 – Zak is now 19 months old. Maureen will celebrate her 21st birthday on August 4 of this year.

Beach Boy Defies Draft
Would Rather Go To Jail

Carl Wilson of the Beach Boys has decided to risk jail rather than report for induction into the Army.

Under a federal indictment charging him with violation of the Selective Service Act, Wilson plans to fight the case through the courts as a conscientious objector.

He faces the same charges as Heavyweight Champion Cassius Clay, although Clay has not yet been formally indicted.

Wilson was ordered to report for induction in Los Angeles on January 3. Like Clay, he refused to step forward to be sworn in.

He was indicted by a federal grand jury in Los Angeles on April 5 and later surrendered to the FBI in New York, where he was allowed to post bond.

Surprise

Carl's decision to fight the draft apparently came as a surprise to most of his friends—and perhaps even to his family.

The singer's father, Murray Wilson, cut short a European trip and returned home immediately after learning of his son's arrest.

"He never mentioned it to me," one close friend told The BEAT. "I don't ever remember hearing him even talk about being drafted, or how he felt about the draft in general."

Appearing before a Federal Judge in Los Angeles, Carl Wilson pleaded innocent to draft evasion charges.

He received permission to join the Beach Boys in England for a previously scheduled European tour. However, he was ordered to return June 20 for a trial on the charges.

Permission to travel abroad for the tour was granted only after he posted a $25,000 bond.

U.S. District Judge A. Andrew Hauk also ordered the singer to report periodically by telephone to Howard Smith, general attorney for the Beach Boys.

At the hearing, Attorney J.B. Tietz solemnly told the court his client "objects to all wars."

Although the arraignment will be June 2, Carl will probably remain free for a long time, even if he should ultimately lose the case.

A source in the U.S. Attorney's office privately estimated that he could remain free on bond for "at least a couple of years" if the attorneys use every legal recourse available.

Carl is scheduled for arraignment in Los Angeles on June 2. He faces a possible $10,000 fine and five years in jail if convicted.

Lawyer Optimistic

But his lawyer is optimistic about Carl's chances of winning the case, possibly on appeal. When asked if Wilson will go to jail rather than submit to induction, Tietz replied, "Oh yes, sure. But I don't think he'll have to."

CARL WILSON WILL GO TO JAIL RATHER THAN SERVE IN THE ARMY.

MICK JAGGER PUNCHED BY CUSTOMS OFFICIAL

PARIS—The Rolling Stones arrived at Le Bourget Airport in Paris following a concert at the Olympia Theater with cries of "Vive les Stones" still sounding in their ears. A quick-tempered customs official flipped when the five Stones' passports were handed to him in a pile. This enraged the guard so that he punched Mick Jagger in the chest and threw a hard blow at Keith Richard, diverted at the last second by road manager Tom Keylock.

Set-Up

The group's London press officer, Les Perrin, said, "It was a set-up. There were five officials waiting for us and one started throwing his weight around."

Another highlight in their roaring Continental tour was two sell-out concerts at the Palace of Culture. Polish police resorted to tear gas and truncheons when 8,000 fans who had been unable to obtain tickets, stormed the auditorium shrieking their disappointment. After the daytime performance, police brought up two heavy-duty water cannons and aimed them in readiness to subdue the evening's mobs. But this proved a futile attempt. Steel-helmeted troops complete with sub-machine guns and police dogs were rushed into action as the frenzied mob waded through the tear gas, lofting bottles and stones at the troops.

Good-bye Chaos

As the Stones left the chaos behind to return home to London, a spokesman announced the group will release a new single, shortly. No new plans have been announced regarding a future American tour for the Stones, although calls and letters from fans asking when and where have been flooding their New York office.

Dylan Dropped, Then Re-hired Same Day!

Bob Dylan, whose personal life is always shrouded in mystery, is now playing a guessing game with two major record companies – Columbia, which has him, and MGM, which wants him.

After dropping out of sight nine months ago, the poet-singer-composer remained secluded in a rural farmhouse last week while:

1. Columbia officially suspended him for "failure to fulfill his contractual agreements."
2. Re-instated him a few hours later announcing he had agreed to a specific recording schedule to satisfy terms of his five-year contract with Columbia, which expired in late 1966, but called for a specific number of recordings.
3. Personal acquaintances, industry sources and Dylan devotees swapped rumors and speculated on the reason for his inactivity, and whether he still plans to sign with MGM.

In July, 1966 Dylan was injured in a motorcycle accident and has made no records or personal appearances since that time. He's been in seclusion in a farm house near Woodstock, New York. This has given rise to the rumors that Dylan has never recovered from the accident.

Mort Nasatir, president of MGM Records, says that he has seen Dylan and that the entertainer appears to be fine. He also announced that MGM has offered Dylan a contract but: "Until he clears obligations with Columbia, he is still technically under contract to them. So that is the problem at the moment."

Dylan may be fine but he certainly isn't working. A special planned by ABC-TV on Dylan which would have run two hours had to be cancelled and Dylan's first book, "Tarantula," scheduled for publication last fall has yet to be seen.

Next Issue in The BEAT: **THE BEATLES** *glorious triumphs   uncertain future* • Exclusive Photos • Unpublished Facts

KRLA ARCHIVES

LETTERS TO THE EDITOR

PLACING THE BLAME

Dear *BEAT*:
You sure have a lot of nerve to say that Terry and the Pack sound like six months back. What do the Monkees sound? About four years back!

Terry and the Pack are breaking up this week and you cutting them down in your magazine really helps a lot! I dont' expect you to ever print my letter because Terry Knight and the Pack aren't popular enough or important enough to you! It makes me sick when you criticize their efforts after all the hard work and determination they've had through the past year and a half!

They never had a chance, thanks to you and others just like you! They are much greater and more talented than a lot of the groups you write up. But you don't care about that. You don't want to know about them. Not while they're new and still struggling. Well, it's thanks to you, as I said, that Terry and the band is breaking up. You make me sick!
Jan Post

Not only are we printing your letter, but we've also printed numerous letters in the past concerning Terry Knight and the Pack. They never made it with a nation-wide hit which would seem to indicate that the majority of the record-buyers did not particularly dig their sound.
The Editor

ADDITIONS TO P.A.T.A.

Dear *BEAT*:
I think your paper is fantastic, especially People Are Talking About. I also have a compulsion to send suggestions for P.A.T.A. to you, so . . . here goes again.

People are talking about false mustaches (of real hair) for boys and if the Simon Shop will take mail orders . . . Lynn Redgrave's marriage . . . the Monkees' movie . . . losing count of the times the DC5 have been on the "Ed Sullivan Show" . . . if Cat Stevens will publish his book and why radio stations have stopped playing "Matthew And Son" . . . the Latin and Egyptian sounds being added to the ever-growing list of pop music's possible paths in '67 and what will finally win out . . . pulling rickshaws in Hobart . . . David Cardwell thinking Davy would go when Chad and Jeremy would return home and deciding the difference is money . . . what happened to Robin Irene Boyd . . . Twiggy coming Stateside to sell her clothes . . . how Jan Berry is . . . whether or not Sheldon Leonard will get to film "I Spy" in Russia and wishing him luck . . . if Peter Tork knows how Huxley feels about "God Is Love" . . . when P.A.T.A. is going to get a by-line and who's writing that pillar.

That's the end of my suggestions from the outside world (actually, it's from behind the bars of a mental institution, but don't tell). Thanks for listening.
Linda Walker

LIVE AND LET LIVE

Dear *BEAT*:
I hate to be the one who says it, but why don't people live and let live? Do people expect to change a person's life by telling them that what they're doing is wrong?

All I hear anymore is, "Why did the Beatles go and grow those stupid mustaches and beards? Why did the Beatles decide to stop touring?" If this is what they want, let them do it in peace without the whole world breathing down their necks.

For the past three or four years, the Beatles have given to us the enjoyment and happiness this world so badly needed. They gave other groups confidence enough to make it to the top. They are still going pretty strong with their latest single. And only a couple of months ago they signed a contract with Capitol to give us nine more years of pleasure.

What happened to our courtesy and manners? Shouldn't we give our warmest appreciation and thanks instead of a "why did you change, I hate you now" attitude.

I think it's disgusting the way people talk about them now. But three or four years ago it was a lot different, wasn't it?

They brought us something new and challenging and we all loved it in one way or another. But now that they're "finished," as some people say, we must turn to something new. Forget what's in the past and conform to the recent trend. Is that what we're doing? I pity the people who think this way.

I, for one, am thankful that I was part of the "Beatle Invasion" that hit. I love them very much and I will always remember them as they are. The four lovable "mop-top" lads from Liverpool; John, Paul, George and Ringo.
Name withheld

AGREEMENT!

Dear *BEAT*:
I would like to thank "Cherry, Cherry" for writing to you about Neil Diamond. I agree with them 100%. I think, I *know*, Neil Diamond is the greatest singer and writer. I like all of the songs he writes and sings. I wish I could watch Neil perform sometime. He has a way of writing all to his own and no one can come close to his way.

The BEAT is just fantastic, cool, out-of-site and great. It seems to get better each issue that comes out. I am glad to see the classified ads and the other new items that you print. When I get *The BEAT*, I take it to school and, well, I don't see it for awhile because everybody likes to read it. Another thing I like about *BEAT* is that there are not too many advertisements but more and more news. Keep up the great work.
Jim Lennon
P.S. Who are the Beatles you talk about??????

THANKS

Dear *BEAT*:
I bestow upon *The BEAT* a multitude of thanks, not only from me, but from the thousands of Seed fans everywhere.

Thanks over and over again and please continue printing pictures and articles concerning the Seeds. Thank you ever so much.
Lynette

WHEELS A FARCE

Dear *BEAT*:
This is the first year that I have subscribed to *The BEAT*. I must say that I find this newspaper a real blast. One column I like is the Letters to the Editor.

I would first like to say something about Mitch Ryder. I think he is one of the best soul singers in the business. I have to say that "Sock It To Me, Baby" is really a song. And as far as the Detroit Wheels "making" Mitch Ryder—well, that is really a farce!

And another thing—I think the Monkees are the most "un-original" group going. I'll admit they put out good records and can sing very well, but that's about as far as it goes. If you left them alone to write by themselves, they couldn't come up with one hit. At least they haven't yet! The main reason most of their fans *are* fans is because of their TV show (which they copied off the Beatles.)

And last, I'd like to say something about the Beatles. There is no group going that can touch them. They're so good that all they need is their name on the label and it sells a million. But there's something else. It's not only the name, but the song. The Beatles (McCartney/Lennon) will undoubtedly go down in history as two of the best composers to come to the music business.
Steve Langlais

HOLY HOROSCOPE!!! WHO COPPED OUT??

Dear *BEAT*:
Holy Horoscope! I can't believe it! You've copped out! I swear you hired my *mother* to write Madame Zena's column. Good grief! My sign (Cancer) read like a tape recording of my old lady's harping!! (Shudder) Get this—"You should avoid: loading up on hot dogs and pizza and ruining your appetite for dinner. Success will be yours by: offering to help your mother with the dishes or the shopping. Avoid: complaining unnecessarily."

That's a horoscope??? Correction: That's *sabotage*!!! So I read on . . . hoping for refuge in my boyfriend's horoscope. Good Grief! Quote: "You will have a close brush with romance, but be careful. It is too soon to begin a permanent relationship. Avoid: Ignoring personal neatness. Don't be lazy: shower regularly."

Needless to say, I nearly choked! So, I read each and every horoscope! My mother wrote the *whole article!!* She told BEAT readers: "You can achieve the greatest success by: accepting advice from your parents, aunts and uncles . . . Avoid: motorcycles and going steady . . . risking your health by staying up too late, filling up on candy . . . dishonesty, especially on tests and written assignments . . . overly-tight bell bottoms . . . being unkind or unpleasant, especially where parents are concerned . . . and now is the time to: cut your bangs, clean out your closet and drawers and limit yourself to two ice creams a day . . . dress conservatively and win more friends . . . avoid too many social activities . . . turn down some dates and pay special attention to finishing your homework."

Dear *BEAT* Editor . . . horoscopes—my foot! Sermons! Please don't trouble yourself with printing my mother's dialogues . . . I hear them enough at home! Get the hint?
Beth Gineok

You'll be glad to know that Madame Zena has been fired, by popular request!
The Editor

JAMESON THE PROPHET

Dear *BEAT*:
This letter concerns the article about Bobby Jameson which ran in a recent issue of *BEAT*. I was so impressed, I couldn't resist writing this. Bobby Jameson is the most wonderful thing that could ever happen to this generation. I, myself, idolize him.

He's one person who really cares. He knows what's happening and what's going to happen. Just because he has long hair, wears a beard, dresses differently and lives for himself; to find out where he's going, people think he's weird and sick. Well, they've got a lot to learn.

Bobby Jameson is one of the most brilliant people in the world. He's so right in everything he says and does. He understands. He truly understands. But, he can't do what he and everyone else in this generation is aiming for alone. He has great courage, but like he says: "We're all a part of each other. It's your decision."
Sandi

VERY MANLY McCARTNEY

Dear *BEAT*:
This letter is important—depending on how you look upon the matter. Well, I guess I better get on with what I have to say. (My deepest wish is for Beatle Paul to receive or read this letter.)

This is what I'd like to tell Paul. I just love Paul with his mustache. Oh, he looks so much more manly and handsome. He looks as handsome as Omar Sharif (Doctor Zhivago). I'd like to repeat in saying that he no longer has that little choir boy look—but now looks very manly.
Vivian E. Lopez

Beat Publications, Inc.
Executive Editor . . . . Cecil I. Tuck
Publisher . . . . Tamyle Tuck
Editor . . . . Louise Criscione

Staff Writers
Carol Deck · Bobby Farrow
Ron Koslow · Shirley Poston
Rochelle Reed

Contributing Writers
Tony Barrow · Sue Barry
Lowrence Charles · Eden
Tammy Hitchcock · Rochelle Sech
Bob Levinson · Jamie McCluskey, III

Photographers
Chuck Boyd · Dwight Carter

Advertising
Dick Jacobson · Jerry Loss
Winona Price · Dick Stricklin
Ron Woodlin

Business Manager . . . . Judy Felice
Subscriptions . . . . Nancy Arena

Distribution
Miller Freeman Publications
500 Howard Street, San Francisco, Calif.

The *BEAT* is published bi-weekly by BEAT Publications, Inc., editorial and advertising offices at 6290 Sunset Blvd., Suite 504, Hollywood, California 90028. U. S. bureaus in Hollywood, San Francisco, New York, Chicago and Nashville; overseas correspondents in London, Liverpool and Manchester, England. Sale price 25 cents. Subscription price: U.S. and possessions, $5 per year; Canada and foreign rates, $9 per year. Second class postage prepaid at Los Angeles, California.

KRLA ARCHIVES

'Oo'—Ethiopean Premier Swipes Twiggy's Fans

LOS ANGELES—The spindly British moppet, Twiggy, blew into Los Angeles International Airport. Clinging to her constant-companion and manager, Justin De Villeneuve, Twiggy knock-kneed her way down the airplane steps and through an almost-deserted terminal to the Hotel Bel Air. Four photographers, two sound men, a body guard and a publicity girl, accompanied the sliver-thin queen of the fashion models.

Unlike New York, where teenage girls mobbed their idol, no enthusiastic screamers and autograph hunters were on hand. Her hotel press conference came close to being a wash-out when none of the press showed until an hour after the announced time. When she was told that most of the reporters were awaiting the arrival of Ethiopian Premiere Haile Selassie at the airport, Twiggy, gloriously uninformed on politics asked, "Oo?"

Basking in the warmth of the afternoon sun, Twiggy wiggled out of two sweaters, revealing her boyish 31-21-32, somehow managing to munch on her fingernails throughout the whole operation.

"It's so nice and warm 'ere," she said mindless of her H's. "I do like it 'ere but I miss me mum and dad."

Twiggy is visiting Los Angeles to film the second part of a three-part TV special. This one will be called "Twiggy In Hollywood" featuring, of course, a trip to Disneyland. She'll be visiting the Warner Brothers movie set of Camelot and model clothes at the Orange County Airport, showing off her 91-pound, million-dollar body.

STONES PLAGUED BY BREAK-UP RUMORS — BUT DENIAL IS ISSUED

The rumor goes: The Stones are breaking up. Mick is sick of performing and wants to concentrate on producing. Brian is even more bored with being a Stone and is quitting completely to go on his own as a solo act.

The answer, from a U.S. representative for the group, denies: "This rumor goes around about every three months. I can definitely say there is absolutely no word on the dissolution of the Stones and there will be no word on their dissolution."

Familiar Story

Really, it's a Beatle story all over again. The Stones, just finished with a European tour that found Polish youths tearing up government property and storming policemen, pelting them with rocks and bottles at the same time, is probably their last.

And Mick has been quoted by a number of papers as stating he will never tour the U.S. again.

Paris Different

The rest of the group agrees, saying that audiences can't hear them, therefore they can't play well. All told, says the group, they are reduced to simply jumping around onstage and yelling a lot.

But in Paris, says Mick, the story was different. People in their forties sat in the audience and they played a proper concert. People were even able to hear Brian's sitar.

While Mick admitted he never wants to do any more tours, he also said he enjoys performing on television and hopes to do so more often.

Plans for the Stones' movie, "Only Lovers Left Alive," have all but been abandoned, he added.

FORGET THE RUMOR that Brian has left the Stones

British Top 10

1. PUPPET ON A STRING ...... Sandie Shaw
2. SOMETHIN' STUPID ...... Frank & Nancy Sinatra
3. A LITTLE BIT ME, A LITTLE BIT YOU ...... Monkees
4. HA! HA! SAID THE CLOWN ...... Manfred Mann
5. RELEASE ME ...... Engelbert Humperdink
6. THIS IS MY SONG ...... Harry Secombe
7. PURPLE HAZE ...... Jimi Hendrix
8. BERNADETTE ...... Four Tops
9. IT'S ALL OVER ...... Cliff Richard
10. SIMON SMITH AND HIS AMAZING DANCING BEAR .. Alan Price Set

Write to:
THE SANDPIPERS FAN CLUB
247 So. Beverly Drive,
Beverly Hills, California

... YARDBIRD—Keith Relf

Yardbirds Set For U.S. Tour

LONDON—The Yardbirds will fly to the U.S. for a six-week midsummer tour beginning July 9 and running through Aug. 20. The group will hit mainly resorts and state fairs. Two early July concerts in Canada will preceed the U.S. visit.

HOLLIES INK EPIC

The Hollies have signed an exclusive recording contract with Epic Records. One of the most popular vocal-instrumental quintets in the world, The Hollies have scored 15 consecutive top-ten hits on the U.K. charts.

Their latest hit single, "On A Carousel," has had swift advancement in England, is a big chart item in other countries and is rapidly making its way to the top in this country.

Increased audience interest in a personal appearance tour in the U.S. was created when the Hollies first U.S singles, "I Can't Let Go" and "Look Through Any Window," zoomed to the top of the charts.

Two more chart-rocking singles followed—"Bus Stop" and "Stop, Stop, Stop" by the time the Hollies made their first U.S. tour with Herman's Hermits.

The Psychedelic In Have The VOODOO-HOODOO® CHARM!

- Keep the one you luv by exchanging the VOODOO-HOODOO!
- The Grooviest Charm!
- Based on the wild Voodoo belief that your heart and soul are tuned in and turned on by a lock of your hair and finger-nail clipping!
- We will personally fashion them into an original voodoo designed charm—surrounded by their own turned on glow!
- Wear it as a necklace ... bracelet ... key ring!
- With heavy mod chain ... silver or gold colored!
- THE VOODOO-HOODOO IS OUTASITE!

ONLY $1.95 PLUS .05 HANDLING CHARGE

SEND TO: THE HU-DO CREATORS, P.O. BOX 4696, PANORAMA CITY, CALIF. 91412
PLEASE RUSH ME THE FOLLOWING ORDERS. I ENCLOSE $2.00 FOR EACH ORDER. (BE SURE TO WRAP EACH SET OF CLIPPINGS SEPARATELY AND IDENTIFY BY NAME WHEN ORDERING TWO OR MORE.)

Send _____ Necklace(s) SILVER ☐ GOLD ☐
Send _____ Bracelet(s) SILVER ☐ GOLD ☐
Send _____ Key Ring(s) SILVER ☐ GOLD ☐

NAME: _____
ADDRESS: _____
CITY: _____ STATE: _____ ZIP: _____

Order Yours Today

KRLA ARCHIVES

Spencer Davis Has New Group

Spencer Davis has a brand new line-up for his new group, disrupted by the departure of the Winwood brothers. The new group is one shy of the originally planned five. The new members are organist Eddie Hardin, 18, and lead guitarist Phil Sawyer, 19, with Pete York remaining on the drums.

The new combo will have no distinct lead voice. Spencer, Eddie and Phil will share the singing. Bass rhythm will come from Eddie's manipulation of the organ foot pedals.

The group is set for a Scandanavian tour in June and then heads for Hungary in July. The group's first U. S. tour will be a five-week series of one nighters starting July 28.

Tremeloes Star On TV

The Tremeloes have definitely been signed to headline 26 color TV comedy shows to enjoy U.S. and world-wide screening. Peter Walsh, the group's manager, is back in England after sealing the agreement with Al Brodak of King Features which also handled the Beatles' cartoon series.

The BEAT has learned that the Tremeloes are thinking about a 40-day tour of this country starting June 11. One pilot for the TV show was filmed in Scotland but the feeling was that the humor was too British to appeal to American audiences. So, some American script writers may be brought in.

Gold 'Spirit' For Raiders

Paul Revere and the Raiders join the million-a-month club by earning three gold records in as many months. The RIAA has just certified the group's smash album, "The Spirit of '67," as a goldie.

Earlier this year, they received one for their LP, "Midnight Ride," and another for their album, "Just Like Us." Their latest LP, Paul Revere and the Raiders' Greatest Hits," became a sales fireball since its release last month, and is a leading candidate for gold record status.

The group's latest single "Him Or Me – What's It Gonna Be?" is climbing to the top of the charts with heavy national airplay.

Currently on a month-long tour of the U.S. and Canada, the Raiders are frequent guests on a variety of TV shows and enjoy constant concert bookings.

LOU RAWLS IS 'TOO MUCH!'

HOLLYWOOD — The audience at Hollywood's Coconut Grove was so much with Lou Rawls, that every gesture and sound the entertainer made brought a response from the three weeks of SRO houses during his recent engagement. Lou is easily at a peak in his personal appearances and also stands at the apex as a recording artist.

To date, the Chicago-born singer's success streak includes ten albums. "Live," recorded a year ago, began it all with certification by the RIAA as a gold record. Later on, in the past year, Rawls recorded three additional albums whose soaring sales records assured him of a rank equal to any of the great singers of our time.

"Live" was followed by "Soulin'," which has now reached the 400,000 mark and is nearing gold record status. "Carryin' On," followed next and has already hit the 200,000 figure.

The soon-to-be-released, "Too much," has topped 100,000 on advance order copies. Total Rawls sales last month have everybody saying, "Too much:" $5 million in albums and singles!

Tears, Tension, Trauma Follow College Letters

Someone had to be disappointed. Of the 45,611 applicants who applied to the prestigious Ivy League Colleges and the Seven Sister Schools in the Northeast only 12,360 got yes as an answer. The story was the same this year only worse: many more applicants than places at the nation's top schools.

The colleges have drifted from their geographic distribution policy which had tried to spread the freshman class evenly over the country. This tipped the scales for applicants from the Northeast who formerly had to face fierce competition from their counterparts in Montana and Texas who often had lower grades.

Most colleges actively scouted up Negro freshman applicants, continuing a recent pattern. Cornell accepted 110 Negroes and Radcliffe 15.

Students from public high schools are running stronger than in the past against their counterparts from private prep schools. Almost 59 percent of Harvard's incoming freshmen come from public schools as do 58 per cent of Yale's – and the proportion seems to be growing, but slowly.

The air was charged and the reaction highly emotional when the all-important letter arrived from college admissions offices of the Ivy schools. "I'm glad it's all over," sighed one Connecticut teenager who received two no's and one yes, "If college has half the pressure in it that's involved in waiting to hear about admissions, then it should be a snap!"

TRINI IS NAMED TOP PERFORMER

MONTREAL — The dust was barely collecting on Trini Lopez' Man of the Year Award which he collected in a celebration at the Dallas hotel where his father worked as a janitor, when he again interrupted a three-week series of one night concerts in the East, to pick up another trophy. He was named Entertainer of the Century in the variety field by the Expo '67 Special Awards Committee. The award, "in recognition of his contribution and status in the entertainment world," was presented at a dinner at the Palace Bonaventure in Montreal.

Film For Dead And Airplane

HOLLYWOOD — Two San Francisco-based rock groups, the Grateful Dead and the Jefferson Airplane have been signed to do sections of "Petulia," a forthcoming Warner Brothers feature film while it is shooting in San Francisco.

New Acts On Sinatra Tour

Sergio Mendes & Brazil '66 and nightclub and television comic, Pat Henry, are booked for the Frank Sinatra seven-city summer concert tour.

The tour kicks-off in Pittsburg on July 2 and will hit Philadelphia, Detroit, Cleveland, Chicago, Madison and winds up in Baltimore on July 15.

PEOPLE ARE TALKING ABOUT the small wave of excitement caused by Paul's visit to the U.S. when before even the rumor that a Beatle was in town won city-wide hysteria ... how unbelievable it is that after all the delays Sonny and Cher's movie is finally out ... the Young Rascals groovin' again after being down ... whether or not the Raiders who split are going to form their own group – or whether or not the other two will really split
... how popular(?) Twiggy is with the teens and coming to the conclusion that she's an adult phenomenon – not a kids' ... whether or not the Stones' movie has been junked permanently and deciding that it has ... this being the year the groups broke up ... Patti Harrison getting her long hair cropped short ... Stone spokesmen denying that Brian Jones is leaving the group along with manager, Andrew Oldham, despite the rumors which keep circulating around
... the charity concerts the Supremes are doing in most of the major U.S. cities this year ... when the entire Sinatra family is going to get together on record ... the Turtles thinking they came out of the popcorn bag ... how old "I Think We're Alone Now" is ... where all the pop excitement has gone ... the possibility that Eric Burdon is mellowing in his old age ... the Beatles and the Monkees having the only two million-selling singles on the national charts.

... whether or not Paul McCartney really did flip for the Jefferson Airplane as one reporter said he did ... Mick Jagger's statement to the press that he will not tour the U.S. again and wondering if it's his decision to save face just in case the Stones don't get work permits ... whether or not England is going back for country and western music and deciding that if Engelbert Humperdinck is any indication, they've already gone

... whether or not Herbie Alpert is losing the popularity he once had among the young set ... Carl Wilson saying "why me?" ... Don Gallucci's hilarious tales of the waitresses and phone operators he ran into on tour .
a few rhythm 'n' blues stations playing the Rascals without knowing who they are ... the Happenings really being the Happenings and now wondering who the Parade are ... David Crosby spend-

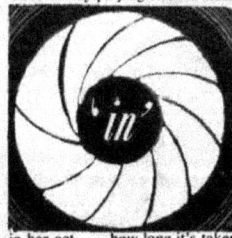

ing more time with the Beatles than he does with the Byrds

... driving to the airport in a chauffeur driven limousine just to interview Dave Dee, Dozy, Beaky, Mick and Tich ... the nice break the Merry Go Round got by being asked to play at Sonny and Cher's party for Twiggy ... sending Diana Ross to Weight Watchers ... Brenda Holloway playing electric violin in her act ... how long it's taken the Easybeats to get a hit record in the United States
... when Neil Diamond is going to get the recognition he deserves and deciding that this day will definitely come ... how the work permit situation is going to be this summer and coming to the conclusion that with the drug investigations in England it's going to be plenty tough to get U.S. work permits this time around ... how sweet the soul music is these days ... Seeds having a hard, hard time getting on the national charts
... the Oogum Boogum man, Brenton Wood, having one of the wildest album covers yet ... Bill Cosby's "take a hike" turning into a "Revenge" but making little difference since it's bound to sell a million no matter what it's called
... Stone's manager, Andrew Oldham, borrowing Stone pictures from The BEAT and what a switch that was ... whether or not the Monterey Pop Festival is going to be a huge success or an even bigger bomb and deciding that it all depends on you ... Cass having a baby girl ... how funny it is to see Frankie Laine back on the pop charts ... how upset Twiggy got because people around the Bel Air Hotel kept thinking she was Mia Farrow.

... Jimi Hendrix playing his guitar with his teeth and how it must have hurt when it blew-up ... Joey Paige going to Vietnam to entertain our troops ... Ala Mod, the new pop film that Tanden Almer (composer of "Along Comes Mary") wrote the music for ... the top rhythm 'n' blues singer who has been slapped with two paternity suits ... jets being the latest thing to buy with the Turtles having one and Dennis Wilson buying one ... Eric Burdon not quite as hung-up over the racial situation in America as he used to be.
... the opera singer who covered the Beatles ... the English group who said pop is dying in England because the kids just go to tear up the theatres and not to hear the act ... Chrissie Shrimpton having a new boyfriend who is not in the business – had enough of them when she broke with Mick Jagger ... the Mothers being in England ... why the chauffeur once threw the Monkees out of their rented limousine ... Chris Britton's leaving the Troggs being nothing more than a publicity stunt

... whether or not Dusty Springfield is really coming Stateside for club dates ... the Dave Clark Five possibly being the only major British group to remain in the touring bag, with the one exception of Herman's Hermits.

PEOPLE ARE ALSO TALKING ABOUT how much fun it is to receive BEAT through the mail – Subscription form is on Page 23. Your name will appear on the cover of every issue.

KRLA ARCHIVES

ON THE BEAT
By Louise Criscione

Whoever said being a pop star is an easy life is out of his mind! When the Rolling Stones landed in Zurich, Switzerland 2,000 fans showed up to welcome them. However, they attempted to get aboard the jet which carried the Stones and the police were forced to use water hoses to control the crowd and get the Stones out of the airport unharmed.

That night a capacity crowd of 12,000 tried to storm the stage of the Zurich Concert Hall while the Stones were performing. They made human pyramids to climb over the the 15 foot high stage and when some of them made it onto the stage the Stones ran off through an emergency exit.

Injured Fans

As soon as the police had the fans removed from the stage, the Stones returned to finish the show—but the trouble was far from over. One fan suffered a fractured skull when he was pushed from the stage, ten other audience members were injured at the end of the concert when the audience smashed seats in the auditorium in an attempt to get the Stones to return for an encore.

Five of the injured fans had to be hospitalized, one of them in critical condition, and the damage to the concert hall was estimated to be more than $2,000.

... KEITH RICHARD

Although Mick Jagger has reportedly told the British press in no uncertain terms that the Stones would never tour America again, Andrew Oldham, Stones' manager, told me today that it all depends on a number of things—the first of which is the outcome of the court hearings in England.

There is another member of the Lopez family on the scene. Trini's younger brother, Jesse, has been signed to make his singing debut at the Bonanza Hotel in Las Vegas for a month beginning July 1. Trini has been helping his brother along with his career and it will be interesting to see if Jesse performs in the same bag his brother lives in.

May's Wendy Ward

Claudine Longet, Andy William's wife, has been named Miss Wendy Ward for the month of May in a promotion sponsored by 1500 Montgomery Ward stores. Herbie Alpert's label, A&M Records, is not crying over Claudine's prize since each one of the stores will feature her album, "Claudine," in their window displays as part of the promotion.

Everyone is busy speculating on how Carl Wilson's refusal to report for the draft will affect the career of the Beach Boys. Carl's attorney says Carl will go to jail rather than be inducted, but he added that he didn't think he would have to. However, the whole thing depends on what the courts have to say about the matter.

I, for one, would certainly like to know the real story concerning the Raiders. It's obvious that Raider spokesmen are not going to admit anything, but very reliable sources continue to say that Fang and Smitty are planning to follow Harpo's decision to leave the group. This would, of course, leave only Paul Revere and Mark Lindsay—or Paul Revere and the Raider if you prefer.

As I said before, Raider officials continue to deny Smitty and Fang's decision to depart. But, then, I seem to remember that they also denied Harpo's leaving right up until he left. So...

The nice thing about American television series is that the two-parters can be put together and sold as a full-length movie in Europe. The latest "movie" to be released in foreign countries is a two-part segment of "The FBI" series which stars Efrem Zimbalist Jr. It will be called, "Cosa Nostra — An Arch Enemy Of The FBI," and will be released by Warner Brothers.

They did this with a segment from the old "Untouchables" and to date the film has grossed between four and five million dollars, which isn't bad when you consider how much cheaper television shows are to make than movies.

... MARK LINDSAY

DON AND THE GOODTIMES ADD NEW GROUP MEMBER
By Sandra Skolnik

His name is Jeff Hawks, and he's the newest member of Don & The Goodtimes.

It happened suddenly, surprisingly, with less notice than the draft boards give. And, Jeff is the first to admit he's not quite over the wonderment of becoming part of the fastest-rising group in the country.

"Meant Me"

"When the Goodtimes recorded 'I Could Be So Good To You,' it's almost as if they meant me," he laughs.

The long and lanky lead singer was confronted with his great career opportunity when Big Don McKinney was taken ill and ordered home to Portland, Ore., by his doctors. It happened in March, just a few weeks before the Goodtimes were supposed to start a month-long nationwide tour for Dick Clark, who'd provided them and first given them cross-country fame on "Where The Action Is."

Coincidence

Jeff was in Los Angeles at the time, by quirk and coincidence auditioning for a new, in-the-works TV series at Dick Clark Productions. (The inside word, in fact, is that he was the leading candidate.)

Lil' Don Gallucci of the Goodtimes was helping out the audition process by playing piano for the candidates, as a favor to his friends in the Clark organization.

Small World

Jeff knew Li'l Don from the days when he was singing with a competing band in the Northwest, Hawk and the Randellas. He was Hawk and (Small World!) Buzz Overman of the Goodtimes was one of the Randellas.

It was only natural that Li'l Don insist Jeff swing over to the Goodtimes house to say hello to Buzzy and the other guys. He did and, while waiting out word on the audition, became a regular visitor to the group's groovy pad in Hollywood.

Then, in the middle of recording their first album for Epic Records, Big Don became sick. Concern for their friend was followed by the realization that a replacement had to be found. And, in a hurry!

All eyes turned to Jeff.

"Groovy Guy"

"He's a groovy guy and a great outasite singer," according to Buzby. "He made my old band go, and I knew the Hawk could really help us out."

Charlie Coe said, "The fans really dug him during our Dick Clark tour, and I feel we're awfully lucky to have Jeff with us."

Jeff commented, "I was really sorry for Big Don when he got sick and a little scared about trying to do his job, because I know how talented he is and how much everyone digs him.

"My Best"

"I hope to prove myself a worthy successor, although I doubt if anyone could ever really replace Big Don. Anyway, I'm just going to get out there and give it my best."

Jeff, 20, celebrates his birthday on August 31. He's an even 6 feet tall and weighs 150 pounds. He has black hair and large, loving brown eyes.

He's from Oakland, where his family, including two younger brothers, still reside. Jeff loves sports of all kinds, writes short stories and songs, and idolizes The Beatles.

He'll be meeting fans in the Los Angeles area for the first time in late May, when Don & The Goodtimes play a few local dates. Then it's off to the Northwest, Southwest and Midwest for the group, a two-month concert swing designed to bring a live version of "I Could Be So Good To You" to everyone who's already heard it hundreds of times over the radio.

... JEFF HAWKS: New Goodtime.

WHERE THEY ARE

SUPREMES
May 11-24, Copa Cabana, N.Y.; May 26, University of Cincinnati; May 28, Hara Arena, Dayton, Ohio; May 29, The Auditorium, Minneapolis, Minn.; May 30, Arena Auditorium, Duluth, Minn.; June 1-10, Shoreham Hotel, Washington D.C.; June 11, Symphony Hall, N.J.; June 13-26, Coconut Grove, Hollywood; June 29-July 19, Flamingo Hotel, Las Vegas.

RIGHTEOUS BROTHERS
May 29 begin one month engagement, Cocoanut Grove.

TEMPTATIONS
May 12, State University, Cortland, N.Y.; June 2-3, Twin Coaches, Pittsburg, Pa.; July 9-15, Steel Pier, Atlantic City.

FOUR TOPS
May 11-20, Basin St. West, San Francisco; May 25-June 4, Whisky A Go-Go, Los Angeles; June 21, Town House, Huntington, Long Island; June 22, White Plains High School, White Plains, N.Y.; June 23-24, Twin Coaches, Pittsburg; July 1, Central Park, New York City.

SMOKEY ROBINSON AND THE MIRACLES
May 12, Montgomery Blair High School, Silversprings, Md.; May 13, Washington College, Chestertown, Md.; May 14, Civic Auditorium, Baltimore, Md.; May 25-June 3, Basin St. West, San Francisco.

JEFFERSON AIRPLANE
May 12-14, Fillmore Auditorium, San Francisco; May 18, Stockton, California; May 19, California Polytechnic College, San Luis Obispo, Calif.; May 20, Birmingham High School, Van Nuys, Calif.; May 26-29, Seattle; May 30-June 2, shooting Warner Brothers film, "Petulia"; June 4, Sam Houston Coliseum, Houston, Texas.

TURTLES
May 12, Hinsdale, Illinois, Central High School; May 13, Coliseum Ballroom, Bend, Illinois; May 14, Wichita, Kansas; May 17, Battle Creek, Michigan; May 18, Township High School, Waukegan, Illinois; May 19, Ashland, Wisc.; May 27-30, Steel Pier, Atlantic City, N.J.; May 31-June 9, tour of England-France-Germany-Denmark; June 24, Lagoon Ballroom, Salt Lake City, Utah.

MARVIN GAYE
May 26-June 3, Beach Club, Myrtle Beach, S.C.

MARTHA AND THE VANDELLAS
May 4-14, Whisky A Go-Go, L.A.; May 26-June 4, Boulevarde Club, Rego Park, N.Y.; May 10, Cornell University, Ithaca, N.Y.; May 12-18, Esquire Club, Montreal, Canada.

JOHNNY RIVERS
June 2-4, Vancouver B.C.; Edmonton, Alberta; Calgary, Alberta.

RICK NELSON
June 29-July 5, San Diego County Fair Show, Del Mar Racetrack, Del Mar, Calif.; August, Steel Pier, Atlantic City, N.J.

JAMES DARREN
June 19, "Wish You Were Here," St. Louis Municipal Opera.

BOBBY RYDELL
Signed for ABC-TV's "Piccadilly Palace," the summer replacement for "Hollywood Palace."

ASSOCIATION
May 11, Riverside High School, Riverside, Illinois; May 12, Niles High School, Niles, Mich.; May 13, Indiana State University, Bloomington, Ind.; May 18, Columbia Basin College, Pasco, Wash.; May 20, Pacific Auditorium, San Jose, Calif.

DON & THE GOODTIMES
May 12, Casey Kasem Dance, Hawthorne, Calif.; May 19, University of New Mexico, Albuquerque, New Mexico; May 26-30, Portland area; May 27, Coliseum, Portland, Oregon; May 31-June 15, Southwestern United States; June 17-25, headlining Teenage Fair, Seattle, Washington; June 26-July 3, concerts in the Seattle area; July 3, three weeks heading a Dick Clark tour through the Midwest.

KRLA ARCHIVES

SPECIAL REPORT BY TONY BARROW

Pop Concerts — Essential Or Obsolete In '68?

...THE JAGGER: "We shall never tour America again."
BEAT Photo: Chuck Boyd

THE BEATLES have decided that it is no longer possible for them to gain anything other than dollars galore from putting on concert performances.

"A group on a stage can't get together with 60,000 people and do anything worthwhile" says John.

"Someday we may work out a way of doing 'live' shows but it won't be anything like a conventional concert format," agrees Paul. "I mean we could go on in funny hats and do a dance. We could switch on fifty tape recorders and try to get something like our recorded sound. Would people want to come? Would they want to listen?"

Bring-Downs

In Paris MICK JAGGER pinpointed other touring problems when he discussed the matter in much depth with *Melody Maker's* Mike Hennessey: "The one-night scene is dead terrible. The people need something much more to watch. I have got some ideas on how to change things — to do something different — but it would be expensive. We shall never tour America again. It is very hard work and one bring-down after another. Every place you go there is a barrage of relentless criticism. You get ten reporters every day who just want to laugh at you and you don't get one even vaguely intelligent question."

In theatres and clubs where the atmosphere must be slightly more intimate and inspiring than it could ever be in the Cow Palace or Dodger Stadium, a performer can feel he is on the same wave length as his audience. But even then the modern electronic recording studio has a thousand special sound facilities which are not available at the average concert or 'live' show venue.

Repeated History

The whole of London's music business is eager to find out what THE MONKEES can and cannot do vocally and instrumentally. Until the end of June we can gauge their potential only from out-of-date records. Yet when they do perform for a total of 50,000 British fans, shall we be any wiser? Shall we hear their voices distinctly or be able to judge their musicianship? Probably not. Instead our eyes will see four familiar figures and our ears will be flooded with the uncouth sound of fan enthusiasms rather than Monkee music. Not that 50,000 fans of the group will worry. They've been through similar experiences for The Beatles, The Stones and The Beach Boys, and the qualities of actual performance and sound reproduction have taken a very secondary place to the brute-force excitement of such occasions. They come to wail and moan, to fling their bodies about and be thrilled. Not to listen or appreciate, not to praise or find fault.

For some years the performers themselves have taken an equally artless view of concerts. They have been willing to put up with professional prostitution in return for substantial financial gain.

Changing Scene

Now, one by one, the world's best groups are taking their stand against the one-night stand. And if only inferior acts are going to be prepared to tour in 1968, perhaps the whole conception of the pop concert will become obsolete. The last remaining medium for the wholly successful purveyance of pop music will be that of the recording tape, in disc, cartridge or other yet-to-be-developed audio or video form.

Yardbirds' TV Special

The Yardbirds filmed their own 30-minute TV special in Paris to be aired over French stations. Earlier this month they put in an appearance at the Cannes Film Festival timed to coincide with the screening of the film "Blow Up" in which they have a featured role.

SPECIAL OFFER TO BEAT READERS!!

TEEN INTERNATIONAL APPROVED

AUTHENTIC MONKEESHADES by DEBS®

* 5 Groovy Colors...rose...yellow... blue...grey...green
* Heavy Mod Golden Chain
* Just Like the MONKEES Wear On Their Swingin' TV Show
* MONKEESHADES are the Wildest!

ONLY $1.98 PLUS .02 HANDLING CHARGE

Send to: MONKEESHADES, 81 W. State St., Pasadena, California 91105
PLEASE SEND ME THE MONKEESHADES AS INDICATED. I ENCLOSE $2.00 FOR EACH PAIR

COLOR_____ NO. PAIRS_____ TOTAL AMOUNT ENCLOSED_____
Name_____
Address_____
City_____ State_____ Zip Code_____

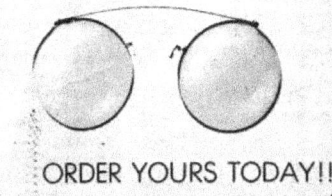

ORDER YOURS TODAY!!

KRLA ARCHIVES

across the board

FROM THE EDITOR . . .

Whether you love or loathe them, think they're preposterous or delightful, you cannot in honesty deny the fact that Sonny and Cher exert a tremendous influence over the young generation. You can chalk the mini-skirts up to London but you can't explain away the abundance of wild-patterned, bell-bottomed pants which appeared on young figures everywhere simply "because Cher wears them."

Hit after hit, mob scene after mob scene, sell-out concerts all over the nation . . . Sonny and Cher Bono are one of the (if not *the*) most popular duos in the music world. They've been consistently pro-young people ever since they started out as Caesar and Cleopatra. Little wonder that young people have remained pro-Sonny and Cher. Little wonder that *The BEAT* is taking this opportunity to salute the Bonos – Sonny and Cher.

Also in this issue we have a fan's own account of her meeting with the Monkees outside of the RCA Victor recording studios in Hollywood; the Righteous Brothers, Bobby and Bill, answer the charges that they've abandoned the teens for the lucrative adult market; and in an exclusive interview, Motown's fantastic Temptations talk about their music, about the successful Motown family, the group who got them started and loads of other interesting topics.

As *BEAT* goes along, we intend to print more and more news stories. We will, of course, continue to run feature articles but we feel that with an increase in news we can keep you better informed on what's going on with the entertainment world, the fashion world and the world of your fellow young adults.

And for those of you who may have been complaining about a lack of Beatle pictures and stories, we plan to remedy that in the next four issues. Each issue will feature a different Beatle on the cover as well as a feature story inside. All our photos are brand new and were taken during the Beatles' recent recording session in England.

Again – if you have any opinions, ideas or suggestions, please let us know.

Louise Criscione

'ROUND THE WORLD

NEW YORK – Alien Actors will find it more difficult to land jobs on Broadway and at Lincoln Center since the membership of Actors Equity at a recent special meeting approved 491-2 a resolution restricting the hiring of actors from abroad (except Canadians) by requiring the consent of the union's 72-member governing council to contracts.

The resolution faces opposition from the League of New York Theaters, composed of producers and theater owners. Equity also voted to set up a strike fund for 1968 in case they find it necessary to carry their ban on foreign performers to the picket line.

LOS ANGELES – Burt Bacharach has signed a producing and recording contract with A&M. His first single release on the label pairs his composition, the theme from "Casino Royale" film, "Bond Street," and "Alfie" which netted him an Oscar nomination.

BURBANK – Grammy Award-winners Ray Charles, The Anita Kerr Singers and guitarist Wes Montgomery began taping "The Best On Record" special at NBC studios here. George Schlatter is producing the Timex sponsored color show.

HOLLYWOOD – Joey Bishop in Hollywood will split the screen with Hugh Downs in New York as emcees of the Emmy awards telecast on ABC June 4. The Hollywood end of the 19th annual event will be held at modern Century Plaza Hotel.

BURBANK – A reported million-dollar price tag hangs on Warner Brothers Records recent purchase of Valiant Records, Sherman-DeVorzon Music and Barbil Music, publishing subsidiaries of Valiant. The Valiant label, founded by Barry DeVorzon and Billy Sherman seven years back, features The Association and two new rock groups, The Collectors and the Six Hard Way. Sherman will remain to manage the publishing concerns while DeVorzon will pick up writing songs and film scripts.

CONSHOHOCKEN – Where? Yes, a small Pennsylvania town, like other small towns, long-ignored by night club owners. Now the town's 14-20-year-olds can buy (for $2.50) a rock-packed evenings fun at Hullabaloo, (named after the TV show), a liquorless teen club which draws 35,000 teenagers a night at 30 franchise locations in U. S. communities.

Hullabaloo founder, John Angel sell $17,000 franchises at the rate of two a week and forecasts a national chain of 500 by 1970. In Conshohocken rigid security measures turn away over 21-ers and refuse readmittance to dancers during an evening thereby nipping in the bud the problem of boys who sneak a nip in the parking lot between dances.

HOLLYWOOD – Nancy Sinatra who has just formed Boots Productions will team up with Sal Mineo to co-star in an independent film feature called, "The Flower Children."

Making The News

Prince Charles had all of England buzzing with the question "Who was that lady?" The leggy blonde's name was practically top secret and the London papers titled her the "Mystery Girl" who was on the prince's arm at the theater. A reporter for London's *Daily Mail* did some investigating and revealed she is 28-year-old **Angela Rau**, an Australian who works for a London advertising agency. "And I'm sorry to disillusion the romantics," wrote the reporter, "but she is not a girlfriend of the Prince's." After the show, Angela, who has ten years on the prince; Charles' little sister, Princess Anne, 16; and Aunt Princess Margaret and Uncle Lord Tony Snowdon all had a not-too-romantic bite to eat.

* * *

Le President Rosko is the hottest bit of Americana rock to bombard the French airwaves. Rosko, who borrowed his air name from a New York Negro DJ, is really 24-year-old Michael Pasternak, son of Hollywood Producer, Joe Pasternak. "I've stolen from the top six disc jockeys in the U.S. and made the result French," said Le President. Multimillionaire Jean Prouvost (whose financial interests include textiles, Paris-Match and Le Figaro) was trying to edge Radio Luxembourg into the number one slot over France Inter, the government station. The teenage market was dominated by a DJ who opened his show with "Hi Friends," which was considered very far out. Using American style jingles and cacaphonous sound effects he is now on top of the DJ scene with his show "Mini-Max" (minimum de blah-blah, meximum de musique.)

* * *

Tunesmith Jeff Barry scored a music-history first in signing an exclusive, three-year songwriting contract with Unart Music, a United Artist music company. The contract's terms guarantee Barry what may be one of the largest fees of this kind ever paid to a composer. Unart will own copyrights on all Barry's new songs, save for songs the Monkees record and special film scores.

Over 50 per cent of his recorded compositions have climbed over the top 40 mark on the nation's best-selling charts. Some of his hits include: "Maybe I Know" (Lesley Gore), "Hanky Panky" (Tommy James and the Shondells), "Doo Wah Diddy Diddy" (Manfred Mann) and "Then He Kissed Me" (Crystals).

* * *

Rex Harrison of Professor Higgins fame, was awarded the Order of Merit of the Italian Republic for "his contributions to the social welfare of the Italian people, for his contributions to the arts, and his distinguished career." The actor, currently filming 20th Century-Fox's "Doctor Doolittle," received the citation, one of Italy's highest honors, from Dr. Alvara Vito Beltrani, Italian Consul General in Los Angeles.

Petula Clark signed a long-term contract with Warner Brothers Records, John K. Maitland, WB President announced. Maitland negotiated the contract with Leon Cabat, President of Vogue Records in Paris who produce Petula's records for U.S. release.

Currently on a concert series tour, Petula has been signed for the lead part in the Warner film, "Finian's Rainbow." Her latest single hit, "This Is My Song," from Charles Chaplin's "Countess From Hong Kong," has topped the 650,000 mark.

David Janssen, who just finished years of "The Fugitive" TV series, will star opposite Barbra Streisand in "Funny Girl" which will begin filming at Columbia in July. Director William Wyler and producer Ray Stark are reportedly near closing the deal with Rosalind Russell to co-star as the mother in the film version of the Broadway hit.

* * *

College Temps, Inc., has given about 3,000 New York teenagers a break and signed them to fill clerical jobs such as typists, accounting clerks, bank tellers and researchers. Teenagers are explored, exploited and entertained. Finally, they're being hired to ease New York's serious shortage of office help. Working schedules are wild and range up to forty hours. Wary employers are pleased to find teens are a good business risk.

* * *

Andy Williams apparently feels the show must go on, even if the performer almost went down. En route to his recent Toronto concert, Andy Williams accompanied by Henry Mancini and his orchestra, were forced to make an emergency landing at the Greater Buffalo International Airport when their charter plane developed engine trouble. Upset but unharmed, the 63-member party was bussed the rest of the way and arrived for an on-time curtain raising. Andy has smashed house attendance records throughout his 16-city tour of the U.S. His Rochester concert was delayed over an hour by the spillover throngs crowding the streets trying to be admitted to the auditorium to hear him perform. Andy set new house records in Toronto, Charlotte, Mobile, Greensboro, Knoxville, Nashville, Indianapolis, Louisville, Cincinnati and Pittsburgh.

"FBI" TV series star, Efrem Zimbalist Jr. visited American troops in Vietnam. Himself a World War II Purple Heart Vet, Zimbalist brought a little bit of Hollywood to battle zones and outposts restricted to larger show units. Returning on a kind of star-shuttle from the war-torn country were Ed Nelson, Tim O'Connor, Chris Connelly and Pat Morrow who resume their roles in 20th Century-Fox's "Peyton Place."

Dave Dee, Dozy, Beaky, Mick and Tich are on what could develop into a world tour for them. Dave Dee & Co. stepped in for the Hollies who dropped out of the second leg of a world tour due to their drummer's illness. After New Zealand and Paris engagements, they're off to the Far-East for live appearances and concerts. "Following this," says leader Dave Dee, "we want to come to the U.S. The way things look now, it won't be long at all."

* * *

The fuzz is in for next season. Six TV police series are planned by the networks for 1967-68 as compared with three last year. "Dragnet," "The FBI" and "Felony Squad" have been renewed while "N.Y.P.D." about the New York Police Department, and "Ironside" and "Mannix", two private eye shows will be introduced.

Spys are slipping. "The Man Who Never Was," "Jericho" and "The Girl From U.N.C.L.E." are all biting the dust leaving the field open to "I Spy" and "The Man From U.N.C.L.E."

The only variety show not axed for next season is "The Smothers Brothers Show." Fall variety starters will be "The Carol Burnett Show" and "The Jerry Lewis Show" joining the returning series starring Ed Sullivan, Dean Martin, Jackie Gleason, Red Skelton and "Hollywood Palace."

Several cowboy shows have been outdrawn. Axed are "The Road West," "Shane," "The Rounders," "Laredo" and "The Monroes." But new entries will be filling the sagebrush trail. They are: "The Cimarron Strip," "The Legend of Custer," "Hondo" and "The Guns of Will Sonnett. "Gunsmoke," "The Virginian," "The Iron Horse" and "The Wild, Wild West," will return.

Spoof shows all goofed. Cancelled for next season are: "Mr. Terrific," "Captain Nice," "Rango," "The Hero," "Run, Buddy, Run," and "Pistols 'n' Petticoats."

"The Doodletown Piper Hour" will fill the summer variety show slot of the vacationing Smothers Brothers. The Pipers, a young singing group who appear frequently on TV shows and other night spots, consist of ten boys and ten girls with an average age of 19. The group served as regulars on the Roger Miller Show and were guests on Ed Sullivan's Show.

KRLA ARCHIVES

Beat Salutes Sonny And Cher

The great American dream of sudden fame and fortune has come true for Sonny and Cher.

In the Youth World of pop blues, kicky clothes, customized cars and new art, Sonny and Cher are top singers who have become super-stars with their first movie, "Good Times." But their success story is not strictly a rags-to-riches tale with some overnight fame thrown in.

Sonny was born in Detroit, Mich., on February 16, 1940, the youngest child of Jean and Santo Bono. He was christened Salvatore, but his parents and sisters, Fran and Betty, called him Sonny from the start.

The family moved to Inglewood, California, where Sonny's father, who emigrated from Italy, was employed by an aircraft company. Sonny wanted a career in show business; to go after it, he quit Inglewood Union High School in the twelfth grade.

For a year he worked as a truck driver, masseur, waiter and at other odd jobs. Then, in 1957, he became a songwriter and later an A&R (Artist & Repertoire) man for Specialty Records. He went on to learn every facet of the business by working for various record companies.

At the time he met Cher in 1963, Sonny had written a number of successful songs including "Koko Joe," "You Bug Me Baby" and "Needles and Pins." He had played and sung on many recording dates, and had acquired a professional knowledge of record production.

Cher is the elder daughter of Georgia and Gilbert LaPiere. She was born May 20, 1946, in El Centro, California, although the family lived in Los Angeles, where her father was a bank branch manager. She has a younger sister, Georgeanne. The girls are of Armenian, Turkish, French and Cherokee Indian descent.

Cher wanted to be an actress, so while she was still in school she studied with Jeff Corey, a well known dramatic coach. Restless for a career, she left Montclair High School in the eleventh grade.

Cher met Sonny on a double date the week she turned 17. She remembers that his Prince Valiant haircut "made him look kind of weird," while Sonny didn't like her at first and thought she was stuck-up. Nevertheless they danced all that night, and after seeing one another for about

(Turn to Page 10)

BEAT ART: Ray Leong & Associates

KRLA ARCHIVES

KRLA ARCHIVES

Tracing Their Career

a year they were married on October 27, 1964. It was Sonny's second marriage.

During their courtship, Sonny was working for Phil Spector, a legendary record producer specializing in rock and roll. They went to a recording session one night, and Cher filled in for a background vocalist who hadn't shown up. Sonny thought she had a good voice, but needed practice. Neither was pleased at the way their careers were going at the time, so working together and inspiring each other they recorded a song called "The Letter" under the name of Caesar and Cleo.

Baby Don't Go

Shortly after their marriage a few months later they recorded one of Sonny's songs, "Baby Don't Go," under their own names. It was a hit, and after one record (Sonny's "Dream Baby," which Cher cut as a soloist) they scored again with "Just You," an early 1965 release.

Their next, "I Got You Babe," was issued in June, 1965. It sold close to three million copies and established them as a top singing duo. Since then they have scored repeatedly with records like "Bang Bang" and "What Now My Love," along with such albums as "Cher," "The Sonny Side of Cher," "The Wondrous World of Sonny and Cher" and "Look At Us."

Fast Fame

Instant stardom in the electronic world of teen can be achieved by two or three smash records and guest appearances on high-rating TV shows. By March, 1966, when they began their screen roles in "Good Times," Sonny and Cher not only were on all the hot record lists, with their albums and singles selling in millions, but they had guested for Ed Sullivan, Danny Thomas, Hollywood Palace, Hullabaloo, Shindig and other big TV shows, and had travelled the U.S. and England on concert tours.

Part of Sonny and Cher's enormous popularity springs from their vivid personalities, and the kind of image they project. Both personify the young "action" generation. Their youthful fans, by identifying with the duo, are able to express something of their own personalities. "Kids appreciate us because everyone wants to be a little individualistic," says Sonny.

Different

"At first we tried to be 'different' and found out fast that wasn't us," he explains. "Then we decided to be ourselves. The kids dig this. They know we are what we are. They also know that we understand them."

Sonny and Cher, by doing what comes naturally, are the super-glorification of the teen mystique. Cher designs her own clothes, which are colorful combinations of bell-bottom pants, pop tops, and ankle boots.

Cher's clothes are marketed throughout the U.S. in major department stores and women's clothing stores and were instantly successful when introduced early in 1966. Sonny wears low-slung pants, Tom Jones shirts, and moccasins. They both appear in matching slack suits for concerts and TV performances.

School Fans

They also feel a deep obligation to their school-age fans. They set an example, personally and professionally, that has earned the approval of youngsters and adults alike. They make many benefit appearances, and are writing a song urging kids to stay in school which will be recorded for the Office of Economic Opportunity in Washington, D.C., and distributed with a message from Hubert Humphrey, U.S. Vice-President.

Sonny writes most of their songs and arranges all of them. He composed and wrote the lyrics for the music in "Good Times." Sonny and Cher sing about love, and their songs are stories set to rhythm and pop music.

(Continued on Next Page)

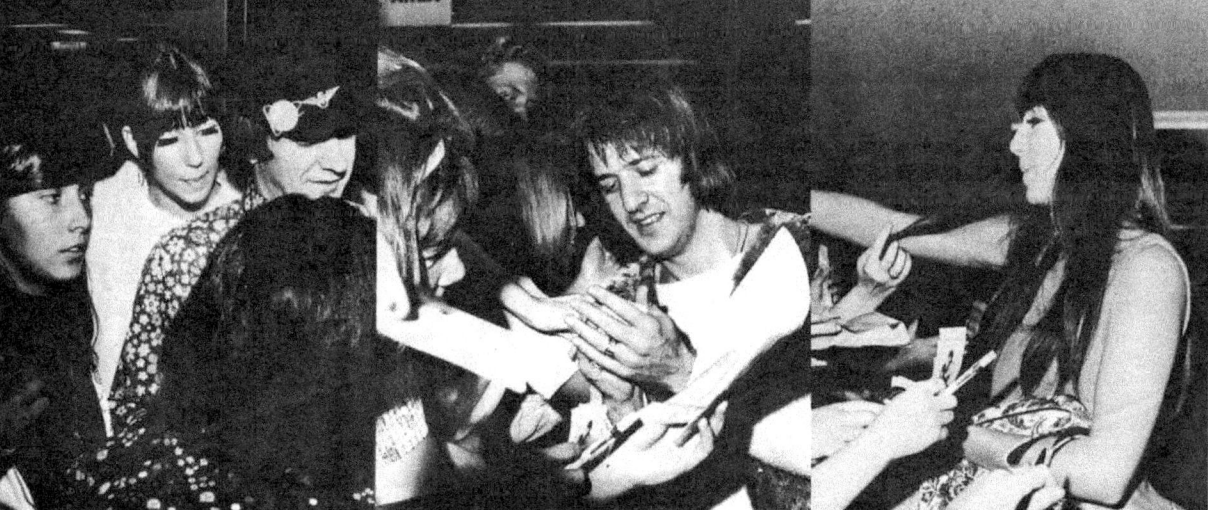

WHEREVER SONNY & CHER APPEAR the crowds are sure to follow and everytime they do Sonny & Cher make it a point to stop and talk to them.

KRLA ARCHIVES

SONNY & CHER wait at airport to fly to Europe for concerts.

Sonny & Cher's Career

(Continued From Page 10)

When they are not performing, Sonny and Cher lead conventional suburban lives. They have a modern, Spanish-style house in the San Fernando Valley, and the fans who ring their doorbell are welcomed graciously. This is not an act. Sonny and Cher are friendly and sociable; they enjoy a close rapport with their public.

Full House

They conduct a good deal of business at home; consequently the house is usually full of people. When he feels like it, which is often, Sonny will cook an Italian meal for as many as happen to be around. He is hard-working, ambitious, and intensely creative. He provides the momentum for Cher, who prefers to let him do the driving.

Neither has much time for hobbies. Cher watches television, designs clothes, shops for material, and collect rings. Her fans know about that, and they toss rings of all kinds on the stage when she performs.

Antique Bug

Sonny collects antique guns, likes to read, and tool around on a motorcycle, with Cher occasionally riding on the back. He doesn't think that girls themselves should pilot motorcycles.

Sonny & Cher's fame has been heralded around the globe, and they have entertained many different kinds of audiences in their travels. They were delighted when Mrs. Jacqueline Kennedy asked them to entertain for a private dinner party in New York and were equally delighted when Princess Margaret asked them to entertain for a charity ball when she visited Hollywood with her husband Lord Snowden.

A BEAUTIFUL STORY
Written by SONNY BONO

WHAT'S YOUR NAME?
IS IT JANE?
WOULD YOU MIND SITTING NEXT TO A SILLY OLD FOOL?
IT'S JUST THAT I'M TIRED OF WASTING MY HOURS
TALKING TO TREES
WATCHING THE FLOWERS GROW
WATCHING BIRDS CHASING BEES
LITTLE BOYS SCRAPING KNEES
EVEN MY TEARS HAVE ALL DRIED
CAN I SIT BY YOUR SIDE

DON'T MISUNDERSTAND ME
I'M JUST AN OLD MAN WITH NO PLACE TO GO
AND IF YOU'LL OBLIGE ME
AND SIT HERE BESIDE ME
I'LL TELL YOU A STORY
A BEAUTIFUL STORY
THAT YOU MIGHT NOT KNOW
PLEASE DON'T GO

PARDON ME MR. TREE
I HOPE THAT I DIDN'T OFFEND YOU BEFORE
YOU WERE MY FRIEND
BUT I WANTED MUCH MORE
NOW I AM BACK ONCE AGAIN
JUST LIKE ALWAYS BEFORE
WATCHING BIRDS CHASING BEES
LITTLE BOYS SCRAPING KNEES
EVEN MY TEARS HAVE ALL DRIED
CAN I SIT BY YOUR SIDE

DON'T MISUNDERSTAND ME
I'M JUST AN OLD MAN WITH NO PLACE TO GO
AND IF YOU'LL OBLIGE ME
AND SIT HERE BESIDE ME
I'LL TELL YOU A STORY
A BEAUTIFUL STORY
THAT YOU MIGHT NOT KNOW
PLEASE DON'T GO

re-printed by permission of Chris-Marc — Cotillion

> "At first we tried to be 'different' and found out fast that that wasn't us. Then we decided to be ourselves. The kids dig this. They know we are what we are. They also know that we understand them."

SONNY & CHER, 1965, at It's Boss in Hollywood.

SO SONNY DANCES with other long-haired buddy.

ONLY TIME CHER ever wore dress — to see Pope.

CHER CUDDLES with one of long-haired friends.

SONNY IN A scene from the movie, "Good Times."

KRLA ARCHIVES

THE GIANT SUNFLOWER BLOOMS AT KRLA. Dave Hull (left) and Dick Moreland are overcome by this awesome display of "flower power." Send a stamped, self-addressed envelope to KRLA for your own free sunflower seeds. Plant a sunflower for someone you love during "Flower Power Week."

GOODTIMERS BUZZ OVERMAN (front) and Charlie Coe are caught in a contemplative mood at a Don & The Goodtimes recording session. They've also been busy answering request lines at KRLA.

Melodyland Theatre
MONDAY, JULY 3 at 8 PM • 1 NITE ONLY
Dave Clark Five IN CONCERT
TICKETS ON SALE at Box Office, by Mail, and at all Ticket Agencies Phone (714) 776-7220

KRLA TOP 40

1. VALERIE — Monkees
2. I THINK WE'RE ALONE NOW — Tommy James & Shondells
3. JUST A LITTLE LOVE — Mike Nesmith
4. LIVE FOR TODAY — Grass Roots
5. PENNY LANE — Beatles
6. HIM OR ME, WHAT'S IT GONNA BE? — Paul Revere & Raiders
7. GROOVIN' — Young Rascals
8. GIRL I KNEW SOMEWHERE — Monkees
9. YELLOW BALLOON — Yellow Balloon
10. LIVE — Merry-Go-Round
11. BLUES THEME — Davy Allen & Arrows
12. CAN'T SEEM TO MAKE YOU MINE — Seeds
13. SIX O'CLOCK — Lovin' Spoonful
14. FRIDAY ON MY MIND — Easybeats
15. CONNECTIONS — Rolling Stones
16. SOCIETY'S CHILD — Janis Ian
17. SUNSHINE GIRL — Parade
18. LITTLE BIT ME, LITTLE BIT YOU — Monkees
19. SOMEBODY TO LOVE — Jefferson Airplane
20. LITTLE GIRL LOST & FOUND — Garden Club
21. SHE HANGS OUT — Monkees
22. RESPECT — Aretha Franklin
23. DOUBLE YELLOW LINE — Music Machine
24. BEAUTIFUL STORY — Sonny & Cher
25. NO MILK TODAY — Herman's Hermits
26. LISTEN GIRL — Giant Crab
27. DON'T YOU CARE — Buckinghams
28. GLASS — Sandpipers
29. SHE'D RATHER BE WITH ME — Turtles
30. I'M A MAN — Spencer Davis
31. ANSWER ME MY LOVE — Ray Stevens
32. SOMETHIN' STUPID — Nancy & Frank Sinatra
33. WHEN I WAS YOUNG — Eric Burdon
34. I NEVER LOVED A MAN — Aretha Franklin
35. SWEET SOUL MUSIC — Arthur Conley
36. HAPPENING — Supremes
37. AT THE ZOO — Simon & Garfunkel
38. LITTLE GAMES — Yardbirds
39. I GOT RHYTHM — Happenings
40. LOVE EYES — Nancy Sinatra

KRLA ARCHIVES

...IS IT A HIT? OR IS IT A MISS?

KRLA PROJECT
Teens Test Discs For Pay

KRLA is using panels of teens and the skills of a media researcher to screen the hundreds of single releases KRLA receives each week.

Rex Sparger, media researcher, had developed a questionnaire covering musical and non-musical areas which the panel members answer before auditioning the singles.

The best part is that the teens on the panel get paid for their efforts! They are organized into six volunteer listener groups who rate the records according to potential sales value and musical quality.

KRLA has been airing some of the singles rated likely hits by listeners and reaction has been good.

John Barrett, KRLA's station manager, stresses that this pre-testing is not meant to replace the station's traditional methods of selecting new records for airplay. He feels the technique can help the labels by indicating a record's strong side so they can concentrate on promoting it.

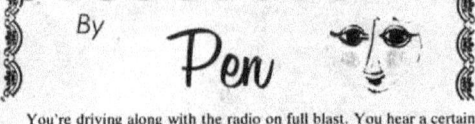

By Pen

You're driving along with the radio on full blast. You hear a certain old song... and pictures start popping into your head about what you were doing when you first heard it. Sound familiar? It should—we've found it happens to nearly all KRLA's Request Line callers.

And, lots of luck if you ever try to buy that "oldie"—when you finally get the money you can't find the record and visa versa, right? Well, now you can *win* your favorite "oldie" just by entering a post-card in KRLA's new "Spring Festival" contest. From 6 p.m. Friday to 8 p.m. Sunday, hundreds of "oldies" are given away to the post-card requesters. Don't miss out.

•

TEEN BAND MEMBERS!—Sign up your group now for the KRLA/Custom Car Show "Band Wagon." This year's Trident's Custom Car and Motorcycle Show will be held at the Los Angeles Memorial Sports Arena, June 2nd, 3rd, and 4th. Thousands of fans will attend this annual show and your band could be prominently featured on a main stage in the Sports Arena. Besides this obvious publicity gain, you'll be mentioned as a contender on KRLA, and you'll be registered in a competition that could win your band a recording contract and $200.00 as a 1st prize winner. And trophies and prizes will be awarded to runners-up by KRLA and the Custom Car Show—so you can't lose.

To sign up, send a post-card with the name of your band, and the name and address of your band leader to "BAND WAGON," KRLA, Pasadena, California 91109. We'll then send you the day and time your band has been scheduled and all the additional information you'll need.

DOUG WESTON IN ASSOCIATION WITH KEN KRAGEN & KEN FRITZ PRESENTS

THE GLENN YARBROUGH SHOW
IN CONCERT
WITH THE FREDDY RAMIREZ TRIO
AND INTRODUCING FOLK DUO MAFFITT & DAVIES

FRIDAY, MAY 19, 8:30 P.M.
PASADENA CIVIC AUDITORIUM
300 E. GREEN, 449-9473

TICKETS: 4.50, 3.50, 2.50. AVAILABLE AT AUDITORIUM BOX OFFICES.
ALL MUTUAL AGENCIES, MUSIC CITY, TROUBADOUR BOX OFFICE AND BY MAIL ORDER

NO, THIS REALLY ISN'T THE KRLA Studios where the popular Merry Go Round answered the request lines.

ICE HOUSE GLENDALE
234 So. Brand Ave. Reservations: 245-5043

ENDS MAY 7
Yellow Balloon
with their hit
"The Yellow Balloon"

THRU MAY 14
an exciting new wit
and singing discovery

Patrick & Paul

MAY 9-14

Tim Morgon

MAY 16-21
Merrilee & The Turnabouts

discover a new sensation

ICE HOUSE PASADENA
24 No. Mentor — Reservations: 681-9942

MAY 2-28

the electrifying
Casey Anderson

Willard & Grecco
as seen on the Johnny Carson Tonight Show & the Ed Sullivan Show

the song & wit of
Mike Smith

ATTENTION!
High Schools, Colleges, Universities and Clubs

CASEY KASEM
May Be Able To Serve You...

Casey can HELP you put on a Show or Dance

Phone: 2-7253

REASONABLE RECORDING RATES

Away From The High Rent District
For
• SINGERS • SONGWRITERS
• GROUPS • COMMERCIALS
• AGENCIES
...THE FINEST EQUIPMENT...
AMPEX — STEINWAY — RCA

FOR STUDIO TIME CALL
EM 3-6901 or EM 3-7770

★ The SOUNDLAB ★

16518 CHATSWORTH STREET
GRANADA HILLS, CALIFORNIA

KRLA ARCHIVES

KRLA ARCHIVES

BEAT EXCLUSIVE
Fan's Tale Of Meeting The Monkees

By Lori Lee

HOLLYWOOD – I could hardly believe my good luck. Within a few hours I would make acquaintance with four of the grooviest guys ever to hit the music world. It was too fabulous a thought for reality. But sure enough it came into being and here are all the exciting details of my meeting the Monkees.

Upon arriving in Hollywood at about 9:15 in the morning, I immediately sped to Columbia Screen Gems (where the television show is taped) only to find out that the Monkees were not presently filming and would not until the beginning of April.

Stick With It

Although discouraged, I refused to give up and went directly to Lenny's Boot Parlor. After hearing so much about its merchandise I wanted to browse around.

The salesman was most helpful because it was he who told me that the boys were to have a recording session at the R.C.A. Building. I rushed over there and asked the guard on duty when the session was to begin. He said that everything was set up for 10:00, which was only a few minutes away. So I waited and waited and waited patiently for a long time until someone spotted Micky's red, white, and blue Volkswagon Bus. The time was exactly 1:17 in the afternoon.

Enter Micky

Well, that just set every teeny bopper off. They all started screaming and crying as if completely out of their minds. I was terribly nervous myself but upon seeing Micky for the first time I knew that everything would turn out just great. He was comfortably attired in a pair of cut-offs, white T-shirt, brown sandals, and policeman's hat. He looked truly out-a-sight!

I hurried up and handed him some gifts picked out 'specially for his character. They consisted of several goofy Car-toon mags, a big chewy dog bone for either himself or You, and a paddle set. He then signed autographs and disappeared into the building.

Only on his second trip out to greet his fans did I notice the big difference in his appearance. Micky had grown a beard! When I later asked why, he replied that it kept his face warm. And as fuzzy as it was, it must of been doing the job just fine.

Other Monkees Arrive

Sometime later Mike arrived on the scene. He had also grown a beard which gave him a very masculine look. And, with his strong Texas accent, he was absolutely groovy. I really dug him!

It was about 3:00 when Peter showed up and brightened everyones' tired faces and spirits. It's sure hard work to have to stand from ten in the morning until three in the afternoon and still look fresh and cheerful. But, when I gave

> *It does happen—fans do occasionally get to meet their favorite entertainers. One such lucky girl is Lori Lee who spent the entire day standing outside of the studio where the Monkees were recording. Her vigil paid-off when Lori met her favorite group, the Monkees.*
>
> *This is her story, exactly as she wrote it. Lori's tale certainly proves one thing—Monkees are human!* The Editor

Peter his presents of a gyroscope top, Mad paperback, paddle-set, and poem made to order about him alone, he smiled and looked so touched that every minute of waiting seemed all worthwhile.

Great Waterfight, 1967

Everyone was now waiting impatiently for the smallest Monkee to arrive and make his grand appearance. But Davy never came. However, there was such a big commotion down at the end of the block, he was temporarily forgotten.

Suddenly, Micky came racing down the street as fast as his size 10 feet would carry him, yelling that they were after him. We all turned around just in time to see him get squirted right in the face with water by two members of the Family Tree, a groovy new singing group.

Squirting Back

Micky, being one who never lets a person get the better of him, started squirting back which was an unfortunate move for yours truly. It just so happened by some unlucky chance, the person for whom the water was intended ducked and take an intelligent guess, at who got all soaking wet. You are 100% correct if you answered me. But in the end it didn't really matter because it was such a hilarious sight to see Micky get so frustrated and wet.

Still, an even funnier sight was his expression when he learned that the whole gun fight was all my fault. After Peter arrived at the building, Micky, Mike, and Rick Klein were just leaving. They returned some time later with a big package containing four or five water pistols, compliments of Mr. Nesmith. You see, besides a paddle-set and little green wool hat for his son, Christian, his gifts also included a gigantic water syringe or hypo-squirt. I wanted to see a water fight and get more than what I had bargained for. Oh well.

Three Of Four

Even with such complications, though, everything turned out just fine. I got to meet three of the four fabulous Monkees and gave them each in person several nutty gifts coming from the mind of an even more nutty person. (Davy never did show up so I left his presents at the studio. I hope he has fun talking up with his extra large box of Corn Flakes).

And now, all I can say is, I just wish that every Monkees fan in the whole world would at some time have the same opportunity I did. And if that lucky person could have only one half the fun I had, it still could be classified as an unforgettable experience for all.

PETER AND MICKY outside Monkee soundstage in Hollywood

DAVY JONES receives combing hand from Sally, Monkee hairdresser

DAVY MAD? Not really

PETER HAPPY? You can bet your life on it!

GENE ASHMAN, couterie for Monkees, straightens Mike's hat

KRLA ARCHIVES

something for everyone

IN THE RECORD DEPARTMENT

KRLA ARCHIVES

BEAT EXCLUSIVE
Righteous Bros. Deny Split With Teens

EXCLUSIVE BEAT PHOTOS

By Eden

The Righteous Brothers are two talented, friendly young men who have paid frequent visits to the pages of *BEAT* in the last couple of years, both in interviews and as members of the Top Ten tunes on our charts. Just the other day, we had an opportunity to sit down and chat for awhile—renewing our friendship and catching up on all the things that have happened since we saw the boys last—and we found Bobby and Billy to be the same warm and friendly human beings they have always been.

Accusation

As friends, they took the opportunity to get a few of their current gripes off of their chests, and one of them involved an accusation which has been hurled at them recently. Bobby explained: "The last couple of months, we've read a few articles in teen-oriented magazines that stated that the Righteous Brothers have *left* their teen following for more adult audiences, and its kinda bugged us! So, we're going to kind of shoot out a little explanation here.

"We have only worked one night club, in the past three years, where teenagers couldn't get in and in the majority of the clubs we've worked, there were many, many teenagers there. The only club that we've ever worked where kids under age couldn't get in was Las Vegas—and they can't even get in the gambling casinos there.

'Never Left'

"Actually, we've never left the teenage kids, 'cause we tour probably as much—or more—as any act in the business today. Another reason for it, too, is that as *we* grow older—naturally the *kids* grow older too. *Every*body grows older at the same time! I think *any* entertainer wants to branch out in as many directions as possible.

"After all, we're 26-years-old and we won't be doing concerts for the rest of our lives; and, if we work our way into the night club scene, which we have done—and I may say we've been very fortunate—we'll have something to fall back on later on in life."

R 'n B

Although Bobby jokingly protested that he should do most of the talking as Willy had very little to say, we turned the conversation over to Bill for a few moments as we discussed rhythm and blues. The Righteous Brothers have been labeled "blue-eyed soul singers" and placed in the R&B bag since the beginning of their career, but when it came down to actually *defining* R&B, Billy began:

"I imagine that it's basically gospel and spiritual music..." "a combination, you mean?" Bobby interrupted, comically taking his turn as interviewer. "Well, not really a combination..." Billy began, then decided "yeah, a combination—it all came out of the same cotton fields! That *is* a very hard question... that's why *I'm* answering that one, and Bobby doesn't want to have anything to do with it!"

Not to be outdone by his blue-eyed friend with the deep voice, Bobby waxed serious for a moment, adding:

"Actually we've never left the teenage kids..."

"There's a very slight difference—a hard-to-define difference—between rock and roll and rhythm and blues.

"Actually, most of your rock and roll singers can't sing rhythm and blues like the authentic rhythm and blues people; but, I would say the difference is that it's more *bluesy* than rock and roll."

Both boys have very definite ideas about their roles as entertainers, especially in the way they treat their fans and audiences. Billy took over the discussion once again to explain this a little. "I think an entertainer should definitely try to live up to how he appears. Like, Pat Boone—if he appears to be a nice gentleman, I think in public he should try and act that way—which I'm sure he does.

"An entertainer should never let them (the public) down, and try to make them as proud of us as we can."

Owe To Public

"And if they've got a number of fans," Bobby added, "I think naturally the people who have been following them expect good records. I think the majority of entertainers owe it to their public to be seen in person, or on television, or in front of motion picture cameras."

Billy added a rather unusual comment here which has got to be one of the nicest things an entertainer has ever said about his audience: "I think both Bobby and I are very *proud* of our audiences. They're very clean, very polite—I couldn't be any happier standing on the stage looking at them. I hope they're as proud of *us* as we are of *them*."

On Tour

The boys have just left on an extensive cross-country tour and are tentatively planning a European tour for sometime this summer. In the immediate future, they will be returning to the Cocoanut Grove in Los Angeles and celebrating the success of their latest hit record, "Melancholy Music Man." Beyond that, there is a movie being *definitely* planned for this September—however, the script has not yet been decided upon, and production awaits the final confirmation.

Before they said good-bye, the boys assured us once again that they *haven't* left their teenage fans—nor are they planning to do so. And as far as they're concerned, they never will. They'll just grow older right along with them.

"After all, we're 26-years-old..."

"Actually, most of your rock and roll singers can't sing rhythm and blues like the authentic rhythm and blues people"

"It all came out of the same cotton fields"

KRLA ARCHIVES

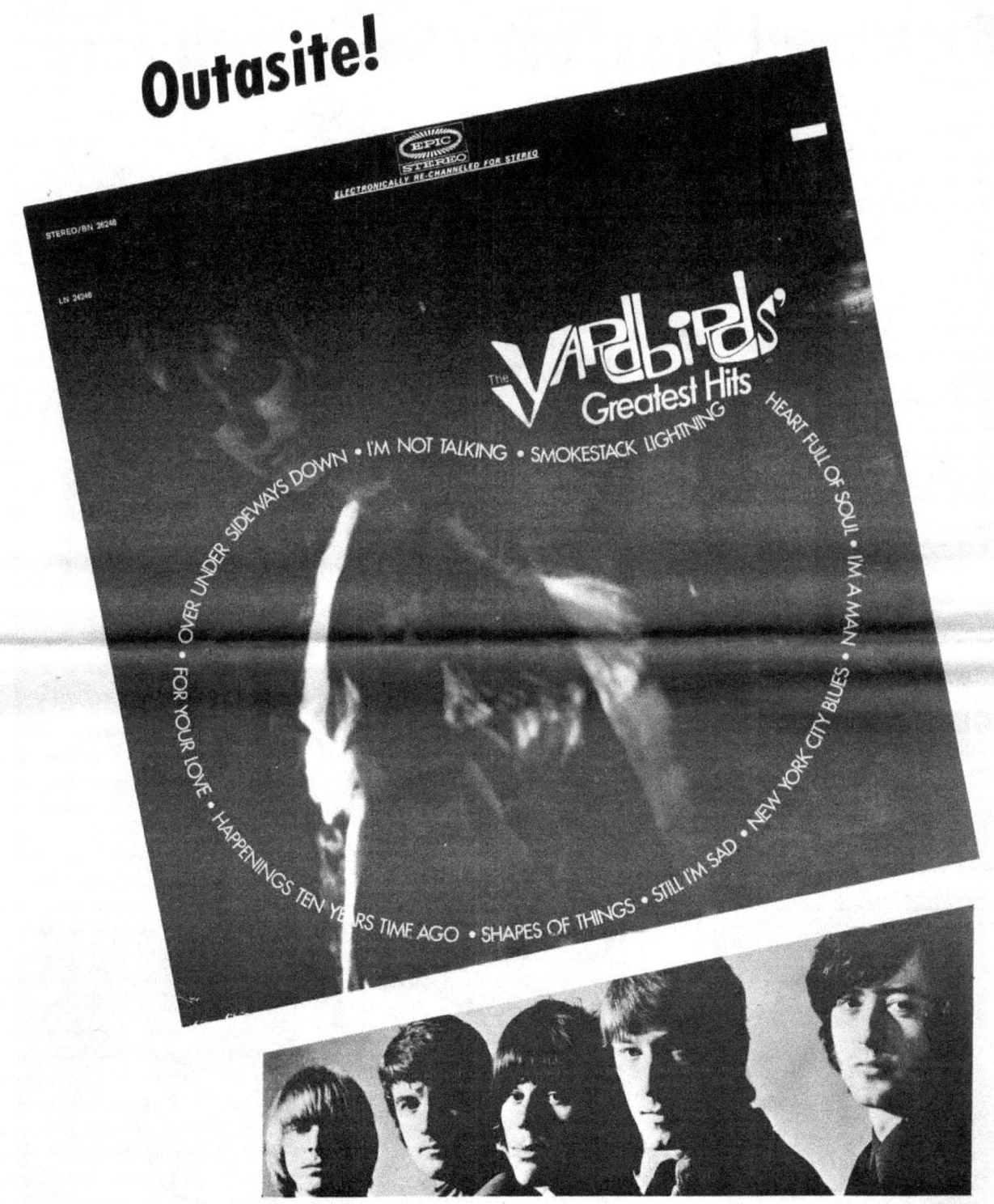

Outasite!

Now Available At **Montgomery Ward** Record Departments

KRLA ARCHIVES

ANTHONY AND THE IMPERIALS
98 Per Cent Heart

By Anna Maria Alonzo

In the popsy-turvy world of the One Hit Wonders, Anthony and the Imperials are one of the most unique wonders ever to hit the pop charts. Although they began their career in a fairly normal way—enjoying hits like "Tears On My Pillow" and "Shimmy Shimmy Cocoa Bop"—it has, in no way, been at all normal since.

Beginning as Little Anthony and The Imperials, the group enjoyed a growing succession of hits during the late 1950's and showed every indication of becoming a "standard" group—one of those groups that consistently produces hit after hit.

Other Ideas

But the U.S. Army stepped in with other ideas, and the group broke up to go their separate ways, each looking for "a new groove." Two years went by before the quartet joined forces once again and it was only after they began to re-organize that they realized their "new groove" was just a "re-modeling" of the *old* one!

The "Little" was eliminated from the beginning of Anthony's name and together, he and the Imperials re-established themselves as a more versatile and polished night club act. Ordinarily, this sort of image would be the first step toward alienating the all-important teen market. But, once again Anthony and friends refuse to conform and they have continued to be just as popular—if not *more* so!—than ever before.

Since their first hit in 1958—"Tears On My Pillow"—right up to their current release—"Don't Tie Me Down"—the group has *continually,* if not consistently, appeared on pop and R&B charts across the nation, and Anthony admits that he has given up worrying when one of their latest singles doesn't make it to the Top 20 on the charts. He explains that the public has continued to be faithful and to support them *in spite of* any charts, and he simply laughs and says "Fate must have her hand on us, so I don't worry about it any more. I just don't understand it!"

Different Forms

In their club act, Anthony and The Imperials combine as many different forms of music as possible, ranging from their own hits to heavy R&B, Broadway show tunes, standard ballads, gospel tunes, and one of the most outstanding and show-stopping versions of "Exodus" ever heard.

Popular in both the pop and R&B fields, Anthony still has his own very definite ideas about music—enjoying all forms—and he tried to explain to The BEAT just what the current rhythm and blues-soul music thing is all about:

"A rhythm and blues song is a song that is basically sung 98% from the heart! It's *pain;* it's the *feeling* of pain. It's an inner pain, or something that you couldn't express, and *musically* is the only way you *can* express it. And you come out with what we call the 'soul sound'; a lot of the riffle of the voice...crying...hollering...which are the things you would do when you're talking—real-life things put into music and you have rhythm and blues. Rhythm and blues is a *feel,* that's all it is. It's taking a note from your voice and pulling it through your heart to make it a feeling."

Anthony and The Imperials are probably one of the hardest-working groups in the country, and if you have any doubts about that, you have only to go and see them perform to be convinced of the amount of time and hard work which has gone into their act. If you wonder how such an act is developed...just ask Anthony.

"It takes *years* and a lot of hard work and constant rehearsing. We rehearse *six* hours a day *every* day...that's a part of life. Our act changes every three or four months—wherever we think there's a song to be added or we feel the whole act should be revamped or needs a shot in the arm—then, we do it! But basically, we practice the art of *singing!"*

With Anthony and The Imperials, singing is definitely an art, and one which *everyone* can enjoy. Next time they're in town, be sure to pick up on some of their "art work;" or stay tuned to your local music charts—they're bound to pop up on them soon or later!

Fast-workin' burn-stoppin' dark-tannin'
SEA & SKI®

SEA & SKI SUNTAN LOTION 89¢ to $2.75

BRAD'S DREAM STAR
Groovy Sugar 'n' Spice

Dear *BEAT:*

Instead of describing a favorite rock 'n roll singer, I think all the guys would be interested in seeing a composite of the all-around female vocalist of their dreams.

My nominee would have the fantastic body of "Sugar" Nancy Sinatra. She would have the strong, radiant voice of Dusty Springfield, but the sweet, delicate touch that Michelle Phillips can add to a song. But most importantly, she would possess that unbelievably innocent look of Marianne Faithful.

Brad Pueschel

Boys seem to be more shy about telling about the girl who fills their dreams than girls are about their heroes. Thanks Brad, for speaking out for the men by putting in a word for the fair sex.

Send us your composite describing your favorite rock 'n roll personality and we'll share it with BEAT readers around the country.

The Editor

KRLA ARCHIVES

Digging The Temptations In Action!

By Ron Koslow

BEAT Photos: John A. Stewart

The performing Temptations are like the mechanics of a finely made watch—all their movements are synchronized and precisioned for maximum harmony.

The Whisky A-Go-Go was packed to capacity and as the lights dimmed, fellow-Motown artist Brenda Holloway was introduced and proceeded to captivate the audience with her beauty, her style and her incredible voice. Singing her past hits like "What Are You Gonna Do When I'm Gone" plus her latest smash "Just Look What You've Done," she then surprised us all by accompanying herself on the violin to a beautiful and sensitive rendition of "Shadow of Your Smile."

Explosion

Now the audience was primed and ready for the main attraction. Suddenly the room exploded in applause as the five elegantly dressed young men catapulted onto the stage; from then on they had control.

It seemed like every song that they sang was just another link in their chain of hits: "Ain't Too Proud To Beg," "Get Ready," "Old Man River" (in a beautiful and dramatic rendition), "Keep On Walking," "Beauty's Only Skin Deep," and of course, "My Girl."

Impossible

It is almost impossible to describe The Temptations' unique style of performance. Their keynote is perfectly timed, completely rehearsed choreography. Every move they make has meaning and lends itself to the over-all effect of their songs. It seems like everything they do is perfect; either all is in utter unison, or there are individual movements which totally relate to one another. But no matter how smooth and well-rehearsed they may be, there is that wonderful and congenial group personality which says to the audience: "Let us entertain you."

Between shows, this wonderful personality became more evident while they relaxed and discussed their career and hopes for the future.

History

Melvin Franklin explained how the group got together and a little bit about their past. "The Temptations have been together almost eight years. Originally, we were two different high school groups, The Primes and The Distants. Otis, Melvin, and David were in The Distants; and Paul and Eddie in the Primes. By the way, we used to sing with another high school group called The Primettes, who are now the Supremes."

... TEMPTATIONS' perfectly timed, completely rehearsed choreography is the keynote of their on-stage success.

David explained the structure of the Motown Corporation, "We did not realize we were creating Motown; we were just a bunch of different groups; but it grew as a lasting relationship. Now Motown is probably the biggest all-American family. Many of us, like the Supremes and The Miracles have really reached the top—everything they do is a hit; and they in turn have done everything possible to help us in our career. The Motown artists have never lost sight of the bit about helping each other."

"Probably the most responsible group for our success in music is The Miracles; they wrote "The Way You Do The Things You Do" and gave it to us as our first hit. They have continued to write some of our biggest hits like "My Girl" and "It's Growing."

When asked about their future, The Temptations admit that they have a long way to go, "We feel that we haven't begun to do the things that we can. Right now the most important thing is a successful engagement at the Copa in New York. We open August 10, for two weeks. This is the pinnacle of our career and we hope all of our fans will be there and will support us."

As The Temptations began to dress for their second show (white shirts, white pants, and orange jackets) David Ruffin turned and said, "You know, show business is our life, and some of our happiest moments are spent on stage; I think people feel this enthusiasm and respond to it as fully as we express it."

KRLA ARCHIVES

to Mother with Love!

Give A Gift Of Music

LAWRENCE WELK'S "HITS OF OUR TIME"
- IN THE ARMS OF LOVE
- SOMEWHERE MY LOVE
- WISH ME A RAINBOW
- I WILL WAIT FOR YOU
- AND WE WERE LOVERS
- GEORGY GIRL
- MUSIC TO WATCH GIRLS BY
- STRANGERS IN THE NIGHT
- Then You Can Tell Me GOODBYE
- THE BEAT GOES ON

DLP 3790

NOW AVAILABLE AT YOUR LOCAL

KRLA ARCHIVES

Shirley You Jest

Someday, when I'm old and gray (I am now *young* and gray), I have a feeling that I'll find a vacancy in my life. I'll discover that I suddenly have so much more time to myself, and pretty soon it will dawn on me why this is happening. I will have stopped spending about twelve hours a day battling about the Beatles.

It seems I have taken it upon myself to become the World's Most Hysterical Beatle Argue-er. And undoubtedly the noisiest.

I'm not quite as bad as I used to be (but I'm still just as *loud*). But that's only because there aren't nearly as many people to argue with. (With whom to argue?) (Aw, you know what I mean). Most anti-Beatle nuts have seen the light and come over to our side.

Unladylike

Thanks to a rather unladylike display on my part, which took place in public (never do anything small) (not to mention right) last Sunday, we can now add another to that list.

I was very surprised by the whole bit because this is someone I've known (known *of*, really) for a long time. What you might call a veteran newspaper type all-round press person.

I don't even remember how the subject of the Beatles came up as the two of us chatted about assorted thingies, but the moment it did, my nice Dr. Jekyl turned into a foaming Dr. Hyde.

He started by saying they put out nothing but noise and trash. I naturally reacted by having a coronary.

Fortunately, he responded by saying something I could really get my teeth into. Namely: "I suppose *you'd* compare them to someone like Leonard Bernstein."

Rather Highly

"No," I simpered. "But did you know that, speaking of Leonard Bernstein, he thinks rather highly of the Beatles and plays quite a lot of their music? As does Arthur Fiedler, the famous conductor of the Boston Pops Orchestra, who appeared on their most recent TV special. Their material has also been recorded by many other orchestras, jazz musicians, etc." (I could have gone on all night, and darn near did).

"Harumph," said he. "I did hear that one of them has written a song," he added. (Please, I know this guy sounds like he's been under a wharf, but this is a working member of the *adult press*, so keep same in mind and realize I was not conversing with an idiot). (He, however, was).

"*One of them has written a song?*" screeched I. (Meet the King of Conservative Estimates).

Getting High

Then, realizing that my blood pressure was doing that thing (I can always tell it's getting high when steam starts coming out me nostrils), I decided to try a calmer approach.

"Look, stupid," I said (okay, okay, I said the "stupid" part inwardly). "I don't care if you don't like the Beatles. It's up to you whether you enjoy their singing. But it isn't up to you to decide whether their music is valid or not. That's already *been* decided. By some of the biggest and best musicians in the world!"

With equal calm, he went into a long dissertation about how a classic is formed, in any area of entertainment. He used as an example, the field of literature, naming Shakespeare, Dickens, Hemingway, more. Then he explained that a classic becomes a classic be-

BEAT Art By Woody Alexander

cause it has universal appeal, and contains truths that don't change from age to age.

Still Popular

Then he posed this question — would, in the future, the Beatles be classics? In other words, would they still be popular years and years from today?

"Not as performing artists," I replied. "But the music they've created *will* be considered *classic*. Some of it already is."

He about fell off his chair. "Why didn't you say so in the first place?"

"I did," I smiled patiently. "But you were so busy talking about something you know nothing about, you didn't hear me."

I'm afraid I didn't convey this seething argument in a very fascinating fashion (sorry about that) (almost as sorry as you are), but I wanted to tell you about it for a reason. Because it'll give me another opportunity to blither about how I just don't understand people.

Beatles

The man I was talking to has undoubtedly never heard much of or about the Beatles, yet he was willing to discuss them as an authority. How can people *do* that? (I arsk you).

I don't know *how* they can do this, but there are certainly enough of them managing to find a way. Personally, when I'm in a conversation where a subject I know nothing about is being discussed (which is painfully often), I at least have enough sense to keep my trap shut, and so do my friends. I wonder why more people don't do the same, instead of blathering on and expressing opinions that are based on hear-say or just plain ignorance. If they did, they might learn something.

My most spectacular Beatle battle lasted three years, and was waged with a certain singer who doesn't like rock. If they gave out medals for thinking out utterly *infuriating* things to say about the Beatles, he'd win top honors. (Course, then he'd have to get a chest to put them on).

So, I tried everything, including tears, threats, tantrums, etc. just to get him to sit down and listen to the Beatles and/or their music. And I got nowhere fast.

Forced-Listener

About a month or so ago, I saw him, and he said: "I take back what I've said about your *friends*. Somebody finally made me sit down and listen to the Beatles."

I know he expected me to rain kisses on his upturned face, but it was too late. Instead, I snarled and replied: "You just want to be on the side that's winning." (Thank you, Bob Dylan, for writing that line so I could steal it from you).

He was another classic example of the typical bad-mouth who talks incessantly but really doesn't know his elbow from a knothole. (No, that isn't quite it). (And here's hoping it *doesn't* come to me later).

An idea for what you can do with this column. (Be calm, I wouldn't dare say that kind of thing in print). If you know someone like the someone's I've just mentioned, circle all this in red (blood would be double effective) and leave it lying about. And then be grateful that we at least *know* we're crazy.

Speaking of George (held off as long as I could), I was wrong about him shaving off his mustache. He shaved his beard, but the cookie-duster remains.

Tickle, tickle.

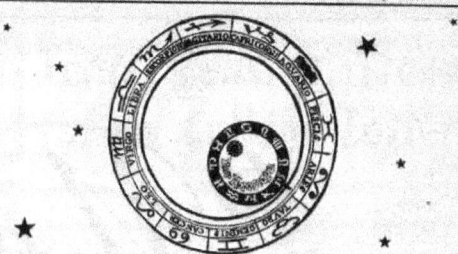

WOULD YOU BELIEVE?
"BRANDI"
is the vintage
mfg. by
"THE SIERRAS"
on Yardbirds - 8005 BMI

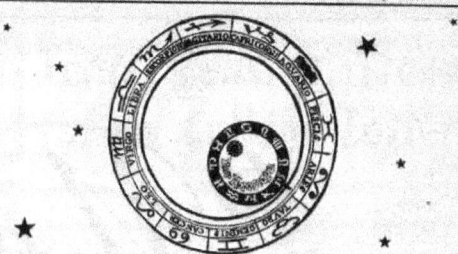

YOUR SIGN IS ARIES IF YOUR BIRTHDAY FALLS BETWEEN MARCH 21 TO APRIL 20

Now is the time to start thinking independently. You will succeed: by challenging traditional views. Read the news but read between the lines. The girl or boy of your dreams is not. True happiness lies with an opposite. Avoid routine. Usually take a shower? Take a bath instead.

* * *

YOUR SIGN IS TAURUS IF YOUR BIRTHDAY FALLS BETWEEN APRIL 21 TO MAY 21

This is not the time to: Argue with friends. You will have to rely on them soon. Avoid: Being greedy. Share your candy bar with a friend. Lay into homework because you will want spare time: Soon: a very groovy person of the opposite sex will blow your mind at a party. Keep your calendar open for steady dates with him or her.

* * *

YOUR SIGN IS GEMINI IF YOUR BIRTHDAY FALLS BETWEEN MAY 22-JUNE 21

Beware: Of trouble ahead in school. You'll be tempted to copy just that one answer on the test from the girl next to you but it will be very unlucky: You'll get caught. Be honest or at least be careful. Plan carefully: It could mean a fabulous summer.

* * *

YOUR SIGN IS CANCER IF YOUR BIRTHDAY FALLS BETWEEN JUNE 22-JULY 23

This is a good month for all moon children. Things may be going smoothly at home unless you argue with your parents. Be diplomatic. Be energetic: Wash your face often otherwise those spots will never go away.

* * *

YOUR SIGN IS LEO IF YOUR BIRTHDAY FALLS BETWEEN JULY 24-AUG. 23

It is important: To show others that you are serious. Do what is expected of you at least half the time. Hang up your clothes, keep your room neat: The sudden change in your sloppy character will confuse everyone and soften your parents' resistance to your desires. They'll give you extra money for records and clothes.

* * *

YOUR SIGN IS VIRGO IF YOUR BIRTHDAY FALLS BETWEEN AUG. 24-SEPT. 23

You are generally very sure of yourself. Your Zodiac says this trait will damage you. Listen to views different from yours. You love the Monkees or the Beatles but find out why others hate them. Learn why so many people oppose the war. You will triumph: If you follow this advice. Others will come to your for advice.

YOUR SIGN IS LIBRA IF YOUR BIRTHDAY FALLS BETWEEN SEPT. 24-OCT. 23

Things will catch up with you this month. Your habit of telling secrets and spreading gossip must end. It will lose friends. Run around the block. If you collapse it's time to get back in shape for summer. If you don't, run around again. What have you been doing all winter? Sleeping?

* * *

YOUR SIGN IS SCORPIO IF YOUR BIRTHDAY FALLS BETWEEN OCT. 24-NOV. 22

You will achieve success: by being creative and following your own intuitions. Don't be afraid to disagree. Say the Monkees are awful and Elvis is great, if you think so. But: Avoid being different just to be different. Back up your views by consulting experts.

* * *

YOUR SIGN IS SAGITARRIUS IF YOUR BIRTHDAY FALLS BETWEEN NOV. 23-DEC. 21

Now is the time to: Decorate your room and yourself. Fabulous bargains in groovy clothes are yours if you act fast. Experiment: Your greatest joy will come from trying new things. Taste the foods you've always disliked: Even brussel sprouts. Read, read, read, your wits are sharp this month and you can learn much about yourself.

* * *

YOUR SIGN IS CAPRICORN IF YOUR BIRTHDAY FALLS BETWEEN DEC. 22-JAN. 20

The time is right: To develop your talents. Begin music or art lessons. You may not think you are very creative, but you are wrong. Try different clothes, mod make-up or a new hair style. You have a real flair and good taste. Now is the moment: To express yourself.

* * *

YOUR SIGN IS AQUARIUS IF YOUR BIRTHDAY FALLS BETWEEN JAN. 21-FEB. 19

Be on the guard for: Your tendency to be snobbish. Go out of your way to consider others. You care more about learning on your own than grades in school. That is a good trait. Concentrate on improving yourself: don't talk so fast so adults can understand. An allowance increase is on the way: But don't wait for it, it's in the future.

* * *

YOUR SIGN IS PISCES IF YOUR BIRTHDAY FALLS BETWEEN FEB. 20-MAR. 20

You must be strong this month: Romance will disappoint you. Be confident in yourself. Others may criticize your schoolwork, appearance, speech, ideas. But stick to your beliefs. Pizza and pickles are fine — if you like them. Awaiting you are: Rewards if you follow this advice.

KRLA ARCHIVES

please send me BEAT
26 issues only
$3 per year

Mail to: **BEAT Publications**
6290 Sunset Blvd. #504
Hollywood, California 90028

☐ New Subscription
☐ Renewal (please enclose mailing label from your last BEAT)
I want BEAT for: ☐ 1 year at $3.00 or ☐ 2 years at $5.00
I enclose ☐ cash ☐ check ☐ money order
Outside U.S. - $9 per year
• Please print your name and address.

Name_____
Street_____
City_____
State_____ Zip_____

CLASSIFIEDS

WANTED

WANTED: Any original snapshots of The Beatles. Will pay cash. Describe and state price. Jeff Peters, 1810 Crone Ave., Anaheim, California.

FORMING ROCK BAND. 365-7223. (Granada Hills, Calif.)

WANTED: WRITERS for a zany HOLLIES mag. Write: Hollies, 2212 Reedie Drive, Silver Springs, Maryland.

WANTED—MOD MALE PEN PAL. 15-18. Marcia Thomas, 603 Whitfield Drive, Natchitoches, Louisiana.

WANTED: AUTOHARP. Call 327-4077 (Gardena, California).

FEMALE DRUMMER looking for job during the summer with group. Call 651-1967 or write Diane Worden, 7906 Colgate Avenue, Cleveland, Ohio 44102. Will answer all letters.

MUSICIANS and vocalists, male or female over 18 yrs. old wanted for new type rock group. If you have talent and creative ability, call or write One Way Productions, Inc., Suite 1804, 260 E. Chestnut, Chicago, Ill. 312-337-7370.

Want to trade records from people from different parts of country. Write Jim Kendrick, 2242 73rd Ct., Elmwood Park, Ill. 60635

Wanted—one outasite guy, answers to name **JOHN SENNE**.

Classifieds
BEAT Publications
6290 Sunset Blvd. Suite 504
Hollywood, California 90028

Prices are cheap! Only 10c a word for personal messages (from you to someone else without an item for sale, trade, promotion, etc. involved). Other classifieds—just 20c a word.

Now what's a word? Well, it's the usual thing plus two groovy exceptions: the number and street (6290 Sunset Blvd.) are one word and the city and state count as only one word (Hollywood, California). Telephone numbers are one word (please include city or area code).

FOR SALE

SELLING BEATLE NEGATIVES to highest bidder—Tracy, 6715 La Marimba St., Long Beach, Calif. 90815.

MAMAS & PAPAS POSTERS, 22" x 28" - $1.00 each postpaid. The Seper Co., 5273 Tendilla, Woodland Hills, California.

PHOTOS FOR SALE. Top groups. Send self-addressed envelope to: Sher, 5325 Central College Road, Westerville.

'65 G.T.O., all perf. equipment, like NEW, NEVER raced! Desperate to sell!!! Call Dave: 213-459-2557 (Pacific Palisades, Calif.)

PERSONALS

WHY? LIVES
Susi — "Jeg Elsker Dig" — Jim
FOREVER JAMESON
Salutations to Gayle, Karen and Susie from Margaret St. Thomas.
FLOWER POWER UNITE!!
TERRY KNIGHT is HAPPENING!! Listen to his albums, TERRY KNIGHT and REFLECTIONS. Geri, California; Sue, Pennsylvania; Kay, Michigan.
"MIKE + DEBBIE" = FOREVER!
Bill Loves Judy
NEKO CHOHLIS did a really **GROOVY PORTRAIT** of DAVID JONES! Pat & Marilyn. San Leandro, California
I LOVE BOB
RANDY OCHOA + CINDY KENNEDY = **GRATEFUL DEAD** (Riverside's a drag and I'm still waiting for you).
"KELVIN + DEBBIE" FOREVER!
"KENT, Don't give up, you'll find her."
STEVE LAINE, Where Are You?
YEA BREU MASTERS!
RICK VOTAW thinks he's something —
JOHN SENNE — Please notice me. I do exist. a fan.
"BOB"
Penny Lane and *Strawberry Fields Forever* Rules
Where Are The Liverpool Five?
JULIE LOVES FANG
DEFINITION OF A BIMBO: a bimbo is a person with lots of hair, soft eyes, an introvert, doesn't speak unless spoken to, one who sits directly in front of a TV set, watching Star Trek, with a can of Colt 45 in one hand and pistachio nuts in the other.
LOUIE—I love you and the car is outasite!! Priss
The Merry-Go-Round goes up not around. A fan.
Curdis Holloway Loves Sherry Millard.
DIANE, VICKI, and LYNN ARE TUVAN!
RONNIE—I LOVE YOU!!! ROSEMARY

"Beatles Come Back PLEASE"
Darrell Loves Donna Bunches!!
FU MANCHU IS PSYCHEDELIC

SANDEE RULES
I love you, Mike Butterfield...
NANCY - I love Ralph Magoo.
TIM AND LISSA FOREVER!
One of these days, mon amour —
I DIG JOHNNY TESORIERO
LOVE ALWAYS, DEE
Holly — "I Love You!" Donnie
The Class of "68" at the Hornell Senior High Schol is the GREATEST!! — Donnie
RINGO AND CHARLEEN
MARY LOVES DAVID
Nancy — I love Sky Saxon.
Barbara loves **ALEXANDER'S TIMELESS BLOOZBAND**, Arelene loves **ALEXANDER'S TIMELESS BLOOZBAND**. Ellie loves **ALEXANDER'S TIMELESS BLOOZBAND**.
WAKE UP, TOM! I luv you.
Kathy
BEATLE RALLY — 12 noon. June 17. Griffith Park near pony and train rides. BRING: Laffs, memories, pics, Beatle-thingies for sale or swap, food for sharing.
OWA TAGOO SIAM
MICHELE...
BEATLES RULE! — Carol
To Mike Shaver and Dave Moor of Thee Difference—We Love You — Kathy & Kathy
"Where is Dylan?"
Mike - Zal
Send Petitions, Letters to:
BRING-BACK THE-BEATLES!
371 E. 152nd St., Apt. 4, Cleveland, Ohio 44110.
"Carol and Mark"
BOB WINKLEBLACK I LUV YOU AND ALWAYS WILL. LOVINGLY YOURS, SANDY LEE!!
Paul FOREVER!!! luv: sue and barb
I.C.B.D. IS COMING!!!
Paul McCartney has "Love Eyes!"
Hi Janice and April — Moby
RIFF RAFF RULE!
ASSOCIATION — WELCOME BACK! LOVE, GAYLE
John—Come back to me!! I need you!! Jackie
I LOVE YOU BOB. LOVE & KISSES (plural!) SANDY
"Randi and Chris"
GO BY "RAPID TRANSIT"
BUDDHA WATCHES CRAIG, JOE, DEE, BRUCE.
I Love You Don Grove — Lynn
I LOVE DENISE HESSON
"THEE DIFFERENCE" RULE!
To the drummer of the Standells: Call Crysi, she has to be straightened out on certain feelings caused by you.
Scaff's Skiffle Band Rules!
MOTHER GOOSE RULES!
THE NOCTURNAL SUNDIAL IS COMING!
Lorelle Loves
James Paul McCartney!!!
Jen Loves
George Hilton Harrison!!!
Pig— Don't you ever stay home? Green Hornet and Kato.
Donovan is love(ly)
Dianka, how'd you get "A" in Chemistry?
PEACE!

INSTRUCTION

REACH COSMIC AWARENESS without drugs—help save mankind from destruction. Write for free booklet, "Cosmic Awareness Speaks." Organization of Awareness, Box 115-E, Olympia, Washington.

MUSICAL FLASH CARDS: Every group needs a good musician—why not you? Easiest way to learn notes, time values, and just good basic knowledge of music. Over 400 facts included in two sets, beginning and intermediate. This is not just a card game for kids! Enclose $1.65 for each set ordered. Immediate delivery. Hollingworth Publishing Co., Rush, Colorado 80833.

SLEEP-LEARNING. Self hypnosis. Details, strange catalog free! Autio Suggestion, Box 24-BT Olympia, Washington.

PEN PALS

BAY AREA BYRD FANS! S.O.S! Please write Jackie, 28 City View Way, San Francisco, California 94131. Enclose stamped, self-addressed envelope.

Look! Everyone! Penpals Wanted. Stonemaniacs, Beatlemaniacs Write: "Ray," P.O. Box 27716, Hollywood, California 90027

RHONDA is lonely. Needs an L.A. boyfriend. Write 4663 Tajo Drive, Santa Barbara, California.

FAN CLUBS

MICKEY AND THE INVADERS FAN CLUB. Send 50c to 232 No. Canon Dr., Suite 206, Beverly Hills, Calif. 90010.

THE SIERRAS FAN CLUB. Send 50c to 232 No. Canon Dr., Suite 206, Beverly Hills, Calif. 90010.

FOR INFORMATION ON THE ROBBS NATIONAL FAN CLUB, WRITE P.O. BOX 350, BEVERLY HILLS, CALIFORNIA 90213.

MARK LINDSAY NATIONAL FAN CLUB, P.O. Box 435, Elgin, Illinois 60120

"**KRUMS**" fan club, 2742 W. 22 Pl., Chicago, Illinois.

LOS BRAVOS FAN CLUB, c/o Miss Jean Tocci, Vice-Pres., 810 Soundview Avenue, Bronx, New York 10472.

BIRTHDAYS

— HAPPY BIRTHDAY DUFI — ALL my love ... TOHDA
HAPPY BIRTHDAY KAREN ... KEITH
VICKY VIELEY — HAPPY BIRTHDAY!
Robbie ... Happy Birthday! Sue

BANDS FOR HIRE

THE FLIPSIDE is the best side. HA 9-5367 (after 4 p.m.) Lakewood, California

KRLA ARCHIVES

RECORDS FREE FROM RC®
You'll Flip at the ZZZIP in RC® Cola

while you swing to your favorite stars! RC and music, perfect partners for the perfect lift

TAKE 1 ALBUM FREE

For everyone you buy... with 6 cork liners or seals from R.C. bottle caps over 100 Capitol LP's available. Order as often as you wish. Nothing to join. Look for this display at your favorite store.

Here's your best way yet to save more on the records you want. In dollars-and-cents terms you get two albums that the Capitol Record Club sells for $3.98 each time you buy one. The savings are even bigger on stereo records! And there are no shipping charges to pay, nothing else to join or buy.

What's more, you choose from top albums by today's biggest stars, including the Beatles, David McCallum, Frank Sinatra, Lou Rawls, Buck Owens, Petula Clark, the Outsiders, Nancy Wilson, Dean Martin, Sonny James, the Beach Boys and many others.

OTHER FINE BRANDS: DIET-RITE®COLA, NEHI®BEVERAGES, PART-T-PAK®BEVERAGES, UPPER 10®
"ROYAL CROWN" AND "RC" REG. U.S. PAT. OFF.; ®1966 ROYAL CROWN COLA CO.

KRLA ARCHIVES

John Lennon—Then And Now

KRLA *Edition* BEAT

JUNE 3, 1967

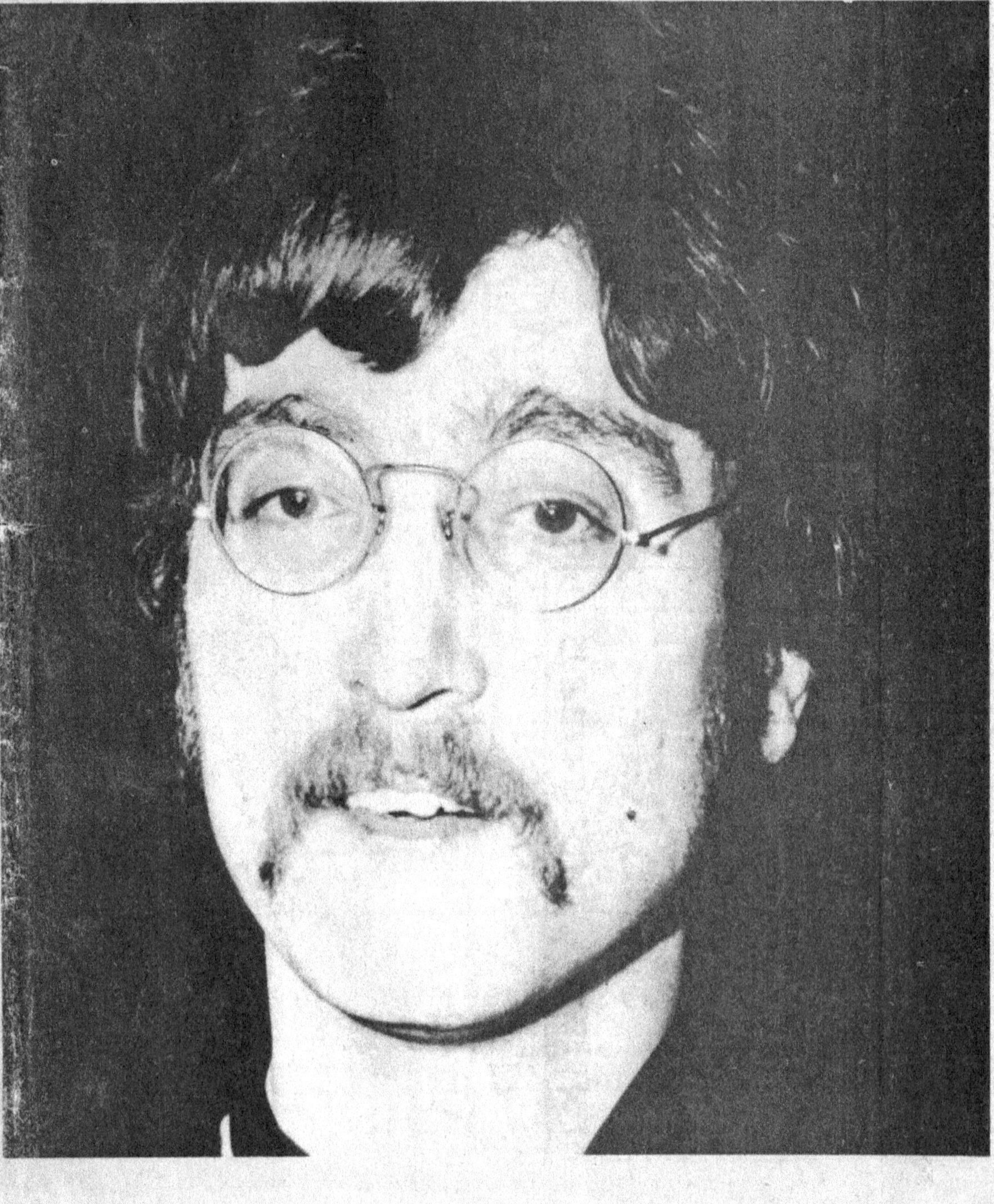

KRLA ARCHIVES

KRLA BEAT

Volume 3, Number 6 — June 3, 1967

TOM JONES TO BECOME ELVIS II?

LOS ANGELES—Col. Tom Parker, the man responsible for the long-lasting and highly successful career of Elvis Presley, may well become Welsh pop star, Tom Jones', American manager!

Discussions have already taken place between the Col. and Jones' personal manager, Gordon Mills. Mills is flying to the U.S. to negotiate further with the Col. and has announced: "If we reach agreement, it would mean that he (Parker) would manage Tom in the States and look after his interests there."

To help establish Jones in America, he is being booked into top clubs in New York, Miami, Las Vegas and Hollywood during the summer.

Jones was originally to have begun a movie career within the next few months but has now postponed his movie debut until 1968.

Stones To Face Jury

DAVY JONES RECEIVES 1-A

HOLLYWOOD—Davy Jones, the only British member of the Monkees, has been classified 1-A by his draft board. Davy will not know until the end of July whether or not he will be called up to serve. It has been reported, however, that Davy has applied for re-classification on the grounds that he is the sole support of his father. His appeal, we understand, will take about three months to consider.

Monkee spokesmen feel that Davy will be re-classified but have stated that if he is not and is actually called up, he will certainly go.

Meanwhile, the Monkees continue filming their television series and preparing for their first concerts in England. While in Britain, the Monkees plan to tape at least one segment of their popular show.

CHICHESTER—Two of the Rolling Stones, Mick Jagger and Keith Richard, have pleaded not guilty to narcotics charges and have asked for a jury trial. The trial date has not yet been set and the two Stones are each free on a reported 100 pound bail.

Party Raid

Jagger and Richard's problems began when a party thrown by Richard was raided by policemen who entered his house on a search warrant issued under the Dangerous Drugs Act.

The seven men and one woman present at the party were not arrested; however, substances were taken from the house and the two Stones were subsequently summoned to appear in court.

The officer in charge of the raid allegedly informed the judge the police received full cooperation from everyone at the party when the officers entered Richard's house.

Both Jagger and Richard showed up for their court date uncustomarily dressed in suits and ties. They did not, however, trim their hair for the judge. Leaving the court, both Stones smiled widely for the photographers gathered outside and appeared not at all upset over their legal tangles.

Stone fans in the United States are considerably more worried than the Stones themselves since it is very likely that the Stones will not be granted work permits in the U.S. Work permits are hard enough to come by but they are virtually impossible to obtain once a foreign entertainer has been linked with narcotics.

Tour Again?

The Stones know this all too well and this is the main reason why they have not scheduled another concert tour of America. Of course, there is always the outside chance that the Stones will be granted work permits and, if so, you can expect them to return for at least one more tour of the U.S. First and foremost, of course, will be the outcome of Jagger and Richard's jury trial in Chichester, England.

THE BEATLES POSE WITH ROAD MANAGERS, Neil Aspinall and Mal Evans, during recording of "Sgt. Pepper." For the full and exclusive details on how each track of the album was recorded. See Tony Barrow's report on page three and discover how John Lennon's young son helped his famous dad come-up with a song title.

—UPI Photo

KRLA ARCHIVES

Letters to the Editor

ASSOCIATION CHANGE

Dear *BEAT*:

This letter was meant to be written several weeks ago when the time came for the sixth in a series of six interviews of the Association came and Gary's interview did not show. I meant to write a letter of complaint demanding it, but then I heard the news—that Gary was leaving the Association.

I think Gary added a lot of personality to the Association and he will be greatly missed (especially by me). Anyway, I was wondering if this was the reason there was no interview, and if you could print one or at least some sort of "farewell" article? I also had two more questions about Gary. 1. When is he leaving for India? 2. Is he on the recording of the Association's new record, "Windy?"

Janet Sawer

Gary is leaving the group as far as personal appearances are concerned. Larry Ramos, formerly with the New Christy Minstrels, is replacing him. Right now Larry is on tour with the guys and Gary is along helping to break him in. Gary will continue to write new material for the Association. He left the group merely because continuously being on the road stifled his creativity as far as writing is concerned. Gary has always wanted to go to India, but has made no definite plans. Maybe he'll make it and maybe not. Gary is not on "Windy." That's Larry and Russ singing lead.

— *The Editor*

HOLLIES

Dear *BEAT*:

In every one of your issues so far, you have always printed something on the Hollies, for which I am very grateful. I have never found a top teen magazine until *BEAT* which has printed much on the Hollies. I would appreciate very much, along with many others, seeing a feature article on the Hollies in a near-future issue of *BEAT*. It's time these guys should get more recognition than they have been getting in other magazines if any.

Thank you again.

Nancy Carlson

COVERS ALL

Dear *BEAT*:

I'm a girl of 15 and I want you very much to make *BEAT* a big hit. I think it's great. It covers everything I'd like to know. Especially of my favorite group, the Monkees.

I spend about $5 a month on magazines and *BEAT* is worth it. My girlfriends think it's fab too and I got them started on it. So I wish that you could keep it a hit.

Sharon Gomez

A DICK CLARK DAY?

Dear *BEAT*:

The following letter is an open letter to the teenagers of the world. I would appreciate it if you would print it in *The BEAT* because your paper is read throughout the U.S. and parts of Europe.

Roberta Franks

A Man of ACTION

If you were to define the word "action" what would you say? Possibly, a type of movement or a happening? No, you'd say what any other normal teenager would say. *ACTION* is a word cherished by many but means nothing to some scrunky people. Action is the third word of a great and cancelled TV show, "Where The Action Is!" And what is the root of Action? Why the talented Dick Clark, of course. He is definitely the man of *ACTION*!! He's been like an angel to the teenagers of yesterday, today and, I'm sure, tomorrow. America should have a national Dick Clark Day to celebrate the many things he has done for teenagers. And anyone who does not think this way about Dick should definitely not admit that he/she is a teenager, because they're not normal!

A Friend

BEAT Photo: Robert Young

STONES

Dear *BEAT*:

I would like to tell you my very favorite feature of all my favorite features of *The BEAT*: The National Top 100 Singles from Cash-Box.

Since St. Louis is sort of a dead city, music wise, I like to know how much farther ahead the rest of the nation is. Now, all you need is a list of the top albums and your magazine will be perfect.

Geoffrey Horner

BLOW IT

Dear *BEAT*:

To "Frenchie" Horn—go blow it will ya!! Mick Jagger is *the* most talented guy around. Also he's very, very, very sexy (sigh). Look kiddo, keep your mouth shut and join the "Swiss Cheeze." Stones 4 ever!

Peggy Shearer

GEORGE'S MOUSTACHE

"*I believe in re-incarnation*"
— *George Harrison*

Of course we've seen you before. You sat for El Greco once or twice. And Warner Brothers gave glimpses of how you laughed and looked when you wailed with Drake.

You're the troubador in our picture books (your love songs had such a different bite).

Brummel, then Beardsley envied your elegance.

Saint, swashbuckler, poet, beau . . . but that moustache has got to go!

Cathy Boyle

MONKEES

Dear *BEAT*:

Maybe on the hippier Coast the Monkees are taken for what they are! . . . actors with "schtick." Here in Chicago, though, they've taken over in a sickening way.

Great groups like the Byrds get no play at all. Request "Strawberry Fields," and the jocks give you a hard time. As far as I'm concerned there are only two good things about the Monkees: Neil Diamond (and even *he* can't pump much originality into those puppets) and Davy Jones looks something like George Harrison in certain angles. And that's it!

Music magazines like *BEAT* should be for and about musicians. Leave the Monkees to ScreenJoys or whatever.

Lynn Gold

P.S. For example, re Chicago's square-ness. The only album cut ever played is that mushy, icky "Valerie." You'd think they never heard of "Revolver." Maybe they haven't. They're too busy remembering Fred Waring.

WOE WE ARE! A MISTAKE!!

Dear *BEAT*:

Well this is the third copy of *BEAT* I've read, and . . . I found a mistake! Woe is you. I hope (!) your office is flooded by mail from all of us Peter and Gordon fans, because in the April 22nd issue, you had an article about good 'ole P&G and a picture of Gordon supposedly. On the same page, you had an article about Paul Jones with the exact same picture! Did you run out of Gordon pictures? If you did, I'm sure that Jo-Anne (our fearless fan club leader) Lucas will be glad to furnish some.

Do you admit to your mistakes?

Chris

PEACE! We admit it! We made a mistake. Apologies to P. & G. fans everywhere.

— *The Editor*

APPLAUSE

Dear *BEAT*:

I'd like to give you a big applause for your great magazine. It seems that there is so much jazz running around about teenagers and what slobs and cruds we are and yet you people express things beautifully and with much knowledge becuz I imagine most of your writers are young people who know what's happening. I'm a happy nineteen-year-old girl on my last leg as a teenager and I regret nothing I've done and think the majority of our generation is outaside kids who live life as we see fit and as time goes by will see our mistakes and better ourselves thru what we know and not what other people try to cram down our throats.

Once again, thanks for a great magazine.

Judy Vitez

THE BALLOON

Dear *BEAT*:

In "In" People Are Talking About you asked "whatever happened to The Leaves? Well, John Beck is now the lead singer of the Yellow Balloon, Tom "Ambrose" Ray is semi-manager of the Yellow Balloon.

The rest of the Yellow Balloon consists of Matthew Andes, Mark Andes, Bob Harris and Eddie Rubin.

These guys are really great so why not give them a chance and print an article on them in *The BEAT*?

Gloria Lopez

CONTRIBUTION TO P.A.T.A.

Dear *BEAT*:

I would like to say first that your mag - er - newspaper - er - publication is the only teen thingy anyone can *believe* anymore! It gets bad when mags make two-page stories out of the time Paul McCartney took a deep breath — real bad! Your - er - your whatever it is (try *BEAT*) reports facts and stuff and you can *believe* what you read. It's for real!

Secondly, I'd like to make a contribution to "In" People Are Talking About:

. . . when they'll start getting people for possession of Chiquitas . . . how unrecognized the Byrds are . . . Paul Simon being the reincarnation of John Marshall . . . why P.S. is like J.M. and deciding maybe he's not after all and it was only a rumor . . . why Ringo grabs a cuppa before going down to the bus and figuring it's only common sense . . . what's in that song that makes it so great besides something stupid.

Thirdly, why can't people close their eyes and listen to the music and decide whether or not they like it *that* way: it's *sound*? Albums look a lot alike and that's what you're buying anyway!

Thanx for reading and I love you, *BEAT*!

Shar

Thank you for reading, Shar, and thanks for the nice comments.

DEDICATED TO HARPO

Dear *BEAT*:

HARPO???
Our smiling Harpo is gone,
Like the caterpillar that
Spins itself a cacoon
Only to emerge as his real self,
James George Valley.

Please print this because this is how I feel and I'm sure Jim would agree with me.

Sue Nation

P.S. I love *The BEAT*. More on the Raiders!

Beat Publications, Inc.

Executive Editor . . . . Cecil L. Tuck
Publisher . . . . Gayle Tuck
Editor . . . . Louise Criscione

Staff Writers
Carol Deck   Bobby Farrow
Ron Koslow   Shirley Poston
        Rochelle Reed

Contributing Writers
Tony Barrow   Sue Barry
Lawrence Charles   Eden
Tammy Hitchcock   Rochelle Sech
Bob Levinson   Jamie McCluskey, III

Photographers
Chuck Boyd   Dwight Carter

Advertising
Dick Jacobson   Jerry Loss
Winona Price   Dick Stricklin
        Ron Woodlin

Business Manager . . . . Judy Felice
Subscriptions . . . . Nancy Arena

Distribution
Miller Freeman Publications
500 Howard Street, San Francisco, Calif.

The *BEAT* is published bi-weekly by BEAT Publications, Inc., editorial and advertising offices at 6290 Sunset Blvd., Suite 504, Hollywood, California 90028. U. S. bureaus in Hollywood, San Francisco, New York, Chicago and Nashville; overseas correspondents in London, Liverpool and Manchester, England. Sale price 25 cents. Subscription price: U.S. and possessions, $5 per year; Canada and foreign rates, $9 per year. Second class postage prepaid at Los Angeles, California.

June 3, 1967

ON THE BEAT
BY LOUISE CRISCIONE

The big subject in the music business is, of course, the Monterey Pop Festival. It happens June 16, 17 and 18 and everyone is pulling for it to be a smashing success. Personally, I don't see how it can possibly miss with the talent they've lined up for the three days. Every facet of the pop field will be represented, so there will be something for everyone, no matter what your musical tastes are. And then, of course, there's the hot rumor that Paul McCartney, who is on the board of governors, will attend the Festival.

Gerry To Solo

Gerry Marsden, who started Gerry and the Pacemakers, has announced that the group will break-up shortly. Gerry plans to begin his career all over again as a solo artist. "As a group we achieved everything we set out to achieve. I have already done quite a bit of solo TV work and I want to write a full-scale musical," said Gerry. "As a group we moved into the cabaret scene over the past 18 months and I'd like to continue doing quite a bit in the way of cabaret appearances."

Gerry Bonner and Alan Gordon, the songwriting team which has composed such pop hits as "Happy Together," "Melancholy Music Man," "She'd Rather Be With Me," have taken a definite stand against psychedelic music. They call it "a musical regression based on writers' misinterpretation of public taste. Even in the dull post-twist and pre-Beatle music period, there was a progression, not particularly impressive, but in the direction which we might expect," said the pair. "And now, the possibilities of fruitful musical experimentation still are not exhausted and, in fact, have as yet scarcely been touched." They added that they did not believe that musical experimentation included "freak-out, freak-in psychedelic noise."

Psychedelic Lennon

It would seem that John Lennon does not agree with Bonner and Gordon since he recently attended the psychedelic "Technicolor Dream" at London's Alexandra Palace.

I saw "To Sir With Love" a couple of weeks ago and although I usually don't say much about movies, I can't help myself this time. It has to be one of the *best* movies to come along all year. It stars Sidney Poitier, who is magnificent, as always, but the surprise is the young supporting cast.

Except for Lulu, popular Scottish singer, the young British cast is unknown Stateside—but I'll bet you even money that after this movie is released *everyone* will be talking about them! It should be out sometime in June—don't miss it.

Talk has it that Tim Rooney has been picked to replace Davy Jones if Davy is actually drafted. However, it seems extremely unlikely that Davy will be called up. He is seeking reclassification because he is the sole support of his father and should have no trouble getting his 1-A status changed.

So, the Walker Brothers are splitting. Scott Walker gave the press an unusually frank answer as to why the group decided that now was the time to break up. "After seeing our last 'Palladium' performance I think I really got things into perspective and made up my mind to quit the group. It's a nasty feeling watching a show like that. I was so embarrassed. I was so full of shame for myself and the rest of the group. It was the last straw. I was disgusted."

Poor Paul Revere. He's certainly had his share of troubles lately. First Harpo left and then Smitty and Fang followed suit. It really got to be a joke in the business with everyone asking how Paul Revere And The Raider were going to get on.

A lot of people are predicting that Revere and Lindsay are not strong enough to carry the group with the others gone. This, of course, remains to be seen. And in the meantime Paul is busy finding himself three new group members.

GERRY MARSDEN

DAVY JONES

BEAT EXCLUSIVE
A Behind The Scenes Story Of Beatles' 'Sgt. Pepper'

By Tony Barrow

LONDON—On the first day of February THE BEATLES began to record a song called "SGT. PEPPER'S LONELY HEARTS CLUB BAND." Paul had contributed the basic ideas for the number so Paul was assigned to handle the main vocal action—with the others joining him for the chorus segments. To add instrumental effect an actual "Lonely Hearts Club Band" was formed—for one time only! It consisted of four horn players, all true and tried session musicians.

Centerpiece

At that point "Sgt. Pepper" was just one of twelve new compositions in line for inclusion on The Beatles' first album of 1967. A couple of weeks later the group began to think of tentative program titles for the finished production. Gradually they began to talk in terms of making "Sgt. Pepper" the centrepiece of the whole thing—a sort of *Lonely Hearts Club Band Show* which would open up with the "Sgt. Pepper" number and, eventually, get back to the same song towards the end.

From here on everything was based on this theme. Instead of being "banded" or broken up into individual tracks, the album would be virtually continuous with no more than a split second of silence between the end of one item and the beginning of the next one. In fact "Sgt. Pepper" runs straight thru into Ringo's solo vocal called "With A Little Help From My Friends," the instrumental link being provided by producer George Martin playing the organ!

Repeat

"Audience reaction" noises were put in behind the "Sgt. Pepper" number, giving an effect resembling that of a live show recording. And before the very last number on Side Two there's a repeat performance of "Sgt. Pepper's Lonely Hearts Club Band" with the same tune, different words, no horn quartet but everyone joining in the vocal and more audience sounds superimposed upon the finished recording.

Before I go any further let me give you an exclusive pre-release run-down on all the other items. After Ringo's specialty number comes "Lucy In The Sky With Diamonds," a title suggested to John by his own son, Julian, who came home from school with a painting he'd just done and claimed that it represented precisely that! John is lead singer and you can hear Paul playing Hammond organ.

Other numbers in which John takes the lead vocal are "Being For The Benefit Of Mr. Kite" (includes quartet of harmonicas played by Ringo, George, Neil Aspinall and Mal Evans), "Good Morning, Good Morning" (which has saxophones, trombones and French horn played by Sounds Inc.) and "A Day In The Life" (in which Paul looks after the solo singing in the middle segment and a 41-piece orchestra provides the series of three fantastic instrumental climax points).

John and Paul are jointly involved in the vocal for "She's Leaving Home" (in which harps and strings form the accompaniment and The Beatles are not heard at all instrumentally).

George Alone

George has a typically off-beat item all to himself—he wrote "Within You, Without You" and he sings it. The other Beatles are not featured at all and the instrumental backing is of strongly Indian influence featuring three tambouras, a dilruba, a tabla, a zither-like Indian table-harp, three cellos and eight violins. George brought a bunch of Indian friends into the session to play the colourful assortment of instruments—and, of course, George himself is featured as solo sitarist as well as tamboura player!

Items in which Paul plays the main role so far as singing is concerned are "Sgt. Pepper's Lonely Hearts Club Band," "Getting Better" (where George plays harpsichord), "Fixing A Hole" (with Paul on harpsichord), "When I'm 64" and "Lovely Rita" (Paul plays piano; John, Paul and George add special effects with combs and paper).

Incidentally Paul got the idea for "Lovely Rita, Meter Maid" from an American visitor who pointed out to him that the young women we call female traffic wardens are known as meter maids on your side of the Atlantic.

So there are twelve new numbers in all—with one of them being heard twice. The longest performances—each just over five minutes—are "A Day In The Life" and "Within You, Without You."

The creation of the very elaborate album cover shows just as much imaginative thinking as the music contained within it. The cover is one of those spectacular open-out jobs with a giant 24-inch by 12-inch colour photograph spread across the inside. For the album cover photographs The Beatles wore specially tailored "Sgt. Pepper" uniforms made up from vivid personally selected satin materials—with lavish braid, equally bright hats and orange and yellow patent leather shoes.

What about the FRONT of the album cover? That's quite amazing in its own way too but you'll see what I mean when Capitol issues "Sgt. Pepper's Lonely Hearts Club Band." For once I understand that every detail of the recordings and the cover will be duplicated precisely by Parlophone in Britain and Capitol in America.

One particularly welcome feature of the cover so far as album collectors are concerned will be the reproduction of all the lyrics in full on the back space. This means that Beatle People wanting the words of all the new songs but NOT the actual music will have the information without paying separately for copies of the sheet music.

More personal effort by The Beatles has gone into the preparation and production of "Sgt. Pepper" than any previous album they've recorded. On other occasions, even if just as much concentration has gone into the music content, there hasn't been the opportunity for John, Paul, George and Ringo to follow thru and take such a close interest in the album cover and other details. Usually they've finished their recording sessions to meet a deadline and gone away on a concert tour. This time they stayed in London and supervised all stages of the album's preparation prior to release.

ART INSTITUTE OF PITTSBURGH
47th Yr. Coed. 18 & 24 mo. Diploma Course: Commercial Art, Fashion, Art, Interior Design, Begin. & Adv. Vet. Appd. Dorm. facilities. College referrals for degrees. Free illus. brochure.
Earl S. Wheeler, Director
635 Smithfield St.
Pittsburgh, Pa. 15222

"The Standel Sound"

"The Nitty Gritty Dirt Band"
Professional musicians throughout the world choose the "Standel Sound," the accepted standard for professional musicians who demand professional performance.

A. P.A. Speaker Column Amplifier
B. P.A. Master Control with Reverb
C. Imperial Line Amplifier — Solid State, Dual Channel

Standel
Solid State Music Systems
4918 DOUBLE DRIVE • EL MONTE, CALIF. 91731

KRLA ARCHIVES

JOURNEY TO OLD BOSTON

J. B. Lansing Sound, Inc. has taken a pinch of dust from the last century and mixed it up with a hefty amount of modern pizzaz in its revival of the Mendelsohn Quintette Club. Five violing, cello and flute-toting old timers with hair parted in the center and curling beards all resemble those famous brothers off the cough drop box.

It wasn't until 1871 that The Mendelsohn Quintette Club of Boston cut their first single, "Meet me at the Liberty Bell, Sarah 'cause you're a ding-a-ling," and it hit big.

The word is out. 'ding-a-ling' hit sounds, sound bigger out. JBL loudspeakers. The rest of the message is being worn by teenagers all over on sweatshirts; "Irving Mendelsohn Swings."

The MQC of Boston (pictured above) signs autographs for the great-great-great-great-great granddaughters of their fans when they first hit big in 1871.

Greek Rulers Okay 'I Spy'

The production company of the TV series, "I Spy," suddenly became involved in some real-life government intrigue while filming the show in the Greek Island of Lindos.

"I Spy" stars, Bob Culp and Bill Cosby were in Marrakech when the Greek army overthrew the existing government in a sudden coup. NBC production manager, Leon Chooluck had gone ahead to Athens, the capital city, to make arrangements for shooting a segment of the show, when the ouster of government heads occurred.

David Friedkin, a co-producer of the series sat stateside chewing on his fingernails unable to get through to Athens since all communications with the outside world were stopped following the coup. However, Chooluck finally sent word that the new government seemed to be big "I Spy" fans, for they renewed the company's work permits and gave the all-clear sign to continue shooting. Cameras, that is!

BUSY MONKEE SUMMER

Monkee fans all over the country mark your calendars for what will be the top rock event of the summer. Dick Clark Productions is sending the fab foursome around the country during July and August for a string of one-nighters, according to an announcement by Rosalind Ross, DCP's executive director.

The Monkees will play some of their many recent hits at 31 single appearances and are set for a three-day stand at Forest Hills Tennis Stadium in New York during mid-July. Here is the Monkee's tour schedule:

July 7, Atlanta, Ga., Braves Stadium; July 8, Jacksonville, Fla., Convention Hall; July 11, Charlotte, N.C., Coliseum; July 12, Greensboro, N.C., Coliseum; July 14-16, New York, Forest Hills Stadium; July 20, Buffalo, N.Y., Memorial Auditorium; July 21, Baltimore, Md., Memorial Auditorium; July 22, Boston, Mass., Boston Gardens; July 23, Philadelphia, Pa., Convention Hall; July 27, Rochester, N.Y., War Memorial Auditorium; July 28, Cinn., Ohio, Gardens; July 29, Detroit, Mich., Olympia Stadium; July 30, Chicago, Ill., Stadium; Aug. 2, Milwaukee, Wisc., Arena; Aug. 4, St. Paul, Minn., Municipal Auditorium; Aug. 5, St. Louis, Mo., Kiel Auditorium; Aug. 9, Dallas, Texas, Memorial Auditorium; Aug. 10, Houston, Texas, Sam Houston Coliseum; Aug. 11, Shreveport, La., Hirsch Memorial Coliseum; Aug. 12, Mobile, Ala., Municipal Auditorium; Aug. 17, Memphis, Tenn., Mid-South Coliseum; Aug. 18, Tulsa, Okla., Assembly Center; Okla. City, Okla., State Fair Arena; Aug. 20, Denver, Colo., Coliseum; Aug. 25, Seattle, Wash., Seattle Center Coliseum; Aug. 26, Portland, Ore., Memorial Coliseum; Aug. 27, Spokane, Wash., Coliseum.

Mamas & Papas Deliver Gold Disc

The Mamas and Papas recent album, "The Mamas and The Papas Deliver" has been certified a gold disc by the RIAA as it moved into the number two spot on the national best-seller charts.

This is the third album released by the talented foursome in less than a year and a half, and all have been million sellers. Their last two singles, "Creeque Alley," and "Dedicated to The One I Love," are both tracks from the album.

Mama Cass Elliott was certified the first genuine "Mama" of the group with the birth of her first baby, a girl, in Los Angeles. The Brunhilde-sized songstress, is separated from the child's father.

Pop Stars In 'Monte Carlo'

Two of Europe's leading female and male popular singers, Francoise Hardy and Gilbert Becaud, have been signed by executive producer Jack Haley, Jr. to guest star with Terry Thomas on "Monte Carlo . . . C'est La Rose." The Wolper Productions special scheduled to be aired over ABC-TV will be hosted by the rulers of the tiny European state, Prince Rainier and Princess Grace.

"C'est La Rose," the title song of the special is Becaud's own composition.

PEOPLE ARE TALKING ABOUT the manager of the Seeds, Tim Hudson, saying: "The Generation of Seeds will overcome the Age of Stones in six months" and wondering if he may be right . . . Paul Revere almost being sued for getting a member of his ailing group from an up and coming group because of a signed contract . . . whether or not George Harrison will follow Ravi Shankar to the United States

. . . the fact that it may be Junior instead of Senior on that record and the one national television show which was hip enough to pick up on it . . . why Florence didn't appear with her sister Supremes at the Hollywood Bowl and deciding that perhaps Florence wants out . . . whether or not that's Neil Diamond plopped into the middle of the Buckingham's "Don't You Care" . . . why Don and the Goodtimes don't appear on a top show like "The Smothers Brothers" . . . what a smash "To Sir With Love" is going to be

. . . the big things now being Chiquita stickers worn on the forehead and Irvin Mendelsohn buttons worn on the lapel . . . the rumor that the Stones have sold-out to the Seeds by perhaps calling their next album "Flowers" . . . whether or not Elmo and Almo really exist . . . the Rascals being one of the best groups in the business and hoping their "Groovin'" will be a million-seller . . . the trouble the Turtles seem to have keeping a publicist . . . the truth being that there is nothing worse than a cold rock group and wondering why publicists can't seem to understand that

. . . the group which has been around for a long time now and finally has a hit along with a personality clash within the group . . . whatever happened to Barry McGuire and finding out that

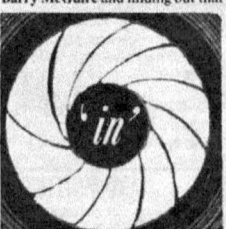

he's joined the love movement . . . the billing now reading "Paul Revere And The Raiders – featuring Mark Lindsay" and what a real coup it will be if the group formed by the ex-Raiders gets bigger than their parent group . . . the popular group who just got over one problem with one of their female members and now has two more in the form of narcotics charges

. . . the new Jim McQuinn look being a hundred percent better than the old one . . . the possibility that the Association may have finally found that elusive one they were looking for . . . Leonard Nimoy being a real gas . . . the maxi-skirts and deciding that they'll never make it . . . the trouble the Hardtimes are having keeping their group members and coming to the very obvious conclusion that this is really the year of the group break-ups

. . . the latest thing in upper circles being wearing a turtleneck sweater with suits instead of a shirt and tie . . . how many members have now been called Grass Roots . . . the Monkees taping a segment of their show in England and how much better Davy looks with his hair cut . . . Mike Nesmith buying a new house . . . what the Spoonful have been doing lately . . . when Johnny Rivers is going to stop recording old Motown hits

. . . how ironic it is that Sidney Poitier played a delinquent student in "Blackboard Jungle" and is now portraying the teacher of unmanagable students in "To Sir, With Love" . . . the rumor that Diana Ross is up for the lead in the movie version of "The Owl And The Pussycat" and wondering what it means to the future of the Supremes . . . whether or not Paul McCartney is really upset about the Bee Gees as London talk says he is . . . the fact that George Harrison is a very lucky man, thanks to that MBE.

KRLA ARCHIVES

SREHTOMS!

No, It's Not "Nature" Spelled Backwards

It's **SMOTHERS** (spelled backwards!)

The perpetuators of tongue-in-guitar tom-foolery

NOW AVAILABLE AT YOUR LOCAL

KRLA ARCHIVES

BEAT EXCLUSIVE

The Chief Beatle – Thru His

By Louise Criscione

John Lennon is the head Beatle. Make no mistake about that. The only question is whether Lennon is best known for his talent or for the quotes he has given the press. And since we're a press-oriented society, the answer is probably the latter.

Lennon was the first Beatle to have his name connected with his face in the minds of fans when the Beatles first appeared on "Ed Sullivan" and the message flashed across Lennon's televised figure: "Sorry, girls, he's married."

Hidden Wife

What American fans didn't know was that while the Beatles were climbing up the elusive ladder of success in England, Lennon's wife, Cynthia, had been carefully hidden.

"I haven't deliberately hidden her from the public," declared John when the "secret" was out. "But I have tried to keep her away from the press. I don't see why they should treat her like a freak just because she married a Beatle."

Perhaps even then the press knew Lennon was a man to be reckoned with. At any rate, neither Cynthia nor the Lennon's baby son were ever treated as "freaks."

As a matter of fact, the press and fans alike thought Lennon and the Beatles could do no wrong. Their careers went jubilently along with more broken sales and attendance records than possibly any entertainer has ever or will ever again be able to achieve.

Lennon was anything but silent during this period, but his statements then did not cause bonfires. On the subject of fan letters, Lennon commented: "You want to see the letters the Japanese write us. You wouldn't believe it. Better than the ones we get from America. You wouldn't believe them either! A lot of American fans are just plain illiterate. You can hardly make out what they're all about."

It wasn't until the Beatles were awarded MBE's that the first hint of uproar reared its head. Beatle fans, were, of course, delighted that their idols had been chosen for MBE's. But some of their fellow award-holders were verbally horrified. Said one war hero: "English royalty wants *me* on the same level as those vulgar nincompoops."

"Better Than Killing"

To which, Lennon answered: "We got ours for entertaining people. Isn't that better than getting it for killing people? But I guess you can't expect everyone to luv us."

Lennon refused to remain undaunted by the uproar, however, and let his wit shine through when he said: "I don't think we got ours for rock 'n' roll. On that basis, we'd have got OBE's (a higher award) and the Rolling Stones MBE's. I reckon we got them for exports and the citation ought to have said that!"

Asked what he planned to do with his MBE, John replied: "I think I'll have mine made into a bell push so that people have to press it when they come to the house."

The first major batch of "Beatlemania dying" rumors were caused by the "greeting" the Beatles received at the Roman airport in July, 1965. One hundred and 50 policemen turned up to protect the Beatles from their enthusiastic fans – the hitch being that only nine fans showed up to greet the Beatles, all of whom were British! The news media had great fun with that one and couldn't refrain from speculating as to the future of the Beatles.

Mob Scene

The fun died a few days later on July 29, 1965 when the Royal premiere of the Beatles' second movie, "Help," was held at the London Palladium in Picadilly Circus. The Beatles were almost mobbed by a 10,000-strong guard of fans. Fourteen ambulances had to be called to carry the injured to hospitals for first aid.

Rumors die hard but by August most people had forgotten that they had only weeks earlier predicted the "end of Beatlemania" and the Beatles were once again "as hot as ever!"

Especially when they arrived on U.S. soil for their cross-country tour in August of '65. Press conferences were held at the Beatle stop-offs and it was Lennon again who received the most attention from inquiring reporters. And again, Lennon let the world in on his quick wit and sometimes-cutting, sometimes-acid, but mostly marvelous humor.

Someone asked him what he thought of Sid Bernstein, the promoter of the Beatles' New York shows, and Lennon replied: "I think 'West Side Story' is his best work."

On the subject of his newly-acquired contact lenses, John quipped: "They're marvelous! I can see things like bus stops and garden gates!"

Serious Lennon

John did, however, become serious when asked about the Beatles' music and about the wave of protest songs which were then hitting the charts.

"There are only about 100 people in the world who really understand what our music is all about," said Lennon. "We try to find a truth for ourselves, a real feeling. You can never communicate your complete emotion to other people but if we can convey just a little of what we feel, then we have achieved something."

On protest songs Lennon spoke frankly: "If there is anything I hate it is labels such as this (protest). The 'protest' label in particular means absolutely nothing – it's just something that the press has latched onto and as usual is flogged to death. Some of the songs which appear to come under this heading are simply good songs – some are not. But, personally, I have no time for the 'Eve Of Destruction' songs."

Stands Straight

Throughout the Beatles' 1965 U.S. visit, Lennon refused to bend to the Establishment whenever he felt they were wrong or out of place. At a Chicago press conference, a distinguished gentleman approached Lennon and haughtily informed him: "I am the acting British Consul General. Are you doing a good job for your country?" "Yes," snapped Lennon. "Are you?"

Returning to England following a highly successful U.S. tour, John Lennon remarked on it only by saying: "The weather's too hot and someone's pinched three of me shirts!"

The Bad Year

No doubt the Beatles will never forget 1966. The first six months of the year were great for them. Their first working date was not until May 1 when they appeared at Wembley Empire Pool outside of London.

After that all hell broke loose. The first thing to go wrong was the original cover of "Yesterday And Today." The Beatles posed in butchers' outfits with decapitated doll heads and raw meat surrounding them. Advance reaction was highly unfavorable and Capitol quickly changed covers at a reported cost of $250,000.

But instead of getting better, things got decidely worse. The Beatles visited Manila in July of '66 and received the first physical maltreatment of their careers. They failed to show up for a luncheon appointment with the First Lady of the country and furious Filipinos sent them off at the airport with kicks, curses and shouts of "get out of our country." Practically all police protection and special considerations were cancelled and the tax bureau threatened for a time to hold up the group's departure.

Apology

The Beatles declared that they had not received the invitation in time to attend but nevertheless Paul, on behalf of the group, apologized. Lennon was not so polite as he told the press: "I didn't even know they had a President." And George let the cat out of the bag when he said: "We're going to have a couple of weeks to recuperate before we go and get beaten up by the Americans."

The Beatles had no way of knowing then that the worse was yet to come. It came in the form of a comment from John Lennon that "The Beatles are more

Controversies

popular than Jesus." The uproar that ensued in America could be heard around the world as a wave of Beatle bonfires, radio station bannings of Beatle records and whispered warnings that the Beatles were certain to get hurt if they tried to make their scheduled tour of America broke out across the country.

Hurried Flight

Epstein made a hurried flight to the U.S. to attempt to calm the roar. Lennon made a formal announcement that the quote had been taken completely out of context, which it had. However, when the Beatles arrived in the U.S. Lennon publically apologized—repeatedly. Still, reporters seemed to get some sort of twisted satisfaction out of making him explain and apologize again and again and again.

When the Beatles held a press conference in L.A., it was the first question asked. "I've explained it 800 times and I think it should be clear," said a tired and disgusted Lennon.

"Well, you made an apology before," snapped the reporter, "can't you say it again?"

"No," answered John, "I can't because I can't remember what I said. Look, I could have used television or anything else. I used the Beatles because that's what I know the best."

Thru the Fire

They dragged Lennon through the fire and they just wouldn't let him go. A middle-aged lady stood up and demanded to know if John was really and truly sorry he had said such a thing, even if he was only using the Beatles as an example.

"I am, yes," said John in an almost-whisper. "Even though I didn't mean it that way, I'm sorry I ever opened my mouth."

But back in England, John snapped out of it and announced: "I hope to get to see more of America because it's the kind of place that might blow up someday by itself, or with the help of some other country."

So, Lennon was still Lennon—despite all the controversy. And thank God he is. Can you imagine what a world it would be if everyone was afraid to open his or her mouth and express their opinions and ideas?

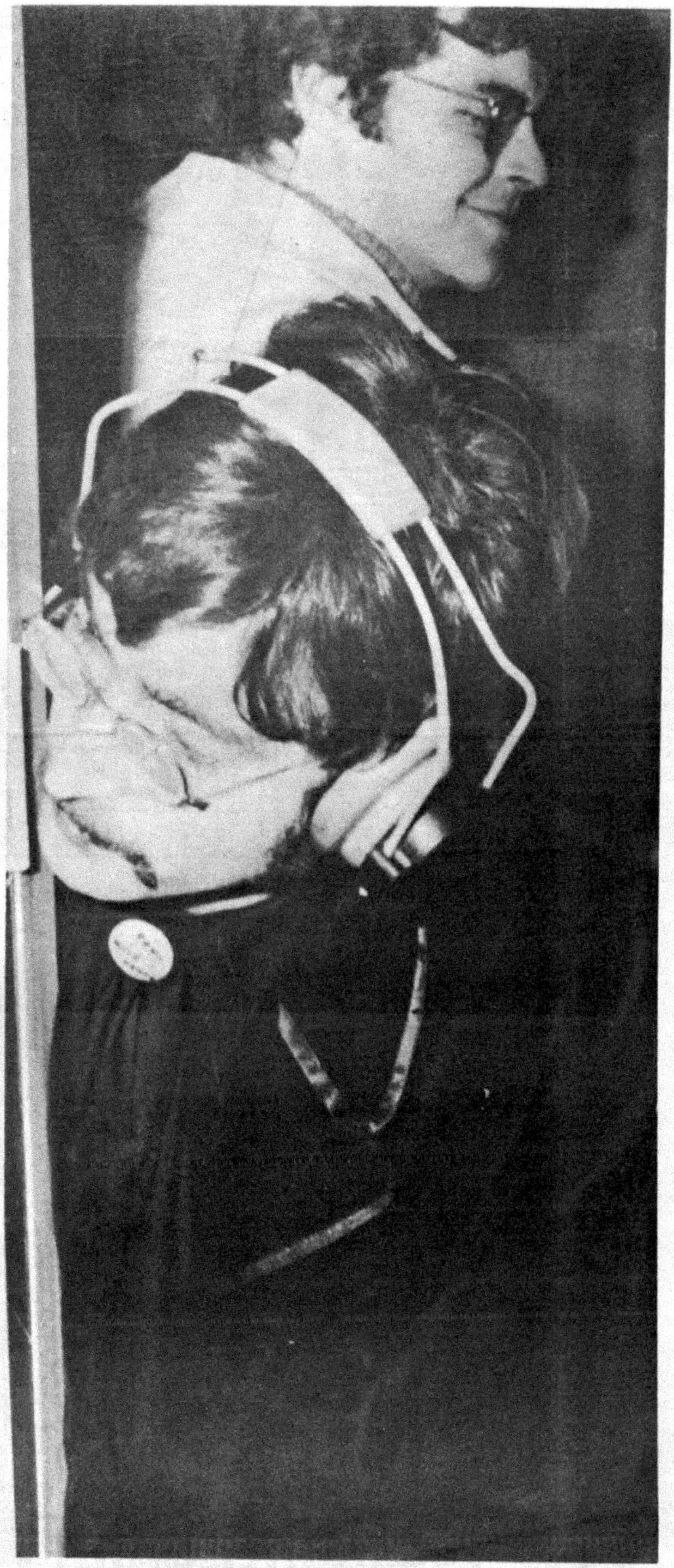

KRLA ARCHIVES

The Fab Foursome!

Including:
'Dedicated to The One I Love'
and
'Creeque Alley'

Instrumental Sounds...

Lots Of Heart...

Now Available At **Montgomery Ward** Record Departments

KRLA ARCHIVES

across the board

Making The News

FROM THE EDITOR . . .

This marks the first of a four-issue salute to the phenomenal Beatles. We've chosen to lead off with John Lennon; it couldn't have been any other way. From the very start, it's been Lennon who has made the front pages of newspapers everywhere. His wit, his satirical mind, his sometimes acid-tongue, his undeniable talent and creativity all make him the stand-out...the leader of the group which filled the terrible void in pop music left when Elvis Presley stopped wiggling his hips and became an actor. Whether or not you like the Beatles is up to you. But it would be a lie not to recognize the tremendous impact they have had on people and music alike. For this, The BEAT salutes them.

Also in this issue we have printed an exclusive, behind-the-scenes story on the recording of the Beatles' latest album, "Sgt. Pepper's Lonely Hearts Club Band." Tony Barrow takes us track by track through the entire album, telling not only how the Beatles recorded the songs but also the ideas and people who inspired each one.

The Jefferson Airplane personify the newly-found musical leadership of San Francisco-based groups. The success of the Airplane has been a long time coming. As much as six months ago we began writing about them, certain that they would eventually make a dent in the nation's charts. And now, months later, we've been proven right as the Airplane take their place as one of the hottest new groups in the pop field. Their story is on page ten. Read it and you'll see that not *all* members of our "upper" society have learned the meaning of the word "class."

Louise Criscione

WHAT NOW ELVIS

Fans and foes alike predicted Elvis Presley's meteoric career would end with his stint in the army. But the resilient 31-year-old pioneer of rock kept his fans and remains a top box office attraction. Now the questions are flying again since Elvis slipped a 21 diamond ring on the finger of his raven-haired sweetheart, Priscilla Ann Beaulieu, 21, at the simple civil wedding cremony at Las Vegas' Aladin Hotel. Priscilla met the millionaire singer when she was a 15-year-old high school student in Germany. Her father, an Air Force officer, and Elvis were both serving Uncle Sam at the time.

Although the lavish champagne breakfast, which reportedly cost $10,000 and included such items as suckling pig and poached salmon flown in from Canada, took two weeks to prepare, the wedding preparations were shrouded in secrecy. This was done to honor a request Elvis' mother made before her death to Col. Tom Parker, Elvis' manager. Mrs. Presley asked that her son's wedding remain a quiet, dignified affair and not be turned into a three-ring publicity circus with screaming fans drowning out the marriage vows.

Elvis' next film has been renamed "Speedway" by MGM. It was originally called "Pot Luck." The film rolls on June 12.

Frank Sinatra took time out from shooting a gangster film, "Tony Rome," in Miami Beach to accept the post of national chairman of the one-year-old American-Italian Anti-Defamation League which is waging a campaign to convince the country that not all citizens of Italian descent are linked to the Mafia network. "It is an honor," began the actor who is currently portraying a thug. "To me any type of discrimination is anti-American."

HOPE AWARD

Mrs. Bob Hope was honored with the title "outstanding mother of the year," at the annual Mothers' Day luncheon of the Helping Hand, a women's charity organization affiliated with the Cedars and Mount Sinai Hospitals.

Mrs. Hope will be awarded the President's Medal at the June commencement exercises at Loyola College in Baltimore.

CLARK WINNER MEETS HERMAN

Lucky 15-year-old Claire Kurz of Bethesda, Maryland, and her father joined Dick Clark on a jet trip to London to meet Peter Noone of Herman's Hermits. A tour of the switched-on capital is the first leg of a European holiday Claire won for correctly naming five historical landmarks aired on "Where The Action Is" and writing the letter picked out of 500,000 entries on "Why I Want To Go To London."

A stay in Paris will wind up Claire's two-week vacation prize and a mod wardrobe from the Cotton Council is ready for her when she returns.

DONOVAN

England's "Mellow Yellow" messiah, Donovan, starts work soon on a 14-week BBC special. For the weekly series, Donovan will set the work of leading poets to music and sing several of his own tunes. Donovan has a June concert tour slated for Brussels and Germany, followed by a British tour.

Barbra Streisand's contract for the title role in the film version of "Hello, Dolly" is the largest money deal for a single film ever made for an artist who has not previously appeared in the movies, according to Twentieth Century Fox. Barbra will play the part created by Carol Channing on Broadway and is the youngest actress ever cast in the part.

Barbra's film debut, however, is in the screen version of "Funny Girl," for Columbia which will screen July 5. "Dolly" starts in January.

HERMITS SET SUMMER TOUR

Herman's Hermits will headline three summer concerts. Supporting acts on the program include The Who.

The concerts, promoted by Dick Clark Productions, are on July 21, in the 11,000-seat Coliseum at Oklahoma City State Fair Grounds; August 29, in the 6,000-capacity Public Hall, Cleveland, Ohio; and September 3 in the 10,000 seat Civic Arena in Pittsburgh, Pennsylvania.

Aretha's Fall Stops Tour

Soul songstress Aretha Franklin who's become a top drawing attraction on the rock best-seller charts with "Respect" and "I Never Loved A Man," has bowed out of her scheduled one-nighter tour with Jackie Wilson and delayed a series of recording sessions since tripping on stage in the middle of a performance in Columbus, Georgia and breaking her elbow.

A jet whisked her to a Detroit hospital operating room. Her doctors are optimistic about the operation and feel confident Aretha's fingers will tinkle over the keyboard when an extended convalescent period is over.

The accident has put her arm in a cast for a month and will keep her off the concert tour during recuperation.

WOULD YOU BELIEVE?
"BRANDI"
is the vintage mfg. by
"THE SIERRAS"
on Yardbird - 8005 BMI

KRLA ARCHIVES

...MARTY

...PAUL

...JACK

...JORMA

By Lawrence Charles

Celluloid fires flicker blue and aqua. Water globules snake and shimmy fuschia and gold. Bearded, beaded, hippie technicians whose fuzzy beards grow into shabby shoulder-length hair are working furiously with projectors, spinning multi-colored discs and shallow bowls of vivid-hued paints creating a visual effect to startle the squinting eyes of millions of television viewers, upsetting the comfort of their living rooms.

It's a light show. Given first breath at the Fillmore and Avalon barn-sized dance halls in San Francisco and now brought to everyone who pauses long enough before flicking the TV dial.

The screamingly vivid colored light show is a backdrop for the latest carriers of the San Francisco sound, The Jefferson Airplane.

They are taping the "Smothers Brothers" show. Crew-cut, pressed shirt CBS technicians tolerate a shaky truce with the sandaled, long-haired hippies who have been imported from what's been called "Liverpool, USA," to create visuals for the Airplane.

Extra-Sharp Flash

A flash of extra-sharp colored pick-up sticks are shot at your eyes as the wailing vibrato of lead singer, Grace Slick, pitches the simple question from the group's latest hit, "Don't You Want Somebody To Love?" Suddenly, Marty Balin, lead singer; Grace; Jack Casady, bass; Jorma Kaukonen, lead guitar; Paul Kuntner, lead guitar; and Spencer Dryden, drums; are all floating like cutouts in a sea of pulsating light and color. TV has scored another triumph. The light show is such an integral part of the Airplane's total impact, that to show them in the steady white lights of a high school gym, senior prom – would be going backwards.

In between numbers, a CBS camera man, rubs his weary eyes,

JEFFERSON AIRPLANE
Booed At Swank Ball

...GRACE, "like a freak side show."

resting his globes from the flashing lights and says, "I made the mistake of having a martini for lunch, now I need dramamine."

Off stage, still keyed up from performing the group has a few minutes to rest before wisking off to a photo session for a national magazine.

Grace strokes damp cinnamon bangs out of her eyes. She is wearing a clinging velvet, floor length sheath with sleeves to the wrist, covered by a shoulder-to-toe orange and red brocade tunic made by fastening two huge towels at the shoulders, cinched by a wide black leather belt, and slit-open thigh high.

"What an unusual outfit, did you design it yourself," someone asks.

"Not really," smiles Grace, "Cannon did most of the work."

The Airplane is enough a part of the San Francisco scene to be invited to play at a strictly white-tie, high-society charity ball recently called the "Fol Der Rol."

"I understand what these people are like," said Grace, herself a product of an exclusive private girls' school, Castilleja. "They hired us to amuse the socialites, kind of like a freak side show."

"We played well," said Marty "and then the audience who were pretty drunk by this time, booed us."

"So we all bowed," said Jack, and we said, 'And now for our first encore!'"

The group dressed no differently for the ball than they usually do – riotously clashing mod outfits. The rich and beautiful people just weren't digging it.

The Airplane is cast to play itself – a rockadelic group – in Warner Brother's feature film, "Petulia." The film, starring Julie Christie and directed by Richard Lester (of Beatle-movie fame) strangely enough, has the Airplane playing at a San Francisco, high society ball. This time they don't get booed, however.

Not Selling Out

The Airplane has gone commercial, without selling out to commercialism. Every West Coast radio listener is familiar with the extended-wail advertisement which is highlighted by far-Eastern musical injections trying to sell that All-American product, White Levis.

"They put us in the studio and said we had to make a 45-second commercial and to get in White Levis," said Marty. The group did mention the dungaree-maker's famous brand name in a commercial that sounds like a toss up between a Gregorian chant and a Muslim evening prayer to Allah. But they did it the only way they will agree to do commercials – their way, without restrictions or guide lines.

The Airplane had some unkind words for the DJ's who refused to play their records in the early days and some grateful ones for their fans who insisted on hearing them. Then they were pulled off by an insistent photographer, to meet the busy schedule suddenly imposed by instantaneous fame.

MOBY GRAPE: AIMING HIGH UP ON THE VINE

The Moby Grape is a San Francisco rock quintet whose stated objective is to "climb high on the vine." They live in Mill Valley, California, a switched-on, sylvan area across the Golden Gate Bridge from San Francisco which functions as a haven for art lovers, boating enthusiasts and week-end tourists eager to sip tall drinks with the hip inhabitants in a beautiful green, hilly setting.

The Grape has just released five singles for immediate distribution around the country in an attempt to storm the best-seller charts with a shot gun approach. They feel their sound is too wide-ranging to be captured on a single disc. They hope DJ's will play them all and let the public pick its favorite.

Groovy Way

Meet the Moby Grape:

Bob Mosley plays bass and writes much of the group's material. A three-sport high school letterman and a dedicated summertime surfer. Bob's sports took second place to music during his second year at San Diego State until he discovered the guitar.

Skip Spence, rhythm guitarist for the Grape and bass and piano player for his own amusement, played drums for a year with the Jefferson Airplane. He left home (Windsor, Ontario) at sixteen and became half of a moderately successful San Francisco folk-rock duo.

Peter Lewis, guitarist, was a commercial pilot until he crash landed a Lear jet at Santa Monica Airport. Raised in a wealthy Los Angeles show business atmosphere, he headed his own rock group, Peter and the Wolves, before the Grape.

Frantic Split

Jerry Miller, guitarist, and Don Stevenson, drummer, both played in a California-based group called The Frantics. After working Northern discotheques and lounges for a while, The Frantics split and Jerry and Don formed a new group, Marsh Gas. Don spent a year hitchhiking around the world and worked some incredibly odd jobs . . . for instance he was a barracks guard for the British in West Germany!

The Moby Grape has played the Fillmore Auditorium and the Avalon Ballroom, two famous headquarters for San Francisco light shows. After much searching and testing, the Grape has become a professional unit, headed, they hope, for the top.

THE MOBY GRAPE: (Standing, from left to right) Peter, Skip (Sitting) Jerry, Don and Bob

KRLA ARCHIVES

U.K. POP NEWS ROUND-UP
Walker Brothers Break As A Group

By Tony Barrow

THE WALKER BROTHERS, one of Britain's most successful American pop imports over the past two years, have ceased to exist as a group! The surprise news that The Walkers were splitting up to follow solo careers came after they had given their final concert performances together via a nationwide tour in which they starred with newcomers CAT STEVENS, JIMI HENDRIX and ENGELBERT HUMPERDINCK.

SCOTT ENGEL, GARY LEEDS and JOHN MAUS are to make individual records in future. Drummer Gary has already sung on two singles. They will retain the group name by calling themselves Scott Walker, Gary Walker and John Walker but they will not appear on radio, TV or concerts as a threesome to promote the last Walker Brothers' record, "Walking In The Rain," which has just been issued here by Philips. They were scheduled to perform the new single on ABC Television's "Eamonn Andrews Show" – a program similar to your "Tonight" show – but the appearance has been cancelled.

Denial
All three artists are emphatic that the break-up was not brought about by internal dispute or disagreement with managers Maurice King and Barry Clayman who will continue to be responsible for their direction as solo singing stars.

Scott Engel told me: "Our musical interests are different. The group had come as far as it could as one unit. Now we see three separate careers ahead, following the different directions of our different inclinations and capabilities. We're still very friendly and we'll each take an interest in seeing what the other two are doing."

During their two years in Britain The Walker Brothers achieved tremendous popularity via chart-smashers like "The Sun Ain't Gonna Shine Any More" and "Make It Easy On Yourself."

Now separate recording contracts, accompaniment groups and fan clubs are being arranged and Scott, Gary and John will begin establishing their separate identities during the summer.

Sinatras
NANCY SINATRA and younger sister Tina claimed terrific press publicity for themselves when they flew into London on a brief visit. Nancy was here to record her first motion picture title song, John Barry's composition for the James Bond movie "You Only Live Twice."

Jones To Parker?
Gordon Mills, manager of TOM JONES, is involved in a current series of important discussions with COLONEL TOM PARKER. If the outcome of his talks is successful Parker will be responsible for the management of Tom Jones in America. Already the star is being contracted to appear at prestige cabaret venues in New York, Miami and on the West Coast during July and August.

Two weeks ago I revealed the possibility that THE MONKEES might film either a TV Special or at least a segment for one of their own shows in England within the next few weeks. Plans along these lines seem to be shaping up substantially and my latest information is that the group, plus its enormous entourage, will be in London for a total of three weeks – before and after the series of five sell-out concerts at Wembley Empire Pool on June 30, July 1 and July 2.

John's Premiere
JOHN LENNON's first solo movie "How I Won The War" will be premiered in London's West End very shortly and general release will follow during the second half of July... DONOVAN is likely to make a TV Spectacular and undertake a series of U.K. concert dates with JOAN BAEZ as his co-star. Miss Baez filled

...THE WALKER BROTHERS

London's Royal Albert Hall at very short notice on May 18, the performance being announced to the public only ten days before that date!... THE BEE GEES in Holland and Germany prior to their 10-day June promotional trip to America when Atlantic Records will help them boost their initial U.S. single "New York Mining Disaster, 1941." Meanwhile the record is heading for the Top Ten here in Britain and an entire album of original compositions is about to be rush-released... JIMI HENDRIX latest addition to list of British probables for Monterey.... Personal to PAT FINN – Goodbye Monument! Good Luck Pat!

CILLA BLACK, still co-starring with comedian Frankie Howard in London's long-running "Way Out In Piccadilly" stage show, topping Palladium TV bill this month... Whoever thought lyrics of "A Day In The Life" included any phrase like "40,000 holes in my arm" should (a) wash out his ears (b) look for the true words on the cover of the "Sgt. Pepper" album!

Gerry To Solo
GERRY MARSDEN, for 8 years the lead guitarist/vocalist with GERRY AND THE PACEMAKERS, soloing on his first CBS single via a big-ballad vehicle, "Please Let Them Be," composed by a name from The Beatles' Hamburg past – TONY SHERIDAN!... Cables of congratulations to the infanticipating MAUREEN AND RINGO STARKEY poured in from America... Expensive jet trip for CARL WILSON when he flew from Los Angeles to join the opening of THE BEACH BOYS' tour in Dublin... Run-out groove of "Sgt. Pepper" album has special sound for dogs, pitched too high for hearing by the human ear... GORDON WALLER may well have married by the time you read this report... More New York recording sessions for THE CREAM whose new single in the U.K. is "Strange Brew"... DAVE CLARK, vacationing in Acapulco, just released "Tabatha Twitchit"... THE TURTLES making their first U.S. visit throughout the first half of June... More press articles "by DAVY JONES" in British magazines than I've ever seen by an other pop star!

Violin Trend From Brenda?

By Rochelle Reed

South African jazz trumpeter Hugh Masekela recently offered Mrs. Holloway 2,000 head of cattle for her daugher, Brenda.

Hugh was kidding, but Ringo wasn't when he asked to borrow

Brenda's hairdryer for his own locks on the Beatles' first tour of America.

Only 17 then, Brenda toured the U.S. and Canada with the mop-topped sensations from the United Kingdom and vividly describes mid-air pillow fights above Montreal and Denver.

"I knew them all well enough to talk to," she says, "and they acted just like people, not like the Beatles. They used to talk about music and playing all the time, it was their whole life. They'd always say how they liked my voice."

Before the Beatles wave hit U.S. shores, Brenda found herself with a commercial sound, several hit records, and a solid singing career. Shortly after the Beatle tour, however, Brenda dropped completely off the pop charts, only having a semi-hit recently with "Just Look What You've Done."

Meanwhile, she says, "I wanted to really find out where my groove was, so I went to drama school and Patricia Stevens Career School, but I decided I like singing better than anything else. I'm glad I've got the acting training in case a part comes along or something, but I don't really want to be an actress."

Recently, Brenda has returned to the nightclub circuit, performing as a supporting act to the Miracles and other Motown groups. She invariably knocks audiences cold with one small part of her act – mid-way through, she pulls out a violin and proceeds to play it.

"When I was in school, I wanted to be a concert violinist or a violin teacher. I love playing. And after twelve years of lessons, my mother said, 'Okay, you better do something with them,' so I always dedicate the songs I play to my mother, 'cause she paid for the lessons."

The Holloway family – Brenda, her mother, brother and sister – are a close knit family from Watts. ("Be sure you say that someplace," she adds.)

"We're really close," she says of her family. "We go everywhere together and if there's something wrong with one of us, there's something wrong with all of us 'cause we don't feel right if one of us is sick or something."

Does Brenda, now 20, feel that being a teenage star kept her from being a normal teen, like so many stars claim?

"No, I know it didn't alter my life any. When I first found out I could sing, I kept asking myself, 'Why am I so different? What do all these people like about me? It makes you feel funny, it really does, to find out you just happen to have a commercial sound. Then you aren't just a singer, you're a servant to the public.

"At first though, I thought singing was all fun and having the money to buy the things you want, and then I went on a tour. That's work! Then you find out singing is a job. But really, I love my work, I like to sing and I like to write too.

"When I fall in love – and I fall in love every week – I write about the experience and what it's taught me, things like 'Oh Boy, I miss you, I can't live without you.' I wrote one song that's sort of a fantasy. I call it 'Land Of 1,000 Boys' and the story is about a place where every girl has her own boyfriend and no one is alone."

"No, I don't think being a singer has really altered my life in any way," she concluded, "I'm still me."

KRLA ARCHIVES

PAUL MC CARTNEY — On the Pop Festival Board of Governors.
BEAT Photo: Howard L. Bingham

KRLA Helps Present Monterey Pop Festival

Radio KRLA, along with Lou Adler, Donovan, Paul McCartney, Terry Melcher, Brian Wilson, Mick Jagger, Jim McGuinn, Johnny Rivers, Paul Simon, Abe Somer, Smokey Robinson, Andrew Oldham and Alan Pariser will present the Monterey International Pop Festival on June 16, 17 and 18.

To be held on the Monterey County Fairgrounds, the Festival will include a number of exhibits, booths and workshops in addition to the concert.

Prices range from $6.50 to $3.00 (See page 16), and accommodations can be obtained by writing to the Monterey Peninsula Chamber of Commerce, Box 489, Monterey, California or phoning (408) 375-2252.

June 16, with a concert featuring The Association, Buffalo Springfield, Grateful Dead, Jimi Hendrix Experience, Laura Nyro, Lou Rawls and Simon & Garfunkel. Saturday afternoon, at 1:30 p.m., the following acts will perform: Big Brother & The Holding Company, The Mike Bloomfield Thing, Paul Butterfield Blues Band, Canned Heat, Country Joe And The Fish, Hugh Masekela, Steve Miller Blues Band, and the Quicksilver Messenger Service.

Saturday evening will feature The Beach Boys, Booker T and the MG's, The Byrds, Jefferson Airplane, Hugh Masekela, Moby Grape and Otis Redding.

Sunday afternoon Ravi Shankar will give a special performance.

Sunday night, the concert will include The Blues Project, The Impressions, The Mamas & Papas, Johnny Rivers, Dionne Warwick and The Who.

Presley & Bono Autos Star

Custom cars prominently featured in recent motion pictures will be among the highlights of the 7th annual International Custom Car & Motorcycle Show, set for June 2-4, at the L.A. Sports Arena.

On exhibit will be Sonny & Cher's "His and Hers" Mustangs, featured in their current hit "Good Times"; the "Mongrel T," used in the Elvis Presley movie "Easy Come, Easy Go," and "The Fireball 500," featured in the American-International movie of the same name.

All three were designed and built by George Barris, creator of the "Batmobile," and the "Munster Koach" among others.

Another "way-out" vehicle to be displayed is the "Ben-Hur" hot rod, fashioned out of the chariot used by Charlton Heston in the movie epic "Ben-Hur." Instead of horses, the chariot is now powered by a super-charged Corvette engine.

In all more than 500 award-winning hot rods, custom cars, dragsters, motorcycles and ski boats, valued at more than one million dollars, will be on display.

The custom creations won't be the only wild things at the show. More than 100 rock bands will perform during the run of the event. In addition, a continuous go-go dance contest will be conducted. Other features include a teen style show and the Miss Teen-O-Rama Beauty Contest.

Show hours are 7 p.m. to midnight, June 2 and 1 p.m. to midnight, June 3-4.

"MONGREL T" — designed and built by George Barris and driven by Elvis in "Easy Come, Easy Go," will be featured at the International Custom Car & Motorcycle Show, June 2-4 at Sports Arena.

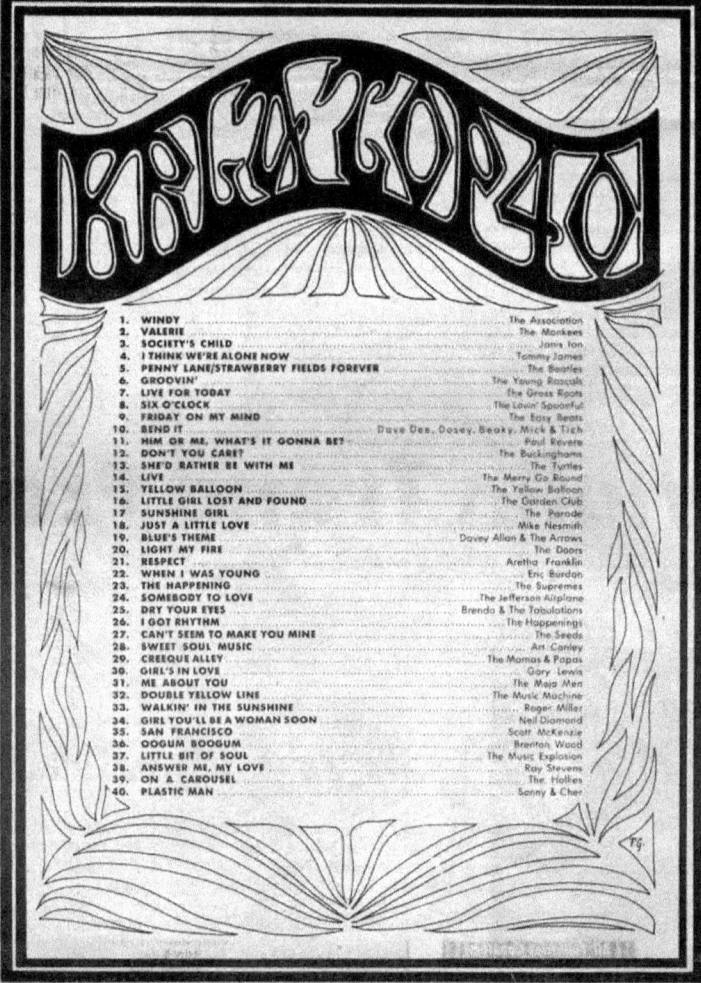

KRLA TOP 40

1.	WINDY	The Association
2.	VALERIE	The Monkees
3.	SOCIETY'S CHILD	Janis Ian
4.	I THINK WE'RE ALONE NOW	Tommy James
5.	PENNY LANE/STRAWBERRY FIELDS FOREVER	The Beatles
6.	GROOVIN'	The Young Rascals
7.	LIVE FOR TODAY	The Grass Roots
8.	SIX O'CLOCK	The Lovin' Spoonful
9.	FRIDAY ON MY MIND	The Easy Beats
10.	BEND IT	Dave Dee, Dozy, Beaky, Mick & Tich
11.	HIM OR ME, WHAT'S IT GONNA BE?	Paul Revere
12.	DON'T YOU CARE?	The Buckinghams
13.	SHE'D RATHER BE WITH ME	The Turtles
14.	LIVE	The Merry Go Round
15.	YELLOW BALLOON	The Yellow Balloon
16.	LITTLE GIRL LOST AND FOUND	The Garden Club
17.	SUNSHINE GIRL	The Parade
18.	JUST A LITTLE LOVE	Mike Nesmith
19.	BLUE'S THEME	Davey Allan & The Arrows
20.	LIGHT MY FIRE	The Doors
21.	RESPECT	Aretha Franklin
22.	WHEN I WAS YOUNG	Eric Burdon
23.	THE HAPPENING	The Supremes
24.	SOMEBODY TO LOVE	The Jefferson Airplane
25.	DRY YOUR EYES	Brenda & The Tabulations
26.	I GOT RHYTHM	The Happenings
27.	CAN'T SEEM TO MAKE YOU MINE	The Seeds
28.	SWEET SOUL MUSIC	Arthur Conley
29.	CREEQUE ALLEY	The Mamas & Papas
30.	GIRL'S IN LOVE	Gary Lewis
31.	ME ABOUT YOU	The Mojo Men
32.	DOUBLE YELLOW LINE	The Music Machine
33.	WALKIN' IN THE SUNSHINE	Roger Miller
34.	GIRL YOU'LL BE A WOMAN SOON	Neil Diamond
35.	SAN FRANCISCO	Scott McKenzie
36.	OOGUM BOOGUM	Brenton Wood
37.	LITTLE BIT OF SOUL	The Music Explosion
38.	ANSWER ME, MY LOVE	Ray Stevens
39.	ON A CAROUSEL	The Hollies
40.	PLASTIC MAN	Sonny & Cher

KRLA ARCHIVES

WORLD'S FIRST CRY-IN — KRLA station manager John R. Barrett was the target of the world's first "Cry-In," a demonstration by 500 youthful fans in protest of the dismissal of popular disc jockey Dave Hull. Hull was removed from his daily program on the station but was restored to his show after his attorneys asked that he be granted an unconditional release or be returned to the air.

By Pen

In the past months you've read a brief out-line of a few of the career opportunities available in the radio industry. D.J., ad salesman, traffic and continuity directors — all of these were covered... but we've left out one of the most important positions held at any radio station — the electronics engineers.

This man (although there are women engineers, too) is the final say about what actually reaches the air-waves and your radios. It is he that controls not only the volume of the sound but whether or not that sound reaches your radio at all. He must be constantly alert, be able to work with various "personalities," be familiar with numerous types of equipment (ampexes, magnacorders, Collins machines, cartridges, electrical transcriptions, etc.), be able to fix any malfunction in the machinery immediately (usually with five or six people yelling at him), and be aware of new advances and technologies within his specialty field.

Interested? Well, this job requires a certain amount of training in electronics which you can find at most colleges and trade schools. Also, basic courses in electronics are sometimes offered in high schools. Check with your school counselor about opportunities in radio electronics.

Youth Split By Extremes

Many young men are daytime, button-down "Joe College" types. At night they don Beatle wigs and mod clothes and head for "where it's at."

Many shy school girls and secretaries explode into nighttime "swingers," said John Milner, a professor at the University of Southern California School of Social Work.

From his ivory tower perch, Professor Milner zeroed right in on what's happening with today's young people. He feels the hippie rebellion touches all of today's young people to some extent. He said today's youth is split by extremes. There are the conformists who are least caught up in the social rebellion, and those who make up the ranks of the hippies, who live in voluntary exile from the mainstream of life — and make the most noise and news. The majority lie in the "vast middle," while many have different daytime and nighttime personalities.

Unlike past rebellions of young people, today's can't be dismissed as a 'youthful fling,' 'just a stage,' or 'something they'll grow out of.' Current youthful protest has already begun to penetrate and change society, Professor Milner said. He sees a decline of the "double standard" of right and wrong, more open-mindedness on racial issues, freer views of sex, breakdown of religious prejudice, and generally more honesty.

EASTSIDE KIDS FAN CLUB: Photos, etc. Discount at Hullabaloo with membership. $1.00. 1984 Addison Way, Los Angeles, California.

WIZARD OF OZ
Sunday nights 8 to midnight

COPPERTONE Suntan LOTION
DO IT NOW! AT All Toiletries Counters

ICE HOUSE GLENDALE
234 So. Brand Ave. Reservations: 245-5043

ENDS MAY 21
Merrilee & The Turnabouts
discover a new sensation

MAY 16-28
Tom & Chet

MAY 16-28
Tim Morgon

ICE HOUSE PASADENA
24 No. Mentor — Reservations: 681-9942

ENDS MAY 28
the electrifying **Casey Anderson** & **Willard & Grecco** as seen on the Johnny Carson Tonight Show & the Ed Sullivan Show, the song & wit of **Mike Smith**

Sears FREE DRAWING
Register Now and Be One of 10 Winners of a $49.95
Duke Kahanamoku
Belly Board

Register through July 5th in any Sears Sporting Goods and Boys' Wear Departments in Southern California. Boys and young men — 6 to 18 are eligible... no purchase necessary.

Sears Employes and members of their family are not eligible

KRLA ARCHIVES

Around The World

NEW YORK — Tommy Roe was presented with two BMI awards at the Grand Ballroom of the Hotel Pierre. Roe won the two BMI citations of achievement for success in the pop field as the composer of "Sweet Pea" and "Hooray For Hazel."

This marked a comeback for Roe, who enjoyed pop success several years ago with BMI winners, "Sheila" and "Everybody." Roe has just finished a national tour and has released his new single, "Sweet Sounds."

WHERE THEY ARE

ASSOCIATION
May 20, San Jose, California; May 26, taping for "The Smothers Brothers Comedy Hour," airing on May 28; May 28, taping for "The Steve Allen Show"; June 16, Monterey Pop Festival, Monterey, California; June 1-14 on vacation; July 24-30, Greek Theatre, Los Angeles, Calif.

SUPREMES
May 24, closing night at the Copacabana, New York; May 26, University of Cincinnati; May 28, Dayton, Ohio; May 29, Minneapolis, Minn.; May 30, Arena Auditorium, Duluth, Minn.; June 1-10, Shoreham Hotel, Washington, D.C.; June 11, Symphony Hall, New Jersey; June 13-26, Cocoanut Grove, Los Angeles, California; June 29-July 19, Flamingo Hotel, Las Vegas, Nev.

TEMPTATIONS
June 2-3, Twin Coaches, Pittsburgh, Pa.; July 9-15, Steel Pier, Atlantic City.

SMOKEY ROBINSON AND THE MIRACLES
May 25-June 3, Basin St. West, San Francisco, California.

JEFFERSON AIRPLANE
May 20, Birmingham High School, Van Nuys, Calif.; May 26-29, Seattle, Washington; May 30-June 2, shooting Warner Brothers' film, "Petulia"; June 4, Sam Houston Coliseum, Houston, Texas; June 17, Monterey Pop Festival, Monterey, Calif.

TURTLES
May 27-30, Steel Pier, Atlantic City, New Jersey; May 31-June 9, tour of England, France, Germany, Denmark; June 24, Lagoon Ballroom, Salt Lake City, Utah.

MARVIN GAYE
May 26-June 3, Beach Club, Myrtle Beach, South Carolina.

JOHNNY RIVERS
June 2-4, Vancouver, B.C., Edmonton, Alberta; Calgary, Alberta; June 20-30, Whisky a GoGo, Hollywood, Calif.

DON & THE GOODTIMES
May 26-30, touring the Portland area; May 27, Coliseum, Portland, Oregon; May 31-June 15, Southwestern U.S.; June 17-25, headlining Teenage Fair, Seattle, Washington; June 26-July 3, concerts in the Seattle area; July 3, three weeks heading a Dick Clark Caravan of Stars through the Midwest.

BOBBY DARIN
July 4-9, Melodyland, Anaheim, California; July 11-16, Circle Star, San Carlos, California; July 28-30, Royal Tahitian, Ontario, California; September 7-16, Rooster Tail, Detroit, Michigan.

NITTY GRITTY DIRT BAND
June 6, Troubadour, Los Angeles, California.

SMOTHERS BROTHERS
June 23, finish taping for first season of their TV show; July 31, begin taping for second season; July 31-August 6, Greek Theatre, Los Angeles, California.

RIGHTEOUS BROTHERS
May 29-June 14, Cocoanut Grove, Los Angeles, California; September 11-17, Greek Theatre, Los Angeles, California.

LEONARD NIMOY
June 10, Edgewater Park, Detroit, Michigan.

JAMES DARREN
June 19, "Wish You Were Here," St. Louis Municipal Opera.

FAMILY TREE
May 19-21, Portland, Crystal Ballroom; May 26-28, Seattle, The Happening, Teenage Fair; June 2-4, Portland, Crystal Ballroom.

BUFFALO SPRINGFIELD
May 20, Evansville, Indiana; May 21, Gary, Indiana; June 2, Conobee Lake, N.H.; June 3-4, Boston, Mass.

FRANKIE AVALON
June 2-11, Sans Souci, New York; June 16, Memorial Coliseum, Portland, Oregon.

HOLLYWOOD — Hugh Masekela has signed a long term, exclusive contract with UNI records. The master of the clean horn sound will continue recording for Chisa Productions. The new agreement gives UNI the distribution job of the recent "Emancipation of Hugh Masekela" LP.

NEW YORK — Paul Butterfield Blues Band has renewed their contract with Elektra Records after completing negotiations with Elektra's business affairs director, Larry Harris.

Since signing with Electra the group has had two LP's on the best-seller charts and worked up a national following. The group is just back from a successful British tour.

SAN FRANCISCO — Is it an artificial flower fad or really the blossoming of something new in pop music? The record industry, always scouting up new themes to sell records, is pushing "flower music" borrowing from recent "Love-Ins," "Be-Ins" and "Happenings" where members of both sexes carry, wear and exchange flowers — the eternal symbol of love and peace.

Among the latest "flower theme" discs are: *San Francisco (Wear Some Flowers In Your Hair)* by Scott McKenzie; *Flower Children*, by Marcia Strassman; *Flower Music*, by the Osmond Brothers and P.F. Sloane's, *Sunflower*, *Sunflower*. The Rolling Stones next album is reportedly titled *Flowers*.

The Seeds, a Los Angeles-anchored group have been preaching the flower gospel with their motto, "Flower Power," and the Giant Sunflower (whose *February Sunshine* is involved in a legal tug-of-war between two labels) seems to be one of the garden varieties. Nancy Sinatra and Sal Mineo have reportedly teamed up to produce a feature length film called, "Flower Children." It looks like everything's coming up roses in the record industry.

LOS ANGELES — Liberty Records, Inc: has signed an agreement with Bob Feldman of Fireplace Productions calling for the release of Jimmy Clanton's forthcoming record, "C'mon Jim"/"The Absence of Lisa," on the Imperial label.

Two of Clanton's gold records are "Just a Dream" and "Venus In Blue Jeans." Clanton starred in several movies before being called into the Army.

THE ROBBS
"Rapid Transit"
Mercury Records
#72678

FREDDIE WELLER, FORMER GUITARIST for Billy Joe Royal, has been signed as a new member for the Raiders. The Raiders have also obtained the services of Charlie Coe, formerly of Don & The Goodtimes. Harpo, Fang and Smitty have all left the Raiders and are reportedly in the process of forming their own group, along with another ex-Raider, Drake Levin. Paul Revere and Mark Lindsay remain Raiders. Speculation is running very high as to which group will do better, the Raiders or the ex-Raiders!

BEAT Photo: Ed Caraeff
THE SEEDS, ORIGINATORS of "flower power" and "flower music" are caught at L.A. International Airport holding, naturally, a huge flower. Leis were gifts from Hawaiian fans.

KRLA ARCHIVES

'To Sir, With Love'

POITIER EXPERIENCES some rough moments before he's accepted.

A DANCE WITH "Sir" and a surprise is coming.

It's not often that The BEAT places a "highly recommended" label on a movie but Columbia's "To Sir, With Love," starring Oscar winner, Sidney Poitier, deserves nothing less. It's theme is not racial—it's simply the relationship between the young generation and the Establishment (represented by Poitier as Mr. Thackery.)

Thackery comes to teach in a London slum school, not because he has a burning ambition to be a school teacher but because he hasn't been able to find work in his chosen field of engineering.

Thackery's class is immediately hostile toward him because he represents authority. Unscrubbed, uncombed and unruly, the class is so far behind their age level that they can barely read, write or do simple arithmetic.

Thackery's attempts at teaching conventionally are continuously thwarted by the class and it is not until he realizes that they are no longer children but young adults, who in a matter of months will be out of school and working, does he begin to be accepted.

He informs his class that they will act like adults, address him as "Sir," call the girls "Miss" and show respect for him as a teacher and for each other as human beings and equals.

School books are discarded as Thackery begins a daily question-answer-and-discussion method of teaching, where members of the class are free to ask questions about anything they wish—love, life, marriage, etc. And except for one student, Denham (played by 22-year-old Christian Roberts), Thackery's plan is enthusiastically received.

It would be unfair of us to divulge any more of the plot except to say that if you enjoy a really well-done movie, don't miss "To Sir, With Love."

Poitier shares the camera with an excellent but virtually unknown British cast. Standouts are Judy Geeson (a young Julie Christie), Christian Roberts and Lulu, popular Scottish pop singer who makes her dramatic debut in the movie. The film is in color and is nicely enhanced by a fine soundtrack which includes songs by Lulu and The Mindbenders.

MONTEREY INTERNATIONAL POP FESTIVAL

THE FOLLOWING ARTISTS WILL PERFORM...

FRIDAY NIGHT / JUNE 16 / 9:00 P.M.
- The Association
- Buffalo Springfield
- Grateful Dead
- Jimi Hendrix Experience
- Laura Nyro
- Lou Rawls
- Simon and Garfunkel

SATURDAY AFTERNOON / JUNE 17 / 1:30 P.M.
- Big Brother & The Holding Company
- The Mike Bloomfield Thing
- Paul Butterfield Blues Band
- Canned Heat
- Country Joe & The Fish
- Hugh Masekela
- Steve Miller Blues Band
- Quicksilver Messenger Service
- ...and many surprises...

SATURDAY NIGHT / JUNE 17 / 8:15 P.M.
- The Beach Boys
- Booker T & the MG's
- The Byrds
- Jefferson Airplane
- Hugh Masekela
- Moby Grape
- Otis Redding

SUNDAY AFTERNOON / JUNE 18 / 1:30 P.M.
- Ravi Shankar

SUNDAY NIGHT / JUNE 18 / 7:15 P.M.
- The Blues Project
- The Impressions
- The Mamas and the Papas
- Johnny Rivers
- Dionne Warwick
- The Who

(Program Subject to Change Without Notice)

a few words for those planning to attend

Be happy, be free, wear flowers, bring bells—have a festival.

1. **HOUSING**—No problem. For ten years, whatever the festival, substantial housing has easily been provided for every guest.

   More than 3000 hotel and motel units are available in the Monterey-Carmel-Pacific Grove-Seaside area. In addition, there are several hundred accommodations within fifteen miles of the Festival grounds.

   For accommodation reservations and information, write now to Monterey Peninsula Chamber of Commerce, Box 489, Monterey, California: (408) 375-2252.

2. **CLOTHES**—Be your own boss. Come as you please, wear what you like. Dress as wild as you choose. But remember that it's sometimes cool in the evenings. Maybe you should bring a blanket and sunglasses.

3. **SEATING**—A matchless hi-fi sound system means that everyone in the new 7000-seat main arena can hear equally well. The sound also carries well beyond the arena into the strolling areas.

4. **TRANSPORTATION**—The Monterey County Fairgrounds are only a mile from downtown Monterey—a ride of less than a quarter-hour; as little as five minutes when traffic is light. The fairgrounds are also situated five minutes from airline, bus and train depots.

5. **EVERYONE'S FESTIVAL**—Bring the family. This is a Festival for all. Everyone. Children of all ages and adults of all attitudes—everyone is welcome at the Monterey International Pop Festival.

6. **EXTRAS**—There are 24 acres of cheerful lawns studded with hundreds of oak trees and family picknicking is encouraged. A tremendous variety of food and drink will be available at very reasonable prices.

In addition to the five main concerts, there will be a number of exhibits, booths, workshops to appeal to every member of the family—including a children's playground.

❋ prices ❋

	Eve.	Mat.
Orchestra Sections 1-2-3 Side Boxes 101-143 & 100-142 Bleachers A-B-C-G-H-J	6.50	5.00
Orchestra Sections 4-5-6 Bleachers C-D-J-K — Side Boxes 145-183 & 144-182	5.00	4.00
Orchestra Sections 7-8-9 Rows A-P Bleachers E & L — Side Boxes 185-199 & 184-198	3.50	3.00
Orchestra Sections 7-8-9 Rows R-ZZ Bleachers F & M — Side Boxes 200-210 & 201-211	3.50	3.00

Check or money order must be enclosed with order; also a self-addressed, stamped envelope. Mail to: Monterey International Pop Festival/325 Mason Street, San Francisco, California/a non-profit organization.

KRLA ARCHIVES

KRLA ARCHIVES

LIKE A THOUSAND COLORS YOU CAN HEAR

A FANTASTIC NEW ALBUM. LN 24304/BN 26304

A GREAT SINGLE. "Please" 5-10117

on EPIC

KRLA ARCHIVES

LYRIC CONTROVERSY
Censor Or Not Censor?

By Sally Standig

To censor or not to censor? That is the question currently blazing in the record business. As of the middle of last month a national radio station chain has been vetoing all records whose lyrics are considered "suggestive."

For scrupulous screening of words, the station chain is requiring all record companies to submit printed lyrics with each record submitted for air play. If one side bumps a censor's roadblock, the other side also fails to get on the air.

Ruby Tuesday

If this ruling had gone into effect a few months back, then the Rolling Stones' hit, "Ruby Tuesday," never would have made it on the particular station chain's outlets because the flip side, "Let's Spend The Night Together" probably would have been tagged "too suggestive."

A different point of view was expressed in a recent interview with the head of one of the major record companies. He said:

"These kids who are writing today's teenage records have something to say... The lyrics represent the thinking of 'young America' and I think that we should listen to them, whether we don't agree with them is not the point."

Negative View

He took a negative view of radio stations muzzling themselves. "I think that censorship on the part of the receiving end of the radio stations could be extremely dangerous and ill-advised."

He conceded however, that radio station self-censorship might act to "remove from the air a lot of the small labels who do not have an attitude of responsibility and probably make things easier for all of us."

But this benefit might be pitifully small compared to the inhibiting effect on the creativity of artists and pop music writers. If teenage music is viewed as an art form, then censorship in this area becomes as harmful and as cramping as censorship in other areas of art.

One of the ways in which the public can lose out when radio station self-censorship is applied was called to the attention of a coast-to-coast audience by Leonard Bernstein on the recent CBS-TV special "Inside Pop – The Rock Revolution." The famed conductor introduced "a marvelous song" called "Society's Child," written and sung by 15-year-old Janis Ian, a New York high schooler.

Reasons Unknown

"It is well-known among the followers of pop radio, but you may not have heard it since it's been withheld by most of the radio stations for reasons unknown to me, although probably having to do with it's subject matter, which is, as you'll see, somewhat controversial." The song deals with a white girl's parents objections to her friendship with a Negro.

Bernstein gave support to the idea that pop music is an art form by expressing a genuine appreciation for songs by the Beatles, the Left Banke's "Pretty Ballerina," which he called a cross between Lydian and Mixolydian modes and the Monkee's, "I'm A Believer" (composed by Neil Diamond).

Leaning Over

The record industry chief said critics of teen music often lean over backwards to find double meanings in the lyrics. He pointed to recent hits like the Beatles' "Norwegian Wood," and Bob Dylan's "Rainy Day Woman" and called criticisms of these songs meaningless exercises of "reading into something."

Asked if there are usually hidden meanings tucked into the lyrics of today's pop music, he replied:

"... somebody's always looking for another meaning that may or not have been there in the author's mind, but whether it was or wasn't, I don't think in any way should influence whether that lyric should be broadcast. Because if on the surface it is a meaningful, artistic, lyrical piece of work, that in itself should be sufficient to allow it to be aired."

When asked if the record industry should adopt a conduct code similar to ones in effect for movies and television, he said, "I don't think that it's necessary nor wise, but I would prefer it to one run by radio stations themselves." He cautioned against "outsiders" trying to impose restrictions on an industry they didn't understand first hand.

TV POP SHOWS COURT TEENS

In their never-ending search to tap the teen market gold mine, American businessmen – from toothpaste makers to telephone companies – have found that the way to a high-schooler's wallet is through his ears. This discovery has produced a rash of television specials dedicated to rock 'n' roll artists and the variety of pop music they produce.

CBS's recent "Inside Pop – the Rock Revolution" caused such a stir that the soundtrack album is now under production and could easily become a modern pop classic.

Herman Spero, successful producer of teen-directed TV show "Upbeat" will do two hour-long specials from Expo 67 in Montreal titled "Swinging Sound of Expo '67."

The shows, scheduled for airing the first week in June and the second week in July, will feature such acts as Gary and the Hornets, Leslie Gore, the Platters, Smokey Robinson and the Miracles, the Pozo-Seco Singers, the New Christy Minstrels and the Vogues.

By Ron Koslow

I just woke up from a long sleep to discover a person I've known (or rather not known) for quite a while is really someone I should have known for a long time.

Karen is a funny looking girl – she is not good looking at all (not on the outside), and she doesn't have many friends. She wears strange clothes and sometimes talks in a language all her own. So she is a loner, I've never seen her with anyone but herself, and never really paid much attention to her.

Yellow Shades

I was sitting on a bench on the Strip the other night and out of nowhere she's sitting next to me, and staring at me through her yellow shades – at 2 o'clock in the morning.

"Hi," she said.
"Hi," I said.
– (brief silence)
"You've seen me around for the last couple of years, but you never seem to recognize me – how come?" she asked.

"Nothing Special"

What could I say? I really had no good reason. Before I could answer, she continued, "You probably think I'm nothing special, huh? In fact, you probably think I'm nothing. Don't be ashamed – I thought I was nothing too. Kind of like being invisible; you walk down the street and people look right through you. And you get used to it. But not really, because it hurts a lot.

"I'm Me!"

"One night last week I was home alone, as usual, and I decided that I couldn't stand it anymore; I wanted to roll up into a little ball and disappear, and that's exactly what I did. I got into the corner, and rolled myself up as small as I could, as tight as I could... and nothing happened ... and I sat there waiting for over half an hour... and still nothing happened. And all of a sudden I realized, 'Hey, it's impossible for me to be nothing, I'm *me*, I'm not nothing.' Don't you see, I tried it and it was impossible; I'm me, and always have been, and I guess that is enough."

And before I could answer her she was gone. There were a lot of things I wanted to say to her, but they will have to wait... till the next time I see her.

Revere Hits Pot-Rock

Paul Revere, leader of the Raiders, fired some hard words at the "crud" recording artists whose records include lyrics praising drugs. He called on DJ's to screen unsavory words and check what he called a menace to youth.

"There's no way to make all DJ's hip to the lingo being used on these records," Revere said, "but the lyrics should be examined carefully."

By taking this stand, Revere has added to the controversy over suggestive lyrics. A large radio station chain has recently required record companies to submit the printed lyrics of both sides of a new release. If one side contains what the station feels is a suggestive phrase, the record receives no air play.

Revere said only a few artists are actually using LSD and other drugs but much of the press spotlight seems to be directed on them. These artists are projecting the image that drugs are "in" and teenagers are imitating them because they think that's where the action is.

"The number of kids approaching me and asking, 'Have you got something to turn us on?' has increased tremendously in the past weeks," said the artist. "Even more painful is when they say that if I don't, they know where they can get it."

Revere has gone on record, musically that is, to protest the "frightening" spread of drugs with his single release, "Kicks," which preaches a drug-discouraging message.

ROUND, ROUND

Words and Music by KENNETH KING

Giggle at whitewash, and laugh at the wall,
 The prancing Pied Piper is not there at all,
But have a gay time and get large when you're small,
 You're doing it 'cos you enjoy it.

Round, round, out of your mind,
 You think you're seeing things –
 I know you're blind
A million bright colors explode in your head,
 Today you're just high, tomorrow your dead.
 Round, Round.

Bounce around happily, float in the air,
 Ride along sky-ways, paint stars with your hair
Don't be perturbed if the world turns to stare,
 You're doing it 'cos you enjoy it.

– Chorus –

Superior being, you'll bubble along,
 When your reflexes weaken, they'll kick you
  back strong,
You're up in the clouds, where you don't belong,
 And you're doing it 'cos you enjoy it.

Round, Round, out of your mind,
 You think you're seeing things –
 I know you're blind
A million bright colors explode in your head,
 Today you're just high, tomorrow just dead.
Round, Round.

Published by permission of copyright owner: Mainstay Music Inc., 101 West 55th St., New York, N.Y. 10019

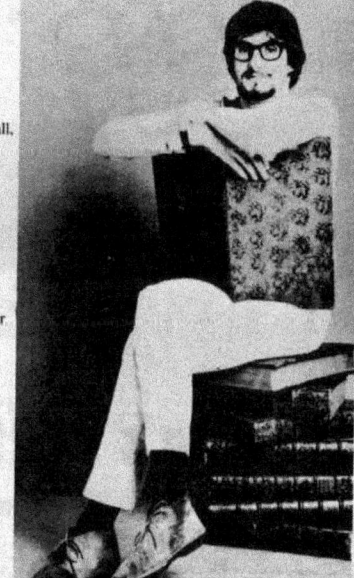

JONATHAN KING puts down the use of drugs in his current hit, "Round, Round."

KRLA ARCHIVES

The latest release of

America's contemporary favorites...

Now Available At Your Local

KRLA ARCHIVES

Merrilee & The Turnabouts Conquer Pacific Northwest

What is the Northwest Sound? It's the sound of happiness, the sound of excitement, the electrifying sound of good times — it's Merrilee & The Turnabouts.

It's vivacious Merrilee belting, blending and working, sparking Turnabout talent into a blaze of music and personality, consuming the entire stage in a burst of senses and sounds.

The Turnabouts fill the stage in back of Merrilee with dancing, song and fun. Showmanship reigns and the evening starts. The lights flare and Merrilee & The Turnabouts explode into a hard rock, up-beat tempo — a lightning rod sending the group's magnetic charge directly to the audience. Contact has been made — *communication* is happening.

The show is on its way. Merrilee reaches out with an intricate ballad that says "soul" and the Turnabouts follow with sensitive musicianship. Merrilee strikes a strong chord on her big Hammond Organ and charges into the next number — hard-hitting blues with vocal backing by the Turnabouts.

The audience is into it and grooving with the mood, music, new arrangements, new songs, soul favorites and *action*. The show goes on, too soon ends and the "Encore!" is finished.

But with the final note of the performance, the story of Merrilee & The Turnabouts just begins.

It's the story of five unique people, who in one and a half years have become one of the fastest rising big sound rock groups and number one concert attraction in the Pacific Northwest.

It's the story of a group who have performed the almost unheard-of feat of grossing over $130,000 without a national hit record in the past 12 months.

Neil Rush is the leader and backbone of the Turnabouts. He originated the group about a year and a half ago in Seattle, Washington with the help of Merrilee. He rules the group with an iron hand and is respected for it.

Neil, 21, is a guy of many talents. He is not only the leader, saxophonist and back-up singer for the Turnabouts, but also switches from a Renaissance recorder to a menagerie of small instruments, or "playing the toys" as he puts it.

A shrewd businessman with the ambition "to be rich," Neil plays the stock market and has created a business out of building and manufacturing the Turnabout's amplifiers, purchased by many of the Northwest groups.

Born and raised in Seattle, Neil likes people and dislikes phonies. His favorite music comes from the Beatles, Bobby Bland and the Raiders.

Merrilee, the 19 year old lead singer of the group, is described by her close friends as a big-hearted, fun-loving person who loves people and animals. She has two cats, a sheep dog and a parrot named Barney. Soon she plans to add an afghan or two to her collection for breeding and show purposes.

When she isn't working or rehearsing, Merrilee can usually be found either out shopping for the latest hip fashions or buying all the new records, dog books and teen magazines on the market.

Brown-haired, blue-eyed Merrilee is a petite package of talent. In addition to lead vocalist chores, she is organist for the group, using a big Hammond organ and standing up while she plays! To top it off, she writes and composes all of the Turnabouts' music.

Merrilee's favorite artists are the Beatles, Aretha Franklin and the Raiders. As a matter of fact, there is really nothing that she dislikes, she says, and her ambition in life is to be "comfortable and warm."

Terry Gregg, bass guitarist for the Turnabouts, is the kind of guy that nothing bothers, so the group always refers to him as "easy going Terry." He is quiet, except when singing, and then you definitely *know* he has a voice.

Terry is a good vocalist and an even better bass player. He's

MERRILEE of Merrilee & The Turnabouts sings lead, plays a big Hammond organ, dances, writes songs

been at it for about 10 years — and credits it as the main support for his tremendous wardrobe of mod fashions.

Terry's main hobby — racing sports cars — was obviously created by his home environment as his father is a car salesman. Terry likes people (especially girls) and clothes (always hip).

Also a native of Seattle, Washington, 20 year old Terry has the sandy blond hair of a surfer. He wants "to be a success" but detests "working too hard."

Karl Peters — with a K not a C — is the intellectual of the Turnabouts and also the musician's musician. Drummer for the group, he carries the rhythm with a hard solid beat which distinguishes him as one of the most outstanding drummers in the Northwest.

Karl, 20, has a very out-going personality which his brown hair just can't hide. The group describes him as a drummer "with lots of soul." One of his favorite pastimes is creating new ideas with strobe lights, which may be one of the reasons The Mothers Of Invention are one of his favorite groups.

He likes girls, especially ones who can cook pot roast. He spends his free time racing sports cars and campaigning against his major dislike — dishonesty.

Vern Kjellberg, 18, is the youngster of the group and naturally the Turnabouts mention it whenever they can. A good looking, sharply dressed lead guitarist, Vern also sings background.

The Turnabouts call Vern the life of the party, except in the mornings when he refuses to wake up. Usually they have to wrap him in a blanket and throw him in the car.

Vern's hobbies are playing pool (he is excellent), girls and more girls, and keeping his Corvette in top shape. His idea of a dinner is a plate full of cheeseburgers, all the better to make his blond hair grow, he says.

Bob Stane, owner of two California clubs which have been launching pads for many top groups (among them the Association, Nitty Gritty Dirt Band, Yellow Balloon and vocalist Gale Garnett), states that his club hired Merrilee & The Turnabouts because of "their spectacular reputation in the Northwest."

"This is the first time that the Ice House Glendale has put in a headline act without an audition or a hit record," he continued.

Individually, the Turnabouts are creative musicians, unique personalities, and blended together, they form one of the best up and coming groups in the U.S. All in all, Merrilee & The Turnabouts total up to an electrifying group from the Northwest, ready to light up the world!

(Advertisement)

MERRILEE & THE TURNABOUTS — a smash Northwest big sound rock group, showcasing for one week at California's Glendale Ice House, May 16-21. (Left to right, Terry, Carl, Vern, Merrilee and Neil). The group will also be appearing at the Hullabaloo After Hours, Friday and Saturday, May 19 and 20.

KRLA ARCHIVES

KRLA ARCHIVES

KRLA Beat

Volume 3, Number 7 — June 17, 1967

FANS FEAR FOR MONKEE'S VOICE

HOLLYWOOD — Millions of Monkee fans have shoved Davy Jones' draft status to the back of their minds and Mike Nesmith's tonsil trouble to the front. Monkee Nesmith entered Cedars of Lebanon Hospital in Los Angeles to undergo a long-postponed tonsillectomy.

Nesmith's personal physician, Dr. Rexford Kenamer, announced that he foresaw a routine recovery period of two weeks but millions of Nesmith's anxious fans are worrying about whether the operation will change Mike's voice.

Said one young fan: "I pray that it won't change Mike's beautiful voice but, you know, sometimes a tonsillectomy will do that and I'll just *die* if Mike sounds even a shade different after this operation!"

During Nesmith's two-week absence, "The Monkees" television show will shoot around him. The recording sessions for their next album have had to be adjusted.

Beatle 'Day' Banned

By Tony Barrow

LONDON — "A Day In The Life," the finest of all the brilliant new "Sgt. Pepper" album compositions, was banned by the British Broadcasting Corporation ten days before the record was released in the U.K.

It is not clear whether or not the B.B.C. followed the example of their American counterparts but the utter folly of the whole thing is that everybody is finding separate yet equally substantial excuses for banishing the ballad from the airwaves.

Apparently your American censors misheard a whole sequence of the lyrics and thought that lines mentioning the town of Blackburn in Lancashire included something about thousands of holes in an arm. So the ban was based upon totally inaccurate information in the first place.

In their announcement the B.B.C. thought that lines about boarding a double-decker bus and going upstairs for a smoke went "a little too far and could encourage a permissive attitude to drug taking." It's difficult to imagine a more unlikely scene than that of a bunch of pot-puffing hippies dreaming away on a London Transport bus, but there you are!

Said deejay Kenny Everett (in whose BBC show the entire "Sgt. Pepper" album was premiered — minus the best item of all): "The B.B.C. have a lot of nice people who just do not know what it is all about."

The most curious fact which emerges from this mass of nonsense is that not one of the self-styled censors on either side of the Atlantic has mentioned the line "I'd love to turn you on" which could be interpreted as a blatant reference to drugs, but has not been. In fact Paul suggests that this refers to turning people on to a better type of pop music.

†††John and Paul have now completed work on the special composition they were invited to write for the worldwide TV show, "Our World" to be screened live via four satellites to a potential audience of 500 million viewers in 31 countries on June 25. The Beatles' contribution to this two million dollar project will take the form of a direct transmission from their recording session at the E.M.I. studios at St. John's Wood in North London. In writing the lyrics, the Beatles have taken into account the fact that the simplest English words should be incorporated in the song so that a maximum of viewers will understand. In addition, they're toying with the possibility of having big boards held up in the studio with some of the words spelt out in different languages. "Our World" will be carried by more than 100 TV stations in America. Nothing will be pre-recorded or pre-filmed but in countries where the time of the "live" transmission is during non-peak TV hours many stations will repeat the entire program hours later.

BEATLES' "Day In The Life" banned ten days before release by BBC because lyrics went "a little too far and could encourage permissive attitude toward drug taking," say the BBC spokesmen.

ROLLING STONES, MICK JAGGER AND KEITH RICHARD, are pictured leaving the Chichester, England courthouse where they pleaded not guilty to charges of possessing narcotics and asked for a trial by jury. The trial date has not yet been set and the two Stones are free on bail. According to the London daily papers, another member of the Stones, Brian Jones, has also been charged with possessing narcotics. The blond-haired Stone was charged separately — he was not at the party thrown by Richards and raided by officers with a search warrant issued under the Dangerous Drugs Act. Jones made his appearance at a West London court and was freed on a reported 250 pound bail. However, he must return to court in early June. Speculation is running quite high as to whether these drug charges will end the successful career of the **Stones** as a group and whether or not they will be granted U.S. work permits.

KRLA ARCHIVES

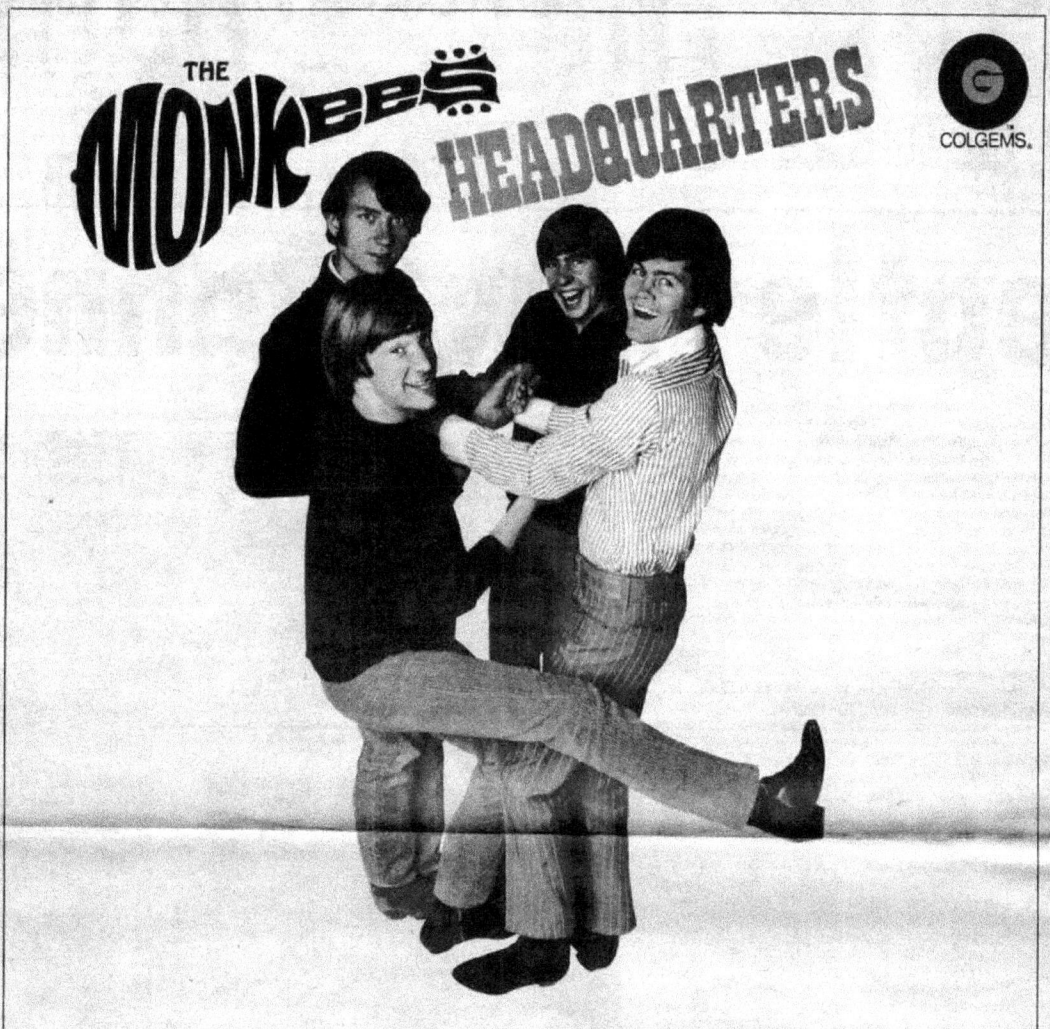

COM-103

"We aren't the only musicians on this album, but the occasional extra bass or horn player played under our direction, so that this is all ours.

"Each one of us has some musical thing, from Manchester to Texas, from the East Coast to the West, and when four people just go with their thing, what comes out is a whole. Don't ask 'a whole what?', just listen. If only the smallest part of how much fun it was to make this record gets heard, it was all worthwhile."

Mike   Davy   Micky   Peter

NOW AVAILABLE AT YOUR LOCAL

KRLA ARCHIVES

across the board

FROM THE EDITOR...

Paul McCartney is the Beatle we've chosen to spotlight this issue. Come along as we take you behind Paul's "charming image" as we let him speak for himself. I think you'll find McCartney has considerably more depth than he is usually given credit for.

We're proud to announce that we've done the impossible! We have managed to get the two Smothers Brothers to sit still long enough to give us their frank and outspoken views on censorship and what they're doing to fight it. You'll be shocked to learn what Tommy and Dickie are forced to go through in order to get anything at all said on their show.

People who are not wise enough to know, believe the Smothers Brothers are vastly popular with young adults because they feature pop artists on their show. Those who are more perceptive believe that Tommy and Dickie mirror the attitudes and ideals of the young generation—and this, coupled with their obvious talents—is the reason for their popularity. Turn to page ten and read what "My Brother and Myselves" have to say on the subject.

We followed the constantly-talked about model, Twiggy, as she spent a day visiting Disneyland. The photos came out so well that we decided to use two full pages to print them all. The art work on the pages was done by one of our staff artists—it took him days to finish, so we hope you enjoy it.

Rod McKuen is probably the most-recorded songwriter working today. We spoke to him in his home perched high in the Hollywood Hills and while his pets played around the house Rod gave us his opinions on everything from money to the protest singers who tell their audiences of "hard times" and then pocket their $15,000 and drive away in their limousines. An extremely intelligent, sensitive and outspoken man—you may not agree with him but if you're broadminded you'll, at least, read what he has to say.

Louise Criscione

Making The News

Bill Cosby Wants Negro TV Comedy

Negro Comic, Bill Cosby, who has been 'passing' very successfully in his traditionally white role on the "I Spy" television series is looking ahead to starring in his own situation comedy series as the head of black but fun-loving, ordinary TV family. He's bucking the same old arguments detractors threw at him when he was cast in the "I Spy" intrigue role.

"They say whites won't identify with a Negro in a part like that," Cosby was quoted recently, "Well Man, the answer is that ever since movies came along, millions of *Negroes* have had no trouble identifying with *white* actors.

Hermits New Film Begins

LONDON — Herman's Hermits have just started shooting a new MGM movie called "Mrs. Brown, You've Got A Lovely Daughter," which is based on an original story by English writer, Trevor Peacock. Morton Da Costa is directing the musical under production at Shepperton Studios.

The group stars in the flick which is a running account of the escapades of an up-and-coming rock group which takes its racing greyhound to London to enter it in the final meet of the yearly Greyhound Derby.

Chaos begins to snowball after they meet the Brown family — Mr. & Mrs. B. (played by Stanley Holloway and Mona Washbourne), and, of course, their lovely daughter, Judy. The film will be shot in color, on location in Manchester and London.

The Hermits will sing eight songs in the film including the title song for which they won a gold record.

WHERE THEY ARE

MONKEES
July 7, Atlanta, Ga., Braves Stadium; July 8, Jacksonville, Fla., Convention Hall; July 11, Charlotte, N.C., Coliseum; July 12, Greensboro, N.C., Coliseum; July 14-16, New York, Forest Hills Stadium; July 20, Buffalo, N.Y., Memorial Auditorium; July 21, Baltimore, Md., Memorial Auditorium; July 22, Boston, Mass. Boston Gardens; July 23, Philadelphia, Pa., Convention Hall; July 27, Rochester, N.Y., War Memorial Auditorium; July 28, Cincinnati, Ohio, Gardens; July 29, Detroit, Mich.

FIFTH DIMENSION
June 8-17, Bimbo's, San Francisco, Ca.; July 3, Disneyland, Anaheim, California.

SONNY AND CHER
June 14, opening of "Goodtimes," Detroit, Mich.; June 14, Steve Allen Comedy Hour, CBS-TV.

JEFFERSON AIRPLANE
June 4, Sam Houston Coliseum, Houston, Texas; June 17, Monterey Pop Festival; June 20-25, Fillmore Auditorium, San Francisco, Calif.

HERMAN'S HERMITS
July 21, Coliseum, Oklahoma City State Fair Grounds; Aug. 5, International Amphitheater, Chicago, Ill.

THE LOVIN' SPOONFUL
July 14-15, Opera House, Chicago, Ill.

SIMON & GARFUNKEL
June 16, Monterey Pop Festival; July 21-22, Opera House, Chicago, Ill.

RIGHTEOUS BROTHERS
May 29-June 14, Coconut Grove, Los Angeles, California; July 25-30, Opera House, Chicago, Ill.; September 11-17, Greek Theatre, Los Angeles, Calif.

ASSOCIATION
June 16, Monterey Pop Festival, Monterey, California; June 1-14 on vacation; July 24-30, Greek Theatre, Los Angeles, Calif.

SUPREMES
June 1-10, Shoreham Hotel, Washington, D.C.; June 11, Symphony Hall, New Jersey; June 13-26, Coconut Grove, Los Angeles, Calif.; June 29-July 19, Flamingo Hotel, Las Vegas, Nev.

TEMPTATIONS
June 2-3, Twin Coaches, Pittsburgh, Pa.; July 9-15, Steel Pier, Atlantic City.

SMOKEY ROBINSON AND THE MIRACLES
May 25-June 3, Basin St. West, San Francisco, California.

LEONARD NIMOY
June 10, Edgewater Park, Detroit, Michigan

BUCKINGHAMS
June 3, Blend, Ill.; June 16, St. Louis, Mo.; June 17, Evanston, Ill.; July 3, Leesburg, Ind.; July 4, South Bend, Ind.; July 7, Lake Schaeffer Monticello, Ind.; July 15, Lake Geneva, Wisc.; July 21, Marne, Mich.

FAMILY TREE
June 2-4, Portland, Crystal Ballroom.

BUFFALO SPRINGFIELD
June 2, Conobee Lake, N.H.; June 3-4, Boston, Mass.

TURTLES
May 31-June 9, tour of England, France, Germany, Denmark; June 24, Lagoon Ballroom, Salt Lake City, Utah.

MARVIN GAYE
May 26-June 3, Beach Club, Myrtle Beach, South Carolina.

JOHNNY RIVERS
June 2-4, Vancouver, B.C.; Edmonton, Alberta; Calgary, Alberta; June 20-30, Whisky A Go Go, Hollywood, California.

DON & THE GOODTIMES
May 31-June 15, Southwestern U.S.; June 17-25, headlining Teenage Fair, Seattle, Washington; June 26-July 3, concerts in the Seattle area; July 3, three weeks heading a Dick Clark caravan of Stars through the Midwest.

NITTY GRITTY DIRT BAND
June 6, Troubador, Los Angeles, California.

SMOTHERS BROTHERS
June 23, finish taping for first season of their TV show; July 31, begin taping for second season; July 31-August 6, Greek Theatre, Los Angeles, California.

PAUL REVERE AND THE RAIDERS
June 8, Lafayette, La., Municipal Auditorium; June 9, Shreveport, La., Hirisch Memorial Coliseum; June 10, Houston, Texas, Sam Houston Coliseum; June 11, Dallas, Texas, Memorial Auditorium; June 12, Corpus Christi, Texas, Coliseum; June 13, San Antonio, Texas, Freeman Coliseum; June 14, Lubbock, Texas, Coliseum; June 15, Amarillo, Texas, Coliseum; June 16, Tulsa, Okla., Assembly Center; June 17, Joplin, Mo., Memorial Hall; June 18, Topeka, Kan., Municipal Auditorium; June 19, Des Moines, Iowa, Veterans' Memorial Auditorium; June 20, Sioux City, Iowa, Municipal Auditorium; June 21, St. Joe, Mo., City Auditorium; June 23, Memphis, Tenn., Mid-South Coliseum; June 24, Jackson, Miss., Fairground Coliseum; June 25, New Orleans, La.; June 27, Columbus, Ga., Municipal Auditorium; June 28, Columbia, S.C., Township Auditorium; June 29, Atlanta, Ga., Municipal Auditorium; June 30, Winston-Salem, N.C., Memorial Coliseum; July 1, Chattanooga, Tenn., Memorial Auditorium

Beatles At 200 Million

LONDON — Beatles, John, Paul, Ringo and George combined world sales have now reached 200 million singles, according to a recent announcement by E.M.I. Records. An album is counted as six singles.

The group's latest album, "Sgt. Pepper's Lonely Hearts Club Band," which has been released illegally by some U.S. radio stations, was officially released in America on June 1.

KRLA ARCHIVES

KINKS HEAD TO LEAVE?

Reports from the British press allege that Kinks' leader Ray Davies will limit personal appearances with the group to devote more time to composing. He may be seeking a position similar to that of Brian Wilson with the Beach Boys—an end to performing with the group and the beginning of a sort of background composer-producer role.

"A substitute would have to take my place on these occasions," Ray reportedly said, "But I intend that all promoters will be made aware of the situation, and I will honor all existing contracts."

Ray said time was too limited to include personal appearances and prepatory work on the group's records. He had to leave his writing half finished to join the group on a recent Scandanavian tour which he said is an obvious handicap to the group.

He will continue to record with the group and said there is no question of his completely severing ties with the group.

However, when reached for comment, the Kinks' co-manager, Robert Wace denied any chance of Ray leaving the group even on a temporary basis. He said rumors indicating Ray's departure "are being put around by people with some sort of ax to grind."

Trini Lopez Tapes Show In London

Trini Lopez has been signed to host a CBS-TV special, "Spotlight," to be taped in London this month. "Spotlight" is the summer replacement for "The Red Skelton Show."

Lopez closes a three-week stint at New York's Basin Street East on June 24, jets to London for the taping and returns immediately for a one-night concert at Asbury Park, N.J., on July 3.

OFF TO ENGLAND for Trini.

Winwood, Davis Join For Movie

Spencer Davis and his former lead singer, Stevie Winwood, have been signed to write ten numbers for 'Here We Go 'Round The Mulberry Bush," currently before the cameras in England as a United Artists' release.

Just over two months ago, the long-time association of Davis and Winwood came to an end when Stevie broke away from the Spencer Davis Group to form his own group, Traffic.

The new Spencer Davis Group will be featured in a dance sequence in "Mulberry Bush" playing the new compositions. Stevie and Traffic will record the title song in addition to the three other numbers he has written for the picture.

"Here We Go 'Round The Mulberry Bush" is being shot entirely on location at Stevenage, Hertfordshire, and stars Barry Evans.

POP MUSIC: NEXT STEP IN RACIAL INTEGRATION

By Sally Standig

The Supremes jolted everyone in the swank Copacabana New York nightclub by tossing off Motown, the million-dollar sound they spread around the world, and doing an all-pop act! Would you believe a night with the Supremes singing, "Michelle," "Yesterday" and material from "West Side Story" and "Thoroughly Modern Millie?" Their old Detroit-sound hits were included, but with rock type arrangements. They sang a medley of "Stop In The Name Of Love," "Baby Love" and others with a sound closer to Liverpool than Detroit.

The Supremes' new image is less surprising viewed against the background of increasing infiltration of white artists onto the R&B charts and Negro artists on rock 'n roll best-seller lists. The kind of integration laws can't achieve, seems to be no problem at all in pop music.

With increasing regularity, white musicians are popping up on the R&B charts. The Young Rascals, Mitch Ryder, the Spencer Davis Group, the Righteous Brothers (they've been nick-named the "blue-eyed soul brothers") Elvis Presley and Jerry Lee Lewis have all swept up in the soul sound market.

One of the big record companies specializing in R&B reports that the bulk of orders for "New York Mining Disaster, 1941" by a new white group, the Bee Gees, are coming in from all-Negro neighborhood dealers. The Dave Clark Five, have seen nothing but sales since releasing "You Got What It Takes" with a R&B arrangement.

The integration of R&B radio programming by white artists is a logical spin-off of the increased exposure of R&B on rock stations. R&B stations have also felt some audience loss with the discovery that up to half their playlists are being aired on traditionally pop-rock stations.

High up on the rock top-seller lists are Arthur Conley, Aretha Franklin, Peaches and Herb, Martha and the Vandellas, the Marvellettes, the Four Tops and the Temptations.

Until recently, an R&B station would scratch a release from it's playlist if it discovered an artist was white. Since all records are black, it was often hard to tell new artist's color from his sound. Now an artist's color seems to be giving way to how close his material is to the R&B vein as a criterion for airing new releases.

YOUNG RASCALS—breaking the color barrier in R & B.

PEOPLE ARE TALKING ABOUT **Nancy Sinatra** being considered for **Elvis Presley's** next movie and wondering whether or not she'll get it . . . up-and-coming groups now being "farm teams" from which the top groups are buying members . . . **Brian Jones** having as much, if not more, trouble than his two fellow **Stones** but is receiving much less publicity about it . . . whether or not the **Beatles** will ever make a third group movie and deciding that they never will

. . . the **Lovin' Spoonful** getting a national hit despite the fact that the Haight-Ashbury crowd doesn't dig them any more . . . the **Seeds** having a good laugh over all the people who are now claiming to have originated the term "flower children" . . . the **Association** bowing out of the "Steve Allen" Show" and thinking that they were smart to come to that decision . . . a certain rock group who becomes upset if they're knocked

. . . **Bill Cosby** turning singer and wondering how that's going to work out . . . when fan riots are going to completely kill personal appearances . . . the fact that MBE's don't stop the banning of records and the radio station which got caught in the middle of a giant publicity stunt to hide the real problem . . . why **"Society's Child"** ever got banned in the first place and deciding that the Establishment is scared to death of any hint of controversy and what a shame that is

. . . **Cher** in her mini-dress and thinking perhaps she should go back to bell-bottoms . . . why that obvious publicity story on the **Jefferson Airplane** got into a national magazine and why they took time to shoot pictures but didn't spend a little time actually talking to the group . . . the possibility of **Gary Alexander** forming his own group . . . **Sammy Davis Jr.** getting on the pop charts alongside **Harpers Bizarre** and the **Bee Gees** . . . Flower power spreading but destined to doom since it will be commercialized and killed just like "psychedlic music" was

. . . taking a "happening" across the Midwest and South . . . why the **Byrds** didn't show up for their Sunset Strip club date . . . why there is such a scarcity of **Neil Diamond** news and photos . . . when the **Rascals** are going to stop groovin' around New York and visit the rest of the country . . . how the **Fifth Estate** know that the witch is dead . . . who is trying to fool who

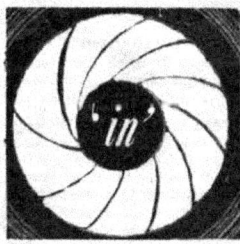

with the new **Dylan** song which isn't new at all but a cut off an album . . . how many times "Respect" is going to make it to the top of the charts.

. . . whether or not the **Everly Brothers** are going to make a comeback . . . **Scott McKenzie's** "San Francisco" being hot on the West Coast but surprisingly cold in the rest of the markets and wondering if it is an indication that the other 49 don', dig flowers worn in the hair . . . **Every Mother's Son** being put on the cover of a rhythm 'n blues paper and deciding that somebody's misplaced their soul . . the tears that will be shed if the **Bee Gees** don't happen in the biggest way possible . . . Screen Gems thinking of pulling another "Monkees" and watching to see if they can do the same thing twice

now that **Tommy James'** situation has been taken care of, how about the **Lovin' Spoonful?** . . . whether or not they're going to land that balloon at the Monterey Pop Festival . . . the fact that if the truth were known a top group would lose just about every shred of respect they've ever had . . . when somebody is going to pick all the fairy tales apart . . . whatever happened to the movie the **Monkees** were supposed to make and deciding that it went the way of the **Beatles'** and **Stones'** movie plans

. . . living for today being better than living for tomorrow and living for yesterday being the biggest waste of all . . . **Tommy Smothers** thinking that consistency is all important, deciding that he's right and wondering why a lot of pop groups don't realize it . . . why Canadian groups can't seem to make it big Stateside . . . the entertainer who offered 2,000 head of cattle to marry another entertainer and whether or not it will be accepted.

Beat Publications, Inc.

Executive Editor .... Cecil L Tuck
Publisher .... Gayle Tuck
Editor .... Louise Criscione

Staff Writers
Carol Deck Bobby Farrow
Ron Koslow Shirley Poston
Rochelle Reed

Contributing Writers
Tony Barrow Sue Barry
Lawrence Charles Eden
Bob Levinson Jamie McCluskey, III

Photographers
Chuck Boyd Dwight Carter
Howard L. Bingham

Advertising
Dick Jacobson Jerry Loss
Dick Stricklin

Business Manager .... Judy Felice
Subscriptions .... Nancy Areno

Distribution
Miller Freeman Publications
500 Howard Street, San Francisco, Calif.

The BEAT is published bi-weekly by BEAT Publications, Inc., editorial and advertising offices at 9121 Sunset Blvd., Hollywood, California 90069. U.S. bureaus in Hollywood, San Francisco, New York, Chicago and Nashville; overseas correspondents in London, Liverpool and Manchester, England. Sole price 25 cents. Subscription price: U.S. and possessions, $5 per year; Canada and foreign rates, $9 per year. Second class postage prepaid at Los Angeles, California.

KRLA ARCHIVES

ON THE BEAT BY LOUISE CRISCIONE

Someone is certainly trying to pull the wool over a lot of people's eyes. A spokesman for Tom Jones issued a statement to the British and American press to the effect that negotiations were going on between Jones' manager, Gordon Mills, and Elvis Presley's manager, Col. Tom Parker.

Said the Jones' spokesman: "If we reach agreement, it would mean that he (Parker) would manage Tom in the States and look after his interests there." Says Col. Parker's spokesman: "There is no basis to it at all. A press agent for Tom Jones wrote a letter and asked if when they visit the States they could come by and say hello. Col. Parker only manages one talent and that is Elvis Presley. We are not discussing, nor do we have any interest in managing anyone else." So ...

The Association are off the road for a few weeks but keeping themselves quite busy finishing up their third album, "Insight Out." They appeared on "The Smothers Brothers," have taped a "Steve Allen Show," and will be the first rock group to ever play the famed Greek Theatre in Los Angeles.

Of course, you've already seen their appearance on the "Smothers Brothers" but in the next issue of The BEAT, we'll bring you exclusive photos of what went on backstage during rehearsals, breaks, etc.

ELVIS PRESLEY

Tomorrow Today

The Quote of the Week comes from the Seeds' manager, Tim Hudson: "The Seeds are playing the music of the now generation – the people who want tomorrow today." The Seeds were, in reality, the originators of the "flower children" tag which is spreading rapidly across the country, picking up originator-claimers as it moves along – but remember it was the Seeds who started it.

The Dave Clark Five have set the dates for their next Stateside tour which kicks off on June 16 in Boston. It then moves on to Portland, Maine (June 17); Chicago (June 18); Fargo, North Dakota (June 20); Minot, North Dakota (June 21); San Carlos, Calif. (June 26); Atlantic City, New Jersey (July 4); Wallingford, Conn. (July 9); Baltimore, Maryland (July 10); Virginia Beach, Va. (July 16); Cleveland, Ohio (July 16); and winds up on July 23 in Camden, New Jersey.

Cosby To Sing?

According to my spies, Bill Cosby is set to make his debut as a singer in August at the Whisky A Go-Go in Los Angeles. Some singers are certainly comedians — should be interesting to see how a comedian/actor becomes a straight singer!

Besides being a successful entertainer, Johnny Rivers is very much a successful businessman. Rivers' Soul City Records has just signed a new contract with Liberty Records, which will run through 1972 and guarantees Johnny approximately $200,000 a year against the net on his own recordings. The contract also gives Johnny free reign to sign any artist he wishes to record as well as song publication rights. Not bad for someone who is only 24.

Well, it looks as if the Monkees are going to receive another one – their latest album, "Headquarters," was not even released when it was ear-marked a million seller! RCA reports that initial orders for the album soared over the million mark and they have requested the RIAA to certify it as a million-seller.

MICKY DOLENZ

The Monkees' first record was released last August and to date they have sold over 6 million albums and 6 million singles in the United States alone – which should set Monkee-haters back a notch or two.

SMOKEY ROBINSON & THE MIRACLES — from a show to a riot.

Smokey Robinson Show Explodes Into A Riot

Critics who charge rock 'n roll concerts inspire violence were given fresh ammunition when a San Diego concert featuring Smokey Robinson and The Miracles, Motown recording artists, ended with hundreds of young people rioting in the downtown convention hall of the Community Concourse.

According to police, rioters threw rocks and bottles at shop windows, police and civilian cars and overturned trash cans. One passerby was knocked down and his wallet stolen. Another was beaten unconscious by a youth swinging a wooden crutch, police said.

Thirty-eight persons were arrested in the two-hour melee. Twenty-seven were juveniles and 11 adults.

Charges ranged from assaulting a police officer to drunkenness, failure to disperse, disturbing the peace, resisting arrest, malicious mischief, curfew violation, battery, assault with a deadly weapon and escape.

The rioting began with the injury of three policemen and three private guards as they stopped fist fights and made arrests at the concert.

The second phase of the rampage began shortly after the capacity audience of 4,000 emptied out the hall. About 100 helmeted police reinforcements wielding riot sticks were just beginning to arrive. They were put into two riot lines, each headed by a lieutenant. Using bullhorns, officers told the youths they were assembled unlawfully and would be subject to arrest if they did not disperse.

The crowd barely budged and police began swinging their sticks and making arrests and chaos erupted. At that point about 500 of the crowd fanned out in the area which also contains City Hall, Civic Theater, an exhibition center and a shopping district.

While police were trying to break up fist fights, the performance was stopped. About 50 young people rushed the stage. But stagehands quickly raised the hydraulic-powered stage to prevent the audience from reaching the performers.

When reached for comment, a Los Angeles representative of Motown Records said, "We can't comment because we weren't there."

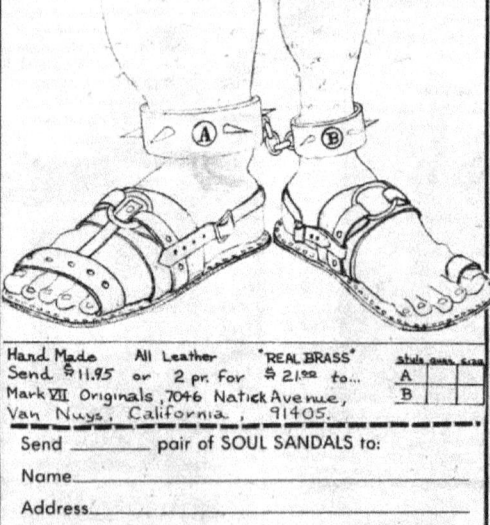

Dylan Poster Museum Pick

The full-color poster of Bob Dylan packaged with his latest Columbia LP has been chosen by the Museum of Modern Art for its permanent collection.

Prominent graphic artist, Milton Glaser, was commissioned by Columbia to design the multi-colored silhouette of Dylan's hawkish profile and curly mane. A number of the artists' other posters are in the museum's collection.

The album, "Bob Dylan's Greatest Hits," was released after nine months of seclusion by the prolific singer-poet following a serious motorcycle accident. Columbia reports that Dylan will return to the recording studio soon.

JOIN THE JBL MOVEMENT

NO LUXURY SO GRATIFYING OR INEXPENSIVE!

Don't be an uninvited...a social outcast ...Don a "MENDELSOHN QUINTETTE CLUB OF BOSTON" T-SHIRT...AND ELEVATE YOUR SOCIAL POSITION!!
THE PRICE ONLY $1.25. A TRULY GRAND OFFER!
They come Small, Medium and Large. ...get one for yourself...get matchmates...get one for your Mother...
YOU'LL FEEL SECURE IN YOUR "MENDELSOHN QUINTETTE CLUB OF BOSTON" high-neck, top quality T-SHIRT!
GUITAR PLAYERS LOVE 'EM...BASS PLAYERS LOVE 'EM...GREEN BERETS LOVE 'EM...SURFERS LOVE 'EM...
YOU CAN'T AFFORD NOT TO OWN ONE!
Fill in and mail the coupon below.

COUPON
Enclosed is $_____ please send me ( ) "MENDELSOHN QUINTETTE CLUB OF BOSTON" T-SHIRTS.
Size_____ Name_____
Address_____
City_____ State_____

JAMES B. LANSING SOUND, INC.
3249 CASITAS AVE., LOS ANGELES, CALIFORNIA 90039
BEAT (B)

KRLA ARCHIVES

Around The World

Beatles On World TV

LONDON – The Beatles will reach an estimated audience of 500 million in 31 countries in a two-hour special to be aired over world-wide television. The Beatles will be seen live, recording a new tune on June 25. The song was written by John Lennon and Paul McCartney especially for the TV program and will be the next Beatles' single release if the foursome like the results.

The BBC will beam the show, called "Our World," around the United Kingdom. More than 100 U.S. stations have agreed to broadcast it. Three American and one Russian communications satellites will participate in the global telecast.

Spector Signs?

LOS ANGELES–Phil Spector, dubbed "the tycoon of teens" for reaching millionaire status by 21 by producing rock 'n roll sounds, is joining A&M records in a top post. The deal reportedly is part of an A&M takeover of Spector's music business concerns, which include Phillies Records. Spector's new job will stress the development of new pop-rock material.

As a record producer and writer, Spector has developed a reputation for consistent success in the teen market. He catapulted the Crystals, the Ronettes and Bob E. Sox & The Blue Jeans, and the Righteous Brothers to smash-selling success. Since moving to the west coast several years ago, Spector has developed an interest in producing movies.

NEW YORK – "Cabaret," the story of the collapse of personal lives in Nazi German based on Christopher Isherwood's "Berlin Stories" and John van Druten's play, "I Am A Camera," was chosen the best musical of the 1966-67 season by the New York Drama Critics Circle last week. The show, which opened to rave reviews eight months ago on Broadway, swept up eight "Tony" awards earlier. The cast includes Lotte Lenya, Jill Hayworth, Jack Gilford, Bert Convy and Joel Grey. The original Broadway cast album of "Cabaret" has been high on the best-seller charts for some time.

HOLLYWOOD – The tender touch of a day that is dead turned Lawrence Welk's venture into pop-rock into a RIAA-certified gold album award. The champagne music maestro won his third gold disc for "Winchester Cathedral." His previous gold albums are "Calcutta" and "Moon River."

NEW YORK – Marshall Mcluhan, "the prophet of television" and noted critic of popular culture, has gone on record (a Columbia LP, that is) with excerpts from his much-discussed book, "The Medium Is The Message." The title is a pun on his central theme, "the medium is the message," an observation on the impact of today's electronic media. Shot through with special sound effects, the LP is meant to be informative as well as entertaining.

Monkee Song Men To A&M

Two songwriters credited with a large share of the Monkees' phenomenal success, Tommy Boyce and Bobby Hart, have just signed long term agreements with A&M records as artist-producers.

Boyce and Hart had a string of hits before writing Monkee songs like "Last Train to Clarksville," "I Want To Be Free" and "The Monkees Theme." The duo will make their singing debut on a forthcoming A&M single release.

Before joining the Monkee team, Boyce and Hart had over 30 of their songs recorded by Dean Martin, Little Anthony, Tommy Sands and Jay and the Americans.

EAST COAST ROCK HAVEN

A kind of east coast Haight Ashbury, minus the publicity ballyhoo, has been quietly emerging since the late '50's in the scholarly environment of Cambridge, Massachusetts. Nestled just across the Charles River from Boston, the area is closely packed with Harvard, Radcliffe and other colleges. Since the start of the Newport Folk Festivals, the heavily weighted student population has provided a receptive audience for a range of young musicians.

A cultural pocket with no-pressure surroundings, Cambridge boasts an unsurpassed proliferation of coffee houses supported by university students looking for low cost entertainment. Blues, folk and rock artists can develop at their own pace while supplying this need.

Petite, dark-haired folk queen, Joan Baez, broke through to national prominence from her Cambridge coffee house warbling sessions. Other lesser names from the area include: the Jim Kweskin Jug Band, Richard and Mimi Farinina (she is Joan Baez's cousin), Jesse Colin Young and the Chambers Brothers.

NANCY SINGS

LONDON – Nancy Sinatra has been signed to record the title song for the forthcoming Sean Connery intriguer, "You Only Live Twice." The song was composed by John Barry with lyrics by Leslie Bricusse.

United Artists has received permission to use the "sugar" singer's vocal on the soundtrack LP of the film from Reprise Records, to which Nancy is under contract. UA is cautiously seeking to avoid the court suits which followed the unauthorized use of Nancy's name and picture on the instrumental soundtrack album of the "Wild Angels," a film about the motorcycling Hell's Angels in which she had a leading role.

Bacharach Inks Musical Score

Burt Bacharach, a double Oscar nominee for his motion picture scores, "Alfie" and "What's New Pussycat," has signed a pact with producer Dave Merrick, to write the music for Merrick's first venture into Broadway musicals, the stage production of the 1960 hit film, "The Apartment."

ROD McKUEN THRIVES ON STEADY WORK DIET

Rod McKuen, multi-faceted singer-writer, left his hillside Hollywood home for a business trip to New York, Paris and London.

He is stopping in New York to discuss his latest book, "Listen To The Warm," with his publisher, Random House. McKuen is the talk of the publishing industry since his first book of poetry, "Stanyan Street and Other Sorrows," published last year sold over 50,000 copies and is the biggest seller poetry collection since Walter Benton published, "This Is My Beloved," over 20 years ago. Poetry books are notoriously poor sellers and advisors told McKuen he would not realize much profit on his work.

After New York, he will jet to Paris for meetings with French singer, Jacques Brel, who collaborated with McKuen on their current hit song, "If You Go Away." He will also confer with Anouk Aimee on her starring in the screen version of McKuen's current popular LP, "The Sea," which he co-authored with Anita Kerr. McKuen is now working on the film treatment.

Before returning to Hollywood, he will produce two LP's from material he wrote with Miss Kerr. The records will be cut in London and Paris using a 100-piece orchestra.

"The Standel Sound"

"The Young Rascals"

Professional musicians throughout the world choose the "Standel Sound", the accepted standard for professional musicians who demand professional performance. (Dept. B)

A. P.A. Speaker Column Amplifier
B. P.A. Master Control with Reverb
C. Imperial Line Amplifier — Solid State, Dual Channel

Standel
Solid State Music Systems
4918 DOUBLE DRIVE • EL MONTE, CALIF. 91731

KRLA ARCHIVES

THE BEE GEES are Brian Epstein's new discovery — which means what?

BEAT SPECIAL BY TONY BARROW

Mining Disaster Gets Bee Gees To America

"New York Mining Disaster, 1941" happened only in the fertile minds of a group called the Bee Gees. It's the self-penned song which has sent 17-year-old twins Maruice and Robin Gibb, their 19-year-old brother Barry Gibb and drummer Colin Petersen (19) high up into Britain's Top Ten. What's more, this was one of several recordings which convinced Ahmet Ertegun, President of Atlantic Records of America, that a quarter of a million dollars would be sensibly spent to secure U.S. record rights of the Bee Gees over the next five years!

Visit To U.S.

This month the Bee Gees are on your side of the Atlantic, their first promotional trip to America with something like 14 cities to be covered in as many days. If you don't get to meet them this time there are sure to be more opportunities. It's a safe bet that the Bee Gees will be back for a bill-topping concert tour before the end of the year.

In 1958, the year that George Harrison joined three potential Beatles in Liverpool, the Bee Gees were already operating as an amateur rock 'n' skiffle trio 30 miles from Merseyside in their hometown of Manchester. In fact they'd made their stage debut entertaining an all-kiddie audience at a local Saturday morning cinema show two years earlier (in 1956) when the twins were 7-years-old and Barry was just nine!

Then the Gibb family left England, emigrating to Australia. In March, 1960 on Brisbane's ABC television channel the Bee Gees had their own weekly 30-minute show. Three years later they were signed by Australis's Festival record label and brought out their first self-composed single entitled "Three Kisses Of Love."

It was not until the early part of 1967 that the Bee Gees decided to head home to England. By then they'd notched up three Number One hits on the Australian charts, been voted top songwriting team of 1965 and 1966 and collected a special award as Australia's best group of 1966!

Contact Epstein

On arrival in London the three boys tried to make contact with Brian Epstein and sent through to his office a series of tapes and albums they'd made before leaving Australia. But it was Brian's Australian colleague Robert Stigwood, Joint Managing Director of NEMS Enterprises, who returned their calls and fixed the meeting which was to result in the signing of a 5-year management contract for the Bee Gees. Simultaneously with that signing, the Bee Gees expanded from trio strength to quartet. They added COLIN PETERSEN on drums. Colin, the only Australian member of the outfit, is the former child movie star who played the title roles in "The Scamp" and "Smiley" ten years ago.

"New York Mining Disaster, 1941" was issued in the U.K. in the middle of April. Considering that the name Bee Gees didn't mean a thing to English fans until this single came on the scene, the group's success was swift, its impact immediate.

On Thursday, May 11, the Bee Gees made their U.K. TV debut on "Top of the Pops" show. The four boys plus most of the dancers in the studio audience wore silver and black badges with the words "Be A BeeGeeBopper!"

Perhaps the most remarkable facet of the Bee Gee talent is songwriting. The three Gibb brothers have an extraordinary flair for creating lyrics which tell curiously off-beat stories. How many other teenage tunesmiths would have though of making a mine disaster and trapped men waiting to die the theme of a chart-aimed pop record? But when you get to hear Atlantic's "The Bee Gee First" album, you'll appreciate the full scope of their creative ability. Every track is an original number written in London over the past few weeks and recorded under the joint studio supervision of Australian producer Ossie Byrne and manager Robert Stigwood. No wonder so many people – experts as well as fans – are beginning to believe in the Bee Gees as the most potent penning 'n performing unit to hit the music business since the Beatles brought out "Love Me Do" in October, 1962!

THE ROBBS "Rapid Transit" "Cynthia Loves" Mercury Records #72678

BEAT EXCLUSIVE
McCartney –

By Tammy Hitchcock

Labels seem to be essential in the music business. The powers-that-be dictate that an entertainer is not truly successful until he has been labeled. Thus we find one Paul McCartney, "the charming Beatle."

It was often said of McCartney that if he hadn't been an entertainer he probably would have been a politician since he could be relied upon to say the right things at the right time, soothe the ruffled feelings caused by his not-quite-so-tactful cohort, John Lennon, and to smile, smile, smile.

Cunning

There is no question about it – Paul has a cunning way with words. Asked if the Stones are more popular than the Beatles, McCartney lifted a questioning eyebrow: "Are they? I don't think so. I wouldn't like to say who is more popular. The Stones have got their publicity agent and we've got ours. It's up to you who you believe. The Stones are good lads and I don't want people to think that it'll come to us sticking our tongues out at each other like school kids."

Responsibility

At the very beginning when adults were blaming the Beatles for their son's stubborn resistance to the barber's shears, Paul announced that the Beatles didn't have any responsibility whatsoever to their fans. "It would probably be a nicer answer if I said yes we have a responsibility to fans, but I can't be noble for the sake of it."

The Beatles had no sooner land-

PAUL LOOKS OVER a lead sheet during one of his recording sessions.

KRLA ARCHIVES

Once Through The Charm

ed in America for their first visit than a nationally-syndicated columnist broke the Jane Asher/Paul McCartney romance and the rumors have haunted Paul to this day. Every reporter asked the same question of McCartney: "Are you married or planning to marry Jane Asher?" He smiled and bore the monotonous questioning until finally he was fed up. "I've no plans but everybody keeps saying I have. Maybe they know better. They say I'm married and divorced and have 50 kids – so you might as well say it too."

Charming

McCartney's "charming" label became a drag as time went on and he concentrated more on saying what *he* felt rather than what others wanted him to say. He disliked the protest song movement intensely and said so. "They make me concentrate too much on the lyric – which I don't like.

"I think Barry McGuire's 'Eve Of Destruction' is rubbish. And when I first heard it I thought it was bad. When I saw McGuire in person leaping around in those boots and growling, I just fell about!

"The Manfreds did a protest number on television which was the end. It was so bad they must have written it themselves."

But to say that Paul completely gave up being "the charming Beatle" would be a lie. He was as charming as he'd ever been – only quite a bit more frank and a little more outspoken.

In 1965 the Beatles turned-down an invitation to appear before the Queen at the Royal Variety Show in London and it was Paul who explained the group's decision to the press. "It's not our audience. If we went on and those people didn't like us everyone would say, 'ha, ha, the Beatles failed, they're on the slide'."

His sense of humor he kept intact; his ability to laugh at himself, at the Beatles and at the world, no doubt, saw him through some pretty rough times. Walter Shensen tells one of the funniest stories about McCartney.

"Boorish"

It seems that once Paul approached Shensen with a newspaper review from one of the London papers. "I don't think it's fair," moaned McCartney. "This chap says we're boorish. That's the one thing we're not – we never bore." Shensen explained that "boorish" does not mean "boring" it means "uncouth." "Oh, uncouth," said the relieved Paul. "Well, I think *that's* fair enough!"

The deafening waves of screams which traditionally accompany a Beatle concert received much notice in the press. Reporters demanded to know how the Beatles felt about performing amid the noise.

And it was Paul who answered: "The fans pay their money to come in and if they want to scream then that's their perogative. We don't mind if they scream. Why should we?

"The only thing that counts is that they are having a good time for their money. Anyway, five years ago we were playing without the screams and, friend, it wasn't half as nice. I mean, the bread is important too, you know."

Although it was Lennon who received the attention for making "How I Won The War," it was McCartney who first left the group to try his hand alone. He wrote "Woman" for Peter and Gordon, but asked that a pen name be used rather than his real name. His idea worked – for awhile.

"I knew someone would find out the truth sooner or later," said Paul, "but I'm glad the story didn't leak out until after 'Woman' had become a hit in Britain and America. I hate to read record reviews which say that so-and-so will have a hit just because a Beatle number is involved. It's not fair on the artists concerned.

"Anyway, my idea worked. Incidentally, this is the only song I've published under a pen name. I don't plan to repeat the idea . . . well, not at the moment, anyway!"

Keeps Cool

Paul is well-noted for his cool. It's amazing how he keeps it when people ask some of the most ridiculous questions imaginable. An "image" is manufactured by a press agent and the press itself. It often times has nothing to do with what entertainers are really like. Yet, during the summer of '66 a reporter stood himself up and asked Paul to explain the Beatles' image.

"I don't know," snapped the hard-to-irritate McCartney. "Our image is what we read in the papers. You people make up our image. We know what our *real* image. is and it's nothing like 'image'."

McCartney once said: "I'm always pleased when somebody has a hit with one of our songs – it's almost as good as us doing it." Yet, a rather well-informed reporter wanted to know what Paul thought of other artists "stealing" the Beatles' material.

Don't Steal

"They don't steal them," fired back Paul. "No, I know they don't," replied the reporter. "But you just said they did," countered Paul, "and besides, we pinch just as much as the rest of 'em."

The Beatles will never tour America again. The press will never have the opportunity to try their hand at making Beatles squirm. But, undoubtedly, McCartney will continue to look through his charm and allow the world an occasional glimpse of what goes on inside his mind.

McCARTNEY peers over the shoulder of a Byrd.

"**BECAUSE IT WAS DARK** and I was looking at the moon instead of the road."

KRLA ARCHIVES

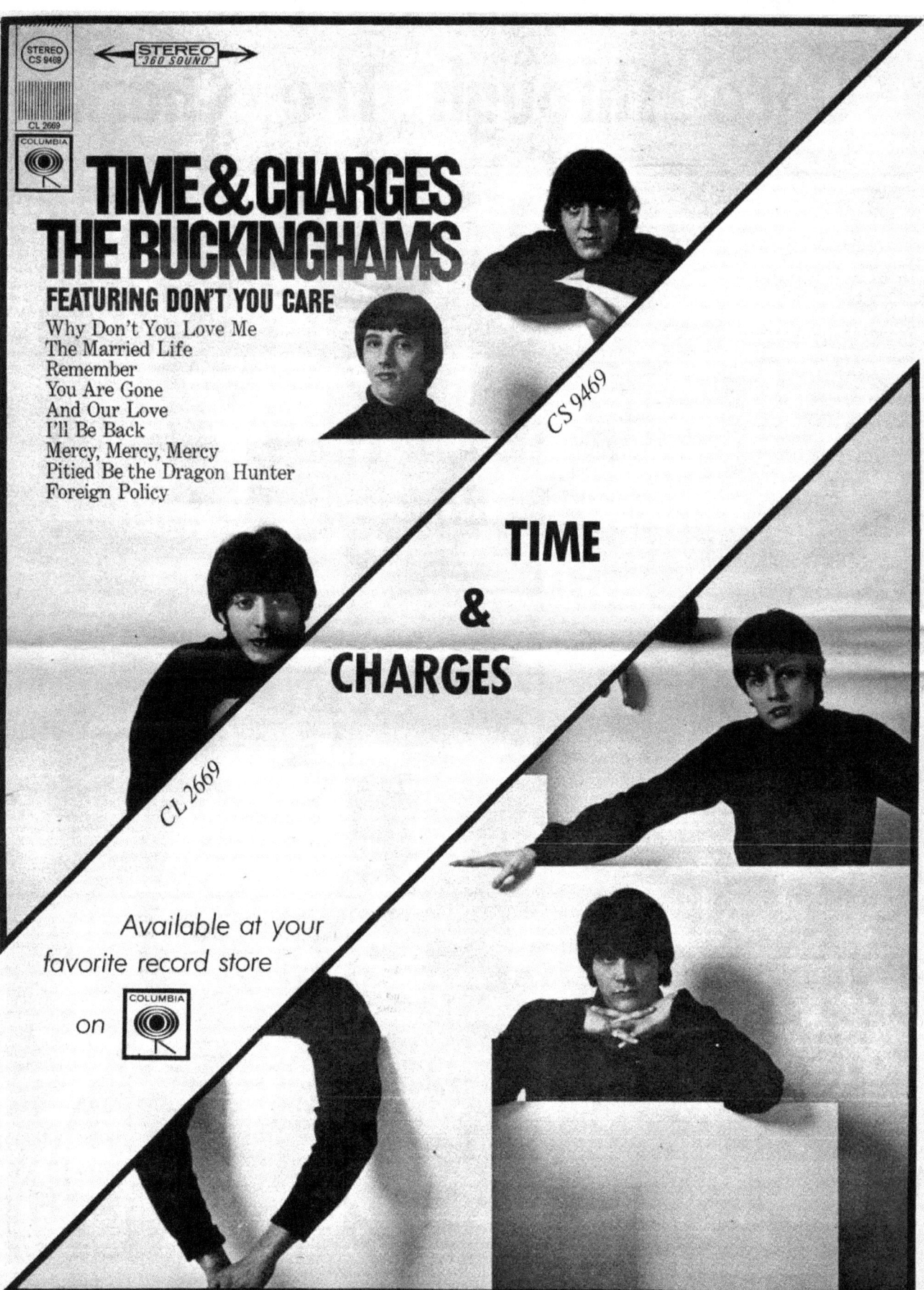

KRLA ARCHIVES

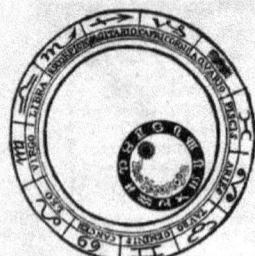

By Michelle

YOUR SIGN IS ARIES IF YOUR BIRTHDAY FALLS BETWEEN MARCH 21 TO APRIL 20
You think that you are very broad-minded but you are fooling yourself. You are really bogged down on a few favorites. To expand yourself listen to different kinds of music; switch to vanilla if you've been a strictly chocolate ice cream addict for years. Change will bring you: increased success. But act fast before you harden into a post-teenage fossil.

* * *

YOUR SIGN IS TAURIS IF YOUR BIRTHDAY FALLS BETWEEN APRIL 21 TO MAY 21
Why do you believe what you do? Now is the time for a deep look at yourself. The position of the moon is good for you. It will keep your mind alert this month. Take stock of your room, your boyfriend, your clothes... do they express the *real* you?

* * *

YOUR SIGN IS GEMINI IF YOUR BIRTHDAY FALLS BETWEEN MAY 22-JUNE 21
Ask questions. People will be especially receptive to you in this month and will feel compelled to respond truthfully. What is really happening in the world? Get behind the newspaper stories from Vietnam. New developments in rock 'n roll, fashion and romance will be revealed to you.

* * *

YOUR SIGN IS CANCER IF YOUR BIRTHDAY FALLS BETWEEN JUNE 22-JULY 23
You are quite attractive but you should stop ruining your looks with too much make-up or affected dress. Girls really don't like long-long hair on boys and the boys are turned off by a girl whose false eye lashes keep her lids weighed down and eyes half shut. Be yourself (if you can stand it). The Result: lots of admiring looks from the opposite sex.

* * *

YOUR SIGN IS LEO IF YOUR BIRTHDAY FALLS BETWEEN JULY 24-AUG. 23
You are a complainer. Continuing this trait: Will cost you important friendships. The world doesn't owe you anything. Be independent and go after things you want. Be creative. This is an excellent time to develop skills you never thought you had. Perseverance will: Bring rewards.

* * *

YOUR SIGN IS VIRGO IF YOUR BIRTHDAY FALLS BETWEEN AUG. 24-SEPT. 23
Things will go smoothly for you in the early part of the month but a stellar coclusion will bring you bad luck toward the middle. Be strong. Keep up your good habits, don't start skipping brushing regularly, and you will come through this dark stretch. Waiting for you: summer fun and personal discoveries.

YOUR SIGN IS LIBRA IF YOUR BIRTHDAY FALLS BETWEEN SEPT. 24-OCT. 23
Pleasant surprises are waiting for you this summer. Be sure to get yourself in shape. Trim up or down those few pounds. You'll want to be in great beach shape when you meet that outasite boy or girl. At first you won't like each other very much. But be patient. He or she is worth it.

* * *

YOUR SIGN IS SCORPIO IF YOUR BIRTHDAY FALLS BETWEEN OCT. 24-NOV. 22
Your greatest joy will be helping others. Look for a summer project working with the poor or helping unfortunates. Unexpected rewards will be yours: if you follow this advice. You tend to be an individual, proud of your opinions. If you really believe you are right: Now is the time to spread your views on controversial subjects like the war, civil rights and pop music.

* * *

YOUR SIGN IS SAGITARRIUS IF YOUR BIRTHDAY FALLS BETWEEN NOV. 23-DEC. 21
Delay no longer. This is the month to do all those things you have been putting off. Clean out your closet. Be sure to throw away the tootsie rolls and chocolate bars forgotten in the pockets of your winter coat. If you continue to be lazy: Your teacher will find out that it's really you who has been scratching initials into the school desks.

* * *

YOUR SIGN IS CAPRICORN IF YOUR BIRTHDAY FALLS BETWEEN DEC. 22-JAN. 20
You have wonderful creative abilities to figure out how not to do homework. If you apply this brilliance to doing it instead of putting it off, unexpected rewards will come your way. Your parents will be so pleased they will offer to chip in on a major purchase you have been wanting to make. You must act fast: Before everyone loses patience with you.

* * *

YOUR SIGN IS AQUARIUS IF YOUR BIRTHDAY FALLS BETWEEN JAN. 21-FEB. 19
The time is excellent: For overcoming your shyness. You are really bright and lively but something made you withdraw. Was it the braces on your teeth, skin problems, or just lack of self-confidence? Others like you but you must be outgoing to find out how much. Girls: try asking the boys to dance. Boys: be the first man at the party to barge in and break up that cluster of giggling girls. They'll love you for it.

* * *

YOUR SIGN IS PISCES IF YOUR BIRTHDAY FALLS BETWEEN FEB. 20-MAR. 20
Prepare yourself for: Serious and important changes coming your way this summer. It may be romance, physical or intellectual but be mature when it hits you. This is a good time to think, if television hasn't made you forget how. Sharpen up your wits or the new things in store for you will snow you.

THE ASSOCIATION have cranked their spreaders all the way to England.

U.K. POP NEWS ROUND-UP

Modern Pirates Bring TV To Britain In September

By Tony Barrow

Before the end of the year Government legislation will scuttle the pop armada of pirate radio ships anchored just out of territorial waters around the British Isles.

The two main stations seem to be confident that they can make alternative arrangements when the new laws prevent the continuation of broadcasting from the present seaborn studios.

Radio London's program director Alan Keen tells me that everything is set. "I can't tell you exactly how we're going to beat the government ban but our plans will be for a permanent commercial station which cannot be affected by the new laws" declares the confident Big L bossman.

Meanwhile I can reveal that arrangements are well advanced for the opening of Britain's first pirate television station! My information is that it will be on the air by September at the latest and will screen full-length movies 24 hours a day! One of Britain's top pop groups is financially involved in the ambitious project. The all-movies policy suggests that the station will operate from a ship at sea where 'live' studio transmissions would be impossible in all but the calmest of weather conditions. The directors of the company are men and women who hold non-British passports. They could not be prosecuted under British law for violation of any regulations designed to banish the pirate radio stations.

The Bee Gees have just expanded from quartet to quintet strength by adding to their line-up 21-year-old Australian guitarist Vince Melouney who has already worked extensively with the group as a session musician during the production of the album "The Bee Gees First." This album, with twelve original Bee Gee compositions, will be released in America via Atco very shortly.

At London's Wembley Empire Pool on June 30, July 1 and July 2, five of Britain's top deejays will share comparing duties – one appearing at each performance – when the Monkees make their eagerly anticipated stage debut on our side of the Atlantic. The selected five are Dave Cash, Alan Freeman, Tony Hall, Peter Murray and Jimmy Savile.

I have received from a thoughtful American journalist/broadcaster, Marilyn Doerfler, a copy of "Crank Your Spreaders," a fascinating little book which is subtitled "The Association Field Guide And Almanac." It includes a collection of Russ Giguere's fave ties, "The Legend Of Roadzilla (What Terrible Passions Drove This Desperate Creature To Its Ultimate Doom)" by Ted Bluechel Jr., the music and lyrics of "Cherish" and "Pandora's Golden Heebie Jeebies," a poem called "Dusk" by Jim Yester and a curious assortment of birds drawn by Terry Kirkman.

Understudy actress Janet Legge took over from an indisposed Marianne Faithfull mid-way thru the short sell-out run of Chekhov's "Three Sisters" staged at London's Royal Court Theatre... Beatles were guests at "Sgt. Pepper" dinner party thrown by Brian Epstein in his Belgravia, London, home. So were a dozen top British and overseas journalists plus deejays Kenny Everett, Jimmy Savile an Alan Freeman... Personal to *BEAT* reader Vivian E. Lopez (Page 2, May 20 issue): Your deepest wish has just been granted!... Promoter Tito Burns has renewed hopes of securing Mamas and Papas for Royal Albert Hall concert in London later this year. ... Latest U.K. chart-toppers the Tremeloes – they hit our Number One spot with "Silence Is Golden" – open a four-week U.S. concert tour in Ohio at the end of June... June single by Cliff Richard couples a pair of Neil Diamond compositions – "I'll Come Running" and "I Got The Feelin'." Mort Shuman in London to attend recording session when Cilla Black taped his "What Good Am I?" ballad... Mitch Ryder in London minus "The Mitch Ryder Show" for a two-week promotional visit – spent time seeing the tourist sites between radio and press appointments.

Four days at San Francisco's Fillmore Auditorium this month should win Jimi Hendrix total appreciation of California's pop people... Paul McCartney shaved off his moustache... First "cover version" single of a "Sgt. Pepper" item in U.K. was "She's Leaving Home" from David and Jonathan whose recording manager is George Martin... Following trade paper stories suggesting that Ray Davies, leader of the Kinks, was considering quitting to concentrate on song-writing, his management issued strongly worded denial. Rumour was that Ray would function rather like Brian Wilson does – guiding and directing the group's activities without performing at all concert dates... Rolling Stones' "Flower" album not issued in Britain where next release is expected to be a July single.

Lyrics of "Heaven and Hell" recorded by the Easybeats altered for U.S. release to avoid anticipated controversy and possible radio banning... New single ("Strange Brew") and upcoming album recorded by Cream in New York.

New "West Coast USA" column for London's *Record Mirror* by David Gooch being dubbed "Britain's first psychedelic journalism!"

ART INSTITUTE OF PITTSBURGH
47th Yr. Coed. 18 & 24 mo. Diploma Course: Commercial Art, Fashion Art, Interior Design. Begin. & Adv. Vet. Appd. Dorm facilities. College referrals for degrees. Free illus. brochure.
Earl B. Wheeler, Director
635 Smithfield St.
Pittsburgh, Pa. 15222

KRLA ARCHIVES

MOD BOD

To: Beat Publications
9121 Sunset Blvd.
Los Angeles, Calif. 90069

Please send _____ sheet(s) Mod-Bod stick ons
(4 psychedelic sheets available at $1.00 each)

Find $_____ enclosed.

Name_____

Address_____

City_____
California residents add 4% sales tax

BE AHEAD WITH MOD-BOD
Turn on your breathin' skin 180 ways
Tune in on the Harvard color spectrum

STRANGE BODY ADORNMENTS
Hearts & Flowers to Psychedelic Phreaqueouts

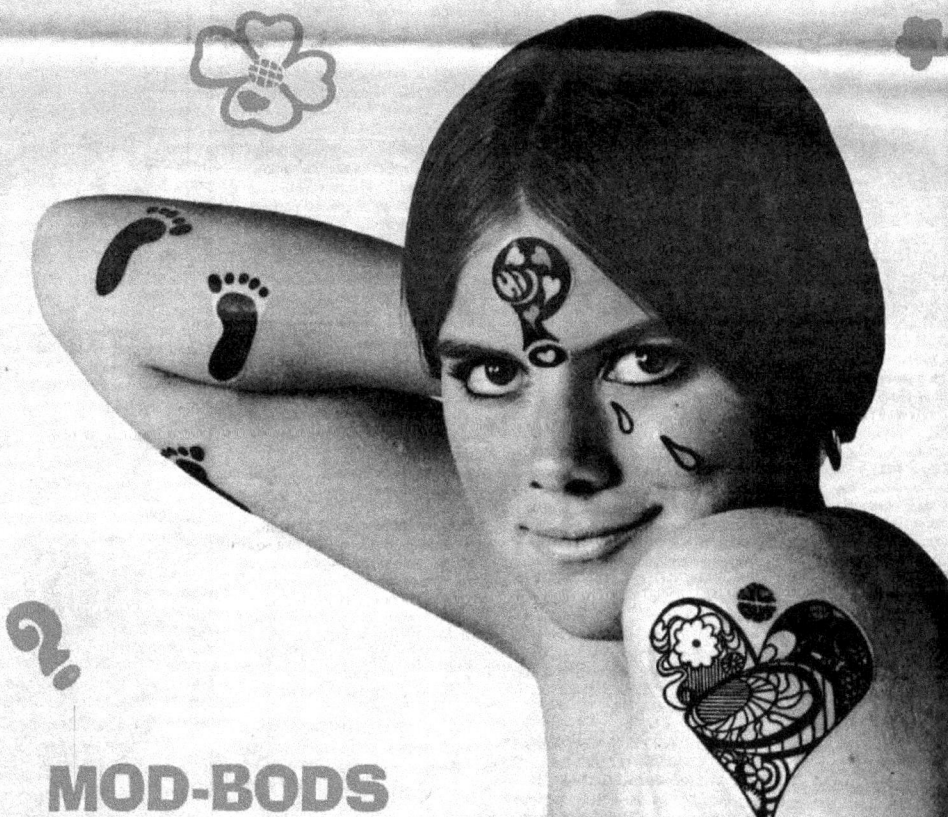

MOD-BODS
Stick on everything, they're reuseable, waterproof, fluorescent, totally tuff, urrrk, supergroovy, bitchen, outta site, cooool, phantazmagoric, uptight, zingo righteous, flashie, too much, mad, conglomerative, pau and et cetera.

KRLA ARCHIVES

Go To Pop Festival Free!!!

KRLA listeners, you can win free tickets and lodging for the fabulous Monterey Pop Festival. Call in on the KRLA toll-free request lines. If your call is selected you will be allowed to guess which Monterey Festival star group is scheduled to come up on a top-secret pre-recorded tape.

You can call in as many times as you wish. If you don't win the first time around you still have lots more opportunity to earn those free tickets and accommodations.

Can you predict which group is next to roll on the Pop Festival tape? Will it be the Mamas and the Papas, Lou Rawls, The Jefferson Airplane, Simon and Garfunkel or one of the other outasite artists who'll be entertaining in Monterey on June 16, 17 and 18.

There is absolutely nothing to buy or send in. You don't need any special knowledge. All you have to do is rub your rabbit's foot and squeeze hard on your four leaf clover and then dial the KRLA request line. You may enter as many times as you wish. Tell all your friends about this fabulous contest...if you all win, it will be party time for you and your friends in Monterey.

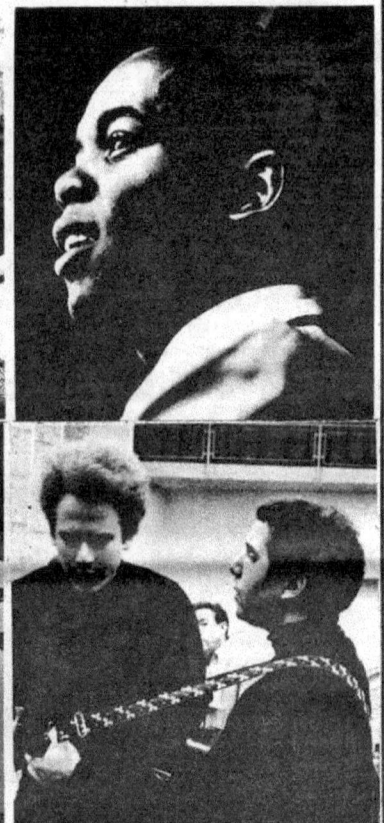

By Pen

Monterey Pop Festival News

Definite information is coming into KRLA daily about the Monterey International Pop Festival to be held in the beach side city June 16th, 17th and 18th. Tickets can now be purchased at all Mutual Ticket Agencies and Wallich's Music City — prices range from $3.00 to $6.50 per concert. Just some of the artists appearing on Friday's concert will be the Association, Buffalo Springfield, Grateful Dead, Jimi Hendrix, Laura Nyro, Lou Rawls, and Simon and Garfunkel.

On Saturday, June 17th, you can see Paul Butterfield Blues Band, Hugh Masekela, Beach Boys, Booker T and the MG's, Byrds, Jefferson Airplane, Hugh Masekela, Otis Redding and more. Sunday — Ravi Shankar, Blues Project, Mamas and Papas, Johnny Rivers, Dionne Warwick and The Who. More artists are being added every day. And, preparations are being made for package tours leaving Friday night and returning Sunday...so make your plans today. And keep listening to KRLA for information about how you can *win* a free trip to the Festival!

'Question Of The Hour'

"Why is it immoral for young people under 18 to dance in Los Angeles — when they dance six feet apart?"

"Why do most of the people who claim to be non-conformists all dress alike?"

These are just two of the questions heard on KRLA's "QUESTION OF THE HOUR"...a once an hour newscast feature which has provoked more than a few listeners to THINK! "QUESTION..." was originated by Cecil Tuck, KRLA's News Director, in an effort to make the listeners aware that today's news affects everyone...that you and I are not just observers but participants.

A Saturday night newscast carried the first questions, and Monday morning's mail carried the first listener reaction. Over one-hundred and seventy questions were supplied by listeners who already knew they were participants...and they had some questions of their own. A listener from Compton asked — "If we drafted 60 year olds first, instead of 19 year olds, would Congress still extend the selective service law?"

WIZARD OF OZ
Sunday nights 8 to midnight

ICE HOUSE GLENDALE
234 So. Brand Ave. Reservations: 245-5043

MAY 30 thru JUNE 11
Tim Morgon
And
Forth & Main

JUNE 30-18
Rainy Daze
with their hit "Acapulco Gold"
— and —
Patrick & Paul

ICE HOUSE PASADENA
24 No. Mentor — Reservations: 681-9942

ENTIRE MONTH OF JUNE
Stone Country
stone: a soft rock
— and —
Biff Rose
as seen on the Mort Sahl Show
— and —
Comedy & Magic of Steve Martin

Casey Issues Astrology LP

Why did we break up?
Will romance come my way?
What am I really like?

Now Casey Kasem, KRLA's sincerest disc jockey, has the answers for pondering young adults in a new album, "Astrology For Young Lovers."

The album, a series of readings for all signs of the zodiac, was especially forecast by Jack Bradford, noted astrologer and syndicated columnist.

"Astrology is the 'now' thing," says Casey, "it's amazing what astrological predictions have come true. Some of our greatest minds have had their own personal astrologists and wouldn't make a move without their consent."

"Astrology For Young Lovers" deals with the traits and predictions of 1967-68, and includes a list of birthdays for almost all of today's recording, movie and television stars.

KRLA ARCHIVES

SMOTHERS BROTHERS
Forcing The Establishment To Bend

By Louise Criscione

While the love-ins, be-ins, chiquita stickers and protest marchers give the Establishment an inkling of what the younger generation thinks, feels and hopes to change, the two Smothers Brothers hit hard into millions of homes each week, pulling the wool from sensitive adult eyes.

Its been said that Tommy and Dickie Smothers reflect the attitudes of the younger generation. "I never thought about it really that much," said Dickie as he sprawled on a couch in their windowless office at CBS. "But I agree with it now that I look at it.

"They're our attitudes basically. We're not trying to identify with any particular group of people but if we have the same attitudes as the younger generation, then we *are* identifying with them," Dickie philosophized.

The tremendous success of their Sunday night show caught most people by surprise. "It surprised us too," admitted Dick. "It has nothing to do with us really. One point is timing. 'Bonanza's' getting old and there are a lot of viewers looking for another show. So, we came on with a variety show which received all the cliches like 'fresh,' 'different,' 'new,' 'exciting.'"

TOM AND DICK SMOTHERS — fighting censorship.
Photo: By Jerry Fitzgerald

DICK, DOM DeLUIS, Nancy and Frank Sinatra Jr.

THE SMOTHERS, RAIDERS, CARL REINER, BARBRA EDEN in the Revolutionary War bit some critics have termed "tastless."

At which point the door burst open and brother Tommy strolled in, dropped his white hat on the coffee table, opened his lunch pail (the type grammar school kids carry) and proceeded to announce to no one in particular that, "the hip people watch our show."

With that out of the way, he plopped himself into the only vacant chair and pulled what was left of a sandwich out of his lunch pail as an undaunted Dick picked up where he had left off. "I think our show is the only variety show which says something. Young people do identify with us because we don't do the stupid things that the Establishment, the adults, do."

As you have no doubt surmised by now, the Establishment is not the Smothers' favorite thing in the world. They wage a continual war with the network censors, a war which as yet has neither side emerging as the victor.

Compromise
"In every show there's something," said a disgusted Tommy. "All year we've fought censorship. Every show is compromises and deletions."

"They're not called censors, though," said Dickie, who had a hard time remembering exactly what they *were* called. "But it's the department which is the view of CBS as to what can go on the air. What it comes down to is the fact that anything *they* don't want on doesn't get on. If it's not acceptable to all the people, they don't want it on."

"I was never aware that freedom of expression and personal opinions are really limited," said Tommy. "You're not allowed to say it if it's not within the realm of the Establishment or adult views. The crime of silence is the worst crime. There are so many things which should be said but all we can do is our best and get as much out as we can.

Buck It
"The artists themselves have very little to say," he continued. "We're probably saying more on our show than most performers have a chance to do. But the only way to buck the Establishment is to join it — but not by being a sell-out."

How does he know that once he joins the Establishment he won't become one of them, think like they think and act like they act?

"As a performer I haven't sold-out, yet. I think I'd do the same thing in a high position, but who knows? You never know what you'd do until you're actually in the position."

The Smothers don't just *knock* the Establishment — they question its validity. Are they asking people to change or merely commenting on what's happening?

Social Comment
"We're making social comment," answered Dickie, "but I don't think you can make social comment on something without asking for a little bit of change."

This social comment has caused some members of the Establishment to cry that the brothers are occasionally "tasteless." Especially drawing fire was the bit they did on the Revolutionary War heroes.

"We don't agree that the Revolutionary War thing was in bad taste," argued Dickie. "The basic premise is wrong but if I defend it, it looks like their basic premise is right.

Handle
"Now the nudist bit Tommy did with Carol Burnett or the KKK thing — at least I can see a handle there. But I can't see where something's tasteless if it's just good fun. 'Tasteless' is a very ambiguous term anyway."

It's all right to poke good, clean fun at someone who is going with the President's daughter, etc., "but to make fun of someone like Cassius Clay would be different," say the brothers.

"Maybe the guy's sincere," believes Dickie, "and we shouldn't make fun of him. He's an underdog and to make fun of an underdog would be in bad taste."

A recent show featured a bit which on the surface was funny while it's underlying "message" (why is killing acceptable while making love is not?) was piercing and legitimate.

"We're brought up on violence and it makes it that much more acceptable to us," said Dickie. "Take my brother's lunch pail (which features war paraphernalia). He sent his maid out to buy him a lunch pail, she went to four stores and that's the only kind she could find.

"Basically, we'd like our comedy to have a purpose. We're on a level now where people either like us or dislike us — love us or hate us. There's no in between."

While those who "hate" them are vocal, they constitute an extremely small minority. "We're bound to bring somebody up with what we say," Dickie continued. "It upsets the network but it doesn't bother us. It's impossible to please everyone and you just have to take the good with the bad."

Impressive List
The brothers have had an impressive guest list since they've been on the air but so far no one has been able to steal the spotlight from the face-making, word-tripping Tommy or the straight-faced, serious Dickie (whom their mom always liked best).

They had Jack Benny and George Burns on one of their shows and all of a sudden people decided they were successful.

"You know the saying, 'guilt by association?' asked Tommy. "Well, this was 'success by association.' Hey, that's a good line, success by association, we'll have to use that sometime!"

Face Value
Much of the Smothers' success, I think, can be attributed to the fact that their comedy can be accepted at face value by the Establishment and dug by the hipper people who are perceptive enough to pick up on the deeper meanings.

"We've always had that," agreed Tommy. "The people who bring their lunch buckets to the factory, the lunch-bucket-bunch, see us on the street and say, 'you guys are okay,' but they don't even know what you're talking about.

"A good line, delivered well, doesn't have to be specific. That's the biggest thing — the attitude of the show. We're always fighting it. Writing always slips in and you know you can get a laugh."

What exactly does he mean by "attitude?" "Attitude is like watching a man on 'Candid Camera.' He's just being natural but he's funny. We try to stay close to that without relying on jokes.

Consistency
"Consistency is so important. That's the flaw in success. The Beatles are consistent but how many groups come along with a good record and then are never heard from again? Or else, how many put out a good album and then follow it up with a bad one? I may be lousy," laughed Tommy, "but at least I'll be consistent!"

Although most variety shows now book rock talent in a desperate attempt to pick up a young audience, the "Smother Brothers" is probably the only show which takes either the time or the trouble to consult the pop acts on presentation.

Ignorant Of TV
"Everytime we have a rock group on," explained Tommy, "we ask them how they want to be presented. They're not performers in a sense, their big thing is sound. We tell them, 'break down your song and let us know who you want spotlighted, where you want the close-ups and then we'll be able to keep with what you want to do.' But most of the time they're ignorant of television."

Despite the fact that the national charts are adhered to in booking their rock acts, the primary requisite is not a hit-record but rather the ability to perform. Lip-syncing is strictly frowned upon "because it would be like 'afternoon dance time' with what's that guy's name?" said Tommy.

The Smothers originally went into television with their comedy series ("Thank God that one went off!" declared Tommy) because they felt they had gone as far as possible with the concert and night club circuit and the only way left for them to go was up. But what's "up" now that they've conquered television?

Fate
"We don't want to stay with it that long," answered Tommy. "We're successful in the media but we don't know what will happen. Personally, I want to get into the producing and directing end. But it depends on fate — whatever fate brings."

So, until fate brings something else, Tommy and Dickie Smothers will go on fighting the Establishment, winning an occasional battle, mirroring the ideas, the attitudes, the frustrations and hopes of the young generation. How long the Establishment will hold out is impossible to predict. But just the fact that the Smothers are making them bend, forcing them to compromise and proving with high ratings that they have a strong and wide support is, at the very least, a step in the right direction.

KRLA ARCHIVES

The LP Everyone's Been Waiting For Is Here!

Complete with full printed lyrics for every song!

PLUS...

Sgt. Pepper paper cut-outs...

and inside—a double size, full color foldout...

NOW AVAILABLE AT YOUR LOCAL

KRLA ARCHIVES

A Romp Through Disneyland With TWIGGY

By Cheryl Halter

Thursday, started out as just an ordinary sunny California day at famous Disneyland. Then the clock struck 12:30 and thru the gates passed the money-making model Twiggy, all aglow with her little girl charms.

All about to embark on a day filled with fantasy and fun, Twiggy was met at the gate by Marcia Minor, Miss Disneyland of 1967, the official V.I.P. tour guide for the park. Also awaiting her arrival were the park public relations and publicity men and press photographers from all over Southern California. When you are a news item it seems the press can find you wherever you go. But Twiggy still claims, "I'm just an ordinary girl." The rest of the world doesn't seem to agree with her.

BEAT Photos: Jerry Haas

Never Suspect

When Twiggy arrived at Disneyland no one could suspect that she was the world's top fashion model if it were not for the press. She was clad in a simple blue bell-bottomed capri outfit, with a halter-type shell, backless and tying at the neck.

Twiggy is rarely seen anywhere without her boyfriend/manager, Justin de Villeneuve and Disneyland was no exception. Justin is known as the man most responsible for Twiggy's fast rise to fame in the fashion world.

Three male escorts accompanied Twiggy and Justin along with Bert Stern, producer of ABC Specials, not to mention the crowd of fans and curious people that followed Twiggy everywhere.

Twiggy's party started with lunch at the Plaza Inn, in the V.I.P. dining room. She then proceeded to take in as many rides and shops as she could before the day ended. As Twiggy moved along Main Street her little girl curiousity moved her big blue eyes into the small shops and stores. She seemed to be lost in a wonderful dream that would never end.

Small Child

Following Twiggy is not like spending a day with any other teenager. It is more like traveling with a small child on a holiday. She seems to enjoy every moment in life, and wants to make sure she doesn't waste any time on unpleasant things.

Now the time has come for Twiggy to leave her holiday at Disneyland. It may well be that she will never forget this day. Nor will the people of Disneyland forget one of the most delightful V.I.P.'s that has come to visit the ever-famous Disneyland.

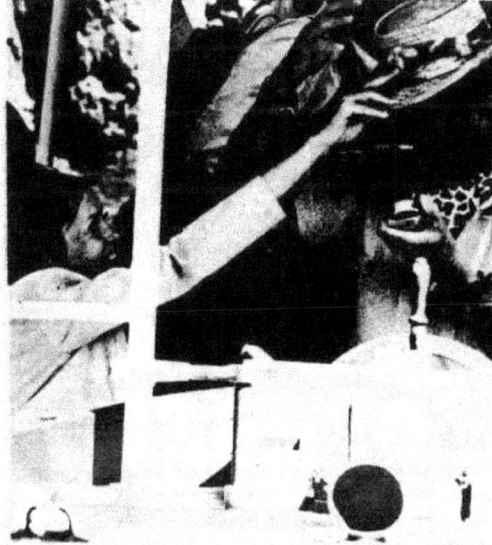

KRLA ARCHIVES

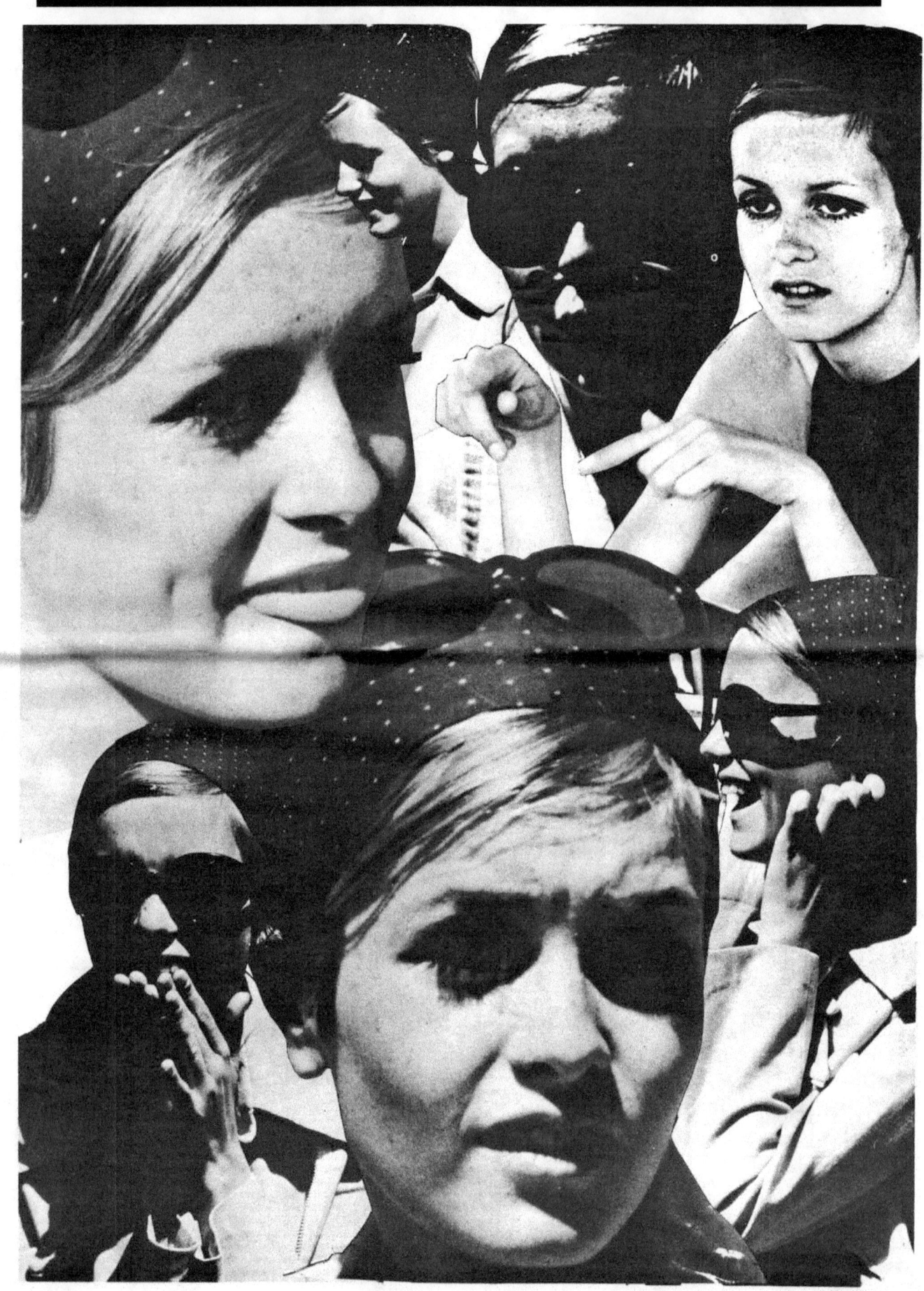

KRLA ARCHIVES

ROD McKUEN:
'Money Is Only Good To Buy Candy Bars'

By Louise Criscione

Nestled on the side of a hill in Hollywood is the home of an extremely talented, highly successful, completely unassuming man named Rod McKuen. A giant cross-section of you know him. Those of you who don't are completely missing out.

Obviously you can't all troop up to his house and bang on the door (though he'd probably let you all in if you did), so we've done it for you.

Rod lives with a giant English sheepdog and two cats, one of which "talks" and the other of which is deaf. If for nothing else, Rod is unique in the fact that he handles just about everything himself. No manager, no publicist . . . just Rod and his animals.

Frankly, it was the easiest interview I've ever done. Rod did the talking; I did the listening. He knows himself, his feelings and his beliefs better than I'll ever be able to. Listen to him. You'll be glad you did.

"There is no such thing as teenagers over nine. The only two teenagers left are Little Orphan Annie and Shirley Temple.

"We live in an adult world. When I went to school it was a lot different and when my brother, who is younger than I am, went to school it was different. The kids of today have a lot more responsibility than we did. Madison Avenue started it. It's not necessarily bad but kids have to realize their responsibility.

"There's always been a generation gap. There's a gap between you and your parents; there are two generation gaps between you and your grandparents. It has nothing to do with today's generation alone but it's more evidenced today because there are more people today.

"There are so many bad songs today because there are more songwriters today. It's supply and demand and somebody to fill it.

REBELLING AGAINST CONFORMITY

"They create their own conformity. They decide to have no conformity and then others draw to it. It's an excuse for not doing anything. The world doesn't owe you and me a living. There's nothing real about Haight/Ashbury.

"The word 'hippies' is kind of a catch-all phrase like 'teeny-bopper.' It's bad—this putting people into a mode. Frankly, I'm delighted with the current generation. I think they're great. They ask questions and maybe if they ask enough questions they'll get some answers — if not from the older generation, maybe they'll be able to find out the answers for themselves.

WHY NO ED SULLIVANS?

"You know, I get offers to appear on these national television shows but I turn them all down because I feel that I have to sing at least 20 minutes to people. I can't do it as a fast act singing one song for three minutes and then coming back on at the end of the show to sing another song.

"I like to play colleges. Usually my college concerts sell-out as soon as they're announced but I don't do it for the money. I feel that if I have an audience of 5,000 and 50 of them go away understanding what I've tried to say I've really done something sensational.

"I hate acting. It was something I wanted to do for awhile. I guess if the right part came along I'd take it but I don't want to just take anything. It's like with my writing. I'd rather write something well and not have it sell any copies. I have all the money I'll ever need. I won't be a millionaire maybe, but I'll have enough money. I came from a very poor family and I've had to support my family since I was 11. I've learned that money is only good to buy candy bars and important things like dog licenses and cat food.

PROTESTING AND DRAFT DODGING

"It's (America) a great country. I think that we owe a responsibility to defend the country we live in. The country defends us. It's not up to entertainers to express political views and we shouldn't send ballerina dancers to Washington. Mort Sahl is a different case in point but it's not right for a singer to sing protest songs and use his power to influence people at a concert and then pocket his $15,000 and drive away in his limousine.

"Take a fifteen-year-old kid singing about hard times. *What* hard times? Have *you* known hard times? I'm a guy who has spent 15 years traveling around the world and it's the same thing everywhere. America is the big thing, American artists, American clothes, American everything. Our entertainers are treated like royalty over there.

"It's very good to protest but I think that outside agitators and people like that interfere with the academic workings of a school. You have to decide for yourself whether or not you're going to school to get an education. College was not necessary for me because I was already doing what I wanted to. College is only good because it prepares you for what you want to do in life. For instance, if you have all the basic talents for writing and all the fundamentals then you're better off writing than going to college.

HIMSELF

"I'm very restless. I like to work 18 to 20 hours a day and as a result everytime I get close to the altar my work scares the girl away. It's very hard for a woman to take second to anything. I can understand that.

"I'm a loner if being a loner means choosing the people I want to be with and spending time alone. Sometimes I spend ten days in a row up here by myself. Sometimes I forget to eat. I eat when my stomach growls. But I'm living the kind of life I want to live. It's very important being my own master.

WRITING

"I took my book of poetry, 'Stanyan Street And Other Sorrows,' to a couple of publishers and they said, 'poetry doesn't sell.' So, I mortgaged practically everything I owned and published it myself. It's sold over 50,000 copies. I was very lucky, it's the largest selling book of poetry in 20 years.

"'Listen To The Warm' is my next book. We get around 300 requests a day for 'Stanyan Street,' and we average about 50 books a week for guys in Vietnam.

"I like doing something if it's a challenge. I have written 900 to 1,000 songs. Maybe 300 of those songs I've never shown to anybody because they're too personal.

"I don't believe in doing anything unless it's to the best of my ability. 'The Sea' (Rod's album with Anita Kerr) was a labor of love. I love working with Anita. She's a remarkable talent.

"I'm writing a movie for 'The Sea' which five or six movie companies are bidding on. I'd like to get Anouk Aimee to play the lead. The unusual thing is that the entire score will be recorded before the movie is made—usually it's the last thing done.

"I was kind of forced into writing but it was through my writing that I became an entertainer.

MUSIC

"Music is definitely a universal language. In my new album most of those songs were originally French. It's a universal market for anything as long as it's well done. You can write a song about anything as long as you do it well and in good taste.

"A writer or an entertainer must be very cautious with the power they have over people. We live in a society which is completely aliented from each other. Sons can't talk to their fathers, brothers can't talk to their sisters. The art of conversation is gone. I don't know where it went but it's gone.

INSPIRATION FOR WRITING

"Almost all of the time I write from personal experiences. They're either something that's happened to me or something that I know about or feel. I think any songwriter relies on personal experiences. I feel this—you do best what you believe in. I am trying to relate man's inability to communicate with man.

"I'm not protesting. One magazine compared me with Bob Dylan but that's an unfair comparison because Bobby is protesting. I'm not—I'm not asking you to change it.

"Every song should have a beginning, a middle and an end. I don't want to write for a market. I write what pleases me and say what pleases me in the best way that I know how. The older you get the more you have to make the very best of it to your ability.

"I haven't noticed any drastic changes in lyrics during the past five years except lyrics like "fly me to the moon and let me play among the stars, let me see what spring is like on Jupiter and Mars" don't make it. Nowadays, they'll believe you only if you say 'let's take a walk, I can't give you the moon, if I could I would, but I'll buy you some flowers at the corner.' There's more reality now and not the sophistication of say, Cole Porter."

So now you know where Rod McKuen lives—whether you agree with him or not, at least now you know a little bit about what goes on in his mind. He deserves at least that much from you.

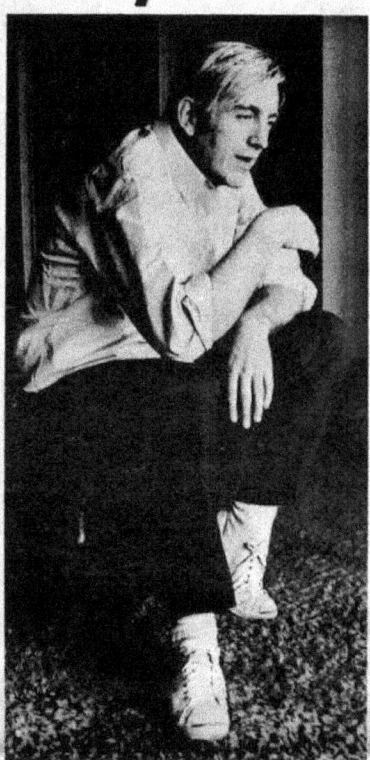

"THE ART OF CONVERSATION IS GONE."

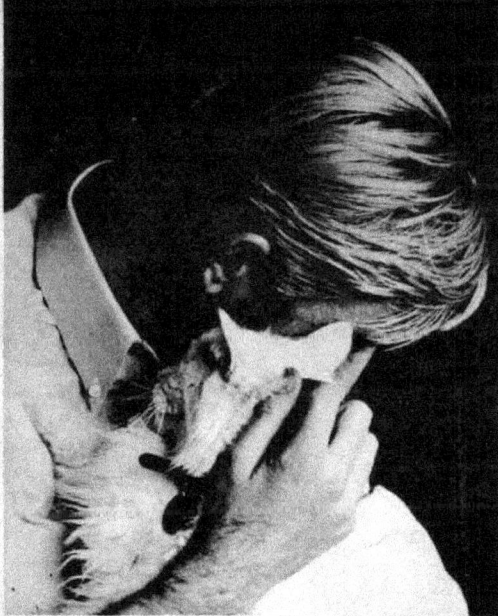

"THE WORLD DOESN'T OWE YOU AND ME A LIVING."

BEAT Photos: Jerry Haas

"It's not up to entertainers to express political views and we shouldn't send ballerina dancers to Washington."

KRLA ARCHIVES

UNIDENTIFIED KRLA listeners mob Gypsy outside KRLA studios after hearing his "Flower Power" speech.

Gypsy Boots: Special Horticultural Consultant

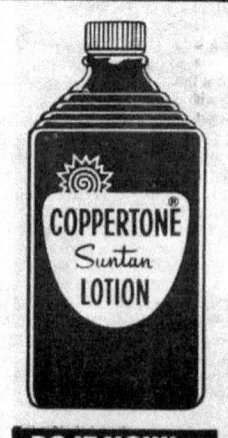

It's the era of the Flower Children. It's the age of "Flower Power" radio. It's what's happening, baby...

Fully realizing the world and especially the younger generations is saying it with flowers, KRLA has hired famed nature boy Gypsy Boots as special horticultural consultant in it's program of "Flower Power" radio.

Boots will be in charge of handing out flowers to listeners and non-listeners alike, regardless of the length of their hair, and otherwise promoting "Flower Power" radio. He will also visit the Monterey Pop Festival with an adequate supply of floral gifts.

It is reportedly a bad year for hay fever sufferers.

GYPSY SWINGS — from a tree outside of his home.
BEAT Photos: Leonard R. Ashmore

Sears FREE DRAWING

Register Now and Be One of 10 Winners of a $49.95 *Duke Kahanamoku* Belly Board

Register through July 5th in any Sears Sporting Goods and Boys' Wear Departments in Southern California. Boys and young men — 6 to 18 are eligible...no purchase necessary.

Sears Employes and members of their family are not eligible

OPENING JUNE 2

A TOTAL ENVIRONMENT NIGHTCLUB
Open Fri., Sat., & Sun.
8:30 – 1:30 $1.75

STROBES • BLACK LIGHT DRINKS • THE BATHHOUSE EMPORIUM •

dancing for over 18's to the Rage Sounds of THE PURPLE PILLOW ABSTRAX, THE RIVER-ON, and JOHNNY & HERB
11441 W. JEFFERSON BLVD.
at the SAN DIEGO FWY.
Culver City 391-7701

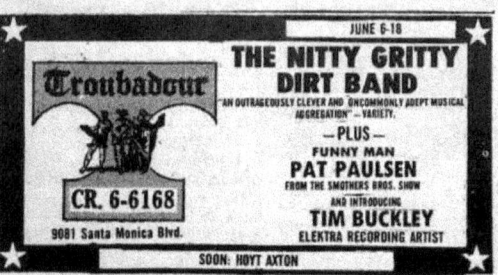

Troubadour CR. 6-6168
9081 Santa Monica Blvd.

JUNE 6-18
THE NITTY GRITTY DIRT BAND
"AN OUTRAGEOUSLY CLEVER AND UNCOMMONLY ADEPT MUSICAL AGGREGATION" — Variety

— PLUS —
FUNNY MAN
PAT PAULSEN
FROM THE SMOTHERS BROS. SHOW

AND INTRODUCING
TIM BUCKLEY
ELEKTRA RECORDING ARTIST

SOON: HOYT AXTON

COPPERTONE *Suntan* LOTION
DO IT NOW! AT All Toiletries Counters

KRLA ARCHIVES

Martha Turns Reporter And Interviews Fellow Vandellas

By Eden

One of the top female recording groups in the country today is Martha and the Vandellas, currently riding high on the national record charts with their latest hit, "Jimmy Mack." In addition to being one of the most successful trios in America today, they are also three of the nicest and most versatile girls we know.

So versatile, in fact, that we decided to let the girls *go for themselves* this time around! Instead of firing questions at them, then, we asked lead singer, Martha Reeves, to interview her two friends, and below you will find the results of the day that Martha Reeves turned Girl Reporter for *BEAT*.

"This is Martha, of Martha and the Vandellas, and with me I have Rosalind Ashford and Betty Kelly.

MARTHA: "Betty, do you plan on taking a vacation soon and where would you like to go on a vacation?"

BETTY: "Well, if we *ever get* a vacation—which we all need!—I think I'd like to go to Hawaii for about a week or two weeks."

MARTHA: "Rosalind, what would you say to a young girl who's interested in show business if she were to ask you whether or not you think it would be best for her to go into show business? What would you say to her, and what kind of points would you give her on entertaining?"

ROSALIND: "Well, first of all, I would let her know that it would be very wise for her—if she hasn't graduated from high school yet—to stay in school and get as much of an education as she can. Then I would go into details as to telling her how hard it is to be an entertainer and let her know that everything isn't *all* fun. It consists of work, and sacrifices, and all sorts of things, and she really has to have a solemn mind to go into being an entertainer. But, after you get into it, and you really enjoy it—it's something that is really beautiful and it's something that you really want to do."

MARTHA: "Betty, what kind of fellows do you like? What do you look for particularly in a man?"

BETTY: "Well, I think I like *conservative*-type men who can be a lot of fun but still keep his composure. I like a quiet-type person—not too loud—and one who likes to do the things I would want to do, or we'd compromise!"

MARTHA: "Rosalind, if you had it to do all over again, would you still choose the singing profession as a career?"

ROSALIND: "Yes, I would! Because, it's gotten to the point where I've been *in* it so long, and I've been trying *at* it so long, that if I had it to do all over again, I would, indeed, go into it again. I love it and I wouldn't give it up for anything in the world."

MARTHA: "Rosalind, do you think, after being in show business five years, that the exchange of what you sacrifice and the hard work, is equal to your success? Do you think it's an even exchange?

ROSALIND: "Yes, I think it is, because—if you take, for instance, if I *hadn't* become an entertainer, maybe I would just be working now and I would have my certain friends and things. But, since I have been in entertainment, it's gotten to the point where I've gotten to be well-known and moneywise . . . I'm not a millionaire yet, but I'm still trying to become a millionaire! Moneywise, I'm satisfied. It's just a thing where we're known by everybody and it's a thing where everybody loves you and you get a chance to meet so many people . . . very many interesting people that maybe I wouldn't have had the opportunity of meeting if I hadn't become an entertainer."

MARTHA: "In the *Vogue* magazine, I noticed recently that all the styles were *mini*. How do you feel about the mini-skirts? Do you think they're going to last or will it be a thing where they'll just go out like the topless bathing suits?"

ROSALIND: "Well, I think they're going to be here for awhile, but I don't think it's going to be a long, drawn-out thing. I don't think they're going to last a *long* time, but I'll give them, maybe another year."

MARTHA STANDS ALONE

MARTHA: "A lot of men turn their noses down at women in pants, but I find that you wear quite a few yourself, Betty. How do you feel about pants?"

BETTY: "I like them, and if you've noticed—whenever I shop, I always try to find a slacks-suit that is unique and yet feminine. I have quite a collection of slacks that I started in England. I think we were the first girls to have bell-bottoms over here — all of us bought them while we were in England, and we had ours about a year-and-a-half before they ever came to the United States. But, usually I get quite a few compliments on my slacks from fellows."

SHIRLEY YOU JEST

Kiele and/or Clang be praised! Bona fortuna (that's Italian for good luck) (which is English for bona fortuna) (phew!) is with you! For the most part, this issue's column (there must be a more descriptive word) (and is) won't be written by me! You have been spared.

Instead, I'll be using a lot of the space to print a thingy composed and sent to me by Sheila Lee of . . . drat, I've lost the envelope. Anytown, Sheila's masterpiece is entitled 25 WAYS TO FEEL LIKE A MORON, and she claims this column was her inspiration while writing this goodie. (I wonder what she meant by that?) (Shhhh....none of your answering.)

And awry we go . . .

1. You are riding in a car with many friends and several enemies. They are playing one of your favorite songs on the radio and you are singing along in your own inimitable (let us hope) fashion. The song stops. You do not. You start singing the next song on the album. But the radio station is not *playing* the album. All stare openly. You get car-sick to distract them.

Very Groovy

2. You are talking to someone very groovy in the cafeteria who has sat down at your table because all the other seats were taken. You flutter your eyelashes for emphasis. One of them falls into your creamed corn.

3. You are walking down a crowded street. You see someone you know. You gather up your courage and call their name loudly. They turn around. So does everyone else. You have never seen *any* of those people before in your life.

4. You are sitting in a darkened movie theater. You are watching a movie starring your fave. You do not scream. But you do wriggle and gasp. You wriggle (and gasp) so much you fall on the floor. As you get up, you see who is sitting across the aisle. It is that boy. The only person you have ever seen who is almost as cute as Paul. And he has noticed you at last.

Missing Purse

5. You drive home and get out of the car. You get out of the car, and put your purse on top of the car while you lock the car. You remember you forgot something. You unlock the car and drive off. Later you miss your purse, while wondering why people are pointing.

6. You are cooking dinner for some of your friends. You are fixing spaghetti. The sauce is bubbling and ready. You keep testing the spaggers (that's what they say in England) (when they've been sick) until it's done just perfect. You place a strainer in the sink. You start to pour the spaggers into same. You miss.

7. You park in a lot where there is an attendant. You go away for a few hours. You come back. You realize you do not have any money left. You begin praying you are better looking than you think you are. Either that or that he needs glasses.

8. You meet someone you have always put up a front in front of (huh?) and acted very sophisticated and grown up. You are in the process of mailing a huge box to the Monkees.

9. You call someone on the phone to find out if he is home. You plan to hang up the moment he answers. You hear his voice. Your arm will not work.

10. You find a bumper sticker (un-used) fluttering about the sidewalk. You pick it up. You can't make out what it says, but it is very attractive. You place it on your bumper. Two months later someone tells you it is a dirty word in a foreign language.

11. You are on the way to a party. It isn't far so you are walking. The streets are icy. You fall down. You get up. You find you have completely split your new tight pants. Later on, your hostess almost succeeds in making you take your coat off.

Good Fairy

12. You go to another party. You heard it was a costume party so you dress like The Good Fairy. You heard wrong.

13. You dive into a crowded swimming pool. You come up for air. Everyone's mouth falls open. You hurriedly check to see that you have not lost half of your bathing suit. You find you have only lost *half* of half of your bathing suit. But you do not sigh with relief. Not for years.

14. You go to a rock and roll concert. Many times in the past you have gotten backstage on phony passes. This time you have a real pass (never mind what you had to do to get it). They will not let you backstage.

15. Your girlfriend is starting to put on a lot of weight. In fact, she is fat. You never mention this. One night you are talking to her at a dance. She asks you why boys never ask her to dance. You tell her. (Whoops.)

Get Smart

16. You meet a member of a rock and roll group you have never heard of. He rather likes you. You think you are smart and don't like him in return because no one has ever heard of his group. He later joins one of the five most famous groups in the country.

17. You go to a slumber party. All of you make buttons with the names of boys you like (who, in most cases, do not like you) and wear them. (The buttons, not the boys.) You forget to take yours off the next day at school. You-know-who is in your American Lit class.

18. You are riding on a bus. Everyone is sour and silent. You think of something funny that once happened. You start laughing. You try to stop. You fail.

Hmmmm.

Hmmmm. Out of room. Would you believe eighteen ways to feel like a moron? Don't worry, I'll print the rest of them soon. By the way, Sheila swears all these things happened to her. In that case, I don't blame her for swearing.

SHAKIN' HER FEATHERS

MARTHA TOOK TIME OUT after this show to interview the Vandellas.

KRLA ARCHIVES

HAPPINESS IS.......
THE TURTLES

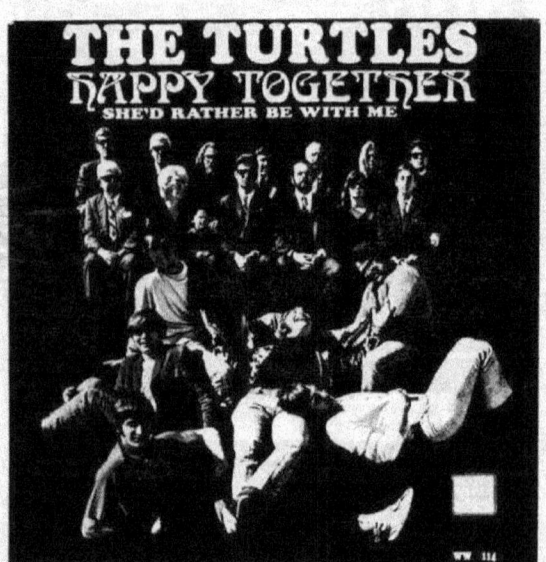

another smash single,

"She'd Rather Be With Me"

Now available at:

MONTGOMERY WARD DEPARTMENT STORES

KRLA ARCHIVES

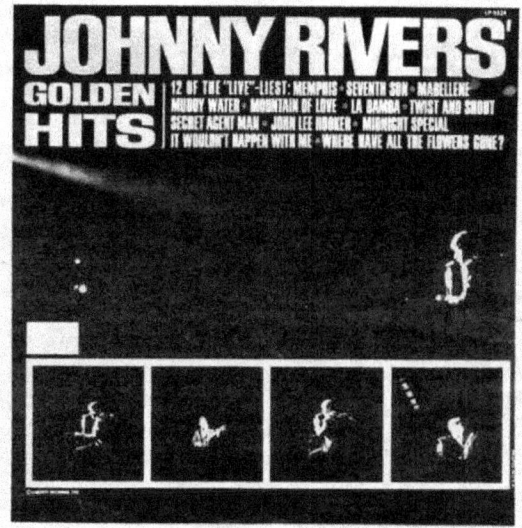

AN URGENT SOUND . . .

. . . FULL OF FEELING

 IN THE RECORD DEPARTMENT

KRLA ARCHIVES

please send me BEAT

26 issues only

$3 per year

Mail to: **BEAT Publications**
9121 Sunset Blvd.
Los Angeles, California 90069

☐ New Subscription
☐ Renewal (please enclose mailing label from your last BEAT)
I want BEAT for ☐ 1 year at $3.00 or ☐ 2 years at $5.00
I enclose ☐ cash ☐ check ☐ money order
Outside U.S. - $9 per year

* Please print your name and address.

Name_____

Street_____

City_____

State_____ Zip_____

National Top 20 Singles
As Compiled By

1. I GOT RHYTHM — THE HAPPENINGS
2. RESPECT — ARETHA FRANKLIN
3. GROOVIN' — YOUNG RASCALS
4. RELEASE ME — ENGELBERT HUMPERDINCK
5. THE HAPPENING — THE SUPREMES
7. SWEET SOUL MUSIC — ARTHUR CONLEY
8. SOMEBODY TO LOVE — JEFFERSON AIRPLANE
10. HIM OR ME — WHAT'S IT GONNA BE — PAUL REVERE AND THE RAIDERS
11. MIRAGE — TOMMY JAMES AND THE SHONDELLS
12. HERE COMES MY BABY — THE TREMELOES
13. SHE'D RATHER BE WITH ME — THE TURTLES
14. HAPPY JACK — THE WHO
15. I WAS KAISER BILL'S BATMAN — WHISTLING JACK SMITH
16. ALL I NEED — THE TEMPTATIONS
17. DON'T YOU CARE — THE BUCKINGHAMS
18. SIX O'CLOCK — LOVIN' SPOONFUL
19. CLOSE YOUR EYES — PEACHES AND HERB
20. SUNDAY WILL NEVER BE THE SAME — SPANKY AND OUR GANG

CLASSIFIED

FOR SALE

FREE LIST OF GROOVY POSTERS — SEPER CO., 5273 Tendilla, Woodland Hills, Calif. 91364

1961 FALCON. $250. (213) 443-6392. Evenings.

GIANT CRAB glowing red bumper stickers, 25 cents each or 5 for $1.00 — Giant Crab Sticker, 448 W. Las Tunas, San Gabriel, California 91776.

GROUPS — Posters made of your group. Lowest prices. This may be just what you need to make it big. (Girls: cut this out and show it to *that* guy). Send name and address plus 5c stamp to: INNOVATION ARTISTS, 246 Cayuga, Elmhurst, Illinois 60126.

WANTED

WANTED: BEATLE INFORMATION, ARTICLES & PICTURES David Royce, 21 Green Street, Monson, Massachusetts 01057.

WANTED — MOD MALE PEN PAL. 15-18. Marcia Thomas, 603 Whitfield Drive, Natchitoches, Louisiana

WANTED: WRITERS for a zany HOLLIES mag. Write: Hollies, 2212 Reedie Drive, Silver Springs, Maryland.

FORMING ROCK BAND. 365-7223. (Granada Hills, Calif.)

FAN CLUBS

THE ROBBS NATIONAL FAN CLUB
Write: P. O. Box 350
Beverly Hills, California 90213

PETER HAMILTON FAN CLUB Send $1.00 to P.O. Box 237, Horsham, Pennsylvania 19044.

INSTRUCTION

SLEEP-LEARNING, Self-hypnosis. Details, strange catalog free! Auto suggestion, Box 24-BT, Olympia, Washington

REACH COSMIC AWARENESS without drugs — help save mankind from destruction. Write for free booklet. "Cosmic Awareness Speaks," Organization of Awareness, Box 115-E, Olympia, Washington.

PEN PALS

TWO MOD, psychedelic, zany female pen-pals, Age 16-21. Pat Untied, 120 Green St., and Bob Michel, RT. Box 74, Zanesville, Ohio.

Raider Rooters Rite! Lee, 4884 Arrowhead, Orchard Lake, Michigan.

WE KNOW! If you want to know, write to: Gina and Nikki, 3190 Simms St., Denver, Col.

BIRTHDAYS

LORINA GALE WALTERS

HAPPY LATE BIRTHDAY COOKIE

HAPPY BIRTHDAY, LYDIA! Love, The Beau Gentrys and Jana and Kathy.

HAPPY BIRTHDAY — JAY COY EGO AMO TE. — JoAnn.

Happy Birthday Paul McCartney!!!! June 18 — Love, Jill Workman

HAPPY BIRTHDAY, SARAH LINDSAY!!!

HAPPY BIRTHDAY to Dee from the Robbs Fan Club, San Jose.

Judy — HAPPY BIRTHDAY! Butch & Charlie

Judy — HAPPY BIRTHDAY! Younkins & Anarchy

PAUL . . . Happy 25th! . . . Sally

HAPPY BIRTHDAY MC COOBY Luv Debbie

PERSONALS

PASSION SUNDAE
PASSION SUNDAE
PASSION SUNDAE
PASSION SUNDAE
PASSION SUNDAE

CHARLOTTE LOVES PAUL

HELLO, HELLO SOUPBONES!!!!

The Liverpool Five *Live!*

PAUL McCARTNEY is *outasite!* — Cindy

Cindy Morris loves Bill Evans

BEATLES! We love you truly... "McCartney LIVES!!!!"

"I LOVE PAUL!!!" *(Lorelle Strikes Again)*

BEATLES RULE, YOU FOOLS!!

To The Woods — May 19 — I stood, stared... enjoyed... Thanks.

PETER TORK . . . JE T'AIME SHARON

The Pack Grooves!!!!!

Teresa — Candy — Linda — Debbie — Saundra — Vevay

I love you Bob Duncan

"ELGIN MARBLE will take over" W.P. Rule

"THE DIFFERENCE" have SOUL!

ANDY — LOVE TO YOU, KAREN

"Super-fantastic are those of ELGIN MARBLE fame"

CLING EASTWOOD You're outasite!!!

Otto Jaks loves Michelle Jaynes

WAYNE...you're OUTASITE!!

CAP HIGH RULES!

Ron Taylor Rules Forever... Pam

KAREN CROFT: Here's looking at you!!?! — GARY

SUE HUNTER LOVES MARK LINDSAY!!

Who is Danzwick?

I LOVE CASS!

GEORGE, JOHN, PAUL and RINGO. Lucky boys! I arrive in London July 5. Expecting to meet you. Stay healthy, happy & home............Love, Leslie (Pres., Chapter 262, BEATLES U.S.A. Limited) P.S. — Happy Birthday to Paul from me.

BRUCE ROBB — Remember Morton West? Luv, SHARON

ATTENTION! Gale, Pam, Terri, Debbie, Joyce, Linda — August Forth!!! Sarah

"ROCKIN' ROBERT of Santa Fe Turns Me On!!!!!" — Loretta of Wilmington

cindy + scott GROOVY!

Yo sheeni hundt!

Ron — Cherish is the word — The Sunshine Girl

"BEATLE-IN" — June 10th — La Jolla!!

I love you Steve Wells

I LOVE YOU BUDDY GREEN — SANDY STERLING

Joe, Debbie, Sharon, Cindy, "Scrufty" — RENNY

After this issue, *BEAT* will no longer accept anything but PERSONAL MESSAGES in the classified section. (We will continue running those classifieds which are already paid in the for sale, wanted, fan clubs, instruction and pen pals sections). Only messages (including Happy Birthdays) will be accepted. We will print names but will not print addresses or telephone numbers.

BEAT has a new address:

**CLASSIFIED
BEAT PUBLICATIONS
9121 Sunset Blvd.
Los Angeles, California 90069**

Prices are cheap! Only 10c a word for personal messages (from you to someone else without an item for sale, trade, promotion, etc. involved).

DEADLINE FOR NEXT ISSUE: JUNE 7

KRLA ARCHIVES

Tax Collectors Chase Beatles

KRLA *Edition* BEAT

JULY 1, 1967

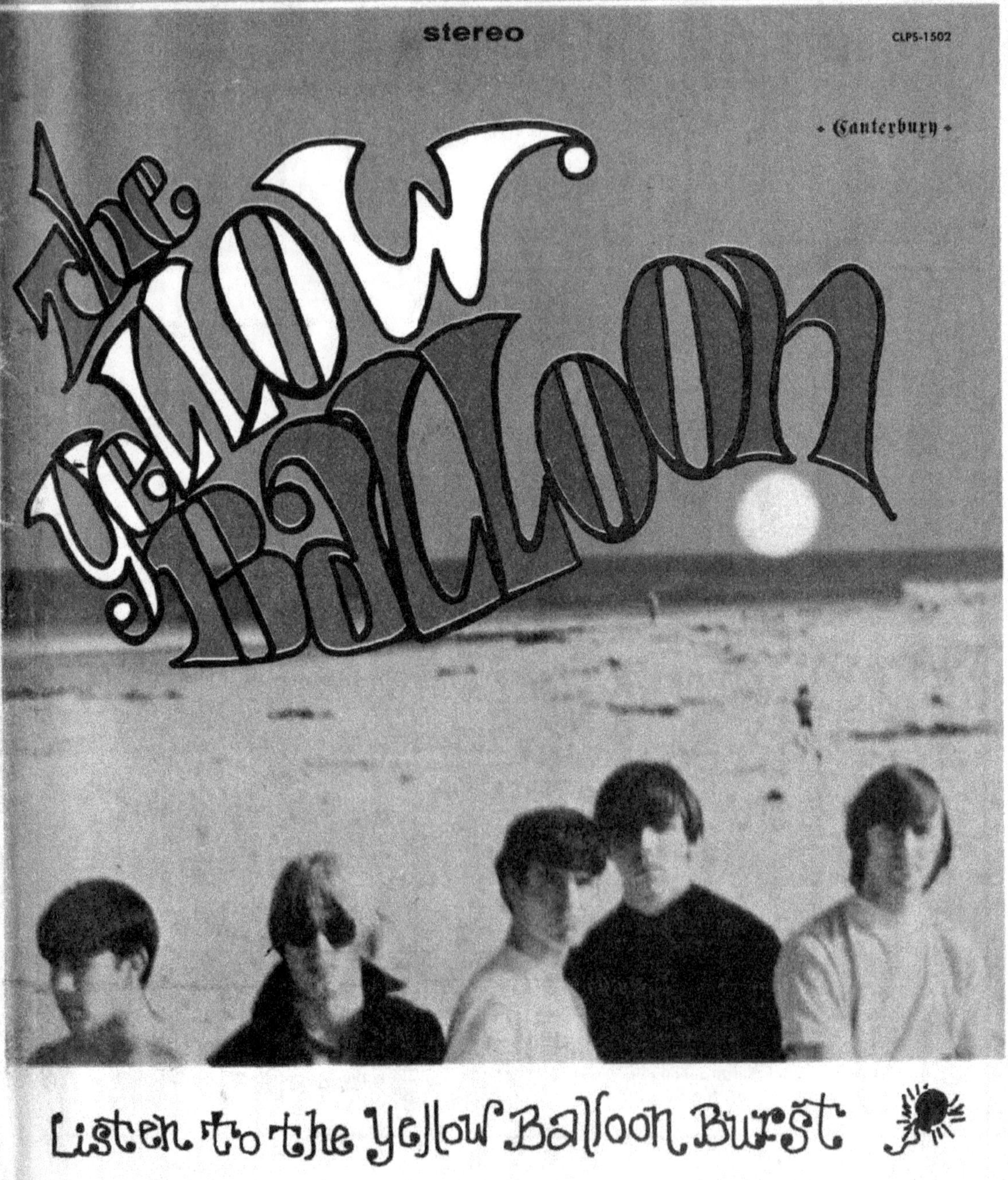

stereo

·Canterbury·

CLPS-1502

The Yellow Balloon

Listen to the Yellow Balloon Burst

KRLA ARCHIVES

KRLA BEAT

Volume 3, Number 8   July 1, 1967

THE CROWDS GATHERED IN SURREY, ENGLAND to get a glimpse of Beatle John Lennon's newly decorated Rolls Royce. John may like it but the Rolls Royce people are furious!

Beatles Face Tax Trouble In Italy

ROME—Tax collectors in Italy are having their problems collecting back taxes from Elizabeth Taylor, Richard Burton, the Beatles, and ballet dancers, Rudolph Nureyev and Dame Margot Fonteyn.

But according to finance minister Luigi Preti, the Beatles appear to be the worst offenders. Preti said the pop quartet earned about $90,000 for eight performances on a 1965 Italian tour and have not even filed a tax return. Under Italo-British convention, the finance chief added, artists are supposed to pay taxes to the countries where they earn money.

The Burton's, he conceded, may have a legitimate excuse for their tax arrears. They never signed a contract with the company which produced "The Taming of the Shrew," in Italy last year (although they were guaranteed $50,000 a piece for it) and it seems they haven't been paid yet.

LONDON—John Lennon has just had his $16,800 Rolls-Royce redone in Beatle colors (pictured above), causing a considerable stir at the famous car maker's London headquarters where muted grays and sedate blacks are the rule.

The new paint job features a yellow background with clusters of flowers with leaves and scrollwork painted in brilliantly constrasting hues rather like a gypsy caravan.

WASHINGTON, D.C.—No, it's not a ballroom; it's the National Cathedral where nearly 3,000 persons attended the first mass musical be-in. The Vagabonds provided the music and the churchgoers danced in the aisles. After two hours of uninhibited dancing, the bell tolled to signal the beginning of church services.

MONKEE MANIA KICKS OFF BEFORE LONDON ARRIVAL

The Monkees' five London concerts were a fabulous success.

Every seat at Wembley Pool concert hall was sold out. The Monkees arrived about a week before their concerts were scheduled to a London primed to an excitement pitch by stories and Monkee promotions in the local newspapers and magazines. Enthusiastic fans were overjoyed that Mike Nesmith was completely recovered from his tonsillectomy and was able to perform with the group.

Reports filtering back from London, claim that the Monkees' London Hotel was exasperated with the chaos generated by the Monkee visit, even before the fab foursome had arrived in Britain. Reporters and fanatical fans tried every way conceivable to stow away in the Monkees' rooms, grab souvenirs of Monkee possessions and give their idols gifts or pay them visits. The effect was very disrupting to the hotel staff and hotel routine in general. Other guests at the hotel had varying reactions to the excited frenzy created by the Monkee visit, but many reportedly were amused by it all.

The Monkees' busy schedule roars into full gear when they return to the U.S. to begin a 31-date concert tour of this country starting in Atlanta, Georgia on July 7 and closing in Spokane, Washington on August 27. The tour, under the direction of Dick Clark Productions is expected to gross about $2,250,000 by filling all of the 386,000 seats involved in all the concert dates. The appearances at New York's Forest Hills Tennis Stadium, the only three-day engagement on the trip, are expected to bring in over $307,000 alone. See page 5 for the complete Monkees' summer tour schedule.

HONOR FOLLOWS SHAME FOR RAY

A smiling Ray Charles heard Los Angeles City Councilman Thomas Bradley officially proclaim June 8 "Ray Charles Day" in recognition of the singers "outstanding contributions to civic affairs, the musical arts, commerce and many other worthwhile causes." Ray was beaming with the honors bestowed on him in the hugh marble-vaulted council chamber. But just over a year and a half ago, Ray was given harsher treatment by officials elsewhere. He was arrested for possession of illegal drugs as he stepped from his plane on a return trip from Canada.

Mrs. Charles looked on proudly at City Hall as the Council took up its first order of business, honoring Ray as "a fine and wonderful human being." He was awarded a scroll citing his achievement of "the highest rank in the entertainment industry." It was noted that he has received seven gold albums and 12 gold singles, each representing one million dollars in sales plus six grammies from the National Association of Recording Arts and Sciences. The Council quoted another famous entertainer, Frank Sinatra, in praise of Ray, "Ray Charles is the only true genious in music today."

Photographers, reporters and TV cameramen heard Ray thank the Council for the honors. Asked what he would do on "his day" Ray answered, "I've got to get back to the office and get to work. I've got to get busy—just like the Councilmen."

KRLA ARCHIVES

LETTERS TO THE EDITOR

MIND AND SENSES FREE OF CHARGE

Dear *BEAT*:

It has been said that with the pill you can see things that ordinarily cannot be seen. Why not use your mind and senses that God gave you free of charge?

For if you use your mind and close your eyes, you can see colors that would have never been thought of in a million years and use your mind and open your eyes and you can see as far as the universe spreads.

Use your mind and your ears and if you wish you can hear the insects talk or use your mind and your taste buds and you can be eating bread and drinking water and it can taste like a three course dinner prepared by the finest chefs.

Use your mind and touch and touch the oceans' waters and you can feel its bottom or again use your mind and your nose and you can take the worst smelling substance and make it smell like the finest cologne or after-shave.

I have tried both, the pill and the mind and senses, and the pill doesn't even compare.

Who needs the pill when you've got your senses given to you by God free of charge?

Name Withheld

WHAT GIVES WITH THREE SUPREMES??

Dear *BEAT*:

Have you ever heard of the Supremes? I admit yours is the only publication I know of that at least has their name mentioned every issue. But how about a two page spread on them? Maybe even have them on the cover!

These girls don't get one-tenth of what they should get in teen mags. What more do they have to do to get to be featured in your great newspaper?

Please, let's have a bit and well-deserved article on the Supremes. How about it?

Don Kornfeind

We'd love to do a huge spread on the Supremes. Now if you can just convince the Supremes...
The Editor

THIS AND MUCH MORE

In all walks of life
In the times of today
Our youth needs a voice
To define what we say.

To express our beliefs
Come what may
Sympathize with the griefs
Of the youth of today.

To view both sides
Free of opinions
Shedding new light
On new formed decisions.

Contributing to teens throughout the lands
Enabling no one to become elite
For this and much more
I send thanks to The BEAT.

— C.O.

AN ADULT TALKS OUT

Dear *BEAT*:

May I, an adult, applaud your fine work on the best musical newspaper going? You see, I'm a music nut. I want to know everything possible about my fave raves and your paper keeps me informed. I can say, at the age of 35 that the Beatles are the best and always will be! The Stones come second in my record collection.

Being a subscriber to *BEAT*, I wish to thank you for not being Monkee crazy! All the other magazines, even the British publications, have deserted our fabulous Beatles. You can not pick up a magazine on the newsstands without having a Monkee staring at you. *BEAT* is at least fair in giving equal coverage to all artists.

After receiving only five or six copies of *BEAT*, I can truthfully say that I can hardly wait for my subscription to end so that I can renew! Thanks again and again for such a great paper and please never desert the Beatles. Long may they reign!

Mrs. Tony Bondad

REPAYING KINDNESS

Dear *BEAT*:

I wish you would please print the following open letter to two young hitchhikers I delivered at a discount mart only because it was hot and I hate to see people broil.

Dear Boys:

I hope you enjoyed the ride and spent the $4 well. Money should not be wasted, especially if it isn't yours. And don't forget: hitchhiking is illegal in California.

The girl whose brother plays baseball

IN PASSING

Dear *BEAT*:

I'd like to say in passing (through the generation gap) that I am aging—but usually on the side of the groovy.

Sometimes, though, it seems as if the kids think their parents invented war and *they* invented paisley...

Lucia Morrison

Beat Publications, Inc.

Executive Editor .... Cecil I. Tuck
Publisher .... Gayle Tuck
Editor .... Louise Criscione

Staff Writers
Carol Deck Bobby Farrow
Ron Koslow Shirley Poston
Rochelle Reed

Contributing Writers
Tony Barrow Sue Barry
Lawrence Charles Eden
Bob Levinson Jamie McCluskey, III

Photographers
Chuck Boyd Dwight Carter
Howard L. Bingham

Advertising
Dick Jacobson Jerry Lass
Dick Stricklin

Business Manager .... Judy Felice
Subscriptions .... Nancy Arena

Distribution
Miller Freeman Publications
500 Howard Street, San Francisco, Calif.
The BEAT is published bi-weekly by BEAT Publications, Inc., editorial and advertising offices at 9121 Sunset Blvd., Hollywood, California 90069. U.S. bureaus in Hollywood, San Francisco, New York, Chicago and Nashville; overseas correspondents in London, Liverpool and Manchester, England. Sale price 25 cents. Subscription price: U.S. and possessions, $5 per year; Canada and foreign rates, $9 per year. Second class postage prepaid at Los Angeles, California.

FEAR OF CENSORSHIP

Dear *BEAT*:

Regarding the censoring of records for "pornographic content," I want to voice my fear of those who would protect me from what they don't wish to see. The danger is that the fear of a phrase can silence a song and that too easily any deviation is seen as a danger.

As an example of what fear can do, look at my pen pal in East Germany. We are both great fans of any rock music and I asked him if I could send him a tape of some albums. He wrote that his government said nein, that "it is a danger for our life, it is a danger for the youth and people of the German Democratic Republic..."

He later added that "they say these things from the West will make us crazy, lazy, and bad people. They say the West tries to kill us in that way. But the people, especially our youth, found thousands of ways to get those unallowed things from the Free World..." We are using one of these ways and regularly exchange tapes.

But the opposition isn't the only home for professional little old ladies. Ever hear the real "Bend It" versus the one that gets air play in the Land of the Free? 'Nuff said.

Name Withheld

OUTASITE!

Dear *BEAT*:

First of all I want to tell you that *The BEAT* is outasite! This is no ordinary "praise" letter but an honest opinion. Your letter department is tuff but the best (by far) articles are "In People Are Talking About" and the national top 100. Keep them!

There is only one complaint that I have. That is the fact that the Mamas and Papas are hardly mentioned except for occasionally in the fad and fashion columns. Except for that, *The BEAT* is perfect in every way. Thanks for such a groovy newspaper.

Greg Burt

CLOSING THE GAP

Dear *BEAT*:

Regarding Ron Koslow's "Notes From The Underground" column which ran several issues ago. I must take exception to Mr. Koslow's column and the opinions expressed in it ("Where Do We Stand?"). His stand that the "generation gap" should be retained and indeed intensified is, I believe, a rather immature stand.

I, as he, am in the communications field (as a commercial writer in broadcasting, sometime poetess and multi-linguist). This is my chosen field because I believe there is a definite lack of communication throughout the world today.

Admittedly, there is a "generation gap" in our country. But is it wise to widen this "gap" through the open rebellion by the young people against their elders which we are experiencing day in and day out all over the nation? Rather, shouldn't we try to *close* the gap? Through communications, try to understand the positions of each other? (I might mention that I am by no means a member of the "older generation," although at 22 I doubt that I can be classified as a "teeny-bopper" either!)

Mr. Koslow expressed the opinion that music, and especially the currently popular music, should serve as a common bond to solidify the young people in their "battle" against their elders. I couldn't agree more that music should (and does) serve as such a common bond. Unification is a good thing. It creates strength and pride. But we must remember that strength without understanding is useless and pride without humility is self-defeating.

And why should music be used for or against someone or something? Music is a precious thing—all types of music, from the new psychedelic variety to the most classical of grand opera—and it is probably the most wonderful form of communication in the world.

Instead of fighting, rebelling against authority, let's try to learn from our elders' mistakes and from their experience-gained wisdom. We'll be taking their place soon enough and then we will, as they seem to be doing now, be able to impose our values on our youth.

Granted, our parents don't always act as maturely as we would expect and like them to act; nor do they always use good judgment and common sense. But how can we of the so-called "younger generation" ever expect to make any headway in the world if we continue to lash out, like spoiled five-year-old brats, throwing tantrums, hitting our heads against brick walls and hurting our own cause?

Communication is the key to understanding and compromise is the gateway to solidarity... whether in music, language, the arts or any human endeavor.

Let's grow up, stop throwing fits and begin to act like the adults we would have our elders consider us. When we do, I'm sure we'll be amazed at just how much progress can be made in *closing* this unnecessary "generation gap."

Brooke-Alison Simons

KRLA ARCHIVES

ON THE BEAT
BY LOUISE CRISCIONE

Nice week for news...**The Turtles** returned from a successful European tour and immediately hit the recording studios to cut a follow-up to "She'd Rather Be With Me" as well as several tracks for their next album...**Nancy Wilson** performed for President Johnson in New York while **Ray Charles** was honored in Los Angeles at a special "Ray Charles Day"...A determined fan of Batman and Robin was booked by police for allegedly stealing photos of his television heroes... Trigg Kelly (Trigg line of fashions) said in New York: "England has completely sabotaged the clean look of American youth. Look on the streets. You can't tell the difference half of the time between the long-haired boys and girls. In fact, many of the girls look more masculine than the boys."

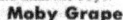

...RAY CHARLES

Moby Grape
Columbia Records must be spending an unbelievable amount of money on the **Moby Grape**. They're releasing five singles simultaneously as well as an album by the Grape. Their press kits arrived in red velvet boxes and they recently flew members of the press to San Francisco for a Moby Grape happening at the Avalon Ballroom.

It was really quite a scene at the Avalon. Hippies mingled with the suit and tie attired Columbia men, flowers were showered down upon the crowd, bottles of "Grape" were given to all the people entering the Ballroom and balloons (grape colored, of course) floated around the room and exploded under dancing feet.

Despite his name, **Engelbert Humperdinck** seems to be doing well. His "Release Me" has already been a hit on both sides of the Atlantic and the gentleman himself is set to make a visit Stateside in September. He is tentatively set for an appearance on "Ed Sullivan," a cross country concert tour, and perhaps a big-money Hollywood movie.

Surprise Harum
The **Procol Harum**, whose "Whiter Shade Of Pale" looks like a huge hit over here, is a British group—not an American soul singer...if you can believe that.

Personal to **Rascals** Felix Cavaliere and Gene Cornish—your new hair styles are outasite!!!

The "I Spy" cast and crew will not be filming in Russia after all. Said Sheldon Leonard, executive producer of the show: "I had discussed it with the cultural attache at the UN who supported my belief. But after 48 hours there I decided it would be ridiculous to try because of the logistics." So, they'll head for Scotland and England instead.

QUESTIONS OF THE WEEK: Is it true that a new member of a well-known rock group went the plastic surgery route so he'd look more like a teen idol?...Which record company was totally embarrassed by the departure of Aretha Franklin to Atlantic and her subsequent "Respect"?...Will the Vanilla Fudge be the next big group?...Who is trying to get in on the action by releasing Mugwumps oldies?...Which group found a sudden decrease of fan mail to the teen publications when word came out they were married?

The **Tremeloes** are supposedly set for an extensive tour of the U.S. during the summer but surprisingly enough their record company doesn't even have the dates, much less the cities. So...

Motherless Brothers??
Ole Hoss Cartwright can be a very funny man. When the Smothers Brothers dumped "Bonanza" off the top of the ratings, panic struck NBC but Hoss (Dan Blocker) remained cool. Just told his producer: "Let's change the name of our show to 'The Motherless Brothers!" Becoming serious, Dan said of the Smothers competition: "It's a pretty good little show. I've seen it and I like them. I think there's room for two shows in a time slot. "Undoubtedly neither CBS nor NBC would agree with Dan.

The great **Righteous Brothers**, Bobby Hatfield and Bill Medley, may or may not be making a couple of films for MGM—the answer you get depends on who is telling the story. They are, however, definitely set to appear at O'Keefe Centre in Toronto July 31-August 5.

...THE RIGHTEOUS TWO

'THE HIPPIE MOVEMENT'

The Word Is Out. The Hippies Are Coming.

This is the cry that authorities are echoing across the country. New York, San Francisco, Los Angeles and other gathering points are experiencing a movement which is growing stronger by the day.

Pictured above are members of The Fraternity of Man who use as their headquarters a mansion in the hills above Los Angeles. Although they are a small group and haven't established a nationwide following, they are in hopes of attracting other like groups to their fold.

Los Angeles has had little problem with gatherings although several love-ins have been staged recently. Primarily the only things disrupting order have been traffic jams and parking violations in the areas surrounding the gatherings.

There is no real settlement of the Haight-Ashbury type and the focal point of interest has remained the Sunset Strip.

New York Scene
A gathering in Tompkins Square Park in New York City of 200 participants turned into a fracas when park attendants informed the group that they were in a forbidden area of the park. The problem apparently began when the music-making hippies refused to leave.

Police were summoned, the hippies locked arms to form a human barricade and the spectators swarmed around them.

Bottles were thrown by the spectators at both the hippies and the policemen. A reported violence ensued. As the injured hippies were loaded into the paddy wagons the only comments were, "but officer, we love you . . ." When the Police Commissioner arrived he reportedly made a few hand signals and the policemen withdrew.

Violence Unnecessary
When asked about the situation, Mayor Lindsay gave the impression that he felt the violence might well have been avoided.

A few days later, another group was staging "peace" skits when one girl was thrown to the ground by either a spectator or participant and some of her clothing was removed. This time, however, order was restored without further incident.

San Francisco officials expect over 100,000 visitors seeking hippie haunts to invade their city this summer. The small area of Haight-Ashbury (15 blocks) is busy readying itself but facilities are few.

The recent incidents involving authorities there have been limited to the breaking up of street dances which have jammed traffic and provoked the residents of the area to slash tires on police cars and other vehicles.

The regular residents of Haight-Ashbury are voicing some concern about the sincerity of the summer visitors. Even the police admit that in the past the society of the area has been love-oriented. But, the new groups coming in are in many cases a different sort, they report.

Some hippies, however, are making plans to welcome the newcomers and have set up free hostels in addition to trying to locate a circus tent for a free kitchen.

The Diggers (who apparently derived their name from the seventeenth century farmers who raised food for the poor) and The Council for the Summer of Love are doing most of the work with help from their followers.

Nationwide
Although most of the publicity given to the probable migration has centered around New York, San Francisco and Los Angeles, other cities are quietly watching the silent invasion of visitors who plan their own type of summer fun.

There are reports from across the country that there is scarcely an area left untouched by the hippie influence and whether the followers number few or many, their devotion to their causes is spreading and their groups are growing in number.

The Hippies are coming. Will the scene be beautiful or . . . ?

THE **ROBBS**
"Rapid Transit"
"Cynthia Loves"
Mercury Records
#72678

ART INSTITUTE
OF PITTSBURGH
47th Yr. Coed. 18 & 24 mo. Diploma Course. Commercial Art, Fashion Art, Interior Design. Begin. & Adv. Vet. Appd. Dorm facilities. College referrals for degrees. Free illus. brochure.
Earl B. Wheeler, Director
635 Smithfield St.
Pittsburgh, Pa. 15222

"The Standel Sound"

"The Nitty Gritty Dirt Band"
Professional musicians throughout the world choose the "Standel Sound," the accepted standard for professional musicians who demand professional performance. (Dept. B)

A. P.A. Speaker Column Amplifier
B. P.A. Master Control with Reverb
C. Imperial Line Amplifier — Solid State, Dual Channel

Standel
Solid State Music Systems
4918 DOUBLE DRIVE • EL MONTE, CALIF. 91731

KRLA ARCHIVES

Beatle Digs Opera Style

Cathy Berberian had no trouble at all understanding Beatle Paul McCartney when they met in England. "I used to think that anyone who was doing anything weird was weird," said Paul. "I suddenly realized that anyone doing anything weird wasn't weird at all, and it was the people that were saying they were weird that were weird."

Paul's unintelligible remark was in way of praise for fellow singer, Massachusetts-born Cathy. It all began when Cathy started singing along with her 13-year-old daughter's Beatle records. The versatile songstress whose expressive voice ranges three octaves from contralto to coloratura started opening her European performances with the Beatles—in bel canto. She even cut an album of 12 Beatles' songs arranged in opera style called "Revolution." The album cover is a careful takeoff of the Beatles' "Revolver" cover design.

CARNABY STREET DIES

Reports from fashion houses across the United States seem to clearly indicate that the Carnaby Street Mod clothing style is "out." Sales have decreased greatly and unsold inventories herald the fact that Mod is dead. And what is taking its place?

Beau Brummell Mod—fancy, dapper, very elegant and somewhat expensive. This will include patent leather spats which are as yet unavailable and much sought after in many large markets, particularly Los Angeles.

The Western Look—currently undergoing a definite promotional upsurge in London. It's the "ranch look"—cowboy boots, cowboy hat and shirt and Levis. The shirt will tend to be "dress" rather than "work" style, meaning pearl buttons and a traditional V-yolk front. Knee length sheepherder jackets will top it off.

The Organic Look—the newest line just now readying itself for a big sprint. "Organic" is increasingly being used to describe the pseudo-hippie, basic natural, "from the earth" look . . . moccasins sans socks, earth-tone "cords" (brown or green), wide belt with brass studs, "cord" shirt with open chest.

As printed in Young American Report

NEW TEEN TV SPECIAL

American Bandstand's Dick Clark is scheduled to produce an hour long television special in the near future titled "The California Scene."

The show will star Paul Revere & The Raiders and several other acts.

Did You Know?

"Beautiful" is the top word on the hippie list. It's an expression of ultimate satisfaction (beautiful man) . . . really not too well accepted in the non-hippie teen crowd.

Dying—"Boss" . . . still frequently being heard in specific parts of the country but slowly being replaced by "bitchin'" (meaning "great" or "fantastic") and groovy.

Dead—"neat," "neato," etc.
Compiled by Young American Report

DON AND THE GOODTIMES CAUGHT IN A NEAR-RIOT

PORTLAND—A record-setting crowd converged on the Coliseum here to turn a concert-dance headlining Don & The Goodtimes into a near-riot, according to eye-witness reports.

Additional police were called out to keep the audience seated and, at one point, to prevent an enthusiastic army of fans from dragging Li'l Don Gallucci off the stage and into their arms.

Closest Squeek

It was Li'l Don's closest squeek since an April adventure in Cincinnati, Ohio, during the Dick Clark "Action" Caravan, when fans rushed him onstage and he sustained a cut lip.

This was the Goodtimes first appearance in Portland since release of the group's current hit, "I Could Be So Good To You." The record has been Number One here for several weeks, a position it has occupied at one or another time throughout the Pacific Northwest region.

The Portland appearance also marked the debut of the newest Goodtime, Joey Newman, who fills the lead guitar spot once held down by Charlie Coe. (Coe has since joined Paul Revere & The Raiders.)

Joey, 19, is blond-haired, blue-eyed, stands 5'11", and is the near-perfect lookalike of Peter (Herman) Noone. He's a Seattle, Wash., native and played with local bands before enlisting with the Goodtimes.

The Goodtimes head out on another tour starting August 4, under the auspices of Dick Clark, who first discovered the Goodtimes and made them regulars on "Where The Action Is." It takes the Goodtimes from Vancouver, B.C., through much of Canada and a number of states in the Midwest and South.

Capacity Crowd

More than 2,000 fans jammed into the Portland Coliseum to see and hear the Goodtimes. Their show included a combination of hits and originals by Buzz Overman, highlighted by "Super Medley," a collection of hits by the Beatles, Beach Boys, Rolling Stones, Lovin' Spoonful, and others. Buzz and Jeff Hawks took turns on the vocal lead, and Joey also had the spotlight a couple of times.

Musical numbers were separated by the bits of humor fans have come to expect, with drummer Bobby Holden heading the laugh brigade. Jeff kept chipping in with imitations of Marlon Brando, Wolfman Jack, and others.

PEOPLE ARE TALKING ABOUT the tax problems the Beatles are having in Italy and recalling their hold-up in Manila because of tax problems and that missed lunch date . . . how far Procol Harum is going to go on the rhythm 'n' blues radio stations before word comes out that they're a British "blue-eyed" group . . . the Rascals receiving an unprecedented salary for playing Brooklyn's Action City . . . the soundtrack album from the movie "Turn On, Tune In, Drop Out" and wondering what the censors are going to say about that one

. . . how long the Mamas and Papas will stick together as a group . . . the speculation that a San Francisco group which has just received national recognition will shortly lose its lead singer due to a personality clash within the group . . . the possibility that Spanky and Our Gang will emerge as one of the hottest American groups within the next six months

. . . Frankie Valli making it on the charts as both a solo and a group member and wondering if that's ever been done before

. . . how long the present day Grass Roots are going to stay that way . . . the fact that not all San Franciscans wear flowers in their hair—some have never even heard of the Avalon Ballroom . . . why "Society's Child" would get banned when "I Think We're Alone Now" wasn't touched and deciding it's not all relative . . . now that the Miracles have a new record out, Johnny Rivers has a follow-up to "The Tracks Of My Tears"

. . . the Doors being huge in L.A. but practically unknown in the rest of the country and wondering what that indicates . . . the Monkees making a poor showing at the Emmy Awards—copping the gold statues but looking and acting so immaturely that even their fans found it hard to say anything nice

. . . the reports that you'd better enjoy "Sgt. Pepper" because that's the last Beatle album you'll get . . . sleeping in the subway being better than sleeping in Golden Gate Park

. . . when or if Neil Diamond is going to make a movie and keeping fingers crossed that he is—and soon . . . the Fraternity of Man and calculating how far and how wide it will spread . . . with the Liverpool sound and the Carnaby fashions dead, it's quite probable that the West will live again . . . the Four Tops being A-Number One bad when it comes to showing up for interviews and deciding exactly where that's going to get them . . . how touchy a certain movie studio got when it appeared in print that one of their movies was about a "thug" . . . how much night is day

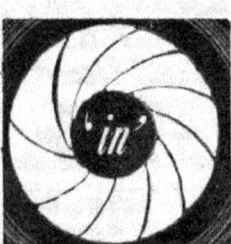

. . . Tom Jones attachment to adjectives and whether or not he will make a successful switch to movies . . . what bad timing it was for Aretha Franklin to break her elbow . . . how much interest the Hollies are paying . . . the unbelievability of a hair dresser making more money than the stars of a television show . . . the bad scene with one member of a hot rock group and what's going to happen if he doesn't return from one of his trips . . . the banana thing being an all-time hoax

. . . whether or not the Elmo & Almo idea is going to go over . . . Chiquita stickers being replaced by mod bod stickers . . . a little bit of soul making for a whole lotta hit, if you can figure that out . . . the heads that are going to roll if a certain group doesn't make it really big after all the money that's been spent . . . whether or not Brenton Wood will be able to fill Sam Cooke's shoes . . . Twiggy being in the news yesterday, out of it today and wondering if Justin is going to change his name again

. . . the New Vaudeville Band being a prime example of what happens when you rely on a fad—Barry McGuire being the other one . . . Giant sunflower trouble . . . whether or not Johnny did pay that money for the honor . . . the fact that a '67 Cadillac may not be as much of a deal as a switched-over group member obviously thought it was . . . what do you really find if you step out of your mind

. . . the Grand Canyon love-in and the fact that you can't plant exotic flowers in a natural setting . . . all the money and publicity in the world not being an absolute guarantee because you can't fool the public all of the time—though it's been done on occasion . . . whether or not Gary Lewis is going to sing "Think Pink" and follow in his dad's footsteps . . . shakin' a tail feather right past the censors

. . . Mama Cass not knowing it but she's going to be on the cover of a new national magazine . . . the latest thing being love sugar—and that's really all it is, sugar . . . how surprising it is that the Turtles haven't changed group members for the last two months . . . Nancy Sinatra getting that role after all . . . the fact that Teddy Neely has a great voice but that the group will probably never make it . . . Phoenix being one city firmly planted in the pocket of the Dave Clark Five . . . the fact that the witch may be dead after all even though the Fifth Estate is definitely alive.

KRLA ARCHIVES

across the board

FROM THE EDITOR...

The biggest news in the music world, of course, is the tremendously successful Monterey Pop Festival. Hopefully, it will become an annual event and those of you who were able to make it to this year's happening will be able to attend next year, or the next year, or...

The BEAT sent a host of photographers and reporters to Monterey and in the next issue we'll be devoting several pages to the Festival as well as exclusive interviews with many of the artists who appeared in the concerts.

The Young Rascals have topped the nation's charts with their "Groovin'." You can hardly do better than that, so we've given them a full page in this issue. We first met the Rascals about a year and a half ago and it's nice to be able to tell you that they're still the same nutty, nice guys today—in other words, for a change success has not gone to the head (only the wallet).

Another long-time favorite of ours, the Association, have finally come up with a smashing follow-up to "Cherish." Of course, it's "Windy" and it stands to be number one in the nation. That, plus the fact that we're admittedly prejudiced when it comes to the Association, prompted us to spend two days at the CBS studios while the group rehearsed and taped "The Smothers Brothers Show." Although we've given them two pages, we still only had room to print half of the unbelievable happenings which took place when six Associates joined forces with two Smothers Brothers.

While we primarily deal with recording artists, we do on occasion interview performers who specialize in other fields of entertainment. Because you've shown you dig him, we journeyed down to the set of "Star Trek" and spoke to Leonard Nimoy. A very nice man with some particularly interesting things to say, you can read his opinions and ideas on page 21.

— Louise Criscione

Making The News

HEMMINGS TO MARRY

ANKARA, TURKEY—"Woe is me" said many a female David Hemmings fan around the world last week. The reason? Another woman.

From this Turkish capitol, British actor Hemmings has announced that he and Hollywood starlet Gayle Hunnicut, a 23-year-old raven-haired beauty, will be married—just as soon as she recovers from the mumps.

The announcements came as the final wave in what might be described as a stormy courtship. The couple flew to Las Vegas in February with every intention of getting married. But they had a quarrel on the way and David (most recently starred in "Blow-Up") changed planes and headed for Turkey to film "Charge Of The Light Brigade."

But apparently he thought better of the move and last week David sent a cablegram to Gayle, asking her to come at once. And she will, she says, just as soon as she gets well.

Righteous Bros. Pack In Teens

LOS ANGELES—The Righteous Brothers opened up the prom season at Los Angeles' famed Cocoanut Grove by pulling in an audience consisting mainly of teenagers and the young Hollywood film crowd.

Backing up the duo were The Blossoms, who reportedly tore up the audience with "Dancing In The Street" and "There's A Place For Us."

WHERE THEY ARE

MONKEES
July 7, Atlanta, Ga., Braves Stadium; July 8, Jacksonville, Fla., Convention Hall; July 11, Charlotte, N.C., Coliseum; July 12, Greensboro, N.C., Coliseum; July 14-16, New York, Forest Hills Stadium; July 20, Buffalo, N.Y., Memorial Auditorium; July 21, Baltimore, Md., Memorial Auditorium; July 22, Boston, Mass. Boston Gardens; July 23, Philadelphia, Pa., Convention Hall; July 27, Rochester, N.Y., War Memorial Auditorium; July 28, Cincinnati, Ohio, Gardens; July 29, Detroit, Mich.

JEFFERSON AIRPLANE
June 17, Monterey Pop Festival; June 20-25, Fillmore Auditorium, San Francisco, Calif.

HERMAN'S HERMITS
July 21, Coliseum, Oklahoma City State Fair Grounds; Aug. 5, International Amphitheater, Chicago, Ill.

SIMON & GARFUNKEL
June 16, Monterey Pop Festival; July 21-22, Opera House, Chicago, Ill.

RIGHTEOUS BROTHERS
July 25-30, Opera House, Chicago, Ill.; September 11-17, Greek Theatre, Los Angeles.

SUPREMES
June 13-26, Cocoanut Grove, Los Angeles, Calif.; June 29-July 19, Flamingo Hotel, Las Vegas, Nev.

JOHNNY RIVERS
June 20-30, Whisky A Go Go, Hollywood, California.

DON & THE GOODTIMES
June 17-25, headlining Teenage Fair, Seattle, Washington; June 26-July 3, concerts in the Seattle area; July 3, three weeks heading a Dick Clark caravan of Stars through the Midwest.

BUCKINGHAMS
June 17, Evanston, Ill.; July 3, Leesburg, Ind.; July 4, South Bend, Ind.; July 7, Lake Schaeffer Monticello, Ind.; July 15, Lake Geneva, Wisc.; July 21, Marne, Mich.

TURTLES
June 24, Lagoon Ballroom, Salt Lake City, Utah.

PAUL REVERE & THE RAIDERS
June 17, Joplin, Mo., Memorial Hall; June 18, Topeka, Kan., Municipal Auditorium; June 19, Des Moines, Iowa, Veterans' Memorial Auditorium; June 20, Sioux City, Iowa, Municipal Auditorium; June 21, St. Joe, Mo., City Auditorium; June 23, Memphis, Tenn., Mid-South Coliseum; June 24, Jackson, Miss., Fairground Coliseum; June 25, New Orleans, La.; June 27, Columbus, Ga., Municipal Auditorium; June 28, Columbia, S.C., Township Auditorium; June 29, Atlanta, Ga., Municipal Auditorium; June 30, Winston-Salem, N.C., Memorial Coliseum; July 1, Chattanooga, Tenn., Memorial Auditorium; July 2, Huntington, W. Va., Memorial Field House; July 5-6, Atlantic City, N.J., Steele Pier,; July 8, Asbury Park, N.J., Convention Hall.

SEEDS
July 1, Covina, Calif., Carousel Theatre; July 19, Minneapolis-St. Paul, Minn.; Minneapolis, Arena.

MARY ANN MOBLEY AND NOEL HARRISON
Starring in "Half A Sixpence" for two weeks beginning July 11 at Melodyland, Anaheim, Calif.

DIONNE WARWICK
June 8-28, San Francisco, Venetian Room of the Fairmount Hotel; July 11-30, Los Angeles, Century Plaza Hotel.

KEITH
June 17, Norfolk, Va.; June 18, Greensboro, N.C.; June 19, Knoxville, Tenn.; June 20, Greenville, S.C.; June 21, Huntsville, Ala.; June 23, Indianapolis, Ind.; June 24, Charleston, W. Va.; June 26, Scranton, Pa.; June 28, Ottowa, Canada; June 30, Canton, Ohio; July 1, Dayton, Ohio; July 2, Cleveland, Ohio; July 3, Canada; July 4, Detroit, Mich.; July 5-6, Canada; July 8, Hampton Beach, N.H.; July 11, Lowell, Mass.; July 12, Old Orchard, Maine; July 13, Weirs, N.H.; July 14, Cape Cod, Mass.; July 15, Riverside, R.I.; July 16, Wallingford, Conn.

4 SEASONS
June 18, Joe Long's wedding, June 23-25, Virginia Beach, Va., The Dome; July 8, Charleston, W. Va., Civic Center; July 17, Owensmill, Md.

LESLEY GORE
Summer stock theater tour of "Half A Sixpence": June 14-24, Valley Forge, Pa.; June 27-July 2, Westbury, L.I.; July 3-8, Camden, N.J.; July 11-16, Baltimore, Md., Painter's Mill; July 18-23, Washington, Shady Grove.

TURTLES
June 15, Nashville, Tenn.; June 16, Memphis, Tenn.; June 17, Birmingham, Ala.; June 19-23, Recording; June 24, Salt Lake City, Utah, June 25, Wichita, Kansas, June 26, Sioux Falls, S.D.

ANTHONY & THE IMPERIALS
July 3, Fallsburg, N.Y., Raleigh Hotel; July 7-13, Miami Beach Fla., Eden Roc Hotel; July 19-Aug. 1, San Juan, P.R., Flamboyan Hotel; Aug. 10-Sept. 6, Las Vegas, Nev., Flamingo Hotel.

Marcia Movie?

HOLLYWOOD — Marcia Strassman, whose first single, "Flower Children," sold over 55,000 discs in Los Angeles and San Francisco alone, has been signed to a multi-picture contract with Universal Pictures. The studio is now looking for the right film script for the actress' screen debut. Marcia is currently working on her first LP.

Shows Added

The Chairman of the Board has added three more shows to his summer tour, making a total of 11 in all.

Added to Frank Sinatra's schedule were matinee performances in Pittsburgh on July 14, Chicago on July 10 and Philadelphia on July 14. It is reported that Sinatra is also considering shows in Cleveland, Detroit, and Baltimore.

Sergio Mendez and Brazil '66, Pat Henry and the Buddy Rich Orchestra are also on the bill.

KRLA ARCHIVES

BANNED, TOO CONTROVERSIAL! AND NOW IT'S A HIT!

Suzy Creamcheese Rides Again! Hear the MOTHERS!

NOW AVAILABLE AT YOUR LOCAL **Thrifty** CUT RATE DRUG STORES

EASY TO WIN PRIZES!!!

PAMELA CARPENTER uses MOD-BOD in the demure fashion for school with only a simple flower beauty mark and butterfly earring.

Don't miss this easy-to-enter, easy-to-win BEAT MOD-BOD contest! Be ahead, be original with MOD-BOD *out-of-sight body adornments* and win fabulous prizes!

Here's a *BEAT* contest that's simple and fun. You can let your imagination run wild. Make up the wildest body and clothing decorations, or even decorate yourself *and your car or bike* with the almost endless variety of MOD-BOD psychedelic designs.

Look at the picture examples on this page and come up with really wild ideas. Then take a picture, either black and white or color and any size. Send it to Beat Publications, 9125 Sunset Boulevard, Los Angeles, California 90069 with your name and address before August 1, 1967.

Anyone can enter. There are no restrictions... boys or girls may enter, there is no age limit. MOD-BODs are printed in 5 wild fluorescent colors on DuPont Mylar with a special adhesive that will not harm the skin. MOD-BODs are waterproof and are even reusable.

Four different 8" x 10" MOD-BOD sheets with up to 60 different designs on each sheet are available at your local department or specialty stores, or you can order direct from Beat (see ad on page 12). Choose from: A. Hearts and Flowers; B. Psychedelic Buttons and Designs; C. Psychedelic Alphabets; D. Psychedelic Phreaquies.

HEARTS AND FLOWERS in 5 fluorescent colors.

AL TROOP adds crazy designs to his guitar and hand.

MORGAN BECKETT goes all out with face decoration... and you should have seen the treatment on the bikini and legs.

LOOK AT THESE FABULOUS PRIZES:

Girls **1st Prize.** 5 Band, International, Fully Transistorized Radio.

2nd Prize. Mirror-Go-Lightly. Regular and Magnifying Mirror surrounded by lights to make your make-up a snap.

3rd Prize. 25 sets of four MOD-BOD sheets.

Boys **1st Prize.** 5 Band, International, Fully Transistorized Radio.

2nd Prize. Pocket size fully transistorized radio.

3rd Revise. 25 sets of four MOD-BOD sheets.

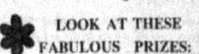

KRLA ARCHIVES

Around The  World

RAVI SHANKAR OPENS SCHOOL

LOS ANGELES — Ravi Shankar, who introduced the delicate sounds of the stringed sitar to the West, opened his first school of Indian music here. Shankar was boosted into wide recognition among pop music fans when Beatle George Harrison chose the sitar for the group's recording of "Norwegian Wood" and then went to sit literally at the feet of the Indian master for months of serious instruction in India's 3,000-year-old music form, "Raga," which means color or tint in Sanskrit. Each Raga is dominated by a single mood, designed for a specific time of day and derived from 72 basic scales.

NEW YORK BEAT

By Lionel Pinkham

Weatherwise, May of 1967 was about the worst — cold, rainy grey days. But one spot in town where the sun seemed always to be shining was at 60th and Broadway, headquarters building for Atlantic Records. That story really started nearly 20 years ago when the then Turkish Ambassador in Washington was trying to keep track of his two crazy kids who dug cool over protocol and the nearest jazz gigs to embassy receptions. With their own money, the kids cut a few jazz dates and when nobody would purchase their masters, they started their own label. Somewhere along the way they ran into Jerry Wexler, Mr. 'sweet soul music' if there ever was one, and the famed Turkish troika of Ahmet and Nessue Ertegun and Wexler took off. Beautiful people! Ahmet seems most into the group scene — The Buffalo Springfield, The Young Rascals, Sonny and Cher, The Cream, The BeeGees, etc., and an incredible new local group called Vanilla Fudge.

Holly Originals

Michael Choan's been around, previewing the first Hollies' platter for Epic. Watch out! Again, like "Stop, Stop, Stop" and "Carousel," it's a Holly original — and word from Graham Nash is that the boys will concentrate on just originals from now on.

Steve Paul's, N.Y.'s half-as-young answer to Elmer Valentine, is finally pulling off a syndicated TV show. First guests are The Young Rascals. Given half a chance, Steve will do two hours on that group. When his club, The Scene, was hot, The Rascals used it as a showcase to help themselves get started. Later, when The Scene came near to losing out on a recent battle with creditors, it was The Rascals who contributed their services and almost single-handedly helped Steve save the club.

Richard Goldstein, hippest of the hippy critics, found a June bride, Judith Mipaas. They interrupted the honeymoon for the Monterey doings. The bride carried lots of flowers.

Lindsay Craftsmen

The *N.Y. Post* really flipped for Mark Lindsay. In a recent profile-interview, they labeled him "Top Teen Idol of 1967," "uncommonly good-looking" and "with the look of being beautifully constructed by the best craftsmen." Etc., etc. While Mark may be used to this kind of adulation from the teeny-bopper books, the byline in this case was Susan Szekely, whose space is usually reserved for The Mamas and Papas, Tim Buckley, and such.

CROSSTOWN BREEZES: David Kapralik's new gig at Epic is good news for that label, probably the best thing that has happened to them since they signed The Hollies ... Shadow Martin, the music man behind Janis Ian and now producer for the Vanilla Fudge, could become the East Coast Brian Wilson ... the BeeGees due in New York on June 29th for a first visit. Four guys when they started, they've just added a fifth, an Australian guitarist ... Lou Adler, John and Michelle at the Hampshire House to talk with network execs about the Monterey affair. If they can work it out, it could be the best thing ever done for pop music on TV. John seems as excited over the success of Scott McKenzie's hit as he is over the likelihood that *Creeque Alley* will hit #1 ... rumblings from Don Kirshner who made Monkees out of a couple of kids and is about to spring some more new plans ... the betting in New York on the Kirshner/Screen Gems tangle is solidly on Donnie ... Hoss Amon, road manager, just axed by the Raiders ... Merv Griffin's office reports that Chris Crosby has signed to do seven TV shows over the summer, which means that Chris will be spending lots of time in N.Y. for Griffin as well as for the first dates on his new pact with Atlantic.

Hippies Get Overexposed?

SAN FRANCISCO — The hippies of this city's Haight-Ashbury district are suffering from over-exposure, on television that is. Locally KPIX-TV, the Westinghouse station, produced an original documentary "The Maze" covering life in the hip community and just aired a second, "Liverpool, USA" which studies the new wave of psychedelic rock coming out of the Bay Area. San Francisco jazz columnist, Ralph Gleason hosts the show featuring the Grateful Dead, Quicksilver Messenger Service and the Wildflower.

National Educational Television's recent nationally aired report, "From Pot To Psychedelics" gathered most of it's material in Northern California.

KQED, the local educational station aired a day-long, seven and one half hour roundtable on the problems of the psychedelic trippers. One of their problems is not, obviously, getting their share of air time.

Sally Field In New TV Role

Sally Field (TV's Gidget) has another TV show in the works. This time, it's as a flying nun in a TV pilot of the same name.

Nightime TV host Joey Bishop highly praises the pilot (it's on the same network as his show) and recently had Sally, with film clips of the show, as his guest.

From the scenes shown, the praise wasn't justified. With upturned faces and astonished expressions the "grounded" nuns watched as Sally (equally astonished) discovered her unusual talent. This scene is probably the "kick off" of the first show.

However, following on the trail of Mary Poppin's success, this show could develop into another of those "family viewing" affairs.

'Diana' Now 10 Years Old

NEW YORK — Singer-composer Paul Anka, an ancient 25 years old, has just celebrated his 10th year in show business.

Paul wrote his first smash disc, "Diana," at the age of 15. The recording sold a fantastic 9,000,000 copies and hit the top of the charts for nearly 12 weeks in the U.S. It also became a near-classic in 20 foreign countries.

Anka has a number of firsts to his name:

He was the youngest entertainer to ever appear at the famed New York Copacabana.

He was the first popular entertainer to be invited to perform in Poland, and the first popular entertainer to tour Czechoslovakia.

Among the some 300 songs Anka has written so far in his career are tunes for many big top stars, plus Johnny Carson's "Tonight Show" theme, "International Showtime" theme, and music for "The Longest Day." He also appeared on Broadway in "What Makes Sammy Run?"

Thus far, the Canadian-born singer has 15 gold records to his credit.

SPOONFUL JOHN SEBASTIAN is flanked by record company officials after copping five awards at the annual BMI dinner. Sebastian now ranks number three nationally. Next to him are Charlie Koppelman (left) and Don Rubin (right), whose music publishing combine, Chardon and Faithful Virtue Music, was the recipient of seven top ten awards to place third among the music publishing firms in the nation.

UK Star Lulu On U.S. Visit

LONDON — Lulu, Britain's newest 18-year-old singing star, has signed an exclusive contract with Epic records and her first single on the label, "The Boat That I Row," is being rushed for U.S. release. The tune was independently produced by Mickie Most who also carved hits for Donovan, The Yardbirds and Jeff Beck.

Lulu makes her screen debut in the forthcoming Columbia film, "To Sir With Love," with Academy Award winner, Sidney Poitier. The red-haired actress-singer, Marie McDonald McLaughlin Lawrie, known to all England as Lulu, also sang the title song of the film.

Canada's Top Group Waxes In Hollywood

OTTAWA — The Staccatos, Canada's top recording group, have just completed a cutting session in Hollywood for Capitol Records under the direction of producer Nick Venet.

The group arrived on the inaugural direct flight from Toronto to Los Angeles, but before leaving, they played at the National Press Club in Ottawa for over 135 U.S. entertainers, writers and producers. Among those attending were Barbara Eden of "I Dream Of Jeannie," Agnes Moorehead of "Bewitched," and Dale Robertson of "Iron Horse."

KRLA ARCHIVES

THE HOLLIES
A GROUP'S GROUP

By Nick Lawrence

The earliest description of the Hollies drifted across the Atlantic from Britain in reports of visiting British artists, American writers and record makers based in London. The comments ran like this: "They're great," "They deserve more recognition," and "They're going to be really big in the U.S." This kind of enthusiastic respect won for the Hollies the special label of "a group's group."

The Hollies pulled off fifteen consecutive hits in England with ho-hum regularity and their records rose to top chart slots in Sweden, Norway and Germany. Even far-away Israel and India reported Hollies discs selling well.

U.S. Success

When the Hollies released their first disc in this country, "I Can't Let Go" b/w "Look Through Any Window" and no one was surprised at its success. Their follow up singles, " us Stop" and "Stop, Stop, Stop" gave the group firm footing as a strong force in international pop music.

Their latest hit in the U.S., "On A Carousel," spun it's way up to the top of the charts fulfilling the safe bets of the chart watchers.

The Hollies string of hits aroused the interest in having them make personal appearances here. Finally they were booked to tour America as a sideline attraction with the Herman's Hermits. The sideline turned out to be one of the show's top attractions.

TV Special

A CBS-TV documentary crew assigned to follow the Hermits on tour for a television special were so taken with the Hollies — on and off stage — that they included them in the telecast.

The Hollies launched their first world-wide tour in April. They were playing to excited, responsive audiences in Europe, but were forced to call off part of the tour when their drummer, Bobby Elliott, fell ill in Germany.

Graham Nash, who plays rhythm guitar and does vocals with the Hollies, is most conspicuous for a prominent personality trait: curiosity. He is the Holly always out in front when meeting new people or grooving new places and ideas. He is aware and sharp. He is constantly asking questions and always listens carefully to the answers.

New sounds and concepts are his passion and he is ever open and ready to pick up on unfamiliar though interesting suggestions. He is a versatile songwriter and music arranger as well as a very quick-witted business mind. He is a handsome 5'11". Twenty-three-year-old Graham has a flat in London but makes frequent visits to his parents' home in Manchester.

Lead singer Allan Clarke is the group's songwriting braintrust. Also 23, he grew up with Graham and together they filtered in and out of various groups while in school. When they finally settled into the five-man groove of the Hollies, Allan, who has been singing professionally for some time, was the natural choice for lead singer. Allan's almost sullen look melts on stage and he becomes a very dynamic performer. He lives with his wife and baby in Salford.

Debut At 12

Tony Hicks, lead guitarist, made his musical debut on a TV talent show at the age of 12. He sang with a group in high school before joining the Hollies. Tony has a relaxed, even languid manner off-stage which is sometimes mistakenly interpreted as irresponsibility. But on-stage that impression is dissolved by his technical and creative mastery of his instrument.

Bobby Elliott, the gutsy drummer of the Hollies, started playing when he was 13. By the time he was 16, he was playing in English jazz clubs and already displaying great musical spirit. His driving drum beat knits the Hollies' music into an insistent and richly textured fabric. The only fair-haired member of the group, gray-eyed Bobby stands a Nordic 6 feet tall.

Almost Shy

Dark-haired, blue-eyed bass guitar and piano player Bern Calvert is quiet, almost shy yet very candid when offering opinions. Tony and Bern played together in high school in a group called the Dolphins. When the Hollies' original bass player, Eric Haydock left the group, Tony went in search of Bern as a replacement. He was playing blues piano in a club working his way through a degree in Aircraft Engineering. After graduation, he left the drawing boards and took off with the Hollies.

ENGELBERT HUMPERDINCK: Perserverance paid off.

THE GOING WAS TOUGH BUT SO IS ENGELBERT

By Bobby Farrow

His name sounds strange and some of his tastes are, well, unusual. Engelbert Humperdinck, one of Britain's top pop singers, counts black cats as lucky charms, dislikes gambling and has frequent cravings for his favorite food, hot, spicy Indian curry. In most other ways Engelbert is as typically British as Yorkshire pudding.

Engelbert's latest single release, "Release Me," has given him firmer footing than ever on the best-seller charts — but his career wasn't always the success story it is today.

Multi-Colored

He was born in May, 1940 in Madras, India, home of the famous multi-colored plaids. When he was six his parents decided to move their ten children back to England. They left the equatorial heat of the Indian subcontinent and set up house in green and rainy Leicester.

Engelbert quickly became the most musical member of his family. As a child he picked up a variety of instruments on his own and studied the saxophone for five years.

On leaving school he became an apprentice engineer. But, his tremendous ambition to make a career in music brought his engineer's job to a quick end. He had saved some money he had won in a talent show competition and decided to make a serious try in show business in London.

But so did thousands of other eager stage-struck aspirants. The going was tough — things weren't happening for him as he had hoped. A few years passed and Engelbert was getting into his twenties and still had not broken through with that all-important hit record.

But the singer was determined and eventually his break came. Engelbert sang a song he had written to his friend Gordon Mills, Tom Jones' manager. Gordon went wild over the number which he thought had sure-hit potential. Mills arranged for Engelbert to record the song and the result was a contract with Decca Records singed in June of 1966. Then he became Decca's representative to the famous International Song Festival at Knokke-Le-Zoute, in Belgium.

Green & Jet

Engelbert has a firm jaw set off by jet black hair and grass-green eyes and measures 6 feet 2 inches. He lives with his bubbly wife, Patricia and two small children, Louise Sarah and Jason Mervyn in a comfortable Hammersmith, England home.

He has made major television appearances in Holland, Belgium, London and Paris. His compositions include "This and That" recorded by Tom Jones. His long range plans include someday making a serious film. Engelbert has nursed one pet ambition since he entered show business: To see his name in lights at the top of the London Palladium bill.

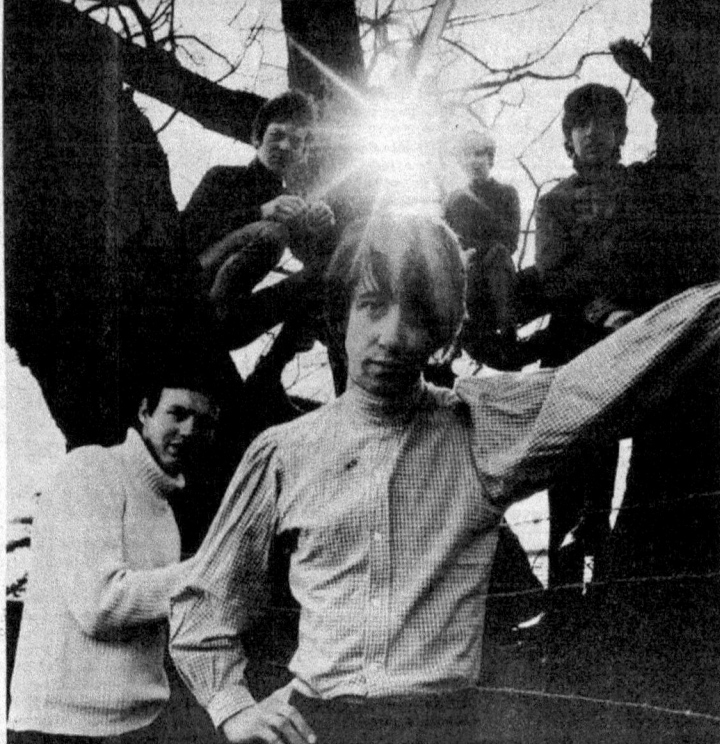

THE HOLLIES: On a carousel that's going nowhere but up.

KRLA ARCHIVES

KRLA ARCHIVES

JEFFERSON AIRPLANE — scheduled for a stint at London's Blaises Club on July 6.

U.K. POP NEWS ROUND-UP

"A Whiter Shade Of Pale" Brings Out Beatles, Oldham

By Tony Barrow

By far the hottest new pop property on the U.K. scene this month is a London quintet calling themselves PROCOL HARUM. The success of their first fantastic single, "A Whiter Shade Of Pale" has taken the business by surprise. It was written by 20-year-old KEITH REID in collaboration with Procol Harum singer GARY BROOKER. Reid wrote the lyrics, borrowed three hundred dollars in order to get a group together and, apart from Gary, discovered lead guitarist RAY ROYER, organist MATTHEW FISHER, bass player DAVE KNIGHTS and drummer BOBBY HARRISON. Gary himself plays piano as well as supplying the mind-blowin' vocal which is some sort of dynamic combination of Eric Burdon and Jimi Hendrix!

When Procol Harum played London's Speakeasy Club after midnight one recent Thursday, an impressive shoal of top names were there. I spotted Eric Burdon, visitor Mitch Ryder, Georgie Fame, all four Beatles plus Pattie and Cynthia, Cat Stevens, Andrew Oldham, Eric Clapton and Chris Farlowe.

Procol Harum, which is Latin for something like "beyond these things," is the name of a pedigree Siamese cat owned by one of Keith Reid's friends.

Walker Debut

June 18, solo debut of JOHN WALKER (ex-Brothers) in concert at Torquay... "Release Me" star ENGELBERT HUMPERDINCK kicks off his first world tour with an Ed Sullivan TV appearance in September. The single has hit the top of the charts in nine different countries and the follow-up, "There Goes My Everything," sold nearly 200,000 copies after six days in British record stores!... Undecided whether or not custom-composed Lennon/McCartney number which BEATLES will be seen recording in June 25 "Our World" global TV program will be issued on publicly-available disc... ENGELBERT HUMPERDINCK may co-star with Steve McQueen in Hollywood movie early 1968... BOB HOPE, in London for "Eamonn Andrews Show" TV appearance, met songstress CILLA BLACK and quipped "I wish I was here more often. On Monday I visit some relatives in Kent and explain to them who I am!"... TOM JONES filming "Spotlight" TV Special for U.S. screening in color... Following operation to repair torn ligament, uncertain whether drummer KEITH MOON would be with THE WHO at Monterey. Keith's collapse and subsequent lengthy convalescence meant cancellation of album recording sessions and Paris concert date.

Monkee Special

THE MOVE will not now tour America in July and their first stateside trip is unlikely to materialize before September. U.S. release of "I Can Hear The Grass Grow" has been postponed... RAY DAVIES (KINKS) directing and financing hour-long pilot program for new TV pop series... MONKEES' answer to "The Beatles At Shea Stadium" due for BBC TV screening June 24... December cabaret season at London's "Talk Of The Town" for songstress SANDIE SHAW... Nearly 300 advertisements splashed around London's subway stations to promote GERRY MARSDEN's first solo record "Please Let Them Be"... Trust there's no truth in the London rumour that FLORENCE BALLARD is about to quit THE SUPREMES... Nude photographs of NANCY SINATRA (courtesy of Ron Joy's prolific camera) adorned a front and inside pages of Britain's top-selling Sunday newspaper, *News Of The World!*... JOHN LENNON became the proud owner of the world's first psychedelic Rolls-Royce at the end of May. Several thousand dollars and a five-week painting job covered the elegant auto in flowers, golden patterns and Zodiac sign for the roof... JEFFERSON AIRPLANE play London's Blaises Club July 6... "We're a very sad group in mood — full of melancholy and despair" says PROCOL HARUM's lyricist KEITH REID... "Sgt. Pepper" album notched up sales approaching 250,000 in U.K. during first week of release, raced direct to No. 1 in *New Musical Express, Disc and Music Echo, Melody Maker* charts... *Disc and Music Echo* "exclusively revealed MONKEES will stay at plushy new Royal Garden Hotel in Kensington during late-June London visit. To my personal knowledge journalists from two national newspapers had made their room reservations a week before the story appeared!... NEW VAUDEVILLE BAND's multi-instrumentalist POPS KERR would like to screen old Laurel and Hardy movies on HENRI HARRISON's drums during combo's stage appearances... "Come and raise your ecstasy count! Freak out at London's newest hippy club!" yelled the opening-night invitations spread about by THE ELECTRIC GARDEN. But the Light Show was a big bring-down and the champagne ran out after the first hour. Still, tall young men in academic robes sold many copies of the *International Times* to a largely un-hip gathering of bewildered patrons.

Jane Returns

New York's top deejay GARY ances... STU SUTCLIFFE, bass-playing Beatle who died in Hamburg 6 years ago, amongst the many people pictured on the "Sgt. Pepper" cover. His face is way over on the left — look directly above the waxwork medal of Sonny Liston.

Must be a cryptic aptness about the title of P.J. PROBY's latest U.K. single — "You Can't Come Home Again"... CREAM guitarist ERIC CLAPTON describing Be-In he attended in New York's Central Park: "There were cops on horses to make sure there was no trouble. The kids offered the cops pop corn and in a couple of hours most of those cops were off their horses walking in the crowd holding flowers in their hands. By sunset they were on the ground listening to the drums."

TAPPY WRIGHT, once THE ANIMALS' road manager, claims he accidnetally gate-crashed a Screen Gems audition and might have become a Monkee!... JANE ASHER returned home to London after her lengthy U.S. tour with The Bristol-Old Vic Theatre Company and PAUL met her at the airport... GEORGE HARRISON's recent visit to Wimpole Street dentist made all the more mournful by the fact that someone let the air out of Mal's tires and George had to take a taxi 20 miles home to Esher... Will U. chart-topper "Silence Is Golden" be just as big for THE TREMELOES in America?

RADIO CAROLINE plan to operate from Amsterdam headquarters if and when Marine Broadcasting bill becomes law... STONES Mick and Keith due in court for jury trial of narcotics charges at the very end of June.

By Ron Koslow

I'm still high (spiritually and emotionally)... went to San Francisco this weekend. That city is too too. Is it for real? I think so, partially, temporarily (until the promoters vulgarize it or the city fathers shut it off). Actually saw people with flowers in their hair, laughing, relaxed, having the time of their young lives. No competition, no material orientation, it's one place, perhaps the only place where "Plastic Man" hasn't struck... yet!!

Martha and the Vandellas at the Fillmore (a line more than two blocks long); Moby Grape (yes, Moby Grape) and Love at Winterland (it used to be a skating rink; now people glide there without the ice).

Speaking Out

Over at Berkeley the kids are speaking up and out. They're out to make things over and they've got the brains to do it.

Back to L.A. — The Doors at the Whiskey... this group is the *heaviest* — have you heard them yet? — If not, do not rest until you have, especially "Light My Fire." You will not believe it!

Word has it that there will be the Be-In to end all Be-Ins at the Grand Canyon this summer. Expecting upwards of 200,000 people. Will you Be there?

Drastic Changes?

This is the summer to do it... to act... to go. This is Our summer and I've got a feeling that there are going to be some drastic changes society-wise taking place.

As Mick says, "You gotta stop, gotta look around" ("19th Nervous Breakdown") — keep your eyes open, babies.

Been getting some great letters from all over — please keep the vibrations happening.

Did you know that the Fairmount Park Be-In in Philadelphia drew over 2,000 people and that a group of hippies have started an underground newspaper there... it's growing!

But the most beautiful thing I've ever seen or experienced in a long time came in the form of a poem from a girl named Jan in Neva, Tennessee. I think it says all there really is to say about what's happening today — and maybe a little bit more.

A DREAM OF SHORT DURATION

Softly, the ethereal light seeps between the blinds and bathes the room in a pale blue gauze, very much like a film of net over the skirt of a young girl's prom dress.
The wind that blew so violently all night has calmed to a soft and gentle breeze, stroking the hair back from the forehead and caressing the skin beneath the open-necked blouse.
The music is urgent — pulsing, pleading, weeping, but always promising, always agreeing that this is the way it should be — this is the ultimate in perfection and in happiness.
The eyes are soft, sleepy, and the light from them spreads a joy over the whole room, a golden mirage, a miracle of love and the power of youth.
Yes, this is the way it should be — forget the war, forget the world and its foolish ideas, forget hate and ridicule, think only of the joy that love can bring.
This is the way it should be. This is the way it will never be.

What more can be said? If you've anything to add, send it along —

KRLA ARCHIVES

GENE CORNISH

EDDIE BRIGATI

The four Young Rascals grow older and more experienced. They progress professionally but they don't change. Wolfing down a raw hamburger in our offices, enthusiastically applauding Smokey Robinson and the Miracles at a club opening, sitting half-still for an interview, strutting down the street in a ten-gallon cowboy hat—none of this has changed.

Off stage they can be pensive or funny, happy or down, fast to make jokes or slow to smile. About the only thing they aren't is big-headed. About the only thing they are is right. Right for their scene, dead center for their time.

If you think their high and low pattern of success has been frustrating, you're correct. And for all their joviality they can, and have been, down. Never basement down, just first-floor down. But the one redeeming quality which makes disappointment liveable is talent. And talent the Rascals own—all of it.

Some say Felix Cavaliere is their leader, and maybe he is. The son of a dentist, he aimed at being a doctor but ended up a musician. Which is just as well. Although intense at his organ, if you only know the Felix Cavaliere you see on stage, you don't know him at all. He merges himself into his music, into the total sound. On stage there is no Felix Cavaliere— only his music.

Off stage, he's much of a gentleman. Rather quiet, articulate, but certainly not the vocal center of attraction.

Eddie Brigati, or "The Mouth" as he is sometimes known, will take over your world if you'd only let him. Amusing, genuinely nice and occasionally ornery—once you've met Eddie you're not likely to ever forget the experience. He is whatever he wants to be. He can light a lady's cigarette or tell her simply that she needs to lose a few pounds.

Both on and off stage, Eddie is a keg of dynamite. Never does he sit still, always he is in motion.

Gene Cornish is not Italian. Ordinarily it wouldn't mean much but in the case of the Rascals it is the only definite trait which separates Gene from his fellow Italian group members. He seems to have a remarkable memory for faces and never forgets anyone who has been nice to him.

Friendly and outgoing, Gene is neither as quiet as Felix or as vocal as Eddie. Spotting a friend in a crowded club, he instantaneously waves a greeting and offers to share his table.

Dino Danelli, without a doubt, is the quietest Rascal in the world. He may also be one of the greatest drummers in the world—though you'd have to from your own opinion on that. He'd never tell you.

If the Rascals have changed at all during their two year career, Dino has changed the most. He's much more open, more eager to talk. He never dominates a conversation but he has now mastered the art of at least getting a few sentences in between the paragraphs of Eddie and Gene.

It's quite appropriate that the Rascals have topped the national charts with a song called "Goovin'." No group grooves more than they do—certainly none has worked harder, picked themselves up better, or deserved world-wide acclaim more than the Young Rascals.

FELIX CAVALIERE

"They are pop . . . blown up, bold, brilliant and tough. They are bang-bang and drop dead. They are super-everything. They don't mess around; they play for keeps."

DINO DANELLI

KRLA ARCHIVES

To: Beat Publications
9125 Sunset Blvd.
Los Angeles, Calif. 90069

Please send _____ sheet(s) Mod-Bod stick ons
(4 psychedelic sheets available at $1.00 each)

Find $_____ enclosed.

Name_____
Address_____
City_____
California residents add 4% sales tax

BE AHEAD WITH MOD-BOD
Turn on your breathin' skin 180 ways
Tune in on the Harvard color spectrum

STRANGE BODY ADORNMENTS
Hearts & Flowers to Psychedelic Phreaqueouts

A. Hearts and Flowers
B. Psychedelic Buttons and Designs
C. Psychedelic Alphabets and Designs
D. Psychedelic Phreaquies
Please specify A, B, C or D when ordering.

MOD-BODS
Stick on everything, they're reuseable, waterproof, fluorescent, totally tuff, urrrk, supergroovy, bitchen, outta site, cooool, phantazmagoric, uptight, zingo righteous, flashie, too much, mad, conglomerative, pau and et cetera.

KRLA ARCHIVES

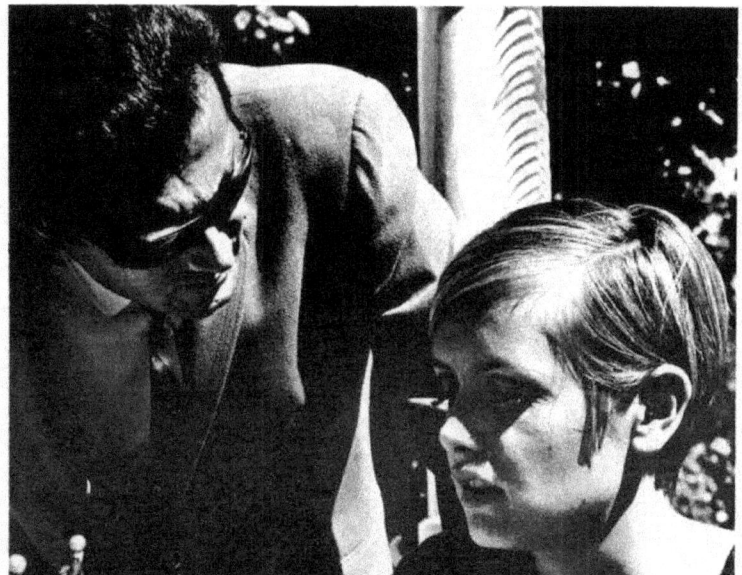

SHE'S GROOVY — but not really worth losing your job over. Rumor has it that the recent dispute between Dave Hull and KRLA was caused by Dave's reportedly skipping his Saturday afternoon show one week to make the party scene with Twiggy at Sonny and Cher's home.

KRLA Brings Love, Flowers, Fans, Fun To Huge Monterey Pop Festival

KRLA — the 50,000 watt Flower Pot — brought love, flowers, fans and fun to the Monterey International Pop Festival ... the world's first king-size musical love-in.

A special KRLA contest task force left Los Angeles early the week before the festival to complete advance work in Monterey so that KRLA's winners and listeners would have the best possible time when they arrived for the big weekend.

Naturally, the KRLA disc jockeys were all on hand during the weekend — all being flown between the Festival and Los Angeles by chartered airliner every three hours so each one could do his show and still turn on to the scene in Monterey.

Also on hand was KRLA horticultural expert and living legend, Gypsy Boots and his Nature Boys. KRLA program director Dick Moreland has announced that plans are already under way for next year's Festival to be held either on the East Coast or in London.

Drugs, Lyrics Documentaries Win Awards

KRLA's "Down The Up Staircase" has been named the best radio documentary of 1966 by the California Associated Press Radio-Television Association. Produced by KRLA newsman Lew Irwin, the program explored the growing use of marijuana and LSD.

A second KRLA documentary entitled "The Language of Rock," also produced by Irwin, was selected for a certificate of excellence Special Award for 1966. This series dealt with the suggestive lyrics of today's music.

KRLA Sends 1st L.A. Man To War Zone

KRLA newsman Roy Holcomb, who left in the first days of the Middle East crisis to cover the war zone for the station, was the first newsman from a Los Angeles independent to be sent to the area.

KRLA pre-empted regular programming four times each hour for special news coverage of the war developments on a 24-hour basis. Newsman Holcomb spent two years in Israel during the late '50's.

By Pen

The father of all flower children, Gypsy Boots, has been named KRLA's official Horticultural Director, Flower Power Expert and Love-In Coordinator. Twenty-five years ago people thought Gypsy was "nuts" when he wore flowers in his hair, but today his precedent is part of a giant movement among today's generation.

The original hippie and first of the nature boys has made his home in the Santa Monica mountains, and Dave Hull remembers Gypsy walking up and down the beaches passing out his own "Flower Power" back in the fifties. You'll be seeing Gypsy at the Monterey International Pop Festival and at all future "Love-Ins" representing KRLA. Look for him — he won't be hard to find.

KRLA'S DOTTED SHORTS

Police protection for the Monterey International Pop Festival cost $25,000 ... KRLA's Reb Foster is in England on tour with the Turtles ... Casey Kasem's new "Astrology for Young Lovers" album is riding high on the LP charts. Famed Hollywood columnist-astrologer Jack Bradford picked the release date and hour according to the stars ... KRLA and Hollywood Bowl Association brass are high (pardon us) on the idea of a classical music event featuring synchronized psychedelic light show in August ... Every Mother's Son folk-rock group had a blast answering KRLA's toll-free request lines last week ... KRLA's Casey Kasem drops his "Mr. Nice Guy" image long enough to play a "Hell's Angels" character in a new movie called "Glory Stompers" ... KRLA is working on a follow-up album to its smash hit "21 Solid Rocks."

KRLA ARCHIVES

Behind The Association

Exclusive BEAT Photos: Jerry Haas

True, you've already seen the Association on the "Smothers Brothers Comedy Hour," but you *didn't* see what went on during rehearsals and lunch breaks when the six Associated men met up with two Smothers men.

You missed the late arrival of Brian (caused by an all-night recording session), Russ perched atop Ted's drums while he waited for his fellow group-members to appear following a lunch break, Ted disappearing *altogether* and Jim Yester attempting to balance a cup of hot coffee on his knee while he probed the inner-workings of a 35-millimeter camera.

Lunch Bucket

The TV screen didn't show you Tommy Smothers wolfing down a sandwich from his famous (infamous?) lunch bucket, Larry Ramos performing an impromptu dance routine or Terry Kirkman trying his very best to keep a straight face while the two Smothers Brothers threw lines back and forth at each other (and anyone else in sight).

You didn't get to see the look on Brian's face when Russ told him he was due in wardrobe to get measured for his costume, "a hairy vest and a loincloth." Actually, it turned out to be a baker's outfit and Brian shook his head in relief.

You didn't get to hear all the words to Tommy and Dickie's banana song because the censors got to it first. Nor did you see Margaret O'Brien strutting around the stage in a yellow-sequined dress topped with rollers in her hair.

Laugh Time

Muffed lines, shirt tails hanging out, jokes interchanged between the cast and crew, the face-making ability of everyone in the studio, last minuted deletions—none of these things reached you. We spent two days at the studio and a lot of it missed us! What we *did* catch is printed on these two pages with a note to enjoy it and the best of luck if you ever happen to find yourself stranded with these eight singers, comedians, musicians, social-commentators, hosts, ad-libbers... all-around great people.

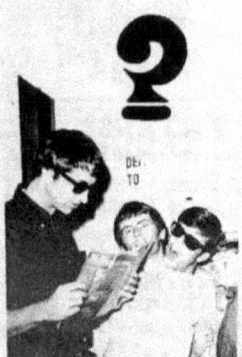

JIM YESTER makes faces

DICK & TOM SMOTHERS speak out on bananas.

AND TOMMY has a good cry.

TERRY KIRKMAN plays flute

KRLA ARCHIVES

RUSS GIGUERE takes a turn on the drums.

BRIAN, JIM

NEWEST ASSOCIATE, Larry Ramos, tunes up.

LARRY DECORATES Tommy with poison ivy.

TED GETS SET for "Windy"

"HOW ABOUT THAT, Dickie?" Yes, indeed.

RECOGNIZE ANY FAMILIAR FACES in this distinguished looking crowd? Like a fireman, a baker, a scholar and a farmer? Would you believe Jim Yester, Brian Cole, Ted Bluechel and Russ Giguere?

BEAT EDITOR, Louise Criscione, and Dick Smothers watch intently as The Association get ready to run through "Along Comes Mary."

KRLA ARCHIVES

KRLA ARCHIVES

The Turtles Are Flying High In Their New DC3

By Sylvia Forman

There's a new species of turtle . . . The flying kind! The top-flight rock group, the Turtles, live a tightly-packed schedule of personal appearances and recording sessions. They've given up crawling and even walking for their new DC 3.

"We've rented an airplane," explained Howard Kaylan, the group's spokesman. "Before we were always worried about getting from one place to another . . . being on time . . . driving through snow . . . rain. Since we went to the air the personal appearances have been twice as easy."

The Turtles have just won their first gold record for their million-selling single, "Happy Together," and their album of the same name is quickly approaching the million-dollar mark. Their follow-up single, "She'd Rather Be With Me," is becoming a hot chart item.

European Visit

The Turtles are presently hard at work on their first European tour spreading their "happy sound" overseas. Their month-long continental tour includes a round of appearances in England, France, Germany, Denmark, Belgium, Ireland and Holland. In England where "Happy Together" hit the Top Ten, they're doing a number of BBC TV shows plus a long list of television, radio and concert performances.

Short On Time

The group scarcely had time to fill out their passport forms and get the necessary shots for their trip. In May they climaxed an impressive series of TV credits with their debut on the "Ed Sullivan Show." They were already familiar to TV viewers from their appearances on "Shindig," "Hullabaloo," "Hollywood Palace" and the "Smothers Brothers Show."

Life zips by at anything but a snail's pace for the Turtles. Upcoming is the release of the Twentieth Century Fox film. "Guide For The Married Man," for which the Turtles cut the title song.

The Turtle's Mark Volman explained the kind of sound the group is trying to project: "Happiness is happening. Unhappiness and sadness are around us all the time, in newspapers, on television. Music is the one thing that can be happy and spread happiness. That's what most people, we think, are looking for now . . . a chance to smile, to grin and laugh."

Musical Chance

The Turtles are giving everyone that chance using music as the medium.

Howard Kaylan, lead singer, spokesman and musical mentor of the Turtles joined a group called The Nightriders (headed by another Turtle, Al Nichol) in high school. The group became the Turtles with their first release "It Ain't Me Babe" with White Whale Records.

Al Nichol started piano lessons at seven but gave them up "Because I didn't like being forced into something." But at twelve he took up other instruments, for fun. He plays lead guitar for the group, but is equally skilled on the trumpet, French horn, organ, piano and harpsichord.

Mark Volman sang with the Turtles before their record hits for only $5 a night. He was after enjoyment and still is – even though the group's pay scale has climbed considerably. He learned to play the sax after joining the group.

"They needed a sax player," says Mark, "and everyone sort of pointed at me."

Before Jim Tucker joined the Turtles as rhythm guitarist, he played with several Los Angeles rock groups. Skilled on the piano and harmonica, Jim never took a music lesson but feels he inherited his musical abilities from his father who is an excellent pianist.

Jim Pons started playing bass for the Turtles a year ago when another West Coast group, The Leaves which Jim organized, broke up after their first success on the charts. Jim quit college after completing three years and has definite plans for returning to earn his degree some day.

John Barbata has never taken drum lessons but has developed a unique show style which adds greatly to the Turtles' impact in concert. He started playing drums while a sophomore in high school and even formed his own group.

John has been flying high with the group since July, '66.

THE TURTLES: Spreading the sound of happiness on a busy seven-country European tour.

Dave Dee, Dozy, Beaky, Mick and Tich: 'America's Great, But Oh Those Hot Dogs!'

By Rochelle Reed

Riding in a limousine is really quite nice, especially when it isn't an everyday occasion. BEAT Photographer Ed Caraeff and I had a ball ignoring people who kept looking in to see who we were – when actually we were on the verge of blowing our cool by yelling, "Hey, this is fun!"

Our chauffer, the perfect stereotype in his special cap, was prepared for pop groups, he said, as in the past week he had driven the Monkees, Twiggy (who was upset because everyone mistook her for Mia Farrow) and the Electric Prunes.

Breezing down the freeways and gliding into 'No Parking' zones, we kept busy practicing the tongue-twisting name of the group we were about the meet – Dave Dee, Dozy, Beaky, Mick and Tich.

It had been almost a month since they left England for the "down under" countries of Australia and New Zealand. They spent one day in Honolulu getting vividly sun-burned but otherwise, this two-hour Los Angeles lay-over was their first taste of America.

The group swarmed into the airport VIP room, where we were camped with cokes, lemonade and peanuts, fiddling with the tape recorder and camera.

Non-Stop Talker

"Oh, 'ello!" they called, grabbing a waitress, dropping their luggage and plopping down on the couch. "So this is America!"

Dave Dee, leader of the group, dominates the five with sheer wordage – he never stops talking.

"It's a good thing, really," he began, "being unknown in the States. You get into a rut otherwise. Like Australia, the kids had never seen us, but then they heard "Bend It" and they were interested."

DDDBM&T as some people call them, reached the ranks of the huge in England, placing six of their discs in the Top 10. They have also had the distinction of having one non-sensical song, "Bend It," banned in places like South Africa and Biloxi, Miss.

No Mustard

Finally, DDBM&T's allotted two hours were up. Their manager came in with a snack – American hot dogs. There was only one problem: he didn't know mustard or relish belonged on them, and consequently DDDBM&T ate their first hot dog very dry.

"Yeeech!" was their general opinion.

Grabbing luggage, coats, plane tickets and what-have-you, the five charming Englishmen yelled a quick "Goodbye, see you soon." Beaky stopped to quickly jot down two words for BEAT readers on my shorthand tablet:

"Love, Beaky."

As Ed, our photographer, summed up: "It was quite an experience!"

DAVE DEE

BEAT reporter Rochelle Reed, Beaky (L), Mick. *BEAT Photo: Ed Caraeff*

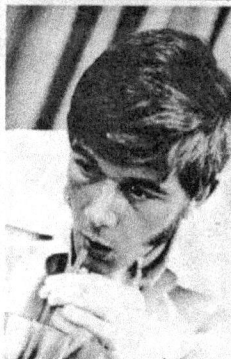

DOZY

TICH

KRLA ARCHIVES

MATCHING HAIR-DO'S — No longer a "fashion don't" for the Switched Ons.

BEAT Art: Linda Bull

with matching hair-do's, bloomer dresses, a new tennis look . . .

■ We did a double take when we saw our first "matching" couple, but after awhile, we decided the double duo look in hairstyles was rather attractive. It's a popular trend in England . . . catching on among the Switched Ons here too.

■ Shoes are news. Some are summer white, delicately styled with lots of straps or covered with flowers.

■ Really shoe news—paper ones! That's right, shoes in paper with big bows on the toes.

■ They aren't really mini-skirts, but next to their old uniforms, the new stewardess outfits worn on most major airlines are above the knee by at least two or three inches. And the male passengers are reportedly very happy about the new look.

■ Dave Dee, Dozy, Beaky, Mick and Tich are "hung-up" as they put it, on scarves rather than ties. They look like silk or chiffon and are pulled through the collar and knotted.

■ Max Factor has come out with a terrific line of lipsticks—Bazazz Frosts. They have all shades of pinks and oranges . . . and best of all, they don't turn color or fade after an hour's wear.

■ Remember the early '60's when yellow, green and lavender nail polishes were the rage? They're back again, especially in light lavender. Beautiful with a summer tan.

■ Beware of too much sun this summer. Tha main cause of skin cancer is from excessive damage from the sun. Stay in the shade or wear a hat at all times. A light tan is wonderful, a "burned up" look really terrible.

■ Bloomer dresses were in, then out, and now they've come back in, despite the fact that they bombed at several Parisian fashion shows. Even pattern books carry bloomer dress designs. They're cute.

■ The latest thing in wristwatches is one for every outfit! Sound expensive? . . . sometimes . . . no! Several fine, inexpensive lines of watches combine craftsmanship with style. Or buy the kind that allows you to switch bands with every whim.

■ Tennis clothes, still traditionally all white, have taken on a more feminine appeal by adding cotton lace. Plain shorts and blouses are out—in are short, shifty tennis dresses.

■ Vacationing? Wear a skirt, or carry a wrap-around with you, for visiting monuments and eating in restaurants. Never wear shorts!

DEAR FASHION EDITOR

Dear Fashion Editor,
 Do you know of any safe and effective way to remove hair from my arms? Creams don't work, I'm sure not going to shave my arms, and those electrolysis things that kill your hair root, well, I've heard that you can only remove a few hairs a day and then it leaves scars.
 Isn't there some way that will remove hair permanently or at least something that will take it away temporarily? Please help me. I've got very hairy arms, and there's nothing uglier. I'm desperate!
                                                                                                Donna

Dear Donna,
 First of all, electrolysis, correctly and completely done, does not leave scars. However, it is true that only a few hairs may be removed at each treatment.
 We suggest that you try bleaching your hair again, but first ask your pharmacist for his recommendation on what to use. If that doesn't work, consult your dermatologist.

Dear Fashion Editor,
 I have a great deal of difficulty applying eyeliner. I use a pencil (I don't want to change to liquid) but I can seldom get it on dark enough. Can you help?
                                                                                                Michelle

Dear Michelle,
 We can help! We found that applying a same amount of cover up cream (we like the lipstick type) to the upper lid will make a smoother surface, so the pencil goes on darker, easier.

SHIRLEY YOU JEST

I feel a whole lot better.
 If you read the last issue of *The BEAT* (and if you didn't, please submit a written excuse immediately, in 5,000 words or less), you may have noticed that the importance of consistency was mentioned in two places. Once by The Brothers Smothers (and my, aren't *they* a groove) and once in the "In People Are Talking About" column.
 And here I've been worrying that my column (humpf) is getting worse and worse.

Consistent

Well, I've ceased worrying. I may not be good, but you've got to admit I'm about the most consistent person (re-humpf) running around loose (consistently ridiculous, that is).
 This column will hardbly by any exception. ('hmmmm).
 First of all, we'll finish up the 25 WAYS TO FEEL LIKE A MORON that I didn't quite complete last time. I got as far as number eighteen and then had to stop gibbering because I'd run out of room.
 The "ways" were sent to me by Sheila Lee of Lost Envelope, North What's-It's-Face. (I just can't seem to hang on to anything these days, my marbles included.) Sheila insists that this column (words fail me) (I know, I know, not nearly often enouh) inspired her witty, and I'm *still* not quite sure how to *take* that.
 Anywry, here they be.

Waterproof Nails

19. You search all over town for a set of "*Guaranteed* Waterproof fingernails. You spend several frantic hours applying them promising never to use that kind of language again. Then you polish them and go to the beach. You swim until tired and come in on a big wave. Your fingernails come in on the next.
20. It's Friday night. All your friends are out of town, and the phone hasn't rung. You settle down to watch the telly and during the commercial you made yourself your favorite sandwich. Your favorite sandwich is made out of cheese and onions. You finish devouring your favorite sandwich. The phone rings.
21. You have learned your lesson. For the next thirty years you do not eat your favorite sandwich. You even refuse to speak to the onions at the supermarket. The phone does not ring.

Scurry In

22. You scurry into a classroom; not realizing that you have a slight rip in the side seam of your dress. You realize this only when you are suddenly impaled on the door knob.
23. It is your first trip on a plane (hmmm). Very groovy people are meeting you. You are afraid you will blow the whole thing and let your queasy tum-tum get the best of you. By practicing great self-control, you do not get sick on the airplane. You get sick in the airport.
24. You are seated at a crowded lunch counter. You are left-handed, which makes things a bit difficult for the right-hander beside you. You accidentally overturn her coke while wrestling with a rare steak (as in rare off the plate). You both stare as the coke pours into her open purse.

Get It Out

25. You are sitting around with friends. Someone you dig very much arrives. You get nervous and start fiddling around with your pop bottle. Three or four hours later you manage to get your finger out.
 Thanks, kiddo, for sending us your most embarrassing thingies. I'd love to tell you about my all-time blusher, but I can't.
 It all started when I found myself in the basement of a crowded department store, clutching a leaky goldfish carton. (That sentence can be taken several ways, none of which are the slightest bit interesting.)
 I edged up to the counter and asked where I could get some water. One of the two clerks saw my goldfish, not to mention my predicament, but the other wasn't paying any attention and thought I had asked for the location of the ladies room.

Hysterics

Therefore, they gave two entirely different answers to my question, at the same time, and the customers standing there (about twenty people) burst into hysterics. When I finally got away from there, I slunk red-facedly (parrdon?) outside. Fortunately, it had started raining, so I opened the carton and stood there looking stupid while said droplets saved my poor fishy's life. (Don't think *that* didn't cause some passers-by to cast terrified glances in my direction.)
 Wish I could tell you what the two clerks said, but I wouldn't dare. (Do you want me to get arrested?) (Shaddup.)
 Come to think of it, there aren't many people who would find themselves in the basement of a crowded department store clutching a leaky goldfish carton. Aren't you glad I'm one of the few.
 I didn't think you would be.

Sioux??

Speaking of George (well, how long do you think I can hold off?) one of my spies in England tells me that he and Pattie have done their house over in a completely Indian motif. (Sioux, I presume.) (A particularly effective word when pronounced Soox.) (I certainly have a ready wit, don't I (Ready for the guys with the long ropes, that is.)
 I was in a state of nervous prostration not long ago when the big rumor about George being in the country was being circulated by people who delight in seeing me break out in hives. (You have just paid a return visit to the world's longest sentence.) (Don't stay away so long next time.)
 Speaking of hives, these were so big they came with their own bees.

(Continued on Page 23)

KRLA ARCHIVES

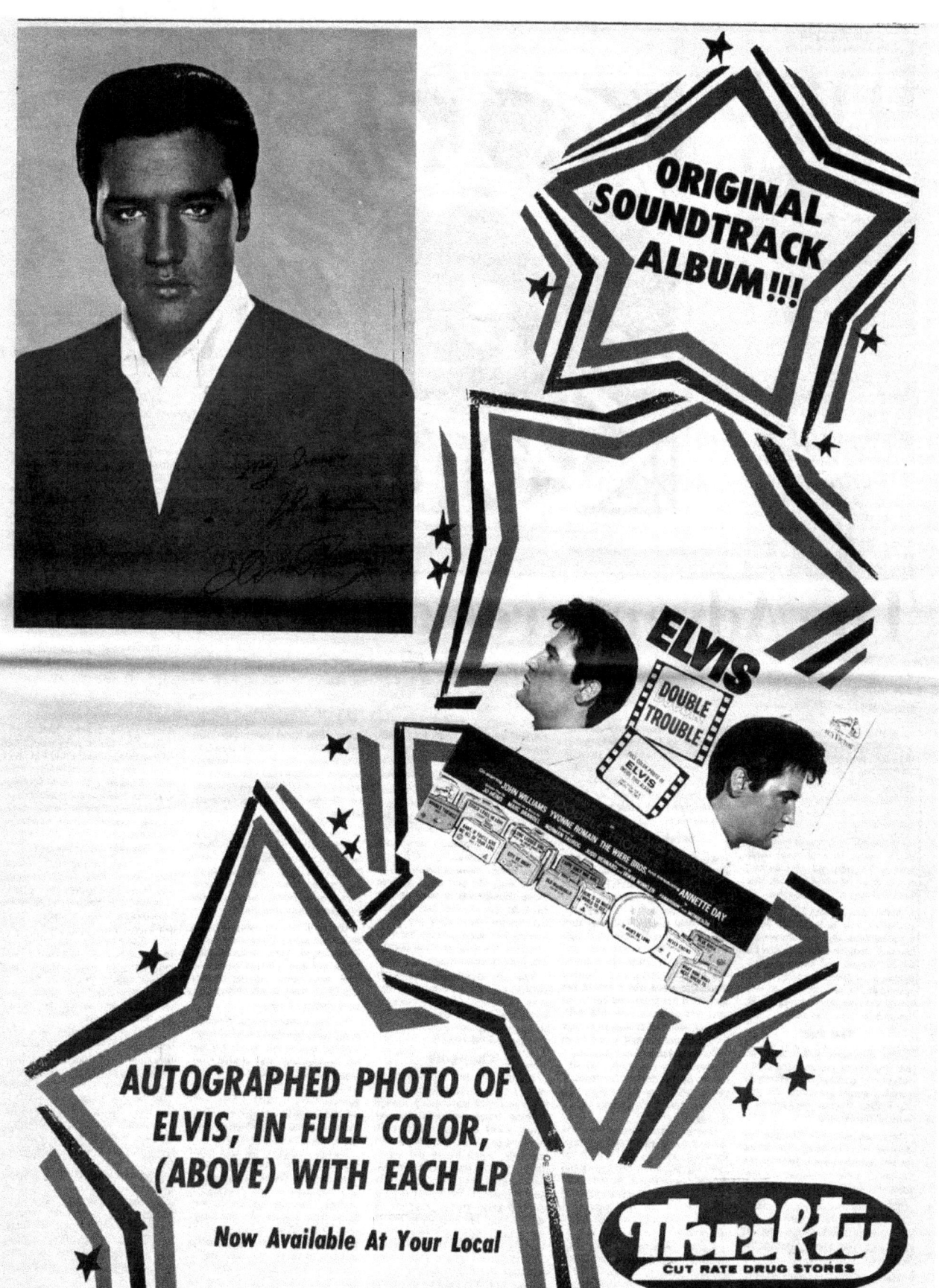

AUTOGRAPHED PHOTO OF ELVIS, IN FULL COLOR, (ABOVE) WITH EACH LP

Now Available At Your Local **Thrifty** CUT RATE DRUG STORES

ORIGINAL SOUNDTRACK ALBUM!!!

KRLA ARCHIVES

By Lawrence Charles

The rumors in the music business have been flying fast and thick. Have the hippies really turned thumbs down on the Lovin' Spoonful? An incident in Northern California in which the Lovin' Spoonful supposedly "sold-out" to the authorities is at the center of the controversy.

"Some hippies have dropped the Lovin' Spoonful," said Eric Jacobson, the group's producer, "and some have not, depending on how well they know the boys and what they are ready to believe about them.

Unknown Details

"There are a lot of details the general public is unaware of and people have been spreading rumors without real knowledge of the events."

If the hippies have left the Spoonful high and dry, it hasn't hurt their popularity noticeably. "On the East Coast where the concentration of hippies is far less than on the West Coast their latest record, "Six O'Clock," hasn't had nearly the success it's had in the West. Of course, losing some friends has hurt them psychologically."

Only Human

No one likes to lose friends, and the Spoonful are only human. But they seem to be picking up new ones every day. Their soundtrack album, "You're A Big Boy Now," from the film of the same name is

selling very well. Despite their movie success, they have no film plans for the immediate future. They find it hard to coordinate record release dates with the film companies and found that conflicting time tables often deny them the exposure they want with their fans.

The Spoonful has been concentrating on week-end college concerts. They are very popular with non-hip, average college-Joe types, whom, fortunately for the Spoonful's commercial health, outnumber the hippies.

The group has been cutting a new album set for release in early August. Publicity has already begun for their big summer show at the Hollywood Bowl.

"Six O'Clock" is the group's ninth record. They've been together going on four years, which on the quickly-changing music business scene, is practically an ice age long.

All New York

The Lovin' Spoonful, John Sebastion, Steve Boone, Zally Yanovsky and Joe Butler, all live in and around New York City. John Sebastion has written more of the songs in the Lovin' Spoonful repertoire than any other member of the group. He often takes the part of lead singer for the group and plays the autoharp and harmonica.

Zally worked with Mama Cass Elliott in a group called the Mugwumps before joining the Spoonful.

The Adventures of Robin Boyd

©1965 By Shirley Poston

The Adventures of Robin Boyd have appeared regularly in print since November 13, 1965, with the exception of the past couple of months. (Robin has been on vacation). (Would you believe a rest cure?) The following chapter is a re-cap of the story so far, and should bring her present and future victims—er—fans up to date.—S.P.

Once upon a thyme (if you think *that's* spicy, stick around) there was a 16-year-old girl named Robin Boyd. She had red hair, blue eyes and long (false) eyelashes.

Robin also had her fair share of problems. For instance, not being a partial bird, she was always exhausted from running fan clubs for all her faves, and she got pneumonia a lot from sneaking to the airport in the dead of night to welcome arriving stars. Additionally, her middle name was Irene.

Tea Pot

One afternoon, Robin spied an old English tea pot teetering atop a neighbor's garbage can. Promptly swiping—oops—rescuing the pot, she carted it home and shined it with an old sweater.

You are probably thinking "oh brother, they're gonna start trying to tell me there was a genie in the tea pot." Your suspicions are correct.

The genie was young, tall, dark, Liverpudlian, and 'andsome. He also looked familiar (and was). In fact, he looked exactly like George Harrison.

George (which by some odd coincidence was the genie's name) informed Robin that he had come to grant her fondest wish to repay her for being such a hard working bird.

Certain that she was either dreaming or had finally lost the remainder of her marbles, Robin admitted that she had several times rather wished she could turn herself into a *real* bird, so she could fly off to visit all her faves and observe them while perched in dark corners.

Wish Granted

Would you believe this wish was actually granted? (Not unless you're mad as a March hare, kiddo). Well, it was. Simply (quite) by saying the word "Liverpool," Robin was suddenly able to turn herself into a *real* robin (with tiny Byrd glasses yet, as she was blind as six bats). When she later found that she was unable to pronounce the magic word which turned her back (and her front, and her front) into her sixteen-year-old self, George was kind enough to change the aforementioned word from "Worchestershire" to "Ketchup." (Incidentally, she made this discovery on the floor of the Beatles' garage after her first "flight" to England, but that's another story). (U hope).

George then snuggled down in his nice warm tea pot and prepared for a long winter's nap. But he had to be kidding. From the day he met Robin Irene Boyd, he was constantly being rousted from his cozy trundle to get his master—whoops—client out of some scrape or another.

Scrape, actually, is not the *word*. In the months that followed, Robin got into some of the most mellish hesses in history. She caused John Lennon to swallow a guitar pick during a performance. She put all of England into an uproar by flapping out of a Rolling Stones concert while in the pocket of Mick Jagger's jacket. She was trapped in a bird cage by a well-meaning Sonny and Cher, and locked in a tea pot by George the genie, his fellow genies John and Pauley, and Ringo the Angel.

When her mother (after much desperate searching through the yellow pages) sent her to a psychiatrist, she immediately terrorized Dr. Alex Andersrag (of Timed Band.fame). Since it takes one to know one, the two soon became close friends and it was through his help that she was later able to talk Ringo (the Angel) out of revoking her magic powers the time she shut his wing in a car door at the local drive-in theater.

The only adventure Robin didn't totally foul up was the time she was allowed, after weeks of hysterical begging and bellowing, to see the Beatles perform at the Cavern. (In *1961,* yet!).

Changing

During all this activity (and more) (you bettah believe it), George found his attitude toward Robine Irene was changing. As time went by, he went from brusque to utterly impossible. For example, when Robin did something he didn't particulary appreciate (which was approximately every hour on the hour) (as the cuckoo clock strikes, that is), he would yank her arm clean out of the socket. And he was violently jealous of other boys, particularly of his fellow genie John, who pinched. But Robin learned to live (it up) with this kind of treatment because all of their battles ended with the words: "Shurrup and give us a kiss."

Robin was just recovering from her most recent (mis) adventure (it was comprised of spending quite some time under the front seat of the Beatles' limousine, which would have been a strange enough position had she not been smeared all over with peanut butter at the time) when tragedy struck.

Pitchfolk!!!

Her father slunk home from work to report that he had been transferred from California to, of *all* places, *South Dakota. Pitchfork,* South Dakota, to be precise (not to mention ridiculous).

Robin, of course, refused to go, as did her sturdy 12-year-old sister Ringo Boyd. This, of course, did them not one whit of good and they were soon tripping toward L.S.D. (Lovely South Dakota, for corn's sake). (I'll say).

To make things worse (if such a thing were possible) (and it was), George was unable to get a transfer immediately and couldn't accompany her to South Da-what's-its-face. Even worse, *her* magic powers were invalid in that state (of mass confusion) and would remain that way until George could work things out and join her.

Robin thought all was lost, especially after the conservative saddle-shoed Pitchforkians gaped and twittered at her "outlandish clothes," but one day, on the way home from school, she and Ringo looked up to see a long-haired, bell-bottomed figure loping along in front of them. Not knowing or caring whether it was a boy or a girl, Robin flang herself into its arms.

The figure (what there was of it) (no one is perfect) turned out to be a girl named Francine, who had been known to take the life of anyone who called her anything but Budgie. As in big-fat-yellow).

Together, the three girls decided to liven things up around Pitchfork by starting the town's first rock and roll group. The only problem was, they had no instruments (except Ringo's drooms, which were actually oatmeal cartons) and even less talent.

Short And Sweet

Then, one morning after a short (but sweet) visit from George, they found themselves the owners of brand new guitars and drooms (Loodwigs). What's more, they could play them, and sing! In fact, they could imitate any group of their choice, and could sound like themselves as well. (Would you believe sick?). Naturally (or, if you prefer—and you might, unnaturally) they named the group The Mockingbirds.

Because she would lose her magic powers were she to breathe one word of same to anyone, Robin explained this phenomena to Budgie only by telling her there were certain things she couldn't tell her. Budgie understood. (Thousands wouldn't). And Ringo was too busy drooming joyously to know or care what was happening.

After a lot of practice, they managed to open a teen night spot called the Neville Club. *How* they managed this is best left unsaid. The police didn't come for them with a long rope the first time the full story behind their club was printed, but leave us not ess-pray our luck.

(Continued on page 23)

KRLA ARCHIVES

...INSTRUMENTALISTS in an age of freak rock.

DAVIE ALLAN AND THE ARROWS

Reluctant Angels

By Bobby Farrow

Suddenly Nancy Sinatra was suing Capitol and Tower Records for $100,000 in damages to stop her picture and name from being used on the soundtrack album cover of the movie, "The Wild Angels." She also flung charges at American International Pictures which produced the film.

Nancy claimed the album was made without her consent and although she had the female lead role, she never Ok'ed the use of her name and picture on the LP jacket.

Freak-rock

Davie Allan and the Arrows, a Los Angeles-based group devoted to instrumentals in an age of freak-rock, who cut the film's soundtrack were as amazed at the album's huge sales success as Nancy was angry.

"We cut *Blues Theme* (the first piece on the LP which opened the film) in about ten minutes. We never knew it would be released as a single because stations were getting so many requests for it."

Blues Theme just squeaked onto the bottom of the national charts and is high on the best-seller lists on the West Coast.

The Arrows agreed to cut the film because they needed work. But says Tony Allwain, rhythm guitarist, "We're hoping we won't be judged on *Blues Theme*. We're more talented than that. It's really very simple. We do a lot more complex and interesting things."

Inevitably the Arrows are now associated with the leather-jacketed, tough-guy motorcycle group, the Hell's Angels, since doing the soundtrack for the film. It's an association they're trying to blot out of their public image.

Revenge

"But don't print that we're against the Hell's Angels," said the group's drummer, Don Manning. "I don't want one of those big, burly, hairy guys pulling me out of bed in the middle of the night for revenge. Actually the Hell's Angels are probably buying most of our records."

The Arrows intend to continue in the instrumental vein. They did the instrumental soundtracks for a second Hell's Angel film, "Devils Angels" and a stock car racing film feature, "Thunder Alley" which are both recent releases. They're currently working on the musical track for "The Trip," a film on LSD starring Peter Fonda.

Different Way

"We're trying to tell a story," said Drew, who uses only his first name. "It could be sung, but we're trying to do it a different way."

The Arrows feel music sets moods, directs thoughts and determines lives. "I couldn't see telling a story with the big band sound of Benny Goodman, for instance, but Bach and Mozart tell stories in their music.

The Arrows admit they're in the same bag as the Ventures but insist they are not carbon-copies of that instrumental group. "Davie has a unique fuzz tone and style of guitar playing," said Tony, "which gives the group a distinct sound."

WHISTLER DUE HERE

LONDON — Whistling Jack Smith, whose "I Was Kaiser Bill's Batman" is gaining on the charts, has lined-up his first American tour this summer.

He is scheduled for radio and television promotional appearances in July and August.

Mr. Spock: Cool Cosmonaut

By Lawrence Charles

Mr. Spock, the star character of the hit TV show, *Star Trek*, is a kind of swash-buckling James Bond of outer space. He's cool, detached, intelligent and human — well, almost human — Mr. Spock looks human but has no emotions, so he rises above the hassle of human passions. He's the winner America loves.

Off camera, Mr. Spock is the very feeling and likeable Leonard Nimoy, handsome, 6-foot father of two equally human children. During a break in filming *Star Trek*, Leonard relaxed in his office at the Desilu studios in Hollywood and told *BEAT* why he thinks *Star Trek* has become so popular and drawn such an avid teen following.

"First of all Spock's physical look arouses intrigue." Daily hour and a half make-up sessions convert Leonard into a fetching astro-man with pointy ears and slanting accent-mark eyebrows. His haircut features bangs cut straight across the forehead and sideburns that taper into points.

Painful Experiences

Leonard feels part of Spock's appeal is that he is in constant control of his emotions. "If adults have an emotional experience or reaction to something," he said, "they have the freedom to express themselves. They don't have to answer to as many authority figures as do teenagers. The kids have the law, parents, teachers and school administrators constantly telling them 'you're too young to know what's best for yourself, so don't react in any ways that we don't approve of.' So an emotional experience becomes a painful thing, a real problem for young people."

Leonard thought for a minute and then zeroed in on what may be Spock's top click factor with teens.

"Spock is very straight. There's no bull about him. He calls the shots as he sees them. He's terribly honest. Kids hate hipocracy. Young people today are asking about things their parents have been shoving under the carpet for years.

Stretching out in his comfortable Spanish-style arm chair, Leonard smiled and said, "When I first came out here to be an actor, the male film idol was Marlon Brando. He achieved fame playing a dumb, boorish, insensitive, crummy guy in *Street Car Named Desire*.

In contrast, Spock is a very intelligent, hip character who knows his work and does it well. The success of *Star Trek* is a sign that women are no longer swooning over the dumb brute in the undershirt who beats up the heroine. It's a welcome change," said Leonard.

Very Much Alone

"Spock is very much alone. On the show there is nobody else like him. A lot of people, especially teenagers, feel isolated." The secret of Spock's success may be his ability to tap this universal feeling, Leonard feels. "Spock seems to thrive on aloneness. He doesn't say 'I wish I were like everyone else.' Instead he says, 'I'm alone and I'm special. I would rather be me than anyone else.'"

One of the show's great appeals is to the ever wondering human mind. The current fascination with unidentified flying objects seems to stem from man's curiosity. "If there really is intelligent life on other planets," said the star, "wouldn't it be groovy if they had all the answers to human problems here on earth?"

Star Solutions

Leonard's performance is so convincing that many of his fan's think he is that great all-knowing problem solver from the stars. During a recent, hectic publicity visit to New York, (where Leonard was mobbed by screaming teenagers in record stores and had to be rescued by the police) Leonard granted some insistent fans a twenty-minute interview in his hotel lobby.

"You know the kinds of questions movie magazines usually ask? What's your favorite color, what dish does your wife cook best? That's sort of what I expected. But these kids hit me with questions like 'What do you think about birth control, the war in Vietnam, capital punishment?' They really thought I was Dr. Spock with all the answers. You know, just lay it on us. They really got down to the nitty gritty."

Spock had one brush with bittersweet romance. But like the cowboy who kisses his horse and leaves the girl behind in tears, Spock escaped.

Spock's space ship, U.S.S. Enterprise, bumped down on another planet. Spock runs into a girl, played by Jill Ireland, he knew a few years ago (not light years, mind you) who had a crush on him. Having the feelings of an eskimo pie, he, of course, never responded.

Suddenly Spock is hit by a spore — his emotions are released — defenses swept away — inhibitions down. Picture this scene — Spock turns to the girl and says, "I love you." She's ecstatic. Spock loses interest in the space ship. He mutinees. His captain flips and puts him down. Spock gets angry. Fantastically, the anger checks the action of the spore and Spock is returned to his emotionless state. He leaves the girl, as tenderly as his non-soul permits, broken up and teary.

The show finishes with Spock back on the job in the space ship. He seems sullen and quiet. The captain asks him what's wrong and Spock answers:

Missing Lovely Things

"All I can say is that for the first time in my life, I was happy." Spock knows he is missing lovely things in life, said Leonard, he feels a sense of loss. You can't have your cool and blow it, says the old proverb.

With space research making a trip to the moon a real possibility, *Star Trek* becomes less of a wild fantasy. On recent visits to Goddard Space Flight Center in Maryland and White Sands Proving Grounds in New Mexico, Leonard was thrilled to find a lot of the scientists designing space equipment are avid *Star Trek* fans.

Science fiction spurs research. If Jules Verne had never written a story about going to the moon, who ever would have thought about visiting that silly old, banana-colored ball anyway?

Hansel And Gretel

Ever since Leonard played Hansel (at age 8) in Hansel and Gretel in Boston's Peabody Playhouse he knew he wanted to be an actor. His no-nonsense, Russian immigrant parents had other ideas. Acting was fine for kids playing around but grown-ups had to do "real" work. "You know what I mean," said Leonard, "that OK-kid-you're-a-man-now-so-go-grab-a-shovel attitude."

"Young people today are questioning that 'work like crazy and love it' attitude." With automation progressively cutting the work week, young people are asking 'If you can enjoy yourself more of the time than working and live with it — if you can adjust to so much leisure time — then why not?'"

Versatile Actor

Leonard's been on almost every television series imagineable playing doctors, lawyers, Indians, Mexicans and bad guys. Back in Boston, Mr. Nimoy, has become Mr. Spock to regular customers at his barber shop. "I guess my parent's know I'm really working now," smiled Leonard.

...LEONARD NIMOY: "no bull about him."

KRLA ARCHIVES

July 1, 1967 — THE BEAT — Page 23

please send me BEAT
26 issues only
$3 per year

Mail to: **BEAT Publications**
9121 Sunset Blvd.
Los Angeles, California 90069

☐ New Subscription
☐ Renewal (please enclose mailing label from your last BEAT)
I want BEAT for — ☐ 1 year at $3.00 or ☐ 2 years at $5.00
I enclose ☐ cash ☐ check ☐ money order
Outside U.S. — $9 per year

Please print your name and address.

Name_____
Street_____
City_____
State_____ Zip_____

Shirley you jest
(Continued from page 18)

I was positive the rumor was true because it seemed like all of a suddy, there were old Beatle songs all over the wireless, featuring an unusual amount of solos by George G. Harrison. (G. as in gnash.)

After doing a lot of checking (would you believe sneaking?) (do you realize we could all become ace detectives after the training we've had stalking pop stars?), I found no George at all and/or short.

I often wonder in these days of Monkee madness... are all of you getting sick of the way I blither about the Beatles?

If so, just remember that at least I'm consistent.

ROBIN BOYD...
(Continued from page 20)

They were also able to entice the teenagers of Pitchfork into the club (again by means better left un-reprinted lest the cuffs be snapped about their sweet young wrists). However... Question: Were they able to get the crowd to stop just standing there and move so much as a muscle? Answer: No.

After a surprise visit from John the genie (who still pinched), Robin knew it wouldn't be long before she would have her powers and her George back.

She also knew what she must do to finally set the teenagers of Pitchfork on their ears. Otherwise known as a nice way of putting it.

(To Be Continued)

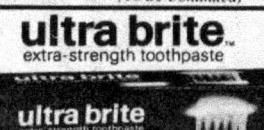
ultra brite extra-strength toothpaste
Ultra Brightens Breath as it Ultra Brightens Teeth

CLASSIFIED

FOR SALE
TAPE RECORDER — Mayfair 1607, New — $42. Rarely used — 6 months. ALL — $42! Inquire, Mary, 7823 Forest Avenue, Munster, Indiana.

FENDER JAGUAR GUITAR — Blonde Custom finish. With case. $195. 870-5960 (Los Angeles, Calif.)

FREE LIST OF GROOVY POSTERS — SEPER CO., 5273 Tendilla, Woodland Hills, Calif. 91364

WANTED
TALENT HUNT. Audition for rock groups, original material preferred. This is your chance to join big record company. Call Rusty Evans, Take 6 Inc., (213) 463-5107.

FORMING ROCK GROUP — 583-3007 (San Diego, Calif.)

MALE BASS GUITARIST looking for job with experienced group. Call 247-7165 (Chicago, Ill.) or write Robt. Perez, 4342 So. Honore, Chicago, Illinois 60609. Will answer all letters.

Flower child with poly-tonal music and happening voice will audition for manager/producer. Abajian, P.O. Box 375, Orange, Calif. 92669.

INSTRUCTION
REACH COSMIC AWARENESS without drugs — help save mankind from destruction. Write for free booklet. "Cosmic Awareness Speaks," Organization of Awareness, Box 115-E, Olympia, Washington.

SLEEP-LEARNING, Self-hypnosis. Details, strange catalog free! Auto suggestion, Box 24-BT, Olympia, Washington

FAN CLUBS
BEATLEMANIACS UNLIMITED c/o Blurps 'n Apesie, 433 Ave. "E", Redondo Beach, Calif. 90277. Only 50 cents!

GEORGE HARRISON FAN CLUB, 3976 Ridge Pike, Collegeville, Penna. 19426.

THE ROBBS NATIONAL FAN CLUB Write: P.O. Box 350, Beverly Hills, California 90213

CYN LENNON BEATLE CLUB, Kathy Burns, 4121 Adair Ave., Crystal, Minnesota 55422. 10¢ monthly. Send SASE for info.

WRITE TO: Entertainers Unlimited, 8135 Rector, St. Louis, Missouri 63134.

"MERRY GO ROUND" 4641 West 132nd St., Hawthorne, California. Enclose $1.00.

BIRTHDAYS
HAPPY BIRTHDAY PITCHIE from Geordie.

HAPPY LATE BIRTHDAY LES THOMPSON!

HAPPY BIRTHDAY PAUL

Happy Birthday Cheryl Aldridge — From Lonabergers

HAPPY BIRTHDAY Paul McCartney — Love, Anne

Happy Birthday to the Jackson boys — Craig & Keith. — Debbie

Happy Birthday Pat. June 27th. D.B.D. & Ken.

"**HAPPY BIRTHDAY** my darling Paul — Love, Lorelle!"

PAUL — Happy Birthday. Please come back to La Jolla. Love, Lynn.

Happy Birthday to **MARY-BIMA**. Love from BENIMBA, BLUMBA, and SUSIE.

PERSONALS
ERIC JOHNSON IS MINE! — Lora —

MARK LINDSAY — I love you. Please call and I'll tell you more. (202) 882-1503 — TEREE (Call soon, OK?)

MICHAEL MELINE loves **CINDY PETZEL**

SOMEONE sent in a dime for mailing my little "Soul Book," and didn't send his address. What shall I do? Malvina Reynolds, 2027 Parker St., Berkeley, California 94704 "La-ta-toe!!"

THE BLACKOUTS turn me on

TURKEY FEATHERS grow on **TURKEY CHINS**

NEIL YOUNG

"**STAINED GLASS**"

"**INSIDE OUCH**"

A RAIDER rooter I'll always be, For the RAIDERS will rule eternally!!!

I LOVE JIM PONS — DEBBIE

CHAPTER ONE is groovy!! Joe and Chris — I was the girl in pink. luv, Sandy

Laurie Upham loves The Monkees

AUGUST 28th is coming!!

Bob — Thanks for your respect — Your Problem Child.

KISSY — I love you — Ding

"I'm here Jack Casady!"

The grooviest guys drive burgundy Corvairs.

ROGER MOBLEY — I love you **NIKKY**

"Thank you, Paul Kantner."

Animal Crackers & Washboards Amalgamated?

WAKE UP, BOB! I luv you. **ELAINE**

within you — without you

MONKEE PEOPLE ARE BASICALLY INSECURE. Beatle People are Groovy!

Pourade and Harrison together — **NO COMPARISON!**

Oh Mama, can this really be the End? To be stuck in California, with the **LONDON BLUES** again.

Barb loves Phil.

JOHN LENNON IS!

HAPPY BIRTHDAY CHA-CHA! Always, Bryan and Barbara and Bosco Rabbitt.

Who are the **PERFECT STRANGES.**

Indescribably Delicious make it! ... **PAM**

I love you, Mike Dunstah ...

REBEL KIND IS HAPPENING! JAMESON!!

"**J.T. NERB LIVES**"

I love you, David Burke!!

WHY FOUR? IS GROOVY... THEY ARE: **CATHY, GINA, KARIN, WENDY.**

Judy + Randy — Love — Norma + Dennis

LOST!!! Two mod boys from West Covina who sat in front of us at '66 Beatle Concert. (Remember Peanut Fight?) Meet at Beatle Rally, Griffith Park, June 17. Michelle & Linda.

I luv Denny Tufano, lead singer of the fab Buckinghams. Nancy Carpenter.

BEWARE!! D & D ARE WATCHING YOU.

Dorothy's in love with Fang.

MONKEE PEOPLE WATCH GIDGET RE-RUNS.

Beatle people are groovy!

Long live Smitty

Sue — **CHER luvs KEITH**

BETULZ 4EVR!! MUNKIZ NEVR!!

MONKEE PEOPLE WEAR BROWN SHOES. Beatles People are groovy!

NAZZ are needed in Phoenix.

Your Friends are our friends.

"**THE WOODS**"

DING lubs KISSY

"**I LOVE YOU, GYPSY — DONOVAN**"

BEAT is no longer accepting anything but **PERSONAL MESSAGES** in the classified section. Only messages (including Happy Birthdays) will be accepted. We will print names but not addresses or phone numbers.

BEAT has a new address:

CLASSIFIED BEAT PUBLICATIONS 9121 Sunset Blvd. Los Angeles, California 90069

DEADLINE FOR NEXT ISSUE: JUNE 21

KRLA ARCHIVES

RECORDS FREE FROM RC
You'll Flip at the ZZZIP in RC Cola

while you swing to your favorite stars! RC and music, perfect partners for the perfect lift

TAKE 1 ALBUM FREE

For everyone you buy... with 6 cork liners or seals from R.C. bottle caps over 100 Capitol LP's available. Order as often as you wish. Nothing to join. Look for this display at your favorite store.

Here's your best way yet to save more on the records you want. In dollars-and-cents terms you get two albums that the Capitol Record Club sells for $3.98 each time you buy one. The savings are even bigger on stereo records! And there are no shipping charges to pay, nothing else to join or buy.

What's more, you choose from top albums by today's biggest stars, including the Beatles, David McCallum, Frank Sinatra, Lou Rawls, Buck Owens, Petula Clark, the Outsiders, Nancy Wilson, Dean Martin, Sonny James, the Beach Boys and many others.

OTHER FINE BRANDS: DIET-RITE®COLA, NEHI®BEVERAGES, PART-T-PAK®BEVERAGES, UPPER 10®
"ROYAL CROWN" AND "RC" REG. U.S. PAT. OFF.; ©1966 ROYAL CROWN COLA CO.

KRLA ARCHIVES

KRLA ARCHIVES

KRLA BEAT
Volume 3, Number 9 — July 15, 1967

Music Love and Flowers

Enter the Young

Words and Music by Terry Kirkman

Here they come
Here they come
Here they come
Some are walkin' some are ridin'
Here they come
Some are flyin' some just glidin'
Released after years of being kept in hidin'
They're climbin' up the ladder rung by rung

*Enter the young... Yeah they've learned to think
Enter the young... More than you think they think
Not only learned to think but to care
Not only learned to think but to dare

Here they come
Some with questions some decisions

Here they come
Some with facts and some with visions
Of a place to multiply without the use of divisions
To win a prize that no one's ever won
Enter the young*

Here they come
Some are laughin' some are cryin'
Here they come
Some are doin' some are tryin'
Some are sellin' some are buyin'
Some are livin' some are dyin'
But demanding recognition one by one
Enter the young*
*Chorus
Reprinted by permission. ©1966 Beechwood Music Corp.

TEN FULL PAGES OF EXCLUSIVE INTERVIEWS AND PHOTOS FROM MONTEREY

KRLA ARCHIVES

How The Happening Happened

BEAT Photos: Rich Schor

The Monterey International Pop Festival was a fantastic success by all accounts. It was a real victory for the art of pop music over commerical exploitation. Artists like the Mamas and Papas, the Byrds, Hugh Masekela, the Association and Simon and Garfunkel came to exchange ideas in almost continuous concerts.

The idea for the first, tremendously ambitious pop convocation was born a scant two months ago one night in John Phillips living room. The evening of April 4, Alan Pariser, dropped in on John, the lanky bearded Papa of the Mamas and Papas, and his wife, Mama Michelle, to try to convince them to headline a profit-making festival in Monterey.

Over Coffee

Paul Simon of Simon and Garfunkel was visiting with the Phillips at the time. Over coffee the two singers talked the promoter into a non-profit festival designed to upgrade pop music. Pariser was convinced it might work and so went along with the non-profit scheme.

The Phillips-Simon team soon picked up support from other major figures in the pop world. The Mamas and Papas' producer, Lou Adler, Donovan, Mick Jagger, Paul McCartney, Jim McGuinn, Andrew Oldham and Smokey Robinson either lent support or joined the festival's board of governors.

Obvious Absence

Some obvious top-pop personalities like the Beatles, Bob Dylan, and the Rolling Stones were missing from the program. They were all invited but couldn't make it for some reason. Folk artists were ignored because it was felt that they are represented at their own festivals. All artists performed free and the proceeds from ticket sales were funneled into a specially created organization known simply as, "The Foundation." The funds will be used to create scholarships for music students, give financial assistance to pop performers and start courses in such pop topics as copyright laws, song composition, agents' practices and other often poorly understood areas, as well as establishing future festivals.

Hard Work

Agents, artists and businessmen surprised themselves at how hard they were willing to work for free. The festival brought out people's hidden creativity. David Wheeler, formerly a part-time public relations man, recruited and unemployed commercial artist, Tom Wilkes to design a program book. The team spent 12, roughly, 18-hour days whipping out an impressive 96 page book. The team had worked together so successfully, they were commissioned to do the cover for the next Rolling Stones' album and ads for the Stones, the Beatles and the Beach Boys.

Phil Turetsky, the festivals 47-year-old unsalaried Business Manager was an important link in making the festival into a reality. He used the previous Monterey Jazz Festival as a model to balance expenses against the festival's intake.

Hang-Ups

Papa John and the rest of the festival's planners worked hard at anticipating possible hang-ups for the June 16-18 event. John put in countless hours at the festival's Hollywood office constantly on the phone with the director or the Monterey fairgrounds or one of the many companies involved in setting up outdoor campsites to handle the overflow crowds. Tugging at his scraggly beard and fingering his ever-present black fur cap, John, the President of the festival's board of governors, arranged for leasing grounds outside Monterey, hiring shuttle buses, making sure food was available and handling complaints and demands from the artists. Not too surprising perhaps, was John's report that most of the artist problems came from the lesser known groups. The stars seemed relatively undemanding.

KRLA ARCHIVES

BEAT: Can you comment about what's happening this weekend in Monterey?
Brian: *Very groovy scene. We've been very busy recording. I just came away for a few days and it's so nice to get on someone else's scene. It's a very beautiful scene happening here.*
BEAT: A lot of people have been sort of critical of this kind of happening in this country. The uptight people.
Brian: *They're frightened of trouble but I don't expect any trouble, do you? It has been wonderful. I have been walking freely amongst everybody. Yesterday I was walking through and joining rings of kids and fans. You know I've never had a chance to do that much before. People are very nice here. I like it.*
BEAT: Would you like to see this kind of thing happen all through the world.
Brian: *We have had one in London and there are going to be more. But of course it should happen. I think it's wonderful. The new generation's expressing itself. This is one way of expressing itself.*
BEAT: Do you like what's happening with the new generation?
Brian: *Yes, very much. There's lots of hassles but things always have to get worse before they can get better. There are mistakes on both sides.*
BEAT: What about the Stones — what's happening with them?
Brian: *We record practically all the time as the Beatles do. We just got about a week off so I came over here with Andrew (Andrew Oldham, Stones' manager). The others have sort of split to various places. I think, I'm not quite sure. But nobody seemed to get it together to come over here. I wish they had 'cause they have missed a very nice scene.*
BEAT: What do you think about the Beatles new album?
Brian: *It's great. It's too much. It's really good. I did a Beatles' session the other night, actually. On soprano saxophone, of all things. Paul's done a couple of ours. You know, it's already happening. I've taken up playing reeds again. I used to play reed instruments. I bought a soprano saxophone the other day and ever since I have been doing sessions on it. There are soprano saxophones on the Stones' records, future Beatle records. You know, it's a funny thing — you get hold of something and put it on everyone's records. It's great. There's a very nice recording scene going on right now in London.*
BEAT: There have been rumors that the Stones and Beatles are going to record together. Could you comment on that?
Brian: *It would be at a certain stage. It would be a very nice thing. We are getting very close as far as work is concerned. Whether actually we could — well we could work something out together. From one point of view it might not be a very good thing because our direction is slightly different from theirs. Lack of distinction because of the joining up of the two might be lost. That's the only thing that could spoil it, I think. There will certainly be schemes. We spend an awful lot of time with each other now. We've got a lot of mutual ideas.*
BEAT: It certainly would be wild from the standpoint of a combination of sounds. It would seem to me that you would come up with something really unique.
Brian: *It's happening already. As I said, I did this Beatle session — mixed on a Beatle session, various things. Paul's done a couple of ours. You know, it's already happening.*
BEAT: It's taking that direction, anyway.
Brian: *Yeah, and that's not a bad direction.*
BEAT: We're glad to have you in Monterey.
Brian: *It's nice to let people know we're still functioning. Still around — still on the scene — still doing all we can.*
BEAT: How long are you going to be over here, Brian?
Brian: *I'm just going to be here for a very few days. Just a little break from recording and everything.*
BEAT: Are there any immediate plans for coming back over after the court stuff is cleared up?
Brian: *No, not at the moment but everything's going to be all right. The big job at hand is to get the L.P. done and we're spending an awful lot of time on it this time. It's going to be more of a production. We've really put some thought into it because people are still liking our albums so we're trying to really give them something that will take them on a stage further. And, so that they will take us on a stage further.*
We feel at the moment that our important work is to be done in the studio rather than in baseball halls and stadiums around the country. You see, once you've been around the country once or twice people have seen you and it's a question of what's to be gained by going around again. But, there's a lot to be gained by letting them share our progressions because we are progressing musically very fast.
BEAT: You're in a position to please yourselves more now, aren't you?
Brian: *Well to a certain extent that's always been true. But, we can't really please ourselves. We have too large a public who depend on us to be able to please ourselves.*
BEAT: That's the best costume I've seen at the Festival. It's beautiful — a work of art.
Brian: *Well, it's Old English and European stuff.*
BEAT: Did you fly here?
Brian: *Yes I flew in the other night. I came by New York and Los Angeles. I spent about one hour in New York and five minutes in Los Angeles. Then I was flown straight out here on a jet. The Mamas and Papas, I think, own it or rent it or something.*
BEAT: Any schedule after the Festival?
Brian: *I've got a few things to take care of at home so I might be leaving as soon as the festival is over. On the other hand, I might just take in Los Angeles and New York on the way back and look up a few old friends. It's nice to come over here. I'm glad I came.*
BEAT: There's a Love-in scheduled for Los Angeles soon. Have you heard about that?
Brian: *It's such a different scene over here from back home. You have more of a problem or at least it's more accute over here than we do.*
BEAT: Which problem is that?
Brian: *The whole problem of social change which is going on around the Western world right now. It's going on in the Eastern world too, but in a different way. We won't talk about that.*
BEAT: Do you think the Pop Festival would look like this or have an atmosphere like this if it had been held in London rather than in California?
Brian: *Yeah. We've had a similar affair in London and there are going to be more. I would like to see these affairs become a regular part of young community life because I think these people here — from what I've seen so far — are acting as a community. They have the community spirit, the community feeling. I haven't seen any signs of any trouble or any emnity. It's very nice. People are showing each other around and it's very beautiful. I'm glad I came. I'll have lots of nice things to say when I get back home.*

BEAT Photos: Ed Caraeff

"I CAME OVER HERE WITH ANDREW"

KRLA ARCHIVES

Inside

TOMMY SMOTHERS: "Before we get started, we want to officially welcome you to the first annual third, the third part of the First Annual International Monterey Pop Festival. My brother couldn't be here tonight because of various reasons and working with someone else like you work with your brother... my brother's a straight man and it's kind of difficult... I'm gonna find it difficult talking and being with you people because no one plays it straight here either.

"Of all the places in the country they could have put this Festival was here in Monterey... where Big Sur and the gorgeous... where the broad Pacific Ocean, crystal blue... sparkling... bring waves crashing against the rocks... strewn shores where majestic pines reach their hands up and fleeting to the sky... where wind torments and the beauty of the rocks and water and trees and green... here in Monterey—in this lousy weather! At least you know it's here in America... where in America we always say 'progress is our most infinite product.'

"But there's nothing to worry about because it is beautiful country and there's a phrase that sometimes when the weather's not particularly the way we want it it's always good to use and I'd like to share it with you. It's kind of a cliche and it goes like this: 'The hills are always greener on the other side of the grass so it really doesn't make much difference, does it?'

"By the way, all the people who've been around for the past couple of days—you've noticed how smooth everything's been going and a great deal of credit is due to about 150 young men around here—the Flower Fuzz—so let's give a hand to Flower Power."

BEAT: Just wanted to get your comments on what's happening here in Monterey this weekend.
MICKY: *Well, it's pretty obvious.*
BEAT: Have you seen anything here that would be a justified criticism of any kind?
MICKY: *Yeah, there are a lot of policemen around that aren't doing anything. They don't have to be here and they look pretty funny in their uniforms.*
BEAT: Do you mean that they look out of place?
MICKY: *Obviously, they look out of place. They're walking around with nothing to do.*
BEAT: Would you like to see this scene repeated?
MICKY: *I'd like to see a place for this to happen every day. Like if there was a big place—a reservation—kind of tribal area where anybody could come anytime they wanted to and do anything they wanted. I'm looking to set up something like that now where people could set up a candle booth. Just a kind of a fair but have it like all the time and there would be slow periods and fast periods—but have it there all the time.*
BEAT: Speaking of tribes. I notice you've got a beautiful costume on. Where did you get it?
MICKY: *I made most of it myself. I tried to get as close as possible to my Indian heritage—the Chickasaw.*
BEAT: Do you have some Indian heritage? I'd like to hear about it.
MICKY: *A lot. Well, my great-grandfather was a Chickasaw Indian and Uh, I've been trying to track down as much as I can, you know.*
BEAT: Have you got any interesting background about some of your ancestors. Some of the things they might have been involved in as far as the white man.
MICKY: *Yeah, they got put on a reservation.*

BEAT: How are you enjoying the happenings here?
OTIS: *"Very great, you know. People everywhere you know and everybody's having a good time. The music's great, too."*
BEAT: What about the people who have been criticizing the fact that this is going to be happening here in Monterey. Have you seen anything here today that would give people a reason to be down on it?
OTIS: *"No, I haven't seen anything that has taken place yet that's very bad. Everybody just out here having a good time. People come dressed just like they want to. Everybody's natural and having a good time, you know. And I think it's a great thing."*
BEAT: Do you think this is something that we should have more of in this country as far as freedom of expression in that area?
OTIS: *"Right. Freedom of expression. Yes."*
BEAT: What about the police. What has your personal experience been with the man?
OTIS: *Well, the man has been very great you know. Nobody has been giving anybody any trouble. There have been no kinds of fights or nothing. Everybody is together and even the policemen are kind of shocked themselves to see what's going on and I think it's very great. I think the end of it's going to be very great, too."*

I'm overwhelmed and I'm especially very happy because this is something that resembles very much the music festivals we have in our country (India). You know, the whole audience sitting outside under the sky and open air thing and very sort of informal. At the same time very well organized. Of course our festivals go all night, you know. They start about 6 o'clock and end about 7 or 8 in the morning. But, beautiful... and these young people are so beautiful... and I love them so very much and I'm so grateful to be loved by them also. I was very happy and very inspired and in some moments I really felt beautiful feelings. Feeling God, as we say. They were beautiful listeners, also—*Ravi Shankar.*

Candice Bergen: "I think the Hippies are getting power and the Establishment's getting worried."

Man, there's so much going on... I couldn't begin to tell you... there's an enormous quantity of people here. Most of them are really grooving. There are very few police. A great deal of enjoyable spirits and good vibrations and flowers and good people. The only thing there's too much of is photographers and there really aren't too many of them. Everything is happening man, music, people, festival and everything. It's beautiful. It's just the nicest scene I've ever seen—*David Crosby.*

KRLA ARCHIVES

Lookin' Out

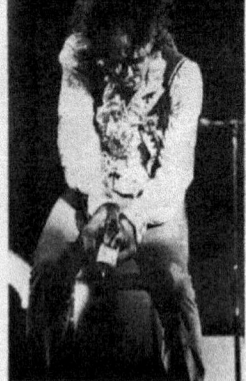

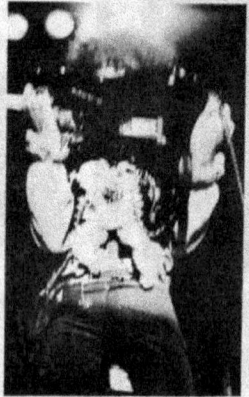

BEAT: How do you feel about being back home, Jimi (Hendrix)?
JIMI: It's very, very, very, very beautiful. Very . . . very . . . very . . . How long can I say this—very, very, very. Keith Altham from England—he says that Donovan wears golden undies. I don't know about that.
BEAT: This is for a pop music newspaper.
JIMI: O.K. Well, he doesn't man, he doesn't, honest, he doesn't.
BEAT: You're on tomorrow night, right?
JIMI: No, (turns to friend) when are we on?
FRIEND: Sunday night.
JIMI: Yeah, not till Sunday. Big build up, you know, blah, blah, blah.
BEAT: This is the first time you're appearing here since you went over to England, right.
JIMI: Yeah, the very first time.
BEAT: Hey, is this guitar especially for here?
JIMI: Yeah, for the show tomorrow—I mean, for whenever we play.
BEAT: That's a groovy outfit.
JIMI: Yeah, look at these little shoulder pads—for American football. You should see the English football (soccer). It's so ridiculous. They run around with their little hands up in the air like little pigeons—run around and kick things, you know. Things pertaining to football.
BEAT: Well, we'll catch you tomorrow night.
JIMI: Yeah, man, dig.
BEAT: (To friend of Jimi Hendrix). Can you tell us a few things about Jimi's stay here. Is he to be here long?
FRIEND: Yes, he's got a week at the Fillmore Auditorium in San Francisco, I think Jimi's going to stay over here for about a week after the Fillmore.
BEAT: A friend of ours told us that he saw Jimi in England recently. We hear that he's very big over there.
FRIEND: Yes, he's a giant over there. He's had three singles in the Top 10 and he looks as if he's on his way to another one. And his L.P. in Europe at the moment is outselling everything except the Beatles' album—which is quite a lot.

ROGER DALTREY OF THE WHO. "This is fantastic . . . the whole of the West Coast . . . the whole of America. At least, where I've been. That' not very much of it but it's just like coming home now. We have a thing like this in England called the Jazz and Blues Festival. We've done it for two years. It's sort of the same situation. It's slightly out of London, in the country. It's similar in a way but not on anything like this scale. It's quite fun but this is completely on its own. I don't think there's anything like this anywhere."

DOUG MC CLURE: Frankly, my reaction to the Pop Festival is that I'm not dressed right. From what I see, I think it's marvelous. Everybody's conducting themselves well, taking pictures and enjoying it and I think it's very good. I guess a lot of people want to find some deragatory remarks for people to make but I certainly can't find anything wrong at all. Parents shouldn't worry too much. It's very good. I think it's a rough time for the teenagers and the young people. Maybe they express themselves in a way that another generation might think is weird or whatever. I think they should, frankly. It's not an easy world to live in today. In any group like this, there are a few things that go on that I can't condone. But you know, on the other hand, there are a lot of things that I really like. There are a few things that I don't care for personally, but nothing that I would really like to give my views on. That happens in any group especially when there are teenagers around. There are always a few who take things and carry them to the extreme. But generally, it's good.

EXCLUSIVE
'It's Drake Myself And Smitty Now

BEAT: We are now talking with Phil Volk. What are your future plans, Phil?
PHIL: Future plans? Everything's kind of like smoke right now . . . up in the air. We have things like contracts and other things going with the record label, but we should be on our way as soon as we can get in the studio, we'll be all right. It's just sewing up the record deal—probably with Columbia or some major label that will believe in us and do the right thing. It's Drake and myself and Smitty now— all formerly Raiders. Like I say, that's pretty illegal, you know.
BEAT: Illegal?
PHIL: Yeah, being a Raider.
BEAT: Why is it illegal being a Raider?
PHIL: I stand on the 5th Amendment on that one because things are in the air. But, anyway, it's (the new group) called The Brotherhood.
BEAT: How much longer will it be, do you think?
PHIL: Summer's really a bad time to release anything. It's really slow except for right now—this is nice here. But, you don't release records here at the festival. Like let's say good things come in 3's, hopefully. That's the triangle we have going now with the Brotherhood and this Fall we're hoping it will be exciting and fun 'cause we've got a lot of ideas that we've never been able to use before because it's pretty illegal being with the Raiders. And now, you know.
BEAT: What do you think of the happening here?
PHIL: It's very tense. It's so new. Such a nice pioneering little effect. I mean it's big—real big.
BEAT: Have you been doing a lot of walking around and digging the other scenes?
PHIL: Well, you have to do a lot of walking just to get here and that's when you really feel like it's happening. Then when you get here you are satisfied and pleased that it's happening and it's big 'cause it's a first, isn't it? I'm really happy about it. I really hope it doesn't get closed down for any reason. Everybody's pretty legit with their motives. Everyboyd's enjoying it. 67's the year for fairs—Pleasure Faire, Pop Fair, it's fun. I'm a small town boy.
BEAT: From where?
PHIL: I used to be a 4-H. That's when fairs were like—oh, Pat Boone and things like that happening.
BEAT: Yeah, like cow shows and blue ribbons.
PHIL: Yeah. Go into the barns at night and talk to the animals.
BEAT: I noticed you were talking with a dog out there.
PHIL: I've always been close to animals.
BEAT: It's a beautiful thing.
PHIL: I think I'll give it all up and move into the woods. On a game reserve just for peace of mind. I think for a year. It's been a pretty freaky world for the last two years.
BEAT: I hope it gets less freaky.
PHIL: Yeah, it's becoming very natural. That's our (The Brotherhood) whole aim—to be very natural. Try to do the best you can at that moment.

KRLA ARCHIVES

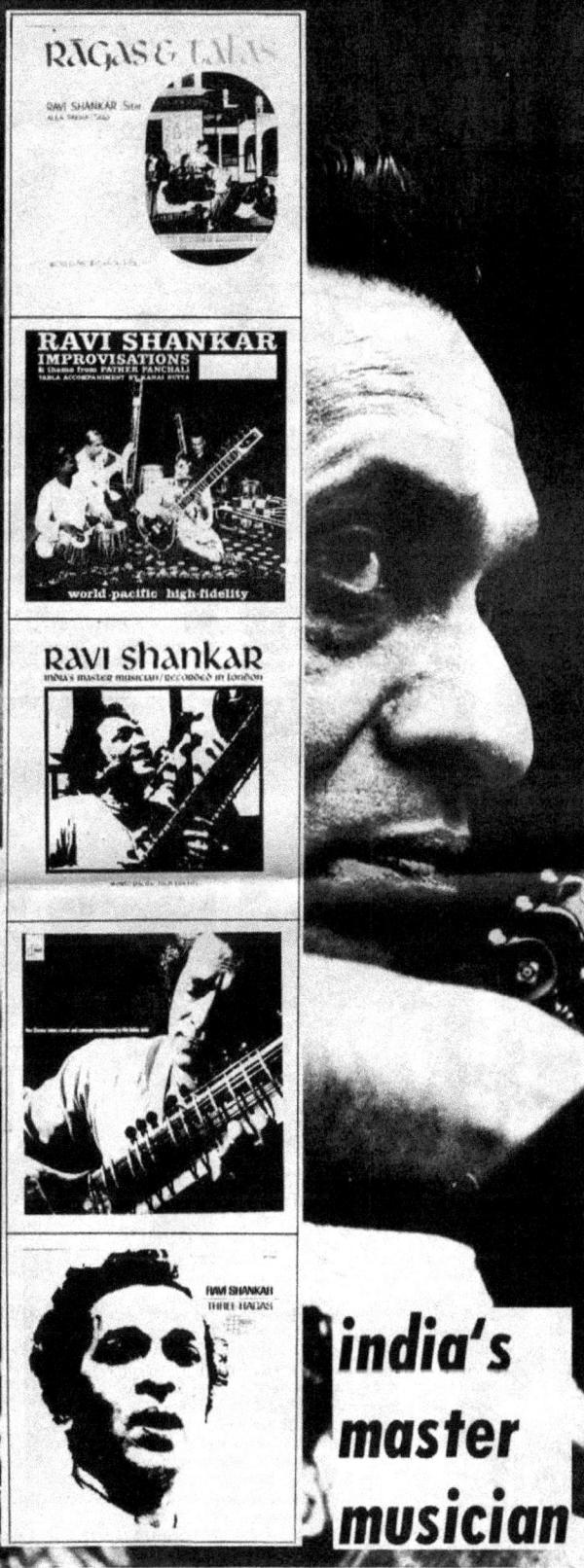

Now Available At:
MONTGOMERY WARD DEPARTMENT STORES

Outside

By Mike Dougherty

An era was born or should I say it blossomed at the Monterey Pop Festival. Tommy Smothers labeled it the era of the Flower Fuzz from the same stage where more than 50,000 new people heard 22½ hours of the grooviest music ever cooked up for a mass audience. The local police who bedecked their motorcycles with garlands of orchids were the friendliest. Their Chief, Frank Marinello said that "I have been through nine Jazz Festivals and when I was told that this would be five times as large I was flatly opposed to it. We have 30,000 citizens in Monterey and 46 regular officers and the Festival people were talking about an influx of three or four times our population. From what I've seen of these so-called hippies I have begun to like them very much. I've even made arrangements to be escorted through Haight-Ashbury district by some of my new friends." The police felt boss vibes and no serious goofs happened. Bless the Monterey Flower Fuzz.

Psychiatrist

As a precautionary measure the County of Monterey provided a tuned-in resident psychiatrist, freakout guide, Dr. Charles Rosewald and, as if to provide an astro-balance, the new Jules Alexander group brought their own out-of-site resident astrologer, Arthur. Dr. Rosewald found no freakouts to administer to and Arthur read the star charts well, because the new Alexander group grooved. Two county nurses, Marjorie Close and Jean Borden officially moonlighted the gig. Marjorie wished aloud that she had been born twenty years later so that she could enjoy "this new kind of music that much longer." She also observed that the entire medical group in attendance was "all tuned in, not turned on." Only a few minor accidents, the kind that happen in any crowd, required first-aid.

The First

Monterey was probably the first huge gathering in modern history involving teenagers, where no transistor radios were visible, the stage was always "live" and so was the audience. Outside of the arena a New Delhi bazaar-like atmosphere prevailed with throngs of new people, many resembling the brawling characters from that scene in "The Way the West Was Won," in a happier frame of mind, and others garbed in the flowing costumes of Hindus on a pilgrimage wending their way to stall after stall that lined the grassy mall.

Overhead orange, pink and red oriental fish kites darted below the blanket of grey Pacific fog and weather balloons taut on their cables proclaimed MUSIC LOVE AND FLOWERS to the world at large. As usual, somebody didn't get the word. During the Saturday afternoon concert which included the Canned Heat, Big Brother and the Holding Company, and Country Joe and the Fish, U.S. Army helicopter #65120 made seven, low, noisy passes over the peaceful music filled arena. Country Joe had an appropriate rebuttal – he invited the crowd to join in on a sing-along to the tune entitled, "Don't Drop That H-Bomb On Me, You Can Drop It On Yourself." Joe, wearing a yellow flower behind his left ear, said, "Want everybody that don't want the H Bomb dropped on them to sing-along." The crowd response was out-of-site and you know, U.S. Army helicopter #65120 had made its last pass for the day.

Transfixed

Later that same afternoon, however, a delta-winged U.S. Air Force fighter buzzed the arena while Big Brother and the Holding Company were on stage. The crowd sat transfixed as their noses told them more about the two worlds that we live in than any writer has yet been able to do. Held in for minutes, by the overcast sky, was the philosophic smog of today as everyone shared whiffs of the residual mixture of burned jet fuel and sandalwood incense. Even the paradoxical fellow wearing a New York State American Legion cap atop his curly rubber-banded tresses stopped running in the center aisle and raised his nose to the heavens as Big Brother, wearing U.S. Army surplus fatigues, punctuated by platoon sergeant stripes, blew the vocal on the Viet Nam Rag. That even zapped the lovely flower girls who came to the concert to boy watch.

Rivers

Johnny Rivers, bathed in purple light, expressed a prevalent phase in psychedelia by wailing the loaded message lyric to, "Help Me Get My Feet Back On The Ground." I suspect that the Beatles are saying almost the same thing in, "Fixing a Hole." They seem to be telling some of the hippies that it's time to pull themselves together and to really do something productive with their new found awareness. If this becomes a question of argument with Timothy Leary, who advocates the drop out, I'll have to go along with Rivers and the Beatles, they really have the viable audience. Creative fulfillment is still the biggest turn on of all.

KRLA ARCHIVES

Looking In

Larry Ramos, newest member of the pleasant sounding Association, who led off the concert on Friday night, recently pleaded with the parents of youngsters in his native Hawaii and their offsprings to take the trouble to listen to the lyrics of the new music. "The sound is groovy," Larry smiled, "but the way to bridge the generation gap is to listen and to understand."

Politeness

Eric Burdon and the Animals, who blew everybody straight out of their minds on Friday night with a super, the-way-things-are-going-to-be-electronic-rock-set, approached the generation gap bridge with a blistering critique of the older folk entitled, "Gimme My Gin." During the entire five concerts I didn't encounter one bummer incident even at the always crowded hot dog stand. It was as though a new era of politeness had been superimposed upon a society which is marked by competitive rudeness. And, during the entire three days I saw one fellow in the arena sipping from one king-sized can of beer. The Eric Burdon rendition of, "Gimme My Gin," should be required listening for old folk who say they want to know what's happening.

The magnificent Lou Rawls took a shot at getting his Friday evening audience into the next highest gear by suggesting that henceforth everybody, "Sock it *toward* 'em." Lou is a guy who grabs you without seeming to want to.

A question that I kept asking myself throughout the performance was, "Why is it that so many electric guitar men also have electric hair?" The only answer I came up with was—those heads must be plugged in too. The Head Light Shows behind the group on the stage were positively plugged in and any attempt to describe them in print humbles me. Perhaps they were a little like coral reefs blown up under a microscope pulsating to the beat of a vital new life force. Amoebas splitting to a better scene and exploding in the process.

A Bug

At first, being a member of the working press without a V.I.P. white ticket bugged me. They told us nomad press that we would have to stay on our feet during the performances and that, "It was okay to be in there, but to keep moving." That is like riding through some areas on a bike with long hair. "It's okay to go through but don't stop here!"

Later, I worked all that out in my head when the P.R. Director told a press meeting that on Friday night Life Magazine was refused admission to the arena but that the Berkley Barb had been admitted.

Even though standing packed in the crowd was a lot like being in a sports car with too many people and not knowing what to do with that awkward arm, the Monterey Pop Festival was the super-groovy event of the year.

KRLA ARCHIVES

Monterey—'It Was A Good Beginning'

AS VIEWED BY ERIC BOURDON

"I think the Monterey Festival was a good beginning for what may follow in the next few years. But I think there were a lot of mistakes made on the organization side of it.

"I'm not putting anybody down in particular. It's just the fact that there was so many restrictions, too many people wearing different tickets of different colors and told that they couldn't go in certain areas and do certain things. Everybody was very paranoic and being on their best behavior and afriad that the cops were going to say something. They just weren't being themselves and I think festivals are for people to be themselves.

"I think people should be themselves all the time—not just at festivals. Everybody seemed afraid of being themselves.

"I don't think there was enough time given to the musicians to play. There was lots of people who felt the same as I did—that when we just got a band started to get through to the audience, we had to stop.

No Laws

"I think there should have been no restrictions—no laws at all. I think everybody should have been able to relax and enjoy things 24 hours a day.

"There was a small fairground on the campus (one of the college campuses) and anybody could go there and play all night long if they wanted to. It was organized by one of the guys from the Family Dog in San Francisco. This seemed to me to be more like the real festival should have been, with people just jamming together and having a ball. The actual Monterey Fairgrounds was sort of stiffled with comments of 'no you can't go in there', 'yes, you can go in there' and 'oh, yeah, you can go in there, you have a pink ticket', etc. I'd just like to see a festival that's more open and free because the music is trying to teach people to be free. The music is teaching freedom and it should be a freedom festival more than anything else, I think.

"We have a festival in England which isn't as big as the Monterey festival. It's the Richmond Jazz Festival. It's jazz and all kinds of music, really. It's just a music festival and it's much freer. I think the main reason is that the police there are much more 'laxed in their attitude.

"We don't have the same kind of police force in England as you do in the United States. They're much more easy going. We don't have the same kind of problems with the kids either—sort of liable to riot as much as the American kids are. Everything there is more relaxed.

Bit of the Two

"I'd like to see a bit of the two mixed together. Maybe if the festival's held in England next year that would be really good. I'd like to see that happen, really. That would be really good.

"The best points of being at the festival for me was just sitting around talking and communicating with the artists that I have wanted to meet.

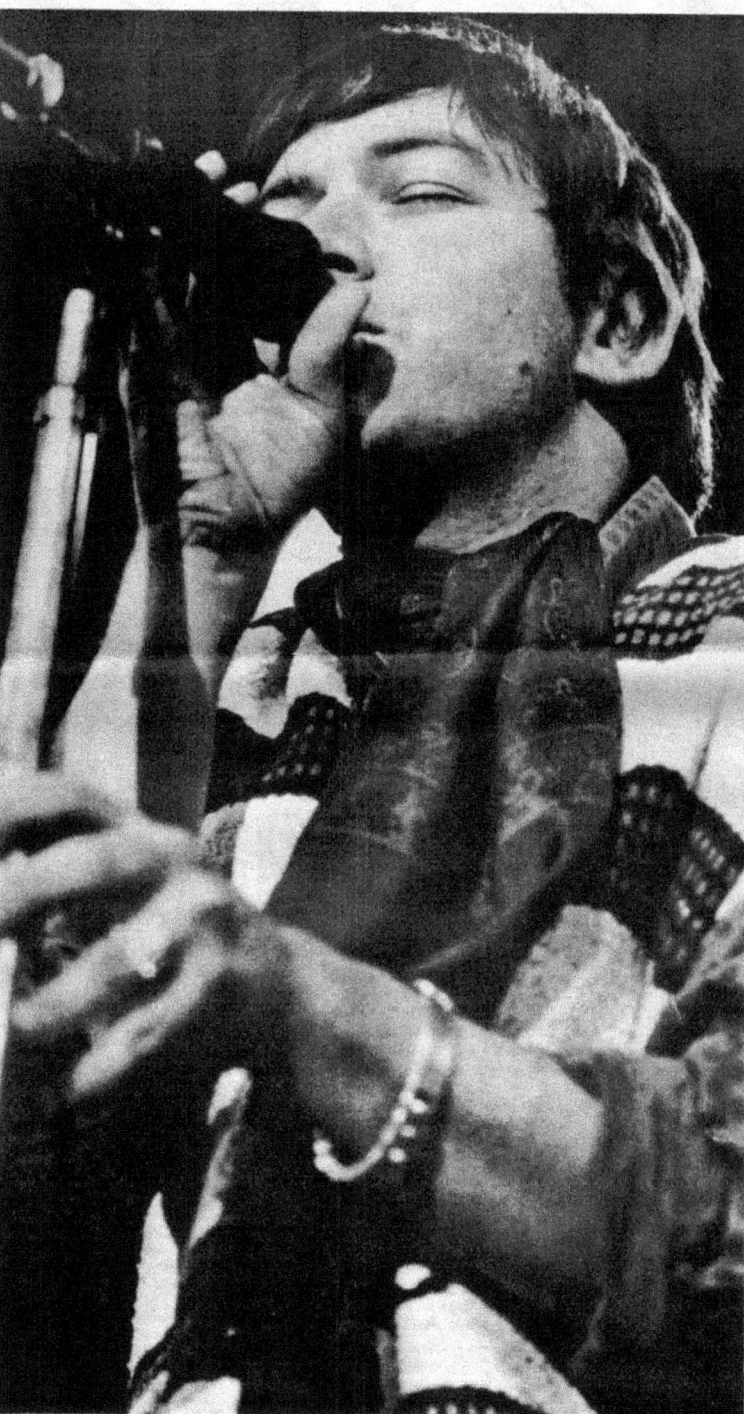

"I was particularly bowled over by the attitude that the Grateful Dead have got towards music and towards life. They are completely free. They live free and there was good incidents and it got through to me and the audience appreciated it. I was sitting in the audience when they were on and the audience really appreciated them, too.

"There was one point when the kids got out of the audience and tried to dance and the organization, which I have been complaining about, tried to stop them and the Dead wanted the kids to dance there. Good.

"If the musicians wanted the kids to dance there, and the kids wanted to dance there, and it's a music festival well who's going to stop them. Who needs to stop them? They don't need to be stopped. This is what causes riots and this is what causes trouble—stopping kids from what they want to do. They are not going to to any harm. All they want to do is dance, that's all.

"I'm kind of proud of Brian Epstein in a way 'cause Brian opened a theatre in London called the Saville Theatre which is strictly for popular music and they had Chuck Berry there. When Chuck Berry appeared there, there was a riot started because the kids wanted to get up on the stage and dance on stage with Chuck—and in the audience. They did not want to touch him or mob him, they just wanted to dance with him.

Manager Sacked

"The management took the strong arm and threw the kids out and Brian sacked the management. This was the first time anybody has done anything like that. It was because the management was to blame. He was the guy who insighted the riot. The kids didn't. Neither did Chuck Berry. It's just free expression and to stop free expression at a jazz festival or a music festival is the most hypocritical think you can do because that's what it's there for. It's a festival of expression.

"At the Richmond Jazz Festival in England, I sat around and watched other people jam and joined in with a few people. Jimi Hendrix and The Who among others.

"We intended to have a 'sit-in' with Pig Pen from the Dead. We went up to his house but we could not find any guitars, unfortunately. Still, we tried. But I learned a lot by just talking to the other acts there and by listening, talking and saying. That was enough.

Religion and Love

"To me, Monterey wasn't a pop music festival. It wasn't a music festival at all, really. It was a religious festival. It was a love festival. It was a demonstration of what we can do if we put our minds to it and how we can impress the people who think that we are incapable of doing things like behaving ourselves and listening to music and acting like human beings instead of acting like savages.

"I think it was all summed up in what the police chief said—that he was really impressed and that he was going to Haight Ashbury and tour it. Also that he really wanted to thank the Hippies for what they did.

"When you can impress a guy like a police chief and leave a mark on his memory, it just won't stop. If you can impress a guy like that, you can impress anybody."

BEAT Photo: Ed Caraeff

"... No Restrictions—No Laws At All"

KRLA ARCHIVES

MAMA CASS catches her breath during "I Call Your Name."

MICHELLE AND DENNY, both in colorful Indian outfits, sat down onstage 'til Cass finished her song.

BEAT EXCLUSIVE
MAMA CASS: 'I Want A Bit Of Freedom Myself'

BEAT: What's your reaction to what's going on here, Cass?
CASS: What do you mean what's my reaction? I'm just as knocked out as anybody else. We've been planning this for a long time and it's really coming off beautifully.
BEAT: You're satisfied with the way everything's happening, right?
CASS: Absolutely. We've had no trouble. Everybody was commenting today while we were walking down by the booths how everybody was so quiet and orderly and having such good vibrations. It's really coming off just exactly like it should have. I couldn't be more excited.
BEAT: What have been your experiences with the policemen here?
CASS: Well, John knows more about that than I do. He was more active on the executive board. I was just having a baby at that time.
BEAT: Congratulations. Did you bring the baby with you?
CASS: No, I didn't, no. She's only seven weeks old and I'm afraid she might be too much for the festival. They're pretty open at that age and I don't want to close her down and bring her. Besides which, I want a bit of freedom myself. It's nice to get out of the house.
BEAT: Back to the subject of the police. You mentioned that John Phillips had handled most of the relations with them.
CASS: The police have been very cooperative. We've had a lot of meetings with them. John was coming up every two or three days to make arrangements. They brought in police from outside counties. With every policeman or plain clothes man on the job there is someone that we refer to as a Hippie and the kids have been very cool. There has been no hassle. It's been very beautiful.
BEAT: What kind of response do you have for the local residents who have been putting this down?
CASS: Oh, I think they ought to be very pleasantly surprised by the fact that there has not been a hassle and that everybody has been mannerly. I think they should be very grooved about it as there's been no disorder whatsoever. There was a little apprehension on the part of the citizens of Monterey but then they have a jazz festival up here, too. Whenever you have a lot of people you have some trouble. But there hasn't been any.
BEAT: So you suggest that the parents who are worried about the generation that their kids are living in should come here and take a look. Then make a decision on that basis.
CASS: Well, I don't know about that. Everybody has to make their own decisions. You can't come to a festival and say "yeah, here's my decision." But I think the parents are getting to know their children pretty well. I don't think there's any misunderstanding. If the parents don't understand their children, don't let them come to the festival. It's not going to help them understand.
BEAT: Have you been up here for any of the other festivals when they were held? The jazz festivals?
CASS: No . . . well, you see, I haven't been in California that long. I've only been here a year and a half, maybe two years. This is my first festival and I'm really excited about it. What can I say? It's a great thing and I wish more people could have come. Everybody is just so nice and quiet. You walk along and look at the booths and all the different things that people have brought to show at the festival and all the art work. I can't complain.
BEAT: Neither can we . . . it's real family.
CASS: Yes, great.

PAPA JOHN, in a black velvet robe, accompanied the big Mama.

SPECIAL TO BEAT READERS

Due to the fantastic amount of photos and exclusive interviews which The BEAT was fortunate enough to obtain at the Monterey International Pop Festival, we know that you'll want to keep this issue as a souvenir and perhaps order another copy for yourself or your friends. So, we have made arrangements to print extra copies which you can purchase for our regular price of 25 cents plus an additional ten cents for postage and handling charges.

Name_____ Address_____
City_____ State_____ Zip Code_____
Please send me _____ copies of the July 15 BEAT
MAIL TO: Special Festival Issue, Beat Publications, 9125 Sunset Blvd., Los Angeles, Calif. 90069

KRLA ARCHIVES

GYPSY BOOTS LOOKS upset, but the rumor that Monterey Pop Festival officials wouldn't let him in for dressing too normal just is not true.

FLOWER POWER — KRLA deejay Dave Hull and a listener fan, Gretchen Langdale, point out that music, love and flowers definitely ruled at the Monterey International Pop Festival.

BEAT Photo: Ed Caraeff

GRACE AND the Jefferson Airplane, who appeared at the Monterey Pop Festival, will perform at the Devonshire Fantasy Fair.

Fantasy Faire, Music Show Headlined By Top Groups

An unbelievable Fantasy Faire and Magic Music Festival is coming to Devonshire Meadows (near Devonshire Downs) Saturday and Sunday, July 15 and 16 from 10 a.m. to 6 p.m.

Continuous music will be provided by these great groups: The Jefferson Airplane, the Doors, the Grass Roots, Country Joe and the Fish, BFD Blues Band, The Mothers, The Solid State, the Iron Butterfly, Canned Heat, Kaleidoscope, the Rubber Maze, The New Delhi River Band, the Transatlantic Flash, the New Breed, the Art Collection, the Second Coming, and the Powers of Evil. All these and many more top bands and vocalists.

But that's only half the story. Other added attractions include more than 100 arts and crafts exhibits, free flowers for everyone, a geodesic Dome light show by the Osley Light Company, Sitar players, flute, food, a gigantic bubbling Buddha, and a stratospheric balloon.

Where else could you find so much music and hippie art, and for only $3 per person a day?

Two Monkees, One Stone Turn On To Pop Festival

Flower petals fell like colored snowflakes, multi-hued lights bloomed in psychedelic patterns of mind-bending geometrics and the music became a living trip.

With concerts by the sea, the Monterey International Pop Festival collected 50,000 pop music pilgrims, hoards of hippies, throngs of teenyboppers and an out-of-sight collection of two Monkees and one Stone.

KRLA was designated the "official" station for the Monterey Pop Festival and had complete access to the super-security dressing room area.

Brian Jones, the only Rolling Stone to make the Monterey scene, didn't bother with disguise and was discovered tripping on the light show opening night. The fans were beautiful. They didn't push, shove or beg Brian for too many autographs. Everyone pretty much let the artists just do their thing when they weren't onstage.

The two Monkees who turned on to the Monterey music scene had even fewer problems. Peter Tork and Mickey Dolenz came dressed in American Indian costumes and had a blast.

Ravi Shankar, whose shimmering sitar drew a two-minute standing ovation after his performance on Sunday, said in an exclusive interview . . . "I'm overwhelmed! I am very happy because this festival resembles very much the music festivals in my country."

Brian Jones, the lone Stone to groove in Monterey, said, "I've just come away from London . . . we've been busy recording. I suppose the very up-tight people have been expecting trouble here this weekend. Personally, I don't. Our people are too beautiful for a bad scene."

"I've been walking freely among the kids," Brian went on, "and that's beautiful, too. I've never really had a chance to do that before . . . you know, with the mobs and autographs and all. The people here are really very nice about all that."

"There are a lot of policemen around that aren't doing anything," said Monkee Mickey Dolenz. "They don't have to be here and they look pretty funny in their uniforms."

The police really didn't have much to do but, actually, they were very cool. They came on with flowers.

HUGE PEACE balloons flew over the Monterey Pop Festival crowds.

Under the stars in the beautiful outdoor concert gardens
JULY 11 to 16
JAMES BROWN SHOW
THE ROYAL TAHITIAN
For reservations (714) 623-2603 or 983-1796
6 miles south of the San Bernardino Freeway in Ontario, Calif. East Riverside Dr. between Euclid and Archibald on the Whispering Lakes Golf Course (Ontario Municipal Golf Course)

KRLA ARCHIVES

KRLA ARCHIVES

KRLA ARCHIVES

KRLA PICKS UP ON THE ACTION AT OUTASITE POP FESTIVAL

"This is beautiful...this is beautiful," Mama Cass laughed over and over again as she sat in the press headquarters on Saturday night at the Monterey International Pop Festival.

Cass was being interviewed by disc jockeys Reb Foster and Johnny Hayes of KRLA, which was sending complete coverage of the fab fest out to a network of 18 top rock stations from coast-to-coast.

"What's your reaction to this scene in Monterey," asked Reb.

"What do you mean 'what my reaction is?'" shot back Cass. "My reaction is the same as everybody else . . . we've been planning this for a long time and it's really coming off beautifully."

Johnny and Reb asked Cass if she was happy.

"No Trouble"

"Absolutely . . . absolutely. There's no trouble . . . everybody was commenting about walking down where the booths are and everybody was quiet and orderly and had such good vibrations . . . it really showed me a lot . . . just like it should have. I couldn't be more excited."

Johnny wondered aloud about the people who were up tight about holding the festival in Monterey.

"I wasn't in on most of the planning," smiled Mama Cass. "I was having a baby at the time . . . but the police are very cooperative . . . we had lots of meetings with them . . . like every few days to let them know what was coming up. They brought a lot of police in from other counties and they have some plain clothesmen dressed like hippies, but the kids have been very cool and the happening is beautiful."

"How about the people in Monterey who didn't want the festival here?" asked Johnny.

Pleasant Surprise

"I think they should be pleasantly surprised. I think they should be very grooved about it. There's been no disorder. . .and there was, I imagine, a little apprehension on the part of the citizens of Monterey . . . but they have a jazz festival up there, too. Any place you've got a lot of people . . . you've got to expect some trouble. So why worry?"

"Well, how about the parents who are up tight about this generation," Johnny went on. "Do you think they'll come to the festival, look around and come to a decision based on what they see here?"

"Well," said Cass, "I don't know about that. I think they really have to make their own decision. They can't come to a festival, take a look at everything and say 'yeh . . . here's my decision.' I think parents are getting to know their children pretty well. I don't think there's any misunderstanding there and if parents won't let their kids come to the festival, it's not going to help them understand."

Next to go on the air was Otis Redding. Otis stepped up to the microphone . . .

"Out-of-Sight"

"What's going on is out-of-sight! I haven't seen anything so far that could make it a bad scene . . . people are just out here having a good time. They're doing what they want to . . . and wearing what they want to . . . they're just being natural . . . and that's cool."

The KRLA disc jockeys asked Otis what he thought about the spirit of freedom reigning at the Monterey Festival.

"Freedom . . . yes," wailed Otis. "Freedom of expression . . . yes. That's what I want to see more of. Everybody is just kind of together . . . I think the policemen themselves must be kind of shocked to see what's going on . . . it's too groovy."

That pretty well summed it up for Otis Redding and all the artists at the Monterey International Pop Festival. Monterey was a very good scene.

KRLA NEWSMAN Jim Steck interviews Brian Jones.

"CHIEF" MICKY NESMITH whoops it up for Festival.

"I COULDN'T BE MORE EXCITED" shouts Mama Cass during break in Festival concerts.

Under the stars in the beautiful outdoor concert gardens
JULY 11 to 16
JAMES BROWN SHOW
THE **ROYAL TAHITIAN**
For reservations (714) 623-2603 or 983-1796
6 miles south of the San Bernardino Freeway in Ontario, Calif. East Riverside Dr. between Euclid and Archibald on the Whispering Lakes Golf Course (Ontario Municipal Golf Course).

ICE HOUSE GLENDALE
234 So. Brand Ave. Reservations: 245-5043

Thru July 2
Stone Country
&
Hypnotist George Sharp

July 4-16
Hearts & Flowers
with their hit "Rock 'n Roll Gypsies"

— Supporting Acts —

July 4-5-6, 11-12-13

Bob Lind
with his hit "Elusive Butterfly Of Love"

July 7-8-9, 14-15-16

The Humane Society
with their hit "Tiptoe Through The Tulips"

ICE HOUSE PASADENA
24 No. Mentor — Reservations: 681-9942

Entire Month Of July

Paul Sykes
fun, songs and wit

Peter Evens
fiery flamenco

The Slippery Rock String Band

KRLA ARCHIVES

KRLA ARCHIVES

AROUND the WORLD

FROM THE EDITOR...

If you stop to think about it, it was amazing how well the Monterey Pop Festival came off. Taking into consideration the fact that there was every conceivable type of person wandering around Monterey—hippies, suit-and-tie parents, young adults from everywhere, entertainers, record company executives, publicity men, disc jockeys, the press, service men—it was almost unbelievable how well everyone got along.

No matter where you went in Monterey, you were bound to run into at least one entertainer—Brian Jones strolling around the Fairgrounds in his fur-collared cloak, Eric Burdon eating a plate of spaghetti at the counter of the La Patio restaurant, Russ Giguere having breakfast in the coffee shop of the Casa Munras Motel. Yet I never saw an entertainer being hounded by autograph seekers, refused service by a restaurant due to long hair or "wild" clothing, or scoffed at by senior citizens of Monterey.

Another interesting thing about the Festival was the civil attitude of the Monterey Police. No doubt there were some run-ins with the law (with that many people in the city, there had to be) but I saw none. What I *did* see and hear were hippies walking up to policemen and prefacing their questions with "exuse me, sir." And the police, for their part, were polite and helpful rather than condescending and brusk. It should prove to the rest of the nation that under-25's (regardless of how they're dressed or how long their hair is) and law officers can, and could, if the audience demanded, get along very well.

Entertainment for the concerts was about as varied as is musically possible. For instance, on one show you'd have the folk of Simon and Garfunkel, the cool of Lou Rawls singing "On A Clear Day," the mixed bag of the Association and the blue-eyed soul of Eric Burdon. Each act usually wound up entertaining for over half an hour and could, if the audience demanded, return for an encore. Individual acts were introduced by everyone from Tommy Smothers to Peter Tork from Andrew Oldham to John Philips.

There were more than enough interesting sidenotes to the Festival: Johnny Rivers dressed as a hippie and was given a very poor reception . . . Brian Jones paced up and down in search of a seat for the opening night's concert . . . The Who shocked the audience by smashing one of their guitars against an amplifier . . . Jimi Hendrix had everyone believing that he was about to burn the entire place down with a can of lighter fluid and a book of matches.

And so the world's first pop festival went its way. Besides being a financial success, it proved something much greater than that. It proved that people, regardless of their race, religion, political and personal beliefs, clothing or hair length, can co-exist with a minimal amount of trouble and a tremendous amount of good times.

That alone made the Monterey International Pop Festival worthwhile.

Revere A Tyrant? Jim Valley Denies It

Former Raider Jim Valley emphatically denied reports that he and three other departed members of the group left because Paul Revere was a tyrant and impossible to get along with.

"Paul wasn't hard to get along with," he told the *BEAT*. "This tyrant image is not really true. He would always explain why he felt strongly about something when he did."

Jim said he left mainly because the Raiders didn't record the kind of material he wrote. "I've written quite a few songs, but the Raiders weren't doing that kind of thing—they did mostly R&B and Stones—type material. I wanted to go out and do other things and experiment. The situation got to be impossible," Jim revealed.

Jim is now recording solo for Dunhill Records.

A stage concert in Birmingham with Herman's Hermits at the end of July will kick off Jim's first series of live appearances.

Going it alone after working for groups most of his career can be hard for an entertainer, but Jim apparently likes it that way. "Dunhill seems to think I'll be successful. If things go right, I would do it," he said.

Jim said he had a record cut over a year ago called "There is Love" released in his home town of Seattle without his knowing about it. "It did fairly well there," Jim said confidently.

He added that he plans to stay solo, at least for the time being, and is not considering joining former Raiders, Smitty, Phil Volk, and Drake Levin in their new group.

FLORENCE BALLARD

NO BREAK UP IN SUPREMES

Florence Ballard, rumored for weeks to be leaving The Supremes, has announced that she will remain with the group.

The possible break from the trio was made obvious last month when Florence skipped a Hollywood Bowl concert and another Motown singer replaced her. This was one of several occasions that Diana and Mary have used another vocalist to replace her.

Florence reportedly had been considering a break from the group for a long time, possible intending to open a shop dealing in either antiques or fashions (she is an amateur decorator and has designed the interiors of both Diana and Mary's homes).

"I felt the time had come when I could not progress any further in show business," she reportedly stated about her almost-exit from The Supremes. However, she reconsidered and is now back in the group. "The decision is final," she said.

Fund Started By Sinatra

Four annual Musical Performance Awards totaling $5,000 have been established by Frank Sinatra in conjunction with the University of California at Los Angeles College of Fine Arts.

First prizes of $2,000 will be given to both a vocalist and an instrumentalist with $500 second prizes in each category. The awards, which are expected to rank among the top music prizes in the U.S., were set up by Sinatra to help promising students develop their talents toward a professional career.

Mick, Stones Rumored To Star in New Movie

LONDON — It is being rumored that Rolling Stones leader Mick Jagger may be the main star in a movie, "Only Lovers Left Alive." Jagger, it is said, will star in the film, and not the group as a whole, but the other four Stones will make appearances in the production.

Allen Klein, the Stones' U.S. business manager and producer of the film, would neither confirm nor deny the rumors. "Wait till the film comes out and see" was the only answer he had for interested Stones' fans and reporters when they asked him about the rumors.

When asked for details of the film, which is due to begin production soon, Klein said "I'd sooner let the film be made then see what's happened."

He said Mick and Keith Richard would write all the music for the film, but he would not reveal where the film would be made.

The film was adopted from a book by English writer Dave Wallis and tells what happens when

MICK JAGGER

a group of teenagers take over control of Britain.

Plans for the Stones to star in the film were first announced last year in May.

Davy Jones Still 1-A

Monkee Davy Jones has not been declared exempt from the U.S. draft, despite the fact that English newspapers have printed that he received a 2A classification because he supports his father.

"It is absolutely untrue," stated a Screen Gems official when he learned of the claim. "We've received no word from Davy's draft board." He added that Screen Gems has no idea when Davy's classification will come up for review. He is now 1-A.

However, speculation is high that the British-born Monkee will be exempted from the draft as he does indeed support his elderly father. But the rumor that Davy may be too short for the Armed Services is unfounded. Though he stands a mere 5'3", Uncle Sam says that is tall enough.

DRAFTABLE DAVY

ART INSTITUTE OF PITTSBURGH
47th Yr. Coed. 18 & 24 mo. Diploma Course: Commercial Art, Fashion Art, Interior Design, Begin. & Adv. Vet. Appd. Dorm facilities. College referrals for degrees. Free illus. brochure.
Earl B. Wheeler, Director
635 Smithfield St.
Pittsburgh, Pa. 15222

KRLA ARCHIVES

across the BOARD

MAKING THE NEWS

Beatles Writing Songs For Full Length Color Cartoon

By Tony Barrow

The Beatles have written and recorded new songs for inclusion on the soundtrack of a full-length cartoon film which will be shown in cinemas throughout the world as a main feature early next year!

The film, produced in color, has the tentative title "Yellow Submarine." The project is a direct result of the highly enthusiastic reception given to The Beatles' television cartoon series which has yet to be scheduled for showing in the U.K.

King Features of New York, the powerful organization behind the TV cartoons, are handling the production of the full-scale picture. The Beatles handed over to production executives the first recordings of the special new songs at a meeting which took place during one of the group's most recent sessions at the Kingsway Studios in central London.

"Yellow Submarine" will include many existing Beatles' hits plus three entirely fresh compositions designed exclusively for the soundtrack. Two of these are Lennon/McCartney creations; the third will be penned by George Harrison.

Current plans are to delay the commercial release of all three recordings until the cartoon film is seen. At that time the Beatles will bring out a single to coincide with the screening of the picture. To minimize the possiblity of copyright leakage between now and the spring of 1968, a full security clamp has been put down on the titles of the three original songs involved.

For all records up to and including their "Sgt. Pepper" album, the Beatles have used studios belonging to EMI Records in St. John's Wood, North London. Since the end of April they have been moving around several independent recording studios including Olympic at Barnes and Kingsway at Holborn. The first of the three cartoon songs was started at Olympic and completed at Kingsway.

MIA ON TV

Mia Farrow is finally returning to television after her departure last year to marry husband Frank. She will star in a two-hour television special, "Johnny Belinda." It is a remake of the movie by the same name and will be filmed in color for viewing on ABC-TV.

Ho Will Guest

Don Ho will put in a guest appearance in a early fall segment of ABC's Hollywood Palace series. Ho will star along with the Don Ho Show featuring the Aliis for the Sept. 29 taping. Reprise is currently negotiating to record the television appearance and include it in one of Ho's soon-to-be-released LPs.

MAKE THIS YOUR BAG!
Tune in on the action with this mod radio-phonograph. Man make with the deep breathing, it's "like" portable. Take it to the beach, phreaque outs, love-ins, play all the groovie sounds. Stay up tight there's more. It's got a bitchin' 2 speed record player and 7 transistor radio. Runs on 2-1½ volt batteries. Has a 3" speaker that gives you a righteous sound. This supergroovy unit carries a 90 day unconditional parts guarantee. Send for it now— you'll LUV it. Clip coupon and mail $19.95. Calif. resid. add 80c sales tax, in cash, check or money order to: JoMar World Imports, 12414 Oxnard St., No. Hollywood, Calif. 91606.

ENCLOSED FIND $19.95 FOR EACH UNIT. PLEASE SEND ME ____ UNITS. FOR CALIFORNIA RESIDENTS ADD 4% SALES TAX.

NAME ____
ADDRESS ____
CITY ____ STATE ____ ZIP ____

WHERE they are

MONKEES
July 7, Atlanta, Ga., Braves Stadium; July 8, Jacksonville, Florida, Sports Coliseum; July 9, Miami Beach, Florida, Convention Hall; July 11, Charlotte, North Carolina, Coliseum; July 12, Greensboro, North Carolina, Coliseum; July 14-16, New York City, Forest Hills Stadium; July 20, Buffalo, New York, Memorial Auditorium; July 21, Baltimore, Md., Memorial Auditorium; July 22, Boston, Mass., Boston Gardens; July 23, Philadelphia, Pa., Convention Hall; July 27, Rochester, New York, War Memorial Auditorium; July 28, Cincinnati, Ohio, Gardens; July 29, Detroit, Michigan, Olympia Stadium; July 30, Chicago, Illinois, Stadium.

JEFFERSON AIRPLANE
July 15, Anaheim, Calif., Convention Center.

HERMAN'S HERMITS
July 21, Oklahoma City, Coliseum; August 5, Chicago, Ill., International Amphitheater.

SIMON & GARFUNKEL
July 21, 22, Opera House, Chicago, Ill.

SUPREMES
June 29-July 19, Las Vegas, Flamingo Hotel.

RIGHTEOUS BROTHERS
July 25-30, Chicago, Ill., Opera House; September 11-17, Greek Theatre, Los Angeles, Calif.

BUCKINGHAMS
July 7, Lake Schaeffer Monticello, Indiana; July 15, Lake Geneva, Wisc.; July 21, Marne, Michigan.

4 SEASONS
July 17, Owensmill, Maryland.

DIONNE WARWICK
July 11-30, Los Angeles, Calif., Century Plaza Hotel.

ANTHONY & THE IMPERIALS
July 19-August 1, San Juan, Puerto Rico, Flamboyan Hotel; August 10-Sept. 6, Las Vegas, Flamingo Hotel.

SPANKY & OUR GANG
July 13, Brockton, Mass., Brockton State Fair; July 15, Birmingham, Alabama, Oporte Armory; July 22, Weymouth, Mass., Weymouth State Fair Grounds; July 28, Indiana Beach, Indiana; July 29, Luxembourg, Wisconsin.

KEITH
July 15, Riverside, Rhode Island; July 16, Wallingford, Conn.

NEW VAUDEVILLE BAND
July 23-29, Atlantic City, New Jersey, Steel Pier; August 6, Davenport Iowa Fair.

SEEDS
July 19-21, Minneapolis, St. Paul, Arena; July 22, Arlington, Chicago, Cellar Club.

SERGIO MENDES & BRIZAL '66
July 31-August 5, headlining at the O'Keefe Center, Toronto, Canada.

DAVE CLARK FIVE
July 5, Knoxville, Tenn., Civic Auditorium; July 7, Tampa, Fla., Curtis-Hixon Auditorium; July 8, Washington, D.C., D.A.R. Hall; July 9, Wallingford, Conn., Oakdale Music Fair; July 10, Owings Mills, Md., Painters Mill Music Fair; July 12, Toledo, Ohio, Sports Arena; July 14, Providence, R.I., Rhode Island Auditorium; July 15, Virginia Beach, Va., The Dome; July 18, Columbus, Ga., Civic Auditorium; July 19, Atlanta, Ga., Muncipal Auditorium; Little Rock, Ark., Barton Coliseum; July 21, Chattanooga, Tenn., Civic Auditorium; July 22, Greenville, S.C., Memorial Auditorium; July 23, Camden, N.J., Camden County Music Fair.

TREMELOES
July 7, Hyannis, Mass., The Surf; July 8, Salisbury Beach, Mass., Surf Ballroom; July 11, Mendon, Mass., Lakeville Ballroom; July 12, Newport, R.I.; July 15, Houghton Lake, Mich., Houghton Lake Casino; July 16, Benton Harbor, Mich., Blossom Lanes; July 17, Saginaw, Mich., Daniel's Den; July 21, South Bend, Ind., Notre Dame; July 22, Leesburg, Ind., Tippicanoe Gardens.

YARDBIRDS
July 10, Theinville, Wisc., Teensville; July 11, Algonquin, Ill., New Place; July 12, Aurora, Ill., Crimson Cougar; July 19, Colorado Springs, Colo., Lakeside Amusement Park; July 21, Santa Rosa, Calif., Fairgrounds; July 28, Sacramento, Calif., Governors Hall; July 29, Concord, Calif., Fairgrounds.

KRLA ARCHIVES

KRLA ARCHIVES

original broadway cast recording ... infectious songs ... vibrant music ... fetching melodies ... a real knockout!

AVAILABLE AT YOUR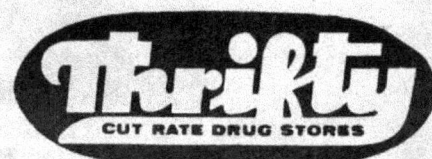

KRLA ARCHIVES

ON THE BEAT BY LOUISE CRISCIONE

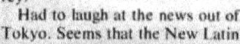

Bill Cosby is finally going to make a movie. The "I Spy" man announced that the film, "Busman's Holiday," will be shot in the Spring and concerns a bus driver (Cosby) in New York who decides to take his bus cross-country to California. The movie stands to be unusual in that there will be little dialogue ("since he's driving alone," says his publicist, "who can he talk to?"). Roy Silver, Bill's manager, will be the producer and the film will be a Campbell-Silver-Cosby Corporation production. Keep it all in the family.

Happy Announcement

Sonny and Cher Bono have happily announced that they're expecting a baby... Dickie Smothers has cut a solo album to be released in the fall. Marks the first time that either of the popular Smothers Brothers has recorded solo... Paul Revere and his new Raiders are doing okay for themselves — $76,000 gross in five dates... the Blues Magoos and the Who are set to go out on the Herman tour this summer. The Who, by the way, were totally knocked out by the reception they received in Detroit, San Francisco and Monterey.

Had to laugh at the news out of Tokyo. Seems that the New Latin Quarter there has hired five skinny, Twiggy lookalikes in order to give the patrons an alternative for the more buxom hostessess. They must be joking...

The idea of girls dancing in cages which has been popular at numerous night spots all across the United States has now spread to Spain. Only thing is — in Spain the girls get payed $5.00 a night for their terpsichorean feats.

For those of you who may have thought otherwise, Roy Orbison is still very much alive. Opens at the Embassy Club in Toronto on July 17 for a two week stand. Meanwhile his movie, "The Fastest Guitar Alive" is getting itself ready to open across the country.

BILL COSBY

Janis Fink????

Funny how entertainers come up with their stage names — Janis Ian's legal surname was Fink. However, Janis decided that Fink would never do so she changed it to Ian — her brother's name... Englebert Humperdinck, decided that his legal name was much too common and so borrowed the name of the author of "Hansel and Gretel" and became Englebert Humperdinck. Strange...

QUESTION OF THE WEEK: Will Johnny Rivers revert back to his old "clean-cut" image since his newly acquired hippie image failed to go over?

Hendrix Surprise

Despite the fact that the world first heard of Jimi Hendrix because of the tremendous success he met in England, Jimi is an American who has been on the music scene for quite sometime.

Chas Chandler, ex-Animal, discovered Jimi in Greenwich Village and brought him to England. Jimi, as you know, took England so much by storm that the latest "in" thing in London is for the guys to have permanents so their hair will resemble Jimi's — whose hair, by the way, is natural.

The Left Banke certainly had their share of inter-group problems — but I hear that they are now all straightened out and the Left Banke should have a record out almost immediately.

Providing, of course, that Tommy Smothers has recovered from the Pop Festival (don't laugh — most of the people who attended still haven't; it was that much of a gas) "my brother and myselves" take something of a vacation before appearing at the Greek Theatre in Los Angeles for a week beginning July 31, and then step into a Sahara stint in Las Vegas on August 8. Their successful television show resumes taping again on August 25.

SMOTHERS BROTHERS

Glad to see that the Four Seasons are doing so well. They're throwing a cocktail party for the Seasons at the posh Beverly Hills Hotel next week which will include a special performance by the group. Next issue we'll have all the photos and story of the party — should be interesting.

Paul McCartney: 'If You'll Shut Up About It I Will'

By Tony Barrow

On the evening of Monday June 19, thirty six hours after the British press had reported and examined Paul McCartney's statement regarding LSD (originally contained in a lengthy interview given by the Beatle to Thomas Thompson for *Life* magazine), Independent Television News sent a reporter to Paul's home to film a follow-up interview on the subject. This was broadcast throughout the UK via the commercial TV network at nine o'clock the same evening.

The following is a direct verbatim transcript of the TV conversation:

REPORTER: Paul, how often have you taken LSD?
PAUL: Er, four times.
REPORTER: And where did you get it from?
PAUL: Well, you know, I mean, if I was to say where I got it from, you know, it's illegal and everything, it's silly to say that so I'd rather not say it.
REPORTER: Don't you believe that this was a matter which you should have kept private?
PAUL: Well, the thing is, you know, that I was asked a question by a newspaper and the decision was whether to tell a lie or to tell the truth, you know. I decided to tell him the truth but I really didn't want to say anything because if I'd had my way I wouldn't have told anyone because I'm not trying to spread the word about this but the man from the newspaper is the man from the mass medium. I'll keep it a personal thing if he does too, you know, if he keeps it quiet. But he wanted to spread it so it's his responsibility for spreading it. Not mine.
REPORTER: But you're a public figure and you said it in the first place. You must have known that it would make the newspapers.
PAUL: Yes, but to say it, you know, is only to tell the truth. I'm telling the truth. I don't know what everyone is so angry about.
REPORTER: Well, do you think you have now encouraged your fans to take drugs?
PAUL: I don't think it will make any difference, you know. I don't think my fans are going to take drugs just because I did. But the thing is that's not the point anyway. I was asked whether I had or not and from then on the whole bit about how far it's going to go and how many people it's going to encourage is up to the newspapers and up to you, you know, on television. I mean you're spreading this now at this moment. This is going into all the homes in Britain and I'd rather it didn't, you know. But you're asking me the question and if you want me to be honest I'll be honest.
REPORTER: But as a public figure, surely you've got a responsibility to not say any...
PAUL: No, it's you've got the responsibility. You've got the responsibility not to spread this now.

You know I'm quite prepared to keep it as a very personal thing if you will too. If you'll shut up about it I will!

A few hours before the ITN newscast Paul repeated his desire to emphasize the point that the last thing he wanted was to encourage or even condone the taking of LSD amongst Beatles' fans or anyone else. He said he did not under any circumstances wish to advocate the use of the drug for anyone else and he hoped people would understand this.

... AND WORLD REACTION

The new Beatle controversy concerning LSD is affecting an astonishing number of people. The *BEAT* sought to obtain a concensus of opinion from people involved in the pop scene directly and indirectly.

A police officer in Los Angeles was appalled at what he called "the irresponsibility of the statement. McCartney should realize his influence on his fans and act accordingly." He went on to express his hope that teens who were undecided about the drug would not now go against their better judgment and experiment with LSD simply "because a Beatle took it."

Teachers seemed equally dismayed over the statement. Christine Frees, a Social Studies teacher at a local high school, said she spent a good deal of her time discussing Paul's statement with her classes. She said although she felt the remarks could have some very detrimental effects on teens, she was relieved to hear that her students did not feel influenced by McCartney's statement.

Without Thinking

The fans themselves seem to be divided between those who think that Paul was just being honest and those who think that he acted without thinking. Susan Lefer, a 17-year-old from Chicago, expressed regret that "her favorite Beatle was endangering his health by taking LSD."

The *London Daily News* tended to agree with Susan when they stated, "Perhaps millionaire McCartney ought to see a psychiatrist who will explain just why LSD is regarded as a dangerous drug. Perhaps he ought to see a psychiatrist anyway."

Unauthorized Possession

"Perhaps Mr. McCartney ought also to consult a lawyer who will tell him it is an offense to be in unauthorized possession of LSD."

However, not all of the comments were antagonistic. Many people felt that Paul was entitled to his opinion and that personal honesty should not have to be sacrificed to public opinion.

Whichever you feel, it is certain that the controversy surrounding both LSD and Paul McCartney's statement concerning its use will not be quieted for a long time.

"The Standel Sound"

"The Lovin' Spoonful"

Professional musicians throughout the world choose the "Standel Sound," the accepted standard for professional musicians who demand professional performance. (Dept. B)

A. P.A. Speaker Column Amplifier
B. P.A. Master Control with Reverb
C. Imperial Line Amplifier — Solid State, Dual Channel

Standel
Solid State Music Systems
4918 DOUBLE DRIVE • EL MONTE, CALIF. 91731

KRLA ARCHIVES

Grace To Get Off Airplane?

BEAT Photo: Ed Caraeff

A rumor that Grace Slick, lead vocalist for the Jefferson Airplane, will leave the group soon were emphatically denied by their American spokesman, Bruce Kane.

"As far as I know Grace intends to stay with the group and will stay with the group," Kane told the *BEAT*. He attributed the rumor, in part, to an article about the Airplane featuring Grace in Look magazine.

Ripe for Rumors

"Now that the Airplane are on top they're ripe for rumors because they're in the spotlight. People are creating these rumors — they aren't based on fact," said Kane.

The Airplane have called off a scheduled tour of England for this month, but no one is sure why. British papers reported that extensive commitments in the U.S. have kept the group here.

Doing Well

The Airplane's British spokesman said "The Airplane are doing so well in America at the moment that they can't make it to England in July."

Kane, however, told The *BEAT* he did not know the exact reason for the postponed tour, but he guessed the group had to finish recording a new album.

Cher To Solo In 'Chastity'

Sonny and Cher are splitting up; but only where records and movies are concerned. They have decided that Cher will solo in a movie written especially for her by Sonny, but he will not be her co-star.

The film will be called, "Chastity," and according to Sonny, who will pen the film, it will be "a serious character study, extremely contemporary with no music. And it will not be the usual type of movie — not the usual plot involvement and resolvement. It will be very contemporary. There's a need for this kind of picture from Hollywood. Europe has been mopping up with it."

"Good Times," the couple's first film together has just been released. Their decision to separate their movie careers parallels a similar decision regarding records. For quite a while now, Cher has been waxing solo on records and albums, while Sonny concentrates on producing and writing.

Humperdinck Runs for Life

BRUSSELS — English singer Englebert Humperdinck, whose "Release Me" is climbing American record charts, had his life threatened after he refused to go on stage for a concert during a tour of Belgium.

After completing two concerts in Brussels, Engelbert was supposed to do a midnight show in another Belgian city. He refused to go on, however, when he learned that promised police precautions had not been taken and his advance fee was not forthcoming.

Engelbert said he was surrounded on a street by several men who told him he wouldn't "get out of Belgium unmarked" if he didn't do the show. Fearing for his life, he ran to his car and made it back to the hotel where he stayed until it was time to fly back to London. He arrived in Britain safely.

'67—Paul's Turn For Putting Foot In Mouth
By Tony Barrow

It's just about one year since JOHN LENNON involuntarily sparked off worldwide controversy via some seriously considered opinions he expressed about stagnation in the church and the contemporary popularity of Jesus Christ and The Beatles.

This year it is obviously PAUL McCARTNEY'S turn! The 1966 Lennon quote was first printed in a *London Evening Standard* feature written by Maureen Cleave and reproduced in America via *Datebook* magazine. The 1967 McCartney quote was first printed in a *Life* feature written by Thomas Thompson and reproduced in Britain via the *News Of The World*, the largest Sunday newspaper.

In gist, McCartney gave the *Life* interviewer a brief but entirely honest answer to a question about LSD. "After I took it, it opened my eyes," he said "We only use one-tenth of our brain. Just think what we could accomplish if we could only tap that hidden part!" He went on to simplify the complexities of world politics by suggesting that if statesmen took LSD there wouldn't be any more war, poverty or famine.

The irony is that Paul's story broke boldly throughout the U.K. national press on his 25th birthday, Sunday, June 18.

The largest headline of all blasted its way across the front page of *The People*. In words two inches tall *The People* screamed: BEATLE PAUL'S AMAZING CONFESSION – "YES – I TOOK LSD."

The *News Of The World* carried a front page picture with the heading BEATLE PAUL SAYS: I TOOK LSD. Inside the paper devoted one entire page to a verbatim reproduction of the Thomas Thompson article from *Life* together with a couple of Henry Grossman's photographs.

The *Sunday Mirror* filled its front page with news of China's H-bomb explosion and a 20-year-old typist accused of taking cabinet office papers. But the main headline on Page 2 shouted: LSD: MIRROR DOCTOR RAPS BEATLE PAUL. The *Sunday Mirror* doctor wrote: "It is not for Paul McCartney to say LSD is or is not addictive. It is a great pity that someone of this popularity should be associated with drug-taking of this kind. Anyone who takes LSD except under proper medical or psychiatric supervision is asking for terrible trouble."

Of course a bunch of Fleet-street reporters invaded Paul's home in St. John's Wood, North London, to invite application of the original *Life* quote.

Paul told them he thought a lot of rubbish was talked and written about LSD. "I had read a lot of sensational stories — like calling it the 'heaven and hell' drug. But that's nonsense" he told the *Sunday Express*.

"I am not, never have been, and never will be a drug addict. The need today is for people to come to their senses. And my point is that LSD can help them. It is obvious that God isn't in a pill but it explained the mystery of life. It was truly a religious experience. It means I now believe the answer to everything is love" he told *The People*.

Confirming that he had taken several trips ("incredible experiences which brought me closer to God"), Paul emphasized at all stages of his press interviews that he was "not advocating that anyone else should try the drug." The last thing he wanted was for his fans to stampede to LSD.

He said "A lot of people talk about LSD without ever having experienced it. I just wanted to understand this drug. I really sincerely hope that people don't get the wrong idea about me. I do not want kids running to take it when they hear I have."

PEOPLE ARE TALKING ABOUT the alleged $40,000 the Beach Boys have thus far spent on their "Heroes and Villains" which may or may not ever be released... how many people have picked up on "Lucy In The Sky With Diamonds"...who would threaten Englebert Humperdinck and why... where Russ Giguere is going to put his gold record for "Windy," providing of course that he gets one... the opening of a top Motown group being absolutely packed with record people and wondering if that's why they received so many ovations

...the fact that Spanky is actually a girl...the latest place for flowers being beards – honestly...how long David Crosby is going to let his hair grow...the 5th Dimension going up faster than most people predicted, especially on the pop charts where they stand back-to-back with the Mamas and Papas...why the Four Seasons keep away from Southern California when they're so hot on the charts

...what bad luck seems to follow the Hollies everywhere they go... the fact that if Davy Jones has been re-classified his studio knows absolutely nothing about it...why that piece of "art" was put on the cover of Janis Ian's album and the fact that she's changed her name from Fink to Ian...the hang-up the Royal Guardsmen seem to have with planes...what is taking Plastic Man so long to make it and wondering if it ever will and what it means if it doesn't...the amazing fact that Frankie Laine just may have a huge hit on the pop charts ...Peter Tork sipping coffee in the Gaiety on the famed Sunset Strip...Micky Dolenz jumping (or falling) into the swimming pool at the Hollywood Bowl...Paul McCartney telling Life Magazine that he's all in favor of LSD...the Miracles never missing...Frankie Valli beating his fellow Seasons by a mile in the pop charts...Percy Sledge singing "Love Me Tender" and

wondering if Elvis should follow suit by cutting "A Man And A Woman"...whether or not there will be open rioting this summer between the hippies and Hell's Angels

...whether or not Holland will be the next "in" place now that London has been declared "out"... the fact that Herman can do much better than that...the fantastic comeback Ray Charles has made

and wondering why no one has yet made a movie based on his life story...the Doors believing that they're representative of America 'cause they're a "melting pot" so to speak...Lesley Gore staying in there

...why the Stones have been so quiet lately and whether or not it's true that Mick cut a single with Marianne Faithfull and that the Stones played on "Sgt. Pepper" and in return the Beatles are going to sit-in on the next Stones' album ...whether or not the Tremeloes are actually going to tour Stateside... who exactly are Jon & Robin and the In Crowd...the unbelievable success of Tommy James and the Shondells and wondering whether or not they've changed their stage act during the past year

. . . John and Paul writing three songs for a full-length cartoon-movie tentatively called "Yellow Submarine" starring guess who? Micro skirts replacing minis and wondering how far things will go . . . Brian Jones attending the Monterey Pop Festival despite his pending trial in London . . . whether or not the Beatles were really at the Pop Festival disguised as Hippies...

. . . Cher making her solo debut in the movie "Chastity" to be filmed without Sonny . . . Ravi Shankar releasing a single, only his second in ten years . . . Dylan's "Don't Look Back" being about as honest as a documentary can be and hoping ABC will do as well with their film of the Pop Festival . . .

. . . John Barry having to rewrite the title song from "You Only Live Twice" because Nancy Sinatra couldn't make the range...

Dunhill going on a talent search with the aid of the Los Angeles City Board of Education . . . the San Francisco papers trying to convince the Hippies to live in Los Angeles instead . . . Sonny and Cher expecting their first child . . . Lulu being so good in her first movie and wondering why "How I Won The War" is taking so long to be released...

KRLA ARCHIVES

KRLA ARCHIVES

THE NEW LOOK in men's hippie fashion emphasizes jeans and a beard.

SWITCHING ON

MINI-SHIRTED KNIT DRESSES with shawls are latest in party attired.

BEAT Photos: United Press International

It All Depends On Where You're Going
or
What To Wear To A Love-In

Company Paperwork

WAYNE, NEW JERSEY — Four employees of the John H. Breck Company in Wayne don't mind taking a good look at some company paper work even during a coffee break. They seem to be studying every detail as a secretary, clad in a miniskirted paper dress, makes her way down the corridor. Breck officials supplied the paper duds for the secretarial staff — but what would **YOUR** employer do?

Winter has been flung, spring has sprung, and thoughts of summer clothes have turned to the psychedelic scene.

Everyone ponders the question of what to wear to the office. But foremost in everyone's mind is what to wear **after** office hours, to late night discotheques and at Saturday afternoon love-ins.

After numerous jaunts to San Francisco's Haight-Ashbury and other hippie happening places, BEAT has been able to compile what shall be known as:

The Hippie Guide To Fashion

Fashion today, according to our experts, can be broken down into three categories — the non-hip, semi-hip and hippie.

Non-Hip

Don't bother to worry about your wardrobe and wear what you wore last summer. So much for this category.

Semi-Hip

You can be found in every office, over every typewriter, behind every desk. You're the work-day square, the late night swinger. Your fashion problem is the greatest.

First of all, follow the fashion forecasts. Wear the demure summer dress, the small stacked heels, the button earrings to work. Do not wear sandals, ponchos, Army surplus jackets or beaded headbands to the office. If you must wear an identifying hippie symbol, sport a hammered silver ring or pin. Under no circumstances should you wear fresh flowers in your hair.

Larger department stores are carrying psychedelic prints in more or less ordinary styles. We suggest that you invest in these if your office will allow shocking colors. Otherwise, stick to the more subdued pastels.

Hair, if it is long, should be worn up on the head, not falling long and straight. Or if you can safely wear it down, keep the ends curled and part it on the side. A center part tends to reveal that perhaps you join those crazy kids in the park when they get together to do heavens knows what at love-ins. Your boss might not like this.

In other words, each day you must strive to preserve the image of the clean-cut American teen. But after work.........

First replace the suit or simple dress with jeans. It is better if you do not wash these too often, for fear of spoiling their appearance. If you only have newly purchased jeans, we offer this formula for getting them into shape: tie in knots, roll down the street, then practice drop kicking them for two blocks. Splatter lightly with paint, then cut small holes in the knees and pull individual threads 'til they look frayed.

Secondly, top your jeans with a knit shawl or denim blue shirt. This can be fairly new, though you must leave it unironed.

Add as many beads, necklaces, bells, buttons, pins and flowers as you wish. (Warning: in some parts of the country, it is passe' to wear more than one button at a time. Be sure you check what is the standard mode of dress in your area before pinning on more than one button).

Headbands are particularly in vogue this season. You can purchase them for as little as one dollar in psychedelic shops.

Footwear, if it is worn at all (Girls, if you go barefoot, do not wear polish on your toe nails. It is a sure giveaway that you are a put-on), should be sandals, or moccasins, preferably hand made. Local sandal makers usually start their prices at about $10. Tire tread soles are the best buy. Moccasins are also in vogue and range in all colors and styles. In colder climates, we suggest the knee-high type, as you can wear several layers of socks under them.

Hair should be worn long and straight, or short and extremely frizzed. Girls usually identify themselves by wearing pierced earrings in both ears, while hippie males wear only one earring.

What to carry. We suggest flowers (these should also be wound in the hair and beard), or a tamborine. Also carry a bowl and spoon to love-ins so that you can share in the food. Do not carry a thermos bottle or lunch box.

Hippie

You already know what to wear. Just carry a Army surplus jacket (Navy is out) in case it rains.

KRLA ARCHIVES

please send me BEAT

26 issues only

$3 per year

Mail to: **BEAT Publications**
9125 Sunset Blvd.
Los Angeles, California 90069

☐ New Subscription
☐ Renewal (please enclose mailing label from your last BEAT)
I want BEAT for ☐ 1 year at $3.00 or ☐ 2 years at $5.00
I enclose ☐ cash ☐ check ☐ money order
Outside U.S. — $9 per year

* Please print your name and address.

Name _____
Street _____
City _____
State _____ Zip _____

Triple Treat!

Available At...

CLASSIFIED

FAN CLUBS

THE ROBBS NATIONAL FAN CLUB
Write: P. O. Box 350
Beverly Hills, California 90213

INSTRUCTION

REACH COSMIC AWARENES without drugs — help save mankind from destruction. Write for free booklet, "Cosmic Awareness Speaks," Organization of Awareness, Box 115E, Olympia, Washington.

SLEEP-LEARNING, self-hypnosis. Details, strange catalog free! Autosuggestion, Box 24-BT, Olympia, Washington.

WANTED

TALENT HUNT. Audition for rock groups, original material preferred. This is your chance to join big record company. Call Rusty Evans, Take 6 Inc. (213) 463-5107.

WANTED! Pop group needing girl singer; plays, dances, designs, odd personality. Write: Niccii, Box 453, Hughes, Arkansas.

FOR SALE

PHOTOS FOR SALE. Top Groups. Send S-A-E to: Sher, 5325 Central College Road, Westerville, Ohio 43081.

BIRTHDAYS

HAPPY BIRTHDAY KURT

Paul is All! Happy late Birthday Luv! — Lynne

HAPPY LATE 25th PAUL. Luv CINDY IRWIN

HAPPY LATE BIRTHDAY ROBIN! Susan

PAUL — Happy late 25th — we'll still send you birthday greetings when you're 64. Love, Susan & Robin

Happy late Birthday Dave Alle Love, Sandy

HAPPY LATE BIRTHDAY JIN of "The Nordics"

ANN BURGHER — Happy Birthday — Kathy and Most Valuable.

HAPPY BIRTHDAY Cyn Walthers. Love, Donna Zielke.

Happy Birthday "Louie Egner" from "C.J. Arnold."

Edith Petillo . . . SPLURGE . . . It's your birthday! Luv, Janice.

Happy Birthday Jeff Hanna!

HAPPY BIRTHDAY PAUL MC.
Love, Elise

Debbie Ferrante,
HAPPY BIRTHDAY, July 14
Janice

PERSONALS

YELLOW BALLOON — remember us? Donnie with a "K". Phyl P-H-Y-L and Sue. From the Teenage Fair.

THESE TYMES swing

Jenny loves a "Krum" . . . Sue

Love is . . . Pride and Joy

Charlie and Traitor — Rocky and Winnie — we're in love.

Steve (James) . . . lesson two?

The Surf stompers are outasite

I love you Terry! Terry Hughey + Skip Nance

I LOVE GEORGE HARRISON — Barbara

"THE DIFFERENCE" have SOUL!

Lee is luv — Mark

Floyd + Jerry's "Love Me Girl" is happening!

Lee rules

Jerry Watts Is Too Superfine — Marcianne

Lee will take over

The Smyle will change your frowns!

THE E.S.P. ARE GROOVY

GEORGE HARRISON FOREVER!

Watch out world, **"LORD TIM HUDSON"** is blooming! Your Flowerchild.

The Scot Richard Case are happening in Detroit!!!!!! Nancy Carpenter

Beatles — Love
Monkees — Blurp!!!

ART — WAKE UP!!!

BEAT is no longer accepting anything but PERSONAL MESSAGES in the classified section. Only messages (including Happy Birthdays) will be run. We will print names but not addresses or phone numbers.

Rates are cheap! Only 10 cents per word.

And remember, BEAT has a new address:

Classified
BEAT Publications
9121 Sunset Blvd.
Los Angeles 90069

DEADLINE FOR NEXT ISSUE: July 5.

KRLA ARCHIVES

RECORDS FREE FROM RC®
You'll Flip at the ZZZIP in RC® Cola

while you swing to your favorite stars! RC and music, perfect partners for the perfect lift

TAKE 1 ALBUM FREE

For everyone you buy... with 6 cork liners or seals from R.C. bottle caps over 100 Capitol LP's available. Order as often as you wish. Nothing to join. Look for this display at your favorite store.

Here's your best way yet to save more on the records you want. In dollars-and-cents terms you get two albums that the Capitol Record Club sells for $3.98 each time you buy one. The savings are even bigger on stereo records! And there are no shipping charges to pay, nothing else to join or buy.

What's more, you choose from top albums by today's biggest stars, including the Beatles, David McCallum, Frank Sinatra, Lou Rawls, Buck Owens, Petula Clark, the Outsiders, Nancy Wilson, Dean Martin, Sonny James, the Beach Boys and many others.

OTHER FINE BRANDS: DIET-RITE®COLA, NEHI®BEVERAGES, PART-T-PAK®BEVERAGES, UPPER 10®
"ROYAL CROWN" AND "RC" REG. U.S. PAT. OFF.; ®1966 ROYAL CROWN COLA CO.

KRLA ARCHIVES

KRLA BEAT Edition
WERE JAGGER AND RICHARDS SCAPEGOATS? 25¢
JULY 29, 1967

- **EXCLUSIVE** Ravi Shankar Interview
- Zal leaves Spoonful
- Harrison & Starr from the beginning
- Supremes On Stage
- Eric Burdon Gives his views on U.S.

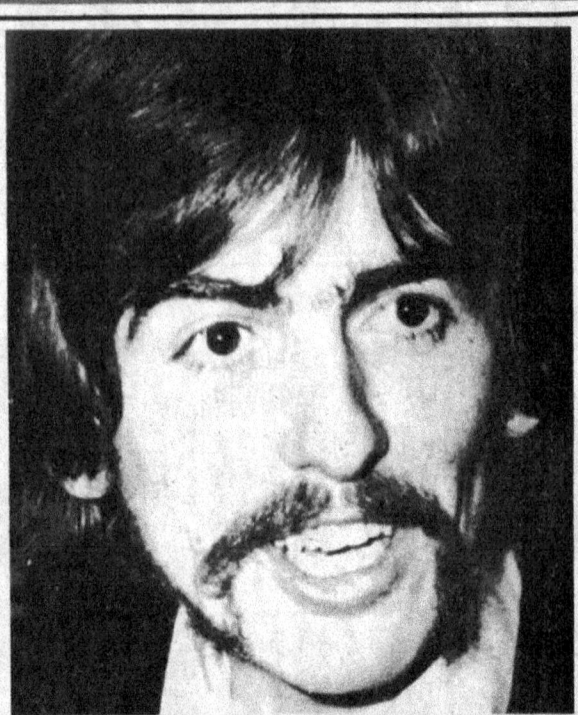

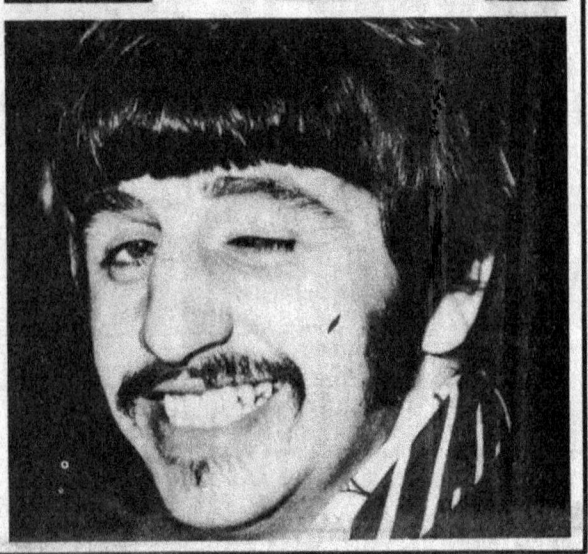

KRLA BEAT

Volume 3, Number 10   July 29, 1967

Wilson Acquitted Of Draft Dodging

LOS ANGELES—Beach Boy Carl Wilson has been acquitted by a U.S. District Court for draft dodging. Carl had appealed his induction notice on the basis that he was a conscientious objector.

Wilson's acquittal, however, was based on a technicality. Judge A. Andrew Hauk, who handed down the ruling, said Carl's local Gardena (Calif.) draft board had acted "irregularly" by ordering the induction from one panel of his board and having the induction papers signed by a member of another panel of the same board.

Not Guilty

"I am not going to find a man guilty of a felony when the board does a thing like this," the judge said.

Anthony Glassman, the assistant U.S. attorney for the case, argued heatedly that any board member or even the board's clerk can sign an induction order. He claimed the board's clerk signed the original induction ordering Carl to report August 9, 1966.

The attorney said that the panel that classified Wilson 1-A allowed induction postponement until Sept. 6, 1966, and the panel member in question merely signed the postponement in his administrative capacity.

Carl's attorney, J.B. Tietz, argued the order signed by the panel member was illegal, and that Wilson was denied due process because he wasn't allowed to personally appear before the board to discuss his situation again.

When the judge asked Carl if he would consent to a non-combatant job, like working in a hospital, the Beach boy replied, "Most definitely—I just want to do something good."

During the trial, Wilson testified, "We were put here to live—killing is very evil and destructive and results in human suffering. I love my country very much, but I won't take part in the destruction of people."

In March, 1965, when Carl submitted his classification questionnaire, he didn't fill out the conscientious objector part. Little more than a year later he did file a conscientious objector application, but it was denied.

Carl was supposed to report for induction last January 3, but when he didn't, he was indicted by a federal grand jury.

Re-Inducted

Since he was acquitted on a technicality, Carl could be re-inducted legally this time. Glassman told *The BEAT* the case was now out of the hands of the federal government. "It's up to the Gardena draft board, now" the attorney said.

The Gardena draft board in turn said that any information about Wilson's case is confidential. A spokesman did reveal to *The BEAT* that Carl was still classified 1-A, so he could be subject to immediate induction.

JAGGER AND RICHARD BOTH GUILTY — are they being used as scapegoats?

Jagger & Richard Guilty; Demonstrations Follow

LONDON—Reaction to the drug convictions of two members of the Rolling Stones has been swift and not unexpected.

Hundreds of British teenagers have been demonstrating against the sentences passed by a Chichester court against Mick Jagger and Keith Richard, lead singer and guitarist of the Stones. Keith was sentenced to one year, and Mick to three months in prison. Both were freed on bail pending appeals.

Even the generally critical British newspapers have expressed doubts about the trial and the stiffness of the sentences. An article in the Sunday *Times* headed "The Stones: A Case Of Social Revenge" said "the sentences were unduly severe . . . these were first offenses normally punishable by probation."

Produced Martyrs

A writer in the *London Observer* said "Far from discouraging others, the case has produced two martyrs . . . emotionally, at any rate, this was in the nature of a show trial."

Demonstrators shouted "Love, love, love" and "Legalize drugs" outside the offices of *The News of the World,* a paper which had pressed for conviction of the Stones.

Richard was convicted for allowing marijuana to be smoked at a party held in his country estate at West Wittering. Jagger received time for possessing four pep pills at the party. Both pleaded innocent.

At a trial held two days before Richard's, Jagger appeared relaxed and smiled at the more than 50 girls who were milling inside and outside the courtroom waiting for the jury's decision. It only took six minutes deliberation. Mick was pronounced guilty of having amphetimine tablets on his person. Dressed characteristically in pale green lounge jacket, and dark green flaring trousers, Mick showed little emotion as the judge announced he would withhold sentencing until Richard's trial was completed.

Testimony during Keith's trial turned up, among other things, that a girl had been found wrapped in a rug during Richard's party. The London Times claimed she was Jagger's girl friend.

Keith was found guilty, and then he and Jagger heard their sentences. Judge Leslie Block told the Stones' guitarist he had been "very properly found guilty by the jury" of an offense which could have carried a maximum sentence of 10 years. Richard was told he would have to pay $1,400 along with his year in prison.

Cries of "Oh, no" came from the public gallery when the fans heard the judge's words, and then again when the judge told Jagger "You will go to prison for three months and pay $280 toward the cost of prosecution."

Police Raid

The evidence against the two Stones had turned up during a raid on Richard's party by police who were tipped off by the *News of the World.*

As of now, Mick and Keith have been released on bail of $19,000, because their appeals could not be completed before the appeal court starts its summer vacation July 31. They are forbidden to leave the country.

Mick is basing his appeal on a claim that he had obtained the pep pills in Italy and his British doctor had approved their use here.

CARL WILSON AND WIFE — will he be drafted again?

ZAL QUITS SPOONFUL

Zal Yanovsky has quit the Lovin' Spoonful. The split with the other three was amicable, and John Sebastian had been advised of the change in advance. Jerry Yester, whose brother is a member of The Association has already been signed as a replacement.

Zal has been quoted as saying, "I was getting bored." He went on to imply that he had lost touch with what was going on around him, and that there were many things that he wanted to do on his own.

Zal's immediate plans include a recording session, and a more intense concentration on making motion pictures. He has stated that he does not intend to form a group of his own.

KRLA ARCHIVES

LETTERS TO THE EDITOR

SOMETHING FOR EVERYONE

Dear BEAT:
It gets me sort of mad to see the prejudices and hates that teen readers voice in your Letters to the Editor column. For instance, those who write and say the Beatles are old-fashioned and the Monkees are the greatest new group in the world.

One other thing many of these readers seem to do is limit themselves to all-out support of one group. Even when it is one of the better ones, this is limiting your entire appreciation of music to one bag. There is so much diversification of music in the pop vein that anyone who bothers to think while listening can find nearly eternal excitement in today's music.

Some examples: the tight sound of Love, the wild sound of the Raiders, the creative sound of the Byrds, the good-time sound of the Lovin' Spoonful, and the basic but good blues introduction from Eric Burdon's Animals.

The frequently risque lyrics of the Stones let Johnny B. Goode know that there is another side to life. Even Herman's Hermits have some worth, helping teeny-boppers across the wide gap between the Chipmunks and the Seeds.

Anyone who hates poetry can listen to a few Donovan (now, for jazz), Dylan (folk) or Simon and Garfunkel (a combination) songs and find out that Sandburg and Jeffers have some modern proteges who really have something worthwhile to say.

All in all, it's nice to know that someone rebelling against Sinatra's bag have something genuinely exciting to turn to, isn't it?
Dan Kelly

IN OR OUT

Dear BEAT:
Who are those so-called "in" people who have been ignorant enough to claim Cher should not wear mini-dresses? Why not open the door for them so they can get out! Undoubtedly you will not answer for you probably are one of those "in" people.

Cher looks totally groovy in a mini-dress. And if you were to be honest with yourself you'd agree. The trouble is, you probably look horrible in a mini-dress and thusly you don't want Cher to wear one.
Jim Canchola, Jr.

Actually opinion is strongly divided as to how we look in mini outfits!
The Editor

BEAT Photo: Ed Caraeff

THE POINT MISSED?

Dear BEAT:
Regarding Brooke-Alison Simons' letter on Ron Koslow's "Notes From The Underground" column.

It seems that Miss Simons is an alarmist of the first order who only stopped to read the headlines before she sat down to write her cliche-filled letter. If she had read the article through, she would have discovered that Mr. Koslow is not advocating that the generation gap be "retained and indeed intensified" but rather is offering some means of reconciliation for the often irrational and "childish" attitudes that the older generation has sometimes imposed on them.

Mr. Koslow was, in fact, suggesting that there was no need for rebellion, since the music and culture of today's youth served in many ways to unite them (not against the adults) as a group and provide for them much of the identity and sense of purpose, which so many adults have failed to do. Being supplied with these two necessities (identity and purpose) there is really no need to rebel.

Miss Simons states that the "unnecessary generation gap" is a product of lack of communication. She couldn't be more wrong! The generation gap is a problem that has plagued civilization since civilization began and stems from the very basic tensions of "the old against the new." It is the efficiency and all-encompassing power of today's communications which has taken this basic problem and magnified it into an almost political issue.

It is through men like Mr. Koslow that the basic implications became apparent and the facts are allowed to be considered.
Tom Monaco

FLOWER OF SKY

Dear BEAT:
He spreads an eccentric sensation of liaison, of being wanted, through poetry of voice and motion. Many revere him, while to others his every gesture induces aversion to even consider him as a moral human.

Another Mick Jagger, or possibly the replacement of such. Quite unlikely to me, for Jagger is my deity of love's existence and freedom and for the time being shall remain so.

But he will be great to all but those who say "another Mick Jagger" with disgust in their voices and eyes. It will also be said with love, tenderness, surprise and gratitude. It will be said as he's seen or heard singing his songs fervently or reposefully. His songs relay his message.

His message: Flower Power
His name: Sky Saxon
Lauri Harrington

READER IS TALKING...

Dear BEAT:
I want you to know that you have a really groovy newspaper. My fave section is "People Are Talking About" and I have compiled a few of them myself.

PEOPLE ARE TALKING ABOUT what name Ringo will give to his expected baby and hoping that it's nothing like the last one . . . the Griffith Park love-in with its plain-clothes policemen, concession stands and wondering just how much love there was and deciding not very much...if "Mrs. Brown" will be an improvement over Herman's last one...just how much longer "Flower Music" will last and coming to the conclusion that once something becomes commercial it's dead...why Dickie Smothers thinks Cassius Clay is an underdog...the Stones probably not getting work permits and wondering if they really care...Shirley Poston's famous relative and her wishing it was you-know-who...how long Sgt. Pepper has been in John and Paul's minds and hoping another develops soon.
Keep groovin'!!!
Marilyn Mangold

Beat Publications, Inc.
Executive Editor .... Cecil I. Tuck
Publisher .... Gayle Tuck
Editor .... Louise Criscione
Staff Writers
Jacoba Atlas Bobby Farrow Gregg Kieselmann
Ron Koslow Shirley Poston
Rochelle Reed
Contributing Writers
Tony Barrow Sue Barry
Lawrence Charles Eden
Bob Levinson Jamie McCluskey, III
Photographers
Ed Caraeff Dwight Carter
Howard L. Bingham Jerry Hoos
Advertising
Dick Jacobson Dick Stricklin
Business Manager .... Judy Felice
Subscriptions .... Nancy Arena
Distribution
Miller Freeman Publications
500 Howard Street, San Francisco, Calif.
The BEAT is published bi-weekly by BEAT Publications, Inc., editorial and advertising offices at 9121 Sunset Blvd., Los Angeles, California 90069. U.S. bureaus in Hollywood, San Francisco, New York, Chicago and Nashville; overseas correspondents in London, Liverpool and Manchester, England. Sale price 25 cents. Subscription price: U.S. and possessions, $5 per year; Canada and foreign, rates, $9 per year. Second class postage prepaid at Los Angeles, California.

FOR the FORUM

The opinions and ideas expressed in the Letters to the Editor or The Forum sections of our paper are not necessarily the opinions of The BEAT. However, we do feel that this is a free country, in which each individual is entitled to hold and express his/her opinions and beliefs. Unfortunately, a limited amount of space prevents us from printing every letter submitted to The BEAT. Consequently, we are forced to print only a general cross-section of the mail we receive.
The Editor

A GRATEFUL DEAD SPEAKS HER MIND

Dear BEAT:
My thoughts . . .
All around me . . .
War, discrimination, hatred, violence, riots, dope, fear . . .
I see it all, yet I am no part of it.
I want no part of it.
Yes, it's the world;
Or so they call it.
better name would be Hell.
To live, you must run.
Don't stop! You may be trampled by the mob.
The world was pure when it was created.
It's sickening how you have corrupted it.
And it's even more sickening to see how you don't care.
This generation gap . . . it's because you don't care.
These kids today are bad you say.
But they have what you lack; courage, hope and love.
They didn't make the world what it is.
They only desire to change it.
But you're too blind to see.
They will win. They must win!
For if the world were to remain as it is now,
Only one thing could be, Total Destruction.
I praise God for letting me have no part in your Hell.
For you see, I am one . . . a grateful dead

When I reread this poem after I finished it, I could not believe that these thoughts were my own and came from my head. But now that I realize I only wrote what I believe, I feel much better. Perhaps I have no right to feel so bitter, but the fact still remains that I do.
Sandi — a devoted teen fan

TAKING A TRIP— IS IT WORTH IT?

Dear BEAT:
This letter is really pointless. I'm not a defeatist nor do I lack confidence in my own ideas, but I say this letter is pointless because I know it will accomplish exactly nothing. But I have to write it because I am mad; mad, disgusted and mainly disappointed. I have just learned that yet another pop musician has fallen into the evil clutches of that number one menace — drugs.

Like everyone else, I have been aware for a long time of the users in the pop world. I've also heard all the arguments advocating pot for musicians: "It helps you perform better," "you need extra pep when you're a musician." There are many others and they are all as lame as the two I have given.

If you need pot to improve your performance, then you don't belong in the business; you don't have the talent. Anyone who works hard for a living would like "extra pep," but do they all resort to drugs?

Many of you are probably thinking, "what a prude!" and maybe I am. But I simply cannot understand why these successful, wealthy and worshipped members of popular groups resort to this. Maybe they have a reason and if they do, I'd like to know what it is. I'd never have written this letter if I hadn't found out about the guy I mentioned earlier. He belongs to my favorite group and he was my favorite member.

I just can't see why he would want to endanger his health, his sanity and possibly his life when he has so much going for him now. For that matter, I can't see why anyone would willingly risk their future for prestige or the experience of "taking a trip" to who knows where. Does anyone who is reading this know why? I, for one, would certainly like to.
Kathy McManus

KRLA ARCHIVES

ON THE BEAT
By Louise Criscione

While Mick Jagger and Keith Richard made all the headlines, Brian Jones' drug problems were kept well in the background. Brian was arrested in May and has already received his preliminary hearing. However, he is not scheduled to appear in court again until this fall.

Meanwhile, Brian was admitted to a nursing home in England but was later transferred to a London clinic "for severe strain." Although Brian is also up on drug charges, he was not at the party at Keith's house and was, therefore, not involved in the same court hearings as Jagger and Richard.

Reversed Judgment

Insiders are now saying that despite the guilty verdict, the two Stones' legal council is confident that they will win their appeal and if the judgment is not reversed they feel the sentences will at least be shortened.

Both the **Young Rascals** and the **Four Seasons** came to visit. The Rascals didn't stay long but they did put on a tremendous show at the Cheetah. It looks as if their newest single, "Girl Like You," will take up where "Groovin'" left off – at the top of the charts. Hope so, they're a group that deserves success.

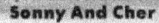
HERMAN

The Four Seasons stayed a bit longer and managed to squeeze in two concerts as well as a party in Malibu at their manager's house. If you've never seen the Seasons, you've missed the most professional group in America. They received two standing ovations at each of their concerts, making it quite understandable as to why they've chalked up 22 gold records. Great people – next time they perform in your area, don't miss 'em.

Sonny And Cher

QUICK ONES: Sonny and Cher are set to guest on the premiere "Jerry Lewis Show" on September 12 ... Screen Gems is going to put a show on television this fall which is an "I Spy" western style, with white and Negro co-stars ala' **Bill Cosby** and **Bob Culp** ... **Frank Sinatra** has been elected to the board of advisers of the Eddie Cantor Charitable Foundation ... the **Smothers Brothers** have signed a three year deal with Harrah's Clubs in Reno and Tahoe ... **Supremes'** concert in Minneapolis drew a near-capacity crowd ... **Sidney Poitier** became the first Negro to ever leave his hand and footprints in the famous cement of Grauman's Chinese Theatre in Hollywood ... **Paul Jones**, formerly with the Manfred Mann, has signed a two-year recording contract with Capitol Records ... the **Tremeloes** have won a Silver Record for 250,000 sales in England for "Silence Is Golden" which, by the way, was written by **Bob Gaudio** of the Four Seasons ... Congratulations to **Jerry Yester** for becoming a **Lovin' Spoonful**.

Jim Valley, one of the ex-Raiders, has been signed by Dunhill Records and his first release is "Try, Try, Try" which he wrote himself.

Budget For Herman

The budget for **Herman's Hermits** latest movie, "Mrs. Brown You've Got A Lovely Daughter," is supposedly set at a million and a half dollars. With that budget, it should be some movie, and if it isn't you can bet everyone connected with the film will hear about it!

What's this? The latest thing seems to be billing a group with the tag "featuring ..." For instance, we have Four Seasons "featuring the sound of Frankie Valli" and Paul Revere and the Raiders "featuring Mark Lindsay." When we get to the Turtles "featuring the tambourine playing of Mark Volkman" we're in trouble.

While others are talking, the record industry is doing something to ease racial tension during the hot summer months. Clyde Otis, a Negro publisher and record producer, is spearheading the drive by supplying record company aid in supplying radio stations with "public service records." Thus far, Aretha Franklin and Dinah Washington records are being shipped to disc jockeys across the nation and Otis is currently talking with James Brown and Ray Charles. The campaign is not, however, limited to Negro artists. They're trying to get white artists on the bandwagon as well.

BRIAN JONES

FIRST PRESS CONFERENCE
Monkees In London
By Tony Barrow

In four days of happy but hectic activity The Monkees met between three and four hundred press, radio and TV people and presented their stage show before a total of 50,000 British fans.

They flew into London from Paris minutes before midnight to be greeted by a roof-top crowd of 300 fans perched high on the balconies of Queen's Building at London's Heathrow Airport. To make sure that those fans had a good chance of seeing the group, Micky, Davy, Mike and Peter broke away from their own ring of security personnel, vaulted over a set of steel barriers and raced across towards Queen's Building with a score of news photographers and TV cameramen in hot pursuit.

During the four days and nights which followed, thousands of fans besieged both the Royal Garden Hotel (where the Monkees' entourage took over most of the heavily guarded fifth floor) and the Empire Pool, Wembley, North London (where the group made its series of five appearances).

The Press Conference, held in the huge Buckingham Suite Ballroom of the Royal Garden Hotel in Kensington, was attended by representatives of almost every European newspaper, magazine and news medium including more than a hundred photographers. As is the convention at these curiously frightening affairs, the standard of questioning was far from high. Yet, the Monkees, facing an ordeal of this type for the first time in their brief group career, coped well with the battery of banality, coming back with brisk ad libs or lengthy explanations according to the mood of each question.

These are assorted extracts from the 20-minute exchange between Monkees and writers:

You come here surrounded by a sort of mythology about being a pre-packaged group and under considerable attack from the critics. Does this matter to you?

PETER: *No, it doesn't bother us that we come under attack. As far as we're concerned you can't help that. These stories about us being a pre-packaged group, I mean in the sense that you mean the words, it is quite true.*

MICKY: (Applauding) *Jolly good!*

MIKE: *It's pretty much the same way everybody else forms a group whether it's John Lennon walking down the street asking Paul, Ringo and George to join him or whether it's someone putting an ad in a paper. You've got to start somewhere.*

What thoughts have you all given to what you're going to do when the series goes off?

DAVY: *We know it's sold for another year in America and we have a pretty good chance of making it another year after that. Then we'll be tired of being Monkees, I should think, in about six years from now but we'll still be playing together I suppose.*

MICKY: *We'll probably go off and do different things – like one of us or two of us, and then three and then four. Whichever way the wind blows.*

Is the feature film you're going to make an extension of your TV series or made on an entirely new concept?

MICKY: *We'd like it to be an entirely new concept. If you've any ideas please let us know. Anybody ... mail 'em in!*

Micky, after you've finished your TV series are you going to continue with your pop career?

MICKY: *I intend to stay in some field of entertainment. I'd like to get in production and movies and records and shows and films and making candle holders on my lathe and I'm getting into electronic music and I've just bought a mock synthesiser and I'm trying to discover anti-gravity and all kinds of things like that.*

PETER: *It took him six months to learn to say "synthesise."*

When you prepare for a press conference like this do you antici-

DAVY AND PETER ARRIVING IN LONDON.

pate the line of questioning and do you agree on a certain line the answers ought to take?

MICKY: *We've never had a press conference like this. It's the first one ever. It's really neat too.*

Did you do any preparation for it?

DAVY: *We had breakfast this morning!*

MICKY: *We've been asked the same questions before but not in this kind of a circumstance.*

I'd like to ask Davy just how far his plans as an independent record producer have gone and if he is recording groups who are they.

MICKY: *The Beatles.*

DAVY: *Yeah, I have a group called The Children. They're a Texas group, six boys and one girl. We cut three tracks at a recording studio in Hollywood. It turned out well.*

Have you any plans to grow any
(Turn to Page 19)

"The **Standel** Sound"

"The Lovin' Spoonful"
Professional musicians throughout the world choose the "Standel Sound," the accepted standard for professional musicians who demand professional performance. (Dept. B)

A. P.A. Speaker Column Amplifier
B. P.A. Master Control with Reverb
C. Imperial Line Amplifier – Solid State, Dual Channel

Standel
Solid State Music Systems
4918 DOUBLE DRIVE • EL MONTE, CALIF. 91731

KRLA ARCHIVES

happening

SAM AND DAVE WIN 'YOUTH PARADE' AWARD

Sam and Dave have been named as the recipients of the sixth annual "Youth On Parade" award presented by The Los Angeles Sentinel in connection with that city's Good Shepherd Baptist Church.

The award cites Sam and Dave for their inspiration to today's youth through their outstanding contributions to popular music.

The presentation is made each year to those who are considered to be 'living examples' of young men and women who have overcome obstacles of racial barriers, poverty and restrictive environment and risen to the height of their profession.

SAM AND DAVE

New Presley Rumor Begun By English

What's going on with the English newspapers? They've spread one rumor after another about Elvis Presley and his famous manager, Col. Parker, and none of them have any bearing in fact.

The first The BEAT heard from Britain was the startling story that Tom Jones was flying to America to become Col. Parker's newest protege. The rumor had it that Parker would establish Jones in the United States and look after his interests here.

Col. Parker's office quickly denied it. "There is no basis to it at all," said a spokesman. "Col. Parker only manages one talent and that is Elvis Presley."

Not long after, the London papers were carrying a story that Elvis had been offered $85,000 to appear at the Statler Hilton Plaza in Miami in Caberet. The papers said that even this record figure might be increased after negotiation.

Again, Col. Parker's office was quick to inform The BEAT, "There's absolutely nothing to it."

"What's it going to be next?" is the only question Elvis fans have for the English rumor-mongers.

Sonny & Cher Plan New Film

Sonny and Cher are beginning plans for their second movie together, entitled, "Ingnaz." Cher told reporters the title is a man's name. "I think it kind of means 'stupid' in German slang," she said.

Billy Freidkin, who produced the couple's first film, "Good Times," will do so again with "Ingnaz." Sonny said the film will give Cher and him a chance to do their first fictional character roles. "This will be easier for me than trying to be natural. I think the hardest role of all to play is yourself."

President In Fat City

President Johnson attempted to close the generation gap by using his version of the teen-age idiom. He was speaking to about 500 students from the Farm Belt urging them to be 'protesters'.

The President later, when speaking to a "happening" for 121 high school students, really "turned on." "When I read about the alienated young radicals, the disillusioned young people, the long hair and short skirts, it hasn't frightened me. I have lived with two teenagers for years ... I keep my cool. I haven't bugged out. I'm still in Fat City."

The gap in the generation is surely closing.

Rocking Bank

Detroit may soon have a new rock 'n roll group. Nothing new you say? Well, they're called The Young Detroiters and the Maximum Interest, and the group is the idea of the Detroit City National Bank which wants to attract young depositors.

New York Hippies Form An Indian Tribal Council

San Francisco is not the only Hippie capital of the world. New York City's Greenwich Village, long the haven of the "beat" generation, is now moving with the times and has become the Hippie center for the East Coast.

Like their counterparts on the West Coast, the Eastern Hippie has dropped out of regular society. However, unlike the San Francisco Hippie, the New York breed has formed a new society of their own, basing their structure on the Indian Tribe System.

Hippies everywhere have long been fascinated by the Indian Heritage of this country. Indeed, there is an Indian prophecy that the Shonshone nation would one day be reincarnated as white men, and Hippies seem to take this to heart for much of their clothing and art objects include Indian regalia.

New Society

This new hippie society is divided into tribes. One such tribe is called the Group Image; others are called The Third World, Pablo, and The Family Store.

Each of these tribes unite to earn money in many different ways. The Group Image has a rock 'n roll band which has just begun to play in uptown discotheques for about $2,000 a weekend.

The Third World has a three story building on the Bowery and they drive a truck. The Tribe also owns a goodly amount of motion picture equipment and additional money is earned by renting this out.

Sells Dresses

Pablo sells dresses and jewelry through a shop called A Joy Dispenseria.

The Hippies themselves readily admit they couldn't function in the so-called 'real world' and are grateful for a place where they can go to live their lives as they see fit.

Invasion Coming

On both coasts of this country the city officials have been discussing this summer when everyone expects a Hippe invasion of New York and San Francisco. So far no solution has been offered.

What do the Hippies think of themselves and the expected 'invasion'? One Village Hippie, wearing a pink belt across his favorite janitors uniform said, "we're all nutballs, basically. Crazies, weirdoes, loonies, who can't cut it in the real world. We're rejects from the middle class, and we stick together because we need the protection."

Hope Or Disaster

He went on to say, "we're misguided, and we're an embarrassment to the nation. But if you go by the papers and the police, then there figures to be 50,000 more kids coming to the east village this summer to drop out. You figure it."

Depending on how you regard the Hippie movement, this increase in the 'sub-culture' of the Hippies will either mean disaster or hope for the young people of this nation. Perhaps this summer will help to clarify the controversy.

HO FORMS CO.

Popular Hawaiian entertainer Don Ho has formed Hana-Ho records as a division of Ho-Brown productions. Hana-Ho will handle its own production, manufacturing and distribution in the state of Hawaii.

H.B. Barnum, another recording star, will be in charge of A&R.

PEOPLE ARE TALKING ABOUT the fact that **Jagger and Richard** were chosen as guinea pigs and wondering why if Britain is sincerely trying to crack the drug scene they didn't catch the other groups ... why **Johnny Carson** didn't talk to the **Association** when they appeared on his show and deciding that it was probably because anyone who attempts to talk to all six of them at once is begging for sheer pandemonium.

... **Johnny Rivers** not changing his image after all because he digs the beard-and-sandle bit ... the **Four Seasons** being able to reproduce their sound as well as, if not better than, any other group currently alive ... the rush to buy "Alice In Wonderland" books ... the funny scene with the toupee wearing member of a top pop group and wondering what's going to happen when one of his fans tries to pull it off

... **Gene Cornish** of the Rascals coming to L.A. with his clothes-spending money and not finding any clothes to buy and the Rascals being late for their Cheetah appearance because of the demonstrators in front of the Century Plaza Hotel ... why the **Supremes** almost invariably refuse to give interviews ... what **Bobby Darin** has to do with Motown ... the Monterey Pop Festival being a complete success because even *Time* and *Newsweek* covered it and *Life* did their best but apparently couldn't get in

... **Lou Rawls** having the widest market appeal—all the way from the hippies to the over-40 crowd—which is a long, long way from the South Side of Chicago ... the green-eyed soul of **Smokey Robinson** still being the best around ... **Stark Naked** and the **Car Thieves** thinking a long time before they came up with that admittedly hard-to-forget name ... what will happen if beards stay "in" and hair styles get longer

... what the big announcement

is that **Tommy James** is about to make and wondering if perhaps he will decide to go solo ... whether or not this batch of "**Herman's Hermits** to split" rumors will prove true, with insiders betting heavily that the group will indeed break up

as soon as their American tour is finished ... what a melting pot the pop charts really are when you have songs like "White Rabbit" and "You Must Have Been A Beautiful Baby" on the same surveys

... **Every Mother's Son** being a group of nice people ... why **Lulu** can't make it Stateside and wondering if "To Sir, With Love" will do it for her ... whatever happened to the **Kinks** ... how the **Monkee** tour is selling ... **Sonny and Cher** appearing in Spain at the 25th Great German Radio Exhibition ... **Frank Sinatra** giving $5,000 to four music students at UCLA and **Duke Ellington** receiving an honorary degree from Yale

... **Terry Kirkman** being one of the most talented young writers on the music scene and if "Requiem For The Massess" doesn't prove it, nothing will ... after flowers in the beard the next thing has to be an orange in the navel ... where, oh where, all the money will really go ... whether or not **Brenton Wood** will be able to take over where **Sam Cooke** left off ... why in the world anyone would ban Margie just because she wanted a G-string for her guitar

... since **Arthur Conley** has revived "Shake, Rattle and Roll" who is now going to be brave enough to record "Rock Around The Clock" and coming to the conclusion that no one is ... the great thing **Mama Cass** has done for overweight females ... why **Mick Jagger** got three months when **Keith Richard** received a whole year ... the mystery surrounding **Dusty Springfield's** relative lack of hit success in the United States ... who the **Fifth Estate** really are

... how **Mitch** is doing minus the **Wheels** ... the camera addicted people who refuse to get out of range when a photographer is shooting an artist and what complete fools they make of themselves ... the strange minds censors have ... how great it would be if **Pet Clark** becomes a huge movie success all over the world ... what *The BEAT* is going to do the next time a group decides to stand us up for an interview.

AROUND the WORLD

FROM THE EDITOR...

Mick Jagger and Keith Richard have been found guilty on drug charges. The judgment was not surprising – merely anticipated. What *is* surprising and what is questionable is why no one has seen fit to arrest the other pop people. The question is – is the law meant for a select few.

We apologize for the delay but we've finally done it – both Ringo Starr and George Harrison have been given a full page in this issue. What began as a four part series on the Beatles somehow became interrupted after Paul and John's articles had been printed. Anyway, we've now picked up where we left off and with Ringo and George our Beatle series is now complete.

It's almost impossible to estimate how many letters we've received concerning the lack of Supreme articles. The reason is simple – the Supremes refuse to give out interviews. This leaves us (and every other publication) with only one choice – we must wait until the Supremes hit town and then send a photographer to cover their appearance. The girls finally arrived, we sent our photographer out to the Cocoanut Grove and the results are on page 14.

We're sort of blowing our horn for accomplishing the impossible – obtaining an interview with Ravi Shankar. Mr. Shankar has been on the music scene for quite some time but it wasn't until Beatle George Harrison took an active interest in Indian music that Ravi Shankar became such a well-known name to American record buyers. Read what Mr. Shankar has to say about his music, American audiences and George Harrison on page 18.

Eric Burdon has always been (and probably always will be) a controversial figure. He expresses his opinions on subjects which most entertainers would never touch. Once again, Eric speaks his mind – this time on America.

I'd like to say once again that although *The BEAT* does not necessarily agree with the opinions and beliefs expressed by the performers we interview, we nevertheless feel very strongly that they have the right to express their opinions publically.

Before space runs out – we were originally planning to include the Four Seasons in this issue. However, we have now come to the conclusion that they are far too talented, popular and intelligent for the space we'd left for them in this issue. With 22 Gold Records to their credit as well as two singles currently in the top ten, the Four Seasons rank as one of the most successful groups ever born. So, in the next issue we'll be devoting a full page to the Seasons including exclusive photos as well as an exclusive interview with the group. Fair enough?

Louise Criscione

MAKE THIS YOUR BAG!
Tune in on the action with this mod radio-phonograph. Man make with the deep breathing, it's "like" portable. Take it to the beach, phreaque outs, love-ins, play all the groovie sounds. Stay up tight there's more. It's got a bitchin' 2 speed record player and 7 transistor radio. Runs on 2-1½ volt batteries. Has a 3" speaker that gives you a righteous sound. This supergroovy unit carries a 90 day unconditional parts guarantee. Send for it now – you'll LUV it. Clip coupon and mail $19.95. Calif. resid. add 80c sales tax, in cash, check or money order to: JoMar World Imports, 12414 Oxnard St., No. Hollywood, Calif. 91606.

ENCLOSED FIND $19.95 FOR EACH UNIT. PLEASE SEND ME ___ UNITS. FOR CALIFORNIA RESIDENTS ADD 4% SALES TAX.

NAME ___
ADDRESS ___
CITY ___ STATE ___ ZIP ___

Banned In Brownfield

Some Texas radio stations are following the McLendon trend of banning popular discs which are deemed to be offensive.

Singles which rate high on the no-no list include "Acapulco Gold," "Sock It To Me, Baby," and "Let's Spend The Night Together."

Even the ordinarily wholesome, red, white and blue Country and Western field is feeling the hot breath of the Texas moralists. Little Jimmy Dickens, popular C&W star, has been banned in Brownsville (Texas), for his naughty hit, "Margie Needs A G-String For Her New Guitar." The Brownsville station, KGAF, said the tune's title, itself, offended it's listeners.

Wilson To Wax Album

Murray Wilson, the father of Beach Boys, Brian, Dennis and Carl Wilson, has been signed by Capitol Records as one of the company's first independent producers.

Wilson, who was the Beach Boys' personal manager in its beginning years, can be credited with a good deal of their initial success. Wilson's new album will be a collection of songs penned by Don Ralke, Eck Kinor and Rick Helm of the Sunrays, as well as by Wilson himself.

Pop Festival Grosses High

The First International Pop Festival has pulled in almost $500,000, according to Lou Adler, one of the main planners of the event. The bulk of this figure came from the television rights purchased by ABC.

All the performers, which included the Mamas and Papas, the Animals, Otis Redding, and the Association, worked free, and the proceeds are supposed to go toward some non-profit causes, although Adler was not specific on this point.

John Phillips, a member of the Mamas and Papas and another head of the Festival, has said that plans are now in the offing to take the Festival to either New York, London, or Stockholm next year. Phillips explained that he wasn't slighting Monterey, but wanted to "attract an even wider international representation."

Adler told *The BEAT*, however, that he had no idea where the festival is headed. "Where the money is going and the future of the Festival, will be ironed out in a board meeting we're going to have in a couple of weeks," he said.

BEAT Photo: Ed Caraeff

Sullivan To Cut Album

Ed Sullivan has just been signed to a long term recording contract by Columbia Records.

Mr. Sullivan, who has long been noted for giving many a pop star an opportunity to be seen and heard on his weekly TV show, will present a series of albums covering such a wide range of themes as countries of the world and Hollywood.

NOTICE

TO YE PUBLIC

HEAR YE... HEAR YE... I, Irving Mendelsohn, a professional musician do hereby proclaim James B. Lansing to be the genius of the sound industry. The great sound "THE MENDELSOHN QUINTETTE CLUB OF BOSTON" brings you is clearly and most definitely due to the great loud speakers made by James B. Lansing Sound, Inc. You know "THE MENDELSOHN QUINTETTE CLUB OF BOSTON" is the greatest quintette club going. You have applauded us at our drug store bashes... clapped and screamed for us at our many personal appearances... praised us noisily at our concerts at Carnegie Auditorium... Lincoln Square... Hollywood Ballroom, etc. These accolades belong to James B. Lansing. We salute JBL... we praise JBL... we honor JBL, the greatest loud speaker maker of all time. REMEMBER AND REFLECT... the very existence of your own "MENDELSOHN QUINTETTE CLUB OF BOSTON" is due to James B. Lansing. A legend in his own time.

Learn more about James B. Lansing. Learn more about the unequaled loud speakers his company produces.

Send 25¢ (coin or paper) and receive the interesting, provocative story of James B. Lansing and his discovery of the greatest quintette club going... "THE MENDELSOHN QUINTETTE CLUB OF BOSTON"

IT'S FREE!! The 25¢ is merely for handling charges.

COUPON
Enclosed is 25¢ for handling charges. Please send me the story of "THE MENDELSOHN QUINTETTE CLUB OF BOSTON"

Name ___
Address ___
City ___ State ___

JAMES B. LANSING SOUND, INC.
3249 CASITAS AVE., LOS ANGELES, CALIFORNIA 90039

KRLA ARCHIVES

across the BOARD

MAKING THE NEWS

Monkees Hold First Press Conference—But In England

LONDON—The Monkees held their first-ever press conference, and in England yet, before more than 400 journalists who showed up for what was to kick off the group's United Kingdom tour.

Bert Rafelson, one of the creators of the Monkees, said he expects the group to gross over $85,000 on the tour. A world tour is predicted for next year, and a for-sure set of concerts has been scheduled for the Orient in February.

Rafelson may film the concerts, although the release date for such a production is not known. There's a good chance that Screen Gems may do the flick for movie-house distribution.

The Danish Kids 'Love' America

A "Love America" campaign has been started in Copenhagen by alienated teenagers called provos. They've started drinking Coca-Cola and eating popcorn so they can feel American. The reason? "Loving is better than hating. It's also more practical because America is so big and powerful," said one of the provos.

The kids are also giving free reproductions of famous Danish paintings to American tourists along with a guidebook.

Mitchum Cut On Way Up

Robert Mitchum's first single in many years, "Little Old Wine Drinker Me," is making headway on the pop record charts and is number one in the country field.

Mitchum would never have re-entered the recording business if he hadn't heard someone else sing the tune over his car radio. He thought it would be good material for his friend Dean Martin to record, but when Dean was reported out of town a friend suggested, "Bob, why don't you record it?"

Barbra Draws Huge Crowd

Over 135,000 people crowded into the Sheep Meadows section of New York's Central Park to hear a concert by Barbra Streisand. It was the largest single audience ever to attend a musical event.

Miss Streisand retired at midnight after three hours and fifteen minutes of continuous singing. Even then, the enthusiastic crowd didn't want her to leave, with frequent shouts of "more," "more" echoing through the huge park grounds.

City officials counted 128,000 people within the park confines and another 7,000 outside who had to listen to the Streisand performance over loudspeakers set up around the fringe of the 98-acre area.

COBURN mistaken by the police.

Coburn Talks Real Beating

Acting is getting dangerous. While filming a chase sequence for his new movie, "The President's Analyst" James Colburn was hit over the head by a policeman who was unaware that the flight was staged.

Colburn who is filming in New York, took a bad beating in the head, and called off shooting for the day. Mayor John Lindsay, who has been promoting the filming of movies in his city, sent his apologies to the injured actor along with a basket of fruit.

The patrolman, Melvin Schwartz, was on his regular beat in Greenwich Village and had not been informed of the days shooting and assumed the escape was real instead of staged.

SPECIAL TO BEAT READERS

Due to the fantastic amount of photos and exclusive interviews which The BEAT was fortunate enough to obtain at the Monterey International Pop Festival, we know that you'll want to keep the July 15th issue as a souvenir and perhaps order another copy for yourself or your friends. So, we have made arrangements to print extra copies which you can purchase for our regular price of 25 cents plus an additional ten cents for postage and handling charges.

Name_____ Address_____
City_____ State_____ Zip Code_____
Please send me_____ copies of the July 15 BEAT
MAIL TO: Special Festival Issue, Beat Publications, 9125 Sunset Blvd., Los Angeles, Calif. 90069

WHERE they are

MONKEES
July 14-16, New York City, Forest Hills Stadium; July 20, Buffalo, New York, Memorial Auditorium; July 21, Baltimore, Md., Memorial Auditorium; July 22, Boston, Mass., Boston Gardens; July 23, Philadelphia, Pa., Convention Hall; July 27, Rochester, New York, War Memorial Auditorium; July 28, Cincinnati, Ohio, Gardens; July 29, Detroit, Michigan, Olympia Stadium; July 30, Chicago, Illinois, Stadium; August 2, Milwaukee, Wisc., Arena; August 4, St. Paul, Minn., Municipal Auditorium; August 5, St. Louis, Kiel Auditorium; August 6, Des Moines, Iowa, Veteran's Memorial Auditorium; August 9, Dallas, Texas, Memorial Auditorium; August 10, Houston, Texas, Sam Houston College; August 11, Shreveport, La., Hirsch Memorial Auditorium; August 12, Mobile, Ala., Municipal Auditorium; August 17, Memphis, Tenn., Mid-South Coliseum; August 18, Tulsa, Okla., Assembly Center; August 19, Oklahoma City, Okla., State Fair Arena; August 20, Denver, Colo., Coliseum; August 25, Seattle, Wash., Seattle Center; August 26, Portland, Ore., Memorial Coliseum; August 27, Spokane, Wash., Coliseum.

FOUR SEASONS
July 17, Owensmill, Maryland; July 19, Central Park, Wollman Memorial Rink; July 28, Harrington, Delaware; July 30-August 1, Steel Pier, Atlantic City.

NEW VAUDEVILLE BAND
July 23-29, Atlantic City, Steel Pier; August 1-5, Washington D.C., Shoreham Hotel; August 6, Davenport, Iowa; August 7-12, Iona, Mich Fair; August 20, Lambertsville, N.J., Music Fair; August 25-26, Louisville, Ky., Fair; August 29-30, Detroit, August 31-Sept. 1, Ohio State Fair.

PAUL REVERE & THE RAIDERS
August 4, Los Angeles, Hollywood Bowl; August 11, Springfield, Ill., State Fairgrounds.

5TH DIMENSION
July 20-30, Whiskey A Go-Go, Los Angeles; August 21-Sept. 2, Vancouver, B.C., Marco Polo Club.

SERGIO MENDES AND BRAZIL '66
July 31-August 5, Toronto, Canada, O'Keefe Center; August 24-26, Detroit, Michigan State Fair; August 28-Sept. 4, Washington D.C., Carter-Barron Theatre.

BLUES MAGOOS
July 17, British Columbia, Agra Vancouver; July 19, Salt Lake City, Utah, The Lagoon; July 22, Houston, Texas, Sam Houston Coliseum; July 23, Dallas, Texas, Municipal Auditorium; July 23, Baton Rouge, La., Redempotriest High School; July 28, Montgomery, Ala., State Colisuem; July 29, Birmingham, Ala., City Auditorium; July 31, St. Petersburg, Fla., Bayfront Center; Aug. 1, Jackson, Miss., Miss. Auditorium.

SEEDS
July 19-21, Minneapolis, St. Paul, Arena; July 22, Arlington, Chicago, Cellar Club.

RIGHTEOUS BROTHERS
July 25-30, Chicago, Ill., Opera House; September 11-17, Greek Theatre, Los Angeles, Calif.

HERMAN'S HERMITS
July 21, Oklahoma City, Coliseum; August 5, Chicago, Ill., International Amphitheatre.

SIMON & GARFUNKEL
July 21, 22, Opera House, Chicago, Ill.

DAVE CLARK FIVE
July 18, Columbus, Ga., Civic Auditorium; July 19, Atlanta, Ga., Municipal Auditorium; Little Rock, Ark., Barton Coliseum; July 21, Chattanooga, Tenn., Civic Auditorium; July 22, Greenville, S.C., Memorial Auditorium; July 23, Camden, N.J., Camden County Music Fair.

TREMELOES
July 16, Benton Harbor, Mich., Blossom Lanes; July 17, Saginaw, Mich., Daniel's Den; July 21, South Bend, Ind., Notre Dame July 22, Leesburg, Ind., Tippicanoe Gardens.

YARDBIRDS
July 19, Colorado Springs, Colo., Lakeside Amusement Park; July 21, Santa Rosa, Calif., Fairgrounds; July 28, Sacramento, Calif., Governors Hall; July 29, Concord, Calif., Fairgrounds.

SPANKY & OUR GANG
July 22, Weymouth, Mass., Fair Grounds; July 28, Indiana Beach, Ind.; July 29, Luxembourg. Wisc.; Aug. 8, Jackson, Mich., Jackson County Fair; August 11, 12, Cinn., Ohio. Moonlight Gardens; August 18, West Allis, Wisc., Wisconsin State Fair.

HERB ALPERT & TIJUANA BRASS
August 11, Winnipeg; August 12, Wisconsin State Fair; August 18, Illinois State Fiar; August 20, Sheep Meadow, Central Park, N.Y..

KRLA ARCHIVES

MORE EXCITEMENT FROM ATLANTIC-ATCO

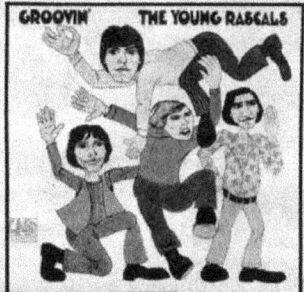
GROOVIN'
The Young Rascals
Atlantic 8148/SD8148

THE SOUND OF WILSON PICKETT
Atlantic 8145/SD8145

THE PERCY SLEDGE WAY
Atlantic 8146/SD8146

THE BEST OF SONNY & CHER
Atco 33-219/SD33-219

SHAKE RATTLE & ROLL
Arthur Conley
Atco 33-220/SD33-220

THIS IS TIM HARDIN
Atco 33-210

THE BEST OF JOE TEX
Atlantic 8144/SD8144

THE SUPER-HITS
Aretha Franklin, Rascals,
Wilson Pickett & other top artists.
Atlantic Group 501/SD501

SMASH SOUNDS
Sonny & Chér, Otis Redding,
Arthur Conley, & other top names.
Atco Group 850/SD850

Ringo Starr—Oldest And Most Unchanged Beatle

By Jacoba Atlas

Controversy and change seems to characterize the Beatles these days, yet one member of the group has remained astonishingly quiet and unchanged. He is the oldest Beatle, the one with the sad-blue eyes, Ringo Starr.

Whereas John and Paul have been creating controversy with their outspoken statements; and George's passion for Indian music and near-Eastern philosophy denotes the enormous change in his thinking, Ringo has said little that would indicate the ways in which his mind has been moving.

This does not mean, however, that Ringo has stayed the same. It would be virtually impossible for him to remain the same person that he was in 1963, when the Beatles first burst onto the scene. It only indicates that Ringo's growth has been less public.

Stand-Out

Ringo has always been a stand-out member of the group. Even in the early days when people were having great difficulty in determining which Beatle was which, Ringo stood out because of his height and his rings.

He joined the group after they had achieved fame in their hometown of Liverpool, and were already established under the banner of the Beatles. Originally Ringo was not the Beatles' drummer, but rather played with another Liverpool group led by Rorry Storm. In those early days, Peter Best was the Beatles' drummer, but due to a controversy still not cleared up today, George and Paul wanted Peter out and Ringo in. Brian Epstein, following the wishes of the majority, arranged for the change.

Least Affected

Ringo immediately became one of the most popular members of the group. Many reasons were given for his personal popularity. He seemed to convey to fans a closeness and a familiarity somewhat lacking in the others. Many felt that Ringo was the easiest to talk to and the least affected by stardom.

With the film "A Hard Day's Night," critics were singling out Ringo as a fine comic actor. In America during those first years, Ringo won the popularity polls and was the most talked about Beatle. Indeed, Brian Epstein states, "America discovered Ringo."

But it was difficult to determine just where Ringo was going, although the direction of the Beatles as a group became evident. Paul and John were writing song after song and each one was receiving more critical acclaim than the last. George also joined the composing field, but Ringo never ventured into that end of the business.

John stunned the world with his widely misquoted statement concerning the relative popularity of Jesus and the Beatles, George went off to India to study with famed musician Ravi Shankar, John soloed in a movie, and Paul scored a film. Most recently, Paul followed in John's footsteps by shocking the world with his views on LSD. With all this going on, Ringo seemed strangely quiet.

While the others have been revolutionizing the pop world with their music and their unconventional ideas, Ringo has remained for the most part, silent. Perhaps, this is the clearest key to his personality. Ringo is simply the quietest, most uncomplicated Beatle of the lot.

It is unnecessary to draw conclusions concerning the Beatles on the basis of comparisons, for they are nothing if not individuals. Therefore, what is Ringo like apart from his famous friends?

Most Mature

He would appear to be very much like his public "image." The oldest, and many believe, the most mature, he has coped admirably with the strains of success. A devoted husband and father, he takes special pride in protecting his young wife, the former Maureen Cox, from the glare of publicity. He delights in telling friends that when they got married her parents "signed her over to me" because Maureen was still a minor.

He is equally concerned over the welfare of their son, Zak, who will be two at the end of the summer. He echos John's statements about a son not owing his father anything, and plans to let the child live his own life, without parental domination. "I will never send my child to boarding school. And I'll never push him. If he passes tests and gets diplomas and everything, well and good, but I'll never say 'you won't get this bike unless you go to college.' And I'll let him decide as he grows up what he wants to be."

He and Maureen spend a good deal of their time with their son, and look forward to the birth of their second child in late August. Another boy? "I do want another boy, but it doesn't matter as much this time. We'll both be very happy whether it's a girl or a boy."

Ringo lives in Surrey in an enormous Tudor house not far from the homes of John and George. The house, which has undergone extensive re-decorating under the close watch of Ringo, has become the gathering point for the Beatles and their friends. For some unknown or unexplained reason, Ringo's home and not Paul's in London or George's and John's in Surrey has become the center for most Beatle activity.

Ringo has always been an avid collector, first of antique guns (Burt Lancaster once sent Ringo a set of pistols) and now of Beatle regalia. He hopes one day to have a thorough collection of souvenirs, photos, articles and other such remembrances tracing the careers of the Beatles from their early days in Liverpool to their present success.

Home Movies

Perhaps borrowing some enthusiasm from Paul, Ringo has also become quite involved with making tapes and home movies. Whether the results of these endeavors will be shown publicly is doubtful, but the interest is there.

Ringo has never claimed to be the world's greatest drummer, and indeed, many music critics have placed him rather low on that achievement ladder, yet his sound is an integral part of the entire Beatle scheme. He seems to know instinctively what the others want, and how to play it. Norman Smith, who has worked on many a Beatle recording session states, "Ringo will start off with one sort of rythmn, then be enlightened by John and Paul as to the particular way they 'hear' it in their original song. Ringo then comes up with it. It's fantastic, the closeness of the group—the way they're all on the save wave length and read each others thoughts."

Many people seem concerned over what Ringo will do if the group breaks up. They need not worry. He is an interested and interesting individual with many directions open to him.

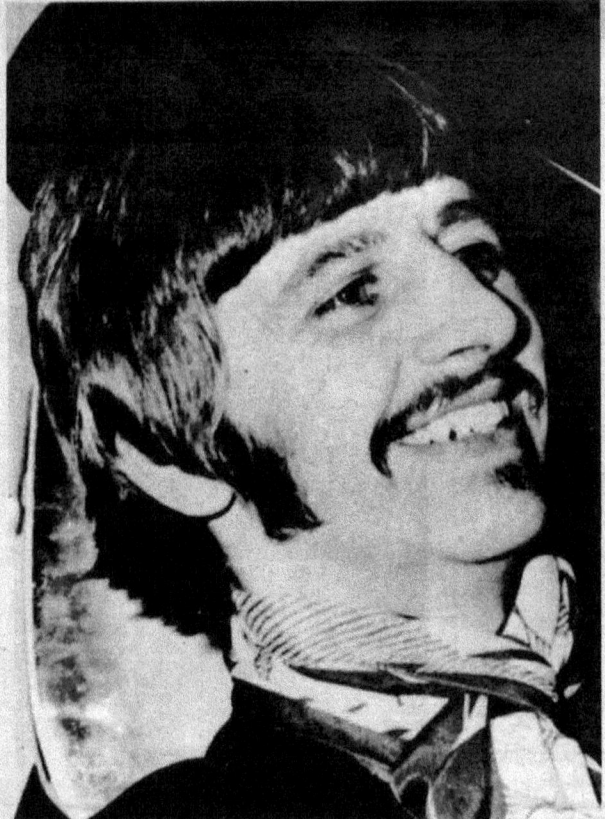

"While the others have been revolutionizing the pop world with their music and unconventional ideas, Ringo has remained strangely silent."

BEAT EXCLUSIVE

George: A Different Face, New Life

By Rochelle Reed

He's a member of Sgt. Pepper's Lonely Hearts Club Band resplendent in an orange braided uniform and flowing hair, with a mustache that somehow grows across his upper lip and drops down on his cheeks to form a beard.

It's been a long time since the days of a silent, sulking George, least obvious of all the Beatles, on the stage of Ed Sullivan.

He's a new George, a different George. A George who no longer spends his free moments "polishing his bottle green Ferrari" as John once put it, but instead packs himself and his wife off to Bombay for six weeks to don Indian garb and master the sitar.

Back in London, he seems aloof, mysterious and introverted. Driving a shiny new Jaguar, he meets his sitar instructor, Ravi Shankar, at the London airport. George, in Indian attire, opens the door for Shankar, dressed in a Western business suit.

Step Back

George, everyone discovered, in 1964, was considered the third Beatle, before Ringo but after writers John and Paul. He was the youngest of the group and news of his 21st birthday traveled around the world from South Africa to Japan.

Onstage, everyone noticed, he had the shortest hair, the shyest smile and the fewest words. He seldom danced around like John and Paul, but stood very still and appeared to be concentrating on his guitar, though those who know him say he was actually eyeing girls in the front row!

He wasn't quoted very much, but reporters managed to discover that he loved cars, hated flying, (he said he was scared of it) and that his favorite dinner—or the food he ate most often in publicity pictures anyway—was eggs, bacon and toast with strawberry jam. He also ate it for lunch.

Meets Patti

Then came "Hard Day's Night" when he met wife-to-be, Patti Boyd, who had a small walk-on part in the movie. She admitted she didn't even like the Beatles until then. So immediately rumors spread that obviously they had married.

George got very angry at newspapermen over the story. But then, he had a reputation for that. Back in 1964, when the Beatles had a few days off in Los Angeles, a photographer nearly received George's version of Waterloo.

Joins Jayne

The Beatles had always wanted to meet Jayne Mansfield and they arranged to join her in a local club where presumably most of the press wouldn't expect them to appear.

However, after a few minutes, the scene turned into a menagerie of fans, press and gawkers. George, particularly annoyed, tossed a few ice cubes towards a photographer. The press, though, stated that it was more like a whole drink.

At the end of the year, he summed up the whole situation and sent out a very personalized Christmas card. The cover bore a picture of George himself, scowling at a cameraman.

But that seems like a long time ago. George hasn't been known to throw anything at a reporter or photographer since. In fact, he waved and smiled to them at his wedding and did the same in Bombay.

So, the question is, what has he been doing lately?

A Lot

Quite a lot, apparently. He was seen at a party by one American pop star who described him as "friendly and talkative. George, along with everyone else, just sat on the floor and discussed all sorts of things and ate a lot and when everyone was quite full, we all went home."

Others have seen him around town — at movies, clubs and his own discotheque, Sibylla's. If he's been traveling (there were rumors that he slipped into the U.S. last month), very few have seen him.

Concepts

Then there is "Within You, Without You," the song George composed for the new Beatle album. Perhaps all the time he was silently staring at the audience back on the Ed Sullivan Show, he was formulating the concepts and ideas he wrote into the song.

In "Within You, Without You" there is the plea for all of us to look within ourselves to find the meaning and the beauty of life. George also re-affirms his belief that all the world can be united through awareness of self. He speaks of going beyond the single person to encompass all living things and people. "We're all one, and life flows on within you and without you."

A DIFFERENT GEORGE — it's been a long time since the Ed Sullivan Show.

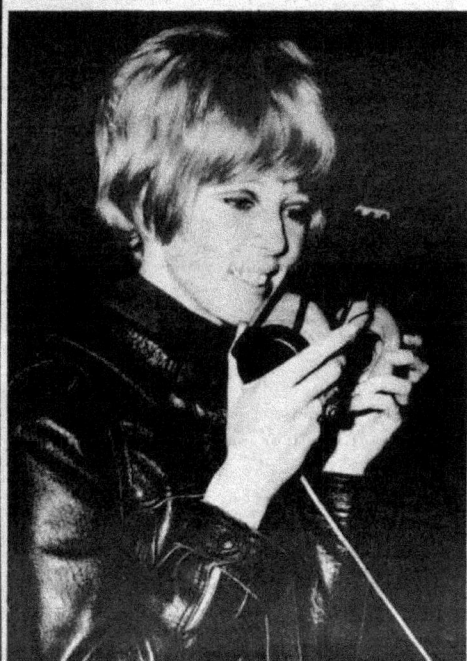
PATTI ATTENDED a Beatle session in jeans and leather jacket.

AT THE SAME session, George unsmilingly posed for the camera.

KRLA ARCHIVES

U.K. POP NEWS ROUND-UP
Bee Gees Pen Two New Potential Hits

By Tony Barrow

By the time you read these words, THE MONKEES will be in London or will be about to jet back to Jacksonville for their U.S. tour opening in Jacksonville. In any event I'll give you a detailed run-down on Monkee business in Britain, complete with a Wembley concert report, for the next issue of *BEAT*.

Meanwhile THE BEE GEES are now on your side of the Atlantic for a couple of weeks. The simultaneous departure of The Bee Gees from London and the arrival of The Monkees was purely coincidental. The simultaneous British and American release of a new record by THE BEE GEES has nothing to do with coincidence. To follow up the swift success of "New York Mining Disaster, 1941" (have *YOU* seen my wife, Davy Jones?) The Bee Gees have penned another pair of marvelous numbers which are potential Top Ten hits. The titles are "To Love Somebody" and "Close Another Door." I'm much excited about the initial impact of The Bee Gees longterm prospects. And it shows I know.

Harum Coming

It won't be long before the PROCOL HARUM come to see you. If they get the chance to do stage appearances rather than just lip-sync promotional things, you must not expect a great deal of showmanship from them. It wasn't stagecraft or visual vitality which sent "A Whiter Shade Of Pale" to Number One in Britain and umpteen other European places. It was sheer audio magnificence. For British concert tours over the years one of the most reliable U.S. visitors has been Roy Oribison, a box office record-breaker time and time again. Orbison just stands there and just sings. Similarly Procol Harum do everything that's necessary without putting on any kind of extra show for hungry-eyed teenyboppers.

Did you believe LULU's mini-skirts?... THE SEEKERS and THE NEW CHRISTY MINSTRELS will perform together as one maxi-group for planned folk-beat finale of "Billy Cotton's Music Hall" TV program in London at the end of August...TRAFFIC a group formed by former Spencer Davis star STEVIE WINWOOD, refusing all bookings to spend summer working on their stage act... KENNY BALL'S JAZZMEN covered "When I'm 64"... GEORGIE FAME recorded composition written by "A Whiter Shade of Pale" team, KEITH REID and Procol vocalist GARY BROCKER, during series of New York studio sessions... SPENCER DAVIS likely to gross 15,000 dollars a week if he accepts singing role in a sci-fi opera to be performed in Germany at West Berlin's National Art Centre!... First avant-garde concert package end of the summer will co-star JIMI HENDRIX and THE SOFT MACHINE with a special lighting planned by Buddy Walters... LULU came home from America loaded with gifts for her 4-year-old kid brother Gordon... JEFFERSON AIRPLANE postponed U.K. visit until late September. Pity...

Neil Cancelled

Sunday concerts, a string of club appearances and several major television dates all cancelled when NAIL DIAMOND shelved plans for June visit to London because of "last-minute Hollywood commitments"... NEW VAUDEVILLE BAND to make guest appearance in movie "The Bliss of Mrs. Blossom" which co-stars Richard Attenborough and Shirley MacLaine... Early next year THE SUPREMES due to make London cabaret debut — probably at internationally renowned Talk Of The Town.

Talking of Flower Power (which we were not really) reminds me that we were promised the blossoming of one SCOTT McKENZIE quite a few weeks ago and his record, "San Francisco (Wear You Know What You Know Where)," is now with us here in London. So is the GIANT SUNFLOWER's "February Sunshine," a little late for the time of the year. It's all Lou Adler product whichever way you look at it so no wonder people are listening and comparing with Mama 'n Papa music.

First In History

What beautiful boldness! RADIO LONDON (Big L to its friends) has made "A Day In The Life" Number One on the Fabulous Forty! This is the first time in the station's short but stormy history that an album track has been placed anywhere on their chart, let alone at the very top like this! Now to consolidate its status as a true ban-banishing, unshy, censorless giant amongst broadcasting companies, Radio London must shed the final vestments of convention and announce the latest U.K. single by THE MONKEES by its original title, "Randy Scouse Git." In case you hadn't heard, RCA Victor Records have released this deck under the meaningless heading of "Alternate Title." I'm sure they wouldn't have offended the least randy of Scouse Gits by letting Micky's single go out without a change of title.

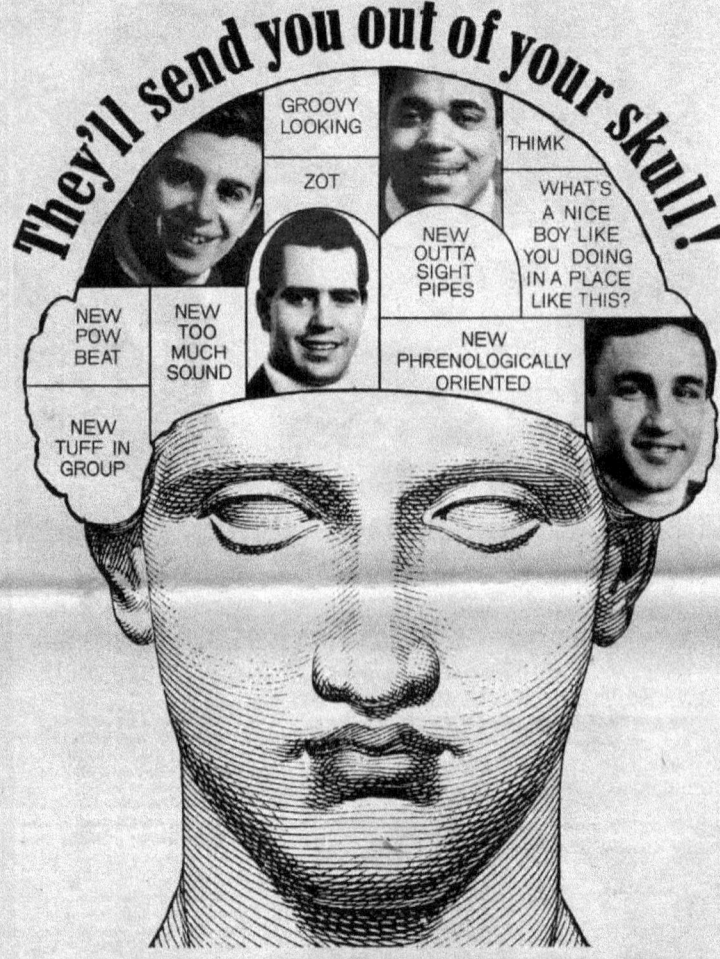

THE AMERICAN BREED
"STEP OUT OF YOUR MIND"
ACTA #804

A HAPPENING HIT
COAST TO COAST
Available at all groovy stores!

Records, a division of Dot Records, Inc.

THE BEE GEES — Not sitting on their laurels.

KRLA ARCHIVES

A Day in the Life of.....

MONKEES, Peter, Micky, Mike and Davy rehearse as Shieks for upcoming television segment.

The MONKEES

Only a couple of years ago, a day in the lives of Davy Jones, Mike Nesmith, Micky Dolenz and Peter Tork would have been a colorless thing indeed. For Peter and Mike, little-known folk singers, Micky, a former child actor, and Davy, an ex-apprentice jockey, one day was pretty much like any other—until, that is, they were brought together as the Monkees.

Today, two years and unaccountable record hits later, they are the most popular vocal group in the country and on the move constantly. A day in the life of the Monkees is divided between recording sessions, screen shootings for their television series, live performances on stages across the nation, and, if they are lucky, an occasional break for rest.

A day in the life of Davy, Mike, Micky and Peter is anything but dull today, as the pictures on this page show.

MIKE—Thoughtful interlude.

DAVY—At poolside break.

ABOARD PLANE, Monkees rest for concert.

PETER—Swinging from a tree.

CROWD meets boys outside hotel.

KRLA ARCHIVES

THE UNPREDICTABLE GYPSY BOOTS, special horticultural consultant to KRLA's Flower Power radio, did field work at a recent Love-In.

Unpredictable Gypsy Boots Startles L.A.

BUT IN BETWEEN THOSE LOVE-INS, GYPSY took time out to put on a tux (unbelievable!) and meet Miss Los Angeles.

8 on the Charts

THE ASSOCIATION

Guest Starring in Person

in The Big Boss

DONALD O'CONNOR SHOW

SPECIAL OFFER TO OUR READERS!
MONDAY, JULY 24 through SUNDAY, JULY 30
A Heavy Evening...... at the Greek Theatre

GREEK THEATRE
UNDER THE DIRECTION OF JAMES A. DOOLITTLE

ESTABLISHMENT EXCHANGE CERTIFICATE

Entitles holder to purchase at GREEK THEATRE BOX OFFICE or BY MAIL, ONE, TWO, THREE or FOUR reserved seats at reduced rate for any ONE performance listed on the back of this certificate. Note Double Discount Nights—a Greek Theatre First!

Henry Mancini Donald O'Connor The Land of Smiles The Righteous Brothers Roger Miller LADO	$5.00 for $4.00	$4.00 for $3.00	$3.00 for $2.00	$2.00 for $1.00
	$5.00 for $3.00	$4.00 for $2.00	$3.00 for $1.00	DOUBLE DISCOUNT NIGHTS
Sweet Charity Andy Williams The Smothers Brothers Tony Bennett Belafonte	$6.00 for $5.00	$5.00 for $4.00	$4.00 for $3.00	$3.00 for $2.00

Send with mail order enclosing self-addressed, stamped envelope or present at box office. Certificate honored until 8 p.m. day of performance; subject to availability of tickets. All ticket sales are final.

NEW, COMFORTABLE SEATS — PARKING IS FREE

GRIFFITH PARK • 2700 N. VERMONT AVE. • LOS ANGELES 90027 • NO 6-6000

KRLA ARCHIVES

DEMONSTRATION OF PROBE SUPPORTED

KRLA will discard the customary radio station practice of staging contests and giving away free prizes during the early weeks of July. This is the period each month during which the radio-audience-rating services conduct their listening measurements and, consequently, the period during which radio stations dispense free airplane rides, free motorcycles and the like.

Instead, the 50,000 watt Los Angeles rock 'n' roll outlet will turn the promotional money allocated for the month over to the American Civil Liberties Union to help finance an investigation of the controversial June 23rd clash between police and some 10,000 anti-Viet Nam war demonstrators at Los Angeles' Century Plaza Hotel during the visit of President Johnson.

Station manager John Barrett has received several thousand pieces of mail since announcing the ACLU donation, the writers being equally divided in their reaction to the station's move.

Congratulations

"The response has ranged from profuse congratulations citing our action as 'fair, intelligent, and stimulating' on one hand, to blistering attacks claiming we are involved in a 'communist-hippie-homosexual' conspiracy on the other."

"From the outset," he continues "our intention was not, and is not, to stir up controversy. We have not taken sides in this issue. We have called for a complete, impartial investigation of the actions of both the demonstrators and the police!"

"We are gratified that a growing number of public officials and well-known citizens who had previously hesitated to become involved are now making similar demands."

KRLA is not the only one in Los Angeles calling for a full and impartial investigation of the demonstrators and the police's actions. State Assemblyman Alan Sieroty of Beverly Hills has asked for a legislative study of the way police are trained to handle crowds.

State Assemblyman Alan Sieroty was joined by City Councilman Ed Edleman who called for an investigation to be conducted by the Police and Fire Commission of which Councilman Edleman is a member.

No Axes

KRLA stresses that it is not taking sides in this issue. The station is simply acting to help find the truth behind the already existing controversy. KRLA news director, Cecil Tuck states, "We have no axe to grind, but whenever this many people are beaten and injured in a civil demonstration we believe the actions of everyone involved should be thoroughly reviewed. Otherwise, it would easily happen again."

KRLA has earned a reputation for dispensing with convention in programming and has won numerous awards, including two Associated Press honors for radio documentaries in 1966. During this past demonstration KRLA news men were present at the Plaza.

"Were the protestors members of a disorderly mob or victims of police aggression," asks Tuck, "we want to find out."

The demonstration was originally conceived to bring the views of the protestors to the President of the United States who was at that time addressing a diner at the Century City Hotel for various members of the Democratic Party. However, this goal was never accomplished, for the President was whisked inside without seeing the protestors, and the demonstration was later forcibly broken up by the police.

SEAN BONNIWELL of Music Machine tells Dick of Machine's new release "The Eagle Never Hunts the Fly."

ARE YOU TAKING A TRIP? TRAVEL TIPS FROM REB

Going to Merry Ole England? KRLA's 9-12 disc-jockey, Reb Foster, has some traveling tips that might help to make you feel just like a Limey.

First and foremost for girls is the mini-skirt. Don't bother bringing anything longer ... they simply aren't being worn. Prices are about the same on both sides of the Atlantic; so either bring your own or wait and see what London has to offer ... it's all the same.

Londoners walk a great deal so bring sensible shoes. But don't overlook the other interesting means of transportation available. Unique for Americans is the double-decker bus, or try the "tubes", London's version of our subways. There are cabs, of course, and surprisingly they are rather reasonably priced.

Rentals for "flats" (apartments) are about the same as in the States, so don't plan on the idea for housing unless you are bringing enough people to split the cost.

Reb, who went to the United Kingdom with the Turtles on their tour says that England is the place for summer travel ... it has everything. He's already planning a return trip.

MARK VII ORIGINALS

50,000 Watt Flower Pot

PAT MOORE! Happy 1/100th of your centennial anniversary with KRLA! Thanks for an outasite year! Luv, Lisa and Pam, Downey.

23 x 30 MONKEE POSTER IMPRINTED WITH YOUR OWN NAME
YOUR NAME_____
1. $ 2.98
2.   5.75
4. 10.00
NO COD's - Add 4% Sales tax in Calif.
TED HILL & CO.
707 Paige Lane
Thousand Oaks, Calif. 91360

ICE HOUSE GLENDALE
234 So. Brand Ave. Reservations: 245-5043

July 15 & 16
Hearts & Flowers
with their hit "Rock 'n Roll Gypsies"
and
The Humane Society
with their hit "Tiptoe Through The Tulips"

July 18-30
Irish Rovers
wild, rousing, Irish crew

ICE HOUSE PASADENA
24 No. Mentor — Reservations: 681-9942
Entire Month Of July

Paul Sykes
fun, songs and wit

Peter Evens
fiery flamenco

The Slippery Rock String Band

KRLA ARCHIVES

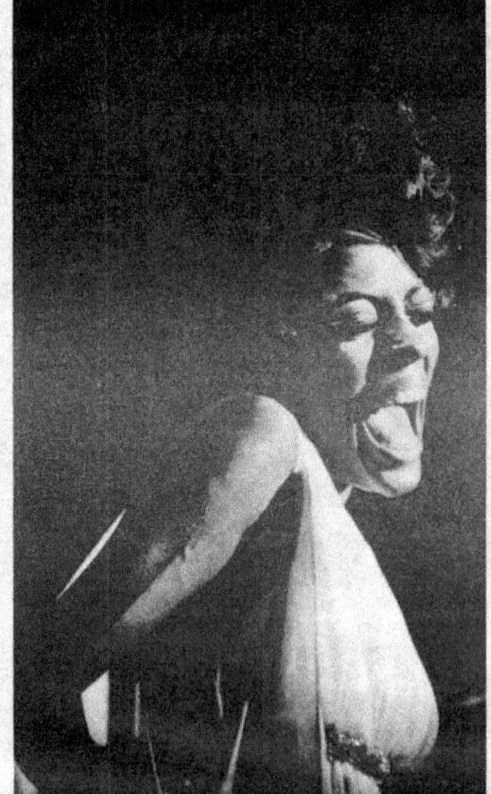

FLORENCE, MARY AND DIANA SING A MEDLEY OF THEIR HITS TO A STANDING ROOM ONLY AUDIENCE
BEAT Photos: Jerry Haas

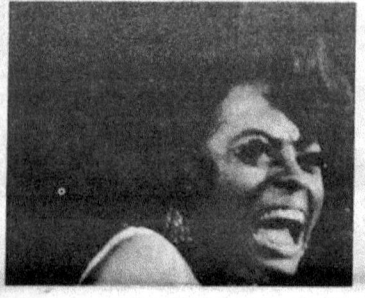

DIANA ROSS:

'Thin Is In!'

DIANA DEDICATES A SONG TO BERRY GORDY

"Thin is 'in,'" says Diana, who maintains she has Twiggy beat in the skinny category. "But fat is where it's at," retorts Florence.

With these light approaches to comedy, The Supremes rounded off an evening of excitement and proof of their professionalism at the famed Cocoanut Grove.

The hallowed halls of the "over thirty" set's favorite Los Angeles nitery were filled to capacity at The Supremes recent opening with representatives from every walk of life except the record buyers who have made The Supremes the most popular female vocal group in the world.

Sing Show Tunes

After nervously rendering their first four songs, The Supremes warmed up and easily delivered the rest of their show, which consisted of about fifty percent show tunes and movie themes, despite the fact that their single records remain of major interest to the young adult record-buying public.

Bobby Darin provided introductions to the evening with a request (in bad taste) for a "flesh pink" spotlight. After a bit of background information by Darin on Berry Gordy, Motown president, Bill Cosby stood up and Darin remarked that the place cards had obviously been switched.

Berry Gordy was there, however, and during the Supremes second return to stage, was honored by a dedication of "You're Nobody Till Somebody Loves You" from Diana. There were no signs of reported tension in the group and Florence, recently rumored to be leaving the group, appeared with them.

3 Standing Ovations

The Supremes received three standing ovations and were given several baskets of roses. After their third standing ovation and curtain call, they closed the show with an obvious plea for better acceptance of *all* people—"Somewhere."

At a small party in another room of the hotel after the performance, the girls appeared wearing pink chiffon floor length dresses with rhinestone trim at the Empire height and were almost smothered by photographers and autograph seekers.

For the audience, micro skirts were the order of the evening with a few floor length dresses in view. Obvious interest of the crowd was the Supremes and the thin eyelet micros (with little else worn). Outlandish costumes, obviously intended to be attention getters, were totally ignored.

BRENDA HOLLOWAY & GIL BOGAS OF MOTOWN.

AN ENTERPRISING YOUNG REPORTER SHARES A TABLE WITH OUR PUBLISHER, GAYLE TUCK.

KRLA ARCHIVES

...Hugh's Latest...

...what can we say...except that it includes a new Hugh...doing 'Society's Child,' 'Baby, Baby, Baby,' 'Here, There and Everywhere'... and eight more...how can anything be so hip?

IN THE RECORD DEPARTMENT

'Insight Out'-asite!

ASSOCIATION

Now Available At:
MONTGOMERY WARD DEPARTMENT STORES

KRLA ARCHIVES

In The News . . .

Four Great Sound Tracks From RCA

Thrifty CUT RATE DRUG STORES

At cut-rate prices, too!

KRLA ARCHIVES

Procol Harum: Beyond A Poem

"Beyond these things" is a blue-eyed British group who named themselves after a Siamese cat, recorded a poem, sent it to number one in England and are being played on the rhythm 'n blues stations Stateside because they haven't yet found out that the group is not genuinely in that bag.

Procol Harum (which translated means "beyond these things") took exactly eight weeks to go from the "unknown" category all the way to the most talked about group on the music scene. The reason is a poem, set to music and called "A Whiter Shade of Pale."

Just Lyrics

Theirs is an amazing story. It seems that one Keith Reid approached record producer, Denny Cordell with the lyrics to "A Whiter Shade Of Pale." No music, just lyrics. Denny admitted that the lyrics were beautiful but he could do nothing until the music was written.

So Keith went off and returned six weeks later with a demonstration record. Although it was accompanied only by a piano, Denny dug it immediately, Keith formed a group and they trouped en masse to the recording studio.

And it was there that Denny Cordell received one of the biggest shocks of his record producing career—the Procol Harum recorded "A Whiter Shade Of Pale" in one take! "I just couldn't believe we'd got it right first time," admitted Denny, "so I said 'Let's try it one more time.' I was wrong."

There are five members in the group. Thus far, Gary Brooker has received the most attention due to the fact that he is the lead singer and also composer of "Pale." Born in 1945, Gary lists both his biggest disappointment and biggest break as "not singing with Andrew Oldham" (Rolling Stones' manager). Besides singing, Gary plays piano with the Harum but is additionally proficient in organ, trombone, cornet, piano accordion and Bengal flute.

'I Don't Believe It'

Says Gary of the group's immediate success: "I don't think I really believe it all yet. What I want to do is get away for a time and organize myself. Think it all out and put it in its proper place. It's all very well people congratulating you and buying you drinks but it doesn't really mean much, does it?"

Mathew Charles plays organ for the group and says his ambition is to receive "recognition from people I admire." He was born in 1946, digs Bach as a composer and John Lennon as a singer. Mathew feels that the Beatles, Bob Dylan and Jimmy Smith were his biggest influences and that his best friend is "my trusty sword."

Says Nothing

Ray Royer handles lead guitar chores for the Harum, was born in 1945 and hates "people spitting at me." He is obviously quite shy since he says almost nothing except that he has had no musical education whatsoever and that in addition to guitar he can also play violin.

Dave Knights swears he was a cowboy before becoming bass player for the Harum, was born in 1945 and has as his professional ambition "to remain." He likes Lennon and McCartney as composers, Marlene Dietrick and Brigitte Bardot as actresses and the Who, the Beatles and the Jimi Hendrix Experience as his favorite groups.

Crime Fighter

Bobby Harrison is the Harum's drummer. Born in 1943, Bobby has the distinction of being the group's eldest member. He believes his biggest break was in joining the Harum and that his biggest disappointment was "not being paid"—though he neglects to say for what! He says his former occupation was "masked crime fighter"—though again he failed to further enlighten us as to whether he rode a horse or a batmobile in his escapades against crime.

And there you have it—the Procol Harum, the group which is threatening to smash the whole music scene wide open. Providing, of course, the censors are agreeable!

PROCOL HAREM—the Latin for "beyond these things" and also the name of a prized Siamese cat. Left to right, Bobby Harrison, Matthew Fisher, Barry Brooker, Dave Knight and Ray Royer.

frankie valli solo

Available At... MONTGOMERY WARD

KRLA ARCHIVES

BEAT EXCLUSIVE

'My Music Not For Addicts'—Shankar

"The message I'm trying to get through is that our music is very sacred to us and is not meant for people who are alcoholic, or who are addicts, or who misbehave, because it is a music which has been handed down from our religious background for our listeners."

The words are those of the famous Indian sitarist, Ravi Shankar, a man whose popularity in the United States has ridden the crest of the psychedelic movement.

But Shankar, in an exclusive *BEAT* interview, made it clear that he didn't want to appeal to drug users or high hippies.

"If one hears this music without any intoxication, or any sort of drugs, one does get the feeling of being intoxicated. That's the beauty of our music. It builds up to that pitch. We don't believe in the extra, or the other stimulous taken, and that's what I'm trying my best to make the young people, without hurting them, of course, to understand."

Shankar refused the label of anti-drug preacher or social reformer. "I have nothing to say. No, it's the people's business if they want to drink, or smoke or take drugs. All I request is that these people just give me a couple of hours of sobriety or sober mind. That's all I request of them. Whatever they do before or after is not my business."

Popular Now

The Indian musician admitted that his popularity has boomed in the U.S. in the past two years, although he had been making tours of the States for the past 12 years.

"Many people, especially young people, have started listening to sitar since George Harrison, one of the Beatles, became my disciple. He is a beautiful person. His attitude toward our music is very sincere. He's very humble, and becoming better and better. His love for India and its philosophy and spiritual values is something outstanding.

Sitar School

Shankar described his music as having different stages in it resulting from many developments made on it over the centuries. "It has got the tremendously spiritual, the tranquil mood, then it drops into romantic, and, in the end, it is very playful and joyous."

Since Beatle George became so interested in the many moods of the sitar, other groups have taken it up, and, says Shankar, "It is now the 'in' thing."

Interest in the sitar has been increasing at such a great pace, Shankar decided to set up a sitarist school in Los Angeles. Indian music in general will be taught there, including a number of other Indian musical instruments and vocal training. "I'm going to be at the school for another two and a half months nearly teaching there," he said. "And even if I go, the school will function, as I'm trying to have a permanent staff."

KRLA ARCHIVES

THE AMERICAN BREED on the way up with new sound, new name.

AMERICAN BREED STEP OUT OF COMMERCIALS

Listen carefully to that next rockin' radio or television commercial — it might be the sounds of the American Breed. The hit recorders of "Step Out Of Your Mind" first made it big doing swinging musical ads for the Pepsi-Cola Company and the Baldwin Piano Company, among many others. The four Chicago-based boys even write some commercials.

The Breed started a couple of years back under the name of Gary and the Nite Lights. They were a pure rock group then, but after months of practice, they got better and better and soon decided a new name would be appropriate for their new sound.

Invites from colleges in the Midwest area started the Breed to circulate their name and music. They made the scene at concerts and dances at Northwestern, Illinois, Wisconsin, Indiana, Lake Forest, Purdue and Notre Dame.

The big lift came at the Teen World Fair in Chicago in the summer of 1966. The guys got such an outasite reception, they were asked to work the entire ten days of the Teen Fair.

Following this, they got an even bigger break when ACTA Records, a subsidiary of Dot, signed the American Breed and released the group's first single called "I Don't Think You Know Me." Their voices really became familiar to the public-at-large when they were retained as the staff band for Pepsi and demonstrators of Baldwin's amplifiers and guitars.

Lead singer and guitarist for the American Breed is Gary Loizzo, blonde haired and 21-years-old. Blinky, as the guys call him, is proficient with the 12-string guitar as well as the organ. He says of all the things he digs the most, it's groovy, fun-loving people.

Mini-skirt-loving Chuck Colbert is the Breed's bassman, but never ask Chuck a simple question such as what he cuts up on the most, because he'll always give you a hip answer. Chuck's garage, incidentally, was recently enhanced by a new Rolls Royce.

Guitarist Al Ciner says he wants to be making groovy sounds until he's 90. Since Al's only 20 right now, it looks like he has a big career ahead of him.

Buddha Graziano, the oldest of the American Breed at 22, has a craving for exotic Italian food, not to mention the drums. Buddha's ambition is a lofty one — he wants to be able to understand girls. Good luck, Buddha!

European Press Meets Monkees

(Continued from Page 3)

facial hair in the near future?

PETER: *I can't stop myself! No, I'd like to grow a beard one of these years.*

MICKY: *We can't. The Beatles did it already.*

PETER: *We'd be accused of imitating. Ha! Ha!*

Mike, do you think it's a good thing for you to take your wife on tours?

MIKE: *I think it would be kinda dangerous.*

Why?

MIKE: *I'll let you figure that out!*

Davy, there have been reports that you're unhappy about being a Monkee, that you're restless and that you feel you could now afford to go solo. Have you any plans to do that this year?

DAVY: *No, I don't. I might as well clear it up now by saying I am NOT leaving the Monkees and I'll be with them as long as they're Monkees. That's all just rumours.*

The Beatles have admitted to taking L.S.D....

MICKY: *Ah! There it is! That was the one we were waiting for!* (Laughter) (continuing) *. . . also two of The Rolling Stones who are on drug charges claim that drugs help them in their work. Judging by one of two of the tracks on the Beatles' LP it gives some people inspiration. Do you think it necessary for pop groups to take drugs?*

MICKY: *Do you like The Beatles album?*

Yes.

MICKY: *Well?*

But do you think it is necessary?

MICKY: *No.*

Do you take them yourselves?

MICKY: *Coffee. I drink coffee. That's about the worst drug I take.*

PETER: *I took aspirin once. It destroyed my head and provided me with a lot of inspiration. I'm gonna write a song.*

MIKE: *I have a real problem. I get high on one-a-day vitamins.*

MICKY: *I drink chlorine with ...*

DAVY: *Ex-Lax does it to me. It keeps me going all the time. No? O.K.!*

MICKY: *No, I don't think anybody needs anything. It's just whatever is right for whoever is involved.*

ART INSTITUTE OF PITTSBURGH
47th Yr. Coed. 18 & 24 mo. Diploma Course: Commercial Art, Fashion Art, Interior Design, Begin. & Adv. Vet. Appd. Dorm facilities. College referrals for degrees. Free illus. brochure.
Earl B. Wheeler, Director
635 Smithfield St.
Pittsburgh, Pa. 15222

DON'T MISS IT!
ORDER YOUR SOUVENIR ISSUE
SEE PAGE 6 FOR DETAILS

BRENTON WOOD IS OUT TO FILL THE SHOES OF TOP SOUL SINGERS

If you want to pay Brenton Wood a huge compliment, ask him if he thinks he can fill the shoes of those giants of soul, Sam Cooke and Jesse Belvin. Critics say he is a likely candidate. Brenton is highly flattered by the comparison, but said recently, "But I've got a long, long way to go." He added that ever since he was a record-buying teenager, Cooke and Belvin have been his heroes.

"I know it takes years of experience to be a Sam Cooke or a Jesse Belvin," said Brenton modestly. "I don't want to fool the people."

Still Studying

So it's natural that he still takes singing lessons. Someday he hopes to become an actor. "Singing I guess, is a form of acting, but my goal is the Broadway stage or the Hollywood screen."

The song that has set critical tongues wagging with comments and predictions is Brenton's single release "Oogum Boogum Man." Asked to define Oogum Boogum, Brenton said,

"They're just two crazy words for a crazy, tongue-tied feeling when a guy sees a groovy gal. And when this nervous cat finally can speak, he tells his girl how much soul she's got and how her mod dress drives him out of his mind, too. It's a very real feeling of today.

Number One

"Oogum Boogum" is now hitting No. 1 in many areas of the U.S. prompting Brenton and his back-up band, Kent and the Candidates to make a national tour.

Brenton is the author of the song with the label credit reading Alfred Smith, his real name.

Brenton's parents brought him to California from his native Shreveport, Lousiana at age 2. He is one of six sisters and five brothers, "none of whom were able to carry a tune." But singing and speed came easily to him.

At Compton High School he made quite a name in track running the 100-yard dash in 9.5 seconds.

At Compton College he became the leader of a singing group, The Quotations, which played "gigs" around the Los Angeles area.

Now 24, Brenton has been singing for almost ten years, "whenever anybody would give me the chance." He left his singing group to become a solo attraction and has been playing the nightclub circuit around the U.S., and Canada.

All the usual talk is circulating about Brenton that always follows the sudden catapulting of a virtually unknown artist into fame and fortune following a hit record. People in-the-know begin to discuss the singer's potential for coming up with another hit. The critical concensus at this point seems to be that there is just no stopping Brenton Wood — either on the track or off.

DICK CLARK TALKS TO BRENTON

KRLA ARCHIVES

'THERE'S SO MUCH BEAUTY HERE, YET SO MUCH ROT HERE' —Burdon

Eric Burdon of the Animals has been to the United States so many times he's lost count. For a person like Eric, who lives in the U.S. as often as he does in his native England, there is a great opportunity to compare countries, and the British blues-rock singer has come to some conclusions that might amaze, and even shock, some Americans who have never given their nation's musical and social institutions much thought.

"I dig it a lot," Eric said of America in an exclusive interview. "Musically, there is no country in the world you can learn from more than the United States. New York has every kind of music there. Los Angeles has specialized in beautiful soft music. Chicago specializes in hard music. The South is just a trip itself because of the blues they have there.

"Most of my time is spent in the United States. I feel like I'm becoming a citizen in a way. When anybody asks where I come from I just say the world, because that's where I do come from."

Mine of Contrasts

Eric characterizes America as a mine of contrasts and, because of it, he says he has learned a great deal about life. "There's so much beauty here, and yet there's so much rot here. There's so many great people here, yet there's so many bad people here. The weather is so hot, yet it can be so cold. The food can be beautiful, and yet it can be lousy.

"I dig it, because it really is a contrast. I never stop learning in America. Whereas in England, everything is just one tone of gray. You never really get into trouble, but you never really get out of trouble. And, you know, it just goes on and on and on in England."

For Eric, the main thing that can't be tolerated about the U.S. is gun-carrying police, a phenomenon which England does not share. "The police don't have guns in Britain, and cops are armed to the teeth here, you know. That's the one thing that frightens me more than anything else in the United States.

Right To Kill

"The policeman has the right to take away someone's life, in particular an ordinary guy who is doing a job of work like any other guy. It's just like giving a postman a gun and giving him the right to take away somebody's life—because some cops are just as intelligent as postmen.

"It's crazy, really. In England we always give people a second chance. Here, it's 'stop or I'll shoot,' and then he squeezes off and a life's gone. That must happen lots of times, and it kind of frightens me.

"When I first came to America, and a policeman entered the room — we used to have a lot of police protection when we first came here — my eyes were continually on the gun he wore on his hip, because in England you never see firearms, never. Even the Army doesn't use guns...it's crazy..."

Eric said the troups who guard Buckingham Palace, where the queen lives, are not allowed to use ammunition in their rifles. "If someone broke into the Palace, they'd have to call for a London Bobby, and he hasn't got a gun either. So, you know, I feel much safer there than here. But as I say, it's worth it . . . to learn and see."

I seem to be making a career of this, and I guess, Paul's.

I'll never forget the day I read John Lennon's now-infamous comment about religion in an American news magazine. I panicked, and sat down and wrote him a long letter, warning him of the possible repercussions of such a statement.

I didn't mail the letter, fearing he would think I was off my nut (or *know* I was).

Six months later, when it was convenient for certain charlatans to use the comment to gain publicity for themselves, the situation erupted into an international scandal.

Several months ago, I read a reprint of an interview Paul had given a reporter from a London paper. In it he mentioned something that could have set off another chain reaction of Beatle-bonfires, because the something could have been misunderstood, or *understood*, as the case may be.

I thereupon re-panicked and sat down to write him a long letter. I almost never got up. When I did, long was not the *word* for what I'd written. Instead of a terse note, I ended up with a novelette.

In my letter, I started by saying things like "Oh, Paul, you've seen what this country can be like when the rabble is roused. Why take chances of it happening again?"

Admire Honesty

But I had to admit, even at the beginning of the letter, that I admired the Beatles' honesty. And when I said that to Paul, my entire mood changed and I started babbling about how much good the Lennon controversy had caused, despite the hassle it had caused them and him.

Good like making people really think about their religious beliefs, and really seeing whether or not they were living up to them. Also good like seeing what some people are *truly* like, and learning to stay away from people who are willing to participate in the passive but deadly violence of burning anything or anyone.

Then I really started raving, and wondering aloud on paper just how honest a person should be. Or better yet, how honest a person can *afford* to be.

Confused State

By the time I got around to the end of the letter (several months later) I had no mortal idea what I was talking about. (Which is certainly nothing new for me.) No, I retract that. I had no idea how I felt about the subjects I'd been blithering about.

Did I want the Beatles to go on being frank and open about their opinions, thereby inciting occasional riots but doing a great lot of good in the bargain, or did I want them, for their own sake, to just cool it and be like others in this business . . . one person when the public is looking and another when they aren't.

Then I got to thinking about how this is hardly limited to the entertainment business. Maybe its more intensified, because more people are watching the actions of a star than witness (or even care about) what an ordinary person is up to. But we're all like that in a way. I'm a perfect example. You probably are, too. Not really the same on the outside as on the inside.

In some ways, this is good. Some things aren't anyone's business. But sometimes, the things you keep under wraps really get to you because you have to bear up under them all alone, or have people react to the outside of you and never know you're not the person they think they know.

Being Sneaky

For God's sake, I don't think anyone on this earth can be more confusing than I can. But I do hope you know what I mean. A friend of mine started smoking a year or so ago, and until just recently she was on this big hysterical kick of keeping it from her folks. She'd practically wash her hair before going home, for fear someone would smell smoke.

After all those months of worrying and being sneaky, her mother finally told her "look, we know you smoke and we wish you wouldn't because it's so unhealthy." She about dropped her teeth. (She also quit smoking.)

On a much larger scale, imagine how the hidden parts of yourself can get to you, if they're really big things, and create a false impression, not only of you, but of society in general because you sure aren't alone.

It seems to me that there's just too much pretense and I don't see how we can solve the real problems of the world until things are really out in the open. Until human beings can stop being duel personalities and be one.

I know this is a pop music paper and hardly the place for all this raving I'm doing, but it also seems like pop music is beginning to be the center of many different kinds of progress. Not just advances in music, but human advances our race should have made hundreds of years ago.

Do I have to tell you that I didn't mail that letter to Paul either?

No Conclusion

I just couldn't. I'd gibbered on for too long and never reached a conclusion as to what I was really trying to tell him.

I only knew one thing for sure. I and a few (million) other Beatle fans were getting a bit tired of the whole world learning social lessons at the Beatles' expense. The John thing was a step forward in human thinking, but he went through hell because of it.

Now I'm glad I didn't mail it. That I had nothing to do with the decision he made not long ago. The decision to be himself or keep his life safely hidden behind velvet eyes and an innocent smile.

I think that his incredible honesty will expand more minds than LSD could ever hope to.

KRLA ARCHIVES

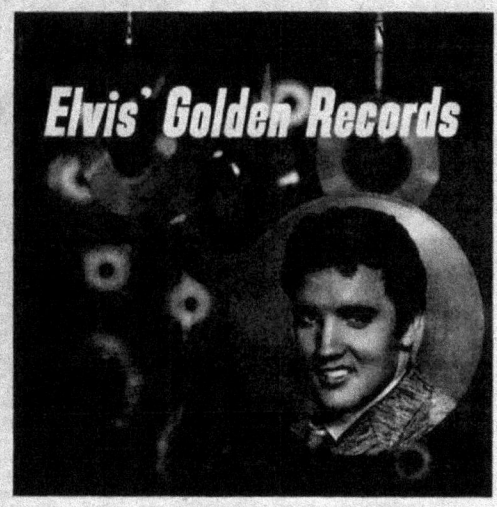

Thirty Six Million Sellers By Elvis!

Like . . .

Houndog
Jailhouse Rock
Love Me Tender
I Need Your Love Tonight
My Wish Came True
It's Now Or Never
Are You Lonesome Tonight?

AND MANY OTHERS . . .

All In These Three Great LP's

AVAILABLE AT YOUR

KRLA ARCHIVES

JOAN BAEZ
Love-Ins Won't Save The World

"I don't talk about music because talking about music doesn't interest me."

(Editor's Note: Undeniably, Joan Baez is a controversial individual. While we do not necessarily agree with what she says, we do believe that she has a right to express her opinions and ideals.)

Joan Baez has just returned from Europe and we were anxious to learn what she found the European attitude to be toward the music scene here in the United States.

"When I meet people and talk," answered Joan, "I don't talk about music because talking about music doesn't interest me. But if it ever ties in at all with non-violence, which is what I *do* talk about and politics, then, I mean, obviously music plays a part somewhere. I think that you can't underestimate the power of music but neither can you save the world by a 'love-in' and a few songs, you know, but I'm a little cynical about that. I know it's impossible. It's a nice idea but it's impossible.

In English

"But as far as the overseas scene goes with music, it's dominated still by the American and English groups and like a group, an Austrian group, has to learn all their stuff in English and they want to try and sell it in the States 'cause there's not much doing in Austria you know."

Music today seems to be taking upon itself the job of questioning. Instead of complimenting the moon in June, more and more of today's pop music is making social comment—asking piercing and legitimate questions. Does Miss Baez think this is a good direction?

"Well, obviously any time anybody begins to question this mess of a world we live in it's a good idea. I've been out of the country for three months so I don't know exactly. In Italy there were some kids writing protest songs. They were pop songs, they're in the top twenty or top forty, and I'm not sure about France or the other places but that was sort of exciting."

Since Miss Baez does not conceal the fact that she believes the world is a "mess," what is her solution for "unmessing" it?

"Okay, for five thousand years we've been doing one repeat after another of the same old thing, which is trying to solve violence by more violence. So what's needed is so huge that it's very questionable whether there's time but it would be a non-violent revolution, which means a tremendous amount of action, a tremendous amount of resistance. But it means you have to stop any co-operation with killing. Now this means it has to be in economics, it has to be social, it has to be institutional—it has to be everything all at once and then, of course, including music.

Any Progress?

Have we made any progress? "No, I think we have barely gotten out of the caves and maybe we should have stayed in them. In a way, with the really terrible disasters that are going on now, some people are so revolted with the amount of violence that in a way maybe it's the time for non-violent action and non-violent talks. They're absolutely so disgusted and fed up you know, that they're willing to listen to anything, even somebody who is nutty enough to talk about non-violence.

"Non-violence has been such a flop and the only thing that's been a worse flop has been violence, so we have that in our favor."

Although she doesn't relish discussing music, it is a very real and important part of her life. "I don't know how I really would survive without music 'cause I couldn't. I would sing anyway, even if I had my tongue cut out. It's terribly important to be able to relax."

The Adventures of Robin Boyd

©1965 By Shirley Poston

To say it was snowing the night The Mockingbirds caused the Pitchfork Freak-Out would be to foist the Paul's-Grandfather of all under-statments off on many an unsuspecting (not if they've been around *here* long) reader.

It happened, to put it blandly (and I usually do), during the blizzardo of the century.

Robin and her fellow (okay, okay, *girl*) (perfectionist) group members Ringo and Budgie were amazed that anyone showed up for their performance at the Neville Club, but despite rain, sleet and all that other post office (ray!) stuff, nothing could keep the teenagers of Pitchfork, South Dakota from their appointed rounds.

Like Cadavers

And, had this been like any other night, nothing could have kept them from proceeding to stand there like a convocation of cadavers throughout the entirety of said performance.

However, this was *not* like any other night. For one thing, Robin had taken John The Genie's advice about discarding their early-Liverpool leather look (she had also taken his Harley-Davidson crack directly to heart) (wait until the next time he tries to pinch *her*) (and she can hardly). Their old out fits had been replaced by matching mini-skirts. (*And* matching tops, *and* matching tops.) (What kind of a girl do you think Robin Irene Boyd *is?*) (Well, try not to let it get around willyah?)

Take Advice

This seemed to set off a few sparks of interest, but the real happening got underway when Robin further took John's advice and decided it was time they stopped saving their Beatle songs for a special occasion and played one for their audience already.

It's hard to say why Robin chose "Little Child" (and it's even *harder* to print). Perhaps it was because she remembered (and was still trying to live down) the effect the song used to have on her. Whatever the reason, they launched noisily into same, sounding so much like the Beatles, they seriously considered mobbing themselves later.

Suddenly, the ghouls-arp-teenagers of Pitchfork were dancing wildly. And smiling, Robin rared back and belted out another chorus (In a ladylike manner, of course.) (Not.)

Then she stopped smiling. "Good grief," she said to herself. "Charlie Brown," she added, feeling particularly witty and original that evening. True, she had set out to make the younger Pitchforkians *unwind,* but she could recall in no way encouraging them to *undress.*

Then she re-smiled, and also larfed hysterically. Underneath the long hemlines and plaid flannel shirts lurked the moddest mini-skirts paisleys and crazy-wild-thingy-type-clothes Robin had ever laid eyes (a painful experience) on. One girl, the very one Robin had suspected was actually a spy from the D.A.R., was wearing a dress made entirely out of soda crackers! (Just the very thing for getting you into a lot of hot soup with your folks.)

This was all the encouragement the Mockingbirds' needed, and they proceeded to play every single Beatle song they'd ever heard (plus a few they hadn't), and their audience clamored for more between frugs.

Surged Out

When it was finally time for either the party of the teenagers and their respective families to break up, everyone surged noisily out the door and braved the hurricane-mit-flakes.

Robin was putting her guitar away when she noticed a stranger standing next to her.

"Why are you standing next to me, stranger?" she shrieked nonchalantly.

But she soon changed her tune when the individual of her non-acquaintance (if I'd said stranger another time I'd have gone ape) handed her a card.

By holding said card about two inches from her eyes (nice enough kid but blind as a at-bay) she was able to read the following inscription . . . Murray Seersucker, West Coast Promotion Man, Hemlock Records.

"*Hemlock Records?*" Robin breathed adoringly. "What are you doing *here?*"

Train Stuck

"My train's stuck in this boig," the stranger (ape, ape, ape) explained. "You gotta good group, kid. I mean, boy, when they started shredding'! Never saw nothing like it before in my life."

Robin blushed. "Why thank you," she said agreeably. (Agreeing, that is, with every word he said. (Modesty ain't everything.) (Fortunately.)

Mr. Seersucker shushed her with a wave. (Or was it a Wac?) "Never mind dat. Be here tomorrow so I can see how you sound minus da strippers. Just the tree of you."

"Just the three - er - tree of us," Robin promised as Ringo and Budgie hovered nearby, clutching their throats. (Never appear too eager, they allus say.)

When the aforementioned tree of them reached the snow-covered Boyd house (with a little help from their friend, Sgt. Pepper of the Yukon and his Wonder Dog, Klang, Robin shouted for her parents to wake up.

Her father, as usual, completely ignored her, but at long last, her mother appeared blearily.

"Mom!" bellowed Robin, not unappropriately. "I think we're going to get a recording contract!" Then, brandishing the card, she told all.

"This can't *be,*" her mother moaned after hearing the story her daughter (make that *his* daughter) babbled.

"Why not?" chorused the Mockingbirds.

"Because this never happens except in old Dick Powell movies," Mrs. Boyd explained patiently. "Besides, you're not even *in* college."

Wondering what on earth she meant by that (if you're in the same ship, ask *our* folks), not to mention who Old Dick Powell was, the threesome retired to the kitchen where they consumed 28 hot dogs. (Their appetites were lessened somewhat by the excitement.) (Thank God.)

But it turned out that Robin's mother was right after all. The thingy *didn't* come off the next day. Not for the reasons she had cited. Because the Mockingbirds, whose talents had appeared in a mysterious manner several months ago, found themselves unable to croak so much as a note into the microphone.

(To Be Continued Next Issue)

KRLA ARCHIVES

please send me
BEAT

26 issues only

$3 per year

Mail to: **BEAT Publications**
9125 Sunset Blvd.
Los Angeles, California 90069

☐ New Subscription
☐ Renewal (please enclose mailing label from your last BEAT)
I want BEAT for ☐ 1 year at $3.00 or ☐ 2 years at $5.00
I enclose ☐ cash ☐ check ☐ money order
Outside U.S. — $9 per year

• Please print your name and address.

Name_____
Street_____
City_____
State_____ Zip_____

THE BEAT WANTS YOU!

ATTENTION ALL BEAT PEOPLE: We need you! Since *The BEAT* is your newspaper, we'd like you to help us. As you know, we are experiencing all sorts of growing pains — adding new columns, discontinuing others. Because we are, after all, a *newspaper* in each issue we attempt to print all the news happening in various segments of the entertainment field.

Now, we'd like to further expand our news coverage by having *you* send us your local happenings. We have correspondents strung across the globe in all the major cities and countries. However, it is difficult to keep in close touch with smaller (though equally important) sections of the nation.

So, we're asking you to help by sending us the news of your city. Please be very brief and include who, why, when and how. Also please include a substantiating source and a phone number to enable us to verify or add to your information if necessary.

We hope in this way to be able to serve you better by printing *your* news, *your* happenings and *your* ideas. How about it?

Send your material to: Beat Publications
9121 Sunset Blvd.
Los Angeles, California 90069

CLASSIFIED

FAN CLUBS

THE ROBBS NATIONAL FAN CLUB
Write: P. O. Box 350
Beverly Hills, California 90213

INSTRUCTION

REACH COSMIC AWARENESS without drugs — help save mankind from destruction. Write for free booklet, "Cosmic Awareness Speaks," Organization of Awareness, Box 115E, Olympia, Washington.

SLEEP-LEARNING, self-hypnosis. Details, strange catalog free! Autosuggestion, Box 24-BT, Olympia, Washington.

FOR SALE

TAPE RECORDER — Mayfair-1607, New — $24. Rarely used — 6 months. ALL — $24! Inquire, Mary, 7823 Forest Avenue, Munster, Indiana.

ROLLING STONES POSTER 2-1/2 feet by 3 feet. $1.50 postpaid. Seper Co., 5273 Tendilla, Woodland Hills, Calif.

WANTED

SONGWRITER needs work. 636 Farragutt St. NW, Wash., D.C. Brainard Hyson (202) TU 2-8970

PERSONALS

Danna Bradford is beautiful — Even when she's MAD!!

Teeny-boppers dig BEATLES: Tubey-boobies dig MONKEES

I LOVE HARRY — Paulette

LOVE — DAFFODIL
FLOWERS — DAFFODIL

Ha! When *weren't* they re-runs!?? FIGHT Monkee-ism! BEATLES FOREVER!

The Jefferson Airplane are the grooviest, especially Jorma!!! Nancy Carpenter

Beatles — Chicago luvs you only!!!

Andy and Rob — WAKE UP!!! Candy and Sandy

Sharon loves Bobby

Vicki, Shari, Kathy, Kathy and Miss Pierce and Cyn, Hi from a lonesome x-California girl Chris

HAPPY ANNIVERSARY to Wally and Linda — from your "problem children"

BEATLES RULE THE WORLD AND EVERYONE IN IT!!!

PHIL, I love you... Janey

BABALOU!!!

S.J.P. Rules!

Steve is the greatest!

SERGEANT PEPPER or GENERAL BLAND?

FIGHT MONKEEISM! BEATLES FOREVER!

Sergeant PEPPER

ATTENTION PETER TORK!! Why Four? Lives and we love u.

BRUTE FORCE LIVES LOVES, LOVES and is HAPPENING!

FRANK: Summ is NICE! Love, PATT

JACUZZI SMITH LIVES!?!

Lynn Neubert, you're the grooviest girl anywhere!

"Indescribably Delicious!"

George Harrison is groovily gorgeous!

Beatles People are SHOT!
"CHRIS LUVS MONKEES"

"Mark LOVES Lynn"

The Yellow Balloon are greatest!

To the R.C.A., Remember my leprechaun the night you went to Phoenix? Diane

"LENNON LUVERS LUV A LOT OF MAN!"

THE NITTY GRITTY DIRT BAND

ROB Luvs Mary Ann

Love is Dave Burgess!!

Life is just a bowl of ANIMAL CRACKERS & WASHBOARDS AMALGAMATED.

THE PEWTER PALS DON'T RUST

Bonnie loves Jim
Maureen loves Jim

The Courtmen Groove!!!

MICKY DOLENZ

SANDY D. Believe me, I'll always like you more than anyone else. Including Shep. — PAT

TOM E. *LUBS* SUE O.

I love ya Dee Robb! — Pattie

BUSSE *loves* BARB — Mike

I'm Karen Diebold's "Sunshine!"

BERT HARRIS loves LYNN ALTMAN

RUBBER STAMPS or SOUL?" Fight creeping creepism! Fight Monkee-ism! Beatles FOREVER!

Anni Rae: The Wild Ones Rule! Right? Love Lee Rae.

BEATLE PEOPLE STEP ON SNAILS
MONKEE PEOPLE ARE JUST ALIVE!

Sis says "HI MARK"

Why walk? Take the RAPID TRANSIT. Love to BRUCE.. Kam

George Harrison is gorgeously groovy!

Eddie Reid, I love you. You're outasite! Sally Dennis

I love you Ed Ledda by Patti Steele

J.H. LOVES B.S! J.H.

Childhood's Eve luvs December's Children

MUSIC MACHINE!

"THE NORDICS ARE HERE!"

Pre-fab or fab? choose now! Fight Monkee-ism! Beatles Forever!

BILL — You broke my heart. Please come back. Love, Jan.

HARRISON — the mystic Beatle, mutable water, infant ancient, send another song when you can, a glimpse of where you've been, a guide throughout beyond within Hi...Bi...

John Lennon — My Soul and Inspiration — I Love You — Cindi

THE MOST ARE INDUBIDIBLY THE MOST!!

NAZZ — Please stay in Phoenix. We need you!

I love you Tommy Spencer

"Jim Lowe, the flower's power is love... Your Flower Child

THE BEAU GENTRY are *HAPPENING!!!!!!*

JWONG!!

Lennon luvvers luv a lot of man!!

SPLHCB is outasite!!

I love Ross' blue Camaro and his brother.

HARTLEY STEVENS... Your slicks are really tuff. Love, Lincoln

GROOVINESS IS:
George Harrison

MARK LINDSAY — I'll *always* love you truly!! Love, Barb Battaglia.

Pat, HI!!!! Write Soon. Love, Lori

Flowers shall bloom and love shall reign on the shores of Legg Lake, Whittier Narrows Recreation Area July 30. — Hollyhock

STYLE IS:
George Harrison

Pat is *happiness*. Kathy is *luv*.

HANDSOMENESS IS:
George Harrison

Pat + Kathy is
love and happiness forever.

Pat is groovy!

"CLEANING POWER!"

Brent — *Forever yours...*

Frodo *LIVES*

Gripweed has clean feet!!!

Genghis Khan lives again in OHN LENNON.

Monkees ROT!

ROBBS: We attack your bods!! Janny and Sandee

WARNING: *THE MAN FROM GLAD IS A TYRANT.*
Neil, Beatnik

KDWB'S JIMMY REED is the greatest ever! Can ya dig him baby — cuz we can! Pete, Mike, Davy, Micky

To Bill Campbell in England. *ALL MY LOVE, Ann Rogers*

ATTENTION!
FRANK RIGJULIO
(off Bandstand) meet me at the American Airlines Terminal in L.A., August 12 — Noelle

WHERE's THE BROTHERHOOD?

WLOF, CHANNEL 95 S CENTRAL FLORIDA'S NO. 1 STATION.

BIRTHDAYS

RINGO, YOU ANGEL, Happy Birthday, July 7th. Sylvia * Laura

JACKIE — HAPPY BIRTHDAY — BONNIE —

HAPPY BELATED BIRTHDAY Paul McCartney!! — Love, Rainy

BEAT is no longer accepting anything but PERSONAL MESSAGES in the classified section. Only messages (including Happy Birthdays) will be run. We will print names but not addresses or phone numbers.

Rates are cheap! Only 10 cents per word.

And remember, BEAT has a new address:

**Classified
BEAT Publications
9121 Sunset Blvd.
Los Angeles 90069**

DEADLINE FOR NEXT ISSUE: July 19

KRLA ARCHIVES

RECORDS FREE FROM RC®
You'll Flip at the ZZZIP in RC® Cola

while you swing to your favorite stars! RC and music, perfect partners for the perfect lift

TAKE 1 ALBUM FREE

For everyone you buy... with 6 cork liners or seals from R.C. bottle caps over 100 Capitol LP's available. Order as often as you wish. Nothing to join. Look for this display at your favorite store.

Here's your best way yet to save more on the records you want. In dollars-and-cents terms you get two albums that the Capitol Record Club sells for $3.98 each time you buy one. The savings are even bigger on stereo records! And there are no shipping charges to pay, nothing else to join or buy.

What's more, you choose from top albums by today's biggest stars, including the Beatles, David McCallum, Frank Sinatra, Lou Rawls, Buck Owens, Petula Clark, the Outsiders, Nancy Wilson, Dean Martin, Sonny James, the Beach Boys and many others.

OTHER FINE BRANDS: DIET-RITE®COLA, NEHI®BEVERAGES, PART-T-PAK®BEVERAGES, UPPER 10®
"ROYAL CROWN" AND "RC" REG. U.S. PAT. OFF.; ®1966 ROYAL CROWN COLA CO.

STONES GAIN BROAD SUPPORT

25¢

KRLA *Edition* BEAT

AUGUST 12, 1967

RAIDER INJURED ON STAGE

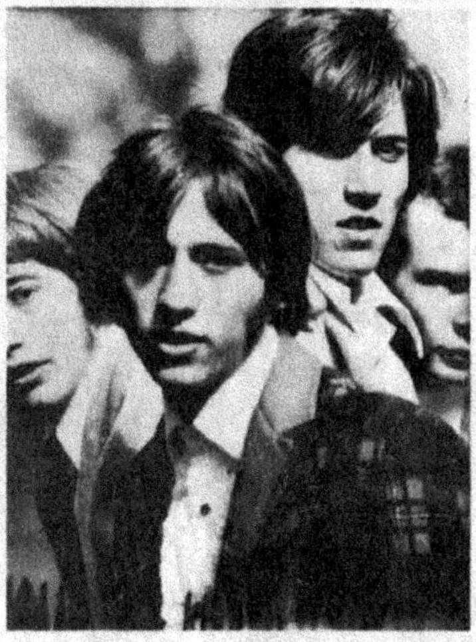

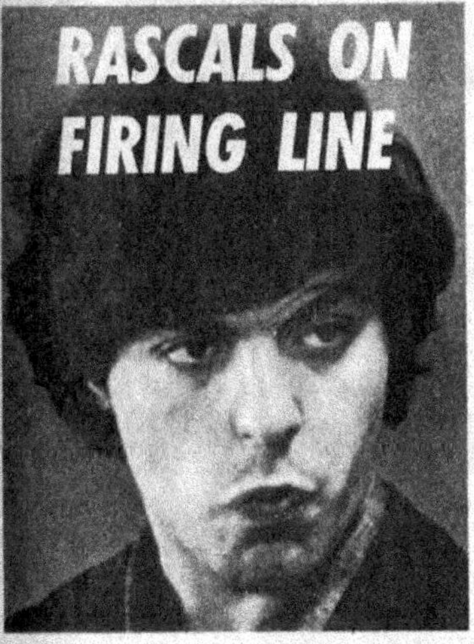

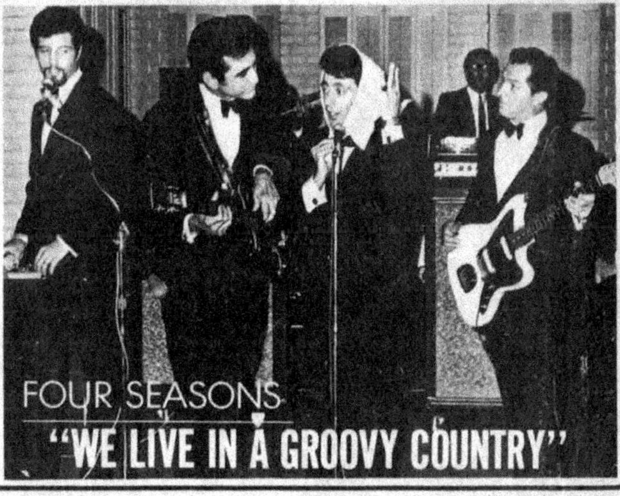

BAEZ TO AID DRAFT DODGERS

monkees plot surprise change

mystery cleared up?

bee gees or beatles?

BEAT Photo: Robert Custer

RASCALS ON FIRING LINE

HERMAN MOVIE HALTED

FOUR SEASONS
"WE LIVE IN A GROOVY COUNTRY"

BEAT Photos: Judy Eldridge

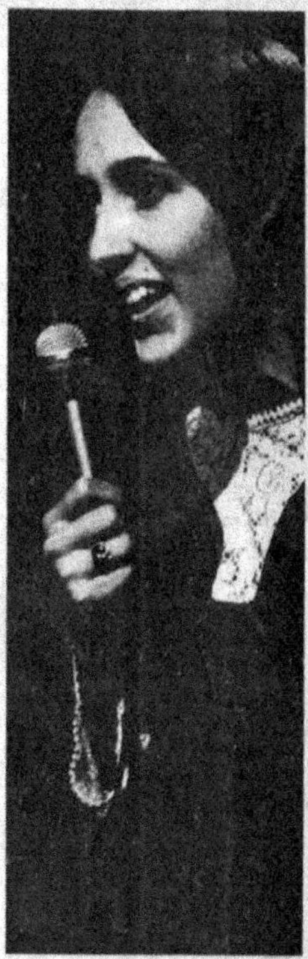

KRLA BEAT

Volume 3, Number 11 — August 12, 1967

PROCOL HARUM CHANGES COLORS
DRUMMER & GUITARIST LEAVE GROUP

LONDON — Procol Harum who have sold over two and a half million copies of their first recording "Whiter Shade of Pale," have had a change of personnel. Guitarist Ray Boyer and drummer Bobby Harrison have left the group and have been replaced by Robin Trowler and Barry Wilson.

Move manager Tony Secunda has also been appointed co-manager. The change follows a disagreement between co-manager Keith Reid, who formed Procol Harum with Gary Brooker, and Jonothan Weston, former Harum manager.

A spokesman for the group said, "The split was on amicable terms. Tony Secunda has been appointed co-manager with Keith Reid. The group will be resuming work this week on recording sessions for a new single and their first L.P."

Baez Joins New Protest

SAN FRANCISCO — Folk singer Joan Baez, a long time advocate of non-violence has just joined a new 70 member committee aimed at encouraging young men to refuse induction into the military.

The Committee which includes four clergymen, an attorney, university professors and Quakers, held a press conference where they stated their intention to "explicitly encourage, aid and abet this civil disobedience on the draft law."

The Committee further stated their position by declaring "the fundamental immorality and increasing brutality of our nations course in Viet Nam compels us to commit our lives to changing that course." The Committee added, "No man's conscience belongs to the state."

Fine & Imprisonment

This public advocation of refusing the draft puts Miss Baez and other members of the Committee in definace of the law. For this defiance there is a penalty of imprisonment up to five years and/or a fine of up to $10,000 for a person who "knowingly counsels, aids or abets another to refuse draft service."

Joan Baez is no stranger to the protest movement or to the threats of courts and fines. Each year Miss Baez has steadfastly refused to pay that portion of her income tax which would go to support the military establishment (about 70% of her income tax). She also has filed a suit against cartoonist Al Capp for what she calls "defamation of character." The charge revolves around one of Capp's cartoon characters called Joanie Phoney. Miss Baez also has run into trouble with the courts with her school for non-violence which is located at her home in Monterey. She has received numerous complaints from her neighbors in the Big Sur Area.

Jail Sentences

When asked at the Committee's press conference what the attitude of the Committee would be to jail sentences, the spokesman, Robert H. Weir, a Palo Alto attorney replied, "no one wants to go to jail. If it means that to get the cooperation of other Americans, you have to run the risk of a $10,000 fine or five years in jail, then you regard this to be the price."

Weir said he would encourage draft resistance but would not advocate "devious" means.

Right To Refuse

"One of man's rights is to refuse to obey the law and accept the penalty," he said. "I would probably so advise young men. But you do not have the right to be fraudulent."

The Committee which is based in San Francisco also includes the Executive Secretary of the American Friends Service Committee, a professor on leave from Stanford University and numerous clergymen.

JOAN BAEZ, noted for protesting, is now set to help draft dodgers.

EDITOR'S NOTE

Due to the fact that our entire staff is taking vacations during the summer, for the next few issues The BEAT has been cut back to 16 pages instead of our usual 24. Most publications merely skip printing for a month to allow their staff to take vacations but we decided that this would not be fair to you, our readers. Therefore, we hope you will understand and bear with us for the next several issues. —The Editor

'Windy' Joins Select Crowd

The Association are currently sitting under the sun in Hawaii enjoying themselves, and they have a lot to be content about. Their single, "Windy," has passed the million mark in sales and is still rising, making them the only group aside from the Beatles and the Monkees to have had two million sellers this year. The Association's first big one was "Cherish."

Raider Hurts Foot & Knee

Mark Lindsay looked as if he had been through the wars when he was finished with the latest Raider tour. At one stop along the way, the lead singer for Paul Revere climbed down from a bus only to be mobbed by fans who had broken through police barriers. Mark tried to sidestep the onrushing crowd, but it wasn't worth it. He twisted his knee in the process, and chipped a bone in his foot when he fell.

Mark's troubles weren't over, however. At a concert later in Memphis, he kneeled down accidentally on a used flash bulb which had been thrown up on the stage by a fan. Mark later said he thought he had felt something but didn't realize until after the concert that he had performed most of the show with a profusely bleeding eight inch gash in his knee.

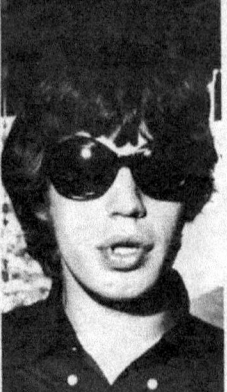

JAGGER: "Not much difference."

STONES WIN SUPPORT FROM ESTABLISHMENT

LONDON — The London Daily Mail has taken up the cause of the Rolling Stones. Without advocating either the Stones' music or their present actions, the Mail has condemned the judicial courts for the "savagery of the sentences passed upon them."

Other noted Fleet Street newspapers such as The Times and the New Stateman spoke of what they called "scapegoatism."

The two Stones spent several days in jail before being released on bail, set at $19,600 each, pending appeal. Jagger seemingly unperturbed at the sentence told newsmen, "there's not much difference between a cell and a hotel room in Minnesota."

The Who have released a single containing two Mick Jagger-Keith Richard compositions in honor of the two convicted Rolling Stones.

At a hastily-called meeting after the Stones' convictions, Who members decided to record "Under My Thumb" and "The Last Time," the proceeds of which would go toward assisting legal costs for Jagger and Richard.

A statement from the group said "There was no time to consider production or arrangements, and what has emerged is a straightforward and very rough cover version of the two songs."

NEXT ISSUE— **A Hippie History**
inside word on a world-wide movement

KRLA ARCHIVES

KRLA ARCHIVES

AROUND the WORLD

Beat Publications, Inc.

Executive Editor .... Cecil I. Tuck
Publisher .... Gayle Tuck
Editor .... Louise Criscione
Assistant Editor .... Greg Kieselmann

Staff Writers
Jacoba Atlas   Bobby Farrow
Ron Kaslow   Shirley Poston
Rochelle Reed

Contributing Writers
Tony Barrow   Sue Barry
Lawrence Charles   Eden
Bob Levinson   Jamie McCluskey, III

Photographers
Ed Caraeff   Dwight Carter
Howard L. Bingham   Jerry Hoos

Advertising
Dick Jacobson   Dick Stricklin
Judy Felice
Business Manager .... Nancy Areno
Subscriptions

Distribution
Miller Freeman Publications

500 Howard Street, San Francisco, Calif. The BEAT is published bi-weekly by BEAT Publications, Inc. editorial and advertising offices at 9125 Sunset Blvd., Los Angeles, California 90069. U.S. bureaus in Hollywood, San Francisco, New York, Chicago and Nashville; overseas correspondents in London, Liverpool and Manchester, England. Sole price 25 cents. Subscription price: U.S. and possessions, $5 per year; Canada and foreign rates, $9 per year. Second class postage paid at Los Angeles, California.

Hermit Flick Has To Wait

Due to their current tour in the United States, Herman's Hermits were unable to complete work on their movie, "Mrs. Brown You've Got A Lovely Daughter." Final sequences of the movie will be filmed when the group returns from the concert tour.

MGM Inks Ryan Bros.

Popular British entertainers Paul and Barry Ryan have been signed by MGM to do a minimum of three starring roles within the next three years. The Ryan brothers, whose "Claire" is high on the British pop charts, will have to postpone their American tour to begin production on their first film, "Sentenced to Sing," in which the Ryans portray two juvenile delinquents.

AIRPLANE FOR TV SPECIAL

The Jefferson Airplane have been signed to headline a television special over the Canadian Broadcasting Company station. A taping will be made in Toronto this year for the special, which will be sponsored by the O'Keefe Centre.

THE AMERICAN BREED LOSES INSTRUMENTS

NEW YORK – No doubt the American Breed literally stepped out of their minds when they had their instruments stolen as soon as they arrived for their first New York appearance.

The theft occurred right in Grand Central Station where the quartet came in from Midwestern bookings to play the Palisades Amusement Park here. It was particularly ironic because the American Breed recently had to purchase a bus to enable them to meet the travel demands created by the large number of dates stemming from their hit record, "Step Out Of Your Mind," but made this New York trip by train.

Bond Nabs Mr. Bond

Sean Connery was issued a summons for speeding which was signed by, would you believe, James Bond.

However, there is somewhat of a difference between Fleming's Bond, and the Bond who nailed "Bond." The London copy is only number 21, and his friends, instead of calling him James as in the noted spy thrillers, is simply known as Jim.

FLOWER CHILDREN

GENTLY BRINGING SONGS OF LOVE AND HAPPINESS

NOW IS THE TIME FOR HEARTS & FLOWERS

The Stone Poneys Poster

OF LOVE
SONGS ☮ AND
SINGING   PEACE
SOFTLY   ENDING
EVER   NEVER
HAPPY

Hearts and Flowers Poster

The Stone Poneys Evergreen Vol. 2

Ahh, Yes! Send a representative of the U.S. Government* to my home with a 20x30 4-color beautiful poster thingy of:
1. ☐ Hearts and Flowers (yes!)
2. ☐ The Stone Ponies (yes!)
(check one)

ORDER ONE
SEND NO MONEY
IT'S FREE!

NAME
ADDRESS
CITY   STATE   ZIP
BLOOD TYPE
SUN SIGN

Fill out, cut out, chant an incantation, and send to:
(2) BEAT
*Postal division, of course

BEAUTIFUL POSTER THINGYS
CAPITOL RECORDS DIST. CORP.
1750 NO. VINE ST.
HOLLYWOOD, CALIF. 90028

ORDER NOW – LIMITED AMOUNT AVAILABLE

HEARTS AND FLOWERS

KRLA ARCHIVES

KRLA ARCHIVES

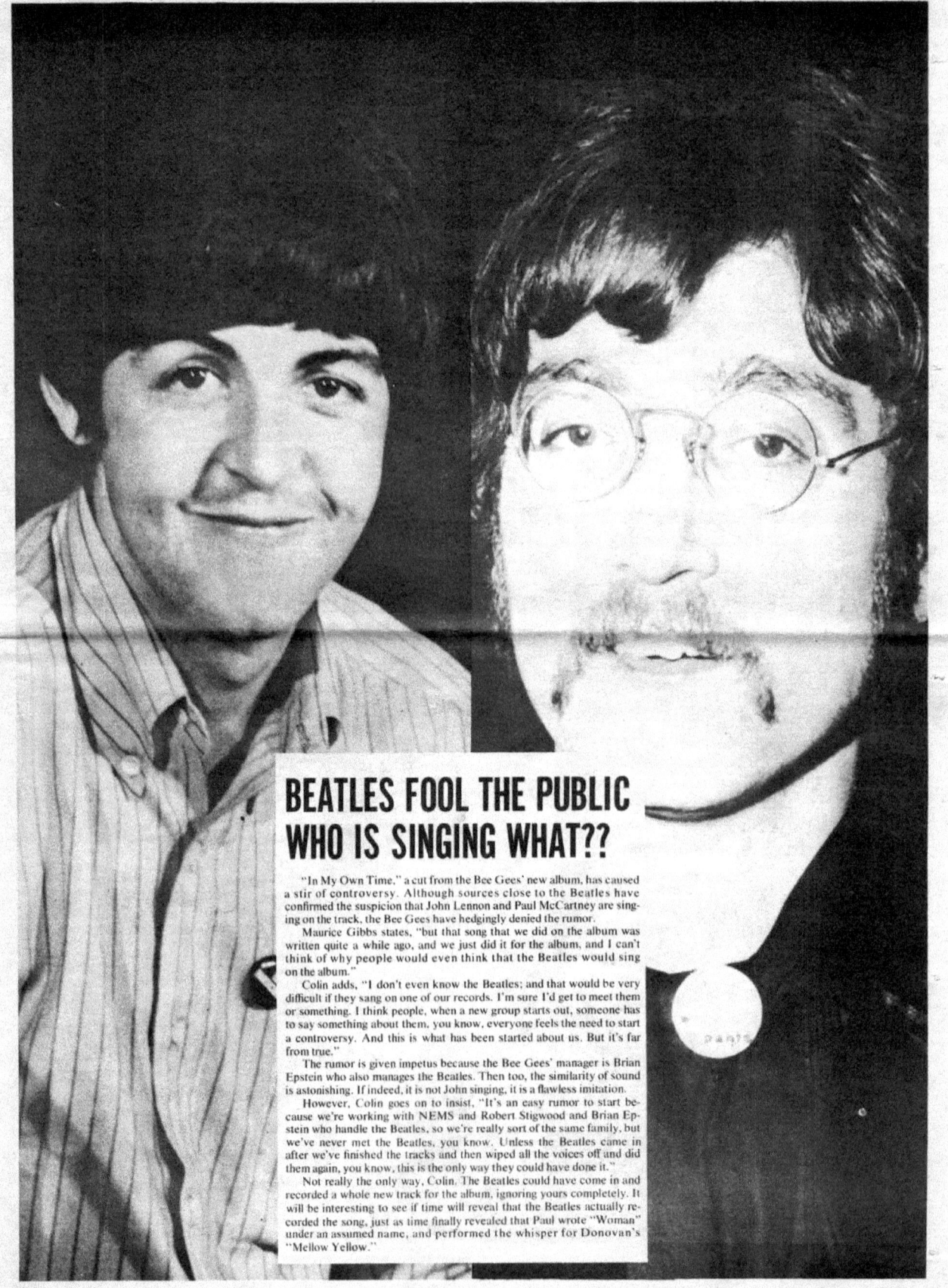

BEATLES FOOL THE PUBLIC WHO IS SINGING WHAT??

"In My Own Time," a cut from the Bee Gees' new album, has caused a stir of controversy. Although sources close to the Beatles have confirmed the suspicion that John Lennon and Paul McCartney are singing on the track, the Bee Gees have hedgingly denied the rumor.

Maurice Gibbs states, "but that song that we did on the album was written quite a while ago, and we just did it for the album, and I can't think of why people would even think that the Beatles would sing on the album."

Colin adds, "I don't even know the Beatles; and that would be very difficult if they sang on one of our records. I'm sure I'd get to meet them or something. I think people, when a new group starts out, someone has to say something about them, you know, everyone feels the need to start a controversy. And this is what has been started about us. But it's far from true."

The rumor is given impetus because the Bee Gees' manager is Brian Epstein who also manages the Beatles. Then too, the similarity of sound is astonishing. If indeed, it is not John singing, it is a flawless imitation.

However, Colin goes on to insist, "It's an easy rumor to start because we're working with NEMS and Robert Stigwood and Brian Epstein who handle the Beatles, so we're really sort of the same family, but we've never met the Beatles, you know. Unless the Beatles came in after we've finished the tracks and then wiped all the voices off and did them again, you know, this is the only way they could have done it."

Not really the only way, Colin. The Beatles could have come in and recorded a whole new track for the album, ignoring yours completely. It will be interesting to see if time will reveal that the Beatles actually recorded the song, just as time finally revealed that Paul wrote "Woman" under an assumed name, and performed the whisper for Donovan's "Mellow Yellow."

KRLA ARCHIVES

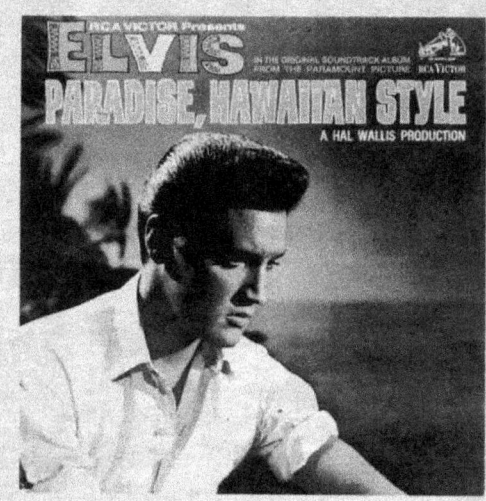

Three Great Soundtracks By Elvis!

Available At...

KRLA ARCHIVES

ON THE BEAT BY LOUISE CRISCIONE

The rumor out of the **Monkee** camp this week is that the group will do some straight dramatic acting on their television series next season. Of course, the zany humor and camera "tricks" will still constitute the majority of next season's episodes but a little bit of drama will also be sandwiched in there somewhere.

It took the **Procol Harum** only eight weeks to top the British charts with "A Whiter Shade Of Pale" — but it's taken them less than that to have two of their members leave. Guitarist Ray Boyer and drummer Bobby Harrison have left "on amicable terms." They have been replaced by Robin Trower, lead guitar and Barry Wilson, drummer.

Association Privilege

A very nice compliment was paid the **Association** by their record producer, Bones Howe: "I consider it a privilege to be asked to work with artists of this calibre who had already proven themselves to be among the nation's best before I joined them." Bones has previously engineered on sessions for Johnny Rivers, the Mamas and Papas, Gary Lewis and the Fifth Dimension.

The **Harpers Bizarre** are certainly moving up in the world. They were the group chosen to provide the entertainment for **Frank and Mia Sinatra's** first wedding anniversary party, which was held in a private dining room of Chasen's restaurant.

Of course, the guest list for the party read like "Who's Who" with such people as Henry Fonda, Lawrence Harvey, Gene Kelly, Natalie Wood and Yul Brenner in attendance. The Harpers were enthusiastically received by the guests and, in fact, stayed to perform three sets. It was sort of a double triumph for the Harpers since their latest single, "Anything Goes," was released the same day.

Righteous Two Buy Movie

The two talented **Righteous Brothers**, Bobby and Bill, have acquired a second motion picture property, "Terrace Of Weeds." Bill and Bob have already purchased "Have You Met My Landlady?"

Under the two-picture deal the Brothers have with MGM, the studio has the first refusal rights on both films. If all goes as Bobby and Bill plan it, they will produce as well as star in both movies.

The **Four Seasons**, who continually have at least one thousand different things going for them, now have one thousand and one. They've just been signed to sing a western ballad in "No God In Saguaro."

Would you believe it? **The Music Machine** is changing their image — slightly. They've cut their hair and Sean Bonnivwell has his hair so short now that he'd be accepted by any school principal in the country! The rest of the members of the group, while sporting much shorter hair than before, would probably still be suspended for "longish" hair.

James Brown has announced to the press that he plans to retire after his European tour in September. His doctor has okayed two shows a week for the master of soul but James says he couldn't just quit part of the business. "I'd have to quit completely."

The **Turtles**, who change group members faster than anyone else alive, have done it again. This time Jim Tucker has gone off "to pursue his own interests." The Turtles have decided not to replace Jim but will instead go with five members rather than six. Jim will not be going solo nor joining another group — says he wants to get out of the business altogether.

Just found out some new dates for you **Young Rascals** fans. They'll be in Hawaii until August 12, then they'll journey to Alaska on August 14, San Francisco on August 18 and 19 at the Fillmore Auditorium, Los Angeles on August 20 and to Europe for two weeks in October.

British singer, **Matt Monro**, will entertain U.S. armed forces personnel stationed in Hawaii from September 13-17. This marks the seventh consecutive year Matt has done such engagements in Hawaii.

MICKY DOLENZ

JIM TUCKER

The Rascals—'Let's Face It, Some Music Is Obnoxious'

By Greg Kiselmann

Felix Cavaliere was puffing casually on his long-stemmed English pipe looking very much like the thoughtful executive — except you'd never catch him in a Brooks Brothers suit.

"The New York scene just isn't different enough," he said in quick response to a reporter's question. "The Doors came out there and it was a good thing. It gave the people a taste of what they'd only heard about in dirty magazines."

Copy What's In

Felix glanced over to his sidekick Eddie Brigati, who started talking as if on cue. "Yeah, most of the groups there just copy whatever is in, and they overplay it. People go on and on and on until it's played out. The kids in New York are really overexposed to pop music."

The two Young Rascals then started joking with the other two members of the group, Gene Cornish and Dino Danelli, and pretty soon the reporters joined in the laughter. The scene was the Century Plaza in Los Angeles, where just two days earlier, President Johnson had stayed and witnessed a massive peace demonstration.

"We saw it all from our window," Dino said. "It really caused an inconvenience getting in and out. We were held up for an hour one night before we could leave for a night club engagement."

"I hope we don't have to see anything like that again," Eddie put in.

The boys then started talking about something they're pretty familiar with — the American music scene.

"Folk-rock, if done well . . . you can appreciate it," Eddie said. "You have to really appreciate music for what's put in it and what the people do for it. Some music is obnoxious, let's face it, but it really depends on how it's done and not what type of music it is. The Beatles linked so many types of music, there's no one bag. They put all music together and created a New Force. It's definitely a progression."

"I think the flower explosion is great," Felix said. "It shows people are still living. When we came out to the West Coast in 1966, I had a feeling big things were going to happen . . . and they did. It's great, because there are so many very nice people involved in it."

Then Eddie caught the ball again. "Through music we're really learning more about people outside of where we live — the English, the French. Younger people these days are opening their scope and appreciating more things. There's a better connection between people."

All the guys admitted they liked the Beatles more than any other group. "The Beatles have really influenced us as far as how to put an organization together," Felix said. "Musically, I guess we've been influenced by Phil Spector and Ray Charles, although we've been influenced by a little bit of everything."

The Rascals said they appealed to people of all ages and really didn't have any preference as far as audiences, "As long as they don't charge or walk out," Eddie said. "Sometimes when the kids start charging, you feel like you're on a football field. All you can do is get up and run away. If they know it's the last song, and you don't have much protection, they might carry your organ away or something. You know, the kids want souvenirs — like hair," he said shuddering as if he were remembering a day when he was almost scalped.

Broken Seat

Dino said his most embarrasing moment on stage came one night when his seat broke beneath him. "I didn't know what to do," he said. "Finally, a friend of mine came from in back and sat on his hands and knees. I sat on his back for the rest of the performance."

But Eddie was the one who had experienced what has to be the worst nightmare for any male entertainer. "I went through a show in front of an audience of almost 6,000 people with my zipper open," he remembered. "I was going through all kinds of motions on stage, and the people were making so much noise, I thought they were eating it up. Then people started cackling, and about half way through the show I caught on. Something like that could really shatter you, but I figured it was just another day. I made a speech about it saying I didn't think it was very funny, but this one girl in front never stopped laughing."

The Future?

How about plans for the future?

"We hope to make a movie," Felix said. "We've had offers to do scores for movies, but we want to make our own movie, if possible."

"We'll never be in one bag," added Eddie. "We want to be very versatile. We hope to do whatever is current, but do it with a lot of our own."

Felix said the Rascals planned to go to the Pop Festival next year. They hadn't gone this year, he said, because "There's a clique among music people . . . but there's other things happening."

And how about their chances of getting the call from Uncle Sam?

"Whenever there's a draft call," Felix said, "we bolt the door. Actually, they don't want us, and we don't want them. I won't explain the situation, but we're going to do something as citizens for our country — like entertain troops."

With that, The Rascals explained they had a rehearsal to go to, and they silently walked out of the room, Felix still puffing gently on his pipe.

CORNERED AT AIRPORT, Rascals Eddie and Dino talk with their fans.

KRLA ARCHIVES

The Love of Peaches & Herb Is Happening.

"FOR YOUR LOVE" is the hit single those Date Sweethearts are making it with. And there's lots more of their love in an album.

date

KRLA ARCHIVES

Cassius Clay Says Boxing Is Becoming A Mere Toy

An exclusive interview with Muhammad Ali by Jim Steck, Sports Director of Los Angeles radio station KRLA.

"This is belittlin' to the American public," stormed former heavyweight champion Cassius Clay, who prefers to be known as Muhammad Ali. It was apparent he is not too happy about the situation himself.

"This is makin' boxing nothin' but a toy! All these fellas runnin' 'round callin' themselves championship contenders an' four of the major ones I have already annihilated. Sonny Liston can whup all of 'em but me an' they didn't even let him in the tournament," Clay fumes.

Regardless of one's personal feeling toward Clay, he makes a very good point. Will the boxing public stand still for a champion everybody knows couldn't carry Clay's gloves?

"How can people sit down to a title fight like that," he asks? "You go lookin' to see the two bes' in the world. How can people recognize these boys as the bes' in the world when they know I can beat 'em and Liston can beat 'em?

"This is belittlin' the sport and makin' it a plaything. Madison Square Garden is makin' them a champion. The WBA is makin' them a champion. Germany is makin' them a champion and England is makin' them a champion."

With the elimination tournament now taking shape and all signs pointing to a world-wide rash of claimants to the heavyweight championship, does Muhammed Ali believe he'll ever be permitted to box professionally in this country again?

"Well," he pouts, "If the Supreme Court, and I'm sure it will, recognizes me as a sincere Muslim, as I am ... automatically I be innocent. And if that happens I'll be back in the ring again."

What if the high tribunal doesn't buy Clay's story and he has to break rocks for a few years?

"I'm just 25 years old, and if I have to spend three or four years in prison I wouldn't be but 28 or 29 when I got out ... an' I'd still whup 'em all! Beat 'em like I was their daddy!"

Now Clay began to sound more like a fighter than a man facing prison.

"The heavyweight champion is the one who done traveled the globe," he exclaimed. "He's the one who beat everybody, regardless of his religion, his race, his color; southpaws, righthanders, tall ones, short ones, fat ones, skinny ones, ugly ones and pretty ones ... the heavyweight champion is the one who can whup every man on earth. An' I can whup every man on earth! An' you never can take it away from me until you whup me!"

Clay's contention here is hard to argue with. To hear Muhammad Ali tell it, Joe Frasier would rather go to Viet Nam with a bee bee gun than get in the ring with the dethroned champ. On the subject of Viet Nam, why doesn't Clay make it easy on himself, accept induction, snag a special services assignment and roll with the punches?

"My reason for refusing induction into the armed forces is on religious grounds," he answers soberly. "I got nothin' against the government, nothin' against the boys in Viet Nam, I'm sorry. Tears come into my eyes to think about the people who are dyin' and bein' killed over there. I got nothin' against the Constitution of the United States. I'm jus' standin' up for what my religion teaches me. That's all."

Would Clay accept induction if this country was attacked?

"Yes, Sir," he answers, practically jumping out of his chair. "I'd fight right now. If someone attacked America you wouldn't have to draft me ...I'd be the first one to grab a rifle."

If Clay is sincere, and I choose to believe he is by virtue of what he stands to lose, his stand on religious grounds could be very costly indeed. Not only to one Muhammad Ali, former heavyweight champion, draft-dodger and convict. The great cost is to boxing and the public. We stand to see three or four years of cream-puff champions, protected from a man who could eat 'em alive by a row of cold, steel bars. There isn't a man alive who can "whup" Cassius Clay ... except himself.

KRLA DISC JOCKEY Charlie O'Donnell and BEAT staffer Heidi Beebe.

NEWSMAN LEW IRWIN accepts his special award for Best Documentary from Associated Press broadcast executive Robert Eunson. Irwin won the award for his series, "The Language of Rock."

FRED PAUL Is Alive

. . . and in Hollywood

23 x 30 MONKEE POSTER
IMPRINTED WITH YOUR OWN NAME

YOUR NAME (Print)_____

1. $ 2.98
2.   5.75
4. 10.00

TED HILL & CO.
707 Paige Lane
Thousand Oaks, Calif. 91360

ICE HOUSE GLENDALE

now thru July 30
Irish Rovers
&
Jonathan Moore

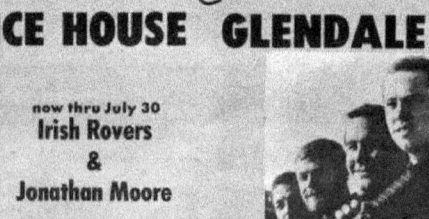

August 1 - 13

Hearts & Flowers
with their hit
"Rock 'n Roll Gypsies"
&
Hypnotist George Sharp

ICE HOUSE PASADENA
24 No. Mentor — Reservations: 681-9942

August 1-13

Maffit & Davies
as seen on the Glenn Yarborough Tour
— and —
Comedian Ken Greenwald
as seen on the Steve Allen Show
— and —
Singer Jean Durand

KRLA ARCHIVES

U.K. POP NEWS ROUND-UP
Hendrix Joins Monkees

By Tony Barrow

Addition of the JIMI HENDRIX EXPERIENCE to THE MONKEES' U.S. summer concert tour a direct result of the tremendous impact Hendrix made in Monterey... JOHN LENNON shaved off his moustache the day before THE BEATLES appeared on the global TV show "Our World"... Within 24 hours of THE MONKEES' arrival in London MICKY DOLENZ made a totally unscheduled personal appearance on BBC Television's "Top Of The Pops" program, chatted with the show's zany deejay JIMMY SAVILE. Responsible for persuading him to be there was "Top Of The Pops" disc girl SAMANTHA JUSTE... THE WHO issued a High Court libel writ against top deejay SIMON DEE. Case involves a Dee feature carried by *Melody Maker*... BBC answer to England's pop pirate radio stations will go on the air September 30 with a "robust music" policy which will mix records with 'live' studio performances by groups, orchestras and solo vocalists. Sounds like a dismal substitute for the lively RADIO LONDON and RADIO CAROLINE!

DC5 Soundtrack

"Hi Hi Hazel," formerly recorded by London's GENO WASHINGTON BAND, is July U.K. single for THE TROGGS... DAVE CLARK completed soundtrack recording sessions for his upcoming movie... "Evolution" album proves HOLLIES striving hard to close gap between themselves and BEATLES where recording progression and sheer ingenuity are concerned... SCOTT McKENZIE for U.K. soon if "San Francisco" is a hit which means he's for U.K. soon... BARRY (BEE GEE) GIBB once thought of calling the group The Petal World... Surprise chart-riser in U.K. this month: "Take Me In Your Arms And Love Me" by GLADYS KNIGHT AND THE PIPS... When PETULA CLARK comes home to London later this year to appear in her own BBC television series possibility she'll star in one-girl two-hour concert at one of our capital's largest venues... Three offers for movie appearances plus the chance of starring in a Broadway musical followed recent visit of LULU to America... PROCOL HARUM cancelled long string of dates to concentrate on recording their first album for swift release in America as well as U.K.

Turtles' Concert

End-of-the-year U.K. concert tour being planned for THE TURTLES following their overdue chart success on our side of the Atlantic... "Our Be-Ins and Love-Ins have really gotten to be something rather ordinary" writes my personal Strip Chick spy "No more nitty-gritty Bohemian beatnik picnics. All commercialised with hot dog stands, bumper stickers and little old men selling false moustaches, plastic freaky buttons, hippy bubblegum and aluminum Indian sticks." Sounds like a drag... For U.K. concert tour in October STEVIE WINWOOD'S new group TRAFFIC planning all-new stereo sound system which will travel with their show.

RAY DAVIES making solo single and album. He's penned twelve new numbers for next KINKS album and solo record ventures do not indicate fresh intention of quitting the group... ANDY WARHOL and THE VELVET UNDERGROUND expect to spend the first week of August in U.K.... DONOVAN'S July album in U.K. made up from titles issued in America as part of "Sunshine Superman" and "Mellow Yellow" LPs... SEEKERS' songstress JUDITH DURHAM re-recorded her solo single "The Olive Tree" several weeks after original version had been released. Second version had slightly faster tempo and was used to replenish dealer stocks as record stores ran out of their initial supplies. Deejays were requested to "use this new version in preference to the one you already have" in unprecedented announcement from EMI promotion department!

BEAT EXCLUSIVE
Four Seasons

By Jacoba Atlas

LOS ANGELES – The Four Seasons came to the West Coast to perform in the area for the first time and completely conquered all who saw them. In two different concerts, the accomplished group received the phenomenal standing ovations so rarely given a pop performance.

Cornering the group at a beach party, they talked openly and freely about their music, their future, and the changes they've gone through.

The group has been going strong since 1962 and when asked how music has changed, Frankie Valli offered his thoughts, "I think there has been a lot of protest music. The world situation has had a great deal to do with the change in music. I get the feeling that many of these songs derive from people's or writer's personal feelings about situations that are happening.

Personal Feelings

"To some extent I would say that personal feelings affect our music. I think there have been many times when we've been pretty far ahead. For instance, in an album we did about two years ago, Bob (Gaudio) wrote a song which was called "Silence Is Golden" and it is now a big hit by a group from England. In an album we also did a protest against protests, because after a while it did get to be a drag. Everybody seemed to have something that they were protesting about and many of these people I guess never got around to realizing that we live in a pretty groovy country and that what they should really do is try to do a little traveling and see how other people live, then they would appreciate our situation."

Are most of Bob Gaudio's songs a protest or a personal feeling or reaction? "I'd say it's basically a personal experience. Protest is not really our bag. We do them every so often when we feel there's a need for something. But basically, they're just personal experience songs."

Unlike many groups, a 4 Seasons' song is finished when the session starts. Bob does not just come in with an idea. "A song is always finished and usually within reason the arrangement is also finished. We usually know what we're going to get and where we're going, give or take a few things. A lot of times things are changed on a date, but we don't go in and just jam and look for sounds; things are usually pretty well predetermined."

Wonder Who

As if their success under the name 4 Seasons was not enough, the boys have also recorded under the pseudonym, The Wonder Who, but the reasons behind this "falsehood" are unusual. Frankie explains that when they were recording an album with Bob Dylan's "Don't Think Twice," the idea came about. "We were in the studio and just kidding around a little, and everybody flipped over the way we were doing it, so we recorded it that way. It was so different from anything that we had ever done, we said why not just for fun, put it out under a different name. And fun seemed to pay off quite a bit."

Frankie is in the unique position of having two hit records on the top ten at one time. His own hit,

FOUR SEASONS — THEY HAVEN'T missed with a record yet!

BEAT Photo: Jody Eldridge

KRLA ARCHIVES

Speaking Of Success

SOMETIMES EVEN YOUR best friends won't tell you, Frankie, but they do make tell-take faces!

FRANKIE: "We live in a pretty groovy country."

which has already been Number One in the nation, "Can't Take My Eyes Off You" and the group's hit, "C'mon Marianne." Why did Frankie feel the need to venture out on his own, while still remaining with the group? "Well, I'd say many people had typed this group for doing a certain kind of thing. However, the biggest reaction we had gotten when we worked college dates or nightclubs, where we do a variety of music, was some of the things we were not recording. They were coming off rather well. So, we had decided since we were a corporation, no matter which way we went, as long as we were thinking of expanding, it couldn't hurt any situation, as long as there was separation between what I did and what the group was doing. This was, I'd say, the basic reason, and with everybody sharing in the profits, we're just one happy family."

College Dates

The 4 Seasons enjoy wide range popularity, never catering to one segment of the population in their music, but could this idea hold over when performing? Tommy deVido stated, "well, actually speaking for the group, as long as their attentive, and usually in colleges they're attentive. They're not drinking, and they're not ordering food and things like that, and you aren't hearing glasses tinkling all over the place, and waiters dropping trays. We kind of like colleges a little better than night clubs."

But Frankie added, "I'd like to say we throw no stones at night clubs because basically our very early experience came from night clubs. It was sort of a show place to give us a chance to do the kind of music that we really felt. So I can't knock night clubs.

"I really see our future in a combination of night clubs and concerts because the young college kid of today will be the night club goer of tomorrow. So there is definitely a place for us in night clubs. I feel the thing that you must constantly re-capture is the teenybopper audience, because that is always brand new, so you have to stay on top of your record situation in order to have everything in hand."

Today's Composers

"I'll tell you, in my opinion, Lennon and McCartney are of our age what Cole Porter used to be 20 years ago," said Bob. "I really think they are fantastic writers, they write some great things, and I think 10 or 20 years from now, they may be known and as popular as Cole Porter is now. I feel that way for maybe 50% of the music that is happening today. I also think there are going to be many many standards made now that you may not think will be standards, but 20 years from now they will be. There has to be new standards made, because the standards of 20 or 30 years ago can't be going on for that long."

The Hippie and the new psychedelic sound in music has affected everyone including the 4 Seasons, but Frankie offered some rather outspoken remarks as to the Hippie Generation and the ability of many of today's groups. "'Hippie' is a very hard word. Some people would like to think they were hippies. They only go along with everybody else.

"Some of the psychedelic music is fantastic. Some of it I just don't understand, and many of these records just don't happen, so you break it down. If I can't understand it how can the public understand it? Unless they're just following and doing what everyone else is doing. But like I say, The Airplane, the Association and many others are fantastic, and the Fifth Dimension. These people have sort of taken this music and brought it to a point of commercialism so that everyone can understand and appreciate what they are doing. I mean if you're doing something that no one understands, what's the sense in it?

"I also believe that many of these performers today are not really capable of performing. I mean if an audience comes out to see you they expect to be entertained and I have gone to several concerts where I have seen groups doing a great job musically, but not communicating with the public. You say, 'well, why, they're doing a great job,' but it's because they seem very disinterested in what they're doing or so completely hung up or involved that they don't care.

Night Clubs

"I can remember, it's only a few short years ago we went out and decided that we should get a night club act. We spent about $10,000 for it and not too long ago we junked it completely. It was a good night club act, but it wasn't us and we decided that the only way to communicate was to be yourself, and never be afraid of being yourself. When we made this change it worked out well.

"I don't say that we've found it to the extent that we've given up searching for new things. I think there's a constant need for changes in the different material that you use and I'd say that we stay on top of it pretty well. We rehearse a lot when we get the opportunity, and I think that's what's really helped us quite a bit."

JOE LONG, TOMMY DeVITO   **BOB GAUDIO,** "the rich one."

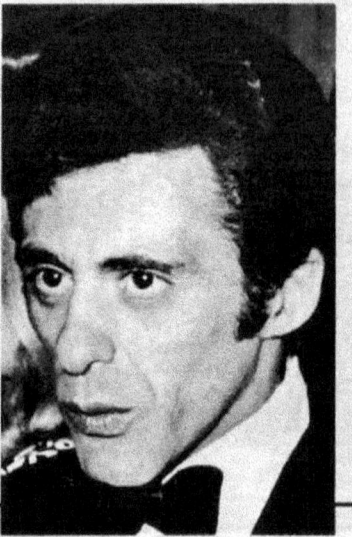

"The thing you must constantly recapture is the teenybopper audience because that is always brand new."

KRLA ARCHIVES

POP MUSIC
Meets The
NASHVILLE SOUND

The Cramer Craze:
Floyd's What's Happening

Available At . . .

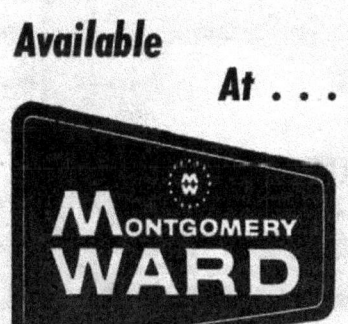

KRLA ARCHIVES

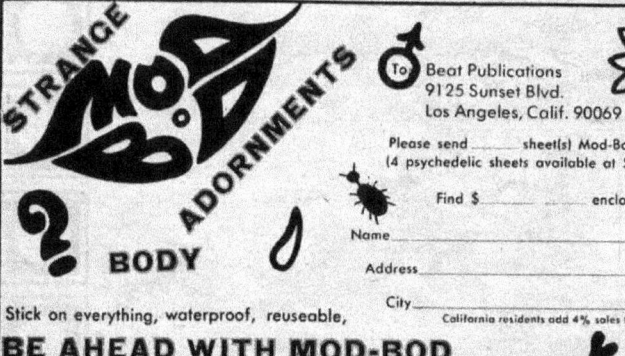

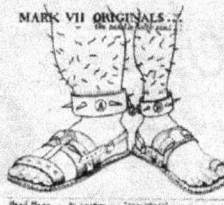

KRLA ARCHIVES

please send me BEAT
26 issues only
$3 per year

Mail to: BEAT Publications
9125 Sunset Blvd.
Los Angeles, California 90069

☐ New Subscription
☐ Renewal (please enclose mailing label from your last BEAT)
I want BEAT for ☐ 1 year at $3.00 or ☐ 2 years at $5.00
I enclose ☐ cash ☐ check ☐ money order
Outside U.S. — $9 per year

• Please print your name and address.

Name_____
Street_____
City_____
State_____ Zip_____

"The Standel Sound"

"The Young Rascals"
Professional musicians throughout the world choose the "Standel Sound," the accepted standard for professional musicians who demand professional performance.
(Dept. B)

Standel
Solid State Music Systems
4918 DOUBLE DRIVE • EL MONTE, CALIF. 91731

A. P.A. Speaker Column Amplifier
B. P.A. Master Control with Reverb
C. Imperial Line Amplifier — Solid State, Dual Channel

CLASSIFIED

FAN CLUBS

THE ROBBS NATIONAL FAN CLUB
Write: P.O. Box 350
Beverly Hills, California 90213

INSTRUCTION

REACH COSMIC AWARENESS without drugs — help save mankind from destruction. Write for free booklet, "Cosmic Awareness Speaks," Organization of Awareness, Box 115E, Olympia, Washington.

SLEEP-LEARNING, self-hypnosis. Details, strange catalog free! Autosuggestion, Box 24-BT, Olympia, Washington.

RUINS — Ed, Curt, Fred, Russ + Mark Rule!! — Mary

No, ONE cannot keep love quiet
LIZ AND HUGH FOREVER!!!
— Gretty-Lou

Flower Girl loves Reeder

POPPY
Strawberry Rock Grooves!!
TULIP

YOUR FRIENDS,
YOUR FRIENDS,
"RUSTIC PATTERNS"
YOUR FRIENDS

I DO BELIEVE IN JIM MAY!

Happy Birthday, Liz — You're the Frosteeist! Luv, DerLingor-Kinder

Beatles *AND* Monkees *RULE*
Danna... Danna Willis... Danna Willis Bradford. WOW!!!!!!!!!

ZALLY POWER
Happy Birthday Mick
SEBBIE, we need ZALLY
NO ZALLY NO

Congratulations to Mike and Joan Kelley — *Luv and Flowers*
— Jill Locas

WEEDS of IDLENESS
hate you!

Cottage Cheese Funeral (wear black)

HERDE IS THE WERDE!!

HAPPY BIRTHDAY TO GRAND-DAD.
Love, Diane

HAPPY BIRTHDAY TO ME! GUESS WHO?

Linda loves Gregor 4 ever, Sissy loves Vinney (she hopes) 4 ever, Lana loves Joey 4 ever, Diane loves Louie 4 ever&ever&*ever*!

Happy Birthday DWIGHT

What became of Linda Makiyama? Linda Makiyama,
I LOVE YOU!

JIM MORRISON... YEA!

Zal... please?

BEATLES ARE LOVE
MONKEES — ESTABLISHMENT

frieda csencitz is here! Hi! Lindy and Freddie from Breinigsville

I PAID $1.00 TO WISH JOHN HODGSON —

A HAPPY BIRTHDAY!

Dave Strazda is BITCHEN — Lani

Let's Stay Weedy

BIGGEST BEATLE PARTY EVER
August 15th — Shea Stadium
12 noon

Flower Power Forever
Mack and his side-kick
WOODY GROOVE
Why, Paul?

The SEEDS are PRIVATE PROPERTY... MINE!!!
— Lynette

Daryl Hooper Grooves

HAPPY BIRTHDAY Dave Burgess from the Liverpool Five Fan Club!

Happy Birthday, CLAUDIA —
Luv Susan

DETROIT: The Rationals, Thyme, Scot Richard Case are slipping through your fingers. Recognize GOOD TALENT.
Good Luck Guys.
Diane Kapanowski.

MONKEE FANS WATCH ZOORAMA!

Happy belated 27th Birthday RINGO!!!! - Lorelle

Monkee fans are illiterate fools.
BEATLES FOREVER!
Joe Lucas

LOVE-IN August 6th Santa Ana Madison Park. God bless you wonderful people

Think GEORGE HARRISON *IS BEAUTIFUL!*

"Happy Birthday, Mindy Stinson, You Devil!!!!" Carole

York, Pennsylvania, EXISTS!

HEY CHICAGO: *"Leave that baby alone"*

BEATLES REIGN FOREVER
Saturday's children... YEAH!!

Nancy, Wise Up! You and Me — *Unbeatable,* C.S.

I love Woody, Sharon

I love you, ELLEN SIEGEL

HNPPY BIRTHDAY - July 17 Dent Franklin and Jerry Smith Marcianne

Joey Robb —
Remember our phone conversation? I hope you enjoyed it as much as I did. I hope I get to meet you someday.
Nancy Carpenter

I luv HARVEY

Joyce — Burgas, Bar, Billiards, and a certain RED car RULES!!

Davy, Have PLEASANT VALLEY SUNDAY'S 4-ever. Paula Taylor

ANNIVERSARY — BEATLES at JFK Stadium. August 16th. True fans will remember. Janet.

"Love" is...................
PAUL McCARTNEY
Hands Off PAUL

Roger is a Sagitarius! Crabs and Fish rule!!

Stamp out Reality Be Happy
Is there life after birth?

Neil Blaze... Hello?

(Larry Stang's method isn't afraid of the dark)

(Larry Stang's method eats lightening)

(Larry Stang's Method loves pickle smiles)

Formality breeds distrust, but the Kallektors from Greenwich Village loves you!

I am the rightful heir to President Polk, yet no one will listen to me — *Tom Cox —*

Rick + Elanina —
Love Forever

"Close your eyes" Ricky + Elania forever

Help keep America Beatlefull!
"CHILDREN (john, robin, joe, jim, joe) ASK"..."CHILDREN ASK is a POWEful song"

Patrick: Like Hippies? Nigel
"Monkees are *outasite* —
— Jackie Trausch"

HAPPY BIRTHDAY! Bob Zinner John York - George Caldwell
Love, Marcy

Mick Jagger — Happy Birthday!!! You'll always be Number One for me. Love and "Flower" forever! Joanie Larsen

David, why the ruin? You've lost me in your restlessness...
CHARLENE *LOVES* **DAVID**

HAPPY BIRTHDAY KARL!!
Love Janice

IF YOUR LOCAL NEWS-DEALER DOES NOT HANDLE THE BEAT — BUG HIM UNTIL HE DOES. HE CAN WRITE TO US FOR INFORMATION, 9125 SUNSET, L.A., CALIF. 90069

BEATLES — Blurps!!!
MONKEES — LOVE!!!!!

WEEDS OF IDLENESS HATE YOU

Happy Birthday to Ringo from Debbie with Luv

THE MONKEES LIVE!
Havershap Spleenbaum will conquer the world!

DON AND THE GOOD-TIMES ARE SO GOOD!!!!

Monkee people are wasting their time and money. Beatle people have a *sound* investment!

Steve outta be SHOT!
— Dave

Happy birthday to somebody groovy
— **HANK PIETRUSZKA** —
Luv from Lin

Beatle — Boobs!

BOLD REBELS ARE HAPPENING!
Beatles — Stick it!!
Monkees — Cricket!!

Free list of groovy posters — seper Co., 5273 Tendilla, Woodland Hills, Calif. 91364

DIANA LYNNE LOVES DARRELL RUSSELL!!

!!Mike Wills!!

Happy Birthday to KYOS' Neil Blaze, a moovy, groovy guy! Sincerely,
Anglia Michaels

Katie Blake is a terrrrible person

THE GROUND FLOOR is vibrating!!!

Happy belated birthday Jerry of the GROUND FLOOR — the girl-next-door

BEAT is no longer accepting anything but PERSONAL MESSAGES in the classified section. Only messages (including Happy Birthdays) will be run. We will print names but not addresses or phone numbers.

Rates are cheap! Only 10 cents per word.
And remember, BEAT has a new address:
Classified
BEAT Publications
9121 Sunset Blvd.
Los Angeles 90069
DEADLINE FOR NEXT ISSUE: Aug. 1

KRLA ARCHIVES

RECORDS FREE FROM RC®
You'll Flip at the ZZZIP in RC® Cola

while you swing to your favorite stars! RC and music, perfect partners for the perfect lift

TAKE 1 ALBUM FREE

For everyone you buy... with 6 cork liners or seals from R.C. bottle caps over 100 Capitol LP's available. Order as often as you wish. Nothing to join. Look for this display at your favorite store.

Here's your best way yet to save more on the records you want. In dollars-and-cents terms you get two albums that the Capitol Record Club sells for $3.98 each time you buy one. The savings are even bigger on stereo records! And there are no shipping charges to pay, nothing else to join or buy.

What's more, you choose from top albums by today's biggest stars, including the Beatles, David McCallum, Frank Sinatra, Lou Rawls, Buck Owens, Petula Clark, the Outsiders, Nancy Wilson, Dean Martin, Sonny James, the Beach Boys and many others.

OTHER FINE BRANDS: DIET-RITE®COLA, NEHI®BEVERAGES, PART-T-PAK®BEVERAGES, UPPER 10®
"ROYAL CROWN" AND "RC" REG. U.S. PAT. OFF., ©1966 ROYAL CROWN COLA CO.

KRLA ARCHIVES

SPECIAL HIPPIE HISTORY ISSUE

KRLA Edition BEAT

August 26, 1967

JON

TOM

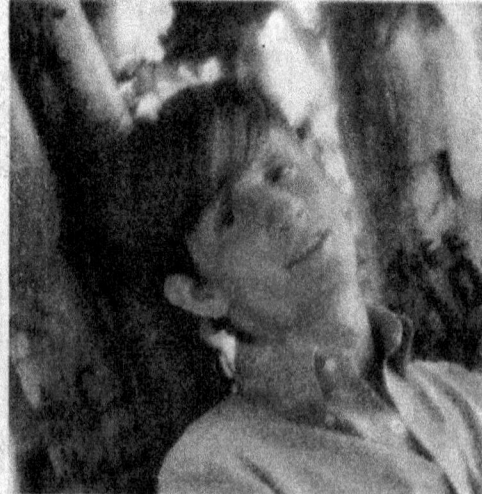

TERRY

young stuff

KRLA BEAT

Volume 3, Number 12   August 26, 1967

Mick Freed; Hero Or Not?

LONDON—Is a popular entertainer responsible only to himself, or does he have a duty to his fans as well? That's the question most being asked now that the Rolling Stones have been freed of their previous drug convictions.

Mick Jagger was quick to lecture reporters after his victorious appeals trial: "In private life my only responsibility is only to myself," he said. "Responsibility is on the gentlemen of the press who publish details of a person's private life."

Opinions Differ

His opinion differed greatly from that of Lord Chief Justice Parker, who presided at the appeals trial. The judge told Jagger, "Whether you like it or not you carry great responsibility because you are an idol to a large number of people."

A number of Britain's establishment newspapers have stated that Jagger, because his actions presumably influence millions of kids, was punished severely in order to set an example. Now that he has been freed, however, the papers are beginning to ask whether smoking marijuana and taking pep pills have become more respectable since the Stones' trial.

Originally Jagger had been sentenced to three months in prison for possessing four amphetamine pep pills. His sidekick, Keith Richard, was given a year for allowing guests to smoke hemp in his country home.

On Probation

In the appeals trial, Jagger argued he bought the pills in Italy and brought them legally to England. The judges lifted his sentence but warned Jagger that he would have to serve the sentence if he were convicted of any other crime in the next 12 months.

Richard was freed because, the judge said, the lower court had made a mistake in telling a jury that police had found a naked girl in his house, clad only in a rug. There was no evidence, they said, that the girl had been smoking hemp.

"Lovely," Jagger told his fans after the trial. Richard, whose face was dotted with chicken pox, said "I feel spotty."

The News of the World newspaper gave police the tip which sent them to Richard's house June 29, and teenagers and hippies have since demonstrated against the paper for allegedly persecuting the Stones.

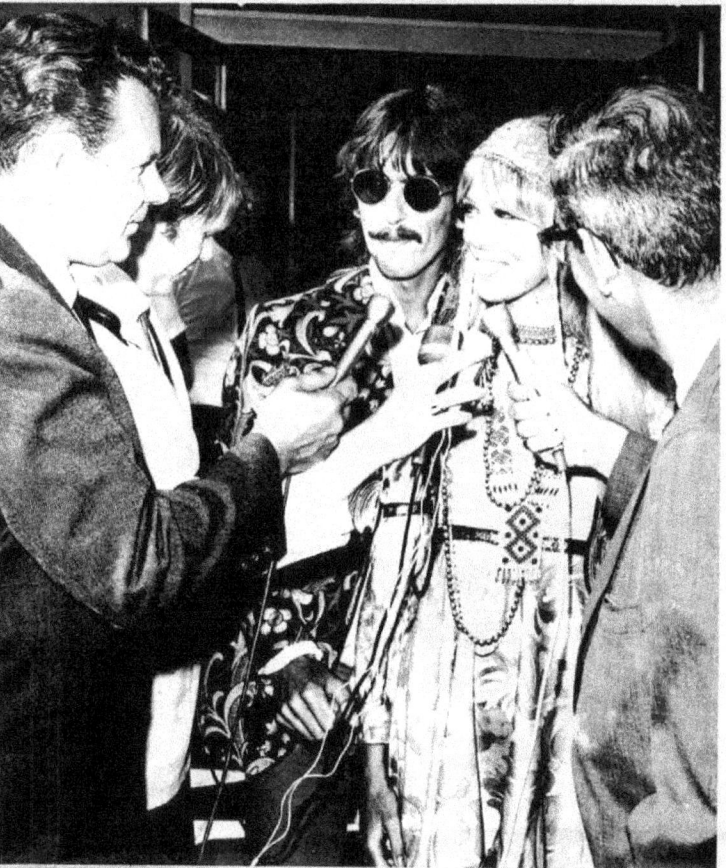

GEORGE HARRISON AND WIFE PATTI step off a Pan American jet at Los Angeles International Airport.

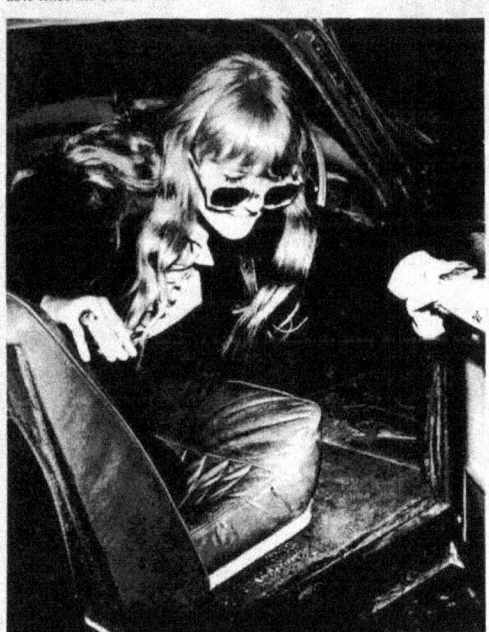

JAGGER'S GIRLFRIEND, Marianne Faithfull, arriving at court.

Harrison Arrives Stateside; Explains Controversial Ad

LOS ANGELES — Beatle George Harrison arrived at the Los Angeles International Airport for what he described as a "little bit of business and pleasure." Accompanied by his wife Patti, who was dressed in the Hippie garb reminiscent of the American Indian, the youngest Beatle was greeted by about 300 fans and a battery of the press.

George admitted that he had no plans for an extended stay in Los Angeles. "I expect to be here no longer than about five days. I have no plans, just come and try and get a bit of peace. You know, I'd like to see a few friends and a few people, that's the only thing I'm here for. And just a few things concerning business."

When asked why the Beatles have decided to give up concert tours, George answered, "It would be hard to pinpoint the problem just in a few words. There's so many different things we'd like. You see, we're all growing sort of physically and mentally and we've got to progress, and concert tours are too much in one rut. I think a lot of people realize this. We're more able to experiment with music and just generally do lots more things that we've always wanted to do.

"You know, in order to do something new, you've got to cut something out, and touring was the thing we were getting the least satisfaction from, because it was getting too big. It was too many politics being attached to it, when all we really are was a pop group coming to sing to the fans. But it was getting into big political things all related to it, that, you know, added up to the decision to stop it."

One reporter mentioned that there was a rumor that the Beatles were going to produce a new album with the "old Beatle sound." However, George denied the rumor, stating, "the Beatles have always been trying to progress with us. So all I can say is the next Beatle album is, well, we don't know. But whatever we do, we try our best."

Legalized Marijuana

Recently Harrison along with the other three Beatles signed a petition to the English Government urging the legalization of marijuana. The petition was also signed by 61 other British citizens and was addressed to the Home Secretary, Roy Jenkins. The advertisement appeared in a full-page story in the London Times. When asked about his reason for supporting the legalization of marijuana, Harrison said, "I think if somebody can go and buy a crate of Johnny Walker whiskey and drink that and be perfectly within the law then I think somebody, particularly within the privacy of his own home, should be able to smoke a marijuana cigarette. You know, I think marijuana is only as bad as ordinary cigarettes or alcohol or tea or coffee or any of those things.

"They're all drugs, all stimulants you know. The thing is to define between something that is merely a stimulant and something that makes your physical body crave for it. There's no comparison between marijuana and heroin."

Increasing Use

Harrison went on to say, "I think the use of marijuana is increasing everywhere in the world. It's not just America and Britain, but it's everywhere, and it's not just marijuana, you know, marijuana is the thing that society has picked up on, but that's not really the problem. The thing is that the young people want something more out of life than just the physically gained things that they get out of society. They're looking for something more, and it's a natural part of evolution that's taking place."

While staying in Los Angeles, Harrison is expected to attend the Ravi Shankar concert at the Hollywood Bowl.

KRLA ARCHIVES

Get Around To The Great Motown Sound . . .

FOUR TOPS

TEMPTATIONS

it's excitement, laughter, soul and music . . .

NOW AVAILABLE AT YOUR

It's Happened. Aretha's Arrived . . . And Everyone Loves Her!

AVAILABLE AT YOUR **Thrifty** CUT RATE DRUG STORES

AND AT CUT RATE PRICES, TOO

KRLA ARCHIVES

FROM THE EDITOR...

What a hassle! *BEAT* reporters and photographers have been scouring the entire city attempting to gather photos and speech from Beatle George Harrison. As often happens, if you try hard enough you can do almost anything and luckily the staff's intensive work has paid off.

Of course, you've already seen and read our efforts on page one but next issue we'll have more photos and more words from Harrison.

Whether you dig or despise the hippies, unless you completely close your mind you cannot discount them. They are a fact. We've waited most of the summer, marking time and watching to see if they would increase, decrease, or drop off the face of the earth. They chose to increase and we've decided to wait no longer. Our analysis of the hippie, his beliefs, his life and his purpose are on pages six and seven.

Every so often we feel that we must go out on a limb and take a stand. On page four you'll see clearly what our view on censorship of pop records, is and why we ask the burning question "mom and dad – has it really changed that much since you stood where we stand?"

In a less serious vein, we've stuck our necks out and predicted that Bobbie Gentry and her self-penned "Ode To Billy Joe" will stand out as the most talked-about and played record of the year. So, we tracked Bobbie down and spoke to her at length over lunch. Read the interview on page six and find out what "Ode To Billy Joe" really means.

— Louise Criscione

AROUND the WORLD

Monkees Hit In New York

NEW YORK – The Monkees were met by less-than-capacity audiences during their three-day stint at the Forrest Hills Music Festival, but were nonetheless well received during their 45-minute program.

The three concerts drew 36,19?, some 6,330 less than the tennis stadium's three-night capacity.

The Monkees sang, mugged and kidded through their show which never let up in its intensity and variety. All of the group's hits were on the bill, including "I'm A Believer" and "Pleasant Valley Sunday," their latest smash.

One of the highlights of the fare came when Micky Dolenz did a takeoff on James Brown. Twice, Micky had Mike Nesmith wrap his prostrate form in a blanket and escort him off the stage.

Despite the screams of thousands of teenage girls, the Monkees powerful amplification enabled the group to be heard by everyone.

The show also included Lynn Randell and the Jimi Hendrix Experience.

MONKEES DAVE & MICKY share a private laugh after performance.

Elvis News Stirs None

MEMPHIS – The news that Elvis Presley will become a father has stirred hardly a soul here in his hometown. No luncheon conversations have been centered on the millionaire rock 'n roll singer and no more than the usual number of curious fans have parked their cars outside Elvis' estate south of Memphis.

Presley, however, rarely gets much comment from city residents. The singer prefers to remain aloof, spending his offstage hours at the Graceland estate or at his new horse farm just below the state line in Mississippi.

He ordinarily leaves the party life alone, although when he does feel so inclined he hires out an entire nightclub or movie house in the early morning hours after the regular patrons have gone home.

Elvis and Priscilla Beaulieu, his bride, are expecting a child in February. According to his friends, the legendary singer is very pleased over the upcoming event, and one; said he had never seen Presley smile so broadly.

ELVIS PRESLEY

Wax 'Groovin' In 2 Languages

The Young Rascals' hit, "Groovin'" will be given a multilingual waxing by Atlantic Records. An Italian and Spanish version of the song, which was prepared for overseas sales, has been released in the U.S. after New York deejays started playing the new cuts.

YOUNG RASCALS

TREMS Len and Dave

Sandie Shaw Film Nixed

LONDON – Plans for British singer Sandie Shaw to make her dramatic movie debut sometime this autumn have been scrapped. Her manager said a part had been found for Sandie, but when the final script was read it wad decided that it was not suitable for her. Three other film offers are being considered, but are not likely to start this year.

Trems Coming To U.S. Again

LONDON – A world-wide tour for the Tremeloes, who only recently returned from an American stint, is currently in the making. The British group has been invited back to the States for three weeks starting November 6. This will be followed by a week of television and personal appearances in Hawaii and seven days in Latin America.

As a result of their tour of the U.S., the Trems have been signed to do a Coca-Cola commercial for TV penned by two members of the group.

Pet Clark Tour

Petula Clark will travel through Canada for two weeks of concerts in late September following completion of "Finian's Rainbow" in which she is co-starring.

PEOPLE ARE TALKING ABOUT whether or not that is really **Paul McCartney** and **John Lennon** singing on the Bee Gees' record . . . why Nureyuv and Fonteyn were given dismissed charges when Jagger and Richard were first given sentences but at least

Beat Publications, Inc.
Executive Editor .... Cecil L. Tuck
Publisher .... Gayle Tuck
Editor .... Louise Criscione
Assistant Editor .... Greg Kieselmann
Staff Writers
Jacoba Atlas   Bobby Farrow
Ron Koslow   Shirley Poston
            Rochelle Reed
Contributing Writers
Tony Barrow   Sue Barry
Lawrence Charles   Eden
Bob Levinson   Jamie McCloskey, III
Photographers
Ed Caraeff   Dwight Carter
Howard L. Bingham   Jerry Haas
Advertising
Dick Jacobson   Dick Stricklin
Business Manager .... Judy Felice
Subscriptions .... Diane Clatworthy
Distribution
Miller Freeman Publications
500 Howard Street, San Francisco, Calif.

The *BEAT* is published bi-weekly by BEAT Publications, Inc., editorial and advertising offices at 9121 Sunset Blvd., Los Angeles, California 90069. U.S. bureaus in Hollywood, San Francisco, New York, Chicago and Nashville; overseas correspondents in London, Liverpool and Manchester, England. Sale price 25 cents. Subscription price. U.S. and possessions, $5 per year. Canada and foreign rates. $9 per year. Second class postage prepaid at Los Angeles, California.

now we possibly know why "Rudy" can jump so high . . . the **Young Rascals** finally making an impact on Britain and wondering why it has taken so long . . . The **Who** cutting two **Stones**' songs to publicly show their support and sympathy for Mick and Keith's legal problems . . . when the **Happenings** are going to cut an original song instead of an oldie . . . the fact that **Glen Campbell** probably makes more money as a session musician than as a performer . . . what a small effect the so-called censoring by some radio stations has had on records becoming nation hits

. . . whether or not the **Supremes** are now going to go in for acting . . . what **Beatle** fans really think about the group's decision not to visit Stateside this summer . . . the fact that while **Neil Diamond** is busy thanking the lord for the night time, his fans are equally busy thanking the lord for Neil . . . how nice it is to see **Tommy Boyce** and **Bobby Hart** getting a hit for them-

selves after all the hits they've provided for the other artists . . . the single artist who just got married and is keeping it a secret using bad logic since no one cared much about his marital status to begin with

. . . the group that never was and still isn't despite a mediocre regional hit . . . **Jr. Walker** and the **All Stars** coming up with the best song titles ever . . . how sad it is when an entertainer signs his life away just to make a buck and wondering 'what price success?' . . . whatever happened to the **We Five** . . . who is going to win the battle of the "Happy" song and deciding that it's a real toss-up . . . whether or not **Jimi Hendrix** is going to make it Stateside now that he's been "discovered"

. . . where you end up if you step out of your mind . . . why **Sandy Posey** has a hit on the national pop charts . . . the fact that someone should definitely rewrite the **Forum**'s biography . . . getting a publicist to admit the truth is almost as hard as trying to water ski in the bathtub . . . what's really happening with the **Byrds** . . . the disc jockey who gets absolutely nothing straight and can't even tell the difference between seven and 22 – which is going some

. . . whether or not **Glen Campbell** has been listening too much to **Bob Lind** . . . the group which a large record company spent untold dollars on and is about to write off as a loss if they don't come through with a huge hit pretty soon

. . . the rap a syndicated columnist gave the **Monkees** for alleged rudeness at their New York press conference . . . whether or not the **Beatles** are really going to change their name to Sgt. Pepper's Lonely Hearts Club Band and deciding that they probably are since Paul McCartney said that any further work done under the name "Beatles" would only go for tax purposes . . .

. . . what's going to happen to the **Four Tops** if they fail to show a second time around . . . why **Phil Everly** is always mistaken for his brother **Don** . . . what a groove the **Fifth Dimension** are . . . who **Robert Stigwood** is and if the rumors that he now has the controlling interest are true . . . how far will flower power go and 20 years from now, will they refer to this as "the flower age."

KRLA ARCHIVES

across the BOARD

MAKING THE NEWS

Diamond Shines In New York

Neil Diamond will open in August at the famed club, "The Bitter End." Diamond is also planning on performing in Central Park under the new policy of summer entertainment in the park.

Recently Diamond has completed work on the Mike Douglas television show, and has also recorded a Coca Cola commercial. He is presently working on perfecting his stage act to include a wider range of material which will allow him more freedom of creativity.

SAM THE SHAM IN A NEW DEAL

Sam the Sham has signed a new contract with MGM Records for another three years. The contract also includes an option for the singer to star in two movies, also for MGM.

BEACH BOYS FORM OWN RECORD CO.

LOS ANGELES – Capitol Records has agreed to produce any new Beach Boy's albums under their own label called Brothers Records. This new label will also produce records made by other artists.

This agreement indicates that the Beach Boys' contract with Capitol Records, which was not due to expire for a few years, has been changed to allow the Beach Boys more freedom.

The first record to be released under this new label is the Beach Boys' "Heroes and Villains."

Hollies Nix Pop Tours

LONDON – It's no more package tours of Britain for the Hollies! Apparently fed up with the conventional pop screamers, the English group is planning instead, a series of "An Evening with the Hollies" throughout Britain's major cities.

In the words of group member Graham Nash, "I'm personally fed up with the screamers. We are putting a lot of effort into our work, and we believe the kind of people who go to concerts – as opposed to pop shows – would be prepared to listen to us quietly."

Surfer Lands Buffy's Hand

HONOLULU – Buffy Sainte Marie, the American Indian folksinger, may inevitably turn to surf music if her husband-to-be has anything to say about it. The lucky man is Dewayne Bugbee, a hawaiian whom Buffy describes as a "Surfer – and he rides horses and loves kids."

A 1965 graduate of Kailua High School, Bugbee met Buffy on the beach at Kauai.

Buffy said she also fell in love with a house in Hanalei (on Kauai Island) which she wants to buy.

"I've got all this money, and if I don't spend it the government will take it. What would I do with a businessman? I wouldn't know how to act," Buffy said.

GAYE HITS ABOVE PAR

CLEVELAND – Marvin Gaye, a man who rarely combines business and pleasure, did so not long ago and came out a winner in both ways.

In Cleveland for a three day nightclub stint at Leo's Casino, Marvin put out a great entertainment show before record crowds. At the same time, however, Marvin decided to enter the 1967 Six-City Holiday Open Golf Tournament just for recreation.

He emerged from the tournament with the first-place trophy to the utter amazement of his friends, including Barry Gordy, president of Motown Records.

HEY MOM & DAD – HAS IT REALLY CHANGED?

Crusading moralists are mounting their most determined campaign to date to censor pop music lyrics with the familiar battle cry that they are "going to pot."

A new wave of anti-pop music sentiment ala' Time Magazine of several months ago is being spread through syndicated newspaper articles and the extreme censorship policies of some radio stations. One such story gleefully predicted that the movement to exclude all "objectional" records from the air waves will become the practice within the near future.

Sight Beyond Nose

Censorship advocates charge that a lot of pop discs contain dirty innuendoes, references to the pleasures of drug taking and general, all-around sinfulness. The same people who find nothing objectionable in Cole Porter's "I Get No Kick From Cocaine" complain that Dylan's "Mr. Tambourine Man" is a reference to a New York junkie; that "Eight Miles High" by the Byrds is an "out and out LSD song;" and that the Rolling Stones' songs are all dirty – just look at them!

The moralists apparently have short memories. Assuming they weren't hermits as youngsters, they undoubtedly thrilled to the songs of the great Cole Porter, such as "Love For Sale" – love for sale/love that's new and still unspoiled/love that's only slightly soiled." And then there's "Making Whoopie." Or possibly they liked George Gershwin – just about every song in "Porgy and Bess" can be taken suggestively; or maybe they're modern enough to like Frank Sinatra – but would you say "All The Way," "It Was A Very Good Year," or "Blues In The Night" are sweet mother and home material?

Vice Removed?

The question you have to ask the moralists is simply "what do you think you will accomplish by banning records? Will sex and drugs then be removed from our lives?" There is only one logical answer, they certainly will not.

The moralists are putting the cart before the horse. Records are not the motivating factors in the lives of American's young people. They never have been. Records (like books and movies) reflect the times, they do not create the times. Songs about drugs were not written in a vacuum. The drug movement was an important fact of life in the Western world long before the Byrds and Bob Dylan arrived on the scene.

And sex was here, we would venture to say, long before the Stones dared to say anything about it.

If the moralists find something disgusting about modern music, they must also find something disgusting about modern life.

There is, of course, the theory that when the under-21's hear the
(Turn to Page 11)

THE GENUINE ARTICLE!

YES, IT'S YOUR OWN FAVORITES "THE MENDELSOHN QUINTETTE CLUB OF BOSTON", yea yea...

AND... You lucky readers of this ad now have the opportunity to possess this priceless masterpiece. A possession like this insures love and a happy home. Through the courtesy of J. B. Lansing Sound, Inc., we offer you this poster of your idolized quintette group at an unbelievable price... NOT $5.00... NOT $3.00... NOT $3.50 but just 25¢ that's right ONLY

GIANT SIZE 22"x35" BARGAIN PRICE 25¢

NO ONE ELSE CAN COMPETE WITH THIS OFFER... COMPETITION ASTOUNDED!!
Take advantage of this offer while it lasts... the demand is great.
Fill in and mail this coupon now.

COUPON
Enclosed please find 25¢. Send me the priceless poster of "THE MENDELSOHN QUINTETTE CLUB OF BOSTON".

Name _____
Address _____
City _____ State _____

JAMES B. LANSING SOUND, INC.
3249 CASITAS AVE., LOS ANGELES, CALIFORNIA 90039

KRLA ARCHIVES

A Fish Story

If you were born February 19 to March 20, you're under the twelfth sign of the Zodiac, Pisces–the fishes. You're governed by Neptune, your best day is Friday and your lucky number, four.

As a Pisces, you're ruled by emotion. You're inclined toward the spiritual and you're a dreamy romantic. You're dignified. And you've a penchant for the arts. Your color is light blue....

That's part of the Pisces tale, as told on Columbia's fascinating new LP *The Astrology Album*. There are eleven other signs in the Zodiac.

You were born under one of them, and this remarkable record reads your very own horoscope, to a way-out musical beat. It's fun.

It's informative. It'll tell you who, why and what you are. And what you should be. You'll learn which of the top stars shares your sign. (Mickey Dolenz, George Harrison, Brian Jones and Mark Lindsay are all Pisces!)

The album is packaged with a huge, handsomely illustrated chart full of facts, fantasies and the birth dates of your favorite stars. Bring it to your next party. For the time of your life.

The Astrology Album on Columbia Records
It's the only one of its kind.

BOBBIE GENTRY REVEALS MESSAGE BEHIND 'ODE'

Who killed Billy Joe McAllister? Or did he jump? What was thrown off that bridge? And why? These are just some of the questions raised by a controversial new song called "Ode to Billy Joe" written by a young Southern girl, Bobbie Gentry. The record is unique; a narrative rather than a song, beautifully depicting life in a small southern town.

"Life in the South is very different from life in California. The church was terribly important in our lives, in every Southerner's life. It was in the church that I learned my music. First in the choir and then advancing to quartets and sextets.

"I had no real playmates as a child (she lived on a farm) and so the piano that we had became my best friend. I began to play when I was three or four, and I used to always try and play on the black keys because I remembered the lady who played in church always played on the black keys. It wasn't until I later studied piano formally that I realized most hymns and gospel songs were written in minor keys."

Southern Life

It is her ability to remember the details of Southern life and relate them in a song that has produced a work of the importance of "Ode to Billy Joe." Her weaving of a mood and re-creation of a situation is flawless. The deep tragedy of Billy Joe tempered with the normalcy of a family eating dinner is remarkably effective.

"The message of the song is to show how little people actually care about other people. How they can discuss this terrible thing calmly as they ask for more food. I wanted to show the casualness and the unawareness of people."

Although there has been a great controversy over what they were throwing off the bridge, Bobbie negates this aspect of the song saying, "It is not really important what they are throwing off the bridge. The important thing is that people don't really care what happens to another person. I don't really know what they are throwing off the bridge, exactly. It is not important. The girl broke up with Billy Joe up on the bridge, so maybe it was some token of their relationship that they threw off the bridge. But it wasn't a person and she didn't push him. That becomes obvious if you listen to all the words in the song.

"Her parents didn't know of the relationship because perhaps Billy Joe was of another religion, which would be very important to a Southern Baptist family, or maybe because he was from the wrong side of town, as the line 'nothing ever comes to any good up on Choctaw Ridge' suggests. At any rate her parents weren't aware of what was going on.

Does He Die?

"Only the preacher knows for sure what had happened, that she was with Billy Joe. I feel he would use that to get close to the family. The Mother wants the girl to marry the preacher, as do all good Southern Baptist families want their daughters to marry preachers. The same was true for me, whenever I would visit my grandparents they would always have the preacher come to dinner, hoping that I would marry him.

"I never say for certain that Billy Joe is dead, only that he jumped. So it isn't necessarily suicide, but it certainly isn't murder. Billy Joe was alone when he jumped.

He jumped because things were too much for him, but the girl didn't have any idea that he would do a thing like that. In the end, everything sort of falls apart for the girl, after she hears about what happened to Billy Joe. Anyway, she sort of goes mad at the end, throwing flowers off the bridge, rather like Ophelia in *Hamlet*."

No Pattern

"But I want to add that not all of my songs are sad or as deep as this one. Many of my songs are happy, in fact, most of the songs on my album are happy. They all deal with life in the South, but I don't want to start a pattern."

"IT'S NOT IMPORTANT what they're throwing off the bridge."

ORIENTAL RELIGIONS greatly influence the flower children whose doctrine is peace and love.

By Jacoba Atlas

SAN FRANCISCO—Five o'clock in the afternoon. The going home traffic already crowding the freeway to a frustrating halt.

The sounds of the busy day still echoing through the ears of the people in their cars. People looking forward to home, a cool drink, some television, any departure from the aggravating competition of the day.

A young girl, fresh from the road, walks into a section of the city ready to put all the city's noises behind her, ready to commit herself to *herself* and not to the *city*.

She is 17, a runaway, one of the hundreds of young people who pour into San Francisco's Haight-Asbury district every day of this summer. They have come in search of a life that will give them more meaning and satisfaction than the one they left. Like some, she may find it for a while at least. Or like others who expected a Utopia, she may find only disillusionment and heartache.

The Hash-berry, as it is called by the papers, is already crowded with people. Hippies stand on street corners, lie down on sidewalks, stroll along the street. They are dressed in strange costumes that immediately give them an identity with the street.

Critics say they are uniforms. Indian head-dresses are worn, hand-loomed materials are made into dresses, flowers are everywhere.

By nightfall, she will find a home, or more likely a small space on a crowded floor, in a "commune." She will become a part of the district, a statistic for Time magazine, another dilemma for the city fathers, and a constant source of aggravation for her parents. But for the moment she feels like a pilgrim who has found Mecca.

American Dream

She has left the American Dream far behind, and entered into a world which preaches no negative doctrines, makes no demands, gives no edicts. The people on the street speak only about love, "trip," other people.

Why young people are flocking to the Haight and streets like it across the world is a question every major publication has sought to answer.

The world's preoccupation with the Hippie is amazing, but not surprising. The love generation scares the Establishment because it cannot understand what is happening, and this lack of understanding creates new fears.

In retaliation the mass media coins phrases to explain away the strangeness of this new culture.

Almost as if to say the Hippies will be less of a threat to middle-class America if one can read about them in the Sunday supplement, the papers relate the love-ins, the pleasure-fairs, and the rock concerts with incredible regularity.

The Hippie movement is a world-wide happening. There are Hippie colonies in London, in Paris, in Amsterdam, in Madrid. Each country brings its own particular culture to the movement, but there is the common theme of love and peace.

There is hardly a section of the country that is not affected in some way by the Hippie culture. Psychedelic stores have opened everywhere. Psychedelic posters advertising everything from movies to restaurants have sprung up.

'Trips Festival'

The first "Trips Festival" organized in San Francisco by novelist Ken Kesey in early 1966 have since developed into the love-ins, be-ins, pleasure fairs throughout the country that have attracted everyone from movie-stars to high school teachers.

The middle-classes have eagerly embraced the light shows, and even Jacqueline Kennedy has purchased psychedelic colored boxes for her children.

Music is the communication for the Hippies, and the pop world has seen the influx of what is now called the "San Francisco Sound" or "psychedelic music."

Groups such as the Jefferson Airplane, the Grateful Dead, Big Brother and the Holding Company are bringing the Haight to the world. Strobe lights create the illusion of "trips," and this com-

KRLA ARCHIVES

SAN FRANCISCO office front shelters hippies for the night.

SAN FRANCISCO Mime Troupe entertains residents of Haight-Ashbury.

What Does It Mean?

bined with music has even been presented on Establishment television.

They have given themselves new names, flamboyant, tender, gentle. A good Hippie name combines both the absurdity and the gentleness in life. An example of this would be the rock group called Iron Butterfly, a name which combines delicacy with strength.

New concepts of masculinity and femininity have also been developed. Gentleness and tenderness are the two most valued human assets. The idea of the super-strong James Bond/John Wayne type man has no place among the Hippie world.

Elvish Language

The poster writing which has become so popular with its curving letters and bright colors originates from a series of books by J.R.R. Tolkin, collectively called *The Ring Trilogy*.

These books which are widely read by Hippies tell of little furry people who live in the "Middle Earth" and speak a language called Elvish.

This Elvish is written in large curving letters, the same curving letters that now inform the world that "Jefferson Airplane Loves You."

The Hippies are an extension of our society, a product of our times. They are perhaps the reaction to a de-humanized culture which puts little value on human life, or human feelings.

Love Cosmology

For the sincere, the love cosmology is a way of life, a solution to the continuing search for something better. They say they have found the alternative to the nine-to-five jobs, to the cold war, to hatred.

They have followed Dr. Timothy Leary's advice and "Turned on, tuned in and dropped out."

Non-Political

The Hippie is essentially non-political, a fact which bothers the left as much as the mere existence of the Hippie bothers the right.

"Political orientation is a waste of energy," one bearded young man declared. Just two years ago this young man was walking a picket line in his home town two thousand miles away from the Haight-Asbury district.

The Hippies also ignore race issues and to a great extent the Negro is excluded from hippie society. This is not due to any hippie prejudice, but because the Negro does not see his place among the Hippies.

This is totally unlike the "Beats" of the 1950's who idealized the Negro to an amazing degree. But the Hippie is a white middle-class happening.

Anti-Intellectualism

Surprisingly, there is a creeping anti-intellectualism among Hippies. Education under the system is scorned, and only spontaneous knowledge is deemed worthwhile.

The written word has been replaced by the driving beat of the rock groups. The new poets are musicians; the new novels are the songs they sing and play.

The Hippie identifies with the American Indian in much the same way that the Beats identified with the American Negro. He wears the clothes of the Indian, preaches the joys of peyote (a hallucigenic drug used by California and Southwest Indians) and organizes his friends into tribes.

New Religion

Some Hippies have formed their own religious order called the Neo-American Church. This church bases its tenets on the Native American Church which is an Indian religious order that uses peyote as a part of its rituals.

So far the courts have not recognized the Neo-American Church as being a legitimate part of the religious community and have refused to exempt its members from legal restriction on the use of peyote.

The Hippie has also discovered the Orient and the Near Eastern Indian. Incense, oriental diets based on the ying and yang principles of masculine/feminine foods and yoga are studied and put into practice.

Indian chants and Egyptian prayers are also used to obtain mental "highs." One prayer is the Hindu chant: "Hare Krishna, Hare Krishna, Krishna, Krishna, Hare, Hare, Hare Rama, Hare Rama, Hare, Hare."

This is repeated for over 20 minutes. The continuous repetition of the proper words is said to produce a "high."

The Hippies' most disturbing trait is his passion for drugs. He seems unable to recognize the danger or else believes it to be a necessary risk to obtain what he wants.

"I know there is an enormous possibility of a bad trip, especially the more I take acid, but it's *my* mind, and *my* body. I consider it unimportant in relation to the mind-expanding experience of a good trip," said one in a typically fervent defense of LSD.

Doctors disagree. Recently UCLA Neuro-Psychiatric Institute published results of genetics and chromosome break-up (a process that happens when a person takes LSD). The results included horrifying cases of schizophrenia and malformed offspring.

There have been other casulties among the drug-taking hippies. Many have believed themselves to possess super-human powers and have taken leaps from high windows in the drug-induced belief that they could fly. Still others, reacting to acid with paranoia have committed suicide.

The Diggers

Sharing is the by-word of the Hippies, not charity. The Diggers, patterned after a group of 17th century English farmers who lived collectively, are a form of Hippie social workers.

They have houses where newly arrived flower children can spend the night free of charge, and they also serve hot meals in parks. Outside San Francisco they operate two farms and run a store in the Haight where clothing is given away.

But many have declared the movement a transient one. And certainly this summer has seen the influx of many pseudo-hippie people into Haight-Ashbury. People who are looking for an easy road to freedom, a superficial escape from pressure, real and imagined.

Many old-time Hippies – people who believed in the love cosmology before it was immortalized by Scott McKenzie – are leaving the cities.

One old-time Hippie put it this way, "These young kids leave their parents' $50,000 homes and come to the city with no knowledge of how to take care of themselves. They're under-age, their parents are frantic, they have no idea of what life is about. They're even panhandling. Begging was

HIPPIE LITERATURE is sold in the midst of rush-hour traffic.

something that was never done in the Haight before this summer."

Many of the older Hippies are moving out to the countryside. Divided into self-proclaimed tribes, they leave the city and its restrictions to find a more comfortable way of life outside the glare of publicity.

Trying To Live

The sincere Hippie is only trying to live, he is not trying to make the cover of Newsweek magazine. In the countryside he is escaping from the watchful eye of the news media, the restrictions of the police, and an influx of the teen-age summer hippie.

The Hippie has been called everything from a degenerate to a saint. One sociologist says the Hippies are an important contribution to the betterment of society as a whole.

"The hippies are a barometer of our sick society. They are dropouts who are turned off by wars, poverty, political phoniness and the 'game' they see around them."

But San Francisco columnist Dick Nolan sees them differently.

"The hip world is the slob world, comprising society's sad sack, traipsing around in Halloween costumes, reciting slogans as meaningless as their barren lives. They are pitiful," Nolan writes.

Pitiful or admirable, the hippies may have provided, in their own unorthodox way, a service to mankind.

They have awakened some of the complacent to a growing need within our culture to re-define our values. To re-define what is meant by success, what is meant by failure.

KRLA ARCHIVES

The Sound Of Music

Thrill To The Music
Of Rogers And Hammerstein
Sung By The Original Movie Cast

AVAILABLE AT YOUR **Thrifty** CUT RATE DRUG STORES

KRLA ARCHIVES

ONE DAY ONLY
Sunday, August 13

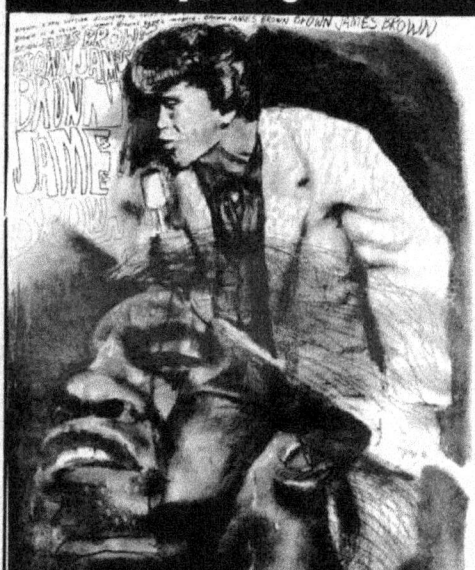

Advance Tickets — $4.00
At The Door — $5.00
Tickets at all Mutual Agencies and Wallich's Music City

TWO BIG SHOWS
8:30   11:00

BY THE SEA
1 NAVY STREET
P.O.P.
STA. MONICA
392-4501

CHEETAH

...BULLETIN...

A large hairy creature has been reported stalking and lurking on the streets of greater Los Angeles and Hollywood. It has been identified as the "KRLApe."

The creature is part of a massive promotion launched by Dick Morland and Associates to promote the successful image of KRLA and its 21 SOLID ROCKS album entitled "Son Of KRLA."

The Ape will participate in a motorcade — with trimmings — on Sunset Strip at an undisclosed time. Beware . . . the KRLApe is here!

BACKSTAGE AT SHEBANG, Casey Kasem and Gypsy Boots crack up over pictures of Gypsy at the Monterey Pop Festival.
BEAT Photo: Bob Hunter

who is FRED PAUL

ICE HOUSE GLENDALE

George Sharp
Hypnotist
Ends August 13

Ends August 13

Hearts & Flowers
with their hit
"Rock 'n Roll Gypsies"

Aug. 15 thru Aug. 27
Bob Lind
with his hit
"Elusive Butterfly of Love"
with
"Mother's Cookies"

ICE HOUSE PASADENA
24 No. Mentor — Reservations: 681-9942

Aug. 15 thru 25
Stone Country
— and —
Comedian Ken Greenwald
as seen on the Steve Allen Show
— and —
Singer Jean Durand

'best under the sun'
Johnson's baby oil
LANOLIN ENRICHED
Johnson & Johnson

baby, turn on a tan!

---

319 No. LA CIENEGA

1 — JOINT EFFORT
2 — PACIFIC OCEAN
3 — ABSTRACTS
4 — OCTOBER COUNTRY
5 — SOMEBODY'S CHILDREN
6 — MUSTARD GREENS
7 — COLORING BOOK
8 — SIOUX UPRISING
9 — FINISHED-PRODUCT
10 — CHOSEN FEW

DANCING 17 — COCKTAILS 21

IF YOU'RE REALLY LOOKING FOR HAPPENINGS, GROOVE-INS, LOVE-INS, DANCE-INS, MOD-BODS — MINI-SKIRTS — AND IF YOU'RE REALLY LOOKING FOR

ACTION YOU'RE LOOKING FOR

9039 SUNSET STRIP

SUNDAY AFTERNOON
GROOVE-IN 4 P.M.
MON. DANCE CONTEST
$500.00 GRAND PRIZE
TUES. — TALENT NITE
WED. — FASHION SHOW

GAZZARRI'S

OL 7-2112   *And That's the Word-in-Hollywood*   CR 3-6606

KRLA ARCHIVES

KRLA ARCHIVES

ON THE BEAT
BY LOUISE CRISCIONE

The racial strife tearing across American cities this summer has caused problems in areas which on the surface do not seem related at all. For instance, the **Monkees** have been "burned" twice. They were set to play dates in both Milwaukee and Detroit but both concerts had to be cancelled due to rioting and curfews. However, they reset the Detroit date but have not yet announced whether or not they will be able to reschedule a Milwaukee date.

Some rather evasive answers from **Tommy Roe** and his associate, Steve Clark, to the question of "has Tommy gotten married?" Said Tommy: "Not so's it shows." And Steve's comment: "If it happened, I'm not aware of it." They both admit, however, that Tommy's latest album, "Phastasy," has been released along with a new single, "It's Gonna Hurt Me" b/w "Melancholy Mood." One of the self-penned cuts off the album "The Executive," is (according to hot rumors) about to be recorded by a top entertainer who shall remain nameless—for the time being.

...TOMMY ROE

Motown Award
Motown has swept the annual Rhythm and Blues Awards conducted by Record World magazine. In the Top Male Vocal Groups category, the **Temptations** took first place, the **Four Tops** second place and **Smokey Robinson and the Miracles** third place. As was expected, **Diana Ross and the Supremes** were named Top Female Vocal Group, followed by **Martha and the Vandellas** and the **Marvelettes**. Jr. Walker and the All Stars were chosen Top Instrumental Combo.

Airplane's Million
Jefferson Airplane, exponents of the San Francisco sound, now leave no doubts in anyone's mind that they are a complete success. Their album, "Surrealistic Pillow," has been certified a million-seller. The Airplane is now busy cutting their third album in the RCA Studios in Hollywood—the same studios, by the way, where the **Rolling Stones** cut many of their hits.

For a group who allegedly hates to travel, the **Association** certainly does their share of it. Having finished up a smash engagement at the Greek Theatre in Los Angeles, they immediately hit the road for Illinois, Michigan, New York, Canada, Massachusetts, Arkansas, Florida, Colorado and Minnesota. On August 19 and 20th they'll tape a Murray The K show in New York and then return home where they're scheduled to tape a "Smothers Brothers Show" on August 25.

Anyone who is planning on being in Los Angeles during the first part of September should definitely make reservations to see the Association when they play the famed Cocoanut Grove from September 5-17th.

Rascal Schedule
Received the **Young Rascals'** personal appearance schedule and to keep it for myself would be destroying the whole purpose. So...on August 22 they'll play the Convention Hall in Asbury Park, New Jersey; August 23, Bushnell Auditorium, Hartford, Conn.; August 25, Canaby Lake Park, Salem, N.H.; August 26, Civic Center, Virginia Beach, Va.; August 28, Colonie Summer Theatre, Latham, New York; August 29, P.T. Barnam Tent Fair, Bridgeport, Conn.; August 30, Civic Auditorium, Knoxville, Tenn.

Personal to Gene Cornish: I am still waiting for your copy and if it's not here by September 1, I'm planning a giant bonfire of Rascal records, photos, etc.!

...GENE CORNISH

Personal to the over-35's: No wonder there's a generation gap. What can you expect when you are rude enough to get up and walk out of a theatre in the middle of a talented pop group's performance? In case it's slipped your mind, it's in extremely poor taste to leave during a performance but it is unforgivable when you insist upon leaving by the front exits so that you can parade out under the noses of a group who is on stage. You've taught your children—why did you forget?

YOUNG STUFF—THE HEIRS TO HERMAN'S POP THRONE??

So you want to be a rock and roll star. Most people do, but few get the opportunity of having a producer from a large record company discover your unknown talent. Just such a phenomenal thing has hap-

REMEMBER?
(Continued From Page 4)

Stones sing "Let's Spend The Night Together" they're going to do it. This theory shoves aside the fact that today's teenagers are more capable of making moral judgments on their own than their predecessors; they are not so naive and empty-minded as to do everything they hear or read. If, as tests have shown, people are not influenced much by real hard-core smut, it's highly doubtful that a few hard-to-detect lyrics in a pop song are going to turn the teen world into one continuous orgy.

Although the headline on this story reads "Mom and Dad" we must admit that not *all* members of the older generation belong to the moralist crusade. Dr. LaMar T. Empey of the University of Southern California's Youth Studies Center sees popular music today as a *positive* influence on the morals of young people.

"The younger generation tends to be the people with a great deal of moral fervor," says Dr. Empey. "I do feel that songs reflect some of the feeling of the younger generation but, interestingly enough, *Time* didn't mention the fact that many of the songs are concerned with civil rights. They're concerned with war. They're concerned with the problems of peace and people getting along together and I think that one would be hard put to demonstrate that the current interest of young people is more with immoral things than with the real problems of our time. Many of the things our young people are being criticized for is for their moral fervor."

Just one last word to those adults who think popular music is dirty and harmful—please have some faith in us.

pened to three young men from Southern California. While playing at their usual high school dance one night, Ken Handler from Canterbury records heard them and in his words "flipped."

"I feel there's a need right now for a young group, to appeal primarily to the teeny-bopper audience. This group will fulfill that need."

The group is called the Young Stuff and is composed of two twin brothers and their friend from high school. They are all accomplished musicians: Jon Tulluis is 17 and plays the drums, his brother Tom plays lead guitar while Terry Waters plays rythmn guitar.

Their image is that of three young, happy uncomplicated boys, who are enjoying what they are doing. When Handler first approached the group, they thought it was some sort of joke. Tom laughed, "We thought he was nuts, we just paid no attention to him." But after a few days they decided they had nothing to lose by trying, and the rest of the time has been spent constantly working on their sound, their performance and their image!

Talk Money
What do these boys do when they're not working, it was a little difficult to get any straight answer out of them. Tom offered some suggestions of what they did with their time off, "we cruise around a lot and let people groove on us." Terry added that they like to go into department stores and when people criticize their long hair or strange clothes, they reply by saying they're rich. Does this work? "We just have to talk about money, and the people shut up, unless they tell us it's too bad we can't afford hair cuts."

Along with promoting their image of happy young men, they stressed that they were not part of the Sunset Strip scene. Terry answered, "we don't put down hippies, but we're not of that crowd." Tom added, "I like light shows and things like that because they're strange, but I wouldn't want to play in one."

They want rather material things for their future, no long philosophical discussions for them. Jon wanted to get enough money together to buy his parents a house – in Greenland. Mostly they just wanted to talk about girls, girls and more girls.

Handler says that he has never handled a group more willing to work and learn the business. The Young Stuff tended to put down some groups who have everything handed to them, who aren't committed to their music. They do all their own arrangements, and although their new single "Poor Boy" is not their own composition they plan to record their own material in the future.

Poor Boy
"Poor Boy" is the culmination of weeks of work. It is a straight rock song about a young man who can't afford his girl friend. The group feels that a lot of teen-age boys will know exactly what they are singing about, and the girls will feel sympathetic.

The song states, "I know its hard times" but that is no longer true for Tom, Jon and Terry. They are the lucky ones, who were "discovered" in the best Hollywood tradition and are now working very hard to live up to the trust the record company and their producer have shown in them.

The future includes radio spots, television appearances and a tour through the Mid-West. An album will be finished in September, and from there, the group, under the watchful eye of Ken Handler, will play it by ear.

ART INSTITUTE OF PITTSBURGH
47th Yr. Coed. 18 & 24 mo. Diploma Course: Commercial Art, Fashion Art, Interior Design, Begin. & Adv. Vet. Appd. Dorm facilities. College referrals for degrees. Free illus. brochure.
Earl B. Wheeler, Director
635 Smithfield St.
Pittsburgh, Pa. 15222

KRLA ARCHIVES

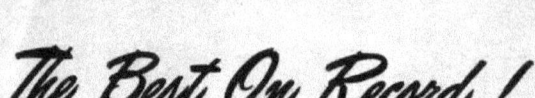

KRLA ARCHIVES

Produced by Richard Perry & Bob Krasnow

Twenty years ago it was Judy Garland with "Over The Rainbow"

Ten years ago it was Elvis Presley with "Heartbreak Hotel"

TODAY IT IS TONY BRUNO WITH "SMALL TOWN BRING DOWN"

"Gotta Fill Myself With More Than Home Made Pie"

CREATIVE FREEDOM FROM BUDDAH RECORDS
7122 Sunset Blvd.
Hollywood, California 90046
469-1101 (213)

Produced By Artie Ripp
BDA 7

KRLA ARCHIVES

Alpert Heads The C/F Charity Drive

Herb Alpert has accepted the post of Honorary Campaign Chairman for the Cystic Fibrosis Foundations "Young People's Walk-In," to raise 50,000 dollars in Los Angeles, Ventura and Orange Counties. Announcement of the appointment for the annual fundraising drive was made by the Foundation's Film Industry Campaign Chairman, Ben Gazzara.

Alpert will spearhead a campaign to raise charitable funds through a door-to-door solicitation September 9 and 10. It is estimated that 10,000 young people between the ages of 18 and 25 will join the Walk-In.

Commenting on the special fund raising effort, Alpert stated, "It gives me great pleasure to head this campaign for Cystic Fibrosis. It provides an opportunity for the young people of Los Angeles to demonstrate their importance to our community in this particular area of social responsibility. I am confident," he continued, "they will respond eagerly to a call for help from the thousands of young C/F victims."

Those joining the Walk-In, Alpert advised, will be invited, free of charge to a special C/F "Op-Hop" at the Hollywood Palladium, Sunday evening, September 10. The "Op-Hop," featuring many popular recording and stage performers, will be staged by Casey Kasem, Chairman of the show and dance. Kasem, KRLA's popular disc-jockey, will also emcee the star-studded performance.

Funds raised by the young adults will be used to help support the Cystic Fibrosis Foundation's two medical centers in Los Angeles, located at UCLA and Children's Hospital. Cystic Fibrosis, a genetic children's disease for which there is no known cure, affects a child born every two hours.

Those wishing to join the Walk-In may do so by telephoning the Cystic Fibrosis Foundation in Beverly Hills: 275-1660.

HERB ALPERT (right) recently appointed Honorary Chairman for the Cystic Fibrosis Foundation's "Young People's Walk-In," meets Casey Kasem and Chris Noel, chairmen of other committees for the door-to-door solicitation September 9 and 10.

KRLA NIGHT AT THE BOWL

The Lovin' Spoonful and Simon and Garfunkel packed the Hollywood Bowl with fans eager to hear these two unusual acts with their varied and different sounds.

Simon and Garfunkel who opened the evening sang in their usual beautiful harmony and impressed the audience so, they received a standing ovation.

The Lovin' Spoonful appeared next, and sang for the first time with their new member Jerry Yester, brother of Association member Jim Yester. Jerry who has flaming red hair was an excellent addition to the foursome, and those fans who were unhappy over the departure of Zal Yanovsky were completely won over.

BY PEN

KRLA's CASEY KASEM has been chosen as Chairman of the giant star-studded Cystic Fibrosis "Op-Hop" to be held at the Hollywood Palladium, Sunday evening, September 10th. The show and dance will climax the C/F "Young People's Walk-In" — a two-day door-to-door effort to raise $50,000 for support of the two C/F medical centers in Los Angeles.

All those joining the September 9th and 10th Walk-In will be the guests of Casey at the "Op-Hop" that Sunday evening. You can help yourself to the FREE evening of fun and entertainment and put yourself in the running for some fantastic prizes (such as a Suzuki motorcycle, a Muntz stereo-pak and more) and help the C/F children all at the same time. Just call 275-1660 and find out how you can join. Do it right now and tell 'em Casey told you to call . . . he'll be looking for you at the "Op-Hop."

Pick me up NOW at your local record emporium

JERRY YESTER, brother of Association member Jim Yester, replaced Zal Yanovsky who said he had grown "bored" with the Lovin' Spoonful.

PAUL SIMON performed his own compositions at KRLA night at the Hollywood Bowl.

KRLA ARCHIVES

please send me BEAT

26 issues only

$3 per year

Mail to: **BEAT Publications**
9125 Sunset Blvd.
Los Angeles, California 90069

☐ New Subscription
☐ Renewal (please enclose mailing label from your BEAT)
I want BEAT for: ☐ 1 year at $3.00 or ☐ 2 years at $5.00
I enclose ☐ cash ☐ check ☐ money order
Outside U.S. — $9 per year

• Please print your name and address.

Name_____
Street_____
City_____
State_____ Zip_____

NATIONAL TOP 25 SINGLES

1. ALL YOU NEED IS LOVE .... Beatles
2. LIGHT MY FIRE .... Doors
3. I WAS MADE TO LOVE HER .... Stevie Wonder
4. PLEASANT VALLEY SUNDAY .... Monkees
5. WHITER SHADE OF PALE .... Procol Harum
6. WHITE RABBIT .... Jefferson Airplane
7. MERCY, MERCY, MERCY .... Buckinghams
8. GIRL LIKE YOU .... Young Rascals
9. SILENCE IS GOLDEN .... Tremelos
10. CARRIE-ANNE .... Hollies
11. BABY I LOVE YOU .... Aretha Franklin
12. CAN'T TAKE MY EYES OFF OF YOU ...... Frankie Valli
13. WINDY .... Association
14. JACKSON .... Nancy Sinatra/Lee Hazelwood
15. WORDS .... Monkees
16. MY MAMMY .... Happenings
17. SOUL FINGER .... Bar-kays
18. HEROES AND VILLAINS .... Beach Boys
19. MORE LOVE .... Smokey Robinson & Miracles
20. I TAKE IT BACK .... Sandy Posey
21. COLD SWEAT .... James Brown
22. THANK THE LORD FOR THE NIGHT TIME .. Neil Diamond
23. SOCIETY'S CHILD .... Janis Ian
24. COME DOWN TO MY BOAT .... Every Mothers Son
25. TESTIFY .... Parliments

As Compiled by Cashbox Magazine

THE ROBBS NATIONAL FAN CLUB
Write: P. O. Box 350
Beverly Hills, California 90213

SKY SAXON — *Happy Birthday!*
Charley's girls: Jan & Sandee
DAVEY DOES...
Liverpool Five Fan Club. Write: 15068 N.E. 13th, Bellevue, Washington
Jim Faire is great!
Bruce of the Revelles is *funny*
BEATLES RULE!!!
Leader of the Buckinghams lives forever. Chicago Loves You.
Monkees AND *Beatles forever*
Dan, You're a groove — Carol
Mick Jagger — Happy Birthday
All Our Love, Alyn & Maureen
Monkee people are purely DUMB! Beatle people are SMART, Beautiful, Stupendous Great — etc., etc., etc.
Happy Birthday Barb — July 22!!
HAPPY BIRTHDAY SKY
Luv, LYNNE
THE HARD TIMES RULE!!
Equal time for *Groovy Monkees*
Normandy Bombsite — *What?*
GEORGE HARRISON HAS STAR QUALITY!!
Psychedelic Invasion is great!
J.S.
Happy Birthday Rick Huxley & Denis Payton
— Love Nancy and Sandy
DAVE CLARK has what it takes
Wanted Desperately:
Denis Payton and Dave Clark!
HAPPY BIRTHDAY PAUL
from Steve
JOE LUCAS *DROP DEAD!!!*
Happy belated from London,
Joni — Lots of Love — Jim Cook
CRYINGTIME IS COMING
August 28th — Beatles we luv you
We hear visions of success
— fans of the —
LOOKING GLASSES
Phyllis Welcome Back — Lorne
See better through the
LOOKING GLASSES
Seattle has the finest CITY ZU in the world! (Naturally)
Gandalf Grooves
T.C. ATLANTIC, TWIN CITIES BAND REALLY HAVE IT!
"Mona" "Shake" — Rick
Debbie Weyers *LOVES* Jim Pilster...*Always*
Hippie Luvs Mike
Bar *Stinks!*
GEORGE HARRISON — WOW!!
Beatles *Disintegrate* — Monkees *Groove*
Stevie — bloom, I *luv* you!
"Frank Sinatra"
Janet from "Philly"
KOREEN GAULD
The "Headstones"
are *Psychedelic*
Lenore Loves Tom Courtenay and the Beatles and the Cubs.
BEATLE FANS MAY *STEP ON SNAILS*, BUT MONKEE FANS *EAT* THEM!!!

TO WALT:
The doll was a joke,
Your curiosity to provoke.
But we want you to know,
No pins do we throw.

CLASSIFIED

Wanted: All Beatle Christmas records except the 1964 edition, will pay. Write Patti Jones, 2722 Foster N.E., Grand Rapids, Michigan 49505
BARBARA LOVES GARY AND SPOCK!
University of Nebraska, Rumbles, Coachmen, Bumbles RATE! Girl named SAM
Is Bjorn McCulloch in?
Andree has *soul!* — Bon
LIVERPOOL FIVE —
Did your amplifiers really blow up?
"Stay stung by the Bee Gees! Join their new fan club! Exclusive photos which were never printed anywhere before are offered to members only! For information write to:
The Bee Gees Clan
c/o Dathy Dakis
1170 Ocean Parkway
Brooklyn, New York 11230
RYDER RIDES 4/EVER!
Billy Levis is fine
Levise Rules
Bari — Cherrychild?
Wuston *Loves* Sunnydown snuff
Happy Birthday Carig Robb
... Karen
Happy Birthday Deddie.
Monkees *Forever!* Luv, Fwease
"RINGO FOR PRESIDENT"
Happy Birthday David Crosby!
— Linda —
Bobby — "Painted Doll" for you alone. *I love you.* Your flower child.
WANTED: Negatives of photos taken of Monkees in concert. Can buy or will return if requested. Notify:
Susan Smith
1111 Wasena Ave. S.W.
Roanoke, Va. 24015
BEETLE People grow up!
"The Museum"
Rick McWilliams rules!
Handsomeness is:
Rick, Tom, Doug — Fang
Dave Clark Says
"Hi Rick McWilliams
Rick luvs CHANCES R
— Peanut shell
Doug — Alligators Sweat out of the eyes — Chintz
BEATLES AND LOVE
forever
Happy Birthday Keith Allison
— Cathy
HAPPY BIRTHDAY SKY
Joyce — didder, didder and happy 13th birthday — Julie
Happy BELATED Birthday to Cris Donahoo in Maryland — *someone you know*
BLOW YOUR MIND with "Mrs. Griffith" by THE RUBBER MAZE — call request lines NOW!
Randy is bitchen! Barbara
Happy Birthday Jackie
— *Love the Scamp*
We're behind you Paul — you're still the *Grooviest!*
Dena Kumitake - Happy Birthday
— *Judy*
"Mick Jagger is..."
Queen Shaz and Project Hill
F. I. G. I miss you — your D'y
Blackhand Conspiracy Wishes
Karen Happy Birthday!
Come — August 28, Dodger Stadium, BEATLES

TO FRAN:
Our floor has a hole,
Our windows need oil,
The smoke came thru both,
And interrupted our sloth.
With Love
Now you drive me!!
H.B. Soupbones.
Nelda Glick is watching us!
"Shades of Sound — BOSS!"
"Parkhursts Forever"
God isn't dead... HE'S just in different places.
Love Birthday Janie. Micky
I care Joey — I really do!
The Monkees only ape the Beatles!
BOB BARTH, WHERE ARE YOU?? WHAT'S HAPPENED ???????
PLEASE WRITE!   Loretta
Beatles are love — Blurbs 'n' apeasie
MIKE — PLEASE?
SONNY & CHER POSTERS
11"x14" — $1.00 each postpaid. Seper Co. 5273 Tendilla, Woodland Hills, California 91364
Joy, My flower child, play "Painted Doll" and remember the love I have for you, Bobby.
Happy Birthday to Dave DeFore, Jim Bunnell, and Jim Burdine of the INRHODES.
Happy Late 5th Wedding Anniversary, JOHN LENNON!!!
Happy Birthday ZAK STARR!
MIKE... *is it love?*
Beatle Fans: Come to cherish memories — August 28th 8:00 p.m., Dodger Stadium
I love James Paul McCartney
BeAtles Rule You Too!!!
"Mature music appreciators appreciate the Beatles."
"John Lennon: *What more can I say?*"
Joe Lucas drinks Kool-aid. Monkees forever!!
To Peter Tork... *I was made to love you... Sharon*
Formality breeds distrust, but THE KOLLEKTORS from Greenwich Village love you!
Pauley
Happy 18th
Your Fren' Debb
Oriental cool = George Harrison
REACH COSMIC AWARENESS without drugs — help save mankind from destruction. Write for free booklet, "Cosmic Awareness Speaks," Organization of Awareness, Box 115E, Olympia, Washington.
SLEEP-LEARNING, self-hypnosis. Details, strange catalog free! Autosuggestion, Box 24-BT, Olympia, Washington.
Now you drive me!!
H.B. Soupbones.
Nelda Glick is watching us!
"Shades of Sound — BOSS!"

BEAT is no longer accepting anything but PERSONAL MESSAGES in the classified section. Only messages (including Happy Birthdays) will be run. We will print names but not addresses or phone numbers.

Rates are cheap! Only 10 cents per word.

And remember, BEAT has a new address:

**Classified
BEAT Publications
9121 Sunset Blvd.
Los Angeles 90069**

DEADLINE FOR NEXT ISSUE: AUG. 15

KRLA ARCHIVES

RECORDS FREE FROM RC®
You'll Flip at the ZZZIP in RC® Cola

while you swing to your favorite stars! RC and music, perfect partners for the perfect lift

TAKE 1 ALBUM FREE

For everyone you buy... with 6 cork liners or seals from R.C. bottle caps over 100 Capitol LP's available. Order as often as you wish. Nothing to join. Look for this display at your favorite store.

Here's your best way yet to save more on the records you want. In dollars-and-cents terms you get two albums that the Capitol Record Club sells for $3.98 each time you buy one. The savings are even bigger on stereo records! And there are no shipping charges to pay, nothing else to join or buy.

What's more, you choose from top albums by today's biggest stars, including the Beatles, David McCallum, Frank Sinatra, Lou Rawls, Buck Owens, Petula Clark, the Outsiders, Nancy Wilson, Dean Martin, Sonny James, the Beach Boys and many others.

OTHER FINE BRANDS: DIET-RITE® COLA, NEHI® BEVERAGES, PART-T-PAK® BEVERAGES, UPPER 10®
"ROYAL CROWN" AND "RC" REG. U.S. PAT. OFF.; ®1966 ROYAL CROWN COLA CO.

KRLA ARCHIVES

BEHIND THE SCENES WITH PAUL REVERE — 25¢

KRLA *Edition*

September 9, 1967

THE BEATLES

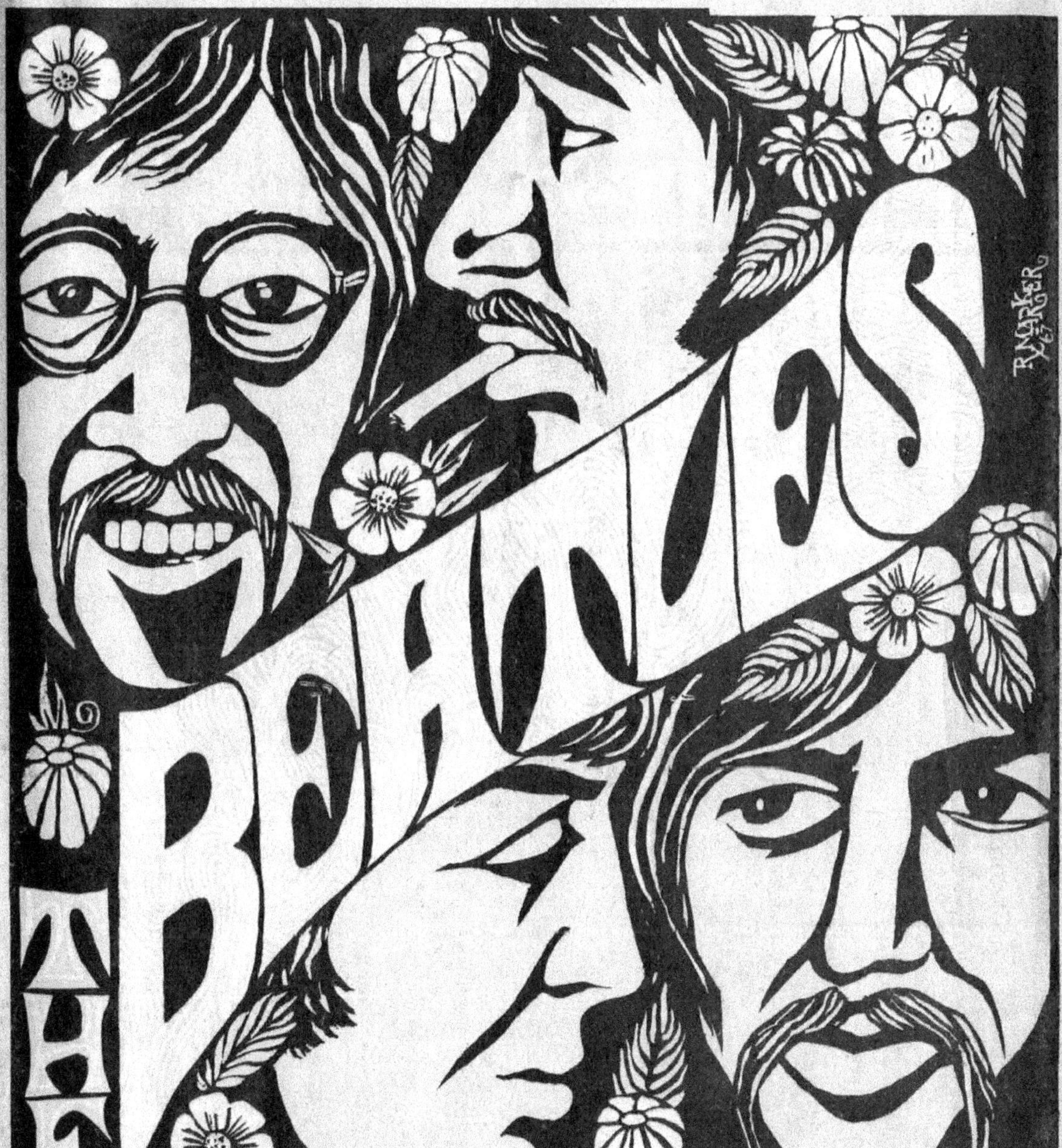

KRLA ARCHIVES

KRLA

Volume 3, Number 13   September 9, 1967

PAUL MCCARTNEY AND JANE ASHER arrive at London Airport in time to read about Mick and Keith.

Following Aftermath Of Jagger, Richard Victory

Tony Barrow

LONDON — Less than 72 hours before the hearing before Lord Parker, the Lord Chief Justice, of appeals by Mick Jagger and Keith Richard against their convictions and sentences, drugs and pop personalities claimed yet another series of front page newspaper headlines in Britain.

In the House of Commons, Miss Alice Bacon, Minister of State at the Home Office, told members of Parliament that she was horrified by the way pop people were encouraging drug taking. She quoted from the pages of Queen Magazine, the luxury glossy which had published statements by Donovan, Radio Caroline chief Ronan O'Rahilly, Marianne Faithfull and others including Paul McCartney and Brian Epstein.

Epstein talked about a marvelous new friendliness which he found around him and said this new mood had originated from hallucinatory drugs. He added, "I'm wholeheartedly on its side."

Among those who had spoken against drugs was songstress Lulu who, along with Epstein, appeared on Independent Television News hours after Alice Bacon's Parliamentary speech.

Lulu said of LSD: "You can never be sure of it as you can be sure of yourself. The idea of hallucination does not appeal to me."

Epstein said, "Alice Bacon's outlook is narrow and singularly ill-informed."

MICK JAGGER is all grins now that he will not go to jail.

JAGGER'S GIRLFRIEND, Marianne Faithfull, elated over news.

Gentry Breaks Beatles' Mark

Will Bobbie Gentry, recorder of "Ode To Billy Joe," be five times as popular as the Beatles? It's doubtful, but Capitol records is acting like it. Bobbie's first album has the largest pre-release pressing in the company's history — 500,000 copies.

The old record was "Meet The Beatles," the Beatles' first LP, which only had 100,000 pressings. The album eventually sold 5,000,000 copies.

Bobbie's single sold 500,000 copies in the first three weeks of release.

GENTRY SCORES a first.

Supreme Loss

NEW YORK — Florence Ballard of the Supremes has quit the singing group for reasons of ill health. She has been hospitalized at Ford Medical Center in Detroit, but there has been no word as to the nature of her illness.

Cindy Birdsong of Patti and the Bluebells has replaced Florence, and this will probably be a permanent arrangement according to Motown officials.

FLORENCE BALLARD has left the Supremes due to bad health.

Spanky says Sunday will never be the same but if brother can spare a dime and you don't hit trouble you can make every minute count by covering the distance in a jet and come to Byrd Avenue on a Lazy Day and open your mind... baby, why can't you be me?

AVAILABLE AT YOUR

"Walk with me and you will see
that our lives were meant to be
And just a touch of love
will make us free."

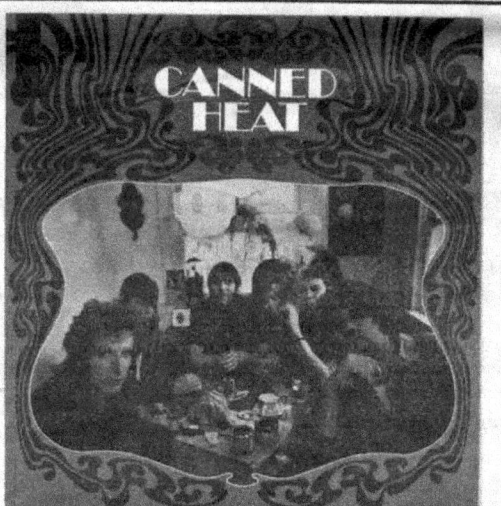

CANNED HEAT

"Canned Heat is imaginative, powerful, tight... in fact, they're simply overwhelming."

A part of today;
  Reflecting the feelings of today
This is the LOVE GENERATION.

NOW AVAILABLE AT YOUR

KRLA ARCHIVES

FROM THE EDITOR...

The Beatles are back on our cover again. The wild poster was designed exclusively for *The BEAT* by Robert Marker, an extremely talented and original artist from Southern California.

Inside this issue we have two full pages on the Beatles—one on George Harrison's press conference in Los Angeles and another which contains the first part of a two-part Beatle history. We certainly hope you enjoy the history since it took one of our staff members months to compile!

We managed to catch the Lovin' Spoonful when they flew into town and on page six you'll find what they had to say about their newest member, Jerry Yester, as well as their music and their future plans.

The Mamas and Papas deservedly received a full page this issue. In an exclusive interview Cass Elliott talks about John Lennon, Michelle talks about her movie plans, John reveals why he left the Naval Academy and Denny simply talks!

The fantastic Four Tops opened at the famed Cocoanut Grove and, of course, we were there to cover it for you. In addition to a review of the show we spoke to the Tops backstage where they were busy recalling the road they took to finally reach the top.

Paul Revere fans will be happy to turn to pages 16 and 17 and find loads of exclusive photos of Paul. The photos were taken at Paul's home with his wife, his children and his dogs. Paul spoke quite frankly to our reporter, touching upon such subjects as drugs, music, the hippie movement and the younger generation.

Also in this issue—the Fifth Dimension, Every Mother's Son, Stevie Wonder, Lou Rawls, Jefferson Airplane, Bee Gees, Johnny Rivers and the Happenings.

AROUND the WORLD

Star Rising In The West

LOS ANGELES—The unplanned rise in interest over a mono-tagged singer named Nilsson has sparked a commotion in the recording industry.

When a radio station played a cut of "You Can't Do That"—a yet-to-be-released medley of 11 Beatle songs—a flood of inquiries poured in asking about the singer and where the record was available. When the word traveled to other areas the same reaction followed.

RCA-Victor was forced to upset its release schedule and bring out the single backed by "Ten Little Indians." An October promotion push had been planned to coincide with the release of Nilsson's first LP, "Pandemonium Shadow Show," before the unexpected interest caused the reshuffling.

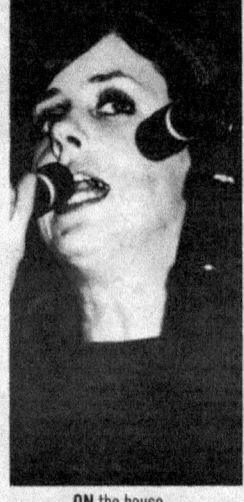

ON the house...

40,000 Take A Free 'Plane

TORONTO—The Jefferson Airplane attracted a crowd of 40,000 at a free concert held on the steps of Toronto's City Hall.

The free concert was given to repay fans who gave the Airplane a warm reception during its stay in the city, according to Marty Balin, leader of the group.

DONOVAN SET FOR U.S. TOUR

A tour of the States by Donovan, beginning the end of September, has been finalized. The tour will consist of 30 coast-to-coast concerts ending in Hawaii. Donovan will take five British musicians to back him up and will also use an American group, the Midnight Strings.

RICKY NELSON hosts Malibu U.

DECCA INKS RICK NELSON

Ricky Nelson has just signed an exclusive contract on Decca records.

The first release will be "Suzanne on a Sunday Morning" produced by Charles Koppelman and Don Rubin. It was written by John Boylan who is a Koppelman and Rubin contract writer.

Nelson has also debuted in "Malibu U," a teen variety show aired on ABC-TV. This television exposure will be a prime factor in promoting the new release.

Koppelman and Rubin, through their Koppelman-Rubin Associates also produces the Lovin' Spoonful, The Turtles, Bobby Darin, The Righteous Brothers and Gary Lewis and the Playboys.

SUPREMES SET FOR TARZAN

The Supremes have been signed for their dramatic acting debut on a segment of NBC's "Tarzan" next season. The three girls will be cast as nuns and will sing several hymns during the one hour segment.

U.A. Signs Goldsboro

United Artist, a Transamerica company has just signed Bobby Goldsboro to a multi-faceted exclusive, long-term contract. Goldsboro will produce many of his own singles and albums under this contract; he will also have the opportunity to produce for other United Artists Recording stars.

His initial production chore for the label was his current single, "Trusty Little Herbert" and his new album, "The Romantic, Soulful, Wacky, Country, Rockin' Bobby Goldsboro."

Michael Stewart, president of Artist Records also expressed the hope that UA could involve the prolific writer/singer in the motion picture industry.

Chubby Twists Cameo Record

PHILADELPHIA—Chubby Checker, who has been credited with popularizing the twist, has filed a $110,000 suit against the Cameo-Parkway Record Co.

Checker, whose real name is Ernest Evans, told a Common Pleas Court that the record company was $32,000 short when it last paid him on April 1.

Chris Borden
SCHOOL OF MODERN RADIO TECHNIQUE
FOR INFORMATION, WRITE: SAN FRANCISCO
ON UNION SQUARE   259 GEARY STREET
AREA CODE 415   YUKON 2-9840
(FURTHER INFORMATION AVAILABLE UPON REQUEST)

Beat Publications, Inc.
Executive Editor .... Cecil T. Tuck
Publisher .... Gayle Tuck
Editor .... Louise Criscione
Assistant Editor .... Greg Kieselmann
Staff Writers
Jacoba Atlas   Bobby Farrow
Ron Koslow   Shirley Poston
Contributing Writers
Tony Barrow   Sue Barry
Lawrence Charles   Eden
Bob Levinson   Jamie McCluskey, III
Photographers
Ed Caraeff
Howard L. Bingham   Jerry Haas
Advertising
Sam Chase   Dick Stricklin
Business Manager   Judy Yelice
Subscriptions   Diane Clatworthy
Distribution
Miller Freeman Publications
500 Howard Street, San Francisco, Calif.

The BEAT is published bi-weekly by BEAT Publications, Inc., editorial and advertising offices at 9121 Sunset Blvd., Los Angeles, California 90069. U.S. bureaus in Hollywood, San Francisco, New York, Chicago and Nashville; overseas correspondents in London, Liverpool and Manchester, England. Sale price 25 cents. Subscription price: U.S. and possessions, $5 per year; Canada and foreign rates, $9 per year. Second class postage prepaid at Los Angeles, California.

PEOPLE ARE TALKING ABOUT the hippies migrating to the Hawaiian Islands and wondering what the natives think of that development... the Doors finally making it to number one in the nation after all these months... the Rolling Stones stealing the British spotlight away from the Monkees ... why Bill Cosby has decided to turn Silver Throat and sing ... Tommy and Dickie Smothers breaking up the over-35 crowd in Las Vegas, not to mention the under-35's and everyone else in attendance... where Patti Harrison got that dress and deciding she must have made it herself... the fact that Van Morrison, formerly of Them, just may make it big on his own... the Sunshine Company winning the battle... Bobby Vee arriving upon the pop scene after quite an absence... the rumor about the Supremes really being true—Florence is gone

... the fact that if all goes as planned Ravi Shankar will make his television debut on the Smothers Brothers' Show... groups getting a "cleaner" image because it's almost impossible to get any grubbier... Brenton Wood making it a solid two... Donovan finally getting back into the States... why "All You Need Is Love" is so far

ahead of "Baby You're A Rich Man Now"... Jay and the Techniques doing all right with their apples and stuff... how come Wilson Pickett thinks Broadway is so funky

... how funny it is to watch the old ladies trying to look young but only succeeding in looking older ... since the Baja Marimba Band has released "Along Comes Mary" it's only fair that the Association release "South of the Border" and whatever happened to Tandyn Almer anyway?... whether or not James Brown will actually retire like he says he will... Simon and Garfunkel faking it pretty well ... Dave Davies having a considerable amount of beard on his face ... the Young Rascals making quite a name for themselves all over the world... why the Checkmates haven't made it as big as they should on record and deciding that talent is no guarantee of success ... the rash of "psychedelic movies" being reminiscent of the "beach party movies" we were treated to awhile back... whatever happened to clean-cut Beatles?

... what's going to happen with the Bee Gees and coming to the conclusion that it will all be worked out... why Peter, Paul and Mary are singing about the Mamas and Papas... how many radio stations are going to play the Association's "Requiem For The Masses"... when the Turtles are going to change members again... how nice it is to see more pop groups bagging big prestige club bookings

... Bobbie Gentry doing quite a bit for the South... what the Stones are going to do now and wondering if they'll be able to get work permits for the States... Fifth Dimension receiving more and more recognition... why Janis Ian hasn't released a follow-up to "Society's Child" since she's had plenty of time to cut one... why the Yardbirds aren't doing too well these days... who is Linda Jones?

KRLA ARCHIVES

Baez Concert Rebukes DAR

WASHINGTON — Joan Baez performed a concert before more than 15,000 people on the steps of the Washington Monument after the Daughters of the American Revolution refused to let her sing in their Constitution Hall.

In what has been called a great personal and musical triumph for Miss Baez, the folk singer invited the audience to attend the performance.

She was denied use of the hall because of her opposition to American participation in the Vietnam war and refusal to pay part of her income taxes in protest. Wearing a simple shift on the stage of the outdoor theatre, Miss Baez drew thunderous applause when she thanked the DAR for "all this publicity" and dedicated a song to that conservative organization. She then sang an old rock and roll song, "Little Darlin'," for the DAR.

"The main point where the DAR and I differ is that they feel the nation comes above all," she told the crowd. "The whole problem is that 123 nations feel the same way."

Pirate DJ's Cause Furor

LONDON — The arrival in London of seven disc jockeys who worked for pirate radio stations outlawed by the British government, was attended by more than 1,000 teenagers who crashed through police barriers and stormed aboard a train to welcome them.

The disc jockeys were employed by "Radio 266," a station specializing in pop music. The mob scene occurred when at the railroad station, the train carrying the dee jays arrived in London from the offshore platform they had used as a broadcast station.

A new law outlawing radio pirates knocked all the renegade stations off the air except for one. The law was designed to starve out the pirates, which operated from ships and platforms beyond Britain's territorial waters, by making it an offense to supply, work for or place advertising with the stations. The BBC, the state-owned broadcasting station, has a monopoly on radio.

The pirate stations had been very popular but, at the same time, dangerous. One pirate chief was shot, another drowned, and there were several battles for the abandoned war-time fortresses on stilts used for stations.

ON THE BEAT BY LOUISE CRISCIONE

Funny scene with **Adam West**, TV's Batman. He was stopped at a traffic light at the beach when he was hit from the rear by a car full of hippies. Said one observant hippie as he spotted West, "Oh man, did we make a mistake!"

Word arrives that the **Monkees** will shoot their movie in January and February . . . **Elvis Presley's** next film, "Stay Away Joe," began filming on August 10 . . . **Bob Vaughn** heads for New York on September 16 for **David McCallum's** wedding as well as an appearance on "Meet The Press" . . . **Monkees** grossed an estimated $55,000 for a one-nighter in the Minneapolis/St. Paul area . . . **Paul Anka** will close the year by headlining at the Hotel Fontainebleu in Miami Beach during the last week of December . . . **Mason Williams** and **Allan Blye**, writers for "The Smothers Brothers Show," are currently writing material for the **Association**.

Davis In Fall

I doubt whether **Spencer Davis** cares much for psychedelic lights after what happened at the Cheetah Club in Chicago. During the first of two scheduled shows at the club, Spencer moved back toward the center of the stage and due to the wild movement of the lights, etc., he misjudged his step and fell off the stage, gashing his left leg in the tumble.

A quick trip to the hospital as well as twenty stitches and Spencer was back on stage for the second show. That performance was unmarred by further accidents.

BILL COSBY, BOB CULP

A crowd of 700,000 jammed the streets of Chicago to greet **Otis Redding** and **Carla Thomas** who reigned as King and Queen of Chicago's 37th Annual Bud Billiken Day parade. Others riding in the parade included **Greg Morris** of "Mission Impossible" and **Ike Cole** (brother of the late Nat "King" Cole.) **James Brown**, **Aretha Franklin**, **Bill Cosby** and the **Supremes** are a few of the entertainers who have previously been featured in the parade.

Petula Clark has signed an exclusive one-year contract to become the radio-television Plymouth girl. Pet's appearances for Plymouth will begin with the introduction of the 1968 models and will include radio and television commercials.

You might be interested in knowing that **Don Grady**, of "My Three Sons," is also Luke R. Yoo of the Yellow Balloon. A bit of stage make-up, shades and long hair changed Grady's appearance to the extent that no one recognized him as Luke. However, now that filming on the series has resumed, the long hair, shades and make-up had to go and Luke R. Yoo lives no more. But Don Grady definitely does and has just been signed by Canterbury Records to produce, write, and sing on his own album.

QUICK ONES: Watch for **Ravi Shankar** to begin scoring American movies. Says the Indian sitarist: "I only want to do sensitive stories. But I don't want to keep it solely for Indian, classical music. I'll do anything from symphony to jazz, or my own music" . . . Everyone should have a buddy like **Bill Cosby** — the comedian/actor, now-turned-singer gave his pal **Bob Culp** a Cadillac for his birthday . . .

DAVY JONES

Four Tops say: "English audiences are more receptive than the ones here in the U.S. They appreciate more what you are — not what you should be" . . . **Simon and Garfunkel** are set to sing three of Paul Simon's compositions in the movie, "The Graduate" . . . **Pet Clark** has been signed for the Fred Astaire television special to be aired in February . . . **Don Ho**, the man so fantastically popular in Hawaii, will have his own hour-long TV special, "Hawaii," either very late in '67 or early in '68 . . . **Paul Newman** is very, very good in Warner Brothers' "Cool Hand Luke."

Cosby Starts Singing Career

Bill Cosby, the comedian, all of a sudden has some competition in the person of Bill Cosby, the singer. His latest album, "Silver Throat," has no comedy in it at all, as a matter of fact.

Instead, the popular comedian takes a stab at vocalizing, and the result may leave Cosby with a hit or two on his hands. Disc jockeys have been playing various numbers from the LP, and Cosby and his producers are waiting to see which get the most response for a possible single release.

Cosby has been flying from San Francisco, the scene of an "I Spy" episode, to Los Angeles, where he has been performing a song and dance routine at the Whisky A Go Go.

Radio Caroline Clashes With Labor Socialism

than T. Kyne

Who is James Wiggs Who is Ronan O'Rahilly? Who is President Roscoe?

Wiggs is the administrator of the Chris Borden School of Radio in San Francisco. Ronan O'Rahilly is the executive director of Radio Caroline, a pirate station on the English Coast. And Roscoe is the number one disc jockey in Europe.

How do these personalities relate?

They met each other this way.

Roscoe wanted to get into radio. In 1964 he enrolled in the Chris Borden School.

During his course in modern radio technique, Roscoe and Wiggs became good friends.

Pirate Radio

In the meantime, Ronan O'Rahilly was initiating a project which is not novel in the history of England but is novel in modern times. He was becoming a pirate. Although Queen Elizabeth (Henry's Daughter) would have smiled benevolently and encouraged him, he became as popular with the Labor Government as a Zulu is to a Boar.

(Turn to Page 15)

Moreno To Tour

Auggie Moreno, 19 years old is currently in the throws of beginning a promising career recording for Manmor Records.

With a single just released, and an album which will be out in just a few weeks, this full-time student of Bakersfield College is looking forward to the future.

In September, Auggie leaves for a thirty day tour of the West Coast and he is also waiting anxiously to hear whether or not he will be able to go on a tour of Vietnam for the United States Government.

"The Standel Sound"

"The Young Rascals"

Professional musicians throughout the world choose the "Standel Sound," the accepted standard for professional musicians who demand professional performance. (Dept. B)

A. P.A. Speaker Column Amplifier
B. P.A. Master Control with Reverb
C. Imperial Line Amplifier — Solid State, Dual Channel

Standel Solid State Music Systems
4918 DOUBLE DRIVE • EL MONTE, CALIF. 91731

ART INSTITUTE OF PITTSBURGH
47th Yr. Coed. 18 & 24 mo. Diploma Course. Commercial Art, Fashion Art, Interior Design, Begin. & Adv. Vet. Appd. Dorm facilities. College referrals for degrees. Free illus. brochure.
Earl B. Wheeler, Director
635 Smithfield St.
Pittsburgh, Pa. 15222

KRLA ARCHIVES

Beatle Meets Stateside Press

George Harrison flew to Los Angeles recently to take in a concert by Ravi Shankar at the Hollywood Bowl. The visit by the Beatle, who has been taking sitar lessons from the famed Indian musician, prompted a press conference at Shankar's school of music in Hollywood.

Sitting cross-legged by his musical mentor, George told reporters he started playing sitar because "I just happened to like this instrument. One obvious reason is because it's a stringed instrument."

"Indian music," George said, makes God come through in a spiritual way. It makes one more aware God can be put into sound. Sitar music is 100 percent spiritual."

Sitar Doubts

With incense burning and sitar music gently playing in the background, George expressed doubts about his chances of mastering the 19-stringed instrument.

"I want to learn a little Indian music and use it in our medium, but I'm not an expert sitar player. If I could sit down and play sitar properly I would. I don't expect to be a brilliant sitarist. I would have to concentrate on playing sitar, but there are so many other things to do, and I want to do them."

The press meeting inevitably got away from the sitar and on to more controversial subjects such as:

The draft. "The draft is diabolical. Anything to do with arms is terrible—a waste of time. If a person wants to volunteer, it's all right but nobody should be forceably made to kill."

Lucy?

Are the initials to "Lucy Is A Sky of Diamonds" an obvious reference to LSD? "It means LSD if you want it to be. Everybody interprets everything in his own way. That's the problem with the world. We didn't realize it could mean LSD until someone mentioned it to us."

George went on to say the song was inspired by something John Lennon's young son said about a girl he knew at school. Then he started speculating about his future.

"All I know is I'm going to carry on being me—I don't know where I'm going. Something else in life has more control over me."

Getting more down to earth, George said the Beatles will be putting out another movie sometime. "We've got a contract to make another movie, but when or how is completely up to us."

'It Depends'

When someone asked George what the Beatles felt about narcotics—a reference to their endorsement of the legalization of marijuana—he answered simply, "It depends on what you call a narcotic."

George put down, however, the idea that the Beatles should watch what they endorse since they influence so many people. "This stuff about the Beatles influencing people is a lot of bull," George said. "It's up to the person if he wants to be influenced—it's their choice."

On the subject of whether he or the Beatles would ever change, George said "Some people think it is a sin to at all. The whole point of life is change. Success has given me every material thing I need, and I realize I need something not material."

Non-Material

George indicated that his interest in Indian music and culture is a part of his effort to delve into the non-material aspects of life.

A day later Harrison flew to San Francisco unannounced and was discovered by some hippies strolling in Golden Gate Park with his wife, Patti. In a short time, several hundred fans were showering the Harrisons with peace buttons, posters, and flowers.

While in the park George picked up a guitar offered to him and performed a short, impromptu concert next to a small lake. He then headed down Haight Street followed like a pied piper by the orderly crowd.

George's reaction to it all? "Wow! It's really great if its all like this."

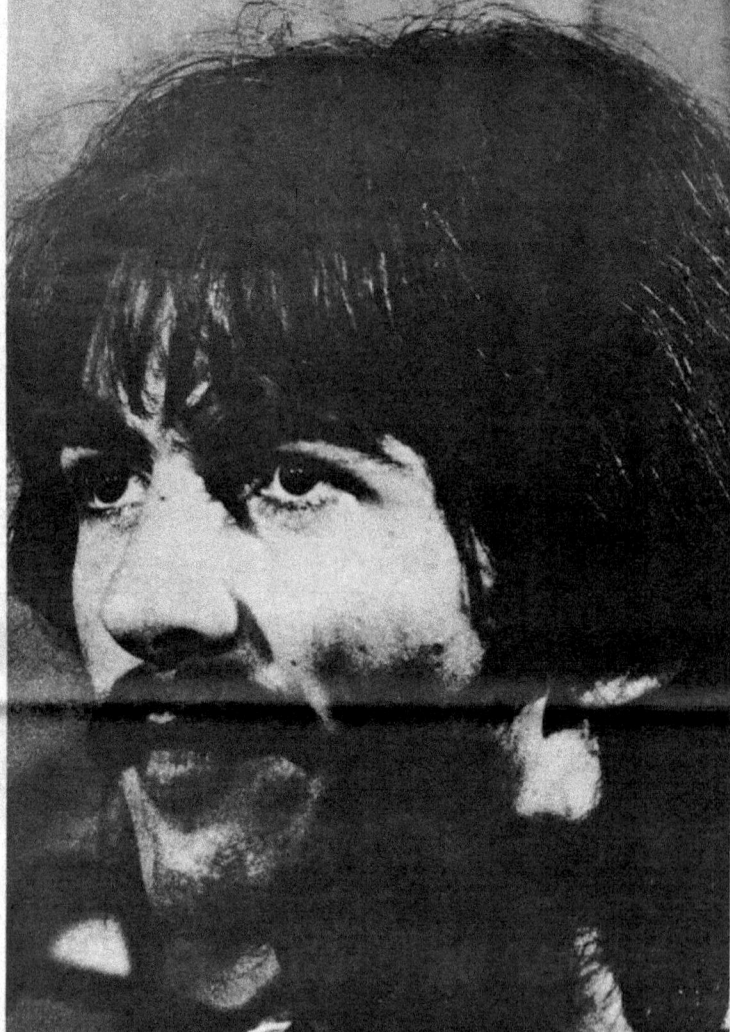

BEAT Photos: Ed Caraeff

"THE DRAFT IS DIABOLICAL," Harrison told Los Angeles reporters.

"I DON'T know where I'm going."

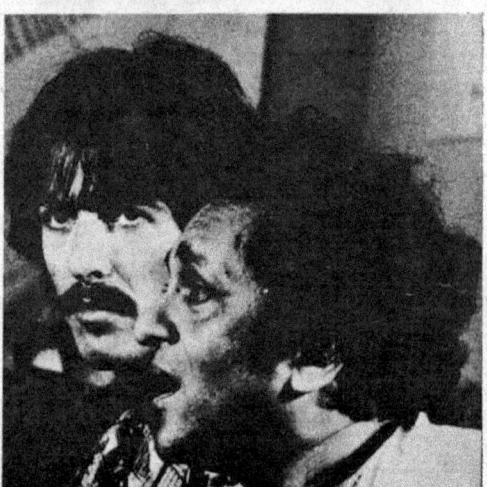

HARRISON SITS with his sitar teacher, Ravi Shankar.

KRLA ARCHIVES

JOHN SEBASTIAN has found a friend in the form of Humpty Dumpty.

JERRY YESTER (replacing Zal) and Steve Boone before a show.

...JOHN ON STAGE

...JOE BUTLER

...STEVE BOONE

JOHN AND HIS luggage wait to be boarded on New York plane.

Lovin' Spoonful Tell It All

A new man has been added to the ranks of the Lovin' Spoonful. He is Jerry Yester, brother of Association member Jim Yester. Jerry replaces Zal Yanowsky who decided to leave the group after two years, in search of greener pastures.

Leader John Sebastian explains the change this way. "This was a mutual agreement that we came to. Zally for a long time was feeling like he didn't know quite what to do, and a lot of the genius that he has wasn't really being put to work and he was kinda feeling like he was lying fallow. So we broke up in a friendly manner, and right now Zally is kind of feeling his way around, acting and directing and producting and trying to decide what he wants to do."

Joining a group that already has established a style and an image is a difficult undertaking, but Jerry Yester with his flaming red hair is taking it all in stride.

"Well, the main difficulty was changing what I'm doing. Just getting adjusted to the new routine, and to the new idea of what I want to do for the time."

How did Jerry meet up with the Lovin' Spoonful?

"About the time they got together I was playing with a group in the village and we even played at the Night Owl together, as a matter of fact. So I've known them the whole time they've been together.

"I am very familiar with the songs and I've seen them quite a bit on stage so that part of it is not really that difficult for me."

Yester is a native Californian and grew up in the suburbs of Los Angeles.

"I grew up here in Los Angeles, went to grammar school in Burbank, Notre Dame High School in Sherman Oaks, and a semester and a half at Glendale College in Glendale.

"I started out singing with my brother in 1960 and then he left to join the service and I joined a few groups and I sang with the In-Group, then a lot of folk groups and I ended up with the Modern Folk Quartet which later became Modern Folk Quintet. When that broke up I started producing records; I produced the Association's second album along with Tim Buckley."

Traveling around the country is a must for any pop group except the Beatles, but this aspect of the pop business doesn't phase Jerry one bit.

"As far as traveling goes, the MFQ did a lot of traveling; we did something like 300 college concerts and a lot of club dates and stuff. So the traveling and the concert situation really isn't a surprise, its just more-or-less back to the old routine, the old grind, as far as traveling goes

"The concerts themselves are a great deal of fun, you know. A great source of something or other, I haven't figured out what yet.

"I prefer writing to anything else, so whatever I can do that will give me the most opportunity to write, I prefer to do. With Buckley for instance I had the opportunity to do a lot of writing and with the group I think I will be able to too."

The other members of the Lovin' Spoonful are more than happy with the addition of Jerry Yester.

Joe Butler states the difference between Jerry and Zal.

"Well, Zal is a very distinct kind of personality and it's really, well, he has the ability to turn people on and to make up little games of things, you know. And that's a lot of fun, but it also can be very hectic.

"Jerry is more easy going, and Jerry and I, we've all known each other for a number of years and we've always been very friendly. That's one of the reasons we wanted Jerry to work with us, because he's a very talented musician and singer and also because we thought that within a group situation he'd really work out fine, and it's really great. A 21-gun salute for Jerry Yester."

Performing the same material with the same people for a number of years can get to be a drag. The enthusiasm of both the audience and the performers begins to wane. Although this hasn't happened to the Lovin' Spoonful, they are aware of the problem and they fight it continually. Now with the addition of Jerry the problem seems to be lessened.

"Keeping the level of performance up is difficult when you do the same material for a couple of years, but if you always keep a fluidness about it you can re-arrange things and change things," states Joe.

"And now with Jerry in the group its a new personality and a new head to work off of and reflect off. That's very stimulating.

"Right now we're going through a period of growth you know. We had gone about as far as we could go with the four people we had been working with, and now there's a new four people in effect.

"Looks like we're over the worst part of it getting the basic show together took a few days, but it's just a matter of grooving with it."

an INfinite assortment of **posters** the world's largest collection

over 600 different designs — rock, psychedelic, personality, art nouveau, and others ad infinitum

Seper Co.

5273 Tendilla, Woodland Hills, California 91364

GREAT NEW TALENT!
AUGIE MORENO
ON
A GREAT NEW LABEL
MANMOR RECORDS
"Very Special Love" # W.B. 2044
B/W "She's Got The Magic" # W.B. 2045

Personal Management — Manuele Bros.
Prod. Hollywood, Calif.
PO Box 349

KRLA ARCHIVES

BEAT EXCLUSIVE
Mamas And Papas Speak Out

The group that was mainly responsible for the amazing success of the Monterey Pop Festival was the Mamas and Papas. Leader John Philips, along with his wife Michelle, and producer Lou Adler worked constantly to make sure that the festival would be a successful venture, both musically and emotionally. Cornering the group in one of their more quiet moments, these four unusual performers spoke openly about the Festival, their future careers, and Mama Cass's new baby.

With all the work that went into the Festival, does John want to get involved in next year's efforts. "I suppose there will be a Pop Festival next year. We all hope so. It was a lot of work for us to be involved with, and for our producer, Lou Adler, and we would prefer someone else to do it next year.

"I think the only people who probably could do it would be perhaps the Beatles in Europe because they can invite all the acts and everyone would show up as they did in Monterey and perform in the same manner.

In Europe
"I would like to see it held in Europe next year myself. As far as improving on the Festival, I think that the physical function of the Pop Festival went very well, and that the only thing that could be improved on would be the programming and other things like that."

Unknown to most people, John Philips attended the United States Naval Academy after graduating from high school. Why did this unconventional young man choose Annapolis? "I went to the Naval Academy straight from high school. My father had been a career officer in the Marine Corps for 20 or 30 years. I had won a scholarship there and so I went.

"I was there about 14 months, I guess. As soon as I was there I realized that I was a misfit. And everyone else realized I was a misfit. It was a terrible situation, but I got hurt playing basketball and I got a medical discharge. It was one of the happiest days of my life."

All of the Mamas and Papas are extremely close to their producer, Lou Adler. John had nothing but praise for the young man who helped create the sound and the image of the group.

Best Producer
"Well, Lou Adler is probably the finest producer, I think, in the world right now. Lou has an extraordinary talent for being able to pick out all the good things you do and to let you know when you're doing the bad things. I guess the main thing about Lou is that he has impeccable taste in music.

"You can play almost any record in the world for Lou and he can tell you exactly where it will go on the charts, it's artistic qualities, right down the line, and just give you a run down on it.

"There are very few people right now who can do this. This is sort of the age of the specialized producer. Andrew Oldham with the Stones, Brian Epstein with the Beatles and Lou with us.

"Lou goes on the road with us 75% of the time and we're very close friends as well as associates. There are very few people who are actually able to do this and still have the ability to be a nice guy, but a bad guy too."

Writes Interpretation
The Mamas and Papas have stated that they don't like recording other people's material, but for very special reasons. John explains it this way, "well, it's hard to record a song that someone else wrote unless the writer himself has given you a tape of his interpretation of it. We're very fortunate in that I write most of our songs, and by the time we get to the studio with the song everyone in the group feels like they wrote it because usually I write a song that's interpreting them and so they feel they're the writers of the song as well as myself. So you get a writers performance and that's really important with any song."

John found it difficult to be both an administrator and a performer at the Pop Festival. This problem also exists throughout the year as business pressure forces the head Papa to turn from being a writer to being a businessman. "You can't turn a businessman off and the artist on because they require two separate qualities. So when you start to write again you find yourself writing songs about tax structures and things like that rather than about things you really want to write."

No Planning
The Mamas and Papas have acquired a reputation for being, if not lazy, then lethargic. To everyone's surprise they worked unbelievably hard to organize the Festival and to the amazement of the "people who know" proved themselves to be full of unending energy. However, when it comes to their careers, they seem to fall back into the first category, and seem incredibly without ambition.

Michelle states, "we haven't done much planning since the group really started. I think we just sort of let everything take its natural course. We just sort of sit around and wait for the next record or the next concert."

Although Michelle is not noted for her planning ahead she did comment on her future as an actress. "Well, I've been offered a couple of starring roles as we call it in the business. I was just called the other day to do Candy, but of course I turned it down because I thought it was dated.

"There is also some interest for me to do the Kazan (director/writer Elia Kazan) film, "The Arrangement," which I might do. I'm interested in movies, and I think after the Mamas and Papas I might do something of that nature."

John Lennon
It is common knowledge that Mama Cass is slightly enamored with John Lennon. "To be honest I have only met him twice and I think he's wonderful and brilliantly talented, as I think all of them are. I especially liked his sense of humor, that was the first thing that captured my interest when I first met him and was exposed to his writings and so forth. I am looking forward to meeting him again and talking."

Then, almost as an afterthought Cass revealed, "We haven't always met under the best circumstances where we can both be relaxed and talk, but I'm looking forward to that."

Cass is the proud mother of a little girl named Owen, which makes her officially a Mama. What does Cass think of this new addition to her life?

Wait & See
"Well my daughter is a giant among babies. She's only 3 months old and she only just started to be aware of things around her, and of being able to recognize people and everything.

"Of course I love her, but I don't know what's going to happen. I don't know what happens when babies get bigger, I just have to wait and see what happens, I have 20 or 30 years to figure it out."

Cass is also famous for possessing very strange items in her house. But Cass maintains that strangeness is in the eyes of the beholder.

"I have a passion for anything strange. I don't know what that means. I mean I know what passion means, I don't know what strange means. I like different things. I like things other than Graham crackers and things you see around us every day like Cheerios."

Asked about her giant stuffed rhinoceris, Cass stated, "Yes, I think my rhinoceris is pretty strange to other people, but it isn't to me. I'm pretty used to having her around. I named her Cynthia (after John Lennon's wife) in a moment of peak.

"I also have a strange cat, she is part Ocelot, but she's not strange to me. But then again, you know, it's all in your frame of reference. It's my environment, you know, I live in it, so it's not strange to me."

Nova Scotia
In their song "Creeque Alley" the Mamas and Papas immortalized the group called the Mugwumps. "All right, what was the Mugwumps like, imagine Zal, late of the Lovin' Spoonful, John Sebastian, Cass, myself, Jim Hendricks (not Jimmy Hendricks) and Art Blakey's nephew on drums and what were they like? I still don't know, I still don't know."

Although there has been a great deal of talk about psychedelic music today, Denny insists that he has not heard any.

"Well, psychedelic music, does that mean who's making the music or who's listening to the music. What does it mean? I've never heard any."

BEAT Photo: Chuck Boyd

THE MAMAS AND PAPAS have gone to the top; now they tell us where they're going from there.

"I have a passion for anything strange. I don't know what that means. I mean, I know what passion means—I don't know what strange means"... Mama Cass

KRLA ARCHIVES

THE JOHNNY MANN SINGERS

FASTEN YOUR SEAT BELTS

AND GET SET TO FLY

Up–Up And Away

Now Available At:
MONTGOMERY WARD DEPARTMENT STORES

KRLA ARCHIVES

THEY HOPE WE HAVE ENJOYED THE SHOW

Two Part Beatle History

By Jacoba Atlas

Once upon a time in the not so mythical sea-coast city of Liverpool, four young men emerged to carry the world along with their music. As in a fairy-tale, they were adored by all and fans eager for personal identification with their heroes clung to their clearly defined public images.

John with his glasses, books and caustic remarks was called the "clever one," he played the role well. Paul with his handsome face and charming manner was called the "sweet one" and fans who found the name Paul a bit too distant endearingly called him "Paulie." George with his high cheek bones and somber demeanor was dubbed the "quiet one," and Ringo with his puppy dog, soft eyes was called the "sad one." They wrote and played songs and called their corporate image—The Beatles.

They broke into the pop scene when it was floundering in poor songs and tired faces. Their songs were better than the other marketable offerings, and their charm and energy completely won over half the world—the younger half.

They wrote simply and sang with a driving beat accompaniment. "I Want To Hold Your Hand," "Please, Please Me," and "I Saw Her Standing There" all set the tone for the fairy-tale to unfold.

Comments

The adult population debated over their long hair, held their ears to the sound of their songs, and more or less generally ignored the Beatles except for condescending comments. Of course they were successes—never before, not even with Elvis—had there been such hysteria, but the charisma would not last; the craze would pass.

With their first movie, originally planned by United Artists to exploit the Beatles' recording popularity with a UA released soundtrack album, the powers-that-be began to take their first serious look at the Beatles and their music.

Such Establishment singers as Ella Fitzgerald and Peggy Lee sang tunes from the movie, "A Hard Day's Night;" and movie critics hailed it as a classic of its kind, likening the Beatles to the Marx Brothers.

As the critics dissected the film, they strengthened the image. John pulled off the wise cracks, Paul looked adorable, George stayed his quiet self, and Ringo emerged as a fine comic actor.

Cinematic Innovators

The film's significance to the motion picture industry was duly noted and Richard Lester, their director, was given an honored place in film hierarchy as a cinematic innovator. The fans, who knew the Beatles were marvelous all along, just enjoyed the exuberance and the honesty of the Beatles—no questions asked.

After "A Hard Day's Night" came a period which although important at the time, emerges in retrospect only as a bridge during which time the Beatles were finding their musical and emotional way. Certainly some interesting songs came out of this time—"I Feel Fine" with that prophetic opening chord, "She's A Woman" with its unique tempo, and "I'll Follow the Sun" with its folk quality; but most of their songs—although streets ahead of their contemporaries—are best kept in our memories.

John himself dismisses this period by saying, "the period I dislike in our career was 'Eight Days A Week' time ... we weren't ashamed of it, and I suppose it was right at the time, but something told me it wasn't us ... looking back we weren't in full control of the music. It was good at the time ... but it was something written for a period—a period of our growth."

Their search for their own musical identity led them to new experimentation and creativity—but they were still hampered somewhat by their image.

More Satire

They made another film, "Help," much more advanced and satirical than "A Hard Day's Night," but still tied to the fairy-tale image of the Beatles. John was again the "clever one," Paul charming, George progressing to an air of mystery and Ringo the comic foil.

The music had gotten better with the lyrics of the title song being especially interesting. With "Ticket To Ride," the Beatles produced a completely new combination of divergent rhythms.

Also the satire of "Help" was a little more subtle and irrelevent than in "A Hard Day's Night." Scotland Yard, religion, drugs, the State, medicine and various social orders all came under the attack of the Beatles, again with the help of Richard Lester. Perhaps their more sophisticated story and use of classical music to underscore the humor of the picture were indications of what was to come.

About this time Paul came up with a lovely-sad ballad "Yesterday," which brought the Beatles firmly into the established "adult" popular scene. Andy Williams, Nancy Wilson, and Perry Como—to name but a few—all recorded "Yesterday." Beatle fans throughout the world fell in love with Paul all over again as he sang solo to the accompaniment of cello and violins.

Eroding Image

Then came the album to end all albums—"Rubber Soul." With this exceptional offering the fairy-tale image of the Beatles was beginning to erode and more mature, more realistic characteristics appeared in their music. Paul's famous quote about not writing fifteen year old songs at twenty, was finally coming true.

Sophistication was beginning to set in. At twenty-five and twenty-three respectively, John and Paul were no longer writing "I'm Happy Just To Dance With You" or "She Loves You." Replacing them were such songs as "Girl" which John wrote after reading a book called *Pain and Pleasure* basing its theme on the Protestant Ethnic of work.

Electronic manipulation of sound in its most simple form could be heard in the simulation of a percussion instrument in the huge intake of breath as John sings the word "girl."

The repetitious rhythms gave way, as they had in "Ticket To Ride," to the more diverse tempos in "I'm Looking Through You" and "You Won't See Me" both of which also contain fine lyrics.

The ballads were well represented with "In My Life," a lovely ode to a present love, borrowing for its bridge from the 17th century baroque period of music, and "Michelle" which like its sister song, "Yesterday" has become a standard.

"Rubber Soul" brought the Beatles the intellectual recognition so often denied them before—despite the books and the movies. It also brought them into a controversy over the meaning of one of their songs, something which had not happened before.

There could be little debate over the message in "I Saw Her Standing There"—unless you want to take exception to the words "she was just seventeen, you know what I mean"—but the protectors of teen-age morality seemed to question just what was really going on in that room made of "Norwegian Wood." One critic went so far as to say it was about a man trying to seduce a lesbian.

When asked about "Norwegian Wood" both John and Paul said that it was simply about a girl who worked in the morning and a man who didn't.

Fidelity & Revenge

Whether that explanation satisfied anyone is doubtful, but the Beatle fairy-tale image of those four jolly lads from Liverpool was beginning to change—at long last. Add to that "Run For Your Life," a contemporary song about fidelity and revenge, and the world had the foundations for the new and brilliant work to come.

(To Be Continued)

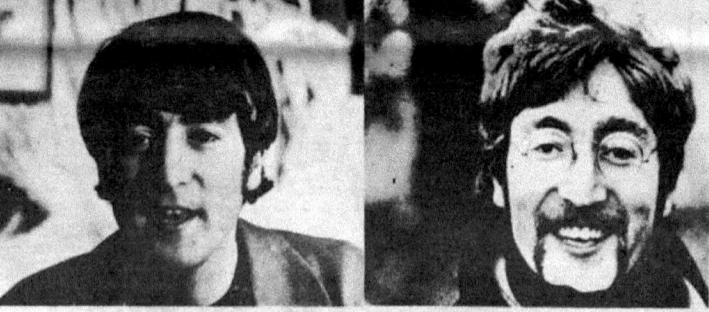

LENNON: Unchanged by success?

READY FOR the long ride to success ...

THE BEATLES in 1964, with one movie behind them and the world at their feet.

KRLA ARCHIVES

'WE'VE INFLUENCED OURSELVES FROM START'—FIFTH DIMENSION

There's a distinctive new sound in popular music, so refreshing and groovy you might call it fifth dimensional, and that's exactly what the people who are making this sound have appropriately named themselves. The Fifth Dimension, which has to be one of the hottest groups in the business, just sounds like nobody else, and they're a far cry from the Motown groove that most Negro groups are in now.

Some observers have called the Fifth Dimension a Negro Mamas and Papas, but the girls and guys in the group are quick to deny the tag.

"We've started something of our own," Marilyn, a beautiful UCLA graduate, told The BEAT. "We want to get away from what the other groups are doing. We're compared to the Mamas and Papas because our first hit 'Go Where You Wanna Go,' was a John Philips composition. Actually, the Mamas and Papas have had very little influence on us."

"That's right," said Billy, the youngest member of the group. "We've influenced ourselves from the start. We had a new sound in mind, and we spent a good five or six months trying to perfect it."

Vocal Experiments

The two girls and three guys got together about a year and a half ago, and were able to get on a tour with Ray Charles. Marc Gordon, Soul City general manager, was so impressed by the group he immediately signed them, and two great hits, the latest being "Up, Up, And Away," have quickly followed.

The Dimension has been able to come up with a sound that is both soothing to the ear and rhythmic, and it may set a trend for the future.

"Other rhythm and blues and rock groups are beginning to follow in our footsteps," according to Billy. "It's probably because we have a restful, relaxing sound that still has a good beat," said Florence, a former elementary school teacher.

General Change

"But, you know music in general is starting a new trend with songs like 'Windy' and 'Can't Take My Eyes Off You,'" Marilyn added. Over 12 other groups, including the Association and Brazil '66, have recorded the balloon song, and others are adding it to their repertoire.

A new single is due from the Fifth Dimension very shortly, but tune has been picked as yet. "We're working on four to six new ideas right now," Marilyn revealed.

But recording sessions will have to come in the spare time between an extensive tour and several tapings for national television. Plans right now call for spots on the Hollywood Palace, Away We Go, The Smothers Brothers, and the Dean Martin Show. A tour schedule will take them to Seattle, Baltimore, Vancouver, Massachusetts and Chicago.

Steady work like this—and highly profitable work as well—is something new to the Fifth Dimension members.

Florence, for example, had worked with some local dance bands and had sung in choirs most of her life. Her musical background was in a classical vein, however, with over nine years study of the violin. Watch for her to make her solo violin debut in the Dimension's next album coming out in September. Brenda Holloway, look out!

Marilyn, who graduated in business administration at UCLA, started singing seriously since her college days. Her interest in singing dates back to when she was 14, and her vocal stylings, she said, have been influenced by both jazz and pop music.

Said mustachioed Ron, "Opera is my field." For three years he sang with the Lincoln Symphonic Orchestra while majoring in music at Lincoln University. He finished third in auditions for the Metropolitan Opera Company's performances of "Showboat" and "Annie Get Your Gun." Ron has directed and sung in several gospel groups, including the Wings Over Jordan, but he considers his greatest thrill to have sung with Dorothy Dandridge and Nat "King" Cole.

When he was 5, Billy started singing in clubs and playing guitar for dance bands in St. Louis, where he, Lamont and Ron were boyhood friends. For a while he even had his own band. "We called ourselves Billy Davis Jr., and the All Stars—that name really shook St. Louis up," he said jokingly.

Baseball Hopes

For Lamont, singing was never an ambition, but baseball was. "I was in the Dodger's farm system and wouldn't even think of starting to sing, although my mother was always trying to get me to. One day, Ron who's my cousin, asked me to back him up for a recording. It took off, and we were in business. I've been learning more and more ever since." In addition to baseball and singing, Lamont has been a photographer for Harper's Bizarre, and was photographic director of Elegant Magazine.

With backgrounds as divergent as these, no wonder the Fifth Dimension are so unique. Like Billy says, "Our sound comes from a great variety of sounds." He couldn't be more right.

5TH DIMENSION — vibrations of their own.

EVERY MOTHER'S SON NOT A TYPICAL GROUP

With all the over-hip, psychedelic groups with their way-out pseudonymes going around these days, it's pretty refreshing to come across a group called Every Mothers' Son. And, at the risk of their careers being injured by a "clean" image, the name applies. These five guys are as polite, intellectually curious, and serious about their music as you could ever find, and their music has the good taste that you might expect from such a group of men.

"We're actually hip," said their spokesman Lary Larden almost defensively. "We're much more hip then the Beach Boys, for example."

Responsible

That may be true, but Every Mothers' Son represents a more responsible type of hippie, a type that's bound to last a long time. As an example, the guys don't smoke — tobacco or anything else won't have a thing to do with drugs.

"I think we're coming out of this drug scene," says bass player Sky Larsen. "Drugs provide a release with no reward—they sap you of your ambition."

The New York-based group also frown on the psychedelic movement in pop music, calling it an often distasteful novelty. "Some groups insult their audiences," said Sky, referring to the screaming, incoherent sounds of some of today's music makers. "I just don't see how people can stay and listen to them."

The boys said they want to appeal to as many people as possible, and not to a small in-group that might be drawn to a psychedelic sound. Said Lary, "Some people will accuse you of commercialism if you try to appeal to a lot of people. But, on the other hand, those groups that fight commercialism too much kill themselves. Because we want to be ethnic."

we're commercial. We just want everybody to enjoy our music."

Well, if two single hits and a top selling album are any indication, Every Mothers' Son are being enjoyed by just about everybody. Their success story is really a switch from the situation a couple of years ago when the boys didn't have enough money to get to rehearsals.

The group was the idea of two brothers, Lary and Dennis Larden, who had made the Greenwich scene for four years as folk singers. One night in a village coffee shop the boys heard a group called the Big Three, which featured a huge vocalist named Mama Cass Elliott. The boys never forgot that experience.

"It was incredible. There was just a wall of sound, and you thought you were listening to 40 people," Lary said. "We really began to realize what we could do, and at that we started away from ethnic."

The Lardens met an organist, Bruce Milner, and soon picked up bassman Larson. When drummer Chris Augustine joined, Every Mothers' Son was complete.

Strong Point

"The strongest point of the group is that, even though the guys have different tastes, we amazingly fit together beautifully," Lary said. The boys prefer to write and arrange their own music, because when they don't, "something's missing." "We want to do it all," said brother Dennis. "It means a lot to a group. If you get someone else's sensations, you can't form concepts of your own."

The boys are their own worst critics when it comes to studio recording sessions. They record, re-record, and record again until they are satisfied the music "doesn't fall down." Then, they play it back 8 to 10 times to make sure no part of the song is boring.

"We don't want to take the easy way out," said Lary knowingly.

EVERY MOTHER'S SON — Meet fans during their recent trip to Los Angeles.

KRLA ARCHIVES

Road Runner

The "Dick Biondi Road Show" really goes on the road starting August 20th. Price, Utah, Nampa, Idaho, Kicking Horse, Montana and Tillamook, Oregon are just a few of the cities Dick and his company will be visiting in an intensive 25 Job Corps camp tour.

The Job Corps, part of the Office of Economic Opportunity, provides training for young men and women between 16 and 21 at camp centers throughout the U.S. Many of the camps are remote and have had no entertainment since they've been open.

With Dick will be Gloria Jones whose hit record "Heartbeat" cannot be forgotten, Mickey and The Invaders, winners of the Teen Fair "Battle of the Bands" and a newcomer Calvin Payne, a California Job Corps member Dick discovered during a previous J.C. tour.

CASEY KASEM told his "Shebang" audience that he had only three more weeks before shaving. Next to Casey is guest Brenton Wood.

ICE HOUSE GLENDALE
234 So. Brand Ave. Reservations: 245-5043

Ends August 27
Bob Lind

Sept. 5 - 10
Standells

KRLA GETS BOB DAYTON

Disc Jockey Bob Dayton has joined the staff of KRLA, it was announced today by program director Reb Foster. Dayton, who will fill the 6:00 to 9:00 p.m. slot, was previously heard on WABC, New York.

THE GOLDEN BEAR
306 OCEAN AVENUE (HWY 101) HUNTINGTON BEACH

CHARLES LLOYD
AUG. 22 - 27

HUGH MASEKELA
SEP. 1 - 10

Reservations PHONE 536-9600 / 536-9102

ICE HOUSE PASADENA
24 No. Mentor — Reservations: 681-9942

Aug. 26 - Sept. 24
Bud Dashiell
(formerly of Bud & Travis)
and
Carol Hedin
— and —
Aeriel Landscape
(Forth & Main)

GAZZARRI'S #1 ON-THE-STRIP — 9039 SUNSET
GAZZARRI'S #2 — 319 N. LA CIENEGA
CR 3-6606 / OL 7-2113

NOW HAPPENING EVERY NITE
1. PACIFIC OCEAN
2. THE ABSTRACTS
3. OCTOBER COUNTRY
4. CHOSEN FEW
5. MUSTARD GREENS
6. SIOUX UPRISING
7. COLORING BOOK
8. SOMEBODY'S CHILDREN
9. DEARLY BELOVED
10. POPCORN BLIZZARD

MORE HAPPENINGS
MON. — DANCE CONTEST $500 GRAND PRIZE
TUES. — TALENT NITE
WED. — FASHION SHOW
SUN. AFTERNOON GROOVE IN — 4 P.M.

Did You Say, "Where's the Action"? What's This... Chopped Liver?!!

DOUG WESTON'S Troubadour
CR. 6-6168
9081 Santa Monica Blvd. at Doheny
★ HOOTENANNY EVERY MONDAY NITE ★

SEPT. 5-17
THE NITTY GRITTY DIRT BAND
AND THE
SUNSHINE COMPANY

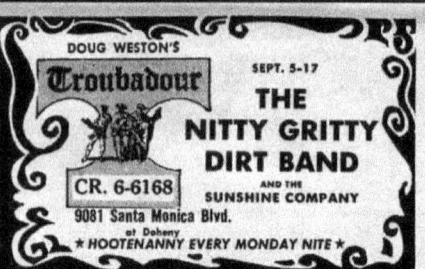

Revlon proclaims SPRING CLEANING TIME FOR SKIN!

Your skin will be fresh as spring time... with 'Natural Wonder's' new medicated Clean-up Crew!

[Revlon ad copy describing Foaming Facial Cleanser, Crystal-Clear Total Care Lotion, New Night Treatment Lotion, and New Under-makeup Lotion]

Medicated 'Natural Wonder' by Revlon
The first complete collection of medicated treatments and makeup.

AUGIE'S BACK!
WITH A GREAT NEW SOUND!
ON
A GREAT NEW LABEL

AUGIE MORENO SINGS!
"Very Special Love"
On ManMor Records #W.B. 2044
B/W "She's Got The Magic" #W.B. 2045

Personal Management — Manuele Bros. Prod.
P.O. Box 349, Hollywood, Calif.

KRLA ARCHIVES

EVERYONE KNEW THEY'D DO IT AGAIN!
JON & ROBIN's 'DRUMS'
c/w "YOU DON'T CARE" – AB 122

IS BEATING ITS WAY TO THE TOP OF THE CHARTS

Jon & Robin

THANKS TO ALL OF YOU GREAT PEOPLE
– WE LOVE YOU –
IT COULD NOT HAVE HAPPENED WITHOUT YOU

FOR BOOKINGS CONTACT:
BANKERS MANAGEMENT
AND SERVICES, INC.
825 OLIVE — RI 2-6111
DALLAS, TEXAS 75201

ABNAK
MUSIC ENTERPRISES, INC.
DALLAS, TEXAS

JON & ROBIN FAN CLUB
c/o ABNAK MUSIC
ENTERPRISES, INC.
825 OLIVE — RI 2-6111
DALLAS, TEXAS 75201

A PRODUCT OF ABNAK MUSIC ENTERPRISES, INC.

KRLA ARCHIVES

– Zip – Zip – Zip – Zip – Zip –

The Five Americans have a new one with extra Zip.

It's as easy as 1-2-3, except it's faster. That's the advice of the postmaster.

YOU GUESSED IT, THE TITLE IS

'ZIP CODE'

b/w "Sweet Bird Of Youth" AB-123

BY THE FIVE AMERICANS

WHO SAY...

'Thanks A Million To All Of You For Putting ZIP Into Our Lives. You're Great'

FOR BOOKINGS CONTACT:
BANKERS MANAGEMENT
AND SERVICES, INC.
825 OLIVE — RI 2-6111
DALLAS, TEXAS 75201

ABNAK MUSIC ENTERPRISES, INC.
DALLAS, TEXAS

THE FIVE AMERICANS
FAN CLUB
c/o ABNAK MUSIC
ENTERPRISES, INC.
825 OLIVE — RI 2-6111
DALLAS, TEXAS 75201

A PRODUCT OF ABNAK MUSIC ENTERPRISES, INC.

John Abdnor, Sr., President

KRLA ARCHIVES

Hits By The Original Artists!

See You In September

Keep On Runnin'

Little Latin Lupelu

Hang On Sloopy

Sweet Talkin' Guy

Chapel Of Love

Ain't Gonna Eat Out My Heart Any More

Leader Of The Pack

Psychotic Reaction

Dirty Water

SON OF KRLA — 21 SOLID ROCKS

Younger Girl

Solitary Man

The Duck

Farmer John

Land Of 1000 Dances

Hanky Panky

You Turn Me On

Little Girl

5 O'Clock World

The Boy From New York City

Thrifty CUT RATE DRUG STORES

Baby Scratch My Back

KRLA ARCHIVES

4 Tops Smash At Grove; Reveal Road To Success

By Sue Doughnym

HOLLYWOOD — The Four Tops reached another milestone in their long climb to acclaim last month, adding filet of soul to the menu at the famed Cocoanut Grove. It was only when they strayed from the familiar R&B bag that rapport was reduced.

Using opening night as the gauge, crowd reaction would peak and the Grove really groove when the Tops worked over tunes such as "Baby, I Need Your Loving," "Reach Out," "Bernadette," and "Seven Rooms of Gloom," supporting their harmony with infectious finger-snapping, hand-clapping and strutting.

Fear Complaints

An upbeat "If I Had A Hammer" had the Ambassador Hotel management fearing complaints from the local Noise-Abatement Society, but least rewarding were the pop tunes. These included "Girl From Ipanema," "Quiet Night," "Mame," and a medley comprising "Born Free, "Alfie," "Georgy Girl" and "Impossible Dream" in a turn that rapped a total 19 titles.

The Tops' Grove debut featured an introduction by Bill Cosby and local television coverage. A City Council resolution had made it "Four Tops Day" in Los Angeles. The night, too, certainly was theirs.

Relieve Frustration

Earlier, reliving the climb to success, Renaldo (Obie) Benson remarked, "We sang all the time to relieve that frustration of being closed in, crowded and bitter."

He was describing how it was, not long ago, when the Tops were growing up in Detroit and groping for escape.

"At that time we started there was a group on every corner," Obie said. "The way our lives were going at that point, we would have given anything to get out of there, man."

The boyhood friends, Abdul Fakier, Lawrence Payton, Levi Stubbs Jr. and Obie, bound by fraternal protectiveness, practiced a crude harmony. Their only formal training was the conviction that show business was the route out.

Starvation

"Our first professional job was Eddie's Lounge in Flint, Mich., and we made $75 for three days, split four ways less 10 per cent," Obie recalled. "We didn't know we could draw on our salary and we had no money, so we starved for three days.

"By then our expenses were $74.50, leaving 50 cents for gas."

They worked the best of the bad clubs, but they worked. And, after hours, they rehearsed for eight or nine hours more. They changed their name from The Four Aims, to avoid confusion with the Ames Brothers. They worked with Basie and Vaughn and Eckstein.

Eckstein Teaches

"We worked with Bill Eckstein for two years and he taught us everything," said Obie. "He taught us shading, how to sing loud and how to sing soft, breath control, how to sell a song musically and lyrically.

"He indoctrinated us in the business completely. We got a million dollars worth of education from Billy."

A couple of records went unnoticed. Then Motown Records produced a contract.

The Tops started climbing the sales charts three years ago, with "Baby, I Need Your Loving," and rarely have been off since.

"The secret is that we radiate from one person to the other," Obie suggested. "And we give our all. Anytime I don't feel like giving 100 per cent it comes back to me, what show business has given me.

"My kids will never come up like me and, you know, we plan as a group to devote more time to helping kids—all who don't have the facility to help themselves.

"We go to Watts or Harlem on our own time. We take records. We talk to them, we do anything just to give them some hope, man. It's a beautiful feeling."

In fact, it's Tops.

LEVI STUBBS — and there was only 50 cents left.

FOUR TOPS PLAYED the best of the bad clubs striving for success but talent finally won out.

Labor VS Radio Caroline

(Continued From Page 4)

He did something very original; and because he did it, he became rich.

He outfitted two ships, took them outside the legal limits, and began broadcasting. He broadcast rock.

He soon had a listening audience of 12,000,000 and all the advertising he could handle.

Roscoe graduated from school, bade Wiggs good-by, and headed for France. With his knowledge of American Radio and the French language (he had attended schools in France and Switzerland), he hoped to make it big and live in style.

He had no luck. He sent a tape to Radio Caroline. O'Rahilly liked it and hired him.

The English liked him. Soon his name was getting around and Radio Luxembourg which broadcasts out of Paris picked up on him and signed him to a contract. Roscoe went to Paris. Speaking French, interjecting Americanisms, and doing a top 40 American Format, Roscoe became a hit with the young set.

Wiggs recently went to Paris to visit Roscoe and explore the job possibilities for Americans in Europe. Roscoe touted him on O'Rahilly, who might be needing American D.J.s because the Labor Government of England was concocting some rare plans for pirate radio.

To England with Wiggs where he was welcomed by O'Rahilly. O'Rahilly told Wiggs about the bill that the Labor Government wanted to pass in order to eliminate pirate radio. The bill would prevent any and all British subjects from broadcasting from pirate stations, prohibit anyone from supplying these stations with materials or supplies or transporting goods and persons to and from the stations. In short, it would be illegal for any Britisher to conduct any sort of affairs with Radio Caroline.

"Do you think that the Bill will go through?" inquired Wiggs.

"It's hard to say," replied Ronan O'Rahilly. "The Torys will try to stop it because they identify with free enterprise. But the Labor Government will try to push it through."

And that is the story of Wiggs, O'Rahilly, and Roscoe, a modern and international story of radio.

Chances are, you like to go without socks. So, we've built *sockless* shoes for you. They're classic-looking sneakers made of our own special *leather*—tough, supple, secret-process steerhide that feels great and outwears canvas two to three times. Socklessnessmanship is here. So are Bare/Foot/Gear sockless leather sneakers. Come in, and put the two together.

ORIGINAL SOCKLESS SHOES

BARE FOOT GEAR

Socklessnessmanship.

©1967, WILLIE LOHAN & SONS, INC.

At these and other fine stores: Anthonie's, Mpls; Bell's College Corner, Asheville N.C; Bodin-Van Dorin, Des Moines; Buffums', Long Beach; Famous-Barr, St. Louis; Frank Stith, Winston-Salem; Frederick & Nelson, Seattle; Harold's, Norman Okla; Hamburger's, Baltimore; Hudson's, Detroit; J. Magnin, LA-SF; Earl Levitt, Williamsburg Va; Julius Lewis, Memphis; Nic's Toggery, Tallahassee; Phelps-Wilaor, LA; Rubenstein Bros, New Orleans; L.P. Shulman, Norfolk; Shoe Shack, Boulder Colo; Walls & Caverly, Syracuse; Yale Co-op, New Haven.

For information, write Bare/Foot/Gear, 522 Veteran, LA Ca 90024.

KRLA ARCHIVES

U.K. Pop News Round-Up
Stones, Beatles Closer

By Tony Barrow

"We love you all for the help from our friends to a happier end" is the slogan which accompanied the unexpectedly early arrival of a new single from THE ROLLING STONES, issued by Decca in the U.K. on August 18. My first striking impression after listening to "Dandelion" and "We Love You," the two Mick Jagger/Keith Richard compositions, is that the musical paths of The Stones and The Beatles have never been closer. It's common knowledge that Stones drop in to watch Beatles make records and Beatles take an equally close interest in the studio activities of Stones. Of course, we are unlikely to see the two groups named alongside one another on a record label since each holds a long-term contract with a different company. But the togetherness of feeling and direction is clear.

We Love You

"We Love You" is the gimmick deck and has the sound of a prison warder's footsteps, the clanky grind of keys turning in a cell-door lock. Of the two sides this is musically more in keeping with previous Stones' records. It features a wild lumpy backing, not a beautiful thing but certainly powerful in its impact. At the end there's a snatch of "Dandelion" played backwards.

Mini-Choir

On "We Love You" the theme of the lyrics runs parallel to that of The Beatles' most recent single. On "Dandelion" the actual presentation moves towards that of John, Paul, George and Ringo in that The Stones form themselves into some sort of mini-choir to provide vast high harmony effects behind Mick's simple, cleanly-delivered solo work. Of the two I prefer "Dandelion" with its brief, repetitive, familiar tune—one of the most commercial productions the group has made since "Get Off Of My Cloud" or even earlier.

The first LP album by THE PROCOL HARUM is on sale in America but NOT in Britain! Before the group issues an album in the U.K. a number of the original tracks will be scrapped and fresh material substituted. But a new single will be released on both sides of the Atlantic within the next few weeks. Probably title on the main side of the record will be the Gary Brooker/Keith Reid number "Homburg Hat" which has a fantastic piano theme to create much the same sort of hypnotic effect which organ playing gave to "Whiter Shade Of Pale."

Carrie To King

JULIET PROWSE stars in the West End stage production of "Sweet Charity" opening at London's Prince of Wales theatre in October... Under the new management of their record producer Ron Richards and publicity man Robin Britten THE HOLLIES now plan a three-week October trip to America to include college concert dates and several major television appearances. Group's "Carrie Anne" follow-up single is to be "King Midas" an original Hollie composition... Randy Newman's "So Long Dad" is latest MANFRED MANN single ... British vocal group and backing band will accompany BRENDA LEE during U.K. cabaret dates in November. ENGELBERT HUMPERDINCK (latest single—"The Last Waltz") goes out on a 40-day U.K. concert tour lasting from the final week of October to the early part of December. Songstress LULU will be a special guest star on most of the dates.

Airplane Movie

At Brian Epstein's Saville Theatre JIMI HENDRIX EXPERIENCE presenting precisely the same act which was considered "too wild" for MONKEES' U.S. tour... During October visit to Britain JEFFERSON AIRPLANE may appear in Terence Cooper movie entitled "Freak Out"... Agent VIC LEWIS who promoted THE MONKEES' London concerts earlier this summer off to Russia to discuss the first-ever East-West exchange of pop talent.

Prior to September cabaret dates in Tokyo DUSTY SPRINGFIELD vacationing in California with her manager Vic Billings... Many TV and radio interviews by BRUCE JOHNSTON in London timed neatly to coincide with Capitol's release of "Heroes And Villains" single in U.K.... Very last record broadcast by RADIO LONDON before it went off the air forever was THE BEATLES' "A Day In The Life"... GEORGE AND PATTI HARRISON flew from London to Los Angeles as "Mr. & Mrs. Weiss" but didn't escape battery of press cameramen. They borrowed their flight name from NAT WEISS, co-manager of THE CYRKLE, who looked after the couple in California.

Answer To Lucy?

JOHN LENNON'S fave new single of the moment is "Hole In My Shoe" created by former Spencer Davis star STEVIE WINWOOD for his new group TRAFFIC. You might say this is Stevie's answer to "Lucy In The Sky"... Revolutionary new concept of pop concert presentation planned by THE PINK FLOYD who will operate circus-style in a mammoth tent and put on a light show. Meanwhile the group is having remarkable success with their first U.K. LP album called "The Piper At The Gates of Dawn"... SPENCER DAVIS had stitches in his knee after falling from the stage of New York's Cheetah Club.

Week-long October stint for THE MOVE at San Francisco's Avalon Ballroom. By then you'll have heard their latest single "Flowers In The Rain"... Quote from NEW VAUDEVILLE BAND'S MICK WILSHER: "Hip groups sneer at us but we're more hip than they'll ever be!"... Once Britain's top teenage songstress HELEN SHAPIRO, now 21, marries in a few weeks time... From Fontana label the new SPENCER DAVIS GROUP moving to United Artists... Says ERIC BURDEN: "San Francisco will be the cultural center of the world in a couple of years. Liverpool was a fallacy—there was only one group, one center of energy. What Frisco is doing where Liverpool failed is to make the scene come to them."

Flower Festival

"Festival of the Flower Children" at Woburn Abbey, one of Britain's most famous stately homes, over August Bank Holiday weekend stars a host of top pop units including THE KINKS, THE ALAN PRICE SET and THE BEE GEES... One of the very last commercials broadcast by the now-dead RADIO LONDON advertised special mail-order records featuring the station's jingles!... Capitol just issued SCOTT McKENZIE'S recording of the Mike Hurst number "Look In Your Eyes" as a U.K. single.

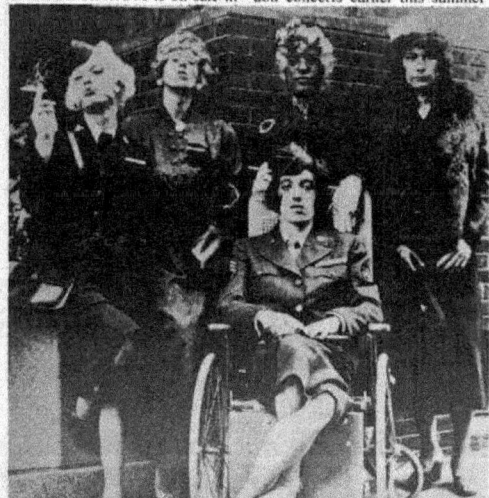
THE ROLLING STONES—sounding more and more like the Beatles.

Paul Revere

PAUL PROUDLY dusts his four gold LP's.

PAUL SEEMS to have something his collie wants.

JODY AND HER DADDY sit on the family Excaliber.

KRLA ARCHIVES

At Home And On The Firing Line

SON, DARRON tunes in his favorite show while Jody and papa Paul wait anxiously. *BEAT Photos: Gino Rossi*

PAUL REVERE — as outspoken as he is successful.

PAUL AND WIFE, SHARON, rest in back yard with family.

DARRON AND JODY try their hand at pop's hobby, Go-Carts.

By Greg Kieselmann

An interview with an entertainer, despite whatever "glamour" might surround him, can often be one of the dullest experiences around, dull because there are so many who are afraid to say anything. Talking with one can often sound like an interview with another since carefully packaged replies are an item on the market in the entertainment business. It's almost with a shock then, that you encounter someone like Paul Revere, the mastermind of the Raiders. Sincerity and frankness so pervade what he says that you almost catch yourself warning him, "Be careful what you say, Paul."

Revere's Concern

Revere, a man who grew up fast, running a barbershop at the age of 17, appears thoroughly domesticated in the surroundings of his beautiful home in L.A.'s San Fernando Valley. With a wife and two children, he has more things on his mind than the average pop singer. "I'm square," he says freely, disconnecting himself from the hippie generation. Yet Revere, whose appeal is basically to the teenybopper, is deeply concerned about today's young people, particularly over their infatuation with drugs and drug music.

"If drugs are a common thing in music, ads, clothes and our language, then your helping it. There's no point encouraging it. Kids are frustrated enough searching for answers. It's hard to have a responsible outlook at that age since kids always try to evade responsibility and not face reality. These things weren't available when I was a kid, but I might have taken them since you always have to have action at that time in your life. Ordinarily you outlive these frustrating periods, but I worry about the harm that can be done during this period if drugs get to your head.

"Ninety percent of the kids in this country have nothing to do with drugs, wouldn't know what you are talking about, or what the lyrics to drug songs mean. The number is minute but getting good press. The word gets around more now than when I was a kid. Now marijuana is talked about like beer was in my youth.

"Why announce banana recipes over television? Why print that morning glory seeds will give you a trip? Fifty percent will go out and try it. The adult world has been putting down drugs, but it turns right around and capitalizes on them. It can't be doing any good. If there's anything to get high on, kids will try it. I'm getting frustrated, there's so much of it in Los Angeles. I don't want to raise my kids here."

Revere is critical of the lyrics of some pop records and advocates a type of industry censorship as the possible cure for objectionable sounds.

"Some songs are obviously rank so you can't miss it; others talk in a hip way about drugs. Of course, any love song can be made dirty, or taken two ways, if you tear it apart.

A Suggestion

"It all goes back to the trade magazines. If records are picked for write-ups, the disc jocks will promote them. However, if the magazines legitimately listened to the records, they could catch anything obviously obscene or unfit to listen to. They could nip it in the bud by throwing the records in the waste basket, and the jocks wouldn't see them. People would then have to be a little more careful and a little less loose. What I can't understand is if the song is not in good taste, why write it? Why don't they have more respect for their fellow man? The only problem with the trade journal censorship, of course, is that they might go on a campaign and abuse their power. They shouldn't go on any kind of campaign."

Although the trend in pop music is leaning toward the electronic psychedelic sound, Revere said the Raiders' basic sound would not change. "If our producer, Terry Melchor, had some extreme plans, though, I wouldn't argue," he added.

Paul's personal bag is funky rhythm and blues. "I dig quality like Otis Redding, catchy melodies with lots of drive and no electronic gimmicks. If I had my way we'd add eight horns to the group and we'd probably starve.

"Everybody in the business right now is interested in looking for strange patterns and concepts. I personally dig hearing something and liking it. Some people take a nothing song and build and build on it electronically, trying to make it into a masterpiece. But 90 percent of the people like something as a whole and don't pick out parts and listen to patterns. Lots of time and money is being wasted trying to give class to rock and roll."

Revere, a well-known and respected businessman, has established a sizeable empire since he started the Raiders 10 years ago. As his business activities take more and more of his time, an obvious question is how long he will continue to record.

"I never will retire, I think. I dig the business and will always be involved in it, less on the stage and more with the business activities. I enjoy being involved with huge sums of money. It's fun to hold on to your money and keep it from the crooks. I love to see talent and hate to see it get gypped. That's why I would like to expand our organization and take on other acts and give them the same advantages we have.

Like Brian?

"In two or three years I'd like to get the organization to the point where I don't have to go out on the road. There are more important things to do at home or working in the background. Let's face it, I'm the organizer of the Raiders, not the star. I could do more good offstage than on stage, but right now, I'm doing both. I'm spreading myself out too much. Brian Wilson removed himself from the road and concentrated on what he did the best. When things get straightened out I want to do like Wilson."

With Paul's enthusiasm and good sense, you just hope he'll never quit the business.

KRLA ARCHIVES

Stevie Wonder — Music And Soul

It's hard to believe, but Stevie Wonder, the 12-year-old musical prodigy who thrilled audiences with his outasite version of "Fingertips," is no youngster anymore. Stevie's now all of 17, ready to enter college, and one of the real pros of the music business.

Since "Fingertips," his first million seller, Stevie's recorded a succession of hits including "High Heel Sneakers," "Castles in the Sand," "Uptight," "Nothin' Too Good For My Baby," "Blowin' In The Wind," and "A Place In The Sun." His style has matured with his years, as exemplified in Stevie's latest smash "I Was Made To Love Her," but this maturity hasn't hurt him a bit. As a matter of fact, Stevie seems to be riding the crest of his success.

More Than Sing

The Motown recording artist can do more than just sing. Stevie can play with real soul, the piano, organ, drums and harmonica, and usually backs himself up with at least one of these instruments, if not all of them during a concert.

But what does "soul" really mean to an exponent of it like Stevie?

"Soul is a feeling," he believes, "it's not soul music, it's music that has soul in it. John Lennon and the Beatles have soul in what they are doing. It's not rhythm and blues, but it is English soul. Soul goes back, back, back," says Stevie hitting his heart.

Stevie, who has been blind since birth, has had few problems coping with the troubles which face every teenager, but Stevie isn't an average boy. He has perceptiveness and musical know-how which you might expect from a 30-year-old.

University Next

In January, Stevie will graduate from Michigan State School for the Blind. He then plans to follow up his studies at the University of Southern California where he will major in composing and arranging.

A man responsible for much of Stevie's scholastic success is his tutor, Ten Hull, a graduate of Michigan University who holds a special degree for teaching the blind.

Stevie's traveling companion, Hull, classifies his pupil as a "dedicated and adept" student with an unquenching desire for knowledge.

Stevie's early development is probably most obvious when you consider he signed his first record-in contract with Motown when he was nine. And he has been moving at a fast pace ever since. Last year Steive was sighted by *Billboard Magazine* as one of the nation's top recording artists and with his latest hit, "I Was Made To Love Her," he is a likely selection for that distinction again.

STEVIE STROLLS with Rita Ross, Diana Ross' sister

STEVIE & RITA study on grass of Wayne University

AND THEN it's off to the library for more study.

The BEAT Goes To The Movies

'BAREFOOT IN THE PARK'

Jim Hamblin

This has to be one of the easiest choices of the year. It's got good direction, good photography, and one of the best casts ever. Currently in exclusive runs in most areas, it's worth hunting down.

Leggy Jane Fonda is revealed with considerable regularity for a closer inspection of her charms, and we thoroughly approve.

Co-star Robert Redford was first seen as the railroad agent in "This Property Is Condemned," and proves himself an excellent comedy actor. The story is about a newlywed couple, which already gives writers enough gags for an hour.

By expanding the action of a very successful stage play, the producers have found a goldmine.

Special note should be made of Charles Boyer, who plays an aged beatnik in the upstairs "apartment." The only way to get to his pad is up a steel ladder.

Probably the most hilarious performance is by Herbbrt Edelman, who was happily chosen to re-create his stage role as the telephone man. You have to *see* it to believe that anything could be that hilarious.

And so as our newlyweds settle down to their first night at home, with snow drifting in the broken skylight, we leave the rest to you, and our delightful memories.

HAPPY Robert Redford

PUZZLED Charles Boyer

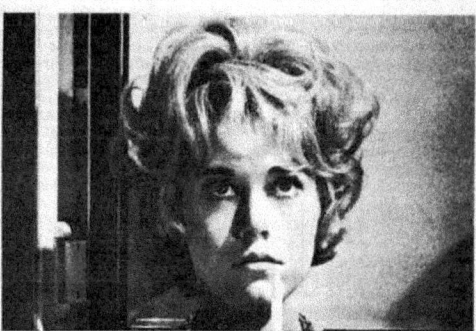

A GLIMPSE of Fonda

JANE FONDA is a newlywed with a definite problem.

KRLA ARCHIVES

Lou Rawls A Misfit?

In a world which insists upon putting people into categories and leaving them there, Lou Rawls is a misfit. He simply will not stay in one bag for long. After kicking about for five or six years, Lou is back again, displacing Frank Sinatra in popularity polls, packing them in at Carnegie Hall, sending the teen-age population to their record stores to buy "Dead-End Street," and impressing the hippie population at the Monterey Pop Festival with his good "Soul" music.

Lou started out singing in Pandora's Box in Los Angeles, and in any club that would hire him in his native Chicago. His main style was the Blues, but for years, Lou couldn't get a hit, and then suddenly the pop music listener discovered Lou Rawls. Why this discovery? Lou has his own opinion as to the reasons for his new found popularity. "I think it's because much of today's rock music was derived from the Blues. Acts like the Beatles and Rolling Stones are singing the Blues and they've shown that the kids not only can dance to it but they dig the sound as well."

"Five years ago, I was singing the same stuff at Pandora's Box on the Sunset Strip in Hollywood. The kids were digging it then and packing the place. But it took groups like the Stones and Beatles to really put it across. They paved the way for Blues, made people aware that the Blues songs make for good listening and dancing."

Carnegie Hall

But Lou is not just popular with those who listen to pop music or "soul" music. His appeal has gone even farther than that. At Carnegie Hall, and in nightclubs throughout the country, Rawls has been playing to standing room only and sold out sets. He has reached the over-thirty, sophisticated people of this country.

This popularity in the night-club circuit is also a new found blessing. Only a few months ago, Rawls had finished what he hopes is his last tour of what he calls the "Chitlin' circuit" of small Negro nightclubs in San Francisco, Cleveland and St. Louis. There he played to audiences that didn't listen, and it was through that experience that Lou developed his quick fire monologues dealing with every subject imaginable; monologues that have become so important in his present success.

Today, savoring the sweet life that fame and money has finally brought him, Lou has nevertheless not forgotten his background and his struggles to reach the top. He knows the dangers of "living off the street" first hand, and has become very active in such programs as "Teen Post" and "Operation Cool-Head," all designed to keep kids out of trouble and the "arms of the police."

Free Concerts

For almost every sell-out concert Lou has played, he's also staged one free one for the kids. Thee were concerts in Cincinnatti, and in Los Angeles as well as in other cities throughout the country.

He knows what he is singing about and knows with what kids from slum areas are faced. He is also aware of the enormous change in American society and emphasizes that kids have to change too. "When I was a kid, you'd hang around the corner and maybe make it. Survive with your 'mother' wit. Not today. Today you've gotta get it out of books, or else you're going to wake up one day and wonder, 'where did it all go to'."

Lou Rawls knows where he's come from and where he's going. The world at large is only too happy to come along.

SUBSCRIBE!
— See Page 24 —

The Airplane Takes Off

The Jefferson Airplane takes off amid whirling lights and the shattering roar of six musicians. The run-way is the Fillmore Auditorium in San Francisco, where the group first formulated their present style that has sent them straight to the top of the pop field.

The Airplane is the leading exponent of the San Francisco Sound; a combination of blues, folk, jazz and whatever else comes to the minds of the musicians. The Airplane is not alone, San Francisco has also been the launching pad for such groups as Moby Grape, The Grateful Dead, The Allnight Apothecary, The Quicksilver Messenger Service, Big Brother and the Holding Company, Country Joe and the Fish, The Loading Zone, and the Yellow Brick Road.

The San Francisco Sound is a free-wheeling endeavor, the outcome of improvisation rather than rehearsal and spur of the moment excitement rather than professionalism. It encompasses particularly every form of music from bluegrass and Indian ragas to Bach and jug-band music. There is no structure involved; the emphasis is on the spontaneous, and songs run on and on, sometimes for over twenty minutes.

But it is not just the music that makes the San Francisco Sound, it is also the total environment. At the Fillmore and other such auditoriums, blinding strobe lights flash in rhythm with the music, the wall seems to squirm with protazoa-type patterns, the 'audience' wears their newest art nouveau and mod fashions, and the aim is total submergence in what is happening. One Fillmore regular puts it this way, "fight it, stay aloof, and critical and you'll suffer one of the most painful headaches imaginable."

The Airplane seek this communication in their music. Paul Kantner, lead singer, believes they have achieved their goal.

"IT DOESN'T MATTER what the lyrics say, or who sings them. They're all the same. They say 'Be free.'"

BRINGING THE BEE GEES INTO FOCUS

By Tony Barrow

It's high time I helped stamp out the rest of the ridiculous rumors about THE BEE GEES. At first many Americans believed that "New York Mining Disaster, 1941" was a Lennon-McCartney composition recorded by The Beatles who, for unstated reasons, wished to conceal their true identity.

Well, that rumor was squashed via the June 17 issue of BEAT which contained my special background story on the group's incredible history of teenage TV and chart success. I believe the photograph I used to accompany my piece for BEAT was the first of the group to be published in America.

Those who are not lucky enough to be numbered amongst BEAT's constantly increasing readership were to see the living proof that THE BEE GEES exist when the group spent the first couple of weeks of July making a promotional tour of America. By now the foursome had been expanded to quintet strength by the recruiting of Australian guitarist Vince Melouney.

But other rumors have persisted. Like: John and Paul produced "Every Christian Lion Hearted Man Will Show You," one of the stand-out tracks on the 14-title Atlantic album called "The Bee Gees First." Like: The album track "In My Own Time" has the Beatles singing and playing alongside the Bee Gees. Like: Paul McCartney travels everywhere with the Bee Gees because he is the group's secret record producer.

So here are the facts. *The Beatles and The Bee Gees have never worked together. "Every Christian Lion Hearted Man Will Show You" was written and arranged by the three Gibb brothers — Robin and Maurice (17-year-old twins) and Barry (19) — who form the core of the Bee Gees. This and all the group's other recordings used as co-producers Australians Ossie Byrne and Robert Stigwood. Stigwood, Brian Epstein's new joint managing director at Nems Enterprises, is the personal manager of The Bee Gees. Despite the fact that many fans telephoned the Bee Gees during their American tour and asked to talk to Paul McCartney, the Beatle was not traveling in the party and has no professional connection with the group.*

It's an established fact that The Beatles admire the songwriting of The Bee Gees and have praised their records. But, apart from off-duty moments in the London clubs, the two groups don't even see much of one another.

Of course there is no denying that there ARE certain similarities between the music made by the two groups. Barry Gibb can sound a lot like John Lennon at certain moments on certain records. What's more The Bee Gees are displaying such remarkable musical progression that one London reviewer sub-titled their album "Son of Revolver!" a thought which The Bee Gees receive with mixed feelings.

It goes without saying that any freshly famous pop group would be flattered and proud to be compared alongside the work of the world's most important quartet.

At the same time I can vouch for the claim of the Bee Gees that Barry, Maruice and Robin Gibb were working together even before The Beatles gained their initial success in Hamburg. I have listened to the earliest Australian-made records produced by The Bee Gees when they were operating as a trio. Vocally there was that same slight but undeniable similarity between Barry Gibb and John Lennon. So I'm quite convinced that the whole thing is coincidence and not carbon-copying.

Perhaps the closeness of their hometowns has something to do with it. The Gibb brothers were born and raised in Manchester, no more than 30 miles from Liverpool. The distinctive local accents in both cities have always shown definite similarities. As a Liverpudlian (Scouser if you prefer the word) I can tell the difference but a man from any other part of Britain might have difficulty in separating the Liverpool and Manchester accents.

††ROBERT STIGWOOD refused numerous tour offers for THE BEE GEES while he was in America with the group. He insists that they should not undertake any series of stage shows, as billtoppers or otherwise, until the early months of 1968 when they can hope to have behind them four or five major American hits. Robert's current plan is to present The Bee Gees in their first U.S. concert at New York's Carnegie Hall.

KRLA ARCHIVES

The Best Play
The Very Best

Lawrence Welk and Billy Vaughn

Superbly Perform

The Hits

Of The Decade

AVAILABLE AT YOUR

KRLA ARCHIVES

HAPPENING

George's House Psychedelic

LONDON — George Harrison has followed John Lennon's lead in painting his Rolls Royce psychedelic colors, but has done him one better — George has painted his house with green, red, yellow and orange psychedelic designs.

Crewe To Pen Picture Score

Bob Crewe has been signed to compose the score for Universal's "What's So Good About Feeling Good?" which stars George Peppard and Mary Tyler Moore. Crewe, who produced the current smash, "Can't Take My Eyes Off You," recorded by Frankie Valli, will be doing his first motion picture score.

Home Jukebox

A new device is on the market now which can program up to 40 hours of music from a remote point. Made by the Seeburg Corp., the world's largest jukebox producer, the machine can store up to 50 LPs in an upright position. It's operated by dialing the storage number of a record on a conventional telephone dial which puts the record's number into the console's "memory bank." Then, by pressing the "Play" button, the memory system electronically has a vertical tone arm move through the line of upright records, playing any side of the cut you ordered. You'll have to dig into your piggy banks, though. The device costs from $795 to $1,500.

KING GRADUATES

LONDON — British pop star Jonathan King has graduated with honors from Cambridge University. He was awarded a Bachelor of Arts degree in English literature.

He is currently at work on a novel which he promises will contain some explosive material. King is also negotiating to have a full-page column in a prominent British magazine. The anti-drug stand he has taken in his music and television appearances have made him very popular with a number of leading British officials.

HIPPIES FORM OWN THEATRE

SAN FRANCISCO — An old movie house located in the heart of San Francisco's Haight-Ashbury district has been converted by hippies into a theatre of performing arts.

The first performance in the new Straight Theatre consisted of a play and music by a folk-rock band. Twenty stockholders pooled their money to buy the old Haight Theatre, according to Hillel Resner, a 25-year-old college dropout who is director of the new theatre.

Harum Split

Procol Harum has lost two of its members — guitarist Ray Royer and drummer Bobby Harrison have left the group.

They have been replaced by Robin Trower on lead guitar and Barry Willson on the drums. The Move manager has been appointed co-manager of the group.

The split was described as amicable, although the disagreement which led to the split was over group policy.

Knight Inks

NEW YORK — Terry Knight has signed an exclusive writing contract with Merlin Music, Inc. Terry, who wrote his current single on the best-seller charts, "Love, Love, Love, Love, Love," also penned eight of the twelve tracks on his latest LP, "Reflections."

Terry's personal manager, Bob Coe, said Terry has composed a special song called "Hang Ten," for use as a promotion tie-in for a new teenage cosmetic.

Dirt Band A Hit

The Nitty Gritty Dirt Band returned to their West Coast base after three very successful weeks at New York's famed Bitter End Club in Greenwich Village. During their stay, the Band also did a gig for the "Tonight" Show

Sinatra Awards

Voices which "The Voice" contributed to train gave their first concert at the University of California at Los Angeles. Frank Sinatra underwrote the cost of annual awards totaling $5,000 for music majors at UCLA's college of fine arts. Two first prizes of $2,000 each were awarded to a vocalist and an instrumentalist, with second prizes of $500 in the same categories.

TJB Gross $162,000

Herb Alpert and his Tijuana Brass walked out of the Northwest recently some $162,000 richer after only three nights work. The group starred in one-niters in Portland, Vancouver and Seattle.

Another Hit For Johnny

Although it's getting a bit repititious, Johnny Rivers has another hit. Of course, it's the old Smokey Robinson song, "Tracts of My Tears," and Johnny sounds better than ever on it. Things seem to be getting repititious because the New York born, Baton Rouge bred phenom has been turning out chart-busters continuously since his first hit, "Memphis," was recorded in 1963.

Along with "Tracts," Imperial Records has released a new Rivers LP, "Rewind," which is climbing the pop album charts. The LP includes the current hit plus Johnny's last single, "Baby, I Need Your Lovin'." The flipside of "Tracts" contains a medley of five tunes from the "Rewind" album, which is an unusual twist.

To say Johnny has done well for himself is an understatement. Just recently he signed a long-term contract with Imperial Records, formed his own publishing company — Johnny Rivers Music — and started Soul City Records. Producing records, however, is just a favorite hobby, Johnny says.

New York, Vegas

Stints at New York's Copacabana and the Riviera Hotel in Las Vegas and guest spots on television shows like "Hollywood Palace" and "The Ed Sullivan Show" have guaranteed his place as one of the top male vocalists in the country.

But despite his fabulous success, Johnny hasn't forgotten his lowly beginnings, and lowly they were. About his early life in Baton Rouge, Johnny says, "We weren't poor, we were double poor." To pick up some money during his school days Johnny would play guitar with his own group at school functions and at local clubs. Working at night, he would come to high school the next day and usually end up falling to sleep in class.

Summers In East

When he was fourteen, Johnny started spending his summer vacations in the Eastern musical capitals of New York and Nashville. On one of these excursions he met the famed R 'n R promoter Alan Freed, who persuaded Johnny to change his name from Ramistella to Rivers.

Later, in Nashville, Johnny met Roger Miller, who was also an unknown then, and the two worked together writing songs and cutting demonstration records for Elvis Presley and Johnny Cash, among others.

But Johnny's successful career really began when he traveled to Los Angeles in 1960, although you'd never know he would be a recording star by the way he started. He had made a decision to give up singing and go into composing strictly, and he did fairly well, writing the Rick Nelson hit "I'll Make Believe."

Los Angeles had really made little impact on Johnny's life until the owner of a small Sunset Strip nightclub called Gazzarri's persuaded Johnny to stand in for a few nights when a scheduled jazz combo copped out. With only a drummer as accompaniment, he became an instant success. Johnny would just sit on a stool and play and sing, but his name got around quickly, and soon Hollywood stars were crowding in to see this new celebrity.

He then took an offer to headline the Whisky A Go Go, L.A.'s first discotheque, and Johnny and the nightclub made each other famous. Since this 1963 debut, he has copped six gold records for sounds as diverse as country and western, motown, eastern rock, and tender ballads.

After his first hit, Johnny bought a house in Los Angeles where he and his mother and father now live. Johnny really bought the house for his parents. After all, it was his father who started him on the road to success, teaching his small son how to pick a guitar and carry a tune on the poor side of Baton Rouge.

STRASSMAN SIGNS

HOLLYWOOD — Marcia Strassman, whose first single, "Flower Children," sold over 55,000 discs in Los Angeles and San Francisco alone, has been signed to a multi-picture contract.

KRLA ARCHIVES

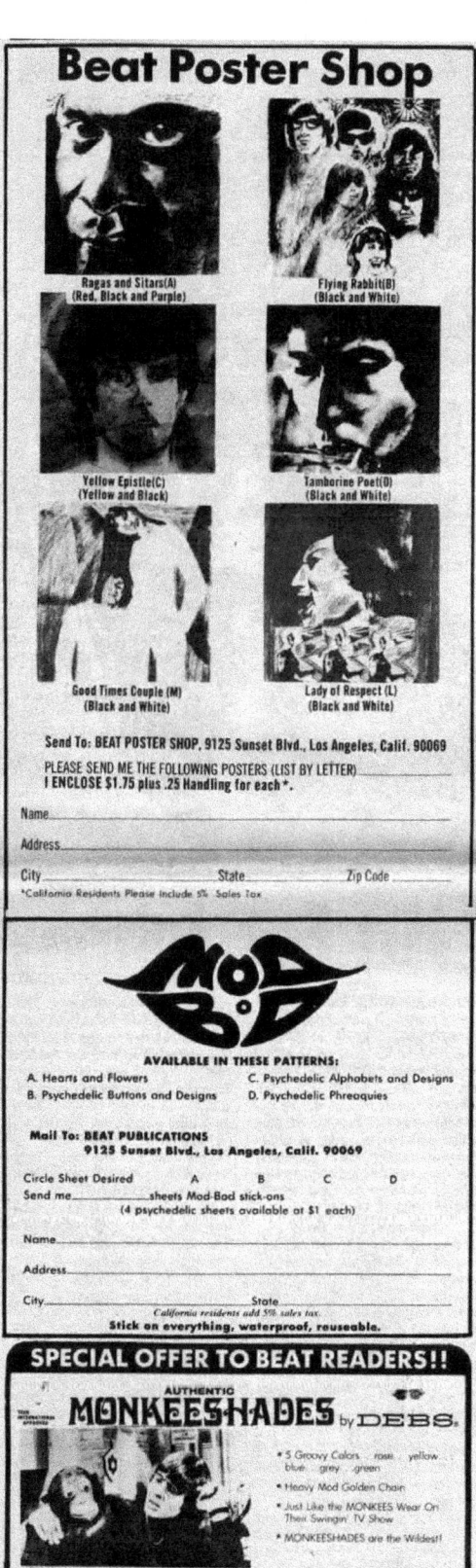

24 ORIGINAL HAPPENING HITS

As Advertised Nationally on Radio & TV

I Think We're Alone Now: Tommy James & The Shondells
Kind Of A Drag: The Buckinghams
Cherry Cherry: Neil Diamond
Turn Down Day: The Cyrkle
Jenny Take A Ride: Mitch Ryder & Detroit Wheels
My Little Red Book: Love
Wooly Bully: Sam The Sham
But It's Alright: J.J. Jackson
Little Girl: Syndicate Of Sound
See You In September: The Tempos
Daddy's Home: Shep & The Limelighters
Why Do Fools Fall In Love: Frankie Lyman
Western Union: Five Americans
Sunny: Bobby Hebb
Daydream: Lovin' Spoonful
Good Lovin': Young Rascals
I Got You Babe: Sonny & Cher
Pushin' Too Hard: The Seeds
Land Of 1000 Dances: Wilson Pickett
Younger Girl: The Critters
I Who Have Nothing: Terry Knight & The Pack
Bermuda: Four Seasons
Gee: The Crows
Maybe: The Chantels

$1.95 BEAUTIFUL FOUR COLOR JACKET
$4.00 FOR 2 ALBUMS (INCLUDES MAILING)
PLUS 50¢ MAILING

24 Happening Hits
9125 Sunset Blvd.
Los Angeles, California 90069

I enclose $_____ for _____ albums.
NAME_____
ADDRESS_____
CITY_____ STATE_____
California Residents Please Include 5% Sales Tax.

SPEC-TRIM SUNGLASSES

UNIQUE SHADOW BOX FRAMES
MOD RECESSED LENSES
TWO-COLOR FRAMES
$4 EACH*

*California Residents please add 5% sales tax

AVAILABLE IN:
Blue and White — White and Pink
Purple and White — Red and White
Yellow and Black — Red and Black
Designate Frame Color

SEND TO:
BEAT PUBLICATIONS
9125 Sunset Blvd.
Hollywood, Calif. 90069

DEBS

SPECIAL ISSUES STILL AVAILABLE

☐ Monterey Pop Festival souvenir Issue
☐ History of the Hippies

25 cents each plus 10 cents for mailing and handling.

SEND TO:
BEAT PUBLICATIONS
9125 Sunset Blvd.
Los Angeles, Calif.
90069

Name:_____
Address:_____
City:_____ State:_____
*California Residents include 5% for sales tax

That's Lou (Capitol) Lou Rawls, *When Love Goes Wrong, Please Give Me Someone To Love, Street of Dreams* and ten other tracks. This is Lou Rawls doing the kind of material that has finally put him on the top. Those who are Rawls fans will find this album excellent. Consisting mainly of Rawls' compositions sprinkled in with ballads like *When Love Goes Wrong* this offering is consistently well done. Unfortunately, Rawls tends to be repetitious in his material and his interesting style becomes tedious after a few songs. But those who consider Rawls to be the greatest blues singer since Ray Charles burst on the scene will find little about which to complain. Two particularly fine offerings are Rawls' *Problems* ("You can only take out what you put in it, that's life) and *Street of Dreams* (All you can hold is the moonbeams").

Paul Jones sings songs from the film "Privilege" and others (Capitol). Paul Jones, *Free Me, I've Been A Bad Boy, Lady Godiva* and nine other tracks. Paul Jones, who is a super-pop star in England is trying for the American audience with this release. Unfortunately, he will not get it. The album for the most part is uninteresting. Jones' best song is "I Can't Hold On Much Longer" reminiscent of the Kinks' "Sunny Afternoon." The songs from the Peter Watkin's film *Privilege* are poorly written and sung without much conviction. Unless the movie becomes a big hit with the record buying public this album doesn't stand a chance. The film concerns the career of a top pop star in England in the near future. *Privilege* has been well-received as a valiant attempt at satire, but critics have generally panned the film as a whole, and Paul Jones in particular. This album cannot survive without the film, and the film does not promise to be of any help at all.

Andy Parks tells about sex, school . . . and like other pressures (Capitol). This is a new comedy album supposedly telling of the trials of a young teen-age boy (15). The album has some very good moments, and a few funny lines, but on the whole it is not very funny. For one thing, it is written by adults with only an eye on teen-agers. "Long As You're Neat" has some good exchanges between father and son discussing long hair and rock groups. Most of the humor has been heard before, with only moderate updating. The discussion of sex between Andy and his girlfriend, Karen, is worth a few smiles, as is Andy's awareness of the importance of being a teen-ager in a youth oriented society that runs throughout the album. If you can catch the album on the radio fine, but it is not worth buying.

Time And Charges/The Buckinghams (Columbia) *Don't You Care, Remember, Mercy, Mercy, Mercy* plus seven other tracks. This is an extremely interesting album, offering many diverse moods and tempos. From the hit rock song "Don't You Care" to the uniquely delivered cover of the Beatles' "I'll Be Back" the Buckinghams prove that they are important performers.

KRLA ARCHIVES

please send me BEAT

26 issues only

$3 per year

Mail to: BEAT Publications
9125 Sunset Blvd.
Los Angeles, California 90069

☐ New Subscription
☐ Renewal (please enclose mailing label from your last BEAT)
I want BEAT for: ☐ 1 year at $3.00 or ☐ 2 years at $5.00
I enclose ☐ cash ☐ check ☐ money order
Outside U.S. — $9 per year

* Please print your name and address.

Name_____
Street_____
City_____
State_____ Zip_____

NATIONAL TOP 25 SINGLES

1. ODE TO BILLY JOE .... Bobbie Gentry
2. ALL YOU NEED IS LOVE .... Beatles
3. BABY, I LOVE YOU .... Arethea Franklin
4. LIGHT MY FIRE .... Doors
5. WORDS .... Monkees
6. PLEASANT VALLEY SUNDAY ...... Monkees
7. MERCY, MERCY, MERCY .... Buckinghams
8. REFLECTIONS .... Diana Ross and the Supremes
9. HEROES AND VILLAINS .... Beach Boys
10. A GIRL LIKE YOU .... Young Rascals
11. SILENCE IS GOLDEN .... Tremeloes
12. WHITER SHADES OF PALE .... Procol Harum
13. APPLES, PEACHES & PUMPKIN PIE ... Jay and the Techniques
14. COLD SWEAT .... James Brown
15. I WAS MADE TO LOVE HER .... Stevie Wonder
16. THANK THE LORD FOR THE NIGHT TIME ... Neil Diamond
17. YOU'RE MY EVERYTHING .... Temptations
18. CARRIE-ANNE .... Hollies
19. COME BACK WHEN YOU'RE GROWN ... Bobby Vee
20. FAKIN' IT .... Simon and Garfunkel
21. LET GOOD TIMES ROLL .... Bunny Sigler
22. WHITE RABBIT .... Jefferson Airplane
23. TESTIFY .... Parliments
24. WORLD WE KNEW .... Frank Sinatra
25. TO LOVE SOMEBODY .... Bee Gees

As Compiled by Cashbox Magazine

HOLLIES RULE ALL!
"EVOLUTION" PROVED IT!
Hollies and DOORS rule!
Hollies, Hollies,
HOLLIES, Hollies!!!!!!!
Jon Jon leader-drummer of the BUCKINGHAMS — you're a "luv"
Lan Roberts, Chuck Boland are weird psychedelic Hippies!!!!! KJR, 950 Seattle
PIGPEN *We love you!*
Monkee Fans wear diapers.
Bob Boemler?
Gail — I think you're the lost and the sweetest. Nickil
John and Janet *forever!*
"I'm So Glad,"
by SCOTT RICHARD CASE is bitchen!
Kent Sanderson, you're outasite ... Sally Dennis
Sue Meyers thinks Larry Bliesner is outasite!
Monkee's scene:
21 inches SQUARE!
BEATLES RULE!
George Harrison: *WOW!*
HAPPY BIRTHDAY! Carl Giammerses Aug. 21, Marty Grebb Sept. 2, Dennis Tufano Sept. 11, LUV, BUCKINGHAM'S FAN CLUB
Saturday's children ... outasite!
"Happy Birthday Sandie Pierce" *Luv, Bill*
HAPPY BIRTHDAY FREDDY WELLER
Ride with the sounds of THE MIDNIGHT RAIDERS — Jonesville, Wisconsin
THANK GOD FOR JOHN LENNON.
Happy Birthday to Carol Weth. Spoon called?
Griffith Park Chirs?
Be saved and believe in JOHN LENNON ... ken johnson
The Wind Cries JIMI
M.P.J.: Maybe the choice you made wasn't really right — Lady a

BEAT cover of The Beatles available in black light, hand screened poster. Pink, green, orange added to make groovy image. Cost is only $1.00 plus 25c tax. Get your order into *The BEAT* now!

REACH COSMIC AWARENESS without drugs — help save mankind from destruction. Write for free booklet, "Cosmic Awareness Speaks," Organization of Awareness, Box 115E, Olympia, Washington.
SLEEP LEARNING, self-hypnosis. Details, strange catalog free! Nutosuggestion, Box 24-BT, Olympia, Washington.
Please Make Pleasanton Happen
At 1420 WHK, Cleveland's weekend midnight to six deejay,
PETE JEBOME,
is the grooviest and most outasite to arrive on the scene. Everybody listen!

Monkee fans: go find your own scene! Too groovey for you here where BEATLES RULE!
STRAWBERRY BEATLES FOREVER!
LENNON *SAVES*

Laurie, Have a HAPPY! Kristy
Please remember 'Younger Girl' I always will. Love, Tommy

DAVY JONES...*I LUV YOU*
Dianne Nelson
luvs Paul McCartney
"Hi Kubieoshe"
PASSION SUNDAE,
PASSION SUNDAE,
PASSION SUNDAE,
PASSION SUNDAE,
PASSION SUNDAE,
Clyde the dragon spits fire ...
WADE!!
Bryan plus Brenda ...
"More Love"
Robyn *Loves* Hal!
Debra *Loves* Frankie!
— The "Four Flowery Children"
Karen LOVES Davy
Is Ron Henley *Real?*
The RAIN *Reigns*
Happy Birthday Craig Robb
— Love Karen
Bob in Madison — remember Jo Ellen and Sheila July 30th? Reminders Zally, "the boys," the Monkees, Stones?
Bay Area *BEATLE FANS*: How can we be together August 29th?????
BEATLE PEOPLE! BLAH!!
JADE electrifies your soul!
Go Army! Pepper and Gripweed want YOU!!
THE BEATLES RULE!
George — Freddy is cool!
Nancy
P.J. Proby forever!!
Donshires
Ripnetzles are better than Zallys
People who wear Red Pants are bitchin'! Consult high tide
Hoppy Burpday Klink Harrison ... Boupsomes
BILLY, I love you. Kathie!
Happy birthday Papa John
Luv Eileen
The 21st Century: Get Going!!!
Lanny is the greatest ever, Luv Ya
HAPPY BIRTHDAY, DAVE
George Harrison has *SOUL*
It's Sterling's fault
Jimmers and Dumbo Forever!
"UMBRELLA EARS" RULE
The Gnarly Beast love you
Luv THE GNARLY BEAST
Hi to the PROPHETS from their Fan Club
"He's HONEST, CUTE, SINCERE, TALENTED INTELLIGENT. His nme ....
PAUL McCARTNEY"
SONNY & CHER POSTERS
11"x14" — $1.00 each postpaid. Seper Co. 5273 Tendilla, Woodland Hills, California 91364
Russ Giguere has eyes that tantalize, mesmerize, finalize, piercifize, and Russifize me!
DETROIT: Think Rational!
Diane Kapanowski
SCOTT RICHARD CASE Swings. Dinane
George 'n Patti are pretty people. To our Freds: The rick, rich, last rights. Mike get a new Tom-Tom
Think — August 28 — is LOVE!
Smart Kitty — Smarter Gail!
Libra (Butch) and Leo (Cindy) want to get hitched. Luv, Leo Luv, Libra
Adopt "Children"
luv, Mary Marin
"Groovin' with
LEWIS & CLARK EXPEDITION
— Michelle S

To my angel — *cherish* is the word forever — P.D.
CHERRYCHILDREN LOVE SPOCK!!!
Philadelphia loves the MONKEES
Long John has soul
Bob, be persistent ..
Bob, be persistent ..
Bob, be persistent ... barnk!
Dickie — Meet me Monday at Chocolate River.
Pheasant Under Glass
"Traci Burke — I love you — " Bobby.
C'mon SPOONFUL people; I love you ZALLY too but if he's happier now — how can we object???
Give Jerry a chance
Lemmon pie is so good!
Bobby — My heart follows you across the endless sea. Joy
The Association are *unparalleled*
Laurie and Kristy
Dan Harrison of Woodland Hills — Where are you? — Love, Tina
Happy Birthday, Dixie Lee Bewick!!! Don't you miss me anymore????
Sunisyde?
Experience Richard Stakey — A splendid time is guaranteed for all ...
Dean Christie, *Dean Christie*, **Dean Christie**
Mod men, Mod men, Mod men
Dean Bonniwell — Happy Belated Birthday
Chuck Sayers — Happy Belated Birthday from Johnney
Big Brother and the Holding Company
Richard Kersulis has funny lookin' feet and very skinny legs.
— Goldie
Hearts and Flowers are blossoming ...
HAPPY LATE BIRTHDAY
Paul and Ringo!!! — Vicky
HAPPY BIRTHDAY
Sharon Taylor — Bill & Margaret
Happy Birthday Joe Butler!! Sept. 16th
Life is PAUL McCARTNEY
Beatles in San Francisco, August 19, 1967 ... in spirit! Beatles we love you!
Krushchev loves Beatles.
Monkees *forever!*
Belated BIRTHDAY GREETINGS to Jodi Sorensen from Savannah's incompatible TIM.
Queen Shaz has power!
Happy Birthdan Michelle Weatherbee, Love, Rick Coleman
"The Association — what's so good about 'em?"
Russ Giguere is *ALIVE!*
Russ Giguere — the man, the boy, the eye, the mind, the soul — is love — Hillary

BEAT is no longer accepting anything but PERSONAL MESSAGES in the classified section. Only messages (including Happy Birthdays) will be run. We will print names but not addresses or phone numbers.

Rates are cheap! Only 10 cents per word.

And remember, BEAT has a new address:
Classified BEAT Publications 9121 Sunset Blvd. Los Angeles 90069

DEADLINE FOR NEXT ISSUE: AUG. 29

KRLA ARCHIVES

www.ingramcontent.com/pod-product-compliance
Lightning Source LLC
Chambersburg PA
CBHW080359170426
43193CB00016B/2760